Second Edition

# Organizational Behavior and Management in Law Enforcement

**HARRY W. MORE, PH.D.**
*Professor Emeritus,*
*San Jose State University*

**W. FRED WEGENER, D.P.A.**
*Late Professor,*
*Indiana University of Pennsylvania*

**GENNARO F. VITO, PH.D.**
*Professor,*
*Southern Police Institute,*
*University of Louisville*

**WILLIAM F. WALSH, PH.D.**
*Professor and Director,*
*Southern Police Institute,*
*University of Louisville*

PEARSON
Prentice
Hall

Upper Saddle River, New Jersey 07458

**Library of Congress Cataloging-in-Publication Data**

Organizational behavior and management in law enforcement/Harry W. More ... [et al.].
    p. cm.
  Includes bibliographical references and index.
  ISBN 0-13-118101-7
  1. Police administration.   2. Organizational behavior.   I. More, Harry W.

HV7935.O742006
363.2'068—dc22

2004065339

**Executive Editor:** Frank Mortimer, Jr.
**Associate Editor:** Sarah Holle
**Executive Marketing Manager:** Tim Peyton
**Managing Editor:** Mary Carnis
**Production Liaison:** Brian Hyland
**Production Editor:** Janet Bolton
**Director of Manufacturing and Production:** Bruce Johnson
**Manufacturing Manager:** Ilene Sanford
**Manufacturing Buyer:** Cathleen Petersen
**Design Director:** Cheryl Asherman
**Senior Design Coordinator:** Miguel Ortiz
**Cover Design:** Amy Rosen
**Cover Art:** Ramin Talaie/Corbis
**Electronic Art Creation:** Integra
**Printing and Binding:** Hamilton Printing
**Copyeditor/Proofreader:** Maine Proofreading Services

**Pearson Prentice Hall™** is a trademark of Pearson Education, Inc.
**Pearson®** is a registered trademark of Pearson plc
**Prentice Hall®** is a registered trademark of Pearson Education, Inc.

Pearson Education LTD.
Pearson Education Australia PTY, Limited
Pearson Education Singapore, Pte. Ltd.
Pearson Education North Asia Ltd.
Pearson Education Canada, Ltd.
Pearson Educacion de Mexico, S.A. de C.V.
Pearson Education—Japan
Pearson Education Malaysia, Pte. Ltd.
Pearson Education, Upper Saddle River, New Jersey

10 9 8 7 6 5 4 3 2 1
ISBN 0-13-118101-7

# DEDICATION

This text is dedicated, in memoriam, to two individuals who made significant contributions to justice education and exemplified a true spirit of professionalism in the preparation of students.

## JOHN PAUL KENNEY, PH.D.

One of the notable pioneers of law enforcement education, Jack Kenney received his doctorate from UCLA and taught at the College of Sequoias; at the University of Southern California; at California State University, Long Beach; and finally at August Vollmer University. His combined careers as a police administrator and academician spanned more than five decades. His expertise ranged from police work with juveniles to planning to organization and management. Kenney started his career in law enforcement as a police officer in Berkeley, CA; from there he went on to become the Director of the Division of Law Enforcement, Department of Justice (State of California). He was also a past president of the City of Los Angeles Police Commission (LAPD). Throughout his career, he was active in professional organizations and was one of the founders of the Academy of Criminal Justice Sciences (initially known as the International Association of Police Professors). Additionally, he served as President of the American Society of Criminology (ASC) from 1957 to 1959.

Jack was an active researcher and consultant to local, state, and federal agencies. Additionally, he published numerous articles in professional journals and was the author or coauthor of six law enforcement texts.

## W. FRED WEGENER, D.P.A.

Fred received his doctorate from Nova University and spent his entire teaching career at Indiana University of Pennsylvania (IUP). He started his career in law enforcement with the Adams County Sheriff's Department (CO) where he attained the rank of Sergeant. Then he became an institutional and field agent with the Colorado Department of Adult Parole. Later he became the Director of the Toledo (OH) Criminal Justice Training and Education Center. For many years, Fred was the Manager of Public Safety at Idlewild Park, Ligonier, PA.

At Indiana University of Pennsylvania, Fred created and became the Director of the Crime Study Center. In addition he was a member and Vice Chairman of the Pennsylvania Deputy Sheriffs' Education and Training Board for the Commonwealth of Pennsylvania. He was always an active trainer, and he presented numerous police training seminars. He served as a consultant for local and state agencies and coauthored two law enforcement texts. One of those books, *Effective Police Supervision*, has been used by law enforcement agencies throughout the United States as preparation for promotion examinations to first-line supervisor.

Jack and Fred had exceptional careers in the law enforcement field as well as in higher education. Their students will remember them as enthusiastic instructors who had the ability to translate theory into the practical realm of the reality of justice operations. Because of the knowledge they imparted, those they instructed will carry on the high standards that they exemplified.

# CONTENTS

## 3 Personality: Understanding the Complexity of Human Behavior in the Organization    54

## 4  Beliefs, Values, and Attitudes: Determinants of Human Behavior    74

## 5  Motivation: The Force Behind Behavior    111

## 6   Stress in Organizational Life: Its Nature, Causes, and Control   145

## 7   Groups and the Group Process: Human Dynamics at Work    180

## 8   Power: Its Nature and Use       216

## 9  Decision-Making: The Essential Element in Applied Management  239

## 10  Managerial Communication: The Vital Process  271

## 11  Leadership: The Integrative Variable  300

## 12   Change: Coping with Organizational Life     344

## 15 Managerial Issues: Considerations for Resolution    409

# FOREWORD

VINCENT E. HENRY, PH.D.
*Associate Professor*
*Long Island University*

Like the day-to-day activities involved in managing a law enforcement agency, writing a textbook about the practice of law enforcement management can be a tremendously difficult and complicated task—especially if one wants to do the job well. From a practical viewpoint, contemporary law enforcement managers confront a daunting array of constraints and challenges. They must vigorously pursue a complex mandate that includes reducing crime and disorder, preserving the peace, and providing social services to the communities they serve, all the while operating within an evolving landscape of legal, social, political, organizational, bureaucratic, and cultural factors that combine and intersect in unique and rapidly changing ways. The priority issues and critical problems one grapples with today may appear far less important in just a few days, but experienced law enforcement managers know that these same issues and problems can easily reemerge—typically with slightly different features or characteristics that demand a somewhat different response—in a week, a month, or a year. At the same time, law enforcement managers in different agencies can encounter issues or problems that appear to be very similar, and yet unique and subtle characteristics within their environments demand entirely different sets of responses. One of the only consistent things about the contemporary practice of law enforcement management, in fact, is that there often seems to be so little consistency to it.

This lack of consistency is not unique to law enforcement management, of course. There are certainly other management fields where priorities change rapidly and where decisions are shaped by a host of factors. Law enforcement management, though, differs from many of these other fields because the human stakes are so high: our society entrusts its law enforcement officers with tremendous powers and responsibilities that are simply not given to members of any other occupation or social institution, and law enforcement managers have the responsibility to ensure that these powers are used properly. There are, then, an ethical dimension and an element of accountability—accountability for the actions or inactions of the organization and for the behavior of those who inhabit it—that further complicate the practice of effective law enforcement management.

Finally, the fact that we live in a time of unprecedented danger from terrorist threats—dangers that either did not exist or were not widely recognized until a few years ago—has imposed an entirely new set of demands upon contemporary law enforcement managers at the local, state, and federal levels. Domestic law enforcement agencies have assumed a new mandate for homeland security, and that mandate requires them to take on a range of responsibilities and functions that extend well beyond the traditional law enforcement responsibilities of reducing crime and disorder, preserving the peace, and providing social services.

Managing a law enforcement organization is no simple task, and neither is writing a textbook that reflects the realities of law enforcement management and organizational behavior. In writing this text, however, Harry W. More, W. Fred Wegener, Gennaro F. Vito, and William F. Walsh have done an absolutely outstanding job of overcoming the obstacles and impediments that beset so many other textbooks in this field. They present a clear, concise, realistic, and very thorough overview of contemporary law enforcement organizations and the issues managers confront, and they do so without becoming mired in unnecessary material or excessive detail. This is a tightly written book that nevertheless manages to cover all the relevant major issues in contemporary law enforcement management, and it does so in an appealing and straightforward style that will be appreciated by both students and teachers. The fact that this book is so highly readable and so well organized speaks to the knowledge, the skills, and the insights of the authors—true professionals who know their subject intimately and can convey its complexity in an intelligible and coherent way that many other academic authors cannot.

One of the difficulties involved in writing a textbook on police or law enforcement management lies in the fact that so much of the literature of management—the primary sources one needs in order to build a framework for understanding—focuses almost entirely on business management rather than police or even public-sector management. Both in theory and in practice, these two fields can be vastly different.

From my own experience as an author and as a law enforcement management practitioner, I know the inherent difficulty of adapting and applying that business-oriented literature to the world of law enforcement. Management principles that work perfectly well in the private sector often do not translate easily to public-sector practice. The authors have done a highly creditable job in adapting broad management principles to the very specific topic of law enforcement, as well as in integrating major works that deal specifically with law enforcement management topics. The references and bibliographies in each chapter are contemporary and relevant, and they reflect the major works in the field. Students and teachers will certainly appreciate the Discussion Topics and Questions and For Further Reading sections that conclude each chapter, since they are also relevant, appropriate, and reflective of the topics and themes discussed within the chapter. The discussion topics can serve as the basis for essay questions or as springboards for in-class dialogue.

In each chapter the authors provide a rather comprehensive review of the historical antecedents to the issues they explore, and I have found that this historic view is of benefit to students because it helps put the issues in their proper context. This approach permits students to appreciate the fact that law enforcement management (indeed, management in virtually every field) is in a state of constant flux, and it helps them grasp how some of the forces, factors, and environments that create the need for evolutionary change intersect and interact to shape actual practice. This approach also permits students to grasp how things got to be the way they are, how various theories and paradigms have shaped management practice over time, and how management personnel have sought to deal with perennial problems. This continual evolution is an intricate process, and the authors do an outstanding job at conveying that complexity without belaboring the point.

Importantly, the authors have a great appreciation for the most current and still-evolving trends in law enforcement management—most notably, the CompStat management style that so many criminal justice agencies are adopting. The book's contemporary focus is further evidence that the authors "know their stuff" and are conversant with the practical realities of current law enforcement practice.

All too often, police and law enforcement management texts do not reflect the most current theories, trends, and practices, and there can be a tendency toward simply repackaging old theories and principles. In sharp contrast to so many other texts, this book provides a realistic and up-to-date view of contemporary law enforcement management theory, policy, and practice. It does so without being prescriptive, didactic, or narrow in its approach.

The authors also have an excellent grasp of the subtle intraorganizational dynamics that are so much a part of police management; this grasp derives in part from their ability to draw upon their wealth of personal experience as practitioners, consultants, and researchers over the years. Readers should know that Harry More is one of the leaders of criminal justice education and management in this country, and whose many texts convey hard-earned knowledge of management issues. W. Fred Wegener was his coauthor on several of these texts, and his study of public administration added depth to the work. Bill Walsh, my former NYPD colleague, enjoyed an outstanding reputation as a police commander, and Jerry Vito's credentials as a scholar of policing are second to none.

As another former practitioner who is now an academic, I have found that many texts on the market seem to simply recapitulate facts and outline the points of major theories. As a result, they often fail to capture the "feel" or the complexity of law enforcement management. Many texts in this area tend to be dry and overly theoretical—they are, essentially, extensive literature reviews—and this is ultimately a disservice to students. It also imposes a distinct burden on conscientious instructors to continually disabuse students of the notion that such texts tell the whole story and to continually emphasize that law enforcement management is a much more complicated endeavor than many theoretical approaches would make it seem.

Whether they are traditional students taking criminal justice or police management courses or experienced practitioners who have returned to complete their education, I have consistently found that my students appreciate the kind of insight a practitioner can provide to the course material. They feel that a practitioner focus adds relevance and meaning to the course material, and they value books and articles written by those with a practitioner background over those written by academics who have less experience working in the field or working with practitioners.

In particular, I found the brief case studies throughout this book to be especially useful and informative, since they provide a glimpse into the essential humanity of the subject matter as well as the human variables that affect actual management practices. These case studies have the ring of truth to them, and they offer students an uncommonly realistic insight into the process of management. Importantly, the case studies do not exclusively reflect either a "big city" or a "small town" approach; there is a good balance to this book, and given the diverse landscape of contemporary American policing, that balance is difficult to achieve. A good text should also seek an appropriate balance between objective recitation of fact and theory and a too-subjective excursion into "war stories," and this text accomplishes that.

In sum, the authors took on a distinct challenge in writing this work, and they have produced a comprehensive, coherent, and very readable textbook. Like the practice of effective law enforcement management itself, their approach is thorough and flexible, rooted in an understanding of historical trends, and reflective of the most contemporary management practices. In every respect, this is an outstanding law enforcement management text—one that I look forward to using in my own classroom.

# PREFACE

Management in contemporary police departments is constantly in flux. As we note in Chapter 1, police management has a rich history that is, for the most part, an integration of knowledge developed originally in the private sector. Most law enforcement agencies have evolved from a highly political style of policing to a more professional model and are currently developing a style appropriately described as community policing.

Within this context, police managers have become increasingly aware of social and individual behavior in the organization. It is generally conceded that when the quality of working life within the organization is good, the organization's goals are more readily met and individual needs accommodated. The creation of positive relationships between line officers, between groups within the organization, and between police managers at every level is critical to the success of any police department. Police managers must recognize the ecology of the organization, accepting it as a dynamic social system. We focus on organizational behavior as a means of understanding both the complexity of the criminal justice organization and the interaction between officers and managers as they work to resolve community problems.

Today's police managers have to develop behavioral and social skills to deal effectively with a rapidly changing community and with the new breed of police officer. The modern police executive must integrate each member of the organization into the managerial process so that the organization can improve both its internal and external adaptive capabilities.

Chapters 1 and 2 of *Organizational Behavior and Management in Law Enforcement* review the antecedents of management thought and consider the dimensions of management, which include problem solving and managerial functions and roles.

Chapters 3 through 6 discuss how characteristics of the individual influence the organization and how, in turn, the organization affects the individual. Behavioral implications include a consideration of personality, attitudes, motivation, and organizational stress. An effort is made in these chapters to present information that provides a real understanding of behavior in the organization.

We are also concerned with social behavior and organizational processes. Groups and the group process are considered in detail in Chapter 7, and extensive attention is given to key elements such as power (Chapter 8), decision-making (Chapter 9), communications (Chapter 10), and leadership (Chapter 11). Each is a natural aspect of the life of the organization, and they condition and recondition the organization.

Chapters 12 through 14 emphasize the interaction process in the organization. Special treatment is given to change, conflict, and developing the organization as a means of improving individual and organizational performance. The last chapter discusses several critical issues with which police managers must deal today, including minorities, women, unions, and the use of deadly force.

The text presents current behavioral theory and its application to the organization. The intent has been to help current and potential police managers understand the different beliefs and assumptions they hold about themselves, others, the organization, and the community. Our goal is to emphasize the importance of human behavior and its relationship to organizational processes.

The transition from theoretical to practical has been accomplished by providing numerous realistic examples throughout the text and by the inclusion of Focuses taken from journals, newspapers, and monographs. In addition, we offer real case studies in all chapters after the first, 45 in all. The instructor should use the issues raised in each case during classroom discussions.

Tables and figures amplify and reinforce important points discussed in each chapter. In addition to a Summary, each chapter has sections entitled Learning Objectives, Key Terms, Discussion Topics and Questions, and For Further Reading.

Each of these features makes the text user-friendly and provides a range of activities to maximize instructor and student interaction. Lastly, the text has been written using an informal writing style. The experience of the authors is that students respond to it with a great deal of enthusiasm.

*Organizational Behavior and Management in Law Enforcement* is the product of many, including all the faculty members who were kind enough to share course outlines and review the text outline. Police departments throughout the nation responded to inquiries and furnished information and data.

# ACKNOWLEDGMENTS

Numerous individuals and organizations contributed to the completion of this textbook by either providing material or granting permission to reproduce material contained in other publications. We would like to thank the following people, who provided information utilized in preparation of *Organizational Behavior and Management in Law Enforcement:* Milpitas Police Department, Milpitas, CA; Joseph A. Bogan, Professor, Indiana University of Pennsylvania; Donald R. Burr, Councilman, Campbell, CA; James D. Sewell; Gary Leonard, Chief (retired), Sandy City, UT; William J. Winters, Chief (retired), Chula Vista, CA; Joseph McNamara, Hoover Institute, Stanford, CA; O. Ray Shipley, Chief, Medford, OR; U.S. Secret Service, Washington, DC; Louis A. Mayo; William Nay, U.S. Department of Energy, Washington, DC; and Charlotte Police Department, Charlotte, NC. We also extend a special thanks to our many students in the Administrative Officers' Course classes in the Southern Police Institute at the University of Louisville.

We would also like to thank Vincent Henry, Long Island University, Long Island, NY and Gordon Frissora, Youngstown State University, Youngstown, OH for reviewing this edition of *Organizational Behavior and Management in Law Enforcement.*

Additional thanks are extended to the following publishers, organizations, and government entities: Madison Police Department, Madison, WI; Albuquerque Police Department, Albuquerque, NM; Charles C. Thomas, Publisher; Commission on Accreditation for Law Enforcement Agencies, Inc.; *Police Chronicle; Teamsters Online; Law Enforcement News*; U.S. Army Research Institute for the Behavioral and Social Sciences, Alexandria, VA; National Institute of Justice, Washington, DC; *Law and Order*; Office of Justice Programs, Washington, DC; National Center for Women Policing; Bureau of Justice Statistics; Department of the Army, Washington, DC; U.S. Census Bureau, Washington, DC; National Executive Institute; The Pittsburg *Press; Success; PCCD Quarterly; USA Today; APB News*; The San Jose *Mercury News*; Alexander Hamilton Institute; Los Angeles Police Department, Los Angeles, CA; The President's Commission on Physical Fitness and Sports; Police Foundation, Washington, DC; Human Rights Watch; U.S. Commission on Civil Rights, Washington, DC; McGraw-Hill Publishing Co.; Scientific Methods, Inc.; Navy Publications and Printing Service, Washington, DC; Gulf Publishing Company; Berkley Books; National Institute for Occupational Safety and Health; and the U.S. Equal Employment Opportunity Commission, Washington, DC.

HWM
WFW
GFV
WFW

# POLICE MANAGEMENT

## Evolving Strategies

## LEARNING OBJECTIVES

1. Identify the focus of the classical school.
2. Define the term *bureaucracy.*
3. List five characteristics of scientific management.
4. Compare the findings of Leonhard Fuld and Elmer Graper.
5. Identify the components of the acronym POSDCORB.
6. Describe why the Hawthorne effect is important.
7. Differentiate between the following terms: input, internal process, output.
8. Compare an open to a closed management system.
9. Identify the characteristics of systems theory.
10. List the key characteristics of the contingency approach to management.
11. Describe the organizational strategy of the political era.
12. Compare the organizational strategies of the reform and community policing eras.
13. List the methods used to organize police departments.
14. Define the term *management.*
15. List the four management functions.
16. Identify O. W. Wilson's nine principles of organizational management.
17. Define *CompStat.*

Police departments are formal organizations that involve the coordination and arrangement of people and resources to achieve a defined purpose. Police managers are expected to achieve the purposes and operational objectives of their departments through the performance of the employees under their command. Managerial and organizational effectiveness depends on the willingness of employees to support and follow direction. However, people differ in knowledge, skills, and abilities as well as in their commitment to their organizational responsibilities. Thus, the behavioral response to managerial direction is a complex phenomenon. To understand it requires critical analysis and knowledge of human behavior by the manager. The intention of this text is to help the reader develop skills in understanding and diagnosing human behavior and problems that occur in the workplace. By learning to understand how people can work both for and against organizational direction, managers can be better prepared to confront these issues in their organizational environments.

The art and science of modern police management did not spring into existence overnight. They are the result of an evolutionary process going back over 200 years. In order to understand this process and put it into its proper conceptual perspective, we will review the evolution of management theory and its impact on police organizations. It is important that students of policing as well as police managers be knowledgeable of the historical developments summarized next in this chapter.

## HISTORICAL ANTECEDENTS

Humans have been thinking about management and organizations since they first started to develop organizations to accomplish specific tasks. Theorists of police organization management, as well as police managers, have repeatedly drawn their ideas from developments in the organizational and business worlds. The theories, names, and concepts discussed here form a foundation for understanding the role of managers in organizations generally and the structure of police organizations in particular. Theories about how to manage organizations have been products of different historical perspectives and value systems. Many of the early management theories were developed by individuals who relied heavily on military and religious models. However, it was the development of the factory system, with its accompanying array of organizational problems, that was the major influence on the thinking and beliefs of individuals who contributed to what is today known as *classical organization theory.*

## CLASSICAL SCHOOL

The organization theories of the classical school dominated managerial thinking into the 1930s and remain influential today, especially in policing. Classical theorists sought to discover the "one best way" to create and administer an organization. They emphasized stable, clearly defined structures and machine-like procedures to control employee behavior and maximize attainment of organizational goals.[1] They believed that organizations should consist of careful-ly designed interrelated parts, rationally working together like a machine. People are parts of this machine, but the organization and its mission take priority over people. Classical theories proposed a closed-system view of organizations and the people in them. The organizational model that best exemplifies this the-oretical perspective is *bureaucracy.*

**Bureaucracy** Max Weber (1864–1920), a German sociologist, provided one of the first sys-tematic analyses of what has become known as the rational–legal organiza-tional model, the "ideal bureaucracy." The bureaucratic organization described by Weber is a centralized managerial authority system based on a logical hier-archical ordering of positions from top to bottom.[2] Weber posited that the characteristics of bureaucratic organization gave it a form of authority that made it technically capable of achieving a higher level of efficiency and effec-tiveness than other organizational forms.

Weber described some of the characteristics of the bureaucratic organization as follows:

1. The organization assigns to its members official responsibility for carrying out its routine activities.
2. The organization distributes authority to those who need it in order to accomplish assigned tasks.
3. The organization vests authority in positions rather than individuals, and the principle of office hierarchy provides for levels of authority.
4. The organization requires thorough documentation of all activity; official records are maintained by staff.
5. The organization considers training to be the best means of ensuring effective performance.
6. The organization requires each manager to devote full-time efforts to managing.
7. The organization considers it essential, for the sake of stability, to reduce management to a set of rules.[3]

In his description of this organizational form, Weber emphasized the rational and legal authority of the organizational staff. He posited that the staff should function according to the following criteria:

1. Offices should be organized hierarchically.
2. Every office is required to have a specific sphere of competence.
3. Open selection of staff is emphasized.
4. Selection should be based on merit.
5. Salary is based on hierarchical rank.
6. The office is the primary occupation of the incumbent.

The bureaucratic model remains viable today because it is a fundamentally logical, rational, and common sense way to organize complex enterprises. Most organizations are bureaucratic to some degree, and this is especially true in the world of policing. Most police departments are structured as bureaucracies, and most police managers have risen to their positions through hierarchical levels like those described by Weber. It is understandable that such managers, having served in bureaucratic organizations for most of their professional lives, tend to hold sacred the concepts of rational authority, hierarchy, specialization, and managerial authority.[4]

The bureaucratic organizational model, with its rational–legal authority structure, is at the core of the professional ideal sought by the early-20th-century police reformers in the United States. During the years 1930 to 1970, police leaders such as August Vollmer, O. W. Wilson, and William H. Parker led a nationwide movement to transform politically dominated police departments into rational–legal professional organizations focused on crime control. Their ideal organizational model subscribed to the following "principles":

1. The primary function of policing is crime control.
2. Police departments should be independent of politics.
3. Effectiveness and efficiency result from a highly centralized command structure and standardized operating procedures.

4. The police organization should be hierarchical and subdivided according to a division of labor and task specialization.
5. Officers are to be selected on the basis of established standards.
6. Officers should be well trained and disciplined.
7. Crime can be deterred by preventive, random motorized patrol.
8. Policing should use modern technology.
9. Police officers should enforce laws impartially.
10. Crimes are solved by scientific investigative methods.[5]

This organizational form met the needs of administrators and reformers of that era who were trying to exclude political interference while at the same time professionalizing policing. Bureaucracy continues to dominate police management because it is designed to ensure organizational stability and permanence and to minimize ambiguity and impreciseness. It provides a means for ensuring control and accountability in the uncertain and sometimes hostile organizational environment faced by many police departments. In a bureaucracy, people can come and go, but the organization always remains intact.

However, many see bureaucracy as the embodiment of everything wrong with government agencies.[6] Many employees of bureaucracies feel that the machine-like quality of this organizational model dehumanizes them and limits their opportunity to express opinions or do anything but conform to organizational rules and regulations. Thinking is reserved for managers, while employees are expected to perform their duties by following rules and procedures.

## Scientific Management

Another classical theorist, an American efficiency engineer named Frederick W. Taylor (1856–1915), is acknowledged as the founder of scientific management. He discovered that in many factories output goals were informally determined by individual workers, who had little incentive to work hard because wage systems were based primarily on attendance.

To remedy this low-efficiency mindset, which he called "soldiering," Taylor advocated a piece-rate system, which he suggested would motivate a higher level of performance if the employees knew it was designed by systematic analysis. He believed it was essential to arrive at the rate by using scientific and empirical procedures to analyze how people work. To accomplish this, Taylor advocated five simple principles that are summarized as follows:

1. Shift all responsibility for the organization from the worker to the manager. Managers should do all the thinking relating to the planning and design of work, leaving workers with the task of implementation.
2. Use scientific methods to determine the most efficient way of accomplishing each task.
3. Select the best persons to perform the jobs thus designed.
4. Train the selected persons to do the work efficiently.
5. Monitor worker performance to ensure that appropriate work procedures are followed and that appropriate results are achieved.[7]

By applying his method, Taylor found he could improve productivity dramatically and at the same time increase the wages of the workers. He also advocated the concept of functional supervision, where each employee would be supervised by no more than one foreman or expert.[8]

Taylor's managerial philosophy involved a complete mental revolution by both management and workers. Employees had to change their attitudes toward work, fellow employees, and managers. At the same time, management had to change their views of workers, duties, and worker relationships. Scientific management was never presented as a complete management theory, but it was the first attempt to use scientific methods to understand task accomplishment by workers. As a result of Taylor's efforts, the role of management changed abruptly from the use of rules of thumb to a more scientific approach that included using scientific principles in selecting, training, developing, and managing workers.[9]

Henri Fayol (1841–1925), a French mining engineer, was the first to attempt to develop a comprehensive theory of administration. He was very successful as a manager, and many responded positively to his writings. He published a monograph on management in 1916, but the first English translation was not available until 1937 and not widely distributed in the United States until 1949.

**Administrative School**

Fayol identified the following as basic functions of each manager:

1. Planning
2. Organizing
3. Commanding
4. Coordinating
5. Controlling[10]

Additionally, Fayol developed 14 principles of management based on his practical experience. A principle is defined by classical theorists as a general truth about the management of organizations—not an infallible scientific law, but an observation that, if applied, would improve organizational performance. Fayol's principles included the following:

1. Division of work, allowing for specialization.
2. Authority (the right to give orders), coupled with employees' responsibility to do their best.
3. Discipline, that is, obedience, application, energy, and respect within the organization.
4. Unity of command: subordinates should receive orders from only one superior.
5. Unity of direction: each objective should have only one boss and one plan.
6. Subordination of individual interest to the general interest.
7. Rewards: bonuses, profit sharing, piece rates, and other methods should be used to ensure equitable payment to employees.
8. Centralization: one point in the organization should have control over all of the parts, but in a large organization, some decisions may have to be made at lower levels.
9. Chain of command: there should be an unbroken chain of managers (scalar chain) from the bottom to the top of the organization. Authority and communication should follow this chain.
10. Orderliness: there should be a well-chosen place for everything, and everything should be kept in its place.

11. Equity: this should be achieved through a combination of kindliness and justice.
12. Stability: management should provide for stability of personnel tenure; mediocre managers who stay are preferable to outstanding managers who come and go.
13. Forethought: plans should be carefully considered before they are executed.
14. Esprit de corps: the group should work as a team, and every member should work to accomplish the organizational goals (esprit de corps).[11]

Fayol's contribution to management was unique and truly valuable. He outshone his contemporaries, and after the publication of his monograph, many others codified his principles. He was responsible for originating the organization chart, job specifications, and the idea that managers should be trained—all concepts that are still used by organizations today. Fayol also pointed out that varying circumstances demanded flexibility in the application of his principles.

Functional management as espoused by Fayol had considerable impact on police departments during the first half of the 20th century. Many of his principles are still taught today, and concepts such as unity of command and esprit de corps dominate the police management scene.[12]

## EARLY POLICE ADMINISTRATION RESEARCHERS

Administrative theory, from the early years of its evolution, was applied by scholars and researchers to police work. In 1906, Leonhard F. Fuld at Columbia University submitted the first doctoral dissertation in the field, a critical study of police organization in the United States. This work was commercially published in 1910 under the title *Police Administration*.[13] In it, Fuld analyzed multiple aspects of police organizations, from the selection of police officers to the structure of police departments and the enforcement of law. He took the position that a police organization could only be effective when it was administered properly by a strong executive. He was especially critical of nonprofessional heads of police departments and of police boards and commissions.

Fuld's study identified numerous problems confronting the police at that time and made a number of recommendations, including the following:

1. Elimination of politics from police administration
2. Specialization of duties
3. Clearly defined duties
4. Constant supervision of duties
5. Strong executive leadership
6. Constant auditing by inspectors
7. Maintenance of discipline
8. Comprehensive training of patrolmen
9. Careful selection of personnel
10. Elimination of non-police duties

Fuld's overall approach placed serious emphasis on management control (close supervision over subordinates) and the necessity of strong leadership from police chiefs. He also stressed the need for continually auditing the activities of all personnel. His work forms the basis of what is known as the "command and control" style of administration in policing today.

In 1915, Raymond Fosdick completed the first comprehensive study of policing in the United States, a survey covering 72 cities with populations over 100,000. He concluded that police departments were organizationally primitive, having developed without design or accurately determined purposes. Many cities were discovered to have police organizations unable to adequately serve their needs. Most departments in his study had two work divisions: the uniformed force and the detective bureau. He also found police departments performing numerous extraneous and unrelated functions such as censorship and collection of taxes. Finally, he observed that departments were burdened with inept leadership. He concluded that for a sound administrative organization to develop, three conditions should be met:

1. The relationship between supervision and work must be well balanced.
2. The different parts of the mechanism must be adjusted to each other.
3. The whole machine must be adapted to its task.[14]

In 1921, Elmer D. Graper published a work entitled *American Police Administration*, which advocated that police departments be administered by one individual rather than a board or a commission. Police organizational authority, Graper said, should be centralized in the hands of a single individual who would be held responsible for the exercise of that authority. Structurally, Graper supported the hierarchical arrangement of officers (military style), as a means of ensuring adequate supervision. He posited that police departments should be functionally organized into divisions or groups specialized according to the specific functions they performed.[15]

The best description of the managerial functions to emerge during the pre–World War II period was set forth by Luther Gulick in conjunction with L. Urwick in 1937. Gulick was the originator of one of the most widely cited and influential acronyms in management and administration—POSDCORB:

**POSDCORB**

| | |
|---|---|
| **P** | PLANNING concerns working out (in broad outline) what needs to be accomplished and then identifying appropriate methods to achieve departmental goals. |
| **O** | ORGANIZING involves creating an authority structure in which work units are established and coordinated for the purpose of achieving organizational objectives. |
| **S** | STAFFING refers to the personnel functions of recruiting, selecting, training, nurturing, and retaining competent human resources. |
| **D** | DIRECTING is the process of making decisions; formulating policies, procedures, rules, and regulations; and performing leadership tasks. |
| **CO** | COORDINATING is the continuous process of developing harmonious interaction between organizational units. |

| **R** | REPORTING requires keeping management and employees fully informed through inspection, records, and research. |
|---|---|
| **B** | BUDGETING involves fiscal control by means of financial planning, resource allocation, and accounting.[16] |

In the decades after Gulick's paper was released, POSDCORB was firmly embraced by police management. It was taught in police training programs and published in police administrative texts, and it served as the basis for test questions on promotion examinations. The influence of the classical theories of management can also be seen in the works of early writers such as O. W. Wilson (police administration) and V. A. Leonard (police organization and management). Another influence on these authors was their mentor, August Vollmer, the father of modern police administration, who served Berkeley, California, as town marshal from 1905 to 1909 and as chief of police (the city's first) from 1909 to 1932. In addition to his law enforcement leadership positions, Vollmer also served on the faculties at the University of Chicago and the University of California.

Vollmer supported the application of managerial, sociological, social work, and psychological concepts in policing. He was the first police leader to support college education for police officers. He advocated the motorization of police patrol units and the development of radio-based communications and records systems. A true innovator and visionary, Vollmer laid the groundwork for the development of the professional policing model that spread throughout policing in the first half of the 20th century.[17]

In the earliest decades of the 20th century, the primary focus of management theory was the structure and authority of the organization itself. During the next phase of the development of the field, greater consideration was given to the needs of individuals within the organization, and human relations and psychological management theories evolved (see Table 1–1).

**Human Relations School**

Human relations are simply relations between people. In management, the term refers to the personnel or human resource aspect of the manager's job. As we have seen, the dominant managerial philosophy in the early part of the 20th century saw management as a production-oriented process grounded in bureaucratic structural control. The employee was considered just another factor in the production effort. In the succeeding years some theorists shifted their focus from organizational structure and managerial control to the interrelationship of the employee and the organization.[18]

The Hawthorne studies, conducted by Elton Mayo and F. J. Roethlisberger between the 1920s and the 1940s, revealed that employee productivity was

Table 1–1  **Historical Antecedents**

Bureaucracy

Scientific management

Administrative management

Early police researchers

POSDCORB

Human relations

Contingency theory

Systems theory

affected not only by job design and rewards for production but also by social and psychological factors.

Employees' feelings, emotions, and sentiments were strongly affected by such work conditions as group relationships, leadership styles, and support from management. These feelings in turn could have significant impact on productivity.

The initial intent of the Hawthorne studies was to identify the relationship between productivity and physical working conditions. It was discovered that no matter how the researchers altered the working conditions, the workers increased their productivity. The researchers determined that employees involved in the experiment were responding to human contact and the fact someone was paying attention to them. In other words, the psychological and social conditions of work proved to be meaningful. This important variable became known as the "Hawthorne effect."[19] Additional investigation was needed, so over a two-year period the researchers studied the conditions of employment, such as work breaks, length of workday, humidity, and the room temperature. They also experimented with changes in the behavior of supervisors, who adopted a coaching managerial style and acted more as work-group resources than as mere order givers. The researchers concluded that the employees as a group controlled the rate of production and had adopted an explicit code of behavior that included the following:

1. The amount of work accomplished should be restricted. If you exceed what is expected of you, then you are a "rate-buster."
2. You should not turn out too little work. If you do, then you are a "chiseler."
3. You should never tell a supervisor anything that would harm a fellow employee. If you do, you are a "squealer."
4. You should never act officious even when functioning as a supervisor.[20]

The importance of the Hawthorne studies is that they demonstrated the critical role of the individual within the organization and the impact of group dynamics on performance. Out of this research developed the "human relations" school of personnel management, which represented a shift in focus to a more supportive approach to the treatment of employees. This theoretical school focused on the most vital of all organizational resources, people.

The "human relations" school and the more authoritarian managerial theorists who preceded it tended to address organizational goals and employee needs as separate and mutually exclusive. The "human resource management" movement that developed out of the human relations school between the 1960s and the 1980s took a different approach. This movement holds that organizational goals and human needs are mutual and compatible: one set need not be treated at the expense of the other. Getting the best from your employees requires that the culture, morale, and psychological environment of the organization be positive. Human resource management involves designing and implementing systems to improve many of these factors.

Human resource management has evolved as a critical management function. All managers spend part of their work time on personnel tasks.[21] Recruitment, selection, training, development, and employee recognition and motivation are considered important factors in creating organizational excellence. The human resource perspective that evolved out of his research requires that a good fit be made between management's objectives and people. However, when two or more individuals work together, the potential exists for problems to arise. Every organization has human problems, and managers must deal not only with their own problems but also with those of the people who work for them. Consequently, a critical focus of the human resource function of management is employee motivation and its impact on performance. The concepts and theories associated with employee motivation are addressed in a separate chapter in this book.

## Systems Theory

The classical organizational theorists were primarily concerned with the internal structure of the organization and creating principles for administrators to follow. The findings of the Hawthorne studies and the development of the human relations school drew attention to a consideration of influences not directly controlled by the organization. The organization was no longer seen as a self-regulating closed structure but as an entity subject to a variety of influences and driving forces in its environment. Researchers began to look at organizations as complex and paradoxical phenomena that can be understood in different ways.[22]

During the 1960s, systems theory, a mode of analysis initially applied in the natural and physical sciences, evolved as a way of analyzing the various environmental factors that influence organizations. In recent years, numerous administrative theorists have made serious efforts to apply systems concepts to management. Systems theory (physical, biological, or managerial) emphasizes the interdependence and interrelationship of each and every part to the whole.[23] It provides a framework for seeing organizational interrelationships not as static "snapshots" but as patterns of change that affect organizations.[24]

A system is an ongoing process that transforms certain specific inputs into outputs; these in turn influence subsequent inputs into the system in a way that supports continued operation of the process.[25] The classical theorist's perspective exemplified by the bureaucracy emphasized a closed-system organizational model. Closed-system organizations are perceived as self-regulating, controlled structures, complete unto themselves, not affected by external forces. This is not an accurate explanation of organizational reality in today's world. Organizations are affected by numerous driving factors in their environments.

The open-system organizational model reflects the dynamic interrelationship of the organization with its external environment. It is characterized by the influence of environmental inputs (external driving forces) that are internally processed (internal capability) and changed into organization products or services that have value for their recipients. Police organizations, viewed as open systems, take a set of inputs (e.g., citizen demands, government mandates, reports of crime) and apply to them a series of processes internal to the organization (e.g., calls for service processing, operational strategies, preventive patrol, investigation, arrest) in order to transform them into outputs (e.g., public safety, traffic control, dispute resolution, justice). However, those who receive the products and services (e.g., citizens, the criminal justice system) also have an impact on the organization. People will not buy products they do not value, and citizens will not support or assist police departments that they believe do not serve community needs.

To apply the systems approach to studying an organization requires awareness of the following features:

1. The basic mission of the organization and the means it uses to set and pursue goals and to measure its accomplishments
2. The specific environmental driving forces that affect the organization
3. The organization's internal strengths and weaknesses
4. The means used by all mission-related components of the organization to set and pursue goals and measure accomplishments
5. The nature of the interrelationships and joint functioning of the organization's subunits

These considerations provide a means of organizing managerial thinking and rechecking it continually. A systems-thinking manager must constantly review the totality of organizational interrelationships and evaluate each decision in terms of its impact on the mission, goals, objectives, and operational delivery of the organization.[26] When a community crime situation changes, the police operational manager must not only analyze when, where, and how this is occurring but also estimate what effects this change may have on that community. The manager must then devise a response strategy, achievable by the appropriate units without exceeding the department's budget, that will meet the objective of crime control while gaining the support of the community and the department's command staff. During the development of this strategy, consideration should also be given to its potential impact on the department, the community at large, the political environment, and other criminal justice agencies. Figure 1–1 sketches some of the possible interactions among system factors that may affect such decision-making.

Systems theory provides a solution to the limitations of the classical mechanistic approach and a rationale for rejecting principles based on relatively closed-system thinking. Systems thinking provides managers with the ability to carefully consider each organizational subsystem and the interrelationships among subsystems. While theoretical, it holds promise as a tool to analyze an organization.

**Figure 1–1**

Simplified Police System.

Adapted from Ernst K. Nillsson, "Systems Analysis Applied to Law Enforcement," *Allocation of Resources in the Chicago Police Department* (Washington, DC: Law Enforcement Assistance Administration, 1972).

**Open-System Thinking and Policing**

Recognition that all organizations are part of larger systems and have an interactive relationship with their environment leads to recognition that police departments, too, do not function in isolation and cannot be perceived as closed systems. Since the 1980s, the "community policing" movement has accelerated the organizational shift in policing from a closed- to an open-system perspective. Before the development of community policing, many police executives chose to operate their organizations essentially as closed systems. The argument was that detachment from the community enhanced professionalism and allowed managers closer control over their officers and better prospects of defending against corruption. Police organizations have not (as a general rule) been totally closed systems, but they have tended to limit input from the environment, community, and other elements of the criminal justice system, and policing has suffered as a result. It became a professionally remote, internally oriented, and rigid profession concerned more with organizational survival and efficiency than with effectiveness and the needs of communities. The closed-system organizational model is increasingly being rejected by police executives because of its rigidity, impersonality, red tape, employee passivity, and centralized control. It is also representative of organizations that reject creativity, limit communication, and can only be described as ignoring their stakeholders' needs.[27]

It is best to view "pure" open and closed organizations as ideal types at opposite ends of a continuum, and to keep in mind that most real-world police departments can be found, not at the extremes but somewhere on the continuum in between. The characteristics of the open-system organizational model are:

1. Tasks are performed in a constantly changing environment.
2. The members of the organization have specialized knowledge.
3. Internal conflict is resolved within the organization.
4. Task accomplishment, rather than process fulfillment, is the most important thing.
5. Every member of the organization is expected to contribute to the organization.
6. Internal interaction stresses problem solving.
7. Excellence of performance is emphasized.[28]

Systems management challenges police managers to become more aware of the interdependence of all systems in their environment. The open model is not a panacea for the police administrator but is a viable frame of reference, calling for positive integration between the organization and the community.

**Contingency Theory**

We have seen numerous attempts to apply organization theories (scientific, administrative, systems, or human relations) to the managerial process. Some applications of some theories have proven highly effective, others less so. Critiques of each theory abound. Some argue that "principles" are dogmatic and unrealistic. Others say that the human relations approach ignores the reality of the organization. Systems theory is viewed by some as being too esoteric and incomprehensible. There are, of course, truths as well as limitations in each of the theories.

What was needed was an integrated approach to management. Just such an approach appeared in the late 1950s and early 1960s, when Burns and

Stalker released a study of British industry that found that differences in the structure of the firms studied resulted from the type of market served and the nature of the technology used. In some instances, a loose organization proved effective; in other cases, a traditional bureaucracy was found to be effective. The two researchers concluded that neither system could be considered superior in all situations, nor there was any single optimal management system.[29]

In general, contingency theorists concluded that in a stable environment, organizations are more effective if they have detailed procedures and centralized decision-making, while in an unstable environment decentralized organizations (which allow for participation and flexible decision-making and place less emphasis on rules and regulations) do better.[30]

It is evident that the contingency approach is actually a blend of different managerial approaches. Its adherents realize that there is no one best way to manage an organization, motivate people, or orchestrate change. Obviously, then, a specific situation can be productively dealt with by any of a variety of managerial responses.

In summary, a contingency management model consists of the following elements:

1. Environmental driving forces
2. The individual
3. The organization
4. The group/team within the organization

Police managers must become adept at analyzing the relationships between the elements just listed when structuring an organization, developing a motivational program, or creating a task force. The major thrust of the contingency approach is to develop a managerial style that maximizes our knowledge of individual behavior, group dynamics, and their relationship to the organization and the environment. Managerial principles are not abandoned but are applied with intuition and practical judgment when the situation requires.

At the same time, increasing emphasis is being placed on the human resource aspect of management. Today's police manager cannot ignore the fact that both sworn and non-sworn employees have needs that evoke different perceptions, values, and emotional responses. Consequently, increasing attention is being devoted to the human equation both within and outside the police organization. It must be understood that there are no simple conclusions for a police manager when organizational behavior is concerned. The contingency approach is widely accepted by behavioral scientists as a viable approach to assessing and dealing with the numerous interacting processes of the elements that make up the contingency model. The key is to consider behavior in dynamic organizational settings. This theoretical model has been incorporated into the "Situational Leadership" training now being received by many police managers.

## POLICE ORGANIZATIONAL STRUCTURE

Unfortunately, through the years police departments have tested few options for organizational structure other than traditional formal bureaucracies. Typically, these are pyramids in which the majority of the organization members find themselves at the bottom. Implicit in such a structure is the identification

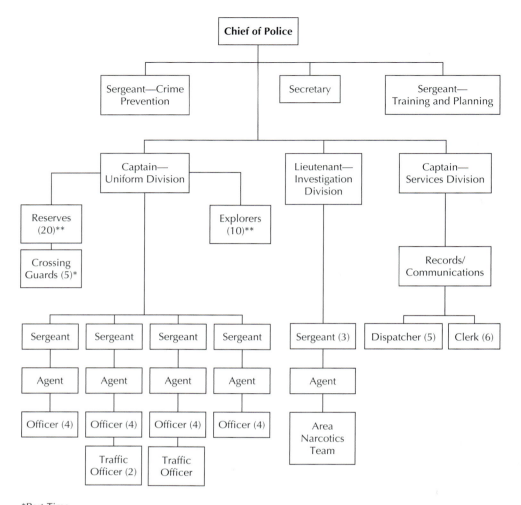

*Part Time
**Volunteers

**Figure 1–2**

Organizational Structure for a Small Police Department.

of those who have power and those who do not (see Figures 1–2 to 1–4). Responsibility is clearly identified by boxes and lines—the higher a box appears in the organization chart, the more knowledgeable and competent the individual occupying that box is presumed to be.

Officers serving in such organizations are rewarded for appropriate behavior with promotions, perks, and fringe benefits that go with the higher positions. All the normal managerial functions such as planning, directing, and controlling are used to direct employee behavior toward the efficient attainment of departmental objectives.

What police executives want is similar to the desire assumed by the classical theorists: to design an organization that will ensure maximum control of both employee behavior and task accomplishment. Organizations design policy and procedural manuals to guide individuals in making appropriate decisions and resolving problems. Although this is a commendable goal, it is seldom attained because of numerous variables and events

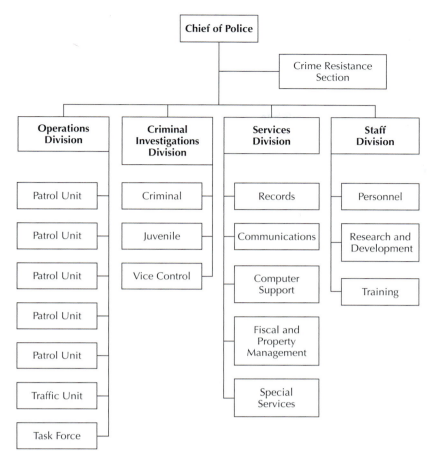

**Figure 1–3**
Organizational Structure for a Medium-Sized Police Department.

that cannot be controlled. People just cannot be fit into boxes or treated as if they were numbers instead of human beings. Many police problems defy predictability. Expertise, training, knowledge, and motivation vary considerably in the many police departments in the United States. In addition, the interaction between individuals in an organization seldom conforms to the rigidity depicted by boxes and lines of authority.

The human equation is forever present. While it might be desirable to always react rationally, it is not always feasible. Emotions enter the picture, and such factors as personality, attitudes, perceptions, power, and group dynamics modify relationships between managers and employees. All these factors influence the decision-making process and alter the organization's response to police problems.

Traditionally, police executives have utilized a number of different approaches to structuring the organization. One approach has been to organize by *major purpose,* such as patrol or traffic, in order to achieve unified control over individuals who are performing similar tasks (see Table 1–2).

A second approach has been to organize by *major process.* Possible examples include the crime laboratory organized to facilitate the examination of evidence

**Types of Organizing**

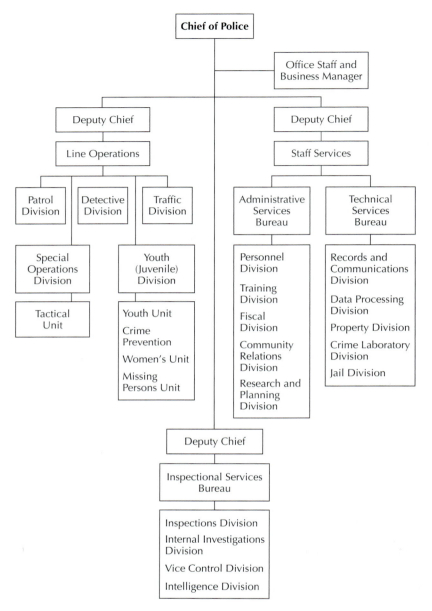

**Figure 1–4**

Organizational Structure for a Large Police Department.

in multiple categories of criminal investigations and the crime analysis unit organized to receive, assemble, evaluate, and analyze data concerning a variety of police problems. It should be pointed out that such function-based organizations often incorporate some aspects of purpose orientation as well.

Another way to organize is by responding to the *clientele* served. Typical of this is the juvenile unit organized to handle all juvenile offenders regardless of age or the crime committed. Foreign language speakers units and narcotics strike forces are other examples of creating special units to deal exclusively with certain groups.

Table 1–2  **Methods of Organizing a Police Department**

Major purpose
Major process
Clientele
Area
Time

The next way to organize is by *area,* or territory. The precinct or district station house has been a part of the large city police organization since Rome created the Vigiles in A.D. 6. This type of organizing was prevalent during the political era, but the centralization efforts of the reform era were aimed in part at eliminating such outposts in order to relieve tax burdens and concentrate on executive control.

The final way of organizing is by *time*. Police departments distribute personnel over three shifts in order to provide around-the-clock operations. The amount, nature, and time of occurrence of offenses supply, in part, the information needed to allocate officers among the shifts.

Executives traditionally used any one of these organizational means, or some combination, in order to provide for the delivery of police service to the community. In recent years, police managers in agencies that operate under a community policing philosophy have sought to decentralize their organizational structure with neighborhood substations. The officers assigned to these substations perform a variety of duties associated with the department's community service efforts. These efforts are a reflection of the transition currently taking place in police management.

## POLICE MANAGEMENT IN TRANSITION

There is general agreement among scholars of policing that American policing has been characterized by three distinct functions throughout its history: controlling crime, maintaining order, and providing services.[31] George L. Kelling and Mark H. Moore, in a 1988 analysis of the strategies used by police management to fulfill these functions, divided the history of policing into three time periods: the political era, the reform era, and the community policing era.[32] They claim that each era has been dominated by a specific strategy. The political era, characterized by the close ties between the police and politics, began in the 1840s and ended during the early part of the 20th century. The reform era that followed arose from a desire to eliminate politics from policing. It lasted in varying degrees until the beginning of the 1980s, when the community policing era began.

**The Political Era**

In the developing American society of the early 19th century, social factors such as violent crime, urban growth, industrialization, immigration, and religious, ethnic and racial violence led to the creation of urban policing systems in the United States. These systems were modeled after the London Metropolitan Police Department, which had been established in 1829 by Sir Robert Peel.[33] However, the Founding Fathers' fear of a strong central government had led them to delegate policing powers to state and local governments. As a

**Table 1–3  Organizational Strategy of the Political Era**

1. Legitimacy and authority were primarily political.
2. Primary functions performed were the control of crime, order maintenance, and numerous social services.
3. Organizationally, police departments were decentralized.
4. Police were intimately connected to the political environment.
5. Demands for police services came from either citizens or politicians.
6. There was extensive use of foot patrol.

result, politics dominated American policing, and departments derived their operational legitimacy and resources from local political parties and politicians. Politicians appointed and dismissed police officers and police chiefs based on party affiliation. The police in turn supported the politicians who appointed them and used whatever means possible to keep them in office.

During the political period, the police were not only actively performing traditional police functions such as crime control, crime prevention, and order maintenance; they also provided an extremely wide range of social services. Leonhard Fuld and Raymond Fosdick both called for the elimination of such functions as running soup kitchens, finding lodging for the needy, collecting taxes, and performing a census. While some of these activities were of a humanitarian nature, they also served as a form of patronage supporting local political authorities.

Nineteenth-century police departments had all the elements of centralized bureaucratic organizations with definite chains of command, but they actually functioned in a decentralized fashion, with each precinct an autonomous unit. (See Table 1–3.) A captain was in command of each precinct, but he owed his position to the local political leader. It was routine for all personnel matters to be cleared with the local politicians.[34] Extensive decentralization and limited organizational control (coupled with the political appointment of officers and managers) led to disenchantment with the police and the role they played in the community. As a result, corruption, inefficiency, political interference, and discriminatory law enforcement characterized policing during this period.[35]

**The Reform Era**   During a period that lasted from the latter part of the 19th century to the first part of the 20th century, politicians and urban reformers were at loggerheads over who would control the police. Abuses of police power were quite common, and the close ties between the police and politicians led to a great deal of corruption.[36] The first attempts to reform the police, led by late-19th-century municipal government reformers outside the police field, failed. Not until the early 20th century were police administrators who wanted policing to be a respected profession actually able to alter the course of policing in the United States.[37]

The first great police reformer of this movement was August Vollmer (1876–1955), the police chief in Berkeley, California. His efforts were carried on by his protégé O. W. Wilson (1900–1972), who through his books on police administration became the primary administrative architect of the movement to professionalize policing. Wilson's organizational perspective was similar to that of the classical theorists. He supported strong managerial control, a centralized command structure, hierarchical organizational structures, specialization of tasks, and operational efficiency. He developed and recommended to police executives nine principles of organizational management:

1. Tasks similar in purpose, method, or clientele should be grouped together in one or more units under the control of a single person.
2. Duties should be defined precisely and made known to all members of the organization so that responsibility can be placed exactly.
3. Channels of communication should be established so that information can flow up and down within the organization and authority can be delegated.
4. The principle of unity of command (one boss) must be applied.
5. Executive spans of control should be limited.
6. Each task should be assigned to a member of the organization.
7. Line personnel must be supervised around the clock.
8. Each assignment of responsibility carries with it a commensurate authority.
9. Persons to whom authority is delegated are held accountable for its use.[38]

As the reform movement came into its own, politics was rejected as the source of legitimacy and authorization. In a few cities, the position of police chief was placed under the civil service. In other cities, the police department's chief executive officer was given lifetime tenure and could only be removed for cause. The purpose of all such changes was to isolate the police from political influence. As a result, law enforcement agencies became the most autonomous public departments in urban government.[39]

This movement established crime control as the primary police function, considerably changing the role of the police. In short order, any proposed police tasking associated with community order maintenance was rejected. The reformers' approach to management and organizational administration was similar to that suggested by the work of Max Weber and Frederick W. Taylor. Management implemented programs linked to economic rewards that, in turn, increased productivity. In addition, principles of division of labor and unity of command became the vogue, and specialization was supported along with hierarchical control. Attempts were made to develop standard policy and procedures in order to reduce officer discretion.

During this era, police administrators sought to enhance their organizations' professional status by narrowing their functions to those associated with scientific investigation and crime control. When special community problems occurred, police management responded by creating special-purpose elements such as tactical patrol units and organized-crime control units. This weakened the patrol function but centralized managerial control. The desire to control the discretionary activities of officers led to structural changes such as additional management layers that shortened spans of control and allowed closer supervision. Meticulous record keeping was emphasized, and the chain of command became the officially preferred channel for communication.[40]

The professional model of law enforcement dominated policing, and citizens became passive recipients of crime-control services. Kelling and Moore placed this in perspective by observing, "The metaphor that expressed this orientation to the community was that of the police as the *thin blue line*." Table 1–4 summarizes the organizational strategy of the reform movement.[41]

**Table 1–4**   **Organizational Strategy of the Reform Era**

1. The authorization for the police was the law, and it was implemented by the professional model.
2. The primary function was crime control.
3. Organizationally, the police were centralized and emphasis was placed on bureaucratic control.
4. Their relationship with the community was characterized as professionally remote.
5. The demands for police service were channeled through central dispatching.

In retrospect, the reform movement can be seen to have swept the country. It made sense that the primary task of the police was to fight crime. Professional law enforcement aimed to avoid the pitfalls of the political era by reducing discretion, providing police services in an impartial manner, and enhancing managerial control over political control. While this model seemed to be effective during the 1940s and 1950s, it was found less than adequate during the subsequent decades.

During the 1960s and 1970s, the United States underwent a series of social changes that altered the relationship between government and citizens. The civil rights and due process movements, followed by the antiwar protests, challenged the way the police handled riots, marches, rallies, and citizens' constitutional rights. Television watchers saw minorities and demonstrators gassed, clubbed, and attacked by dogs, and police tactics and interrogation procedures were brought into disrepute.[42]

Other changes were just as significant. During the 1980s, researchers determined that the fear of crime was more closely correlated with disorder than with crime.[43] Unfortunately, order maintenance had been downplayed for years. In fact, few departments collected data on "disorderly" offenses; police management did not train officers to handle such activities, nor did they reward officers for successfully performing order-maintenance activities. The focus was on serious crime, not on offenses that created disorderly neighborhoods.

The professional reform movement resulted in police managers becoming increasingly remote from line personnel. The problem was management style. While professionalism was the key word of the reform era, it did not extend to the lowest level of the organization, the patrol officer. Management maintained the fiction that the total organization was designed to support patrol, but such was not the case. The reality of the situation was that management continually tried to control the behavior of patrol officers. The police bureaucracy stifled initiative, and everything had to be done by the procedural manual. This perspective even extended to personal conduct of the officer off duty. Specific rules and regulations were developed to ensure compliance with departmental policy. In many agencies any assignment except patrol was eagerly sought after, and over time, patrol was performed by the youngest, most inexperienced officers and those who had been reassigned back to it as punishment for rule violations. In fact, it became a dumping ground in many departments.[44]

**The Community Policing Era**

Beginning in the 1980s, police administrators who were not satisfied with prevalent police service delivery models began to experiment with different operational approaches. These efforts drew financial support from the National Institute of Justice, the Police Foundation, the Police Executive Research Foundation, and the Charles Stewart Mott Foundation. Departments resurrected the

Seattle Mayor Paul Schell introduces Police Chief Gil Kerlikowske (left) during a press conference. Both men said they were pleased to announce that crime overall in the city had dropped by 10 percent, with dramatic declines in both murder and theft, down 10 percent and 15 percent, respectively

Associated Press

strategy of foot patrol, involving decentralization of patrol units and an emphasis on community outreach and problem solving. In some of these experiments it was found that citizen fear of victimization was reduced and citizen satisfaction with the police was enhanced; on the police side, attitudes toward the public improved and officers found that foot patrol was both personally and professionally rewarding.[45]

During this time the term *community policing* came into use, implying a partnership between the police and the people they serve. This partnership is designed to improve the quality of life in a community by introducing strategies designed to enhance neighborhood solidarity and safety. Community policing envisioned that the police through a variety of strategies could work closely with citizens of a community to address issues of crime and social disorganization. The police discovered that citizens responded positively when asked about their priorities and concerns with crime and disorder. This in turn led to the police obtaining valuable information and, in some instances, identified problems that were unknown to the police.

Community policing encourages police departments to develop a close bond between the patrol officer and the community. Officers are urged to get to know the citizens on their beats, to understand their needs, habits, and wishes. The underlying assumption is that the police must be truly able to relate to a community in order to understand its problems and offer creative responses. Community policing is the actualization of the concept that in a democracy the police are not supposed to be insular, self-contained, or cut off from the communities from which their power is derived.[46]

Community policing encouraged police departments to adopt proactive strategies and tactics in order to repress crime, fear, and disorder within neighborhoods. In return, community members were expected to take a proactive

Table 1–5 **Organizational Strategy of the Community Policing Era**

1. The authority for this strategy stems from community support, law, and professionalism.
2. The control and prevention of crime are considered the major functions of the police.
3. The organizational design emphasizes decentralization and the use of task forces.
4. This period is characterized by a consultative relationship with the community.
5. Community policing tactics include foot patrol, problem solving, information gathering, counseling, and education.

role in helping the police and other government entities set and implement community-oriented policy. The goal was for citizens, through this exchange process, to have input in setting organizational goals and objectives as well as in establishing priorities for action. In principle, each community or neighborhood should be policed in accordance with neighborhood needs and values.[47] In its ideal form, community policing envisions police assignments and strategies being set in accordance with local needs, norms, and values. This decentralized approach to operational strategy is assumed to provide citizens with protection that is tailored to meet the needs of diverse communities (see Table 1–5).

In contrast to the traditional bureaucratic model, community policing shifts the focus of police work from handling random calls for service to the resolution of community problems.[48] In essence, community policing places more responsibility on the department. Agencies committed to community policing must perform their traditional duties of law enforcement, order maintenance, and service as well as attempt to solve local problems. The police function is expanded to include a proactive response to maintaining order, dealing with quality-of-life offenses, and fixing "broken windows." All of these add to the complexity of the police role in society.[49]

In sum, community policing is not just a program but an operational and organizational philosophy designed to promote police-citizen, community-based problem solving. This problem-confronting approach contradicts many of the key features of the reform era. Foot patrol creates a closer relationship between officers and members of the community. Problem solving was found to be totally foreign to previous efforts by police management to standardize the tasks performed by patrol officers. Lastly, relying on citizen endorsement of order maintenance (as a means of justifying police activities) acknowledges dependence on the political process and the broadening of the police function.[50]

During the latter part of the 20th century, many police departments, encouraged by federal funding, decentralized a portion of their patrol resources into community-oriented operations. Ideally, community policing is a bottom-up strategy that places emphasis on the police officer's ability to use information, judgment, wisdom, and expertise. Simultaneously, it encourages police administrators to actively engage their external environment and develop strategies to address threats and opportunities the community is facing. In this way, community policing represents a significant shift in organizational power and control, from administration to operations and from closed- to open-system organizations.[51]

This organizational shift requires that police management adopt a new strategic and flexible leadership style in organizations that have traditionally exercised centralized command-and-control management.[52] The police management culture that emerged out of the reform era emphasizes adherence to internal rules and procedures and promotes efficiency rather than effectiveness. However, research has found that the process of organizational change needed to support this philosophy and make community-oriented strategies work is often incomplete.[53] In many police departments community policing is the responsibility of an organizational subunit, not the whole department. For example, the Office of Justice programs reported that 65 percent of departments serving 50,000 or more residents indicate that they have a full-time community policing unit responsible for this activity.[54]

Community policing, for all its support by the national government, has never fully achieved what its advocates hoped it would. Today, almost every specialized program developed by a police department is labeled community policing. While many police departments claim they are engaged in some form of community policing, the majority of them are still bureaucratically structured and delivering their services based on the strategies of the reform era–bureaucratic model of policing.[55]

## CompStat

As community policing evolved to become the dominant police organizational philosophy in the latter part of the 20th century, a debate emerged regarding what is the appropriate way for police managers to direct their organizations' service delivery function. Some administrators favored the traditional bureaucratic model of the reform era, with its emphasis on efficiency and organizational control. Others believed that community and/or problem-oriented policing was a more appropriate way of addressing the needs of the nation's diverse communities for public safety. However, voices of doubt were raised by others who questioned the ability of community policing strategies to achieve their stated objectives of community stability.[56]

In the last decade of the 20th century, there emerged in New York City a group of police executives who proposed that crime prevention, order maintenance, and community safety are the products of integrated problem solving, strategy development, and intense managerial oversight of the entire organizational process.[57] William Bratton, then New York City Police Commissioner, together with his command staff developed a goal-oriented strategic management process that uses information technology, operational strategy, and managerial accountability to effectively control crime and police communities. This process evolved out of the weekly Crime Control Strategy meetings the New York City Police Department began holding in January 1994 as a means to increase the flow of information between the agency's executives and the commanders of operational units. These meetings placed particular emphasis on the dissemination and analysis of crime and quality-of-life enforcement information. Bratton and his command staff designed these CompStat (for "computer statistics") meetings as a way to make his 76 precinct commanders and their officers accountable for the crime rate. During these meetings, CompStat combined a comprehensive, continuous analysis of current crime with strategy development and assessment.

Computer technologies allow for the mapping of crime patterns and of causal relationships among different crime categories. This information is disseminated to operational managers in periodic CompStat reports that contain crime complaints and arrest activity at the precinct, patrol borough, and city-wide levels, as well as concise summaries of these and other important performance indicators. During these meetings, crime patterns and selected strategies are discussed and analyzed, results are evaluated, and resources allocated. CompStat has transformed the NYPD from a reactive organization that settled for the status quo to a vigorous, motivated police department that works actively to achieve its mission. Operational managers are held accountable for addressing the crime and disorder issues and trends associated with the CompStat Report's data for their areas. Under CompStat, operational managers are empowered to focus, manage, and direct their units' problem-solving process. Traditional, community, and problem-oriented policing strategies are integral parts of their operational tactics. A principal objective of the CompStat process is not just to displace crime but to reduce it and create a permanent change in the community.[58]

The underlying principle of CompStat is that police officers and police agencies can have a substantial positive impact on crime and the problems facing the communities they serve. The program challenges police executives and managers to take a different approach to the way they manage police organizations and police activities. It is radically different from the accepted concepts and practices that have guided police administrators through most of their history, and it points to new methods and strategies police agencies can use to fulfill their mission. CompStat emphasizes the vital link between command accountability, information, operational decision-making, and crime-control objectives. However, its impact extends far beyond crime fighting; it is a management process that can adapt to constantly changing conditions and can be applied in any organizational setting.[59]

To date, CompStat has been deemed by some the single most successful crime-fighting management tool in the nation. The New York City Police Department is credited with turning the city around from a place that once represented the ultimate in urban lawlessness into a city now safer than the 23 other largest cities in the United States. Police statistics for New York City indicate that since NYPD changed its operational strategy in 1994, major crime in New York City has dropped by 43 percent; murder has dropped by 60 percent. In 1996, CompStat won the prestigious *Innovations in American Government* award from the Ford Foundation and the John F. Kennedy School of Government. CompStat is in the process of being replicated by a number of police departments around the nation.

Emerging from this process is a new police strategic leadership model, similar to models found in business organizations. This leadership style—built around vision, mission, values, goals, engagement, empowerment, accountability, outcomes, and evaluation—represents a change in how police organizational managers conceive of their departments. The police executives exercising this style are a new kind of strategic leaders; they proactively develop and implement organizational directions that allow their departments to successfully initiate and reshape their activities in order to effectively meet the demands of their operational environments. Through this process, each strategic leader seeks to align his or her external and internal environments in order to fulfill the organization's mission. They are creating open-system adaptive-learning organizations.[60]

At the heart of this new strategic police management process are the following basic tasks:

1. The chief executive creates a *strategic vision* that motivates the organization with a sense of purposeful action toward accomplishment of the basic mission and functions of the department. The purpose of a strategic vision is to provide long-term direction to the organization and its members.

2. Senior management sets performance objectives—translating the strategic vision into *specific performance outcomes* for the organization to achieve. The emphasis is on outcomes, not outputs.

3. The organization develops a process of *information gathering, analysis, and dissemination* that provides operational managers with the timely information they need to make informed decisions.

4. Senior management fixes managerial *accountability* for the development of plans, strategies, and the accomplishment of results.

5. Operational managers *craft a strategy* to achieve desired outcomes.

6. Operational managers *implement and execute* the chosen strategy efficiently and effectively.

7. Managers at all levels *evaluate performance,* initiating corrective adjustments in vision, long-term direction, objectives, strategy, or implementation in light of actual experiences, changing conditions, new ideas, and new opportunities.

Whether this new strategic management process will have a long-term effect on crime rates remains to be empirically tested. Creating responsive and effective police organizations will require organizational changes that demand more than quick adaptations and limited structural changes. A properly designed CompStat process will establish accountability at all managerial levels of the organization under the direction of the executive staff and will focus the entire organization on the department's mission. Thus CompStat, by involving the whole organization, can go far beyond the incremental structural changes that occurred during the adaptation of community policing, while retaining an organizational leadership style similar to those established during Sir Robert Peel's police reform of 1829 and the American professional reform movements of 1930–1970. Time will tell whether CompStat is the appropriate method that police executives should adopt to govern their departments and provide public-safety services.

## SUMMARY

Police management as we know it today is the result of an evolutionary process nearly two centuries old. Many of the early management theorists relied on military and religious models. Other theories were developed in business and industry and later were adopted by the police field. These theories include ideal bureaucracy, scientific management, functional management (including POSDCORB), human relations, systems, and contingency management.

During the early part of the 20th century, police departments in the United States were at the focal point of numerous pressure groups that worked diligently to control the police. During this political period, the police provided not only traditional police services but also a wide range of social services that included collecting taxes, running soup kitchens, exercising census responsibilities, and finding lodging for the needy.

Disenchantment with political control of the police and the resulting widespread corruption led to the reform era in which the goal was to isolate the police from political influence. Services that could be described as social work were eliminated, and the primary goal of the police became enforcement of the law. Professionalism became the dominant cry of the reformers, and every effort was made to reduce officer discretion and provide services in an impartial manner.

The reform movement dominated the police scene during the 1940s and 1950s, but during the following decades a series of social changes altered the relationship of the police with the public. The civil rights and antiwar movements challenged the way the police handled marches, disorders, riots, and rallies. There was a cry for police review boards; television watchers saw minorities and demonstrators gassed, clubbed, and attacked by dogs, and police tactics were brought into disrepute. The reform movement resulted in the police becoming detached from the communities they served.

Today's approach is called community policing. It contradicts many of the key features of professionalism advocated during the reform era. Under the community approach, crime control remains as one of the functions of law enforcement, but equal consideration is also given to order maintenance, conflict resolution, problem solving, and the provision of services. Officers at every level become involved in the decision-making process, and input from members of the community is actively sought. Under this concept, officers are assigned to a specific beat for an extended period to conduct crime-control meetings, engage in problem-solving activities, and work diligently to improve the relationship between the police and the public.

However, through the years police departments have preferred to organize themselves bureaucratically, by structuring their organization according to major purpose, major process, clientele, area, and time. The dominance of the bureaucratic organizational model in policing, with its control-oriented management culture, has resulted in a limited adoption of community policing by many police departments.

In the latter part of the 20th century, a new strategic management process called CompStat was created by the New York City Police Department. This process is currently being adopted by many police agencies in the United States and Europe. How this process will affect policing remains to be empirically tested.

## KEY TERMS

bureaucracy
community policing era
CompStat
contingency management model
functional management
Hawthorne effect
line and staff
organizing by area

organizing by clientele
organizing by time
political era
POSDCORB
reform era
scientific management
strategic management tasks
systems theory

## DISCUSSION TOPICS AND QUESTIONS

1. What were the classical school theorists trying to accomplish?
2. What are the characteristics of a bureaucracy?
3. What are the limitations of a bureaucracy?
4. List Henri Fayol's elements of management.
5. Describe the findings of the Hawthorne studies.
6. How would you apply the open organization model to a typical medium-sized police department?
7. What are O. W. Wilson's nine principles of management?
8. What are the distinguishing features of a CompStat organization?
9. How are police departments organized?

## FOR FURTHER READING

Vincent Henry, *The Paradigm: Management Accountability in Policing, Business and the Public Sector* (Flushing, NY: Looseleaf Law Publications, 2002).

Henry provides a detailed analysis of how CompStat operates and its potential applicability to other departments and businesses.

George L. Kelling and Catherine M. Coles, *Fixing Broken Windows: Restoring Order & Reducing Crime in Our Communities* (New York: The Free Press, 1996).

Kelling and Coles provide examples of the implementation of "Broken Windows" theory in different locales and departments. They offer a clear presentation of the difficulties and promises of this approach.

**Eli Silverman, *NYPD Battles Crime: Innovative Strategies in Policing* (New York: Northeastern University Press, 1999).**

Silverman's analysis of the CompStat process places it firmly in the history of reform efforts in the New York City Police Department. It provides a broad context of how CompStat is aligned in the timeline of police administration.

# NOTES

1. Hal G. Rainey, *Understanding & Managing Public Organizations* (San Francisco: Jossey-Bass, 1997), p. 29.

2. Max Weber, *The Theory of Social and Economic Organization* (New York: The Free Press, 1947), pp. 329–341.

3. H.H. Gerth and C. Wright Mills, *Max Weber, Essays in Sociology* (New York: Oxford University Press, 1946), pp. 196–224.

4. V.A. Leonard and Harry W. More, *Police Organization and Management* (Mineola, NY: Foundation Press, 2000).

5. Herman Goldstein, *Problem-Oriented Policing* (New York: McGraw-Hill, 1990).

6. David Osborne and Peter Plastrik, *Banishing Bureaucracy: The Five Strategies for Reinventing Government* (New York: Addison-Wesley, 1997).

7. Gareth Morgan, *Images of Organization* (Thousand Oaks, CA: Sage, 1997), pp. 22–26.

8. Frederick W. Taylor, *Principles of Scientific Management* (New York: Harper & Row, 1911).

9. Roy R. Roberg, Jack Kuykendall, and Kenneth Novak, *Police Management* (Los Angeles: Roxbury, 2002), p. 25.

10. Claude S. George, Jr., *The History of Management Thought* (Englewood Cliffs, NJ: Prentice Hall, 1968).

11. Henri Fayol, "General Principles of Management," in Jay M. Shafrits and J. Steven Ott, eds. *Classics of Organization Theory* (Pacific Grove, CA: Brooks/Cole, 1992).

12. Thomas A. Reppetto, *The Blue Parade* (New York: The Free Press, 1978), p. 156.

13. Leonhard F. Fuld, *Police Administration* (New York: Putnam, 1910).

14. Raymond B. Fosdick, *American Police Systems* (Montclair, NJ: Patterson Smith, 1969).

15. Elmer D. Graper, *American Police Administration* (New York: Macmillan, 1921).

16. Luther Gulick, "Notes on the Theory of Organization," in Luther Gulick and Lyndall Urwick, eds. *Papers on the Science of Administration* (New York: Institute of Public Administration, 1937), pp. 3–31.

17. James J. Fyfe, Jack R. Greene, William F. Walsh, O.W. Wilson, and Roy C. McLaren, *Police Administration* (New York: McGraw-Hill, 1997), p. 13.

18. Evan M. Berman, James S. Bowman, Jonathan P. West, and Montgomery Van Wart, *Human Resource Management in Public Service* (Thousand Oaks, CA: Sage, 2001), p. 13.

19. John W. Newstrom and Keith Davis, *Organizational Behavior: Human Behavior at Work* (New York: McGraw-Hill, 1993), p. 273.

20. F.J. Roethlisberger and William Dickson, *Management and the Worker* (Cambridge, MA: Harvard University Press, 1939).

21. Gary Dessler, *A Framework for Human Resource Management* (Upper Saddle River, NJ: Prentice Hall, 2004), p. 4.

22. Morgan, *Images of Organization*, p. 13.

23. Daniel Katz and Robert L. Kahn, *The Social Psychology of Organizations* (New York: John Wiley & Sons, 1966), pp. 14–29.

24. Peter M. Senge, *The Fifth Discipline: The Art & Practice of the Learning Organization* (New York: Doubleday, 1990).

25. Rainey, *Understanding & Managing Public Organizations*, pp. 28–29.

26. David K. Banner and T. Elaine Gagne, *Designing Effective Organizations: Traditional & Transformational Views* (Thousand Oaks, CA: Sage, 1995).

27. Ronald W. Glensor, Mark E. Correia, and Kenneth J. Peak, *Policing Communities: Understanding Crime and Solving Problems* (Los Angeles: Roxbury, 2000).

28. Tom Burns and G.M. Staler, *Management of Innovation* (London: Tavistock, 1961).

29. Banner and Gagne, *Designing Effective Organizations*, pp. 159–160.

30. Morgan, *Images of Organization*, pp. 44–50.

31. Jihong S. Zhao, Ni He, and Nicholas P. Lovrich, "Community Policing: Did It Change the Basic

Functions of Policing in the 1990s? A National Follow-Up," *Justice Quarterly,* Vol. 20 (2003), pp. 697–724.

32. George L. Kelling and Mark H. Moore, *The Evolving Strategy of Policing* (Perspectives on Policing, Washington, DC: National Institute of Justice, 1988).

33. Fyfe, Greene, Walsh, Wilson, and McLaren, *Police Administration,* p. 10.

34. Erik H. Monkkonen, *Police in America—1860–1920* (Cambridge, England: Cambridge University Press, 1981) and James F. Richardson, *Urban Police in United States* (Port Washington, NY: National University Publications, 1974).

35. Kelling and Moore, *Evolving Strategy of Policing.*

36. Mark H. Haller, "Historical Roots of Police Behavior, Chicago 1890–1925," *Law and Society Review,* Vol. 10 (1976), pp. 303–323.

37. Reppetto, *The Blue Parade,* pp. 93–114.

38. O.W. Wilson and Roy Clinton McLaren, *Police Administration* (New York: McGraw-Hill, 1972).

39. Herman Goldstein, *Policing in a Free Society* (Cambridge, MA: Ballinger, 1977).

40. George L. Kelling and William J. Bratton, *Implementing Community Policing: The Administrative Problem* (Perspectives on Policing, Washington, DC: National Institute of Justice, 1993).

41. Kelling and Moore, *Evolving Strategy of Policing.*

42. Fyfe, Greene, Walsh, Wilson, and McLaren, *Police Administration,* pp. 16–18.

43. William Spelman and Dale K. Brown, *Calling the Police: Reporting of Serious Crime* (Washington, DC: PERF, 1981) and George L. Kelling, *Police and Communities: The Quiet Revolution* (Perspective on Policing, Washington, DC: National Institute of Justice, 1988).

44. Malcolm K. Sparrow, Mark H. Moore, and David M. Kennedy, *Beyond 911: A New Era for Policing* (New York: Basic Books, 1990), pp. 3–125.

45. Robert Tojanowicz and Bonnie Bucqueroux, *Community Policing: A Contemporary Perspective* (Cincinnati: Anderson, 1990).

46. J.H. Skolnick, "On Democratic Policing," *Ideas in American Policing* (Washington, DC: Police Foundation, 1999).

47. George L. Kelling and Catherine M. Coles, *Fixing Broken Windows: Restoring Order & Reducing Crime in Our Communities* (New York: The Free Press, 1996).

48. Kenneth J. Peak and Ronald W. Glensor, *Community Policing and Problem Solving: Strategies and Practices* (Upper Saddle River, NJ: Prentice Hall, 2002).

49. Herman Goldstein, *The New Policing: Confronting Complexity* (Washington, DC: National Institute of Justice, 1993).

50. Kelling and Moore, *Evolving Strategy of Policing.*

51. Peak and Glensor, *Community Policing and Problem Solving: Strategies and Practices.*

52. Mark H. Moore and Darryl Stephens, *Beyond Command and Control: The Strategic Management of Police Departments* (Police Executive Research Forum, Washington, DC, 1991).

53. Zhao, He, and Lovrich, "Community Policing: A National Follow-Up," pp. 697–724.

54. B. Reaves and A. Goldberg, *Local Police Departments 1997* (U.S. Department of Justice, Office of Justice Programs, Washington, DC, 2000), p. 16.

55. Jack R. Greene and Stephen Mastrofski, eds. *Community Policing: Rhetoric or Reality* (Prager, New York, 1988); Howard Safir, "Goal-Oriented Community Policing: The NYPD Approach." *The Police Chief* (December 1997), pp. 31–58; and Wesley Skogan, *Disorder and Decline: Crime and the Spiral of Decay in American Neighborhoods* (New York: Free Press, 1990).

56. William Bratton with Peter Knobler, *Turnaround* (New York: Random House, 1998) and Jack Maple with Chris Mitchell, *The Crime Fighter: Putting the Bad Guys Out of Business* (New York: Doubleday, 1999).

57. Vincent Henry, *The CompStat Paradigm: Management Accountability in Policing, Business and the Public Sector* (Flushing, NY: Looseleaf Law Publications, 2002); and Eli Silverman, *NYPD Battles Crime: Innovative Strategies in Policing* (New York: Northeastern University Press, 1999).

58. Silverman, *NYPD Battles Crime.*

59. William F. Walsh, "CompStat: An Analysis of an Emerging Police Managerial Paradigm," *Policing: An International Journal of Police Strategies & Management,* Vol. 24 (2001), pp. 347–362.

60. Senge, *The Fifth Discipline,* p. 13.

# DYNAMICS OF MANAGEMENT

## Managers and Organizational Behavior

## LEARNING OBJECTIVES

1. Identify the elements of the police managerial process.
2. Define *management*.
3. Identify and describe the four management functions.
4. Identify and describe the three levels of organizational management.
5. Describe how middle managers influence their organizations.
6. Explain the difference between line and staff managers.
7. Describe the skills managers use to achieve their objectives.

8. List the competing role expectations managers face in the workplace.
9. Identify the manager's role in the CompStat process.
10. Define what is meant by organizational behavior.
11. Identify the four types of behavior with which a police manager should be concerned.
12. Compare individual and interpersonal behavior.

Police departments are government organizations that are created to provide public safety for defined jurisdictional areas such as towns, boroughs, cities, counties, or states. The Justice Department's Bureau of Justice Statistics reported in 2000 that there were nearly 800,000 full-time sworn law enforcement officers serving in a total of 17,784 state and local police departments in the United States.[1] Police officers are responsible for safeguarding lives and property, maintaining the quality of community life, and protecting the constitutional rights of everyone, regardless of political or social persuasion. They fulfill this mission by providing a variety of services that include responding to emergency calls for service, preventing crime, rendering first-responder aid, enforcing laws and ordinances, resolving disputes, regulating traffic, investigating criminal events, and arresting violators. A police department's chief executive and his or her management team are expected to provide organizational direction and performance oversight in order to achieve the department's mission in an

In a large metropolitan police department, two sergeants were promoted to lieutenant at the same time and both were assigned to field operations. Within six months, Lt. Marge Smits proved to be a very competent and effective manager. Unfortunately, Lt. Roger Miles was less than successful. Upper management is becoming genuinely concerned about Lt. Miles's inability to function as a manager. Capt. William Proctor is completing six-month reviews for each of the lieutenants and is truly perplexed about this situation. Both officers had performed outstandingly in their former positions, but Smits has risen to the challenge of her new position while Miles demonstrates an inability to adjust to his.

Lt. Smits finds that the demands of her new position contrast sharply with what was expected of her when she was a sergeant. When she was a first-line supervisor, she was expected to function as an operational expert, leaving command or managerial decisions to upper management. Smits views her role as something entirely different than anything she has ever done; she relishes the interaction with the personnel she supervises and the challenge of accomplishing goals and objectives through others. On assuming her new job, she immediately reviewed the personnel files for each of the officers in her unit and became familiar with their knowledge, skills, and abilities. Utilizing this information, she has little difficulty in attaining unit objectives, starting to identify individual weaknesses, and working with employees in order to improve their performance. When officers successfully accomplish assignments, they are given immediate feedback as she works diligently to improve her coaching skills and provide positive leadership.

Roger Miles, who had an exceptional record in his previous position, is clearly lost as a lieutenant. His primary concern is to scrutinize every officer's performance to such an extent that he can always find an error or omission. In each instance, the officer is made aware of inadequate performance. Lt. Miles intensifies his supervision style by paying careful attention to every incident and report. Nothing is too small to correct. As a result, unit objectives fall by the wayside; intensive supervision dominates the relationship between Lt. Miles and the officers in the unit. Errors are not tolerated because Miles believes that they reflect poorly on his leadership skills. Lt. Miles personifies the "See Me" syndrome where subordinates find their mailboxes filled with memos asking for further information or clarification. The officers have reached the point where it seems to be more important to respond to memos than to perform police work.

Lt. Smits is clearly functioning as a manager. Lt. Miles is performing as a technician. Obviously, Capt. Proctor prefers the former. Management is a unique activity requiring the application of distinct skills. Lt. Miles feels comfortable performing tasks best done by first-line supervisors. The situation in which Lt. Miles finds himself is typical. It continually challenges managers such as Capt. Proctor. This is a dilemma that demands a solution.

Capt. Proctor expects Lt. Miles to accomplish departmental goals through the officers he is supervising and to refrain from performing non-managerial tasks. What should Capt. Proctor do to get Lt. Miles to perform as a manager? Some managers feel this is "Who Wants to Be a Millionaire?" question—one that is easy to ask but difficult to resolve. Our purpose here is to help you understand why such leadership problems arise, how they can be analyzed, and what techniques are available to resolve the problems.

To understand why an employee does not perform at the assignment level (or performs inadequately) will probably require a manager not only to view the employee as an individual but also to examine his or her relationship to the group and the organization.

*In this instance, does Lt. Miles have the necessary skills to perform as a manager? Has he been trained? Does he need additional resources to accomplish his job? While these questions do not address every aspect of why Lt. Miles performs as he does, they illustrate the complexity of problems a manager encounters.*

*This case focuses on the reality of how and what occurs in an organization. Employees adapt to their position differently, and it is evident that a police manager must learn to deal with human behavior effectively.*

effective and efficient manner. The direction and oversight are accomplished through a process that involves the following managerial activities:

1. Development of a departmental mission, vision, organizational goals, and operational objectives.
2. Creation of strategic, operational, procedural, tactical, and budgetary plans.

3. Creation of an organizational structure focused on ensuring fulfillment of mission and performance objectives.

4. Employment of a leadership direction and style that, while focused on mission fulfillment, will also achieve willing compliance and support from employees of the department and members of the community.

5. Controlling and assessing departmental activities through measurement, evaluation, and—when necessary—redirection.

6. Ensuring that all members of the department are competent and adhere to the highest standards of integrity and ethics.

The importance of this managerial process cannot be underestimated. It is hard to imagine any department operating effectively without it.

Police departments are characterized by authority relationships and by a division of labor that, depending on their size, can be simple or complex. Research has consistently found that police work influences the behavior of those who perform it.[2] Through their daily work, officers can develop a sense of pride, belonging, and accomplishment, or they can experience hostility, anger, stress, and frustration. Organizational design and management styles can enhance, limit, or inhibit employee coordination, cooperation, and mission fulfillment.[3] However, managers must understand the effects of individual behavior on their organization as well as the impact of the organization on individual and group behavior. The more managers understand their role and the impact of human behavior in the work setting, the more effective they will be at achieving organizational objectives.

Police managers are becoming increasingly aware of the need to understand human behavior in the workplace. Through the study of organizational behavior, they can begin to understand not only why organizations are such complex entities but how their behavior as managers and their interaction with their officers can affect the organization.

## MANAGEMENT DEFINED

A manager is a person who plans, organizes, leads, and controls the work of others so that the organization achieves its goals.[4] The manager serves the critical function of linking the organization's mission, its desired goals, and its operational accomplishment. In this text, *management* is defined as *a continuing process that includes all activities focusing on the identification, refinement, and attainment of objectives by the effective application of resources.*

This definition is dynamic and is based on the fundamental concept that positive management of a police organization is the only way of maximizing the effectiveness of resources, both human and technical, to achieve departmental goals. It defines the concept of managing in terms of what managers *do*.

**Management Functions**

Our definition of management can be accepted and understood much more readily through an understanding of the responsibilities of a manager. The primary purpose of all managers is to achieve results effectively and efficiently through the individuals under their command. In addition to achieving performance results, the police manager is also responsible for the manner in which these results are achieved. The sensitivity of the police role, in a democratic society with its legal constraints on police use of authority, means that the method used is as important as the ends achieved. Accountability for the conduct of subordinates is such an important managerial function that it is usually clearly defined in department manuals and guidelines.

Four primary functions clearly represent the types of activities managers engage in to fulfill the responsibilities of their positions. These basic functions include planning, organizing, leading, and controlling. The time spent on each activity will vary, depending on the managerial level within the organization. However, these functions are part of all managerial levels, and they must be performed to some degree on a continuing basis if the department is to function effectively.

1. *Planning*. A plan is the careful development of activities to achieve desired goals or control projected conditions.[5] Planning involves the translation of mission, vision, and unit goals into specific operational objectives and the identification of the resources needed to achieve these objectives. It is a problem-prevention as well as problem-solving activity that prepares the department for the future. Police departments operate in demanding and changing environments. They cannot function effectively if they strive to consistently maintain the status quo or if, because of a lack of planning, they must continually respond to one crisis after another. Police managers must be aware of and evaluate external and internal environmental forces affecting their departments. Managers plan in order to develop strategies and methods for addressing the demands placed on their organizations. However, plans cannot be etched in granite; they must be continually evaluated and altered to meet changing conditions.

One plan will not accomplish all things. Police departments develop a variety of plans that address issues associated with operational control, procedural requirements, tactical strategies, fiscal accountability, personnel allocation, and managerial projects. Planning is an organizational necessity that must be strongly supported by the police executive if it is to be effectively supported throughout the department. It allows the manager to answer the following questions:

1. What should be done?
2. When should it be done?
3. How should it be done?
4. Who should do it?

2. *Organizing*. The organizing and coordinating function of management involves the structuring of an organization and the deployment of resources designed to achieve the organization's goals and objectives. Management organizes to achieve the alignment of strategy, structure, process, information systems, reward systems, employees, and operational service delivery.[6] Organizing is necessary in order to establish accountability, distribute the department's workload logically, and create a mission-focused, unified organizational effort.

In policing, the decision to group related activities usually takes into consideration such variables as the major purpose of the activity or function, the services demanded, the process or method to be utilized to achieve objectives, the nature of the clientele, the geographical distribution, and time. Most of these factors operate simultaneously. A well-organized department acts as a unified team, with each unit focused on mission accomplishment and service to the community.

3. *Leading*. Managerial leadership is the ability to influence others to perform their duties willingly. It is the essential function for the achievement of a department's mission, goals, and objectives. Leadership must be provided by all managers at all levels of the police agency. Managers are ultimately judged

by the quality of their leadership as reflected in the performance of their subordinates. The complexity of relationships between managers and police officers requires unique insight and a special awareness of individuals, groups, and the needs of the department. Leaders must have an understanding of their department's driving forces, resources, and positive motivational factors (not fear). Leadership is a social contract predicated equally on the leader's desire to lead and on the consent of those led.[7]

Police managers must work with and through people to establish a positive organizational culture focused on mission accomplishment. All managers must maintain a serious and continuing effort to direct the creation of a results-oriented working environment. The manager who strives on a daily basis to provide leadership will find that it is contagious, and officers will respond to his or her positive direction. Successful leaders, by their daily actions, convince their subordinates that the interests of leader and subordinates are the same.

4. *Controlling.* Controlling involves fixing accountability, establishing policy and procedures, setting performance standards, comparing actual behavior with these procedures and standards, and then taking corrective action where needed.[8] All police managers are accountable for the competency and commitment of the people they command. It is the managers' responsibility to know what is happening with the resources, both technical and human, entrusted to them by the organization. This requires that managers make a point of checking on progress in an effort to determine if previously agreed-upon objectives have been attained. The control function involves the following activities:

1. Identifying goals and objectives
2. Developing and maintaining performance standards
3. Monitoring performance
4. Evaluating personnel
5. Rewarding when appropriate
6. Disciplining when necessary

Control begins at the level of monitoring the performance of the subordinates who are accountable for accomplishing tasks. However, the manager must ensure that those subordinates have the knowledge, skills, and ability to perform their duties. Control will never be achieved if those responsible for task accomplishment are improperly informed, ill-trained, or ignorant of the level of performance expected.

Monitoring performance is essential to control. Effective managers obtain, and share with superiors and subordinates, the hard data needed to review operational progress. Data-based management uses fact, not subjective opinion. When conditions change, or when specific deviations from previously agreed-upon standards are identified and measured, corrective action should be taken.

The four managerial functions just discussed are not mutually exclusive, but highly interrelated. They do not necessarily occur in the sequence we listed but can happen at the same time. Keep in mind that managerial performance of these functions is continually modified by any or all the following factors:

1. Changing environmental demands
2. Managerial knowledge and competence
3. Organizational level
4. Nature and type of activity
5. Knowledge, competence, and commitment of employees

# MANAGERIAL LEVELS

Police organizations vary in size and complexity, from micro-departments with fewer than 25 officers to multilevel macro-departments employing a thousand or more people. As organizations become larger and more complex, the number of managerial levels increases. In a very small police agency, the chief of police and one sergeant will often be the only managers; in a very large agency, there can be 15 or more managers at the executive level alone. In general, all organizations have three distinct but overlapping managerial levels: the executive/strategic level, the middle management/administrative level, and the supervisory/technical level (see Figure 2–1).

Police managers at the *executive/strategic level* have a variety of titles, such as commissioner, director, chief, colonel, or superintendent. They are assisted by other top-level managers who have titles such as assistant chief, deputy chief, assistant director, deputy commissioner, colonel, or lieutenant colonel. These senior administrators deal with strategic issues, on the order of how the goals and objectives of the department interrelate with the needs of government and community. The police executive's role is inherently political because he or she is appointed by the controlling governmental authority and represents the department to that authority and to the community.[9] In many departments the chief executive occupies a demanding, high-profile position and must be available 24 hours a day, 7 days a week.

Managers at this level are primarily responsible for planning, setting direction, maintaining organizational integrity, creating goals, developing policies, ensuring fiscal accountability, and responding to political and community inquiries. A key requirement for police executives is leadership: the organizational direction they develop must effectively meet

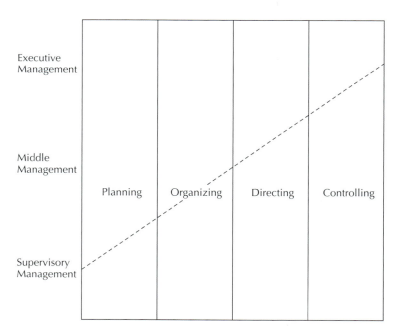

**Figure 2–1**
Relationship of Level of Management to Functions Performed.

current organizational and community needs while simultaneously preparing to meet future needs.[10]

An assistant chief, second in command, normally functions as the alter ego of a police chief executive and is a key figure in the management team, with in-line administrative responsibilities. Generally, deputy chiefs are responsible for supervising major functions such as line operations, technical services, investigations, or staff services. They may recommend goals and objectives; assist in the development and administration of policies and procedures; manage, direct, and organize operational services; and conduct internal investigations as directed by the chief executive.

Managers at the *middle management/administrative level* in policing are captains, lieutenants, or civilian managers in administrative positions. They manage divisions or units carrying such titles as patrol, traffic, records, communications, personnel, or research and development. Managers at this level are responsible for interpreting policies and procedures and for creating programs that translate departmental goals into the day-to-day tasks of operational units. They are responsible for converting the chief executive's vision into operational reality. These managers organize, coordinate, and control departmental resources and personnel. In the exercise of their control function, they evaluate supervisory accountability and unit performance.[11]

In their analysis of the administrative problems associated with the implementation of community policing, George L. Kelling and William J. Bratton contend that captains and lieutenants gained control of the practice, knowledge, and skill base of the police occupation during the development of the professional reform model of policing in the early 20th century. During this reform period, middle managers became the main proponents of centralizing control over the police organization's internal environment and operations.[12] Their success in establishing central control and their continuing role in exercising it make them the critical actors in the implementation of the organizational change required for the adoption of community policing and CompStat programs. Failure to win middle management's support is cited as the primary contributor to the demise of team policing in the 1970s.[13]

Malcolm K. Sparrow, Mark Moore, and David Kennedy identified six ways that police middle managers influence their organizations. First, middle managers operate at the boundary between knowledge and power in the department. Because of their positional authority, they translate the executive's vision and direction into operational strategies. Second, middle managers largely control the nature of the department's professional environment. The procedures they develop and the actions they take in dealing with subordinates define and reinforce the core cultural values of the department. These core values let the officers know what is and what is not acceptable operational behavior. Third, middle managers are the ones who can determine how employees view the department's procedural manual—as a means to justify command-and-control discipline, or as a source of knowledge, guidance, and inspiration. Fourth, middle managers have the power to quash new ideas (and they have been routinely accused of doing so, especially ideas that they believe challenge their authority). Fifth, middle managers have the ability to define work in a way that encourages their officers to tackle harder, broader problems: they can empower their officers by letting them know that the organization values their knowledge and expertise. Finally, middle managers control the extent to which discretion can be built explicitly into the department's value system.[14] In summary, the middle managers' organizational position gives them the power to choose what they will do: passively resist, tolerate, or lend their support and lead in the reengineering of their organizations.

The managers who operate at the *technical/operational level* of the department are the supervisors. Sergeant is the principal rank held, except for integrated police-fire organizations, where the title is lieutenant. They constitute the first level of management in the department. These first-line supervisors are generally held responsible for accomplishing short-term goals and exercising oversight of day-to-day operational activities.

Supervision of police personnel is the critical factor in achieving departmental performance objectives and officer compliance with procedures, policy, and law. It is each supervisor's responsibility to make certain that the individuals under his or her command perform their duties and accomplish organizational objectives according to law, departmental procedures, and ethical values. In the daily performance of their duties, supervisors make important decisions that affect the quality and manner of police operations—both the type of service provided to a community and the commitment and competence of the employees who provide that service. As a department's principal quality-control agents, supervisors have significant impact on the effectiveness and financial liability of the law-enforcement organization.[15]

Supervisors are accountable and responsible not only for their own performance but for that of their units: they are evaluated on the basis of their subordinates' accomplishments. However, a work unit's outcomes cannot simply be understood as the sum of individual performances. Work groups develop their own dynamics, problem-solving processes, and cultures, which have an impact on their performance. The supervisor's success will depend on how effectively he or she can build a positive relationship of mutual respect and trust with his or her work unit.[16]

In addition to managing their own teams of employees, supervisors are also part of the department's management team. Being promoted to a position on this team calls for a radical change in operational philosophy and outlook. Supervisors are required to develop skills and abilities that will allow them to manage the variety of people and performance challenges that occur daily in policing. Thus, becoming a supervisor requires that the new manager commence a personal and intellectual transformation that will change his or her organizational perspective, basic concepts of work, and relationships with others in the department. This adjustment takes time and effort. It is further complicated by the fact that the supervisor is often required to exert authority over individuals who are his or her social and professional colleagues. In many departments, new supervisors find themselves supervising officers whom they have closely worked with for years. Directing the performance of a former close colleague from patrol days is not an easy task.

The supervisors' organizational position places them in a unique and somewhat conflicting role. They are caught between two organizational worlds: management and operations, bosses and cops, the office and the street. In some departments these two worlds view each other with great hostility; in others there is mutual respect and cooperation. Where the organizational climate is negative, this in-between position can be a source of conflict for the supervisor. The differing expectations of the two sides, if not understood and responded to correctly, can develop into contradictory pressures that create conflict and role ambiguity for supervisors.[17] Of the three managerial levels in police departments, the operational/technical (supervisory) level is the largest.

Another way of viewing managers and the functions they perform is to distinguish between *line* and *staff*. *Line managers* have the authority to give orders to achieve organizational goals. *Staff managers* assist and advise line managers in accomplishing these goals. Recognizing the line/staff distinction is the initial step to take when a department arranges related functions under unified supervision and command. Once this step is accomplished, it becomes readily apparent how to allocate effort between the department's two principal functions: preparation for the delivery of police services and the actual delivery of those services.

The accepted classification of staff functions and line operations in police departments can be seen in Figure 2–2's depiction of the structure of a medium-sized department. Staff functions deal exclusively with supporting activities. In some larger agencies they have been broken down into various administrative and technical services, but in all cases the key is that they function to support line operations and the attainment of organizational goals. Line operations

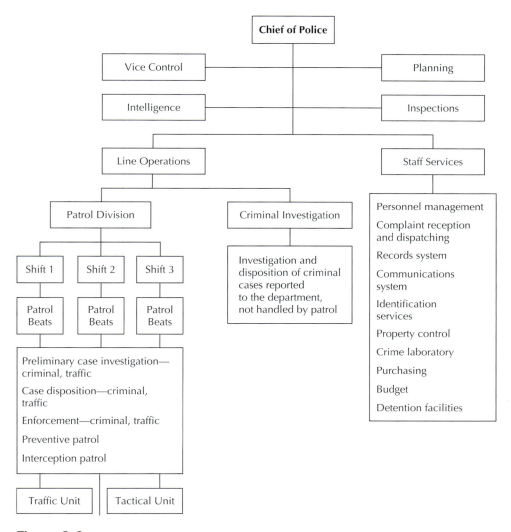

**Figure 2–2**

Organizational Structure of a Medium-Sized Police Department, Distinguishing Line and Staff.

translate policy into action. Ultimately, the delivery of police services to the community is the responsibility of the line, but it is staff elements that provide the personnel, technical expertise, records, material support, and other services that enable the line to accomplish its job.

The variety of activities included on the staff side can be seen in the following list of functions into which staff services are often subdivided:

1. Administrative Services
   Personnel
   Training
   Budget
   Community Outreach
   Research and Planning
   Crime Analysis
2. Technical Services Records
   Communications /Dispatch
   Property
   Crime Laboratory/CSI units
   Prisoner Holding Facility

The distinction between line and staff services allows for the orderly arrangement of elements within the structure of the police organization. Such an arrangement provides for a clarification of lines of authority and the chain of command, and it facilitates the distribution of power within the organization. A clear distinction between the two allows each service to devote total energies to the accomplishment of its functional objectives.

The effectiveness of a police organization generally depends on the quality of working life within it. In the short run, managers can attain objectives by threatening employees (ordering them to do something or suffer the consequences), but experience has shown that in today's working environment, officers do not readily accept authoritarian management that uses coercion or executive fiat. Effective organizations are characterized by a positive working environment that reflects mutual respect, trust, and ethical relationships between managers and officers.

# MANAGERIAL SKILLS

Successful managers not only have the right traits to know what they are supposed to do; they also have the skills to accomplish their objectives. A *skill* is the capacity to translate knowledge into action in such a way that a task is accomplished successfully.[18] In order to achieve objectives and goals, which is what management is all about, managers need to have three essential kinds of skills—technical, human, and conceptual—and to exercise them effectively.[19]

**Technical Skills**    All managers must be technically proficient in order to ensure that specific duties are performed correctly. Technical skills are based on craft experience, training, knowledge, operational procedures, laws, and techniques of policing. Every police manager must be current on the changes in the law, policy, procedures, and standards of performance that affect themselves and their subordinates. All managers should also know how to create a plan, organize, lead, and control.

Every managerial position has technical skills directly related to its responsibilities. For example, the manager of an investigative unit has to be knowledgeable in such areas as case management, legal aspects of interviewing and interrogation techniques, proper utilization of informants, legal rights of suspects, and surveillance techniques.[20] The CompStat process requires that operational commanders and managers have the technical knowledge to ensure that crime data are gathered constantly and analyzed quickly and accurately.[21]

## Human Skills

This skill set involves working with people and includes being thoroughly familiar with what motivates employees and how to utilize group processes. Good human skills enable a police manager to provide necessary leadership and direction and to ensure that tasks are accomplished in a timely fashion, with the least expenditure of resources. The interpersonal skills managers need include knowledge of human behavior and group dynamics, understanding of attitudes and motives of employees, and the ability to communicate clearly and persuasively.[22] Managers must know how to build positive interpersonal relationships with their employees, peers, superior managers, and stakeholders outside the organization. All of this requires the managers not only to possess knowledge and understanding of human behavior but also to employ this skill on a daily basis.

## Conceptual Skills

Effective managers have more cognitive ability than less effective ones, and they are perceived as more intelligent by their subordinates.[23] Conceptual skills help a manager take a system's view of his or her department's mission and goals. An effective manager uses his or her conceptual skills to understand the organization as a whole and assess the working relationships of its parts. When the interrelatedness of units and tasks is clearly understood, actions can be taken that are truly beneficial to the organization. Coordination is enhanced and effectiveness is the result.

As shown in Figure 2–3, all three of these skills are required in varying degrees at each of the managerial levels. As one moves up in the hierarchy, conceptual skills become more important and technical skills less so, but the common denominator for all levels of management is human skills. Supervisory managers in particular will find that human skills are a dominant factor in their working environment, since for the most part they will be required to manage rather than perform technical tasks themselves. Executive managers will find themselves using conceptual skills extensively as they plan and make decisions affecting the entire organization and its future, but they too will be only as successful as their ability to attain goals and objectives through the efforts of others. The importance of human skills cannot be emphasized too strongly.

## Managerial Role Expectations

A *role* is a set of behavior patterns expected of the person occupying a given position in a social unit such as an organization.[24] No matter what level of the organization they occupy, managers usually find themselves dealing with conflicting role expectations. The police organization expects that the manager will act and make decisions on its behalf, but employees—who have their own desires for fair treatment and their rights in the workplace—also expect the manager to act on their behalf.

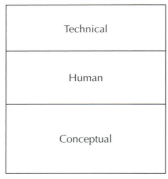

SUPERVISORY MANAGEMENT

| Technical |
| Human |
| Conceptual |

MIDDLE MANAGEMENT

| Technical |
| Human |
| Conceptual |

EXECUTIVE MANAGEMENT

| Technical |
| Human |
| Conceptual |

**Figure 2–3**

Managerial Skills Needed by Managers at Different Organizational Levels.

Adapted from Robert L. Katz, "Skills of an Effective Administrator," *Harvard Business Review*, Vol. 52 (5) (September–October 1974), pp. 90–110.

More specifically, on the organizational side every police manager is expected to be competent, loyal to his or her department and its mission, and committed to the department's goals and objectives. The manager is expected to be in command of his or her organizational unit, to be accountable for the employees assigned to the unit, and to achieve results. This means that the manager must have a clear understanding of the department's mission, vision, policy, procedures, and objectives.

On the employee side, police officers expect support, respect, and fair treatment from their managers. They expect their managers to understand them and treat them in a rational, consistent manner. The interrelationship between managers and employees forms the foundation upon which mutual trust and respect are built. Management based on mutual trust and respect is the most effective way to deal with people. How managers act toward their employees, while responding to the needs and demands of the organization and displaying competence as a manager, is critical to their success. The potentially competing expectations listed below can be sources of uncertainty and stress for the manager, but it is important to understand that between them these two lists present all the essential elements of good leadership.

Police organizations expect managers to:

1. Manage day-to-day operations
2. Work for the attainment of organizational objectives
3. Maintain a well-trained, motivated work unit
4. Use authority responsibly
5. Adhere to and administer the department's policies and procedures
6. Keep superiors, employees, and peers informed
7. Prevent problems as well as solve them
8. Be creative and flexible
9. Provide leadership and use initiative
10. Be accountable

Police employees expect their manager to:

1. Let them know what is expected
2. Give them timely and accurate feedback about their performance
3. Recognize and reward good performance
4. Listen to them
5. Provide them with the opportunity to grow and develop in their positions
6. Treat them equitably and fairly
7. Use authority appropriately
8. Provide support, resources, knowledge, and understanding[25]

Managers at different levels in the organization handle each set of expectations differently and to different degrees of intensity. Lower-level managers spend a great deal of time concerned with employee needs and expectations, whereas police chief executives are more apt to concentrate on the organizational expectations. In every instance, it should be kept in mind that a manager's personality may affect *how* a role is performed, but not *whether* it is or should be performed.

## THE NEW EMERGING POLICE MANAGEMENT ROLE

In police organizations during the professional reform era of the early 20th century, the primary function of the manager was to control operations and personnel. Managers sought guidance and direction from their department's policy and procedures manual. Whenever an employee asked for direction in a situation the standard response was, "do as the policy and procedures manual directs you to do." Oversight and control, with an emphasis on maintaining the status quo, were the prime directives of the police manager.

However, as noted in Chapter 1, substantial societal change has challenged earlier methods of police administration and management. Police departments are restructuring in order to respond more effectively to the forces of change. The emergence of concepts like community problem-solving policing and CompStat has resulted in the development of a new set of roles for police managers. Today, the primary role of the police manager is to be effective and achieve results. However, effectiveness as a manager means effectiveness in and through an organization.[26]

Effective organizations are ones in which people work at their full potential to achieve the mission. Peter Senge[27] identifies effective organizations as those that are skilled at creating, acquiring, and transferring knowledge and at modifying their behavior to reflect new knowledge and insights. He calls organizations that do this and develop the intellectual capabilities of their people "double-loop learning organizations." Double-loop learning involves questioning basic operating assumptions, entertaining different approaches, and experimenting with different arrangements. Managers in these organizations are creative and open to new information; they are system thinkers and self-confident learners. In contrast, adaptive or "single-loop" learners focus on solving problems in the present without examining how these problems may affect the entire police department or its future.[28]

Senge's theoretical construct appropriately describes the CompStat management process that is currently emerging as the dominant paradigm of police organization management.[29] A variety of organizational adaptations of CompStat are currently taking place in policing throughout the United States, Canada, and Europe. Each adaptation is a system that first identifies and focuses on emerging crime trends or quality-of-life issues and then attempts to effectively and efficiently use operational resources to control these trends. CompStat is based on the long-held managerial value of maximizing every asset of the organization, including each individual employee.[30]

Organizations using CompStat employ a strategic management process that uses organizational strategy to unite the decisions and actions of executives, operational commanders, and front-line officers into a coordinated and compatible pattern. In this process the crafting, implementing, and execution of operational strategies become critical managerial functions. Another critical management function in this type of organization is the capacity to manage human intellect and to apply it to useful organizational activities.[31]

Strategy is the means by which an organization responds to environmental conditions such as crime, disorder, citizen demand, and public safety. Strategy development must consider the critical managerial issue of how to achieve performance objectives given an organization's capabilities and resources. Objectives are the ends and strategy is the means of achieving these ends. An organization's strategy should be both proactive (intended) and reactive (adaptive)—a combination of planned actions and on-the-spot reactions to unanticipated changes in conditions. An organizational strategy is something that is shaped and reshaped as events take place and operational demands change.

For CompStat to be successful and for police departments to become effective learning organizations, operational managers must be empowered with the authority to develop clear, effective tactics to address crime and quality-of-life conditions in their operational areas. Managers must be flexible and ready to change their plans when crime conditions change. CompStat requires that all commanders be accountable for

- The quality of their plans
- The quality of their efforts toward crime reduction
- Their managerial oversight of operations (including evaluation and feedback) and results obtained

CompStat requires that a department's management develop an ongoing process of rigorous follow-up to ensure that the desired results are actually being achieved. Executives as well as operational managers must constantly follow up on what is being done and evaluate results. Evaluation makes it possible to assess the viability of particular strategic responses and to incorporate the knowledge gained into subsequent strategy development efforts. By knowing how well a particular strategy worked on a problem, and by knowing which specific elements of the strategy worked most effectively, departments will be better able to construct and implement effective responses for similar problems in the future. The follow-up and assessment process also permits the redeployment of resources to meet newly identified challenges once a problem has abated. Operational managers are expected to follow up on tactics and deployment by

- Getting out of their offices and seeing what conditions and operations are really like in their areas of responsibility
- Asking the operational personnel questions about current cases of interest, crime patterns, or situations requiring attention
- Reviewing crime reports daily
- Paying special attention to daily reports of serious crime
- Reviewing crime analysis materials (daily or weekly, depending on production schedules)
- Communicating daily with operational personnel about crime conditions
- Frequently discussing specific cases and crime conditions with their sub-unit managers and key personnel

Eli B. Silverman[32] has identified CompStat as an agent of organizational change that generates key reform processes such as new strategies, reengineering, and reorganization. In his view, CompStat serves as the glue that binds all these changes together because it involves double-loop learning. CompStat Crime Strategy meetings are forums where creative problem solving can take place and be turned into action. At Crime Strategy meetings, difficulties and obstacles are discovered, positions clarified, ownership and responsibility demanded, problems diagnosed, alternative strategies designed, and solutions defined and delivered. CompStat lets agency managers at all levels see their results every week and permits them to change tactics and deployment based on what they see and know. Because of this double-loop learning process, a deeper organizational transformation takes place.

CompStat forces police managers at all levels of the organization to be concerned with how they and their units are contributing to the department's mission. This concern is translated into a skill set that involves information management, planning, strategy development, measurement, and ongoing communication. The department's executive team must be able to help operational managers develop strategies and tactics to meet objectives. Both of these levels of management must be able to accept failure and, rather than punishing staff for it, use it to modify or replace tactics. The ability and willingness to reallocate resources, support creative solutions to problems, track progress, and integrate functions within the agency require a strategic management orientation similar to that found in successful business organizations. This style of management began to be adopted by police organizations during the last decade of the 20th century.

## ORGANIZATIONAL BEHAVIOR

It is clear from the foregoing discussion that management is a people-related function. Organizations are made up of people; they are not collections of interrelated mechanical parts. Managerial success and organizational effectiveness depend on how well managers understand human behavior in the workplace. If police managers are to be effective, they must pay increasing attention to the interpersonal aspects of their managerial roles. This is especially true as more and more police agencies expect managers to develop operational strategies and strategic management practices that depend on other individuals to be effective.

Work is a fundamental and natural aspect of everyday life in our society; it is central to our social, economic, and psychological existence. An adequately paying job provides not only the necessities of life but also a sense of personal identity and accomplishment. Most people describe themselves in terms of a work group or organization, and police officers are no different—their identities are often defined through their work. Achieving work-related goals is just as important to most officers as material rewards.

Personal interaction in organizations gives members a sense of belonging. In the case of police departments, the result is a social bond unique to the police culture. The sharing of duties and responsibilities heightened by the presence of danger generally results in officers becoming strongly committed to police work, which for them is more than just a job. The tasks to be performed become highly significant when properly accomplished and provide a feeling of well-being and fulfillment.

Police managers have great success when managing highly motivated employees. However, not all officers fit into this category. There is no simple explanation of why some employees are highly productive and others are not, any more than there is of other aspects of human behavior. There has been no shortage of theorizing about why employees do what they do and why the same situation can provoke different responses. Some theorists argue that participation in the decision-making process is the answer to the problem of motivating employees.[33] However, some organizations have found that when this recommendation is implemented, some previously highly motivated individuals prefer simply to follow instructions and not be involved. Other experts recommend continuous communication from top management. They posit that effective communication tends to encourage better performance and leads to job satisfaction.[34] Some employees respond positively to this technique and want to know what is going on. Others seem to care less and only want to hear from the top when the message has to do with compensation or perks. Obviously, human behavior is a complex phenomenon.

Police managers are increasingly aware of the need to understand human behavior in the workplace. They generally have a definite view (usually based on personal experience and observation) of how officers behave within the organization. However, if those views are based on myth or misinformation, their dealings with their employees will be less productive and less efficient, and they will find themselves expending more time and effort on personnel performance issues than if their understanding were better.

Through the study of organizational behavior we can begin to understand not only the complexities of organizations but also something about managerial behavior and the interactions between officers, managers, and the organization. Such study will also help us develop a better work-related understanding of ourselves and other people.[35]

If police managers are to deal effectively with all the critical aspects of organizational behavior, it is essential that they develop and utilize motivational skills in addition to enhancing their conceptual skills. (It is generally assumed that police managers, particularly the more senior ones, are not lacking in technical competence and that any weakness they may have is in areas other than operational application.)

Organizational behavior is the systematic study of the behavior and attitudes of individuals and groups in organizations.[36] The behavioral sciences, such as sociology, psychology, and anthropology, provide a basis for understanding human behavior at both the individual and group levels. Police managers utilize knowledge of human behavior to manage individual and group behavior.

**Organizational Behavior Defined**

To really understand behavior in an organization is difficult because it involves understanding not only individual behavior but also the impact on individual behavior of the groups to which he or she belongs. Such an understanding requires that we view the organization as a social system that is conditioned and reconditioned by its environment. According to this perspective, police organizations are not isolated entities but are part of a large societal environment. Thus, it is becoming increasingly apparent that law enforcement agencies cannot function in isolation.

Police managers are faced with many challenges, including understanding individual differences (in such areas as skills, motivation, and learning abilities). When concerned with individuals in groups, managers must also consider factors like communication, decision-making, power, and leadership. With this understanding as a basis, the manager can focus on work itself and can consider such variables as attitudes toward work, conflict, stress, and work design.

When tasks, individuals, and groups are interrelated, organizational design becomes a means of maximizing performance. The more successful a manager is in dealing with human behavior, the more successful the unit and the organization will be.[37] To understand organizational behavior, police managers should concern themselves with the following behaviors: individual, interpersonal, group, and organizational (see Table 2–1).

Table 2–1 **Types of Behavior in the Organization**

| |
|---|
| Individual |
| Interpersonal |
| Group |
| Organizational |

**Individual**    Individual behavior in the work setting has a highly significant impact on the effectiveness of an organization. People are different from each other; their behavior influences the behavior of other individuals, the attitudes of the small groups of which they are members, and the performance of the organization as a whole. Individuals have different perceptions of organizational reality and they react accordingly. Therefore, it is important to understand how individuals develop their beliefs, attitudes, and values (see Chapter 4). It is also a continuing challenge for a manager to understand what motivates an individual (see Chapter 5). Another factor is that the values, attitudes, and perceptions officers bring to the job or those they acquire after employment become exceedingly significant when managers strive to achieve agency goals.[38]

Another aspect of individual behavior is the personality of each officer. While his or her personality can be analyzed from many viewpoints, our concern here is the influence of other individuals, groups, and the organization on the personality of the officer (see Chapter 3). A law-enforcement agency exerts considerable influence on each individual officer, and this process of occupational socialization continues throughout the officer's career. Everyone makes assumptions about their peers, supervisors, and managers, and these assumptions influence individual behavior toward others. It is essential that managers become truly aware of individual differences as they attempt to understand individual and organizational needs. Finally, individuals and especially police officers who work in high-service demand areas can suffer from stress created by organizational life (see Chapter 6).

**Interpersonal**    The interpersonal behavior that arises when two people interact can be of considerable concern to managers. This interaction may occur between two police officers, between a superior and a subordinate, or between two managers. In most instances it involves such factors as leadership style, power, influence, and communication (see Chapters 8 through 11).

Interpersonal communication is a critical factor affecting both behavior and performance in police organizations. Effective communication is essential, and it seldom just occurs—it must be cultivated. Poor communication can lead to poor decisions; in most instances it is closely tied to such managerial variables as power, leadership, and influence. Power is a natural phenomenon in organizational life, the thing that makes it possible to influence people's behavior in order to achieve objectives and goals. In some police departments power serves as a positive feature, allowing people to control their own destinies while accomplishing the mission. However, power inevitably modifies interpersonal relationships within the organization. When individuals compete for it, conflict can occur, and it is difficult to imagine an organization where power is not a key variable in the relationships among members. Leadership is the catalyst that makes an organization effective. The interpersonal skills that police managers possess directly affect individuals and groups, as well as the total organization. Finally, managers are continually challenged by the need to reduce and manage interpersonal conflict in an effort to achieve departmental objectives and goals.

**Group**    Even though most police officers perform their duties singularly or in pairs, group behavior is becoming increasingly important to police managers. SWAT teams, task forces, and unions are examples of formal groups found in policing. Chapter 7 discusses in detail the dynamics of the group and the group process. Groups, both formal and informal, are powerful forces working for the attainment of goals and assisting in the adaptation to change (see Chapter 12).

Groups exert influence over the attitudes and behavior of each officer. As members of a work group, officers often feel or act differently than they would alone. The group can foster teamwork that results in the attainment of objectives, or its members can sabotage innovative programs. A manager can be more effective through understanding how groups are formed, what types of groups there are, and how groups found in the work environment operate. Groups have a strong influence on individual behavior. The manager who does not understand the role they play within the organization will be less successful than the manager who directs group behavior in such a way that there is a positive contribution to the organization.

## Organizational

The structure of the organization itself is significant, because faulty organizational design can limit or inhibit coordination and cooperation between employees. Organizational design brings together like functions and provides for formal internal communication. In some instances police departments become fragmented, and individual units within a department function with total disregard for other units. This was especially true in the early part of the 20th century, when detective units operated independently; in some instances the heads of detective units were political appointments.

The complexity of the organizational work to be performed also influences behavior: managers have to be especially concerned with how individuals and groups adjust to their assignments, and all managers should be aware of the need to deal with job stress, conflict, turnover, and absenteeism.[39]

It is increasingly apparent that police organizations continually react to the external environment and that the nature of this ongoing reaction modifies the internal environment of the organization. It is the task of the police manager to enhance the working relationship between the external and internal environments and effectively manage resultant behavior. This is not an easy task, so managers must utilize every resource at their command in order to identify, understand, assess, and resolve organizational problems. The current trend toward community policing places an exceptional demand on all police personnel, as the organizational structure becomes increasingly decentralized and the department focuses on attaining the goals set forth in departmental value statements. The demands can become especially urgent when temporary task forces come and go with the appearance and resolution of community problems.

## Historical Foundations of Organizational Behavior

The growth of organizations and their increasing importance within society resulted in greater attention being given by researchers to employees and their needs in the workplace. Probably the most lasting of the early research products are Abraham H. Maslow's motivation studies. Maslow studied what he called the "self-actualized individual," a superior character whose personality was harmonious and whose perceptions were less distorted than those of other people by desires, anxieties, fears, hopes, false optimism, or pessimism.[40]

From his analysis of the self-actualized individual, Maslow created a theory of human behavior. He identified five levels of human needs within a motivational hierarchy. When basic needs (physiological well-being and safety) were fulfilled, the growth need came into play, influencing the individual to seek belongingness, esteem, and self-actualization (see Chapter 5).

Another researcher, Douglas McGregor, believed that all management acts are based on specific assumptions, generalizations, and hypotheses about employee behavior. He suggested that if a manager holds workers in relatively low esteem, he or she will see the majority of workers as somewhat limited in their commitment to the organization (in contrast with managers, an elite group whose focus is the organizational needs).

Such a manager assumes that most employees are inherently lazy, want to have someone take care of them, and work best when subjected to firm control and positive direction.[41] This managerial perspective is known as "Theory X." In contrast to this is the "Theory Y" perspective that sees workers as committed, intelligent, responsible, and basically honest.

A manager functioning under a positive set of assumptions about worker behavior is concerned about relationships and the creation of an environment emphasizing the development of initiative and self-direction. Theory Y assumptions challenged the fundamental tenets postulated in the "ideal bureaucracy" and "scientific management" theories. However, its basic assumptions support the premises of community policing and the CompStat management process (see Chapter 5).

Frederick Herzberg postulated a two-factor theory of worker motivation. His research was concerned with job satisfaction or dissatisfaction. In other words, what do employees want from their work? When subjects of his investigation reported feeling unhappy with their jobs, he found that they identified conditions external to task accomplishment.[42] The factors that lead to workers being motivated include work itself, advancement, achievement, and recognition. This is in contrast to "hygiene" factors such as administration, supervision, salaries, and working conditions. Herzberg encouraged managers to create a working environment emphasizing "satisfiers" rather than "dissatisfiers" (see Chapter 5).

Other researchers directed their attention to leadership. In what have become known as the Ohio State leadership studies, Rensis Likert identified management styles in organizations as lying along a continuum from authoritarian to participative.[43] He found that, with few exceptions, the highest-producing units within an organization were those in which the management style was participative.[44] According to Likert, human resources must be handled as a significant asset.

During the same period, the 1950s, Robert Blake and Jane Mouton developed the highly popular "managerial grid." The grid identified five different styles of leadership: "impoverished," "task," "country club," "middle-of-the-road," and "team." Each style was defined in terms of the relationship between a concern for production and a concern for employees. The most desirable style was found to be team management[45] (see Chapter 11).

As behavioral researchers reviewed the numerous studies on leadership and motivation, they found them to be highly prescriptive and, in many instances, mutually contradictory. These researchers declared an end to efforts to identify universal principles, the best leadership style, or optimal motivational factors, and the "contingency approach" was born.

Fred Fiedler, Martin Chemers, and Linda Maher's discussion of leadership suggested the adoption of a contingency approach, which would recognize that different situations and conditions require different management approaches.[46] They identified three dimensions determining the situational control of a job:

1. *Relationship between the leader and followers.* Do they get along together?
2. *Nature of the task structure.* Are the procedures, goals, and job evaluation techniques clearly defined?
3. *Amount of position power.* How much actual authority does the leader possess to hire, fire, and discipline?

Chris Argyris set forth (in a series of articles and texts) his theories concerning the difficulty of adjusting the individual to the organization. Argyris's view is that an organization that emphasizes task specialization, chain of command, unity of direction, and limited span of control is fostering "immaturity" among its employees and that the leadership style of such organizations tends to create conflict and frustration by pressuring "maturity-directed" employees to behave immaturely. Argyris viewed an effective organization as one requiring employees to be self-responsible, self-directed, and self-motivated. He argues that motivation can be maximized when each employee pursues goals and experiences psychological growth and independence.[47]

The contingency approach came into existence as a consequence of the frustration that behavioral scientists and consultants experienced in implementing ideas set forth by the traditional theories. For the most part, the business world has been more receptive to evolving managerial theories than has the world of public administration.

The implementation of organizational development (OD) programs in law enforcement agencies has received mixed responses. While OD has been highly successful in some situations, in other situations it has been overwhelmingly rejected. Chapter 14 describes techniques for improving performance through the use of OD.

Seeking ideal management concepts is something like the search for the Holy Grail that, in ancient times, proved to be so difficult. Many of us are still looking for the "one best way" to do things, but those who accept the contingency approach believe that differing situations require different management approaches. Contingency supporters reject the concept of "one best way" to accomplish something and prefer an eclectic approach. For example, in one situation work simplification might prove highly successful, whereas in another, changing the relationships within a work group could be the best solution.

The approach taken by this book is to include contributions from most of the major theories of management, with a primary focus on organizational behavior. Our review of the history of management theories makes it clear that the traditional assumption that there was only one best way to manage people in organizations has received less and less support through the years. The foundation for a new approach to management was laid by later theorists who began to emphasize the necessity of understanding organizational behavior.

As previously indicated, law enforcement managers for the most part still emphasize traditional management approaches, but progressive police organizations are turning to managerial approaches that are currently more widely accepted by organizations outside the law enforcement world.

Cindy Miller was appointed to the position of chief 6 months ago, after serving in a neighboring police department for 12 years. The last rank she held there was lieutenant. Miller's predecessor as chief had served for many years. His managerial style may be described as "don't do anything that rocks the boat."

Soon after assuming the position, Chief Miller instituted a program of personally reviewing the daily reports of officers by randomly selecting them from different shifts. This new program went over like a lead balloon. Shock waves permeated the whole organization. The typical reaction was that the chief was treating everyone like children. The chief's position is that while some officers might find it demeaning to be made accountable in detail for their activities, in her judgment daily reports should be a managerial tool, not a meaningless form.

The chief's review program created such dissent that several officers complained to members of the city council. The media soon picked up on the issue. The chief became very defensive and pointed out that it was an in-house matter and officers had no business taking it outside the department.

*Faulty communication may or may not have been at the center of this problem. What do you think? What might the chief have done to prevent this conflict? Is it a question of organizational behavior that is a function of interpersonal relations or of group dynamics? Did the officers have a right to challenge the chief? If you agree, explain why.*

Police managers should be fully aware of both the advantages and the disadvantages of different managerial theories. Although the pragmatic police executive might feel somewhat uncomfortable with how many competing theories there are, there is a definite need for managers to be aware of new theories and ideas when implementing new programs. Change is always with us and rapid change places urgent demands on the organization's ability to respond. What was good enough yesterday is quite likely not to work as well today. The eclectic approach we have chosen provides the law enforcement manager with tools benefiting not only the organization but also the employees and the public.

Max D. Kenney had previously served as a chief in two other communities before being appointed chief of Websterville, a city with a population of 110,000. The department has 120 sworn personnel and 21 civilians. Websterville can be described as a bedroom suburb in a large metropolitan area.

Chief Kenney when initially employed was known as a visionary, and the officials who hired him expected him to make the department the most professional in the area. Kenney has a master's degree in public administration, has been a police officer for 14 years, and is considered by most to be a comer.

As chief, Kenney spends the majority of his time performing the roles of figurehead, liaison, and spokesperson for the department. Operational activities are supervised by the assistant chief; Chief Kenney's internal supervision is limited to issues that might threaten the integrity or reputation of the department.

Chief Kenney holds numerous press conferences and does everything possible to maximize positive press relations. As a matter of policy, reporters are required to deal directly with the chief on any case of significance. The chief is also deeply involved in three major professional organizations and spends a great deal of his time attending meetings and serving on committees. In addition, he attends every city council meeting, plus neighborhood association meetings and every cultural or social event his busy schedule allows.

*From the preceding description, it is apparent the chief believes the chief executive should spend most of his time engaging in activities external to the department. Do you think the chief is truly performing the roles required, or should he be more concerned with internal roles such as monitor and disturbance handler?*

# SUMMARY

Police managers are becoming increasingly aware of the need to understand human behavior in the workplace. Through a study of organizational behavior we can begin not only to understand why organizations are such complex entities but also to learn something about managerial behavior and the interactions among officers, managers, and the organization. In order to really understand organizational behavior, it is essential to become aware of behavior at the individual, interpersonal, and group levels. Organizational behavior as a field of study did not appear out of nowhere—it was a product of evolution, and its historical antecedents included ideal bureaucracy theories, scientific management research, and the human relations movement.

In order to perform effectively, a manager must develop three areas of skills: technical, human, and conceptual. The common denominator for all levels of management is human skills—they are of the utmost importance. It is evident that managers are most effective when goals and objectives are attained through the efforts of others.

Management is a continuing process that focuses on the identification, refinement, and attainment of objectives by the effective application of resources. Operationally, a police manager accomplishes this by articulating value statements that guide the department in its effort to attain defined goals.

# KEY TERMS

CompStat managerial responsibilities
group behavior
individual behavior
interpersonal behavior
learning organizations
line manager

management
management functions
managerial levels
managerial skills
organizational behavior
staff manager

# DISCUSSION TOPICS AND QUESTIONS

1. Generally, what behaviors must be considered in order to fully understand the concept of organizational behavior?
2. Why is it important to understand the concept of organizational behavior?
3. Differentiate between the managerial skills needed by a manager at the supervisory level and those needed by middle managers.
4. Describe what a manager should do to understand his or her subordinates.
5. Why does a police chief spend a great amount of time on the interpersonal role?
6. What are the responsibilities of a manager in a CompStat organization?

# FOR FURTHER READING

Gary Dessler, *Management: Principles and Practices for Tomorrow's Leaders* (Upper Saddle River, NJ: Prentice Hall, 2004).

Dessler provides an in-depth analysis of the role of the manager in today's organizational environment.

David H. Freedman, *Corps Business: The 30 Management Principles of the U.S. Marines* (New York: HarperCollins, 2000).

Excellent analysis of a winning leadership and organizational management process.

Malcolm K. Sparrow, Mark Moore, and David Kennedy, *Beyond 911: A New Era for Policing* (New York: Basic Books, 1990).

Good basic analysis of traditional and innovative management in the operational world of policing.

# NOTES

1. Bureau of Justice Statistics. http://www.ojp.usdoj.gov/bjs/

2. Michael E. Cavanagh, *Policing Within a Professional Framework* (Upper Saddle River, NJ: Prentice Hall, 2004), pp. 73–104.

3. Richard M. Ayres, *Preventing Law Enforcement Stress: The Organization's Role* (Washington, DC: Bureau of Justice Assistance, 1990).

4. Gary Dessler, *Management: Principles and Practices for Tomorrow's Leaders* (Upper Saddle River, NJ: Prentice Hall, 2004), p. 3.

5. James J. Fyfe, Jack R. Greene, William F. Walsh, O.W. Wilson, and Roy C. McLaren, *Police Administration*, 5th ed. (New York: McGraw-Hill, 1997), p. 212.

6. Jay R. Galbraith, Edward E. Lawler III & Associates, *Organizing for the Future: The New Logic for Managing Complex Organizations* (San Francisco: Jossey-Bass, 1993), p. 2.

7. David H. Freedman, *Corps Business: The 30 Management Principles of the U.S. Marines* (New York: HarperCollins, 2000), pp. xii–xiii.

8. Dessler, *Management*, p. 3.

9. Gary W. Cordner, Kathryn E. Scarborough, and Robert Sheehan, *Police Administration*, 5th ed. (Cincinnati: Anderson, 2004), pp. 179–209.

10. Albert J. Reiss, Jr., "Shaping and Serving the Community: The Role of the Police Chief Executive," in William A. Geller, ed. *Police Leadership in America: Crisis and Opportunity* (New York: Praeger, 1985), pp. 61–69.

11. Malcolm K. Sparrow, Mark Moore, and David Kennedy, *Beyond 911: A New Era for Policing* (New York: Basic Books, 1990), pp. 213–214.

12. George L. Kelling and William J. Bratton, *Implementing Community Policing: The Administrative Problem* (Perspectives on Policing, Washington, DC: National Institute of Justice, 1993).

13. Lawrence W. Sherman, Catherine H. Milton, and Thomas V. Kelly, *Team Policing Seven Case Studies* (Washington, DC: Police Foundation, 1973).

14. Sparrow, Moore, and Kennedy, *Beyond 911*, pp. 213–214.

15. William F. Walsh and Edwin J. Donovan, *The Supervision of Police Personnel: A Performance-Based Approach* (Dubuque, IA: Kendall Hunt, 1990), pp. 1–13.

16. Cordner, Scarborough, and Sheehan, *Police Administration*, pp. 301–302.

17. Walsh and Donovan, *Supervision of Police Personnel*, p. 5.

18. Robert L. Katz, "Skills of an Effective Administrator," *Harvard Business Review*, Vol. 52 (1974), pp. 90–110.

19. Dessler, *Management*, p. 10.

20. Charles R. Swanson, Neil C. Chamelin, and Leonard Territo, *Criminal Investigation*, 6th ed. (New York: McGraw-Hill, 1996).

21. Vincent E. Henry, *The CompStat Paradigm: Management Accountability in Policing, Business and the Public Sector* (Flushing, NY: Looseleaf Law Publications, 2002).

22. Gary Yukl, *Leadership in Organizations* (Upper Saddle River, NJ: Prentice Hall, 1998), p. 252.

23. Shelley Kirkpatrick and Edwin Locke, "Leadership: Do Traits Matter?" *Academy of Management Executives* (May 1991), p. 49.

24. Stephen P. Robbins, *Managing Today* (Upper Saddle River, NJ: Prentice Hall, 1997).

25. The two sets of role expectations have been developed by William F. Walsh through the use of interactive training exercises during 30 years of training police managers throughout the United States.

26. Peter F. Drucker, *The Effective Executive* (New York: Harper Colophon, 1985), p. viii.

27. Peter M. Senge, *The Fifth Discipline: The Art & Practice of the Learning Organization* (New York: Doubleday, 1990), p. 13.

28. Ronald G. Lynch, *The Police Manager* (Cincinnati: Anderson, 1998).

29. William F. Walsh, "CompStat: An Analysis of an Emerging Police Managerial Paradigm," *Policing: An International Journal of Police Strategies & Management*, Vol. 24 (2001), pp. 347–362.

30. Walter Schick, "CompStat in the Los Angeles Police Department," *The Police Chief*, Vol. LXXI (January 2004), pp. 17–23.

31. William F. Walsh, "Policing at the Crossroads: Changing Directions for the New Millennium," *Policing: An International Journal of Police Science and Management*, Vol. 1 (1998), pp. 17–25.

32. Eli Silverman, *NYPD Battles Crime: Innovative Strategies in Policing* (New York: Northeastern University Press, 1999), p. 190.

33. Susan E. Jackson, "Participation in Decision Making as a Strategy for Reducing Job-Related Strain," *Journal of Applied Psychology* (February 1983), pp. 3–19.

34. J. David Pincus, "Communication Satisfaction, Job Satisfaction, and Job Performance," *Human Communication Research* (Spring 1986), pp. 395–419.

35. John R. Schermerhorn, Jr., James G. Hunt, and Richard N. Osborn, *Organizational Behavior*, 6th ed. (New York: John Wiley & Sons, 1997), p. 3.

36. Ibid.

37. Gary Dessler, *A Framework for Human Resource Management*, 3rd ed. (Upper Saddle River, NJ: Prentice Hall, 2004), p. 15.

38. Robert E. Worden, "Police Officer Belief Systems: A Framework for Analysis," *American Journal of Policing*, Vol. 14 (1995), pp. 49–81.

39. Abraham H. Maslow, *Towards a Psychology of Being* (New York: Van Nostrand, 1962).

40. Douglas McGregor, *The Human Side of Enterprise* (New York: McGraw-Hill, 1960).

41. Frederick Herzberg, Bernard Mausner, and Barbara Snyderman, *The Motivation to Work*, 2nd ed. (New York: Wiley, 1959).

42. Rensis Likert, *New Patterns in Management* (New York: McGraw-Hill, 1961).

43. Rensis Likert, *The Human Organization Patterns* (New York: McGraw-Hill, 1967).

44. Robert R. Blake and Jane S. Mouton, *The Managerial Grid* (Houston: Gulf, 1964).

45. Fred E. Fiedler, Martin M. Chemers, and Linda Mahar, *Improving Leadership Effectiveness: The Leader Match Concept* (New York: Wiley, 1976).

46. Chris Argyris, *Understanding Organizational Behavior* (Homewood, IL: Dorsey Press, 1960).

47. Chris Argyris, *Personality and Organization* (New York: Harper & Row, 1957).

# —3———

# PERSONALITY

## Understanding the Complexity of Human Behavior in the Organization

### LEARNING OBJECTIVES

1. Define *personality*.
2. Identify personality determinants.
3. List the various personality theories.
4. Describe the concept locus of control.
5. Compare and contrast the defense mechanisms of projection and avoidance.
6. Identify the personality traits of a Type A personality.
7. Describe the relationship of personality to work.
8. Identify the characteristics of a High-Mach personality.
9. Describe an individual who has a strong bureaucratic orientation.

What makes one police officer behave in consistent ways in a variety of situations while the behavior of another officer is often unpredictable? An individual's personality is an answer that easily comes to mind. Personality is an important element of behavior and cannot be discounted. At the same time, each person is influenced by others as well as by the particular complex array of circumstances surrounding an event or a particular situation. No two people are exactly alike, and each person brings his or her own unique characteristics to the work environment.

Since personality is often the determinant of the way people react to the same situation, it is an important concept that police managers must understand in order to manage the behavior of their subordinates. Personality is often described in terms of how we perceive someone. For instance, we describe some managers as "hard-nosed" and authoritarian, others as really fair and "nice guys." Patrol officers describe their peers as "great street cops" or "wimps," depending on how they behave when confronted with a difficult situation. This process of employee personality labeling, if carried to extremes and not addressed by the manager, can lead to misunderstanding and interpersonal conflict in the workplace.

Police managers must continually attempt to analyze human behavior. This is a difficult but necessary task—vital to their effective management of people, with their various personality traits. Unfortunately, there has not been universal

Jane Cooper is a member of the Sea View Police Department and is in her ninth year of service. She is married and has two children, three and six years old. She is a graduate of the local community college, with a degree in law enforcement. As a college student she interned in three different local law enforcement agencies. She was an explorer scout, and as a youth she spent weekends riding a dirt bike, which influenced her career goal to become a motorcycle officer.

The Sea View Police Department has 642 sworn positions including 14 motorcycle officers who make up the traffic unit. Officer Cooper had been on a waiting list for six years before passing a series of rigid coordination and safety tests and receiving the appointment to the motorcycle unit.

As a patrol officer, she enforces the law aggressively and her orientation is almost totally legalistic. In her view, the law is "absolute" and a violation is a violation. There is no room for consideration of the spirit of the law. A transgressor of the law should always be arrested or cited, she feels; social consideration should be left up to social workers.

Officer Cooper really enjoys her work and finds days off to be boring unless she is riding her bike in the countryside. She had refused to take a promotional examination prior to her assignment to traffic, because it was more important to her to become a motor officer than to receive a promotion. Within the department, the motor officers are looked upon as a different breed. They are viewed as highly aggressive and always in the thick of things, with a real love of facing danger. The unit members consider themselves the real elite unit in the department. All members have a great deal of pride not only in the work they perform, but in their uniform, which sets them apart from other members of the department.

Officer Cooper has been in three accidents since her appointment to the motorcycle unit. In every instance she was fortunate enough not to be seriously injured, but the motorcycles were totaled. Top management in the police department is becoming increasingly concerned about the aggressive behavior of the members of the motorcycle unit—not only in their contact with the public, but in the increasing number of accidents and injuries to officers. During the last calendar year, motorcycle officers have been involved in nine accidents. As a result of injuries, one officer has been retired on disability and three officers have been on sick leave for a total of 61 days. Unfortunately, during the same period of time, the number of citizen complaints against motor officers has doubled as compared to the average for the previous five calendar years.

*The officer in charge of the traffic unit, Captain Roger Miles, has been asked to devise a program for reducing motorcycle accidents and citizen complaints. The chief questions Miles's selection of Jane Cooper because of her aggressive nature, the number of accidents she has been involved in recently, and the fact that she has received four citizen complaints during the last year. If you were Captain Miles, how would you handle this problem? Do you think motor officers should be selected because they are aggressive? After reaching a conclusion, keep it in mind, and then after reading this chapter, review this case and see if your solution changes.*

agreement on the exact meaning of personality. This is because psychologists disagree as to how personality is acquired and what causes it to change.[1]

Nevertheless, a manager must deal with the reality of each situation and the different personalities of the employees involved. A police department (in the final analysis) is a group of people joined together in order to achieve organizational goals and satisfy their personal needs. The methods used to achieve these goals, and the presence or absence of competition among the goals, depend in part on the personalities of the managers and employees involved.

## PERSONALITY

**Personality Defined**

The term *personality* is usually used to mean the unique combination of ways of thinking and behaving that make an individual who he or she is. Many people make loose use of psychological terms like "introvert" and "extrovert" to describe the personalities of others. Such labels convey a brief impressionistic description of the person being referred to.[2]

Although attempts to categorize personalities have pitfalls, the process can be useful to managers because there is evidence to show that personality can influence behavior. A realistic awareness of personality can be helpful to managers because it can allow them to predict the behavior of employees, peers, and superiors. Here is one formal definition of personality:

> Personality is a stable set of characteristics and tendencies that determine the commonalities and differences in the psychological behavior (thoughts, feelings, and actions) of people, having continuity in time, and that may not be easily understood as the sole result of the social and biological pressures of the moment.[3]

This definition expresses a general theory of human behavior. It applies to everyone, not just to one individual or a class of individuals in a given situation. Personality, so defined, describes a person's total behavior under varying circumstances and at different times. Some feel personality is so important that it describes the very essence of what it means to be a *Homo sapiens.*

Another feature of this definition is it addresses both commonalities and differences. Our personalities include some features that we have in common with everyone else and some that are exclusive to us, not seen in others. Managers must look for and understand the features that all employees share, as well as the ones that make each individual employee unique. This combination of similarities and differences is what makes humans unique and what makes managing the human resources of an organization so challenging.

Admittedly, personality is relatively stable. Although it can change, this usually happens gradually over a period of time. At the same time, situational factors can have a definite influence on personality, as is clearly apparent from studies of individuals who have completed police academy training. These studies discovered how much the graduates were influenced by the peer socializing process of the organization once they spent time in the work setting with other officers.[4] Many officers have commented on the difference between what they were taught in the academy and what was expected of them by officers with greater field experience. In this field training stage, the new officer learns to conform to the informal socialization process of peer values rather than to the organizational values taught in the academy.[5]

**Personality Determinants**

How does one's personality develop? There are a number of theories describing the process. The following four basic assumptions about human behavior are drawn from one of those theories, known as *interactional psychology:*

1. Behavior is a function of a continuous, multidirectional interaction between the person and the situation.
2. The person is active in this process, both changing the situation and being changed by it.
3. People differ from each other in many characteristics, including cognition, affect (emotion), motivation, and ability.
4. Both the objective situation and the person's subjective view of the situation are important.[6]

Interactional psychology attributes human behavior jointly to the personality of the individual, the nature of the situation, and the continual interaction between the two. This makes personality a very important consideration for managers within an organization because it influences how employees react to and evaluate the demands of their work setting. For example, an officer who is achievement oriented will, in all probability, evaluate each working situation in terms of its potential to aid his or her career advancement. Such an individual is more apt to volunteer for assignments, pursue special training or higher education, and develop an expertise needed by others, all with the intent of achieving the highest possible recognition or advancement in the shortest possible time. However, officers who are strongly influenced by the officer peer group culture will adjust their behavior to conform to the work group's often anti-organizational view of the world.[7]

## Heredity

Early research into personality stressed the importance of genetically determined characteristics. Heredity refers to factors present at birth, such as physical stature, gender, energy level, muscular composition, reflexes, and temperament. Beth Azar concluded after a review of 20 years of research with twins and adopted children that there is a genetic component to just about every human trait and behavior, including personality, general intelligence, and behavioral disorders.[8] This perspective views heredity as the final arbiter of how one acquires a personality.

Research that is more recent suggests that while heredity is one of the major determinants of behavior, it might not be as important as was once thought. The brain—which we still know relatively little about—may or may not hold more answers for personality than does heredity. In fact it is currently believed only a limited part of behavior can be definitely attributed to heredity. Current research in the field of genetic engineering may eventually answer many of the questions regarding the part heredity plays in determining personality, but as of today those questions have not been answered.

Managers should consider that, based on our current knowledge, non-hereditary factors probably exert more influence on personality development and the subsequent behavior of employees than do hereditary factors. If all personality characteristics were fixed at birth and solely the result of heredity, then one could not be influenced by experience, environment, or the variety situations encountered during one's lifetime. In summary, heredity is a limited explanation of personality and cannot fully explain why individuals behave the way they do.[9]

## Culture

Another determinant of personality is culture. Culture is a system of shared beliefs, values, attitudes, and meanings that guide individual behavior. This system is acquired by individuals through their interactions with significant others such as parents, teachers, and peers in a process called *socialization*. Over time, cultural socialization conditions and reconditions individuals, providing them with an accepted system of norms that structures their day-to-day behavior.

Organizational theorists believe that culture is the hidden meaning behind behavior and that it must be observed and understood by managers, if they wish to change behavior.[10] In a strong culture, the organization's core values are intensely held and widely shared. The more members who believe in and accept these core values, the greater will be the organization's commitment to those values and the stronger will be its culture. A strong culture will have greater influence on the behavior of its members by creating a climate of intense internal behavioral control and group commitment. For example, World War II Japanese soldiers killed themselves rather than surrender and admit defeat, which meant failure and disgrace in their culture. An increasing body of research indicates that a strong culture is associated with successful organizational performance.[11]

Organizational culture theorists claim that formal rules, authority, and procedures designed to govern behavior do not restrain the personal preferences of employees, but cultural norms, values, beliefs, and assumptions do.[12] For example, the veteran police officer who tells the rookie, "Never mind what the manual says, this is the way we do it in the real world," is instructing the new officer in the accepted way of behaving in that department. In order to understand or predict how an organization member will behave under different circumstances, one must know what the patterns of basic beliefs and values are that form the employee's *organizational culture* (see Chapter 4).

In an organization, culture serves four basic functions:

1. It provides a sense of identity to members and increases their commitment to the organization or their work group (a sense of belonging or esprit de corps).
2. It provides a way for members to interpret the meaning of organizational events and the organization's external environment (a way to structure and make sense of what they can't control).
3. It reinforces the core values of the organization (everybody knows what counts and what is the right way to do things).
4. It serves as a behavioral control mechanism for organizational members (if you don't conform to the accepted ways of acting, you are an outsider or outcast).[13]

People's concepts of what actions should or should not be exercised in a given situation are strongly influenced by the culture in which they were socialized. Cultural influences are especially noticeable in employee motivation.

For example, many young men and women currently entering the police service are less oriented to authority and less competitive than their predecessors; their lives can be complete without relying heavily on job satisfaction. These changing employee expectations may require managers to consider assigning work in different ways.[14]

Cultural diversity places unique demands on managers. Police departments are having difficulty recruiting members of minority cultures (as mandated by the courts in order to make departments reflect the ethnic compositions of communities being policed). One of the problems is that some cultures foster a disdain for the police and in some instances have mistrusted the police for many years (see Chapter 15 for a discussion of minorities and law enforcement). Nevertheless, members of different cultures—such as Chinese, Japanese, Mexicans, Cambodians, and Vietnamese—are becoming police officers with increasing frequency. The need to assimilate them into the working environment is another challenge for police managers.

Learning to recognize how the traits we are born with and the beliefs and attitudes we acquire through socialization influence us will add to our understanding of the human personality. The person-situation interaction is another factor influencing personality. As we noted, personality is usually relatively stable, but that stability can be altered by situations. Unfortunately, our knowledge is somewhat limited in this area, and there is not a system for categorizing specific situations and how they impact personality. Each situation is different. Differences may seem very small, but when filtered by a person's cognitive mediating processes (such as perception), they can lead to quite large subjective differences and diverse behavioral outcomes.[15]

**Situation**

What we do know is that under certain circumstances an individual can react in ways seemingly almost foreign to his or her personality. In numerous instances officers have performed heroically, placing their lives in jeopardy, when if they had considered the event logically and rationally, they may never have reacted as they did. Conversely, in other instances officers fully aware of what is right, and of the potential outcome of doing wrong, have acted unethically or engaged in illegal behavior for personal gain.[16]

Managers should be careful when generalizing about the way employees behave unless they take into account the nature of each situation. They must be knowledgeable about the strengths and weaknesses of each employee being supervised. Rather than spending a great deal of time addressing those weaknesses, a reasonable alternative may be altering the situation. For example, a first-line supervisor, when handling new employees, may choose to organize their work assignments so as to minimize their involvement in situations requiring close supervision.

Although the public generally views the police force as a unit, it is important to note that a force is made up of individual personalities who are each affected by heredity, culture, and situation.

Spencer Grant, PhotoEdit

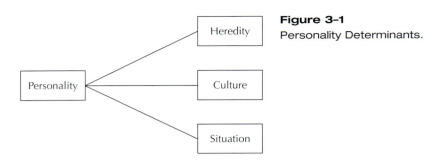

**Figure 3–1**
Personality Determinants.

More study remains to be done of situational factors and their influence on personality. What we do know is that people are not static, acting the same way in all situations, but instead are changing and flexible. Figure 3–1 illustrates how the three determinants work together to create personality.

# PERSONALITY THEORIES

The organizational behavior approach to management stresses the importance of managers thoroughly understanding the various theories of personality in order to assess the way people behave in their organizations. Numerous theories have been proposed during the last two centuries. Most prominent among them are the *psychoanalytical theory, trait theory,* and *humanistic theory.* Each presents a different view of personality, and each has both supporters and detractors. No one theory of personality development totally explains all variation in behavior, but a manager who understands various theories has taken the first step in dealing with the complexity of human behavior—individual, interpersonal, group, or organizational.

**Psychoanalytical Theory**

Sigmund Freud (1856–1939) developed the first comprehensive theory of personality. He believed that the human mind is dominated by the unconscious and claimed that to truly understand a person's behavior it is necessary to analyze the unconscious motivations that underlie many of his or her thoughts, wishes, feelings, and memories.[17] According to this perspective, personality results from a dynamic process that involves a constant state of tension and conflict between the conscious and the unconscious.

Freud theorized, based on observing and listening to his patients, that personality results from the interaction between three parts of the mind: the *id,* the *ego,* and the *superego.* Each of these performs a different function and develops at a different time.[18] Freud viewed these three components as constructs, not physical entities. The basic component of personality is the *id,* which is present at birth and is the source of impulses that operate in an uncensored manner. The id strives to fulfill such basic needs as hunger, thirst, and sex. It operates on the pleasure principle and demands immediate and complete gratification. The individual is not aware of the id because it is not expressed consciously. The id is primitive, uninhibited, and not subject to rational control. At birth, the id is the total personality of each person.

The second component that develops is the *ego.* It begins to develop shortly after birth, when the child realizes that not everything wanted is immediately available. The task of this construct is to mediate between the needs expressed by the id and the real world. It is the only personality component that, in Freud's theory, has access to and a relationship with the actual environment.[19]

The ego distinguishes between what exists in the subjective mind and what exists in the reality of the external world. It may be described as the rational cognitive process that decides one's course of action. It serves as the manager of an individual's personality structure and has the capacity of recognizing, evaluating, and testing reality. It reasons and learns from experience. Like the id, the ego generally functions at the unconscious level; Freud believed that none of the three components of personality operates solely at the level of consciousness.[20]

The ego functions as the problem-solving element of personality as it deals with the real world and copes with life. This process becomes increasingly complex as the third component of personality, the *superego,* begins to develop.

Up to this point, the ego need only check with reality to see whether the demands of the id can be met, but the superego adds a new dimension. The superego is shaped by society's concepts of what is right and what is wrong, what conduct is acceptable and what is unacceptable. These ideals and values are acquired by everyone (either through being taught or through learning from example) during childhood. Over the years each person develops his or her own norms and standards of behavior, which are reflected in the superego.[21]

Thus, the superego is concerned with morality, with what is right and what is wrong. It is formed early during childhood and influences reality via the ego. It is like a conscience that contains values and a control system telling us what we should and should not do. The superego permits the fulfillment of id impulses only when they are found to be moral, regardless of whether the ego determines that such fulfillment would be safe and reasonable.[22]

Generally speaking, when the id is in control, an individual tends to act in a selfish manner, is easily angered, and can be impulsive. If one's superego is overdeveloped, an individual will tend to feel guilty and unworthy. When the ego dominates an individual's personality, there is a more realistic behavior pattern, the person tends to react logically, and life is generally more satisfying.[23]

Freud's psychoanalytical explanation of personality is based on the idea of conflict; it involves constant interplay between the id and the superego, moderated by the ego. The behavior patterns of individuals are viewed as the result of defense mechanisms that respond to the anxiety created by the conflict.

Managers may encounter various defense mechanisms as they deal with employees and other managers. Each mechanism is designed to reduce the anxiety created in an individual by conflict among the three components of his or her personality.[24] One of the most common defense mechanisms is *projection*. Individuals using this mechanism tend to see in others the traits or characteristics they have themselves. For example, an officer might project his or her own personal feelings, emotions, anxieties, and motives when judging other officers or supervisors. A supervisor who is highly judgmental and critical of everything done by subordinates will, in many cases, view his or her own immediate manager as too strict and demanding in never allowing freedom to perform assigned tasks. Projection also occurs when managers assume all employees being supervised are like themselves, hardworking, industrious, goal oriented, and totally devoted to work. It can be a shock when a manager realizes that some employees have a greater orientation to their family or to personal activities than to work.[25]

*Avoidance* is another defense mechanism. Managers who consistently withdraw from conflict situations involving their subordinates are using this mechanism. This can be costly not only to the officers involved but to the organization. Patrol officers who practice this form of behavior have been known to respond too slowly to calls for service involving potential physical confrontations or danger. It is also common to find an officer who is harboring a deep feeling of resentment toward his or her peers to handle this feeling by avoiding social interaction with other officers. Such officers may at times resort to e-mail as their only means of communication with others. Still others will use all their available sick leave (but not to the point of jeopardizing their job) as a means of avoiding organizational conflict and reducing anxiety.[26]

For police officers in the performance of their duties to exhibit anger, hostility, or aggression is considered unprofessional conduct. However, anger is a very powerful feeling, and many officers have trouble dealing with either their own anger or that of others. It should be kept in mind that anger, like any other feeling, is not good or bad in and of itself, but police officers are expected to repress or deny any anger they may feel when dealing with others.

The fact is that almost all people become angry from time to time, and some act on this feeling by becoming aggressive. The improper use of force by an officer is often a reaction to deeply repressed feelings of anger and fear. There is no one correct way to respond to anger. Police managers must be constantly aware of the psychological well-being of their officers. Line supervisors are the closest to their subordinates and are usually the first to sense problems in their officers' behavior reactions.

Police managers should receive training in counseling. It is their responsibility to investigate incidents in which their officers' behavior has violated department regulations or the law. However, through training and counseling they may be able to act in a positive manner through early intervention to prevent this type of incident from occurring. Generally speaking, the first sign of a problem of this nature is not physical but verbal aggression.

Freud's psychoanalytical explanation of personality is not accepted by all behavioral scientists, but his early works have had a strong influence on others who have investigated the concept of personality. At the very least, the theory points out the complexity of human behavior and provides managers with a way of understanding how subconscious conflicts can lead to anxieties that affect the behavior of their officers.

## Trait Theory

Another approach to analyzing human personality, called trait theory, focuses on specific attributes peculiar to individuals. Each individual's personality is viewed as growing out of a particular collection of traits, such as ambition, loyalty, and aggression, which remains consistent from situation to situation. Some of the trait approaches identify distinct personality categories against which individuals are matched. Other approaches see personality differences more as a matter of degree than of the distinct presence or absence of certain traits.[27]

In contrast to Freud's emphasis on the unconscious, Gordon Allport and H. S. Odbert believed that conscious determinants of behavior were what really counted. They theorized that each person's unique behavior could be accounted for or predicted based on the lasting, stable presence of certain specific traits.[28] These traits are basic descriptive terms for how each individual interacts within both society and organizations. They include such attributes as being quick-tempered, aggressive, or social.

Oscar Williams has been a patrol officer for seven years in the Metropolitan Police Department. He is a graduate of the local university, where he majored in political science. During his college years he was an outstanding football player and could favorably be described as a big man on campus. After graduation, he served in the Army for six years and was discharged with the rank of first lieutenant.

In the police academy he was considered by his instructors to be the best cadet ever graduated from the program. Williams passed the field-training and probationary periods with flying colors, and each of his supervisors anticipated that he would move rapidly through the ranks. After his second year in patrol, he served successfully as a member of the department's SWAT team and then as a member of a special task force that monitored the activities of paroled offenders with extensive criminal records.

Officer Williams has taken the sergeants examination twice but failed the written portion both times. He responds by continually criticizing the promotion examination, pointing out that it is not actually a true measure of the skills an individual needs in order to be an effective supervisor. Over the last two years, he has slowly but surely become disgruntled with the police department's management. He criticizes many of the department's policies and constantly questions the promotional process.

He has begun to function at a minimum level and only does what is necessary to keep out of trouble. He arrives late for roll call, but not late enough to be disciplined. He takes coffee and meal breaks exceeding the time set forth by departmental policy. His general negative attitude is rubbing off on younger officers, and some of the older officers refuse to work with him. During this same time, he has become very active in the local police union, and he uses his membership as a platform for criticizing department management. He constantly finds fault with every immediate supervisor, saying that they are exceedingly strict and refuse to give officers the freedom needed to perform effectively. Officer Williams is increasingly viewed as a thorn in management's side and a real problem employee.

His immediate supervisor has become increasingly strict in her supervision and is documenting the times he is late for roll call or takes too much time for meal and coffee breaks. Every arrest Officer Williams makes is reviewed with careful scrutiny, and reports he prepares are rejected with increasing frequency. Officer Williams filed a grievance against his immediate supervisor, charging that he has been singled out for punishment because he is active in the police union.

*If you were Officer Williams's supervisor, how would you deal with this distressing person? Is there something in Officer Williams's conduct that suggests he has a personality problem? If so, what is it? How should a manager work with an employee who is constantly negative? Can something be done to change the negative traits that Officer Williams exhibits?*

---

Allport and Odbert identified three modes in which traits influence behavior: *cardinal*, *central*, and *secondary*. They described a *cardinal* trait as a single trait dominating the behavior of an individual; they believed such individuals to be rare. A possible example of an individual with a cardinal trait would be a police executive who displays a calm, secure, and unworried demeanor in all situations, no matter how out of control his or her words or actions may seem to others involved.

More typically, according to Allport, an individual's behavior will be the expression of a larger group of *central* traits. Allport felt that an evaluator could form an accurate understanding of an individual's personality by knowing as few as five to ten of his or her traits.

The third level Allport identified consisted of *secondary* traits, which are sometimes displayed by individuals but which fluctuate and change from time to time. These "surplus" traits are not strong enough to influence individual behavior successfully. In general, Allport's efforts were directed toward finding a way to describe or identify personalities rather than trying to explain what causes them.[29]

Recently, the "Five Factor" model, a different personality theory also based on predispositional traits, has been found valuable in understanding personality and work behavior.[30] Table 3–1 identifies the five personality elements

**Table 3–1  The "Five Factor" Personality Traits**

| Core Traits | Descriptive Characteristics of High Scores |
| --- | --- |
| Conscientiousness | Dependable, hardworking, organized, self-disciplined, persistent, responsible |
| Emotional stability | Calm, secure, happy, unworried |
| Agreeableness | Cooperative, warm, caring, good-natured, courteous, trusting |
| Extraversion | Sociable, outgoing, talkative, assertive, gregarious |
| Openness to experience | Curious, intellectual, creative, cultured, artistically sensitive, flexible, imaginative |

used in this model and their major characteristics. There is now considerable agreement on which personality trait predispositions lie at the core of personality, and there is also accumulated research that these five best predict performance in the workplace.[31] Although the five traits are largely independent factors of a personality, like primary colors, they can be mixed in countless proportions and with other characteristics to yield a unique personality whole. However, also like colors, one may dominate in describing an individual's personality.[32]

Of the five factors, *conscientiousness* has been identified as the one with the strongest positive relationship to job performance. Individuals who are dependable, persistent, goal directed, and organized tend to be higher performers, especially in police work.[33] Conscientious police officers and managers set higher achievement goals for themselves, hold higher performance expectations, and respond well to empowerment. They are also less likely to be absent from work.[34]

Although conscientiousness has received the most attention because of its impact on employee performance, the remaining traits are also important. Equally important, especially for managers, is *emotional stability*. Police managers who maintain a calm, secure disposition in emotionally charged situations are highly valued. Their behavior serves as a model to the officers they supervise.[35] Recently, it was found that the five factors might also be predictive of team performance. Higher-performance teams were found to have better than average scores on traits of conscientiousness, agreeableness, extraversion, and emotional stability.[36] In conclusion, depending on the situation, all five of the traits measured by this model warrant attention when analyzing organizational behavior.

**Humanistic Theory**

Humanistic theory is a positive approach that views each individual as important in determining his or her own growth. It is represented by psychologist Carl Rogers, who had a very optimistic view of human strength and who believed self-concept was the core of personality. Rogers believed that all people have a basic drive toward self-actualization, that is, toward being all they can be. Self-concept includes the attitudes, values, thoughts, and beliefs that individuals have developed during a lifetime of experience. Rogers viewed the workings of the unconscious mind as a positive motivator for individual behavior. He said that the concept of self evolves from one's early experience in dealing with the environment, from the regard shown by others, and ultimately from reaching a point where the ideal self and the real self are congruent.[37]

Police personnel should be selected based on their ability to shift gears psychologically as they adapt to the demands of changing situations.

Michael Newman, PhotoEdit

The *congruent* individual functions at the very highest level. Such a person is open, does not react defensively, gets along well with others, and possesses high self-esteem. Rogers suggests this individual is one whose fundamental desire is to become everything he or she is capable of being. This means that for each individual, self-actualization is something unique, specific, and totally individualized.[38]

Other individuals may have an *incongruent* personal view, may become tense or anxious, and may react defensively as a means of protecting and preserving the view they have of themselves. From a managerial perspective, humanistic theory would suggest that such employees need to be treated positively, that is, understood and respected as individuals. In the humanistic view, employees are positive assets of the organization; if it becomes necessary to discipline or criticize them, the focus should be on the unacceptable or inadequate behavior and not on the individual. Under no circumstances should an employee be rejected as an individual. Feedback should emphasize tasks to be performed, with the aim of helping employees improve their job performance. The key is not to attack an employee's self-esteem, because that will result in many undesirable effects.[39]

Humanistic theory, like other personality theories, has both supporters and detractors, but its value is that it focuses on the positive aspects of human nature, acknowledging that the human organism seeks growth, self-actualization, and pleasant, productive relationships with others.

Personality is exceedingly complex, as is evident from the personality theories discussed above. Each of these theories makes a significant contribution to the understanding of personality. Depending on his or her education, preparation, training, and background, a manager may feel most comfortable with the explanations offered by one of the theories and find that that theory

## Table 3–2  **Personality Theories**

| Theory Type | Motivation for Behavior | Primary Interest |
| --- | --- | --- |
| Psychoanalytical | Unconscious | General behavior |
| Trait | Conscious | The individual |
| Humanistic | Conscious or unconscious | The individual |

meets his or her specific needs. What is essential is for managers to choose one or more of the theories to use as a means of gaining insight into organizational behavior (see Table 3–2 for a comparative chart of the theories). A manager might use the psychoanalytical approach by working to identify the nature and extent of conflict exhibited by employees and the defense mechanisms they employ. Some managers might feel comfortable in evaluating personality by utilizing observable traits such as self-sufficiency, control, or conscientiousness. Another manager might find the most satisfactory approach is to assist employees in achieving goals and enhancing their self-esteem. Each of these approaches can be used to provide insight into an individual's total personality—including the actual character, behavior, and temperament of the employee.

## DIMENSIONS OF PERSONALITY

Researchers have identified a number of personality dimensions that have special relevance in the work environment. The significance of these dimensions varies from organization to organization and from situation to situation. Each is related to the overall concept of personality rather than to any specific personality theory. The dimensions we discuss here are locus of control, Type A/Type B behavior, Machiavellianism, and adapting to Bureaucratic Orientation.

**Locus of Control**  According to the concept of *locus of control*, people can be broadly divided into those ("internals") who believe that they themselves are responsible for what happens to them and those ("externals") who believe that what happens to them is determined by situations or other people.[40] These expectations are learned. Internals believe they control their own fate; externals believe luck and chance control their fate.

Consider the following situation. Officer Cole has been studying for the promotional examination to be given next Wednesday. How should she approach the test? With the idea that passing or failing will be primarily determined by how well she studies the course material? Or with the idea that her results will have much less to do with her academic preparation than with factors totally beyond her control, such as the validity of the test? Or, perhaps, with the idea that her test results will depend on her ability to obtain a copy of the test in advance?

If Cole believes that her results will depend on her own efforts, she is said to have an *internal* locus of control; if she perceives passing or failing as beyond her ability to influence, she is said to have an *external* locus of control (see Table 3–3).

Locus of control is a continuous personality dimension, and employees actually are arranged somewhere on a continuum ranging from high external to high internal. Research on locus of control has strong implications for

**Table 3–3   Characteristics of Employees Who Have an Internal Locus of Control**

| | |
|---|---|
| Information seeking | Involvement in decision-making |
| Goal oriented | Self-control |
| Social | Limited risk taker |
| Extroverted | Achievement oriented |
| Responsive to motivation programs | Persuasive |

organizations. There is some evidence that internals have greater control over how they behave in any given situation, are more social, and actively search out information needed to accomplish a task. Internals have been found to have higher job satisfaction, to be more willing to accept managerial responsibility, and to prefer participative management.[41]

Internal locus of control has additional implications for police managers. Internals have been shown to display higher work motivation and to believe more strongly that effort leads to accomplishment. They are more likely to want some control over their jobs and will generally exhibit a strong desire to assume some responsibility for decision-making. They want to be part of the organization and control as much of their working environment as possible.[42]

Internals enjoy work over which they have some control and usually gain satisfaction from the work itself. They exhibit a great deal of self-control, conform to reasonable guidelines, and limit risk taking. Internals, as a group, are more extroverted in interpersonal relations and more apt to relate to fellow employees as well as to the public. They are responsive to motivation techniques and programs, and their careers advance more rapidly than those of individuals with an external orientation.

Locus of control has serious implications for police managers. Internals want to be involved, so each manager should strive to create an inclusive working environment that seeks officer input. The working environment should foster individuality and reduce employee dependency. It should also be kept in mind that people's expectations can change; they are not set in concrete. Managers can make a difference, and this is best done when the organization continually acknowledges and rewards outstanding performance.

An effective manager can change the expectations of employees, thereby improving morale and making a positive impact on employee performance. As employees become aware that hard work and the attainment of objectives are adequately rewarded, they are persuaded that what they do and how they do it can make a significant difference. The goal of the manager is to affect performance positively by demonstrating that each individual has the potential to influence outcomes. Subordinates must be made to feel that the things they do are significant.[43]

## Type A and Type B Behavior

Another personality dimension of interest to police managers is one that distinguishes what is called *Type A* behavior from *Type B* behavior. Both of these types intrigue behavioral scientists because of their impact on the organization and its employees.

The Type A personality is characterized by a competitive striving for achievement, an exaggerated sense of time urgency, and a tendency toward aggressiveness and hostility. Individuals who exhibit Type A traits are more than three times as likely to experience serious heart disease.[44] Type A individuals tend to

Table 3–4  **Type A Personality**

| | |
|---|---|
| Competitive | Hard driving |
| Achievement oriented | Impatient |
| Tendency toward aggressiveness | Easily irritated |
| Tendency toward hostility | Detail oriented |

work rapidly on assigned tasks, and their working relationships with others are often uncomfortable, impatient, irritating, and even aggressive. Police managers described as "Type A" typically set high performance standards, are hard driving and detail oriented, and thrive on routine (see Table 3–4).

Type A individuals work fast even when there is no need to do so. When this tendency is carried to the extreme, their concern for details can become more important than the results they are trying to achieve. In addition, Type A individuals dislike being interrupted and show outward signs of annoyance and impatience such as frowns and grimaces when it happens.[45] When work becomes all-important, this type of person will resist change, tightly control the activities of subordinates, and behave in a way that has a negative impact on interpersonal relations.[46]

The impatient nature of Type A personalities causes them to perform poorly when the task requires a delayed response. Current research suggests Type A's perform better when they function under the pressure of a deadline, when they are required to respond to multiple demands, or when they are performing solitary work. On the other hand, they function below par when they have to perform tasks requiring complex judgment and when required to work as a member of a team.[47]

The Type B personality can be described as easygoing and not especially competitive. Current evidence suggests that about 40 percent of the general population is Type A and 60 percent Type B.[48] Obviously, the two types have different impacts on a police organization and have to be handled differently. Type B personalities are more easygoing, relaxed, unhurried, deferential, and satisfied. They are easier to manage because their behavior is predictable. Because they are noncompetitive and prefer to work with others, they are good candidates for team assignments or for working in two-officer patrol vehicles. When they assume supervisory and managerial positions, they prove to be people oriented and interact well with peers and with those they supervise.

Some Type B personalities have refused promotions because moving to higher ranks would force them to function as administrators rather than as managers continually interacting with subordinates. Type B managers are more apt to delegate authority, let employees work at their own pace, and provide detailed supervision. The ability to get along with others and the desire to work as a team are significant characteristics of Type B managers. On the other hand, the Type B personality needs closer supervision to ensure that deadlines are met and organizational objectives achieved.

**Machiavellianism**

Naturally, the personalities of police managers vary considerably. Occasionally a supervisor or manager exhibits the characteristics attributed to Niccolo Machiavelli (1469–1527), who more than 400 years ago wrote a book

Table 3–5 **High-Mach Personality**

| | |
|---|---|
| Power hungry | Deceitful |
| Manipulative | Logical |
| Pragmatic | Adept at identifying weaknesses in others |
| Emotionally distant | Influential |
| Not concerned with morality | Detached |

entitled *The Prince*, which outlined a strategy for obtaining and keeping power.[49] This book is still required reading in several business schools.

Machiavelli's book advocates a strong leadership style, including manipulation of others as a way to attain goals. He admonishes readers that "It is better to be feared than loved," and "Humility not only is of no service, but is actually harmful."[50] Clearly, Machiavelli believed that ends always justify means. A true Machiavellian manager is pragmatic, maintains emotional distance, and manipulates others for personal gain.[51] Making friends, being loyal, and expressing anything resembling ethics or morality are all viewed as inhibitors of true success.

Two psychologists, Richard Christie and Florence Geis, developed a short questionnaire termed the *Mach Scale*. Those who score high on the test are termed *High-Machs* and behave in ways consistent with the principles espoused by Machiavelli.[52] High-Mach managers are not the least bit concerned about whether they lie or not and will use deceit in their relationships to achieve their desires. In their view, morality can be ignored if necessary to achieve desired objectives. High-Machs are usually convincing liars and are adept at identifying weaknesses in others. In general, others are viewed as being gullible and not aware of what is best for them. Thus, High-Machs will likely justify their behavior as ethical because they were acting in the best interest of others[53] (see Table 3–5).

Managers with a High-Mach personality orientation approach tasks logically and thoughtfully, do not respond to persuasion, and have little regard for the opinions of others. They consider their problems with cool detachment and never allow emotions to enter into the equation. High-Machs function best when they control the situation and operate in a nonstructured position.[54]

Interestingly enough, High-Machs feel no guilt as they manipulate others for personal gain. It is a game, and the winner takes all. They perform at their zenith when dealing with others face to face, when emotions cloud the judgment of others, and when the situation is loosely structured.[55]

Managers of this type are quickly identified by patrol officers, who see through their deceit and manipulations and respond with passive resistance and minimum work output. The officers know that the High-Mach manager is only concerned for his or her own personal objectives, and they resist through small actions, such as working strictly according to rules and regulations, refusing to perform work outside their job title, and generating just enough citations and arrests to meet minimum productivity standards.[56]

**Bureaucratic Orientation**

Police departments, for the most part, are bureaucratic organizations that foster top-down management control systems. Many agencies hold sacred the concepts of rationality, hierarchy, specialization, and positional authority. Rules and regulations dominate daily operations. It is the view of many that a bureaucracy thwarts communication and stifles innovation and creativity. Many people also feel that such an organization demands conformity and group thinking but limits personal growth.[57]

Is there such a thing as a bureaucratic personality? That is, are there certain personality features that best describe those who achieve rank in bureaucratic organizations? Bureaucracies are very demanding in their own special way, and it appears that individuals who exhibit the following attitudes and behaviors seem to be the best-adjusted individuals within such organizations:

1. They exhibit absolute conformity and adherence to rules and regulations. Individualization is minimal; abstract rules dominate operations.
2. Their social interactions are impersonal and are not allowed to interfere with their decisions and other organizational processes.
3. They accept higher authority without question. The chain of command dominates and must never be violated, so acquiescence to authority is essential.
4. They are traditionalists and supporters of the status quo: members are expected to identify with the department and accept the traditions developed over the years.
5. They operate deep within the box of rules, focusing on what was and is, not on what could be.[58]

Those who are out of step with the demands of a bureaucratic organization are more apt to seek employment elsewhere. It is also quite apparent that some personalities have no difficulty in accepting bureaucratic standards and adjusting well to such an organization. Many individuals find bureaucracies meet their personal needs because rules dominate, positional authority is viewed as important, and the organization is looked on as more important than the individual.

---

**CASE STUDY**   Lieutenant Robert F. Taylor

Robert F. Taylor has been a member of the Continental Police Department for eight years. He is currently assigned to the chief's office and is responsible for supervising the investigation of complaints against sworn personnel. He has been a lieutenant for two years, having assumed his current position after serving as a watch commander in the patrol division. Lt. Taylor graduated from the local university where he majored in public administration. Within the department, there are a number of officers and supervisors who feel Taylor achieved his current rank because of his skill at manipulating people and his total disregard for the feelings of others.

Lt. Taylor is viewed as someone who clawed his way to the top in a relatively short period of time, and the general consensus is that he is power hungry, using deceit without any thought of the moral consequences. He is very pragmatic in his approach to decision-making and has demonstrated a special ability to influence the brass in the organization. Many feel he is being groomed for an early promotion to captain.

Taylor goes by the book and is a stickler for the application of each and every rule or regulation. He may be described as a real traditionalist and is totally devoted to the job. Whatever comes down from the top is viewed as gospel and is never questioned. There is considerable anxiety about whether Taylor will use his new position in such a way as to ensure his next promotion.

Taylor is aware of how he is viewed by some of the members of the department. He says he believes some of it is sour grapes, but he is still concerned about the potential negative influence on his career.

*How would you describe Lt. Taylor's personality? Does he have a strong bureaucratic orientation? Would you describe him as a Type A or as possessing a High-Mach personality? If you were Taylor, how would you deal with those who object to the way you operate? Would it be counterproductive for you to try to change your behavior in your new position? If you were Taylor's immediate supervisor, how would you relate to him?*

# SUMMARY

Police managers must continually analyze personality and its impact on employee behavior. There are a number of theories describing how personality develops. Each of these makes the following assumptions about human behavior: (1) Every individual possesses specific personality characteristics; (2) Life experiences influence personality characteristics; and (3) Each individual develops a distinct personality as a result of life experiences.

Early research into personality postulated heredity as the final arbiter of how one acquires personality, but it is currently believed that heredity plays a limited part in determining behavior. Culture is another factor influencing personality development. Culture exposes everyone to certain norms, attitudes, and values that are passed from parents to children. Culturally based factors exert a great deal of influence on organizational behavior, and police managers must respond not only to cultural variance but also to the different ways culture influences each person.

Another factor influencing personality is the situation. A situation may alter the behavior of an individual, causing a manager a great deal of difficulty when trying to supervise an employee. Unfortunately, much research remains to be done on situational factors and their influence on personality.

There are numerous theories of personality development. The most prominent are psychoanalytical, trait, and humanistic. Each theory can provide a manager with useful insights into the complexities of human individual, interpersonal, group, and organizational behavior.

Researchers have identified a number of personality dimensions that may have special relevance in the work environment. These dimensions include locus of control, Type A/Type B behavior, Machiavellianism, and bureaucratic orientation.

# KEY TERMS

bureaucratic orientation
culture
ego
heredity
High-Machs
humanistic
id
locus of control
Machiavellianism

personality
personality determinants
psychoanalytical
situational
superego
traits
Type A behavior
Type B behavior

# DISCUSSION TOPICS AND QUESTIONS

1. How does personality develop?
2. How important is culture in the development of the individual?
3. Why do individuals who have a bureaucratic orientation seem to perform effectively in police organizations?
4. Differentiate between individuals who have an external and an internal locus of control.
5. How would you deal with a manager who uses avoidance as a defensive technique?
6. In what ways do situational factors determine personality?
7. Differentiate between psychoanalytical and trait theories.
8. Describe three kinds of traits.
9. What are the characteristics of employees who have an internal locus of control?
10. Describe the personality orientation of a High-Mach employee.

# FOR FURTHER READING

Elizabeth Reuss-Ianni, *Two Cultures of Policing: Street Cops and Management Cops* (New Brunswick, CT: Transaction Books, 1983).

Classic study of the distinctly different organizational cultures that exist between line and management cops in the same department.

Victor E. Kappler, Richard D. Sluder, and Geoffrey P. Alpert, *Forces of Deviance: Understanding the Dark Side of Policing* (Prospect Heights, IL: Waveland Press, 1998).

A thought-provoking analysis of police deviance that raises serious questions about management operations and ethical issues.

# NOTES

1. Fred Luthans, *Organizational Behavior,* 9th ed. (New York: McGraw-Hill, 2002), p. 215.

2. John R. Schermerhorn, Jr., James G. Hunt, and Richard N. Osborn, *Organizational Behavior* (New York: Wiley, 2002), p. 51.

3. S.R. Maddi, *Personality Theories: A Comparative Analysis* (Homewood, IL: Dorsey, 1980), p. 32.

4. Larry K. Gaines, Victor E. Kappler, and Joseph B. Vaughn, *Police in America* (Cincinnati: Anderson, 1994), pp. 241–242.

5. Roy Roberg, John Crank, and Jack Kuykendall, *Police & Society* (Los Angeles: Roxbury, 2000), pp. 129–131.

6. J.R. Terborg, "Interactional Psychology and Research on Human Behavior in Organizations," *Academy of Management Review*, Vol. 6 (1981), pp. 561–576.

7. Elizabeth Reuss-Ianni, *Two Cultures of Policing: Street Cops and Management Cops* (New Brunswick, CT: Transaction Books, 1983).

8. Beth Azar, "Nature, Nurture: Not Mutually Exclusive," *American Psychological Association Monitor* (May 1997), p. 1.

9. J. Steven Ott, *The Organizational Culture Perspective* (Pacific Grove, CA: Brooks/Cole, 1989), pp. 1–12.

10. Debra L. Nelson and James Campbell Quick, *Organizational Behavior: Foundations, Realities, and Challenges* (St. Paul, MN: West, 1995), pp. 494–497.

11. Terrence E. Deal and A. Kennedy, *Corporate Cultures* (Reading, MA: Addison-Wesley, 1982).

12. Y. Weiner and Y. Vardi, "Relationships Between Organizational Culture and Individual Motivation: A Conceptual Integration," *Psychological Reports*, Vol. 67 (1990), pp. 295–306.

13. Nelson and Quick, *Organizational Behavior*, p. 494.

14. Ron Zemke, Clair Raines, and Bob Filipizak, *Generations at Work: Managing the Clash of Veterans, Boomers, Xers and Nexters in Your Workplace* (New York: AMACOM, 2000).

15. Luthans, *Organizational Behavior*, p. 218.

16. Victor E. Kappler, Richard D. Sluder, and Geoffrey P. Alpert, *Forces of Deviance: Understanding the Dark Side of Policing* (Prospect Heights IL: Waveland Press, 1998).

17. David G. Myers, *Psychology* (New York: Worth, 1986).

18. Peter Gay, *The Freud Reader* (New York: W.W. Norton, 1995).

19. Samuel E. Wood and Ellen G. Wood, *The World of Psychology* (Boston: Pearson Allyn and Bacon, 2001).

20. Nelson and Quick, *Organizational Behavior*, pp. 79–80.

21. Alan O. Ross, *Personality: The Scientific Study of Complex Human Behavior* (New York: International Thomson Publishing, 1987).

22. Jerald Greenberg and Robert A. Baron, *Behavior in Organizations: Understanding the Human Side of Work* (Upper Saddle River, NJ: Prentice Hall, 2002).

23. Donald A. Laird, Eleanor C. Laird, and Rosemary T. Fruehling, *Psychology: Human Relations and Work Adjustment* (New York: McGraw-Hill 1993).

24. Duane Schultz and Sydney Ellen Schultz, *Psychology and Work Today: Introduction to Industrial and Organizational Psychology* (Upper Saddle River, NJ: Prentice Hall, 2001).

25. Donald D. White and David D. Bednar, *Organizational Behavior: Understanding and Managing People at Work* (Boston: Allyn & Bacon, 1986).

26. Schermerhorn, Hunt, and Osborn, *Organizational Behavior*, p. 387.

27. Stephen P. Robbins, *Managing Today* (Upper Saddle River, NJ: Prentice Hall, 1997), pp. 354–360.

28. R. Richard Bootzin, Gordon H. Bower, Robert B. Zajonic, and Elizabeth Hall, *Psychology Today* (New York: Random House, 1986).

29. Gordon W. Allport and H.S. Odbert, "Trait Names: A Psychological Study," *Psychological Monographs*, Vol. 4 (1936), pp. 211–214.

30. J.M. Digman, "Personality Structure: Emergence of the Five-Factor Model," *Annual Review of Psychology*, Vol. 41 (1990), pp. 417–440.

31. Robert J. House, Scott A. Shane, and David M. Herold, "Rumors of the Death of Dispositional Research Are Vastly Exaggerated," *Academy of Management Review* (January 1996), p. 203.

32. Luthans, *Organizational Behavior*, pp. 220–222.

33. Michael K. Mount and Murray R. Barrick, "Five Reasons Why the Big Five Article Has Been Frequently Cited," *Personnel Psychology*, Vol. 5 (1998), pp. 849–857.

34. T.A. Judge, J.J. Martocchio, and C.J. Thoresen, "Five-Factor Model of Personality and Employee Absence," *Journal of Applied Psychology*, Vol. 82 (1998), pp. 745–755.

35. Paul M. Whisenand and R. Fred Ferguson, *The Managing of Police Organizations* (Upper Saddle River, NJ: Prentice Hall, 2002).

36. Murray R. Barrick, G.L. Stewart, M.J. Neubert, and M.K. Mount, "Relating Member Ability and Personality to Work-Team Processes and Team Effectiveness," *Journal of Applied Psychology*, Vol. 83 (1998), pp. 377–391.

37. Carl Rogers, *On Becoming a Person: A Therapist View of Psychotherapy* (Boston: Houghton Mifflin, 1970).

38. R. Richard Bootzin, Gordon H. Bower, Robert B. Zajonic, and Elizabeth Hall, *Psychology Today* (New York: Random House, 1986).

39. Whisenand and Ferguson, *Managing Police Organizations*, pp. 288–308.

40. Nelson and Quick, *Organizational Behavior*, p. 80.

41. T.R. Mitchell, C.M. Smyser, and S.E. Weed, "Locus of Control: Supervision and Work Satisfaction," *Academy of Management Journal*, Vol. 57 (1975), pp. 623–631.

42. P. Spector, "Behavior in Organizations as a Function of Locus of Control," *Psychological Bulletin*, Vol. 93 (1982), pp. 482–497.

43. Ronald G. Lynch, *The Police Manager* (Cincinnati: Anderson, 1998), pp. 27–42.

44. Myer Friedman and Ray H. Rosenman, *Type A Behavior and Your Heart* (New York: Knopf, 1974).

45. Robert E. Franken, *Human Motivation* (Pacific Grove, CA: Brooks/Cole, 1988).

46. Schermerhorn, Hunt, and Osborn, *Organizational Behavior*.

47. C. Lee, L.F. Jamison, and P.C. Earley, "Beliefs and Fears and Type A Behavior: Implications for Academic Performance and Psychiatric Health Disorder Symptoms," *Journal of Organizational Behavior*, (1996), pp.151–177.

48. Jerald Greenberg and Robert A. Baron, *Behavior in Organization: Understanding the Human Side of Work* (Upper Saddle River: Prentice Hall, 2002).

49. Niccolo Machiavelli, *The Prince* (New York: Simon & Schuster, 1970).

50. Ibid, pp. 71–75.

51. James Bowditch and Anthony Buono, *A Primer on Organizational Behavior* (New York: Wiley, 1994), p. 115.

52. Richard Christie and Florence L. Geis, *Studies in Machiavellianism* (New York: Academic Press, 1970).

53. R.A. Giacalone and S.B. Knouse, "Justifying Wrongful Employee Behavior: The Role of Personality in Organizational Sabotage," *Journal of Business Ethics*, Vol. 9 (1990), pp. 55–56.

54. Schermerhorn, Hunt, and Osborn, *Organizational Behavior*, pp. 54–55.

55. Robbins, *Managing Today*, p. 356.

56. See William F. Walsh, "Patrol Officer Arrest Rates: A Study in the Social Organization of Police Work," *Justice Quarterly*, Vol. 3 (1986), pp. 271–290.

57. Mark H. Moore and Darrel W. Stephens, *Beyond Command and Control: The Strategic Management of Police Departments* (Washington, DC: Police Executive Research Forum, 1991), pp. 1–6.

58. David Osborne and Ted Gaebler, *Reinventing Government: How the Entrepreneurial Spirit Is Transforming the Public Sector* (New York: Penguin Group, 1993), pp. 212–214.

# —4—

# BELIEFS, VALUES, AND ATTITUDES

## Determinants of Human Behavior

1. Define *operant behavior.*
2. Define *culture,* and identify the steps involved in the socialization process.
3. Discuss the nature of and need for introspection.
4. Compare and contrast ideas, beliefs, values, attitudes, opinions, and motives.
5. Identify various levels of existence, and discuss them in terms of value conflict.
6. Demonstrate the relationship between attitudes and job satisfaction in complex organizations.
7. Define *perception.*
8. Identify the principal components in the perception formation process.
9. List and describe the steps involved in perception formation.
10. Describe the sources of perceptual distortion.
11. Define *motivation,* and show how it is affected by prior experience, beliefs, values, attitudes, opinions, and expectations.
12. Show how behavior is a function of the interaction between people and their environment.
13. Describe the manager's role in changing improper attitudes and behaviors that are exhibited by employees.
14. Identify the steps involved in a planned intervention designed to produce a change in employee attitudes and behaviors.
15. Illustrate the complex relationship between environmental stimuli and goal-directed behavior.

Police departments are dynamic, organic organizational social systems created by and composed of human beings. They are microcosms of the society at large and provide a sociocultural setting in which people interact with, react to, and influence one another as they pursue common goals and objectives. However, it is common for many officers to refer to their organization as a distinct separate thing—"the department." They fail to recognize that they and their activities *are* the organization.

The individual is the fundamental subsystem upon which organizations are built. Individuals consist of interdependent physiological and psychosocial systems that work in concert with environmental factors to produce distinctive behavior. The dynamic interdependence between human (internal) and environmental (external) factors helps to account for the complexity of human behavior.[1]

Harvey Adams is a captain in charge of the midnight patrol shift in a large urban police department located in the Midwest. The captain is 57 years old and has been a police officer for nearly 30 years. Once considered progressive and even radical, he has been having great difficulty dealing with many of the social changes taking place in society. Adams is, in fact, being investigated by the State Human Relations Commission. He has been charged with sexual discrimination against a female police officer.

Officer Jo Andleman, 26 years old, has been with the department for 2 years. She is the only female officer on Adams's shift. Andleman has been working the midnight shift for about 8 months. An avowed feminist, she "marches to her own drummer." She is outspoken in her support of equal rights and comparable pay for women. Officer Andleman is also a pro-choice activist.

When Capt. Adams heard rumors that Andleman was living with a male police officer assigned to the same shift, he called her into his office and ordered her to sever the "immoral" relationship immediately. Even though she had a "clean slate," he gave her a written reprimand for "conduct unbecoming an officer." When she objected, he criticized her for "living in sin" and subjecting the police department to ridicule. Adams told Andleman that if she had to "shack up" with a policeman that she should "make it legal" and become his "little mama." Adams told her that he would do all he could to get her fired if she failed to heed his "advice."

Because the department's rules regarding conduct do not prohibit fraternization or cohabitation with other police personnel, Officer Andleman filed a grievance to have the written reprimand removed from her folder. She also filed a sexual discrimination charge with the Human Relations Commission. Capt. Adams is upset by the incident and has put in for retirement. He told the chief he could no longer stand to work in the same department with "morally bankrupt people."

The Human Relations Commission investigation revealed that Harvey Adams was raised in a traditional and very religious family. As a fundamentalist, he interprets the Bible in literal terms. Adams was taught that women are subservient to men and should function as homemakers. He feels that women have no place in a "man's job" like police work. Thus Capt. Adams has a very negative attitude toward female police officers. He belittles them and expresses his opinions in overtly sexist terms.

*Is Capt. Adams a dinosaur and out of step with society? Or is he representative of the male chauvinists who were attracted to police work in the past? Prepare a memo for the mayor explaining—based on the information contained in this chapter—what you think happened in this situation. Indicate whether or not you feel that the captain's resignation was in the best interest of the police department.*

## HUMAN BEHAVIOR

Human beings are social animals who exhibit recurrent, regular, and recognizable patterns of behavior. In a general sense, *behavior* can be defined as anything an individual does that involves self-initiated action and/or reaction to a given stimulus. From an organizational point of view, behavior consists of adaptive adjustments people make as they cope with one another, with problems, with opportunities, and with synergistic aspects of specific situations.[2] All human behavior involves the conscious or subconscious selection of particular actions from among those that are possible and over which a person exercises some influence, control, or authority. At times, the selection of alternatives is almost automatic and is made without very much thought. For example, a police sergeant who responds to the scene of a traffic accident will quickly direct his officers to set out cones or place their vehicles in a manner that will enhance the safety of the people at the scene. In other cases, behavior is the product of a complex chain of activities that involves planning and designated operational activities by specific officers.[3] A police officer learning to qualify with her department's weapon, for example, engages in a series of behavioral adaptations during firing practices that are keyed to internal as well as external factors designed to achieve a successful outcome.

Normal human beings exhibit two basic types of behavior simultaneously and are able to integrate them into a stable persona. These are (1) inherited behavior and (2) learned behavior.[4]

1. *Inherited behavior.* Inherited, or innate, behavior refers to any behavioral response or reflex exhibited by people due to their genetic endowment or the process of natural selection. The survival of the species is contingent on behaviors like breathing, ingesting food, voiding wastes, mating, and defending oneself. These behaviors are modified through adaptation as the environment acts on the individual.
2. *Learned behavior.* Learned, or operant, behavior involves cognitive adaptations that enhance a human being's ability to cope with changes in the environment and to manipulate the environment in ways that improve the chances for survival. Learned behaviors (such as verbal communication, logical problem-solving techniques, and job skills) give people more control over their lives. The importance of learned behavior lies in its consequences for the person and for the environment.

It is learned (self-initiated and goal-oriented) social behavior that sets human beings apart from other animals. Abstract thinking leads to vicarious learning and activates the adaptive process.

**Social Relationships**

Human beings are social animals who live and work in groups. Throughout their existence, humans have learned that by forming groups they can accomplish more than they can by working alone. A group is ordinarily defined as a collection of individuals who derive satisfaction from interacting with each other in some consistent and coordinated way as they strive to achieve a common goal or objective. Groups are held together by a variety of social relationships (see Figure 4–1). A social relationship exists when people have reciprocal expectations about one another so that they act in relatively patterned ways. This concept is important because almost all human behavior is oriented toward others. Not only do people live and work together, they share common beliefs, values, attitudes, and normative understandings. They continuously interact with and respond to significant others. People shape their (conscious and unconscious) behavior in relation to the behavioral expectations of significant others within groups.[5]

Groups, like the societies they belong to, develop distinctive ways of interacting with their internal and external environments. These group cultures define appropriate ways of feeling, behaving, and thinking for group members. Culture reflects the shared language, events, symbols, rituals, and values indigenous to a particular group. It is developed by groups to help them cope with the demands of their environments. While culture is derived from past behavior, it is perpetually reconstituted in current members via the socialization process. From a pragmatic point of view, culture embodies shared beliefs (how things work) and values (what is important) that are internalized by members of a group to produce behavioral norms (the way things "ought to be done").[6] Culture must be learned

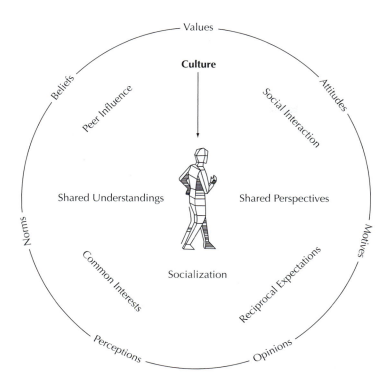

**Figure 4–1**

Group Dynamics, Social Relationships, and Learned Behavior.

before it can be internalized (see Figure 4–2). In this context, learning is defined as a dynamic process that manifests itself in changed behavior that is based on prior experience.[7] People possess few—if any—instinctive skills and no instinctive knowledge that will enable them to survive. They survive only by virtue of what they have learned. The central idea is that culture is learned from other human beings in group settings, shared with them, and modified through interaction with them.

As groups mature, they develop their own unique personalities. In other words, each group evolves its own ways of behaving, which cannot be identified solely with the biography of any specific group member. In fact, individual characteristics are usually overshadowed by those of the group itself. A police work group such as a patrol shift that has worked together for several years, for example, will usually exhibit characteristics apart from and beyond the mere sum of the characteristics of its members. However, people cannot be directed to work as a productive group. People have to want to work together and have to develop, through their daily interactions, closeness to each other and to what they are doing. This is the basis for teamwork. It is the role of every manager to create an environment in which teamwork will develop. However, to have a successful team, each member must place the team's objectives first, ahead of his or her individual objectives.

The performance of a work group is, or should be, more than the simple sum of the individual efforts of its members. By coordination across individuals, activities, or functions, it becomes possible to create a high-performance group whose performance as a whole is greater than the sum of its parts. This is known as the "synergistic effect."[8]

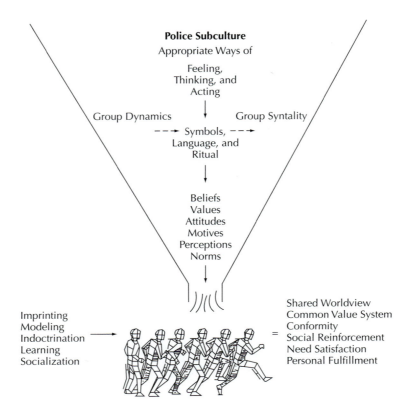

**Figure 4–2**
Learning, Internalizing, and Exhibiting Culture.

Every group attempts to socialize its members as they move through the cycle from initiation to full participation. Socialization is the process by which group-shared beliefs, values, attitudes, and norms are inculcated into each member's psyche (see Figure 4–3). Once these beliefs, values, attitudes, and norms have been internalized, they serve as prescriptive guides to appropriate behavior (see Table 4–1 for a definition of these terms). Consistent beliefs, values, attitudes, and norms produce conformity with group-shared expectations. Inconsistency creates ambivalence and conflict. Conflict and ambivalence about norms of behavior can result in anomie, a sense of normlessness which frequently leads to deviant behavior.[9]

By the time young men and women become police officers, most of them have developed a stable worldview and fixed personality structure. They have a repertoire of beliefs, values, attitudes, and norms that they bring with them into the workplace.[10] As these individuals become police recruits, they begin to acquire new ideas, beliefs, values, attitudes, motives, and norms and to incorporate these into their preexisting frame of reference. Consequently, a police officer is a dynamic composite of experience as modified by current events. Research has consistently found that the police operational experience and how individuals adjust to it are the most important factors in the development of good or bad individual police officer behavior.[11]

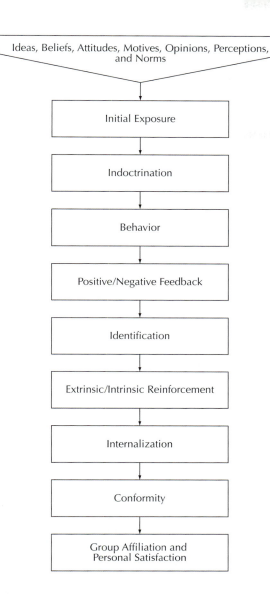

**Figure 4–3**
The Human Socialization
Process.

Ideas, Beliefs, Attitudes, Motives, Opinions, Perceptions, and Norms

Initial Exposure

Indoctrination

Behavior

Positive/Negative Feedback

Identification

Extrinsic/Intrinsic Reinforcement

Internalization

Conformity

Group Affiliation and Personal Satisfaction

## PEOPLE-ORIENTED MANAGEMENT

It is also clear that the beliefs, values, and attitudes of individual police administrators help to determine their capacity to work effectively with subordinates. Modern police management became more people oriented in the latter part of the 20th century. The philosophical base of this managerial approach lies in the following beliefs:

1. Human beings are social animals who engage in purposeful (goal-oriented) behavior.
2. People exist in terms of their interrelationships with other human beings and life forms.
3. The welfare of individual workers and that of the work group cannot be separated from one another.
4. Every employee possesses intrinsic worth as a human being.

| Table 4–1 | **Glossary** |
|---|---|
| Ideas | Abstract mental images of something imagined, seen, or known. |
| Beliefs | Ideas accepted as true and acted on as an article of faith. |
| Values | Strong and enduring beliefs about appropriate conduct and/or end states of existence (e.g., goals), which are preferable to opposite or inverse conduct or end states. |
| Value System | Enduring values arranged hierarchically in terms of relative importance to a particular individual. |
| Attitudes | Predispositions, based on one's beliefs and values, to react either positively or negatively to various ideas, persons, events, or things. |
| Motives | Cognitive variables that activate, direct, sustain, or inhibit a person's goal-oriented behavior. |
| Opinions | Judgments about ideas, persons, events, and things translated into words that reflect one's ideas, beliefs, values, attitudes, and motives. |
| Perception | Filtering processes through which individuals transform, attach meaning to, and structure information coming from their experience or memory. |
| Norms | Shared beliefs, values, attitudes, expectations, and rules—spoken or understood—that guide human behavior in specific situations. |

5. Every human being has the need to grow and develop toward the realization of his or her own unique potential.

6. Workers and work groups have an inherent propensity for change.

7. People are not by their nature passive or resistant to organizational needs.

8. The individual and the sociocultural environment can be understood through use of scientific methods.

9. The essential task of management is to arrange organizational conditions and methods of operation in such a way that individual workers can achieve their own goals best by striving to accomplish organizational goals and objectives.[12]

Managers who subscribe to this philosophy are known as "organizational humanists." They believe in achieving productivity through people and seek to instill in all employees an awareness that their best efforts are essential for the success of the enterprise.

Thomas J. Peters and Robert H. Waterman, Jr., became the leading proponents of organizational humanism in America with the publication of their book, *In Search of Excellence* (Warner, NY, 1982). Based on their research, Peters and Waterman conclude that there is hardly a more pervasive theme in excellent organizations than respect for the individual. Such organizations, they found, use an abundance of structural devices, systems, styles, and values interacting to reinforce one another, which enable them to "achieve extraordinary results through ordinary people."

Peters and Waterman believe that workers should be permitted control over their own destinies, but they do not advocate mollycoddling people. They are talking about tough-minded respect for individual workers and a willingness to develop their ability to set clear and reasonable expectations for themselves. These authors hold that employees should be given genuine autonomy to step out and make a meaningful contribution to the organization. Peters and Waterman contend that managers in excellent organizations are quite different from their counterparts in less healthy organizations. They are more open and trusting. They treat people as partners in the collective enterprise. They respect their subordinates and see them as the wellspring of productivity. They make people feel like winners, and they celebrate winning ways with a variety of nonmonetary psychosocial rewards.

In a sense, all intentional behavior is the product of intrinsic motivation. People, based on psychosocial needs and/or environmental stimuli, set their own goals and expend the amount of effort necessary to demonstrate to themselves that they can reach, or nearly reach, these goals. There is an implicit question of values in all goal setting. Setting personal goals and activating goal-oriented behavior are inextricably linked to one's judgment of good and evil, right and wrong, and desirable and undesirable. These judgments are rooted in each person's cultural heritage, ethical perspective, and normative orientation. The heterogeneous nature of modern American society helps to reinforce ethical relativity and anomie. Since police administrators perceive reality in terms of their own values, attitudes, and expectations, they must learn a great deal more about themselves in order to minimize distortion and prevent interpersonal conflict.

In order to become truly effective managers who have the ability to get things done through others, police administrators must learn to understand themselves as well as their subordinates. Introspection is the process of looking inward through the process of self-examination of one's inner thoughts, feelings, and beliefs. It is the key to self-understanding and leadership, the first step in what Peter Senge calls "personal mastery."[13] The individual who achieves personal mastery has developed an understanding and control of his or her emotions, strengths, weaknesses, needs, and drives. Managers can achieve high levels of personal mastery by continually clarifying what is important to themselves and their organizations. In this manner, they can develop a clear understanding of how they and their individual units fit into the overall mission and strategy of the organizations to which they belong. This knowledge provides them with a special sense of direction that enables them to clarify their visions and goals.

Effective managers understand that who they are (in terms of background, experience, beliefs, values) usually determines what they do with the organization's human resources. Self-awareness allows them, when necessary, to reevaluate their style and to adjust their behavior accordingly. Being comfortable with their role as administrators in a complex organization is much easier when police managers can do the following:

1. Be aware of and have the ability to accept themselves as fallible human beings with strengths and weaknesses.
2. Develop realistic expectations so as not to demand perfection from themselves or subordinate personnel.
3. Have the capacity to recognize and deal effectively with negative attitudes and less-than-acceptable behavior exhibited by some others within the organization.
4. Come to realize that self-esteem is dynamic and subject to change.

Successful police administrators know that their own personal beliefs, values, attitudes, and expectations have a substantive influence on perceptions, interpersonal relations, and work-group dynamics. Thus good managers:

1. Understand that they are a "walking system" of conscious and unconscious values, which are so much a part of their personality that they are scarcely aware of their existence or influence.

2. Use all means at their disposal to identify personal predilections or biases that reduce their own objectivity in assessing the on-the-job behavior of others.

3. Strive to evaluate themselves and their personal values in a rational and objective manner.

4. Endeavor to change any of their own values (and concomitant behaviors) that, based on serious self-evaluation, need to be changed.

If police administrators are secure within themselves, have adequate coping mechanisms, and understand their own feelings, beliefs, values, attitudes, and motives, they ordinarily will not find it difficult to identify with and respect healthy differences in other people.

## IDEAS, BELIEFS, AND VALUES

Human beings are intelligent social animals with the mental capacity to comprehend, infer, and think in rational ways. People convert raw physical and social data into psychological imagery. They use the power of reason to draw conclusions, make judgments, and guide their goal-oriented behavior. A healthy mind produces a continuous stream of ideas. Ideas are generated during the thought process and can be described as relatively abstract mental images of something imagined, seen, or known. They are cognitive representations of what is or what could be. Ideas are untested concepts that may or may not reflect reality. Creative people have the ability to translate good ideas into positive action.

Ideas, once formed, are cycled through the mind for (conscious or subconscious) evaluation. Some seem implausible and are discarded outright. The rest are arranged along a continuum of support ranging from *some* to *complete*. Beliefs are ideas accepted as good or true (whether they are or not) and acted on as an article of faith. Since the person involved makes an emotional commitment, beliefs take on an existence of their own. Selective perception is used to confirm and reinforce them. Consequently, they can withstand virtually any challenge. Facts become irrelevant! Logic becomes irrelevant! A Theory X police administrator, for example, who believes that his or her officers lack ambition, dislike responsibility, and prefer to be led will reject Peters and Waterman's assertion that giving employees respect and autonomy will help police departments achieve extraordinary results through ordinary people. Theory X administrators find it difficult or impossible to share power with, rather than exercise power over, their subordinates.

As human beings, we learn and share the values by which we live. Values represent the ideas and beliefs through which we define our personal goals, choose particular courses of action, and judge our own behavior in relation to that of others. Values are not specifically defined rules for action but general precepts to which people are expected to give their allegiance and about which they are likely to have strong sentiments. Values are very important in that they have a direct influence on our perceptions, preferences, aspirations, and choices. In addition, personal fulfillment depends in large measure on how well our values find expression in our daily life.[14]

Paul M. Whisenand, one of the best-known police management theorists in America, along with coauthor R. Fred Ferguson contends that "we are what we value." They argue that police administrators need to know and understand their own values because values are the foundation of one's character, personality, management style, and on-the-job behavior. Past values help determine who we are and what we want out of life. Current values give substance to our personal and professional being. Future values will influence our behavior at some point down the road. Values are mental constructs representing behaviors and end states of existence (goals) that are important to us as individuals.[15]

From a practical point of view, a value is a strong and persistent belief that certain behaviors and/or end states of existence are preferable to other behaviors or end states. A *value system* is an enduring set of beliefs, ranged in order of importance, about preferred conduct (instrumental values) and end states of existence (terminal values). Because all people possess more than one value, managers need to adopt a broader perspective and think in terms of value systems. Those managers who value honesty and openness in human relationships will do everything in their power not to manipulate or appear to be manipulating their subordinates.

Values are enduring yet changeable beliefs about appropriate ends (goals) and acceptable goal-oriented behaviors (means). Basic values are acquired through imprinting, modeling, and socialization in a group setting (see Chapter 7). These values influence virtually every aspect of life. There is evidence to support the following general propositions concerning human values:

1. The actual number of values that people possess is relatively small (typically between 30 and 60).
2. Values are organized into value systems.
3. Each person's values can be traced back to his or her formative years; to the culture, institutions, and society he or she belongs to; and, to some extent, to his or her unique genetic makeup.
4. The consequences of our values will be manifested in virtually all that we think, feel, and do.
5. A large part of a police manager's effectiveness or lack of it results from his or her value system.
6. Enhanced or continued leadership is linked to our awareness of our values and the values of our co-workers.[16]

Individual values and value systems are critically important variables in that they automatically filter the way people perceive the world around them. They serve as ethical as well as moral standards. Values and value systems help resolve internal conflicts and facilitate the decision-making process. They encourage analytical thinking about legitimate goals and the socially acceptable means for achieving those goals. Values and value systems also motivate people to get off dead center and move toward the accomplishment of important organizational goals and objectives. Individual values and value systems are manifested in the behavior of police officers at work.

Normal people, regardless of their intelligence, evolve through various levels of existence. As a person develops psychosocially, he or she moves away from a very limited set of values to a more expansive system of values that gives much more meaning to his or her life. Old values are replaced by new values

**Evolving Value Systems**

more appropriate to a higher level of existence. Clare Graves has identified the following seven levels of psychosocial existence (see Figure 4–4):[17]

1. *Reactive*. This is the basic level of existence in the evolutionary sequence. Reactive people are childlike. They exist in the here and now and have no conception of cause or effect. They are not aware of themselves or others as individuals. Their only real interest is in the physiological aspects of work (pay, benefits, safety, working conditions, and so forth). Relatively few people become fixated at this stage of development.

2. *Tribalistic*. This is the first established "way of life." Employees at the tribal level are mainly concerned with their own safety; their principal value is tradition. People at this particular level have a strong need for direction from the boss. They are impressed by the use of power and authority in the workplace. Group values are considered to be binding. Violation of group-shared expectations elicits strong negative sanctions.

3. *Egocentric*. Rugged, self-assertive individualism is prevalent at this level. Egocentric people are inclined to be suspicious and disruptive at work. They are often selfish, thoughtless, unscrupulous, and dishonest in dealing with others because they have not learned to live within the constraints imposed by the group. Rights become absolute and are perceived as the prerogatives of management. Power is viewed as the inalienable right of those who have claimed it. Egocentric employees respond well only to managers who are strong and willing to exert control.

4. *Conformist*. Conformists accept their position in life and accept inequity as a fact of life. They subscribe to the work ethic and believe in self-sacrifice, duty, loyalty, and the ideal of achieving perfection in one's assigned role. Conformists accept department policy, procedures, rules, and regulations. They go by the book. They have very low tolerance for ambiguity, resist innovation, and seek to perpetuate the status quo. Conformists tend to judge themselves and others in terms of absolute moral law.

5. *Manipulative*. Manipulators are wheeler-dealers who constantly strive to get ahead. They are ambitious, pragmatic, and utilitarian in their efforts to achieve recognition, status, and material rewards. Manipulators see everything as a game. They are on the lookout for the surest and best way to beat the system. They excel in unsettled situations in which they can use ingenuity to achieve, advance, and garner psychological as well as economic rewards. Manipulators are goal-oriented moral entrepreneurs with a desire to meet their own needs regardless of the cost to others within the organization.

6. *Sociocentric*. In a sociocentric state of being, people feel that getting along with others is more important than getting ahead of them. Their value system centers on interpersonal relationships, positive human relations, empathetic supervision, and goal-oriented collaboration within the work group. Emphasis is placed on sensitivity and collegiality rather than utilitarian exploitation. Sociocentric police administrators share power with, instead of exercising power over, their subordinates.

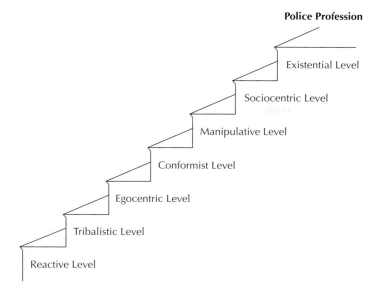

**Police Profession**

Existential Level

Sociocentric Level

Manipulative Level

Conformist Level

Egocentric Level

Tribalistic Level

Reactive Level

**Figure 4–4**

Seven Levels of Existence.

Adapted from Clare W. Graves, "Levels of Existence: An Open System Theory of Values, *Journal of Humanistic Psychology*, Vol. 10, No. 2 (1970), p. 143.

7. *Existential.* At the existential level, people focus their attention on themselves as autonomous individuals. They believe in meaningful work through job enrichment. They value spontaneity over conventionality. Continuing growth and development are very important to them. People at this level have a need to set their own performance standards, to seek opportunities to solve problems, to participate in the decision-making process, and to perform work that is imaginative as well as challenging. They are at the highest stage of development and have a distinctively different value system than those at the other six levels. They are intolerant of closed systems, overly restrictive policy, and the arbitrary use of authority. People who are existential are quite often viewed as troublemakers and may be forced out of work groups because they do not or will not conform to culturally mandated expectations. People at the existential level of existence have difficulty dealing with rigid structure, formal roles, rules, and regulations.

Some people, for a variety of reasons, do not move up the evolutionary ladder from one level of existence to the next. They become fixated at a particular level or, for any number of reasons, actually regress from one level to a previous level. This process is fluid. When managers find themselves out of sync with their subordinates in terms of basic values, it is frequently because they and their subordinates are on different levels of existence.

In many police departments, bureaucratic values shape organizational goals and set performance standards. Utilitarian values like efficiency, effectiveness, productivity, and accountability stress the rational aspects of work and virtually ignore what Douglas M. McGregor called "the human side of enterprise." Police administrators who are preoccupied with control values are badly cast to play the exceedingly complex managerial roles assigned to them today. Their ineptitude in dealing with human resources leads to internal strife and a demonstrable reduction in the problem-solving capacity of the complex organizations they administer.

**Humanistic Values**

While mechanistic values like efficiency, effectiveness, productivity, and accountability are still very important, in many organizations much more emphasis is now being placed on the quality of work life. This shift in values is based on profound dissatisfaction with the traditional bureaucracy and its emphasis on the principles of scientific management. The shift is also related to the rising influence of humanism in contemporary American society. Humanists place a great deal of emphasis on goal-oriented communication, interaction, and collaboration. Effective managers are viewed as pragmatists who understand they must temper bureaucratic values with genuine empathy (for employees and clients) if they are to accomplish the mission, goals, and objectives of the police department.[18]

Humanism has been nurtured by the following trends:

1. Generally higher levels of education in the workforce.
2. New technology that frees most people from routine physical labor yet makes them much more dependent on goal-oriented social interaction.
3. Sociocultural change that is more challenging than threatening.
4. Increasing opportunities for experiences never before so readily available to the population as a whole.
5. Escalation in the revolution of rising expectations.

As police managers adapt to a more existential/humanist philosophy of work, more and more of them are questioning and moving away from traditional bureaucratic values. They are constructing new multidimensional value systems that stress service, efficiency, effectiveness, productivity, and accountability while addressing employee needs for personal growth, self-esteem, competence, and autonomy.[19]

Since management is often defined as "the art of getting things done with and through the efforts of other people," all credible management theories have a humanistic component. They are based—to one degree or another—on the value-laden assumption that organizations should be designed to meet the legitimate needs of people (including employees) as they seek to accomplish their missions, goals, and objectives. Even the infamous "paramilitary mentality" of traditional police administrators is not impervious to humanistic values. Most mainstream police managers know that the effectiveness of their organizations depends upon the effective use of human resources. They understand the importance of autonomy, empowerment, shared decision-making, and team management. Little by little, their values are shifting away from the typical Theory X belief system.

Police organizational management is moving toward its own unique brand of industrial democracy. These new values have provided an impetus for unionization and are usually incorporated into collective-bargaining agreements. Some of them have been factored into community-based policing strategies and collegial organizational models like the one depicted in Figure 4–5.

Modern progressive police administrators have abandoned the overly simplistic view of man embodied in bureaucratic theory. They have replaced it

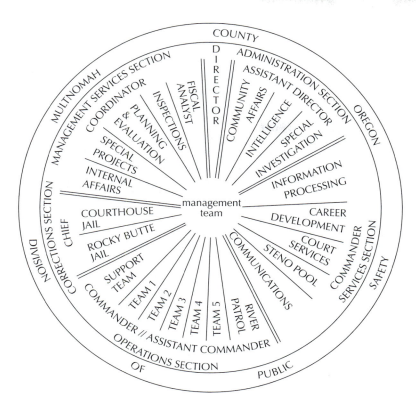

**Figure 4–5**
Collegial Organizational Structure.

with human resource management concepts that envision the manager's primary responsibility as creating an organizational environment in which employees can grow, develop, and perform effectively. In the organizations led by such administrators, power is based on competence, collaboration, and teamwork. Such administrators believe that most police officers want to be good at their job and have a need to exercise self-direction and self-control. Under the right set of circumstances, they encourage their officers to seek out and accept responsibility. They mentor their officers in order to develop the knowledge, imagination, creativity, ingenuity, and practical skills necessary to help the police department accomplish its mission, goals, and objectives, today and in the future. A police administrator's primary job is to get things done through others. In order to do this, he or she is expected to marshal resources, motivate personnel, supervise employees, set the moral tone, and perform all of the other specialized work required to keep the organization in operation.

## ATTITUDES AND OPINIONS

As noted earlier, the term *culture* refers to the characteristic values, traditions, and behaviors a particular group shares. Police officers are members of a unique occupational group and share a distinctive cultural orientation.[20] Beliefs are major components of that culture. *Beliefs* are ideas that people in a group share about themselves and the physical, biological, and social world in which they live. Beliefs, regardless of their accuracy or merit, influence perception and regulate our relations with other human beings, society, and nature itself. *Values* are very strong beliefs about what is good and/or what is bad. A *personal value system* is a relatively permanent perceptual framework that influences and shapes our attitudes, opinions, motives, and behavior.[21]

Values and attitudes are similar in that both are beliefs about appropriate ways of feeling, thinking, and behaving. Values are much broader, however, and cut across specific situations to which personal attitudes are tied. Values are also more enduring than attitudes. They transcend attitudes and serve as a guide to our attitudes, judgments, choices, and behavior.[22]

An attitude is a general point of view that is a composite of our beliefs concerning a particular person, object, event, or situation. It represents a way of looking at someone or something and is coupled with a predisposition to react to that person, object, event, or situation in a predetermined manner. An attitude can also be described as a state of mind in which one's likes and dislikes are translated into a judgment about the intrinsic worth of a certain person, event, or thing. An opinion is the verbal expression of this judgment and reflects the personal beliefs, values, and attitudes of the person doing the expressing. Police managers can learn a great deal about the beliefs, values, and attitudes of the people who work for them if they take the time to analyze their behavior, language, and opinions. This is true because *values* (general principles) generate *attitudes* (favorable or unfavorable feelings) that are translated into our *opinions* (personal judgments) and lead to specific *behavior* (cognitive response to stimuli). This process is illustrated in Figure 4–6. Table 4–2 gives examples and demonstrates the dynamic interaction between these variables.

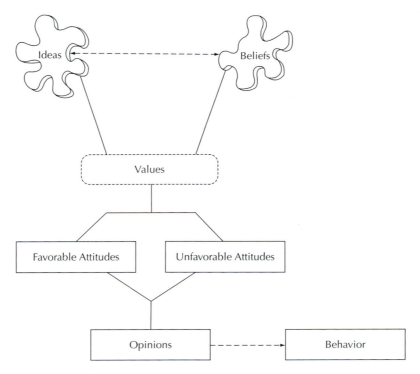

**Figure 4–6**
Values in Action.

## Table 4–2  Behavior Formation

|  | Example 1 | Example 2 | Example 3 |
|---|---|---|---|
| **Value** | Belief in the ethical use of police power to protect and serve the community. | Belief in and respect for people regardless of their station in life. | Belief in the legitimate use of authority to accomplish management goals and objectives. |
| **Attitude** | Feeling that criminal activity by police officers violates the Law Enforcement Code of Ethics and should not be tolerated. | Feeling that empathetic understanding and support will help others to achieve their full potential. | Feeling that police officers are to carry out all legitimate orders given to them by their superiors. |
| **Opinion** | "Blue coat crime" should be rooted out and police officers who violate the criminal code ought to be prosecuted to the full extent of the law. | Police officers should have an opportunity to be involved in making those decisions that directly affect them. | Insubordination should not be tolerated and must be dealt with in a forthright manner. |
| **Behavior** | A police officer reports his partner for stealing jewelry from the body of an accident victim. | The police chief forms a task force to recommend ways to improve the overall quality of work life in the police department. | An acting lieutenant suspends a senior patrol officer for failure to follow a direct order. |

Paul Whisenand and R. Fred Ferguson[23] have analyzed the relationship between values and attitudes. They point out the following distinctions between the two:

1. A value is a single belief; an attitude grows out of several related beliefs concerning a single object or situation.
2. A value ranks objects and situations; an attitude focuses on a specific object or situation.
3. A value is a standard; an attitude may or may not function as a standard.
4. Values are enduring beliefs, few in number; attitudes are multiple and tend to change as new objects or situations are encountered.
5. Values are central to the personality and the cognitive makeup; attitudes are less so.
6. Values are very broad, whereas attitudes are more overtly linked to particular objects or situations.
7. Values reflect adjustive, ego-defensive, and knowledge functions explicitly, whereas attitudes do so implicitly. Attitudes are identifiable predispositions to react in a favorable or unfavorable way to a particular person, event, or object in the environment.

**Acquiring Attitudes**

Attitudes are learned, not inherited. People acquire positive as well as negative attitudes as the result of their personal experiences, and they maintain them if there is sufficient reinforcement to justify doing so. Police officers, like all other human beings, acquire their attitudes in three distinct ways: (1) direct experience, (2) association, and (3) the social learning process.[24]

1. *Direct experience.* Attitudes can develop from a personally rewarding or painful experience with a person, event, or object. A rookie police officer who has lost several criminal cases may—whether he or she was at fault

or not—develop a very cynical attitude toward due process and argue that public safety is in jeopardy because the courts are too lenient on criminals.

2. *Association.* Attitudes toward a person, event, or object may develop from associating them with other persons, events, or objects about which attitudes have already been formed. A detective may be predisposed to think that all patrol officers are sloppy investigators because he has received several case assignments in which preliminary investigations had been poorly conducted by the reporting officers.

3. *Social learning.* Attitudes may also develop based on what someone is told about some person, event, or object by another person. A patrol supervisor may employ very close supervision over women police officers because his peers have convinced him that "most women have less physical ability than males" and cannot perform the physical aspects of patrol work as well as their male counterparts.

Attitudes which are value-specific and have been acquired through personal experience are usually more resistant to change than those learned through association or from other people. When attitudes that are formed as the result of association and/or the vicarious learning process are integrated into a mutually reinforcing cluster of values and attitudes, they become much more stable and resistant to change.

**Functions and Characteristics**

Attitudes are idiosyncratic and reflect an individual's beliefs, feelings, and behavioral predispositions. They serve four very distinct functions for the individual:

1. *Knowledge function.* An attitude can help people organize and make some sense out of their knowledge, experiences, and beliefs. As such, an attitude serves as a standard or frame of reference. A stereotype, for example, is an attitude that ascribes certain traits or characteristics to all members of a particular group regardless of their individual differences. Accuracy is irrelevant.

2. *Instrumental function.* An attitude may develop because it (the attitude) or its object (person, event, or thing) is instrumental in obtaining rewards or avoiding punishments. Attitudes serve as means to an end. A lieutenant's positive attitude toward police work and co-workers could be instrumental in achieving a promotion (reward) or in helping to avoid rejection by other command personnel (punishment). In other cases, the object itself becomes a means to an end, and attitudes develop from associating the object with its outcome. For example, a sergeant may develop a very favorable attitude toward police officers who are easily controlled and a negative attitude toward subordinates who question the need for so much control. The sergeant clearly associates "success" with the ability to exert control and "failure" with the lack of control.

3. *Value-expressive function.* Attitudes may serve as a concrete expression of one's basic values or self-image. A police officer who places great value on social order, for example, may display a negative attitude toward ambiguity, individuality, and the so-called excesses caused by too much freedom. While on the other hand, a captain who considers himself a firm, fair, and unbiased manager may exhibit a very positive, unbiased attitude in all his interactions with his officers, no matter what their sex or ethnicity. A person's real values can be inferred through the analysis

of personal attitudes only if the attitudes displayed are, in fact, genuine. Any type of game playing is detrimental in that it distorts the process and reduces the accuracy of the analysis.

4. *Ego-defensive function.* Attitudes also serve to protect people's egos from unpleasant or threatening knowledge about themselves and their psychosocial environment, Accepting this kind of negative data induces stress and emotional anxiety. Consequently, we develop and deploy defense mechanisms Rationalizations are used to (1) block or (2) alter these negative data in an effort to control physical stress and emotional anxiety. Under these circumstances, rationalizations function as a device to control cognitive dissonance (e.g., tension that arises when a person holds cognitions—ideas, beliefs, values, attitudes, motives—which are psychologically inconsistent) and create a dynamic equilibrium between different yet interrelated elements of the thought process. Thus, the tension within the individual that is causing the opposing attitudes is controlled. A police chief who views himself or herself as a natural leader yet treats uniformed police patrol officers harshly, without regard for their personal feelings or professional competence, may adopt an ego-defensive attitude. He or she may rationalize that this manner of treatment reflects the strong leadership that officers expect. This particular rationalization makes it unnecessary for the chief to come to grips with the fact that as an autocratic person there is a compulsive need to control subordinates. It tends to justify the chief's innate, psychologically well-camouflaged need for superiority based on differential psychosocial status. Police officers who develop ritualistic attitudes about their work may be trying to protect themselves against deep-seated feelings of inadequacy, insecurity, inequity, and so on.

An attitude is a psychological mindset that influences our opinions, perception, and behavior. Attitudes are the positive and negative predispositions that people interject into virtually everything they do. An individual's attitude has a number of identifiable characteristics. They are ordinarily discussed in terms of their valence, multiplicity, relation to need, centrality, and determinance:

1. *Valence.* The valence, or magnitude, of a particular attitude is indicative of the degree to which it is positive or negative toward a particular attitude object. For the purpose of this discussion, an attitude object is an idea, person, place, or thing. Most attitude research involves the empirical measurement of valence. We want to know the intensity of feeling. Valence is easy to quantify.

2. *Multiplicity.* Multiplicity refers to the total number of factors incorporated into one's attitude. Police officers might have a very positive attitude toward the department (because it takes care of its own) yet feel free to criticize it when their sense of fair play is violated by the arbitrary actions of some administrators. Other officers in the department may feel loyal, respectful, and totally dependent. Criticizing the department would be equivalent to a mortal sin. Due to the dynamics involved in formulating and maintaining attitudes, it is nearly impossible to find a one-dimensional attitude. The more factors we incorporate into and use to support a particular attitude, the less susceptible it will be to substantive change.

3. *Relation to need.* Attitudes differ widely in terms of their relation to individual needs. As we indicated, attitudes are keyed to and reflect our

level of existence. A humanist police administrator's attitude about sharing power with instead of exercising power over subordinates is the manifestation of his or her personal needs for social interaction, collaboration, achievement, and self-actualization. Other attitudes are more peripheral in nature and cluster around aesthetic, intellectual, occupational, and recreational interests.

4. *Centrality*. Some attitudes are, for various reasons, more central or salient than others. They cluster around high-priority values. They are fully integrated into our personality. Central attitudes become motives or cognitive variables that activate, direct, sustain, or stop goal-oriented behavior. They are easily reinforced and usually resistant to change. Racial prejudice is an attitude built on our predisposition to react very negatively toward other human beings due to their race or ethnicity. Discrimination, on the other hand, involves prejudicial action or treatment. While a particular attitude may change, our central attitudes are almost never changed with reason alone.

5. *Determinance*. Determinance measures the degree to which our attitudes directly influence our personal behavior. A police officer's negative attitude toward procedural due process could lead to apathy, mechanistic performance, and absenteeism. Countervailing factors may be more influential, however. The fear of being fired may act as a constraint. Under these circumstances, fear keeps the negative attitude in check. Male police administrators with a negative attitude about women may bend over backward not to discriminate against female police officers because the administrators have developed strong feelings about equity, equal employment opportunity, and affirmative action. The stronger the attitude, the more likely it is to evolve into a motive for goal-oriented behavior.[25]

Attitudes are important variables in the psychosocial landscape of collective behavior. They influence perception and serve as guides for human conduct. Police administrators must learn how to identify and analyze their own attitudes vis-à-vis those of superiors, subordinates, and society. This knowledge will help individual managers to understand themselves and should provide them with a vehicle to identify their own values, understand their own motives, explain the behavior of others, develop healthy (empathetic) relationships, and avoid interpersonal conflicts caused by the misinterpretation of someone else's motives (see Table 4–3).

Table 4–3  **The Benefits of Attitude Analysis**

Introspection and attitude analysis help police managers to:
1. Identify their basic beliefs.
2. Clarify their personal values.
3. Explore their attitudes.
4. Understand their motives.
5. Accept individual differences.
6. Understand behavior of others.
7. Develop healthy relationships.
8. Avoid interpersonal conflict.
9. Manage personnel effectively.

Work plays a dominant role in our life. It occupies most of our time and consumes more energy than any other single activity. It is a critical factor in development of the self-concept. Most people learn to define themselves, in part, by their occupation, profession, or career. Job performance is influenced by factors such as (1) individual levels of aspiration, (2) pride in one's work group, and (3) interest in the job itself.[26] While there is no clear-cut scientific evidence to show that job satisfaction and job performance are directly related, there is no doubt that a police officer's attitude toward work can have a positive or a negative effect on how well the job gets done.

In simple terms, job satisfaction is an attitude. It is a reflection of our general attitude toward work (composed of beliefs, feelings, and a predisposition to act) and a set of relatively specific attitudes concerning certain aspects of a particular job. From a conceptual point of view, job satisfaction and dissatisfaction are a function of the perceived relationship between what employees expect from their job and what they actually get.[27] Morale (job satisfaction) is the degree to which the needs of individuals are satisfied and the extent to which they attribute that satisfaction to the job.[28] The main components of job satisfaction are as follows:

1. Relevant and meaningful work
2. Acceptable working conditions
3. Positive work-group dynamics
4. Satisfaction with the agency
5. Adequate general supervision
6. Accessible and fair rewards
7. Intrinsic satisfactions

While these components may not be applicable to all work environments, they appear to be significant aspects of job satisfaction in complex criminal justice organizations.

Poor morale (job dissatisfaction), like any other bad attitude, is contagious. It can spread throughout a police department just like a virus. Poor morale tends to lower the efficiency, effectiveness, and productivity of human resources. It often manifests itself in forms such as (1) apathy, (2) disruptive behavior, (3) interpersonal conflict, (4) absenteeism, and (5) employee turnover. It is the police manager's job to counteract the job dissatisfaction that leads to these behaviors. In order to carry out this responsibility, managers use a variety of techniques:

1. Job analysis
2. Job redesign
3. Job enlargement
4. Job enrichment
5. Participation
6. Job rotation
7. Organization development

These techniques are normally incorporated into a motivation strategy.

# PERCEPTION, MOTIVES, AND HUMAN BEHAVIOR

Human beings are rational animals who have the ability to convert raw data into conceptual representations of reality. Beliefs, values, attitudes, and opinions help to shape a person's understanding of the physical, social, and psychological world. People do not react to each event in their lives as something unique. They construct a perceptual frame of reference that establishes a sense of order and gives meaning to their experiences.[29]

People assume that they possess a clear and relatively undistorted view of reality. They believe ideas, people, places, and things are pretty much as they perceive them to be. This belief is so strong that it is given little or no thought. The problem is that our perceptions are not always accurate. As human beings, we do not experience the world around us in simple and direct terms. Our cognitive picture of it is synthesized and constructed out of information derived from the five senses. The process by which people organize and interpret sensory input is known as perception.[30] Due to the subjective nature of this process, reality exists only in the eye of the beholder. Truth becomes relative and is merely a reflection of an individual's point of view.[31]

Perception is a mental screen or filter through which information must pass before it can be integrated into human thought processes and behaviors. People use this perceptual apparatus to help them do the following:

1. Relate their past experiences to current situations.
2. Choose the various stimuli to which they will react.
3. Group stimuli into a manageable number of categories.
4. Fill in missing data about persons, places, or things.
5. Defend themselves against serious threats to the ego.

It is through the manipulation of perception that we create and maintain a sense of consistency and order in a complex world where rapid change is the rule rather than the exception. Perception is used to process environmental stimuli. This process of selecting from a number of available stimuli is called *accommodation*. Accommodation is one of several processes that determine what stimuli will be converted into useful information, perform the conversion, and then link the resulting information to an appropriate behavioral response. In this context, perception helps to protect the human mind from systemic overload.[32]

**Perceptions**  Every perceptual event has three components. Perceptions are formed based on interaction between (1) the perceiver, (2) the target, and (3) the situation in which the perceptions take place. These factors influence the perceiver's interpretation of all sensory data related to an idea, event, person, place, or thing:

1. *Perceiver*. While there is some disagreement, most social scientists contend that there is no such thing as objective reality. They operate on the assumption that what is perceived as "reality" depends largely on the personal characteristics and background of the perceiver. Research in

organizational behavior (OB) indicates that emotions, beliefs, values, attitudes, motives, interests, experiences, and expectations skew perception. They also help to determine the actual behavioral response in any given situation.[33]

2.  *Target*. In addition to the factors just noted, perception is affected by the characteristics of the target itself. Two of the most important characteristics are the degree of ambiguity of the target and the target's social status. Since perception involves the attribution of meaning as well as interpretation, ambiguous targets are particularly susceptible to perceptual distortion. Research clearly indicates that in the perception of persons, the social status of the target influences the perceiver's perception of the person as much as the target's words and actions do. Status and perceptual distortion go hand in hand. Because targets are not looked at in isolation, the relationship of a target to its background (or perceptual field) also influences perception.[34] People have a natural inclination to group close things and similar things together. Proximity is frequently translated into cause and effect. Stereotypical thinking may be the rule rather than the exception.[35]

3.  *Situation*. There are a number of situational variables with the potential to influence an individual's perception of people, places, and things. The physical surroundings, social setting, emotional atmosphere, and time frame are important factors in perception formation.[36] While the perceiver and the target might remain unchanged, the perceiver's *perception* of the target is anchored to the situation and changes with it. Perception is an inherently complex psychosocial process by which human beings attach meaning to those things they experience through the senses. There are forces in each of us (perceivers), in the stimuli (targets), and in the environment (situations) that cause perceptions to differ. It is no wonder that sincere people adopt opposing points of view and exhibit radically different behaviors.

**The Perception Process**

Behavior can most simply be viewed as an individual's response to a stimulus in a given situation. This view is known as the stimulus-response (S-R) model and is often used to explain reflex actions. In more complicated behaviors, however, there is a chain of discrete events between the stimulus and the operant (intentional) response. The chain includes three intervening subprocesses—*reception, organization,* and *interpretation*—that work to convert information input into decisions or behavioral outputs.[37] The perception process is illustrated in Figure 4–7.

*Sensing* is the first step in the perception formation process. In other words, a stimulus is encountered by one of the five senses: touching, tasting, seeing, hearing, or smelling.

Since people simply cannot deal with all of the stimuli in the physical, social, and psychological environment, they become selective in picking out those stimuli they feel are important and tuning out the others. This is known as *selective perception*, which is the psychological predisposition to see and evaluate raw data (about people, places, and things) in light of our own ideas, beliefs, values, attitudes, opinions, motives, and past experiences. People sort through the data related to sensory stimuli and consciously or, more likely, unconsciously select information that is supportive and satisfying. They tend to ignore information that is painful and/or disturbing.[38] Whether

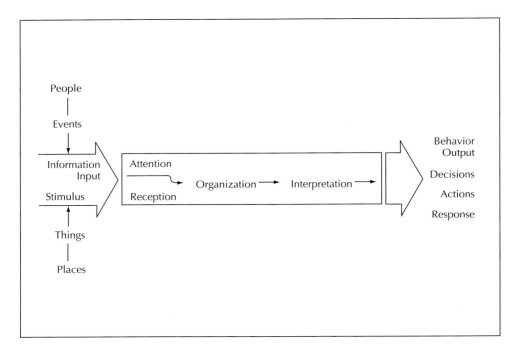

**Figure 4–7**
The Perception Process.

a particular stimulus captures our attention and elicits a behavioral response will depend on:

1. The properties of the stimulus itself (size, intensity, contrast, repetition, motion, and so forth).
2. Past experience with the given stimulus and other competing stimuli within the environment.
3. Our inclination (based on our personality, values, motives, and past learning) to see certain things and not others, regardless of the properties of the target itself.

Selective attention leads to selective perception and serves as the springboard for all purposeful human behavior.

Once attention has been focused, the bits and pieces of information derived from both the target and the situation must be organized in such a way that they can be incorporated into one of the perceiver's cognitive systems. (A cognitive system is a set of interrelated perceptions and cognitions about people, places, and things.) Our perceptual mechanisms operate to organize the information into patterns and categories that make some sense. This process is known as perceptual organization.

*Perceptual organization* is the psychological predisposition to avoid the discomfort normally associated with unorganized information by reconfiguring and attributing meaning to it based on each person's beliefs, values, attitudes, interests, motives, experiences, and expectations. Our mind automatically sorts all sensory information into patterns or categories in an effort to avoid systemic overload. Consequently, there is a natural tendency to do the following:

1. Distinguish a *central object* (person, event, place, or thing) from its surroundings. Leaders tend to stand out more than support players do in crises.

2. Respond to people, things, and situations based on *anticipated rather than actual* information input. A mindset is a compulsive proclivity to think and act without rational analysis.

3. Combine bits and pieces of information into wholes by creating *groupings* based on proximity, similarity, closure, and continuity (see Figure 4–8).

4. Perceive the characteristics of a target (person, place, or thing) as remaining relatively *constant* despite variations in the stimuli that produced the original information. This helps people deal with the instability caused by change.[39]

5. Predict behavior and *ascribe meaning* to the motives of others. This process, called attribution, is designed to make the behavior of others more understandable.

These perceptual organizers are beneficial most of the time. There is a downside, however. They add to and distort reality. When it comes to the perception of persons, several other perceptual tendencies influence how

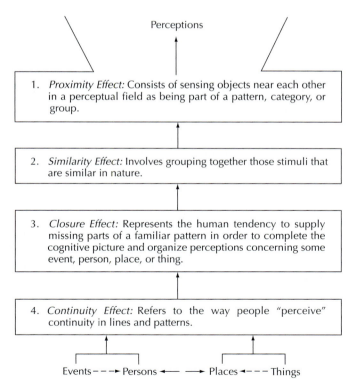

**Figure 4–8**
Perceptual Organization Through Grouping.

people organize their perceptions and convert them into cognitive systems. Following is a discussion of these further perception organizers.

1. *Frame of reference.* A frame of reference is a perspective, or vantage point, from which people view people, events, and things. Frames of reference are both windows on the world and lenses that bring the world into focus. Perception is dependent on the context in which it occurs and on the frame of reference used by the perceiver. Managers, consultants, and policy makers draw upon a variety of frames of reference, or paradigms, in their efforts to change and improve organizations.[40]

2. *Stereotyping.* Since it is impossible for one person to know everyone else in terms of their distinctive traits, people develop and use stereotypes. One way to simplify the management and organize sensory data about other people is just to assume that they all have the same characteristics because of some category (or group or pigeonhole) they fall into. For example, one could put police officers into mental categories based on their ethnicity and respond the same way to everyone in the same category. This might conserve cognitive energy but is likely to result in a loss of information and the spread of misinformation. Stereotypes based on race, gender, and age skew perception if they predispose the perceiver to ignore specific information concerning the individual and rely on preexisting stereotypical images.[41]

3. *Halo effect.* This occurs when one personal trait or attribute is used to develop an overall impression of another person. It involves generalizing from one characteristic to the total person. The halo effect, like stereotyping, tends to obscure individual differences. People are perceived as being either good or bad. Once they have been assigned to a particular category, we tend to ascribe only good qualities to those labeled as being good and all bad qualities to those labeled as bad. Selective perception is used to confirm our expectations.[42]

4. *Projection.* In this mode of organizing perception, the perceiver ascribes his or her own characteristics to other people and uses himself or herself as the norm for judging others. It is much easier to comprehend the behavior of others if we assume that they are similar to us. Consequently, our own characteristics influence what we are likely to see in others. A classic projection error is for managers to assume they and their subordinates have the same unmet needs or motives.

5. *Expectancy.* Expectancy is the tendency for people to find or create in another person what they expected in the first place. This is also known as the *Pygmalion effect* and is similar to selective perception in some respects. People often see what they want to see in order to validate their original expectations.

Once sensory stimuli garner attention and are organized in a way to facilitate their integration into the thought process, normal people use the power of reason to interpret the already-processed data, generate further useful information, and select appropriate operant responses. Perceptions are interpretations of sensory data.[43]

Mike Byrne was, at age 29, the youngest detective sergeant in the history of the Milesburg Police Department. Byrne's meteoric rise in the police hierarchy began three years ago. As we might say, it was "in the cards." Byrne was a relatively undistinguished patrol officer in this industrial city of 38,000. After five years on the street as a patrol officer, he was temporarily assigned to the five-member detective bureau to fill in for another officer who was on sick leave. As duty officer on the midnight shift, he was dispatched to investigate the abduction of a three-year-old boy who had been taken from the home of his mother's boyfriend. The child's body was found a week later. It had been dismembered and discarded in a landfill in another county. After an extensive investigation, the police came up with the name of a prime suspect and put out a bulletin on local radio stations. A confidential informant contacted Officer Byrne and told him where the suspect could be found. Byrne and his partner, Leonard Smitts, went to the suspect's hideout. After several gunshots were exchanged, the suspect surrendered. Because he captured the suspect, Byrne became the darling of the media.

The trial itself became a media spectacular. Officer Byrne seized the opportunity and used the media to his advantage. He made local news almost every night for two weeks. The suspect was convicted, and after an emotional episode in which he admitted he had killed the boy, he was sentenced to death by electrocution.

The trial took place in an election year. The leading candidate for mayor liked Byrne and, sensing his popularity, announced publicly that if elected he would promote Byrne to the rank of detective sergeant. The candidate won the election. The incumbent detective sergeant was transferred to a new assignment, and since all command officers are appointed by and serve at the pleasure of the mayor, Mike Byrne was promoted to the exempt rank of detective sergeant. The other detectives resented the fact that the mayor was politicizing the bureau. They saw Byrne as an opportunistic political hack. There was an informal work slowdown and an escalation in the level of interpersonal conflict, and productivity declined drastically. Byrne was like a fish out of water. He was not a leader and had no real experience as a supervisor. Things became intolerable. After ten months of continuous rancor, Mike Byrne was reduced in rank and quietly reassigned to the patrol division. He resigned from the department after three years. He now owns a private security company.

*What happened here? Was a perceptual distortion involved in this case? What is the lesson to be learned? How would you as the police chief executive deal with the mayor in this type of situation?*

*Interpretation* is the psychological process by which people evaluate information input concerning a particular stimulus and choose an operant behavioral response. The cognitive context for interpretation is in the mind and consists of the concepts, theories, and cause-effect models we use to construct our own versions of reality. How police officers interpret sensory stimuli will depend in large measure on their past experience, their value system, and their attitudinal propensity to think or act in certain ways. This helps to explain why different people "see" different things even when they are looking at the same person, event, or object. In a sense, as we noted before, there is no such thing as objective reality. Sensory inputs are transformed through perception into interpretive or "normative" reality and complete the perception formation process.[44]

It attaches meaning to our experiences in relation to other people, events, and things. Figure 4–9 illustrates the dynamics involved in perception formation.

In order to survive and thrive in a complex sociocultural milieu, we must be prepared to receive, organize, interpret, and react to all kinds of environmental stimuli. The accuracy of our perception is a critically important factor in the struggle for physical as well as psychosocial survival. The inability to interpret cues correctly and cope with dangerous situations can lead to tragedy in police work. Overestimation of danger cues in some situations can lead to the unnecessary use of force while

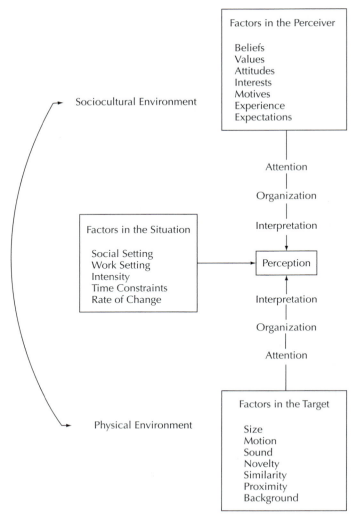

**Figure 4–9**
Dynamics of Perception Formation.

in other instances officers can suffer serious injury or death as a result of underestimating danger cues.

Successful police administrators understand the psychosocial dynamics involved in perception formation and are aware of the inherent potential for perceptual distortion. They have learned that personal beliefs, values, motives, experiences, and expectations put subjective constraints on perception. Truly perceptive managers:

1. Have a relatively high level of self-awareness and know how to avoid most of the perceptual pitfalls that we discussed earlier in this chapter.
2. Seek information from a variety of sources to confirm or disconfirm their personal impressions of a given person, event, or thing.
3. Tend to form empathetic relationships and are often able to see situations as they are perceived by others.

4. Know when to intervene and how to influence the perceptions of significant others who are drawing incorrect impressions about people, events, or things in the work setting.

5. Appreciate individual differences and seek to avoid those perceptual distortions that bias performance evaluations.[45]

There is no doubt that perception has an effect on managerial decision-making, and these decisions affect work unit efforts to accomplish the police department's mission, goals, and objectives. It is also clear that values and value-based perceptions are motivators. They trigger and shape operant behavior.

Motivation is the inner state that causes a person to take actions to satisfy **Motivation**
a need. In other words, motivation explains why we as human beings act the way we do.[46] The motivation process begins with physical or psychosocial needs (or deficiencies) and ends with the accomplishment of certain goals. A *motive* is a stimulus arising out of a need that produces an action. An intensely felt set of interrelated needs is known as a *drive*. Perceived needs that are linked to basic values give rise to potent motives and are always accompanied by powerful drives. Perception is the psychodynamic variable that activates goal-oriented behavior.

Stephen Robbins argues that unsatisfied needs stimulate people and usually exert a strong influence on their interpretation of sensory stimuli. Intense primary (instinctive) and secondary (learned) needs command attention. They are the focal point of our interests and a catalyst for action. Some psychological studies have shown that a sufficiently hungry person may perceive food in sensory data that are not actually food-related. In one experiment, subjects who had not eaten for 16 hours and subjects who had eaten only a short time earlier were both shown a series of blurred pictures. The hungry subjects perceived the images as depicting food far more frequently than did the well-fed ones.[47] In an organizational context, police administrators who are insecure often perceive a subordinate's efforts to do an outstanding job as a threat to their own position. In other words, personal insecurity can be incorporated into a perception that other people are out to get your job, regardless of their real intent. Machiavellian personality traits can also affect perception: people who are devious and/or manipulative themselves are prone to see the same traits in others. This way of attaching meaning to sensory stimuli is known as selective attribution. It is not surprising that traffic officers are more likely to notice and react to moving violations than are absentminded professors. A sergeant who has just been reprimanded by the lieutenant for the sloppy way subordinates handled a burglary investigation will in all probability try to identify the cause of the problem and be more on top of things than he or she was before this incident occurred.

Good managers understand the psychodynamics involved in motivating their subordinates. They know that their own motives, tucked away in the subconscious mind and difficult (if not impossible) to define, turn them on, influence their perceptions, and serve as springboards to purposeful behavior. This self-awareness, based on introspection, is a key ingredient in effective management. Good managers also make it their business to anticipate how significant others will behave in given situations. In order to do this, they learn to understand other people in terms of their unique characteristics, including:

1. Wants
2. Needs
3. Beliefs
4. Values
5. Attitudes
6. Motives
7. Experiences
8. Expectations
9. Perceptions
10. Perspectives
11. Situations

This anticipation helps managers understand why the behavioral response to a given stimulus differs from person to person and for the same person at a different time or under a different set of circumstances.

**On-the-Job Behavior**    Behavior refers to the conduct of human beings as they react to environmental stimuli and includes the actions people take or things they say with regard to:

1. Objects
2. Events
3. People
4. Problems
5. Opportunities
6. Situations

Based on knowledge derived from the behavioral sciences, there is every reason to believe that behavior is (1) caused (2) motivated, and (3) goal oriented. In other words, most human behavior is purposeful.[48] Operant behavior is intentional behavior involving some choice among alternative responses. In very simple terms, behavior is a function of the interaction between people and their environment. The basic equation is as follows:

$$B = F (P \times E)$$

This means that factors within the individual (P) and the environment (E) determine behavior (B), both directly and indirectly due to their effect on each other.[49] Purposeful human behavior is produced by a sequential process involving a feedback loop. The essential steps in the behavior formation process are outlined as follows:

1. There is an implicit or explicit goal to be achieved.
2. The behavior aimed at goal accomplishment is caused by reaction to an environmental stimulus of some kind.

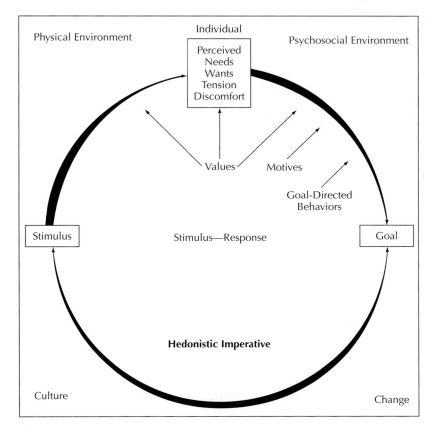

**Figure 4–10**

Steps in the Behavior Formation Process.

Adapted from H.J. Leavitt, *Managerial Psychology*, 4th ed. (Chicago: University of Chicago Press, 1978).

3. The stimulus is generated by needs (or wants) which, if not satisfied, cause tension and discomfort.

4. The reduction of tension and discomfort becomes a hedonistic imperative, or goal.[50]

The steps in the behavior formation process are illustrated in Figure 4–10.

While the behavior formation process is the same for all human beings, actual behaviors vary substantially. Because people are unique (with different backgrounds, value systems, perceptions, and motives), they react idiosyncratically to environmental stimuli. This is compounded by the fact that an individual's needs, wants, and expectations are subject to change. Consequently, a person's response to the same stimuli will ordinarily deviate from time to time. A patrol captain, for example, may give a subordinate a verbal warning for a minor infraction one day (depending on the captain's needs, wants, and expectations), whereas he or she might write up the subordinate for the same behavior in a different situation or at a different time. Good managers know that because of individual and situational differences with respect to needs, wants, tension, and discomfort, human behavior—even under similar circumstances—is difficult to predict.

# MANAGEMENT'S ROLE IN CHANGING ATTITUDES AND BEHAVIOR

As noted earlier, attitudes are the product of related beliefs and values. They are incorporated into our motives, opinions, and behaviors. Positive attitudes toward work in general, one's job, and the department (as a whole) are indicative of high morale. High morale produces an esprit de corps that is conducive to cooperation and collaboration.[51] Negative attitudes, on the other hand, often lead to interpersonal conflict and have been linked, at least indirectly, to poor on-the-job performance. It is the police administrator's job to accentuate the positive and minimize the influence of negative attitudes.

Police administrators have three basic options for dealing with employees who exhibit negative attitudes:

1. *Do nothing.* They attempt to contain negative attitudes through benign neglect. This "let the sleeping dog lie" strategy seldom works and usually makes the situation worse. Doing nothing allows the employee to think that the administrator approves or condones his or her behavior.

2. *Intervene.* They seek to transform negative attitudes into neutral or positive attitudes. The success of any attempted intervention will depend on the strength of the negative attitude and the skill of the change agent.

3. *Terminate.* They try to fire the employee. In a unionized and litigious environment, discharging someone for having a bad attitude is a very difficult task. Managers are required to make a good-faith effort to change the person's unacceptable behavior before they are permitted to hand out a pink slip.

In order to do their job properly, police administrators must learn to be effective change agents. This is not an easy task. Since attitudes are anchored to beliefs and values, they are always resistant to change. Two principal barriers tend to limit the extent to which employees are likely to change their attitudes. These are (1) insufficient justification and (2) previous commitments. In the absence of a compelling need to change, people prefer to maintain the status quo. This inertia is very difficult to overcome. The second barrier encompasses past promises and gut-level values. A person's link to the past may be powerful enough to block a change in attitude and accompanying behavior. People are prone to take a position and defend it. They invest their ego, reputation, resources, and sometimes their job maintaining their position.[52]

**Change Agents**  Change agents know that personal dissatisfaction and significant emotional events can modify a person's negative attitudes. They can change the attitudes and behavior of others by using these forces (which stem from people's values and relate to their needs) in one or more of the following six ways:

1. *Leadership by example.* The police chief executive and other members of the management team are in an excellent position to change attitudes by setting an example for their employees. They must model the way they want their officers to behave at all times.

2. *New information.* When employees receive new information they accept as truthful and significant, they are apt to change their attitudes about ideas, events, people, places, and things.
3. *Intimidation.* While it might be temporary, fear and the use of threats can bring about a change in attitudes.
4. *Individual discrepancy.* When attitudes and behavior do not mesh, people experience cognitive dissonance and have a need to change one or both of them to make them congruent.
5. *Organizational discrepancy.* When employee attitudes are at odds with those that are part of the organizational culture, they experience the need to alter their own attitudes, alter the cultural attitudes, or remove the discrepancy by leaving the department.
6. *Participation.* When employees are allowed to participate in events and decisions that affect them, their attitudes are exposed to either confirmation or challenge.[53]

Whether or not police administrators succeed in changing the attitudes (and behavior) of employees will depend largely on their credibility and believability as *communicators*. We see others as credible and believable when we perceive them as expert, unbiased, and likable. Success will also depend on the *intervention techniques* used to effect attitudinal change (see Table 4–4). The *audience* is the third variable. Some groups—based on their history and cohesiveness—are much more resistant to change than others.

Table 4–4  **Intervention Techniques**

1. *Force field analysis:* Study of the dynamic relationship between the "driving forces" that promote change and the "restraining forces" which inhibit change.
2. *Effective communications:* Opening up channels of communications for employees, peers, and outside specialists in an effort to deal with fears, negative attitudes, and the lack of motivation.
3. *Persuasion techniques:* Methods designed to convince employees to change attitudes and/or behavior. Here are some examples of effective techniques for use by change agents:
   - Explain why change is necessary.
   - Explain how it will affect them.
   - Be honest and tell them the truth.
   - Try to reach a realistic compromise.
   - Give them examples of past success.
   - Plant seeds and let them germinate.
   - Seek information by asking questions.
   - Offer them a choice of alternatives.
   - Present change as a challenge.
   - Promise to evaluate them regularly.
   - Request cooperation and avoid orders.
   - Give them a demonstration.
   - Involve them in the decision.
4. *Participation techniques:* Methods designed to keep subordinates informed about departmental activities and let them participate in making those decisions which affect them.
5. *Training programs:* Formal methods for teaching personnel the skills, knowledge, attitudes, and behaviors needed to do their job efficiently, effectively, and productively.
6. *Organization development:* OD is an educational strategy intended to change the beliefs, values, and attitudes of people and organizations as they seek to improve their ability to achieve common goals and objectives.

*Source:* W. Richard Plunkett, *Supervision: The Direction of People at Work*, 3rd ed. (Dubuque, IA: William C. Brown, 1983).

**Initiating Change**   Managers can usually bring about a change in their subordinates' attitudes (and accompanying behavior) if they use the following five-step process. Once managers observe improper behavior or hear improper attitudes expressed, they should (1) identify the improper attitude, (2) determine its root causes, (3) weaken the root causes, (4) offer a practical substitute, and (5) reward all those employees who exhibit the new attitude or behavior:

1. *Identifying the improper attitude.* Once managers determine that a subordinate's behavior is improper, they must look for the attitude behind it. The attitude should be defined in specific terms. By investigating an improper attitude, showing genuine concern, and making constructive comments, managers are frequently able to resolve the problem without further intervention. Employees may come to the realization that their behavior is unacceptable and change it to conform to the general expectations of the manager.

2. *Determining the root causes.* The manager should collect and analyze relevant information in an effort to determine the roots (or primary causes) that support and feed the attitude in the employee's mind. The best way to accomplish this objective is to get employees talking about their beliefs, feelings, attitudes, motives, and expectations. Some of the root causes that nurture and support improper attitudes are listed here:

   • Group pressures
   • Faulty logic
   • Ambiguous standards
   • Prior experiences
   • Selective perception

3. *Weakening the root causes.* Once the root causes have been identified, they can be analyzed in terms of strength and vulnerability. A program of action should be developed to attack these causes systematically, using reason. One way to attack an improper attitude (and the accompanying behavior) is to point out flaws in the employee's assumptions or draw attention to the changes that have taken place to weaken those assumptions since they were originally formed.

4. *Offering a substitute.* While managers may be able to change an employee's attitude by constant harping and the use of criticism, this approach takes too long and leaves some noticeable scars. It will also lead to the employee fixating on the manager's behavior instead of his or her own. As a rule, people will change only when they determine that the attitudes they hold are no longer worth keeping. Orders and threats tend to suppress natural and observable behavior and drive it underground. Employees become wary and do what managers want only when management personnel are present. When managers are absent, old attitudes and behaviors will resurface. Permanent change comes about when employees begin to question their own beliefs, values, attitudes, and motives.

5. *Rewarding proper attitudes.* Change is normally reinforced by positive social sanctions. Managers should remember that *"Things that get rewarded get done."*

While these five steps sound simple enough, good managers know it takes a great deal of time, energy, skill, and expertise to bring about substantive attitudinal change on the part of personnel in any complex police organization.

The traditional view held by most police management theorists is that changed beliefs and/or values produce new attitudes that lead to changes in on-the-job behavior. Some management theorists contend that, on the contrary, it is more sensible to change a person's behavior first. This is based on research indicating that people realign their attitudes in support of their behavior. A few management theorists argue that people should be taught specific behaviors that they can apply on the job and that correspond to the desired attitude change. When the trainees learn that they will be rewarded for their behavior, their attitudes will change to agree with the newly learned behaviors. In order to teach these appropriate behaviors, trainers use modeling techniques, role playing, and social reinforcement.

---

**CASE STUDY**   Chief M. Lawrence Glick

Corona is a small yet relatively prosperous city located in the corridor between New York City and Washington, D.C. The police department has an authorized strength of 113. Virtually all of the officers on the force have taken college courses, and a large percentage of the younger officers hold BA degrees. Some of them are working toward an MS in criminal justice. Sworn police personnel are covered by civil service. All members of the department except the chief and commanders in exempt positions (with the rank of captain or above) are represented by the same labor union. Commanders have formed a team to serve as their bargaining agent.

The former chief of police was a politically astute autocrat who maintained power through tight administrative control and manipulation of the reward system. He was, in terms of his values system, anything but an organizational humanist. He found it impossible, regardless of the composition of the workforce, to share power with others rather than exercise power over them. The chief used selective perception to protect his ego and vilify those with the audacity to question his authority and/or style of management. Everything "hit the fan" when a study conducted by the State Department of Community Affairs concluded that the police department was "plagued by

labor/management conflict, bad attitudes, low morale, and disruptive infighting." As a result, the city manager asked for and received the chief's resignation.

Larry Glick, an administrative lieutenant with 22 years of experience, was promoted to chief. He was given a mandate from the mayor to "clean up the mess at police headquarters." Chief Glick is a pragmatist. He is convinced that the only way to increase the efficiency, effectiveness, and productivity of the police department is to improve officer attitudes and morale. The chief knows that he does not have the expertise to accomplish these objectives by himself. He has been authorized to hire a consultant/change agent. The person he has chosen is an organization development (OD) specialist with experience in law enforcement. Dr. Karl Helms is set to begin the project later in the month.

*Did Chief Glick make the right decision? If you were Dr. Helms, how would you approach this project? What type of intervention seems most appropriate? Prepare a memo for the chief in which you explain, compare, and contrast the traditional approach and the behavior modification approach discussed at the end of the chapter. Outline some of the change strategies that can be used to achieve the goals of the project.*

# SUMMARY

Human behavior involves the conscious or subconscious selection of actions over which the person exercises some degree of influence, control, or authority. People are social animals that live in groups and engage in purposeful (self-initiated and goal-oriented) behavior. Each group develops a unique way of interacting, or culture. Culture is the cement that holds a group together and defines appropriate ways of feeling, thinking, and acting. Beliefs, values, attitudes, motives, and expectations are passed from one generation to the next through the socialization process. Values are the linchpin in one's personality, character, management style, and goal-directed behavior.

Police administrators at the existential (or humanistic) level of existence find themselves questioning and moving away from traditional bureaucratic values. They adopt multidimensional value systems that stress efficiency, effectiveness, and productivity while responding to each employee's need for personal growth, self-esteem, competence, and autonomy. Good managers try to cultivate positive attitudes in their subordinates because employee attitudes are critical variables in the success or failure of any goal-oriented enterprise. Attitudes reflect values, express feelings, and indicate a predisposition to act in a certain way with regard to a given stimulus.

Human beings are rational animals with the unique ability to convert sensory data into cognitive representations of reality. Attitudes (which are based on values and past experiences) influence perceptions and are factored into the motives that produce operant behavior. Motivation is the inner state that causes a person to behave in ways designed to satisfy a need. Perceived needs that are linked to basic values become potent motives and are always accompanied by powerful drives. Good managers understand the links between values, attitudes, perception, and motivation.

Positive attitudes toward work, the job, and the organization are indicative of good morale and may lead to increased productivity. Negative attitudes, on the other hand, can lead to interpersonal conflict and have been linked, indirectly, to poor job performance. Good managers work to transform negative attitudes into positive attitudes. Some use the traditional five-step process in which they identify improper attitudes, determine root causes, weaken the root causes, offer substitutes, and reward those who exhibit appropriate new attitudes and concomitant behaviors. Other managers reverse the process. They seek to change behavior first, on the assumption that people will realign their ideas, beliefs, values, attitudes, motives, opinions, and expectations to support the new behavior. They emphasize the importance of modeling, role playing, and social reinforcement.

# KEY TERMS

attitudes
behavior
behavior modification
B = F (P × E)
beliefs
change agents
cognitive dissonance
culture
group dynamics
ideas
introspection
job satisfaction

morale
motivation
motives
operant behavior
opinion
perception
perceptual distortion
socialization
value conflict
value system
values

## DISCUSSION TOPICS AND QUESTIONS

1. How do organization/management theorists define behavior and differentiate between inherited and operant behaviors?

2. Where do our beliefs, values, attitudes, and motives come from, and how are they transmitted from one generation to the next?

3. What is introspection? Explain why an officer needs to do it in order to become a truly effective police administrator.

4. Define ideas, beliefs, values, attitudes, motives, and opinions. How are these psychological concepts related to one another?

5. What does it mean to say that attitudes are cognitive, affective, and conative?

6. What is an attitude? Explain its functions.

7. Define perception. Explain the impact perception has on our decision-making.

8. What are motives? How are they formed? How do they influence our expectations, perceptions, and behavior?

9. Discuss the six strategies police administrators use to modify the attitudes of their subordinates.

10. How does the behavior modification/attitude change approach differ from the traditional five-step attitude/behavior change process?

## FOR FURTHER READING

John Crank and Michael Caldero, *Police Ethics: The Corruption of a Noble Cause* (Cincinnati: Anderson, 1999).

Crank and Caldero succinctly hit the nature of police corruption—the ends justifying the means—the traditional "Dirty Harry" problem.

Peter M. Senge, *The Fifth Discipline: The Art & Practice of the Learning Organization* (New York: Doubleday, 1990).

The management Bible of the nineties, Senge introduces the concept of a "learning organization" that adapts to its changing environment in order to achieve a competitive advantage.

## NOTES

1. Gary W. Cordner, Kathryn E. Scarborough, and Robert Sheehan, *Police Administration, 5th ed.* (Cincinnati: Anderson, 2004), pp. 216–223.

2. Gary Dessler, *Management: Principles and Practices for Tomorrow's Leaders* (Upper Saddle River, NJ: Prentice Hall, 2004), pp. 282–213.

3. Herbert A. Simon, *Administrative Behavior* (New York: The Free Press, 1997), pp. 77–78.

4. Joseph H. Reitz, *Behavior in Organizations* (Homewood, IL: Richard D. Irwin, 1981).

5. Paul Hersey and Kenneth H. Blanchard, *Management of Organizational Behavior: Utilizing Human Resources* (Upper Saddle River, NJ: Prentice Hall, 1993), pp. 19–52.

6. Stephen P. Robbins, *Essentials of Organizational Behavior* (Upper Saddle River, NJ: Prentice Hall, 2000), pp. 241–246.

7. Linda K. Stroh, Gregory B. Northcraft, and Margaret A. Neale, *Organizational Behavior: A Management Challenge* (Mahwah, NJ: Lawrence Erlbaum, 2000), pp. 74–75.

8. Stephen R. Covey, *The Seven Habits of Highly Effective People* (New York: Simon & Schuster, 1990), pp. 262–270.

9. Robert K. Merton, *Social Theory and Social Structure* (New York: The Free Press, 1957), pp. 131–195.

10. John Crank and Michael Caldero, *Police Ethics: The Corruption of a Noble Cause* (Cincinnati: Anderson, 1999).

11. Roy Roberg, John Crank, and Jack Kuykendall, *Police & Society* (Los Angeles: Roxbury, 2000), p. 267.

12. Douglas M. McGregor, *The Human Side of Enterprise* (New York: McGraw-Hill, 1960).

13. Peter M. Senge, *The Fifth Discipline: The Art & Practice of the Learning Organization* (New York: Doubleday, 1990), pp. 7–8.

14. Ramon J. Aldag and Loren W. Kuzuhara, *Organizational Behavior and Management: An Integrated Skills Approach* (Mason, OH: South-Western, 2002) pp. 346–347.

15. Paul M. Whisenand and R. Fred Ferguson, *The Managing of Police Organizations* (Upper Saddle River, NJ: Prentice Hall, 2002), pp. 3–22.

16. Ibid., p. 13.

17. Clare W. Graves, "Levels of Existence: An Open System Theory of Values," *Journal of Humanistic Psychology*, Vol. 10 (1970).

18. Warren Bennis and Bert Manus, *Leaders: The Strategies for Taking Charge* (New York: Harper & Row, 1985).

19. Ronald G. Lynch, *The Police Manager* (Cincinnati: Anderson, 1998).

20. John P. Crank, *Understanding Police Culture* (Cincinnati: Anderson, 1998).

21. Joel A. Barker, *Future Edge: Discovering the New Paradigms of Success* (New York: William Morrow, 1992).

22. Gary Dessler, *Management* (Upper Saddle River, NJ: Prentice Hall, 2004), p. 38.

23. Whisenand and Ferguson, *The Managing of Police Organizations*, p. 9.

24. Aldag and Kuzuhara, *Organizational Behavior and Management*, p. 115.

25. Dessler, *Management*, p. 287.

26. Fred Luthans, *Organizational Behavior*, 9th ed. New York: McGraw-Hill, 2002), pp. 126–139.

27. Craig Pinder, *Work Motivation in Organizational Behavior* (Upper Saddle River, NJ: Prentice Hall, 1998), p. 245.

28. Roy R. Roberg, Jack Kuykendall, and Kenneth Novak, *Police Management* (Los Angeles: Roxbury, 2002), pp. 185–211.

29. Lee G. Bolman and Terrence E. Deal, *Reframing Organizations: Artistry, Choice and Leadership* (San Francisco: Jossey-Bass, 1991), pp. 309–320.

30. Luthans, *Organizational Behavior*, p. 183.

31. Thomas S. Kuhn, *The Structure of Scientific Revolutions* (Chicago: University of Chicago Press, 1970).

32. Stroh, Northcraft, and Neale, *Organizational Behavior*, p. 33.

33. Luthans, *Organizational Behavior*, pp. 195–197.

34. Robbins, *Essentials of Organizational Behavior*, pp. 23–25.

35. Robert P. Vecchio, *Organizational Behavior: Core Concepts* (Mason, OH: Thompson, 2003), p. 39.

36. Aldag and Kuzuhara, *Organizational Behavior and Management*, pp. 96–100.

37. Luthans, *Organizational Behavior*, pp. 183–195.

38. M.J. Waller, G.P. Huber, and W.H. Glick, "Functional Background as a Determinant of Executives Selective Perception," *Academy of Management Journal*, Vol. 38 (1995), pp. 218–235.

39. Alvin Toffler, *Future Shock* (New York: Bantam Books, 1972).

40. Bolman and Deal, *Reframing Organizations*, p. 11.

41. Claude M. Steele, "A Threat in the Air: How Stereotypes Shape Intellectual Identity and Performance," *American Psychologist* (1997), p. 617.

42. Kevin R. Murphy, Robert A. Jacko, and Rebecca L. Anhalt, "Nature and Consequences of Halo Error: A Critical Analysis," *Journal of Applied Psychology* (April 1993), pp. 218–225.

43. Cordner, Scarborough, and Sheehan, *Police Administration*, pp. 233–235.

44. Richard M. Hodgetts and Fred Luthans, *International Management: Culture, Strategy, and Behavior with World Map* (New York: McGraw-Hill/Irwin, 2002).

45. John R. Schermerhorn, Jr., James G. Hunt, and Richard N. Osborn, *Organizational Behavior* (New York: John Wiley & Sons, 1997).

46. Luthans, *Organizational Behavior*, p. 249.

47. Robbins, *Essentials of Organizational Behavior*, pp. 241–245.

48. Roberg, Crank, and Kuykendall, *Police & Society*, pp. 265–267.

49. Luthans, *Organizational Behavior*, pp. 25–27.

50. Harold J. Leavitt and Homa Bahrami, *Managerial Psychology: Managing Behavior in Organizations* (Chicago: University of Chicago Press, 1988).

51. Dan Carrison and Rod Walsh, *Business Leadership: The Marine Corps Way* (New York: Barnes & Noble, 1999).

52. Harry W. More, W. Fred Wegener, and Larry S. Miller, *Effective Police Supervision* (Cincinnati: Anderson, 2003), pp. 305–313.

53. Paul M. Whisenand and George E. Rush, *Supervising Police Personnel: Back to the Basics* (Englewood Cliffs, NJ: Prentice Hall, 1988), pp. 22–23.

# MOTIVATION

## The Force Behind Behavior

## LEARNING OBJECTIVES

1. Discuss the etiology of goal-oriented human behavior in the workplace.

2. Define *motivation* and those terms associated with the motivation process.

3. Describe the interplay between individual, social, and situational factors related to human motivation.

4. Explain needs and the adaptive behavior they elicit in the motivation process.

5. Differentiate between content theory and process theory as they relate to the human motivation to work.

6. Compare and contrast major content and process theories.

In a generic sense, modern-day management can be defined as the proactive process of getting things done with and through other people by guiding their individual efforts toward the accomplishment of common goals and objectives. While police administrators are expected to allocate and manage time, equipment, material, and money, the most significant aspect of their job is the management of people. Human beings are far different from any other type of resource they are asked to deal with. This is because each person is truly unique and brings various attitudes, values, sentiments, motives, behaviors, and skills with him or her into the workplace. According to Paul Whisenand,[1] a police supervisor is responsible for first releasing and then directing an employee's motivation to accomplish the mission of the department.

David Gunther was the new chief of police in a small rural community in upstate New York. The department had an authorized strength of six full-time and four part-time police officers. Chief Gunther was anxious to fill the vacant sergeant's position created when he was promoted to chief three months earlier. The sergeant is second in command. Since the department was not covered by civil service, the chief had the authority to promote whoever he chose, subject only to the advice and consent of the mayor.

After a very careful review of the situation, Chief Gunther concluded that Charles Zanich, a five-year veteran, was the best person for the job. Officer Zanich was a personable, energetic, and talented man with excellent analytical skills. He was a natural leader with a commitment to public service. Officer Zanich was always a high achiever. He was the (1) Top candidate on the eligibility list the year that he was hired; (2) Outstanding trainee at the academy based on academic achievement, marksmanship, self-defense, and professionalism; (3) Officer of the Year for a heroic rescue of three drowning children; (4) Recipient of four commendations for exemplary police work; and (5) Coordinator of the police department's in-service training program. As far as the chief was concerned, he really had no alternative but to offer the position to Charles Zanich. He felt that he and Zanich were simpatico and would complement one another.

After securing the mayor's authorization to fill the vacant position, Chief Gunther asked Officer Zanich to stop by his office. They exchanged pleasantries and then the chief told Officer Zanich he would be promoted to the rank of sergeant (at a higher pay grade) effective the first of the month. Much to the chief's surprise, Zanich declined the promotion. The chief did everything he could to get Officer Zanich to change his mind, but the officer maintained he was simply not interested in taking on the responsibility of a first-line supervisor. He said pay was not the issue. He thanked the chief, left the office, and returned to work.

Chief Gunther's surprise turned into anger. He felt Officer Zanich was being selfish. He considered him an ingrate with no sense of loyalty to the department. He swore that he would never do anything for Officer Zanich and that Zanich would rue the day he had refused "to stand up and be counted." Although he was unhappy with the situation, Chief Gunther promoted James Wooten.

The chief's hostility toward Officer Zanich festered to the point where it turned into open conflict. He watched Officer Zanich closely and frequently criticized him behind his back. Over a period of time, Officer Zanich became increasingly dissatisfied with his job. He became a chronic complainer. Poor morale reduced his performance and led to increased absenteeism. Charles Zanich found himself in a box. He got so frustrated that he resigned from the police department and left police work altogether.

*What happened in this particular situation? What assumptions did Chief Gunther make, and why did he become so angry with Officer Zanich? If you were the chief of police, how would you deal with an officer who does not see promotion per se as the preferred path to job satisfaction and/or career advancement?*

## PURSUING EXCELLENCE

Leading others as they pursue an organization's mission, goals, and objectives is the essence of police management. Leadership does not exist in a vacuum, however. There is a symbiotic relationship between leadership, motivation, and performance in complex goal-oriented police departments. Most management theorists believe that highly motivated individuals, working smarter, are more productive and produce a better quality product or service than their less motivated co-workers.[2]

Human motivation is a fascinating topic. Motivating people to work has become one of the most pervasive concerns in contemporary management theory—a buzzword in industry and an "in" term in the lexicon of police management. Increasingly it is adopted as the goal of staff development. There is probably no other topic in which police administrators express more interest. The motivation of police personnel is viewed as an antidote for poor performance, a magic key to productivity, and the answer to all sorts of organizational problems—even the external constraints, like funding limitations, under which police agencies operate.[3] However, the application of simplistic solutions to very complex social problems rivals baseball as America's favorite pastime.

The motivation perspective just discussed is not the panacea it was made out to be by the theorists and practitioners who argued that it had ushered in a new era of enlightened human resources management. After nearly a half-century of rigorous scientific inquiry, we still do not know what motivates a human being to act in a certain way. It is very difficult to tell why some police officers are self-starters and seem to be high achievers in almost everything they do, whereas other police officers need prodding and external incentives to do anything productive. It is hard to explain why activities that generate enthusiasm and energy in one person might well trigger boredom and apathy in someone else.

Motivating human beings to work, to produce more, and to seek excellence is one of the simplest yet most complex tasks in management. It is simple in the sense that people are hedonistic. They have been programmed socially as well as genetically to minimize pain and to maximize pleasure. Consequently, motivating them should be easy. It is up to management to determine what a person wants and to use it as a reward or incentive. Whenever people act in any way, good or bad, it is because they have been motivated to act.[4] Reward people for proper behavior, and you usually get the right results. Fail to reward the right kind of behavior, and you will most likely get the wrong results. Things are not as simple as they may appear at first glance, however. Different people have different desires and needs. Rewards one police officer considers important may be viewed by others as undesirable or merely superfluous. In some cases, the needs of employees are not the same as those of the organization; if the differences are irreconcilable, they can lead to dysfunctional conflict, disorganization, and deterioration in performance. Even an enticing reward is not a sure-fire motivator. Rewards, in themselves, do not ordinarily motivate people unless there is a belief that an effort on their part will lead to a payoff. Police personnel, like all other human beings, differ from one another in how they size up their chances of earning meaningful rewards or achieving their own personal goals.[5]

Police administrators have a managerial responsibility to recruit, screen, select, and develop human resources with the potential to be efficient, effective, and productive employees. Unless these individuals are motivated to draw on this potential, however, they are not likely to achieve the level of performance that is desired from them. Managers at all levels are faced with the problem of motivating subordinates to unleash their own potential so that the mission, goals, and objectives of the organization can be accomplished. One way to deal with the so-called motivation problem is to create conditions in which people acting to satisfy personal needs and to achieve their own goals act in such a way that the work desired by the organization gets done as well.[6] Police managers must learn to recognize symptoms of flagging motivation and to design jobs and reward systems to alleviate the problem. Failure to act will only compound the motivation problem and could eventually destroy the organization.

**Motivation to Work**

# ORGANIZATIONS AS SOCIAL ENTITIES

Organizations are unique social entities that are created by human beings in order to accomplish certain goals that require cooperative effort. A formal organization is a social unit that has been designed to achieve a common objective or set of objectives. As instruments created for a specific purpose, all formal organizations have similar structural characteristics, including (1) a fairly distinct division of labor; (2) built-in mechanisms to regulate, coordinate, and control the activities of members; and (3) the capacity to replenish depleted human resources. Healthy organizations have the ability to adapt to changes in the environment, alter internal processes, reconfigure job assignments, and withstand the influx of replacement personnel. Consequently, a typical formal organization acquires an identity independent of its members, a distinctive persona of its own that—while it will change based on situational factors—tends to perpetuate itself from one generation to the next.[7] An unhealthy organization, like an unhealthy animal, is very likely to wither away and risks death. In order for a police department to survive and thrive, management personnel must learn to deal effectively with the behavioral requirements of individuals who work for them.

In order to become effective managers, police administrators must learn to understand and appreciate the importance of their role in the motivation process. They must also develop a repertoire of motivational techniques that will encourage qualified people not only to join and remain in the police department but also to perform their duties in an enthusiastic, competent, consistent, and professional manner. Motivation is the pin that connects employee needs and job performance within organizations. It is the key to a productive and satisfying life. In particular, highly motivated, productive, and satisfied employees are the mainstay of quality police service. As Whisenand notes, "The supervisor-as-leader is in a pivotal position to recruit, get the best out of, and retain police employees."[8]

Organizations should be viewed as living organisms rather than inanimate things. Police departments, for example, are deliberately constructed social systems, with structures and processes designed to coordinate the activities of workers as they seek to accomplish group-shared goals and objectives. An organization is a coalition of many participants with diverse needs, values, attitudes, and behaviors.[9]

Organizations are social entities in which members take part and to which they react.[10] An organization consists of people with formally assigned roles who work together to achieve stated goals.[11] For the purpose of our discussion, motivation is the energizing force that brings people together and that serves as the springboard to individual effort as well as goal-oriented group interaction.

# MOTIVATION AND THE MOTIVATION PROCESS

The study of motivation and the motivation process can be traced back to antiquity. There have always been attempts to describe, explain, and predict goal-oriented human behavior. The ongoing interest in motivation is based on the assumption that those in authority need to know what turns people on or off about their work. Until quite recently, the emphasis was on the use of coercive power to increase individual productivity and/or organizational output. Things began to change several decades ago. Most police administrators now subscribe to the old adage, "You can lead a horse to water, but you can't make it drink."

"Motivation" is not a particularly easy term to define. While just about everyone agrees that it has something to do with human behavior, no one has been able to formulate a single definition that is acceptable to all of the behavioral scientists and management personnel with an interest in this topic. Some writers avoid definitions altogether. They are content to focus their attention on the consequences of human behavior. Others, in the classical tradition of Frederick W. Taylor (see Chapter 1), explain motivation in terms of economic rationality. They see human beings as goal-oriented individuals who have been programmed to avoid pain (punishment) and to seek pleasure (rewards). Still other organization/management theorists reject utilitarian views and contend that motivation is a subconscious psychological process that evolves in people as the result of personality, background, environment, and cultural factors.

**Defining Motivation**

Motivation is defined as the intensity of a person's desire to engage in some activity.[12] The process of motivation is often described in terms of a simple stimulus-response model.[13] But the process is not that simple: between the stimulus and the response are a number of mediating factors that differ with each individual worker. They include

- *Personality* (as presented in Chapter 4). The characteristic and distinctive traits of the individual.
- *Abilities.* The set of skills workers bring to the job. These interact with motivation to create performance.
- *Self-Concept.* The perceptions people have of themselves and their relationships to people in other aspects of their life.
- *Perception.* How our personalities and experiences cause us to interpret stimuli.
- *Attitudes.* Predisposition to respond to objects, people, or events in either a positive or negative way. Job satisfaction is one example of an attitude.

Again, it must be emphasized that these factors differ with each individual. The law of individual differences states that people differ in their personalities, abilities, self-concept, values, and needs.[14] Still others are convinced that motivation is a conscious and continuous process in which individuals make choices about what they will or will not do in given situations.[15]

There are conflicting definitions of motivation based on etiological considerations. In much simpler times, motivation was thought of as the means, methods, and techniques used by management to stimulate workers to engage in activities designed to achieve the organization's mission, goals, and objectives. Leaders, managers, and other authority figures were expected to use extrinsic motivators (motivators external to the person) such as pay, promotion, fringe benefits, and camaraderie as carrots to induce employees to increase their output and to upgrade overall quality of their product or service. On the other side of the coin, the famous Hawthorne experiments conducted during the mid-1920s clearly demonstrated that intrinsic factors also motivated people to behave in certain ways. Intrinsic innovators like instinct, drives, desires, values, feelings, and needs are internal to the individual and, as such, are largely unaffected by environmental stimuli. People strive to achieve, to be competent, to contribute, and to derive real satisfaction from work. The theorists, researchers, and practitioners who subscribe to this human relations school of thought place most of their emphasis on internal, as opposed to external, variables. The primary function of management is to create a situation in which worker needs and organization needs are not only congruent but mutually reinforcing.[16]

Police officers, like all other human beings, are motivated in reality by a combination of intrinsic and extrinsic factors. Both are necessary. According to Stephen P. Robbins,[17] the motivation to work is caused by a set of energetic forces, originating within and beyond the individual, which initiates work-related behavior and determines its form, direction, intensity, and duration.

Motivated employees are in a state of tension created by an unsatisfied need. This tension leads to creation of drives until the need is satisfied and tension is reduced. Motivated behavior is aimed at reducing these tensions. Thus, motivation to work can be described as dynamic forces within an individual that account for the intensity, direction, and relative persistence of the energy expended at work.[18] Researchers have found a direct link between motivation and effort. In fact, motivation is a predictor of overall effort. In the long run, effort, individual ability, and organizational support determine the level of people's job performance.

Motivation is the drive within people to alleviate the discomfort caused by internal tensions. A drive is an energetic force fueled by human needs. These needs become a motivator for action. Mental and physical actions are conscious and unconscious efforts to achieve goals. Goals are desired outcomes an individual feels will lead to a reduction in internal tension. Once their needs, desires, and wants are fulfilled, people experience a measure of personal satisfaction.

**Related Terminology**

Before proceeding with a discussion of the motivation process itself, let us review some basic terminology one more time. A precise vocabulary is very important because ambiguity leads to confusion and helps perpetuate misunderstanding.

1. *Needs.* Something within people that moves them to engage in work-related behavior in an effort to accomplish personal goals.
2. *Drives.* Dynamic inner forces created and energized by needs.
3. *Tension.* The frustration or discomfort caused by unfulfilled needs.
4. *Motives.* Inner impulses, drives, needs, and abstract values that energize, activate, move, and direct behavior that is designed to achieve specific goals.
5. *Goals.* Objects, conditions, or activities toward which a particular motive is directed.
6. *Incentives.* Internal and external stimuli, such as anticipated satisfaction (positive as well as negative), social reinforcement, and financial rewards, that bring about goal-oriented behavior designed to reduce the tension caused by unfulfilled human needs.
7. *Performance.* The purposeful activity that results from an individual's goal-oriented behavior and that is normally evaluated in terms of specific outcomes.
8. *Motivation.* A psychosocial process that produces an attitude that results in an action leading to a particular result.
9. *Internal motivation.* Motivation that comes from within a person (based on needs, drives, feelings, desires, and values) and that activates certain conscious and unconscious behaviors designed to produce satisfaction.
10. *External motivation.* Motivation resulting from the application of incentives to encourage patterns of behavior that will contribute to accomplishment of an organization's mission, goals, and objectives.

While there is no simple answer to the question of what "turns on" human beings or motivates them to act as they do in a given situation, police administrators will be ahead of the game if they learn to view motivation as a dynamic interactive process rather than as a collage of marginally related managerial tasks. It is through knowledge and the skillful use of motivation that modern managers attempt to mold their people into productive units capable of achieving new and much higher levels of performance.[19]

**Motivation Cycle**

According to Calvin Swank and James Cosner,[20] the motivation cycle or process consists of needs setting up drives to accomplish goals. They argue that the intensity of the drive toward a goal is always proportional to the severity of the need. A police officer's absolute need for peer acceptance, for example, could supersede his or her desire to be considered a professional, leading him or her to elect to conform to the "code of silence" rather than testify against a fellow officer involved in a brutality case.

Again, Stephen Robbins[21] describes the motivation process in terms of unsatisfied needs (see Figure 5–1). He sees unsatisfied needs as a motivator that prompts people to engage in work-related behaviors that are directed toward the attainment of goals they feel are capable of satisfying their needs. Thus the motivation process consists of six sequential steps: (1) unsatisfied need, (2) tension, (3) drives, (4) search behavior, (5) a satisfied need, and (6) reduction of tension.

Equipped with the necessary skills, knowledge, and uniform, these recent police academy graduates will look to management for motivation.

David M. Jennings, The Image Works

Unsatisfied → Tension → Drives → Search → Satisfied → Reduction
Need                              Behavior   Need       of
                                                        Tension

**Figure 5–1**

Basic Motivation Process.

Adapted from Stephen P. Robbins, *Essentials of Organizational Behavior* (Upper Saddle River, NJ: Prentice Hall, 2000), p. 44.

The simplicity of the diagram is somewhat deceptive, however. Behavioral scientists and experienced police administrators know that human behavior is "multimotivated," in that any number of conscious, subconscious, and at times conflicting needs demand satisfaction simultaneously. It is the intensity of a need or the relative mix of needs that determines behavior in a given set of circumstances. We will never know, for example, exactly what motivates an otherwise passive police officer to become a supercharged hero in a dangerous or life-threatening situation involving very young children; it is always difficult to isolate a single causal factor in relation to job-related behavior in complex criminal justice organizations.

While many police administrators still believe that motivation is something they do to their subordinates, they are wrong. Motivation is a dynamic and goal-oriented *internal* process. It is—in essence—what individual officers feel and do in relation to their own particular needs. Seen from this standpoint, the only true form of motivation is self-motivation.[22] Almost all successful police managers have the unique ability to elicit self-motivation in their employees and reinforce it. They do this by creating environments in which police personnel are able to satisfy needs through affiliation, competence, recognition, and productive police work itself.[23]

**Motivating Yourself and Others**

Motivated people continuously set new goals because their needs, desires, and wants are nearly insatiable. It is only human nature to want more, to strive to progress. People want to improve themselves and their condition, to acquire new things, and to improve their position vis-à-vis others within their organizations. Robert B. Denhardt and his colleagues have raised the issue of motivating public-sector workers. Motivation in the public sector, they say, is *aimed at the achievement of public purposes* and it is critical if public workers are to fulfill their responsibilities to the citizens and communities they serve.[24] The "conventional wisdom," however, is that public-sector workers are fundamentally lazy and unmotivated. Denhardt and colleagues suggest three basic reasons for this popular belief:[25]

1. Rewards and incentives available for use by public-sector managers, particularly in terms of pay and promotion, might be limited.

2. People who pursue public-sector careers may be less achievement oriented than people in the private sector, that is, they may by their very nature be a not very highly motivated group, primarily attracted to public service by job security.

3. Motivation in public organizations may be complex because of ambiguous goals (unlike the private sector, where the clear and fundamental goal is profit).

Of course, these authors do not adhere to such beliefs; in their view, public employees are clearly the equals of their private-sector counterparts.

Whisenand squarely puts the job of motivation in the lap of police managers: "When I encounter unmotivated police employees, inevitably I see an unmotivated supervisor."[26] He defines worker motivation as the psychological forces within a person that determine

- The direction of a person's behavior in an organization.
- A person's level of effort.
- A person's level of persistence in the face of obstacles.

The job of supervision is to facilitate and sponsor employee motivation.

Even though motivation is something inside each person, police administrators activate and guide the motivation process as they seek to improve the performance of a department's human resources. Performance—the results of workers' behavior—is the bottom line in management. Motivation is only one of the factors that contribute to those results.[27]

Based on the preceding discussion, it is evident that there is no satisfactory simple answer to the question, "What motivates people to act as they do in a given set of circumstances?" Behavioral scientists have developed an array of different theories to explain the dynamics involved in human motivation. Fortunately, most of these theories tend to reinforce each other to some degree. We devote the remainder of this chapter to categorizing and describing some of the major theories. Our purpose is to provide information, not to say a particular theory is right or wrong. It is, in the final analysis, up to each police administrator to abstract, synthesize, and reconfigure this information in such a manner that it will work in a given environment with a specific clientele. Broad generalizations usually lack substance and are of little or no real value in motivating personnel to work in complex criminal justice organizations.

## APPROACHES TO MOTIVATION THEORY

As noted earlier, the motivation to work has been the subject of serious scientific inquiry for more than a half century. Behavioral scientists normally approach the study of human motivation from two general perspectives of content theory and process theory:

1. *Content theories.* Content theories attempt to explain *what* motives (needs, desires, and wants) are and how they influence human behavior. In addition, these theories provide ways to profile and analyze people in order to identify their motives. They have little or nothing to say about the process by which needs arise and are manifested in actual behavior. As seen by these theories, understanding motivation is primarily a matter of recognizing basic needs and the process by which they are satisfied.

   The centerpiece of content theory is that unmet needs motivate people to act. People seek to reduce inner tension by fulfilling these needs. Satisfied needs do not motivate. While content theory does not explain how people are motivated to do some particular thing, it does provide some insight into individual needs and may help police administrators understand what their subordinates will or will not value as work incentives. Content theory helps us understand what people want.[28]

2. *Process theories*. Process theories explain *how* people are motivated. These theories examine goal-oriented behavior based on the degree of satisfaction associated with particular rewards used to initiate it. Process theories focus on the motivation process rather than on motives per se. They strive to shed light on the cognitive (mental) processes by which human beings choose to engage in certain behaviors designed to satisfy their own needs. While content theories emphasize needs themselves, process theories zero in on decision-making as it relates to job performance. Process theories are built on the assumption that people make conscious and subconscious evaluations of contemplated behavior and assess the consequences of their actions. These personal expectations are critical in determining how a person is motivated to perform in any given situation.[29]

These theoretical approaches are not mutually exclusive. In fact, most content and process theories reinforce one another and provide police administrators with an information base which can be transformed into action designed to help subordinates become more efficient, effective, and productive workers. The theories provide clues about people, explain why people (do or do not) work, and examine how the psychosocial environment influences job performance. Job performance is the bottom line in management and is the key factor in determining the long-term health of any complex criminal justice organization.

Content and process theories represent a radical departure from the classical concept of motivation advocated by Frederick W. Taylor in the early 1900s, as discussed in Chapter 1. Taylor was a utilitarian looking for practical ways to increase the productivity of available human resources. He believed identifying the one best way to do each particular job and segmenting each task into a series of simple operations or steps could achieve maximum organizational efficiency. Each worker would be trained to perform a few task-related operations. The combined efforts of all workers would then maximize efficiency and productivity. Taylor also believed that workers were not capable of self-motivation. They had to be motivated by external forces (managers) in order to overcome their natural inclination for "soldiering" (his word for doing just enough to get by). Increased productivity would be achieved by creating incentives (in the form of financial rewards) to work harder during a specific period of time. Taylor devised a bonus system to reward and reinforce the behavior of those who exceeded the minimum expectations set for them. In a Pavlovian sense, improved performance and increased productivity reflect a conditioned response activated by external reward systems.[30]

## CONTENT THEORIES

Interest in content theory can be traced back to the Hawthorne studies conducted in Chicago during the mid-1920s. The researchers wanted to know how productivity is affected by negative environmental factors, but they found fewer negative effects than they expected. They concluded that unanticipated "psychological factors" had somehow influenced the productivity of the experimental group. While the researchers were unable to find a direct relationship between physical working conditions and worker outputs, it became clear that organizations do not exist for production alone. They are organic social settings in which people seek to satisfy their own intrinsic psychological and social needs. The experiment itself became a motivator. The assembly workers felt they were being treated as people rather than machines. Management's interest in their situation made them feel special. It was a recognition of their worth as human beings. The researchers concluded that when human needs are met, workers develop a very positive attitude toward work, management, and their organization. The need for achievement often leads to greater job satisfaction, improved performance, increased productivity, and commitment to the goals and objectives of the organization.[31]

Content theories attempt to explain what motivates people to behave as they do in relation to their work. While most of the theories are consistent with one another, there are some important differences. The theories presented here are representative of this genre.

Abraham Maslow's "progression" theory of employee needs is one of the best-known content theories. As a positive humanistic theory of motivation, it stresses the importance of both biological drives and psychosocial needs. According to Maslow,[32] five basic human needs activate, fuel, and shape the internal drive to overcome inertia affiliated with the status quo. He classes them as physiological (survival) needs, safety (security) needs, belonging (social) needs, self-esteem (ego) needs, and self-actualization (fulfillment) needs. These terms are ordinarily defined as follows:

**Hierarchy of Needs Theory**

1. *Survival needs.* The most basic of all human needs is to sustain life. Biological maintenance requires food, water, air, shelter, sex, and so on. Due to the nature of the life cycle, the satisfaction of physiological needs is of limited duration. As soon as one need is satisfied, another replaces it. When police managers concentrate on meeting survival needs to motivate personnel, they are operating on the assumption that most people work based on economic incentives. Emphasis is placed on pay increases, improved working conditions, and better fringe benefits as the best way to motivate their personnel.[33]

2. *Security needs.* Security needs emerge once basic survival needs have been met. People have an intrinsic need to be relatively free from fear, to feel safe, and to have some stability in both the physical and interpersonal events involved in day-to-day living. According to Frank Goble,[34] these needs can be grouped into two categories: (1) the need for order and stability and (2) the need for freedom from anxiety and insecurity related to personal safety, job security, financial survival, and the capricious actions of others. Police administrators who place primary emphasis on meeting the security needs of their personnel rely on policies, procedures, rules, and regulations to produce order, promote safety, improve performance, and increase productivity.

3. *Social needs.* Once physiological and security needs have been satisfied, social needs emerge as a very important source of motivation. Human beings have an inherent need to interact with significant others. People derive personal satisfaction from group membership. Groups fulfill their need for human companionship, love, affection, and a sense of belonging.

Police administrators who understand and appreciate the importance of the social needs of subordinates know that employees have a strong tendency to identify with and internalize the norms and values of the work group. Effective managers facilitate communication, promote purposeful interaction, and encourage meaningful participation in order to improve job performance and the individual productivity of their human resources.[35]

4. *Ego needs*. Ego-esteem needs have two dimensions. First, people have a need to be respected by significant *others* for who they are and what they can contribute to the work group. They have a desire to be competent, and they look to the work group as a source of recognition, acceptance, prestige, and status. Second, people have an absolute need for self-esteem. In other words, they need to feel they are worth something to themselves as well as to others. Self-esteem is manifested in feelings of adequacy, worthiness, fulfillment, and self-confidence. Managers who understand the importance of ego-esteem needs do everything they possibly can to ensure that their employees become competent and exhibit self-confidence, harbor few self-doubts, and have a good self-image. Effective police administrators help their subordinates to realize that "public service offers distinct opportunities for motivating people to do excellent and often extraordinary work."[36]

5. *Self-actualization needs*. The need for self-actualization is triggered when people have to some extent satisfied their physiological, security, social, and ego needs. The need for self-actualization is the need to grow, to be creative, and to fulfill one's potential. While this need varies from one person to another, in all cases it causes people to pursue interests and knowledge for their own sake and for the joy of becoming the persons they feel they have the potential to become.[37] Self-actualized people have successfully met a need to become increasingly competent and to gain mastery over their own life. All of their talents and potential are put to use. At this stage, motivation has become an internal process. External stimulation is unnecessary. Management's job is to provide resources and to create an environment in which self-actualizing people are given the freedom to make truly significant contributions to the organization.

The order in which Maslow listed his five human needs, shown above, amounts to a hierarchy ranging from the most basic instinctive drives to the most abstract psychosocial motives (see Figure 5–2). Maslow divided this hierarchy into lower-order (survival, security, and social) needs and higher-order (ego and self-actualization) needs.

According to Maslow's hierarchy of needs theory, the effect of human needs on job performance is governed by three basic principles: (1) countervailing needs, (2) satisfaction deficit, and (3) progressive fulfillment.

1. *Countervailing needs*. Human beings are viewed as multidimensional social animals that sort through, prioritize, and strive to satisfy a variety of competing (lower- and higher-level) needs on a simultaneous basis.

2. *Satisfaction deficit*. Unsatisfied human needs create a state of tension, a perception of deprivation, and an impetus to act in a way to satisfy those needs.

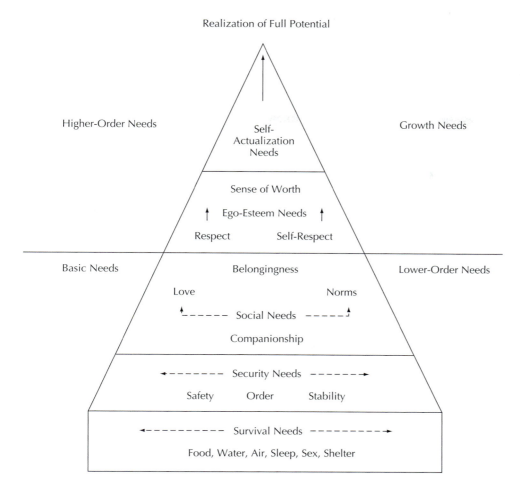

**Figure 5–2**
Maslow's Hierarchy of Needs.

3. *Progressive fulfillment.* The five-level hierarchy of needs determines the order in which needs will serve as motivators: needs at any given level can affect behavior only after needs at the lower level below have been satisfied.

An unmet need creates a satisfaction deficit that commands individual attention and determines goal-oriented behavior. When deficits at one level are reasonably well satisfied, they cease to act as motivators, allowing people to focus more attention on the next higher level of needs. This move up the hierarchy as needs are satisfied is known as "satisfaction progression."[38] The key to understanding the dynamics of this process lies in accepting the progression principle, the idea that people are motivated by the lowest level of unsatisfied needs. If all of a person's four lower levels are reasonably well satisfied (in terms of that person's expectations, personality, and past experience), he or she will move on to seek self-actualization. It should also be noted that once a need is satisfied, there is a natural tendency to reevaluate the definition of what is reasonable and to upgrade expectations.

Consequently, people cycle back to lower-level needs when the reasonable level of satisfaction is defined upward or when the status of a previously satisfied need is jeopardized.[39] A police officer who accepted a low starting salary to launch a career, for example, will likely redefine what is reasonable pay as he or she becomes more competent and moves up the career ladder. A new definition of what is reasonable may create a satisfaction deficit and motivate one to seek a promotion or look for another, higher-paying, position.

According to Maslow's hierarchy of needs, police administrators should identify the unfulfilled needs of their subordinates. This will give them a better understanding of why police officers may or may not perform as expected. Management must find incentives that will stimulate and reinforce desired work-related behavior. In practical terms, police departments should provide employees with sufficient financial compensation to meet their basic needs, a reasonably safe environment in which to work, and a nonmonetary reward system that reinforces individual self-esteem. Enlightened police administrators recognize the need for the personal growth of their subordinates and support it by providing opportunities for career advancement, encouraging self-development, and creating environments in which police officers are allowed to explore their own talents and dreams.[40]

While very few people (probably less than 10 percent of the general population) achieve self-actualization, most professional police officers are acutely aware of their higher-order needs. As they have moved in the direction of self-actualization, their need structure has changed. Growth needs (for competence, fulfillment, and respect) have displaced survival needs as primary motivators. Consequently, modern police administrators must be willing to de-emphasize their short-term goals and pay more attention to developing human resources. Failure to meet the growth needs of professional employees is certain to have a negative effect on the efficiency, effectiveness, and productivity of the police department. As Thomas Peters and Robert Waterman pointed out in their book, *In Search of Excellence*,[41] outstanding companies go to great lengths to meet the higher-order human needs of professional employees. This type of proactive management strategy is designed to counteract the dysfunctional influence of stress, absenteeism, shoddy workmanship, interpersonal conflict, and poor morale.

While there has been little or no scientific validation of Maslow's theory, it is still accepted as an article of faith by organizational humanists and theoreticians who subscribe to the human relations school of management. Maslow's concepts have been repackaged in many ways, and they serve as a foundation for most content theories.

**E.R.G. Theory**     While Maslow's theory has a great deal of humanistic appeal, there is simply no consistent evidence to prove his contention that satisfying a human need at one level actually decreases the motivational importance of that need so that the satisfaction of a person's needs is a process that becomes less and less concrete as time goes on.[42] Consequently, some motivation theorists have attempted to modify the hierarchy of needs concept to make it more realistic in terms of its application to goal-oriented behavior. Clayton Alderfer's "E.R.G." (existence/relatedness/growth) theory has become one of the better-known content theories. Alderfer developed his E.R.G. theory in an effort to simplify Maslow's hierarchical model. E.R.G. collapses Maslow's five human need categories into just three and contends they are active in all human beings:

1. *Existence needs*. These include all of the drives, desires, and wants related to a person's physiological and material well-being. Maslow's survival and security needs are combined into a single category focusing on the need for food, water, shelter, safety, pay, fringe benefits, working conditions, and so on.

2. *Relatedness needs*. These involve the innate sociability of human animals as they search for meaningful and mutually satisfying relationships with significant others, individually or in groups. The satisfaction of social (interaction) and ego (esteem) needs grows out of the process of sharing.

3. *Growth needs*. These are directly related to the psychosocial processes that produce a sense of self-esteem (personal worth) and/or self-actualization (personal fulfillment). When growth needs are reasonably well satisfied, people exhibit confidence in themselves and engage in tasks that not only require the full use of their existing capabilities but may also require the development of new skills.[43]

People are very complex social animals; they exhibit a myriad of behaviors as they consciously or subconsciously strive to satisfy a variety of competing (even, at times, conflicting) needs.

E.R.G. theory has no hierarchical progression component. There is absolutely no assumption that lower-level human needs must be satisfied before higher-level needs can be activated. In fact, any need may be activated regardless of whether or not any other needs are satisfied.[44] As a result, people may be multiply motivated at any given time. This makes it very difficult to tell exactly what motivates people to behave as they do in a particular situation.[45]

Alderfer's E.R.G. theory is straightforward and simple to understand. It is built on three basic principles: the need-escalation principle, the satisfaction-progression principle, and the frustration-regression principle.

1. *Need-escalation principle*. The less any level of need has been satisfied, the more the individual will desire satisfaction at that level.

2. *Satisfaction-progression principle*. The more that lower-level needs have been satisfied, the stronger will be an individual's desire for satisfaction of higher-level needs.

3. *Frustration-regression principle*. The less that higher-level needs have been satisfied, the more likely will be a renewed emphasis on previously satisfied lower-level needs.

E.R.G. theory is based on dynamic interaction between perceived needs. The combination of satisfaction-progression and frustration-regression can result in cycling as a person focuses on one need, then another, and then back again.[46]

David McClelland, a psychologist, used the Thematic Apperception Test (TAT) to identify and measure basic human needs. The TAT asks people to look at pictures and write about what they see. Based on extensive data,

**Acquired Needs Theory**

McClelland and his colleagues identified three basic human drives: (1) need for achievement, (2) need for affiliation, and (3) need for power. He defined these needs in the following way:

1. *Need for achievement (abbreviated by McClelland as nAch)*. Human beings have a basic need for achievement. This relates to each person's desire to be competent, to solve problems, to accomplish complex tasks, and to make a meaningful contribution to the organization. People with this need will want to do well no matter what goal they pursue.
2. *Need for affiliation (nAff)*. The human need for interpersonal contact and group affiliation is insatiable. It is reflected in a person's desire to establish and maintain meaningful social relationships with significant others. People rated high on nAff welcome tasks that require interaction with others; those rated less high prefer to work alone.
3. *Need for power (nPower)*. People strive to acquire power in order to influence or control the behavior of others. People rated high on nPower might be overly concerned with personal power. Those with less of a need for power might not take the necessary actions if they could offend the group.[47]

These three needs (nAch, nAff, and nPower) exist in all people all of the time. One need is predominant in each person, however. It motivates people to act and shapes their job behavior.

McClelland's theory is based on the fundamental assumption that the needs for achievement, affiliation, and power are acquired over time and because of various life experiences. They are learned motives that are given substance by an individual's personality, background, and values. People are normally motivated by their dominant need. This dominant need is usually translated into a person's work preferences. People with a high nPower usually become much better managers than the high achievers. They have a sincere desire to influence others in an effort to accomplish the organization's mission, goals, and objectives. They thrive on ambiguity, seek responsibility, and feel comfortable being involved in the executive decision-making process. McClelland's theory encourages managers to learn how to recognize dominant needs in themselves and others and how to create work environments that are responsive to the personal need profile of each employee; managers are also encouraged to learn how to help identify the characteristics of people who may be best suited for particular kinds of jobs in the organization.[48]

McClelland's nAch, nAff, and nPower are needs very similar to those identified by Maslow and Alderfer. They can help police administrators understand why people act the way they do and what determines their work preferences (see Table 5–1). Identifying an employee's dominant need could give managers a unique opportunity to match the right person with the right job in the right set of circumstances—ideally taking much of the guesswork out of the motivation process and increasing the likelihood that management will achieve a harmonious balance between the psychosocial needs of the individual and the needs of the organization.[49] Finding the right balance is critical in determining the productivity of a complex criminal justice organization.

L. J. Clayborn is the chief of police in a wealthy suburban community of 21,000 located just outside a large midwestern industrial city. He was appointed chief 31 years ago, when the municipal government was first incorporated. The chief is a very powerful man with an institutionalized political base. His word is law and has never been challenged.

Chief Clayborn is autocratic in that he distrusts the judgment of his subordinates and makes virtually every decision that affects the police department but paternalistic in the sense that he takes care of those officers who are loyal as well as obedient. The department has the highest pay scale and the best equipment in the metropolitan area. On the surface, it is a model police agency.

The older officers (who refer to themselves as "donkeys") are content to let the "old man" run the show. Most of them have retired intellectually and want to avoid responsibility like the plague. They have absolutely no desire to jeopardize their lucrative pensions by making "decisions." Most of them are ritualistically counting the days until they can "hang 'em up."

Younger officers—who are ordinarily better educated, more participative, and often risk oriented—have been challenging the status quo. They want more input into the decision-making process. Several of the renegades have formed an association and are calling for an election to identify an exclusive bargaining agent. Chief Clayborn, in a knee-jerk antiunion move, fired the president of the police officers' association. This action only fueled the fire of discontent. Members of the police officers' association have voted no confidence in the chief and asked for his resignation.

The chief is being pressured by the news media to resolve the police department's internal problems. He believes that his job may be in jeopardy. Consequently, he has approached the city council and the mayor with a final proposal designed to reduce the tension. His plan calls for the "prompt resolution of all grievances by the chief of police," "a substantial increase in pay and fringe benefits," and more "job security." The police association's board of directors has labeled the chief's plan as a sham designed to perpetuate the status quo and to "camouflage the real issue."

*What is the real issue? How would Abraham Maslow and Douglas McGregor describe the dynamics of the situation? If you were the chief of police, what would you do to defuse this problem? Is it time for the chief to go? Why or why not?*

Table 5–1 **Work Preferences Based on a High Need for Achievement, Affiliation, and Power**

| Individual Need | Work Preferences | Exemplar |
| --- | --- | --- |
| High need for achievement | Skill Competence Responsibility Autonomy Challenging goals Feedback Competitiveness | A rookie police officer with a dominant need to master his/her craft and be a true professional. |
| High need for affiliation | Interaction Relationships Communication Participation Camaraderie Sharing Group orientation | A community relations specialist assigned to help ease the conflict between the police and inner-city minority community. |
| High need for power | Manage Influence Control Direct Decide Instruct Motivate | A newly promoted major with the will to manage human resources in order to achieve a police department's goals and objectives. |

Taking his cue from Maslow and other content theorists, Douglas McGregor developed a different humanistic theory of management. It is based on two distinct sets of assumptions about human nature (he called them Theory X and Theory Y) and the idea that managers tend to fall into one of two groups depending on which of the two assumptions they make about their employees. Theory X (the traditional approach to direction, control, and management) is based on a negative view of people. Theory Y (a more modern humanistic view) sees people as innately motivated and improvable. According to McGregor, managers organize, control, and attempt to motivate employees based on one or the other of these assumptions.

Theory X, the framework for much of traditional management thinking, includes the following negative assumptions:

1. The average human being has a natural dislike for work and will avoid it whenever possible.

2. Because they really dislike work, most people must be coerced, directed, controlled, and threatened with punishment in order to get them to work toward the achievement of organizational goals and objectives.

3. Most humans lack ambition, avoid responsibility, and need constant direction. Their chief concerns are survival and job security. Consequently, employees are viewed as expendable resources with little or no value in and of themselves. They simply become a means to an end.

The tragedy of Theory X is that it is a self-fulfilling prophecy. Theory X police administrators treat their subordinates in a suspicious and authoritarian manner. They threaten them, exploit them, and look down on them. New employees soon learn that their drive, ideas, initiative, and commitment are neither respected nor rewarded. They learn to behave the way they are expected to behave. Police officers who find themselves in Theory X environments adapt quickly. They adopt a nonproductive, "What's the use?" attitude. As poor morale robs an organization of vitality, the organization becomes progressively more dysfunctional.

Theory Y represents the other end of the continuum and is based, in large measure, on Maslow's hierarchy of needs. Theory Y assumes that once people's lower-level needs (for survival, security, and belongingness) have been reasonably well satisfied, they are motivated by higher-order needs for self-esteem and self-actualization. If they are deprived of the opportunity to satisfy these higher-level needs at work, they become frustrated. They often react to this frustration by becoming indolent, passive, resistant to change, nonproductive, and unhappy. Poor morale creates a dilemma for proactive managers, and its resolution calls for a totally different set of assumptions about what motivates people to work. Douglas McGregor offered Theory Y as a "modest beginning for a new theory" with respect to the day-to-day management of human resources. Theory Y is built on the following set of assumptions:

1. The average human being does not inherently dislike work. In fact, the expenditure of physical and mental effort is as natural as play and rest.

2. External control and the threat of punishment are not the only means by which to elicit individual effort. Employees exercise self-direction and self-control in order to achieve goals to which they are committed.

3. Motivation, the potential for development, the capacity to assume responsibility, and the readiness to direct one's behavior toward organizational goals are present in every person. Management does not put them there.

4. Commitment to goals is a function of the rewards that are associated with their achievement. The most important rewards are to be found in the ego satisfaction and the self-fulfillment aspects of commitment.

5. The most important function of management is to create an organizational environment and arrange internal processes so people can achieve their own goals best by directing their own efforts toward organizational objectives. The manager's job is to create opportunities, release potential, encourage growth, and provide guidance.

6. The capacity to exercise a relatively high degree of imagination, ingenuity, and creativity in seeking solutions to organizational problems is widespread throughout the population.[50]

Intrinsic motivation is viewed as the key to improved performance and increased productivity. Theory Y, in sharp contrast to Theory X, emphasizes managerial leadership through motivation by objectives—that is, by permitting subordinate personnel to experience need satisfaction as they contribute to the achievement of the organization's mission, goals, and objectives. If workers are not motivated, it is because of poor management practices that do not allow employees' natural positive attitudes toward work to emerge.[51]

Theory Y managers respect their personnel and use rewards to enhance performance. They also seek to motivate their people through allowing them meaningful participation in the organization's decision-making process. Police officers who feel like part of the team and who receive psychosocial satisfaction from their job are much more likely to invest time, talent, energy, and expertise in the organization.[52]

As with Theory X, Theory Y may have a Pygmalion effect. Assuming the best about people often results in their giving their best. All other things being equal, people learn to give what they are expected to give. By treating subordinates as mature, fully functional human beings who are capable of making a significant contribution to the police department, Theory Y administrators frequently motivate police personnel to achieve extraordinarily high levels of performance.[53] Theory X and Theory Y are not mutually exclusive managerial strategies; they represent the assumptions on which managerial strategies are built. While McGregor did not argue that either Theory X or Y is always correct, he did suggest that managers tend to adopt Theory X assumptions more often than can be justified by the characteristics of their employees. He argued that where and whenever appropriate, management practices that are consistent with Theory Y would produce much greater personal and organizational benefits. His typology suggests that police administrators should tailor their managerial approach to meet the profile (X or Y) exhibited by police personnel. Perhaps the optimal theory would encourage the police administrator to employ either of the approaches at one time or another, depending on the behavior patterns of his or her personnel and the demands of the situation.[54] Figure 5–3 explores the relationship between McGregor's concepts and other content theories.

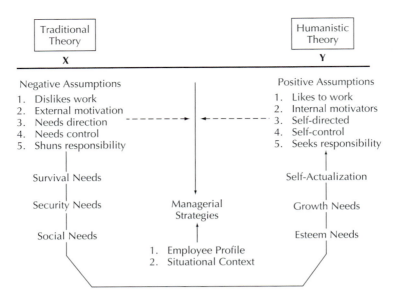

**Figure 5-3**

McGregor's Theory X and Theory Y.

Adapted from Douglas M. McGregor, *The Human Side of Enterprise* ( New York: McGraw-Hill, 1960).

**Motivation-Hygiene Theory**

Frederick Herzberg developed another view of human needs. His "motivation-hygiene," or "two-factor," theory was originally derived from an analysis of critical incidents reported by 200 engineers and accountants. They were asked to describe the times when they felt exceptionally good and exceptionally bad about their jobs. Based on the different things respondents identified as sources of satisfaction and dissatisfaction in their work, Herzberg identified two themes characteristic of all jobs: (1) "maintenance" or "hygiene" factors and (2) "motivational" factors. He explained these terms as follows:

1. *Maintenance factors.* Maintenance or hygiene factors are those things in the work environment that meet an employee's hedonistic need to avoid pain. They include the necessities of any job (e.g., adequate pay, fringe benefits, job security, decent working conditions, supervision, interpersonal relations, managerial practices, and realistic policies, procedures, rules, and regulations). Hygiene factors do not satisfy (or motivate); they set the stage for motivation. They are, however, the major source of job dissatisfaction when they are perceived to be inadequate.

2. *Motivational factors.* Motivators are those psychosocial factors in work that provide intrinsic satisfaction and serve as an incentive for people to invest more of their time, talent, energy, and expertise in productive goal-oriented behavior. The primary human motivators are (1) achievement, (2) recognition, (3) advancement, (4) the work itself, (5) the potential for growth, and (6) responsibility. The absence of motivators does not necessarily produce job dissatisfaction.[55]

While these concepts are obviously related, they represent completely different dimensions of satisfaction.

In terms of motivation, hygiene factors provide the milieu within which motivators (or satisfiers) function. They create a neutral state by meeting lower-level human needs and preventing negative or dysfunctional behavior. Actions designed to improve hygiene factors can prevent or help to eliminate job dissatisfaction but cannot increase job satisfaction per se. Whisenand offers the following suggestions based on needs theory:

- Do not assume that all police employees are motivated by the same needs or values.
- To determine what will motivate any given worker, determine what needs that individual is trying to satisfy on the job.
- Make sure that you have the authority and power to administer or withhold consequences that will satisfy a person's need.
- Design job situations so that the officers and civilians can satisfy their needs by engaging in behaviors that enable the department to achieve its mission.[56]

The least desirable situation from a management point of view is to have police officers experiencing low satisfaction (of higher-level human needs) and high dissatisfaction (with the organization's efforts to meet lower-level survival, security, and social needs). The best mix involves high satisfaction and low dissatisfaction (see Figure 5–4). The police administrator's goal under the two-factor theory is to minimize job dissatisfaction and to maximize job

| Job Satisfaction* (Satisfiers) | Job Dissatisfaction* (Hygiene) | Adaptive Behavior |
|---|---|---|
| High ← - - - - - - - - - - - → High | | Competition<br>Conflict<br>Normlessness<br>Wheel spinning<br>Individualism |
| High ← - - - - - - - - - - - → Low | | Cooperation<br>Self-direction<br>Self-control<br>Responsibility<br>Productivity |
| Low ← - - - - - - - - - - - → High | | Stress<br>Low morale<br>Poor workmanship<br>Absenteeism<br>Turnover |
| Low ← - - - - - - - - - - - → Low | | Ritualism<br>Apathy<br>Status quo<br>Soldiering<br>Resists change |

\* Motivational factors interact with hygiene factors to produce adaptive behavior.

**Figure 5–4**
Satisfaction/Dissatisfaction and Adaptive Behavior.

satisfaction. Once improved hygiene factors reduce job dissatisfaction, managers must be prepared to shift their attention to motivational factors if they are to create more job satisfaction.

The best way to motivate workers (to be more efficient, effective, and productive) is to give them a bigger stake in the job itself. In fact, upgrading the job itself is the core component of Herzberg's theory. According to Herzberg, managers motivate their subordinates by eliciting their input, encouraging participation, involving people in the decision-making process, and enlarging or enriching the job.[57]

Frederick Herzberg's motivation-hygiene theory draws heavily on Maslow, Alderfer, and McGregor. It emphasizes the importance of dynamic interaction between maintenance needs (hygiene) and motivation needs (satisfiers). Like all other content theories, it has been criticized for its methodological imprecision. A major debate concerns Herzberg's contention that hygiene factors function only as dissatisfiers, not as satisfiers. Researchers have found little or no support for this position. Nevertheless, there does seem to be some substance to the rest of Herzberg's theory. According to Lyman Porter and Raymond E. Miles,[58] much of the evidence supports the conclusion that job content factors are considered to be critically important to those workers who are asked to report their most highly satisfying experiences.

**Content Theory Revisited**

While it is virtually impossible to tell exactly what motivates people to act as they do in a given situation, theorists such as Maslow, Alderfer, McGregor, and Herzberg have made important contributions to our knowledge of the psychosocial processes that produce goal-oriented human behavior. They have provided us with food for thought and a springboard to further inquiry. In sum, the content theories address the following "bottom line" requirements for managing employee motivation:[59]

- Assess employee needs.
- Identify the most active needs of employees.
- Develop specific strategies to satisfy active employee needs.
- Implement strategies.
- Evaluate the plan.

## PROCESS THEORIES

Many behavioral scientists have been frustrated by the seeming subjectivity and introspectiveness of the content theories.[60] They are much more interested in how people are motivated to engage in goal-oriented behavior. Some of them subscribe to behavior modification approaches based on classic reinforcement theory. With Pavlovian zeal and Skinnerian logic, they believe workers can be trained to be more efficient, effective, and productive through the use of stimulus-response techniques, with money as the primary reward. Some behaviorists recommend the use of what they call "operant conditioning" to make people operate in a certain way to receive a certain reward.

They contend that people are what they are and do what they do because of environmental factors rather than internal drives, needs, or abstract intellectual calculations.[61] Operant conditioning theory is based on the assumption that when an operant response (the desired behavior) is followed by a pleasant incident (a reward), it causes people to associate that pleasant outcome with the desired behavior. Since human beings are hedonistic animals who prefer pleasure to pain, people usually behave in a way that brings them pleasure. Operant conditioning theorists encourage managers to avoid the use of punishment as the primary means of motivation; more effective, they say, is the following approach:

1. Specify the desired behavior in clear operational terms.
2. Use positive reinforcements (rewards) whenever possible.
3. Minimize the time lag between desired behavior and reinforcement.
4. Use a variable-ratio schedule as opposed to continuous reinforcement.
5. Determine the response level, and use shaping techniques to obtain appropriate behavior.
6. Manipulate environmental factors so that they will all reinforce the desired behavior.
7. Keep the positive reinforcement at the lowest level needed to maintain performance.[62]

The operant conditioning process became the centerpiece of Frederick W. Taylor's scientific management and is still popular in some management circles. Most newer process theories stress the decision-making dimension of work performance. Newer process theories represent a dynamic alternative to the more descriptive content theories discussed in the last section. They have been designed to help police administrators understand the cognitive (thought) processes by which individual workers choose to engage in specific behaviors in order to satisfy their personal needs. Two of the most popular process theories are expectancy theory and equity theory. Both are based on the assumption that people make conscious and subconscious assessments of contemplated actions and the consequences of those actions. Personal expectations of the outcomes associated with goal-oriented behavior are critical variables in determining how people are motivated to perform at work. Let us take a closer look at these two theories.

## Expectancy Theory

Expectancy theory assumes not only that people are driven by intrinsic needs but that they also make subjective decisions about what they will or will not do based on what they think will result from their effort. The motivation to work is determined, in large measure, by what the individual believes about effort-to-performance relationships and about the desirability of the work outcomes (rewards) associated with different potential levels of performance. In other words, police officers will evaluate behavioral alternatives and choose the one they believe will lead to the best ratio of reward to effort.

The higher the expectation that a given behavior will pay off (in terms of an anticipated reward), the more likely people are to invest their time, talent, and expertise in order to do it well. Victor Vroom's expectancy theory is designed to explain the dynamics involved in this type of choice behavior.[63]

Vroom, a well-known management consultant, introduced his expectancy theory in the early 1960s. He identified five critically important variables: (1) expectancies (beliefs about performance capabilities), (2) valences (beliefs about outcome desirabilities), (3) outcomes, (4) instrumentalities (beliefs about outcome contingencies), and (5) choices. Vroom discussed these variables as follows:

1. *Expectancy.* Expectancy is a probability estimate made by a person concerning the likelihood that a particular behavior will be followed by a particular outcome. The degree of expectancy ranges from zero (none) to one (absolute certainty). There are two levels of expectancy: Expectancy 1 (E → P) is a person's perception of the chances that a certain level of effort (E) will lead to first-level outcomes that result in adequate job performance (P). Expectancy 2 (E → O) is a person's perception of the chances that performance (P) will lead to desired second-level outcomes (O).

2. *Valences.* A valence is the strength of one's preference for a particular outcome. Unlike expectancies, valences can be positive or negative and are measured on a scale from −1 (very undesirable) to +1 (very desirable). The level of motivation will depend on how much someone wants the ends (goals) of work effort as well as the means (or tools) needed to achieve these ends.

3. *Outcomes.* An outcome or reward is any need-related consequence of a behavior. First-level outcomes are the outcomes of successful job performance (a sense of accomplishment, feelings of competence, goal achievement, and so forth). Second-level outcomes are the consequences to which first-level outcomes are expected to lead (a pay increase, promotion, professional status, and so forth). Some outcomes are intrinsic to the person; others are extrinsic.

4. *Instrumentality.* An instrumentality is the belief that if the necessary level of performance is achieved, the anticipated outcome (reward) will be forthcoming. The overall strength of an instrumentality ranges from zero (none) to one (certainty).

5. *Choice.* A choice concerns the selection of a particular pattern of behavior. People weigh the potential value and consequence of each action they contemplate in order to estimate the probability that certain outcomes can be attained by choosing a particular behavior.

These variables interact with each other to affect motivation. The interactions of three of them in particular—expectancy (E), instrumentalities (I), and valence (V)—determine the extent of the motivation to perform (M). All three must have high positive values to produce goal-oriented choices. If the value of any one of these three variables for a person approaches zero, the probability that he or she will be motivated to perform well also approaches zero. Vroom contends these factors are interrelated multiplicatively, as expressed in the equation $M = E \times I \times V$. When people believe they have the ability to accomplish a certain task if they perform at a particular level, their self-confidence may produce a high level of expectation (expectancy).[64]

This belief will not, in and of itself, motivate goal-oriented behavior, however. They must also have a high level of confidence that if they put forth the necessary effort and perform at a high level, they will be rewarded (instrumentality), and they must place high value on the reward or other anticipated outcomes (valence). A patrol officer, for example, may have the skill, steady performance, and the intradepartmental support for appointment to the SWAT team but may turn the opportunity down because this special assignment is far less important to him than maximizing the amount of time he can spend with his terminally ill wife.

Managers play a key role in operationalizing expectancy theory in the workplace. The multiplier effect (just discussed) requires police administrators to attempt to maximize expectancy, instrumentality, and valence when they seek to use work-based rewards to create high levels of work motivation among their subordinates. In order to make effective use of expectancy theory in motivating their personnel, police administrators should:

1. Establish reasonably high expectations and a climate of police professionalism.
2. Recruit, screen, select, and retain well-qualified personnel.
3. Create an incentive system based on equal access to meaningful rewards.
4. Supervise subordinates in such a way that they are always learning, growing, and expanding their horizons.
5. Implement an effective in-service training program keyed to the concept of staff development.
6. Forge a direct link between job performance and positive reinforcement.
7. Analyze the total situation for conflicting expectancies, and take appropriate action to minimize conflict.
8. Check to make sure there is an equitable distribution of rewards based on actual performance levels.
9. Perform the executive function of keeping the motivation system in a state of dynamic equilibrium.

From an expectancy perspective, *the things that get rewarded get done!* Establishing the proper link between job performance and meaningful rewards is the single most effective way to improve organizational efficiency, effectiveness, and productivity.[65]

Expectancy theory has evolved into a very complex explanation of motivation, built around the assumption that human beings are rational animals who voluntarily choose to engage in those behaviors that their expectancy calculation tells them will consistently produce anticipated rewards (see Figure 5–5). The complexity of the expectancy model has made it very difficult to validate it through applied research. The lack of supportive data does not invalidate the concept, however. Common sense tells us that motivation depends on the dynamic interaction between our expectations, opportunities, desired outcomes, and the intensity of our desire for particular rewards. While they may not be able to explain it in technical terms, most effective police administrators have incorporated expectancy theory into their overall philosophy of management.

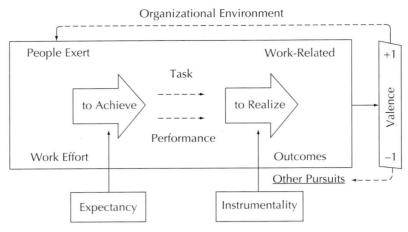

Organizational Environment

People Exert | Work-Related | +1

Task

to Achieve ----→ to Realize | Valence

Performance

Work Effort | Outcomes | −1

Other Pursuits ←----

Expectancy

Instrumentality

Human beings are rational animals who voluntarily choose those behaviors their expectancy calculation tells them will consistently produce anticipated rewards.

**Figure 5–5**
Simplified Version of Expectancy Theory.

**Equity Theory**     One of the most sensitive issues confronting modern management is achieving equity in rewarding individual workers for their job performance. Equity means fairness. From a motivation standpoint, equity refers to the perceived fairness of rewards and of the reward system itself. J. Stacy Adams[66] formulated one of the best-known equity theories. He contends that a feeling of inequity is a motivating state of mind. In other words, when people feel that there is an inequity in the way they are being treated, they will be moved psychologically to eliminate the discomfort and to restore a sense of equity to the situation. Inequities are perceived when people believe the rewards or incentives they receive for their work output are unequal to the rewards other workers appear to be getting for comparable output. This violates the widely accepted norm that people should be treated equitably (not equally). Workers expect meaningful rewards that are commensurate with their job performance. Equity theory is based on the idea that people want to maintain balance. They are especially interested in maintaining *distributive fairness*. This exists when employees think people are getting what they deserve—not more, not less.[67]

According to Adams's equity theory, a key element in determining the fairness of a particular relationship lies in this type of social comparison. A perceived inequity involves the comparison of an existing state or condition with a given standard. Employees instinctively compare themselves and their particular situations with others in the workplace. It is common for officers to compare the work their jobs require of them with the work of other employees—for example, sergeants assigned to what are often perceived as "rubber gun squad," details requiring little or no real police work. Comparisons of this type tend to lower morale. It is often impossible for management to justify the allocation of work. It does not matter what managers believe is fair and equitable, because pay and equity are in the minds of those affected. Even if police officers and sergeants were rewarded in exactly the same way, inequities would still be found. Inequity exists when unequals are treated as equals as well as when equals are treated as unequals. The bottom line is that perceived inequities are inevitable whenever large numbers of people interact with one another in complex criminal justice organizations. They are caused by factors such as:

1. Pay differentials and discretionary monetary incentives.
2. Racial, religious, sexual, and social discrimination (actual or perceived).
3. Variable access to organizational resources.
4. Political as opposed to merit-based promotion.
5. Favoritism and selective communication.
6. Preferential assignment based on length of service.
7. Differential status and the distribution of perquisites.

Equity theory is based on the assumption that all workers have been socially programmed to compare themselves and other employees with respect to what they get out of their job (outcomes) and what they invest in their job (inputs). Outcomes include pay, fringe benefits, prestige, feelings of achievement, a sense of personal satisfaction, and so on. Inputs are factors such as special skills, training, ingenuity, perseverance, and hard work. These comparisons are then translated into ratios that reflect their inputs and outcomes vis-à-vis those of others within the workforce. A negative inequity exists when a police officer feels that he or she is receiving relatively less of a valued outcome than other officers in proportion to work inputs. A positive inequity, on the other hand, exists when an officer feels that he or she is receiving relatively more of a valued outcome than others doing the same type of work. If an individual's input/outcome ratio is equal to that of the others, the person will experience a sense of equity. Both negative and positive inequity are motivators.[68]

When the reward for performance equals or exceeds what is considered fair, the satisfaction will produce repeat behavior.[69] If a reward falls short of perceived equity, dissatisfaction will reduce the motivation to continue the effort. Adams noted that when employees perceive either positive (overpayment) or negative (underpayment) inequity, they will suffer cognitive dissonance and disequilibrium; to reduce these psychosocial discomforts they will consciously or subconsciously engage in one or more of the following behaviors:

1. Increase performance, workload, and other kinds of inputs to justify higher rewards when they perceive a positive inequity.
2. Decrease performance, workload, and other kinds of inputs when they perceive a negative inequity.
3. Change outcomes (or rewards) through personal persuasion, collective bargaining, legal action, or dysfunctional behavior such as misappropriation, employee theft, and outright corruption.
4. Change comparisons by persuading low performers with equal pay to increase their efforts and by discouraging high performers from being rate busters.

Ramon J. Aldag and Loren W. Kuzuhara[70] contend that managers can maintain control of the equity dynamic in their work unit if they follow these rules:

1. Assess employee perceptions of equity in their work situations.
2. Identify employees who perceive inequities.
3. Identify the basis for employee perceptions of inequity. Openness is critical because it tends to reduce suspicion and helps defuse the perception of inequity.

4. Evaluate management policies and practices to determine the validity of employee perceptions.

5. Identify specific changes that can be made to address employee equity concerns.

6. Implement changes and communicate them to employees.

While these relatively simple rules will not cure all of the very complex problems associated with psychosocial equity comparisons, they should help to make the process more objective. Since most Americans equate objectivity with fairness, there could be a genuine reduction in labor-management conflict.

Even though recent research has consistently demonstrated that the perception of inequity leads to reduced output, more absenteeism, and higher employee turnover, some motivation theorists feel that equity theory is of limited value because it is a special-purpose theory rather than a general theory of motivation.[71] They argue that equity theory does not explain how people select a person to compare themselves with or how they arrive at the value placed on inputs and outcomes. Nevertheless, equity theory provides police administrators with an intellectual framework for thinking about issues such as equity, fairness, and justice in the allocation of rewards. In fact, feelings of inequity and injustice have served to motivate human beings throughout all of recorded history.

## IMPLICATIONS FOR POLICE MANAGEMENT

Police administrators today must come to grips with one simple fact of life—they are dealing with a new breed of employee. Modern police personnel are more sophisticated than their predecessors. They are better educated, more participative, and much less resistant to change. They demand respect and expect to be treated as professionals. While money is still a magical word in the police subculture, it has a much different meaning than it did a generation ago. Salaries and fringe benefits have been improved to the point where more money, in and of itself, no longer serves as the primary motivator. Police officers demand more than just money. Most of them want to do meaningful work that meets their conscious and subconscious higher-order needs for growth, self-esteem, and a sense of fulfillment.[72]

Police managers, who are expected to get things done through others, are in a position to help satisfy the higher-order needs of their subordinates. Their job is to translate individual effort into collaborative action. Effective managers tend to be proactive people developers who subscribe to the Theory Y assumptions of Douglas McGregor. They emphasize the importance of (1) participation, (2) job design, (3) job enlargement, (4) job enrichment, and (5) job rotation.

1. *Participation*. As police officers move up the professional ladder, they have an increased need to become involved in charting the course of an enterprise. They experience a strong desire to help shape its mission, set its goals, and determine its objectives. Meaningful participation in the organization's decision-making process gives them a sense of ownership in, and a strong commitment to, the decisions it produces. Since collective decisions are often superior to those made by a single individual, managers should solicit input from their personnel and employ strategies designed to facilitate full participation. A police department will be much stronger when management is comfortable sharing power with, rather than exercising power over, its professional employees.[73]

2. *Job design.* A job consists of a task or series of tasks a person performs in support of the organization's mission (purpose). Job design involves deliberate and purposeful planning in order to bring both the structural and psychosocial aspects of the activity together in one basic process. It is the police administrator's responsibility to design the task and the work setting so that employees will have intrinsic motivation to perform and will derive satisfaction from a job well done. Properly designed jobs are interesting, challenging, achievable, and rewarding. Managers usually prepare job descriptions that spell out the duties, processes, authority, responsibility, and accountability inherent in a given job.[74] Managers can sometimes address morale and motivation problems by designing jobs to make them more meaningful.

3. *Job enlargement.* One of the first modern methods of motivating employees through job design was job enlargement.[75] This involved injecting some variety into a fairly repetitive, boring job by introducing different, yet related, kinds of tasks. Instead of doing just the same repetitive task for eight hours, police patrol personnel might do three or four different, but related, tasks requiring the same level of skill. The team approach to motor vehicle assembly is a very good example of job enlargement. The "police agent" concept in law enforcement represents another practical application of this idea. Police agents are patrol personnel who have responsibility performing many of the routine duties usually assigned to detectives. Patrol officers are often allowed to conduct preliminary investigations in misdemeanor and lower-level felony cases. These job enlargement strategies are built on the assumption that variety is the spice of life. Job enlargement motivates employees to improve job performance and increase their productivity.

4. *Job enrichment.* Job enrichment is a different job design strategy, which aims to counteract the negative aspects of specialization by building motivating factors into job content. Frederick Herzberg called this "vertical loading"; it is calculated to meet higher-order human needs for autonomy, growth, and self-actualization. Both job enrichment and job enlargement add variety to a job by introducing new tasks, but enlargement adds them "horizontally," at the same skill or decision-making level, whereas enrichment adds them "vertically," requiring higher levels of skill or decision-making ability. According to Herzberg,[76] the purpose of job enrichment is to motivate people by

1. Removing some controls while maintaining overall accountability.
2. Increasing the accountability of each person for his or her own work.
3. Giving employees responsibility for performing a natural and complete unit of work.
4. Granting additional authority to people in their area of responsibility.
5. Encouraging autonomy in decision-making as it relates to the task being performed.
6. Introducing new and more difficult tasks not previously handled by employees at a particular level.
7. Assigning individual police officers to enhanced or highly specialized tasks to help them become experts.

Because of the rigid bureaucratic structure of most American police departments, job enrichment programs have not been widespread. Where such programs have been implemented, they have produced encouraging results. They motivate police personnel by targeting their higher-order needs for achievement, responsibility, recognition, advancement, and personal growth.

As police departments' personnel become more and more sophisticated, it will take innovative strategies like job enrichment to motivate them to become team players whose personal goals coincide with those of the organization.

5. *Job rotation.* Job rotation is a motivation strategy in which people are moved into different jobs, usually on a temporary basis, in order to give them additional experiences, understandings, and challenges. It is most often used to cross-train employees so that they gain a better appreciation for the importance of different jobs and the relationships between jobs in an organization. Employees who become involved in job rotation programs are usually more valuable to themselves and their employers because they develop the ability to perform more than one limited function.[77] Job rotation tends to give employees more self-confidence and helps prepare them for promotions and transfers. While many police departments have experimented with job rotation programs, they have not been as effective as originally envisioned. The enemy is bureaucracy and the lack of good management. Bureaucracy prevents police administrators from becoming leaders by turning them into paper shufflers rather than people developers.

Almost all of the available evidence suggests that these motivation strategies work if managers are careful about when, how, and with whom they are used. Their success in improving efficiency, effectiveness, productivity, and morale will depend on the composition of the workforce, the managerial skill of the police administrator, and the dynamics of the situation. These motivational strategies will probably have more influence on quality than on quantity.

---

**CASE STUDY**   Captain Marsha Darley

Captain Darley is the commander of a patrol division in one precinct of a very large city. Based on tradition and operational policy, the department has a rigid bureaucratic structure keyed to job specialization. Patrol officers answer calls, do preliminary investigations (when minor crimes are involved), and engage in preventive patrol when time allows. The Bureau of Criminal Investigations conducts all other investigations. Job descriptions are specific and binding. Deviation from a job description results in immediate disciplinary action. The workload is used to justify this particular division of labor.

The dehumanizing aspect of bureaucratic specialization has taken its toll on the personnel assigned to the patrol division. Statistics indicate the extent of the problems in the division (as compared to the specialized work units within the police department):

1. The job is viewed as dissatisfying.
2. Morale is low.
3. The crime rate is up.
4. Response time is long.
5. The clearance-by-arrest rate is down.
6. Use of force is at a record high.
7. The number of citizen-initiated complaints is up.
8. More officers are filing disability claims.
9. Absenteeism is rampant.
10. Abuse of sick leave is epidemic.
11. Employee turnover is exceeding projections.

The situation has become critical and imperils the division's ability to function efficiently, effectively, and productively.

Captain Darley has just returned from a four-week FBI Academy course on the quality of work life. She has been asked to devise a plan (and motivational strategies) to counteract the overspecialization in her unit. If this pilot program is successful, it will be transplanted to other precincts of the city.

Captain Darley is being given financial support as well as moral support to carry out this project. Management has finally come to the conclusion that increased productivity can only be brought about by improving the motivation of line personnel. Police work is labor intensive. Most of the budget (between 75 and 85 percent) is spent on human resources. Dissatisfied employees are a liability. The solution is to design a motivation program that meets the needs of both the department and the employees.

*What philosophical approach do you believe Captain Darley should take in carrying out this project? What specific motivational strategies would you recommend that she consider? Give several concrete examples.*

---

# SUMMARY

Management can be defined as getting things done with and through the efforts of others. Thus, it is the police administrator's job to create an environment within which professional employees motivate themselves. This can be done by establishing a concrete link between appropriate job behavior and meaningful rewards. Motivation is a psychosocial process. It produces an attitude that generates actions that lead to anticipated results. All other things being equal, well-motivated police officers are more efficient, effective, productive, and satisfied than unmotivated ones.

Most motivation theories are based on the assumption that psychosocial tensions caused by intrinsic and/or extrinsic factors are translated into human needs. Needs elicit instrumental behaviors that are designed to reduce the tension. Of course, different needs generate different and unique adaptive responses. The intensity of a felt need (or needs) activates and energizes people as they interact with one another in the workplace.

The motivation theories discussed in this chapter fall into two very distinct categories: (1) content theories and (2) process theories. Content theories attempt to explain exactly *what* motivates people to act as they do in a given set of circumstances. Process theories, on the other hand, deal with *how* people are motivated. While none of these theories provides a complete explanation of motivation or the motivation process, they tend to supplement one another and provide the police administrator with a comprehensive perspective on this very complex psychosocial phenomenon.

## KEY TERMS

acquired needs theory
caused behavior
content theory
drives
equity theory
E.R.G. theory
expectancy theory
hierarchy of needs theory
incentives/rewards
job design
job enlargement
job enrichment

job rotation
motivation
motivation-hygiene theory
motivation process
needs
organizational humanism
organizations as social entities
participative management
performance
process theory
psychosocial adaptation to tension
Theory X and Theory Y

## DISCUSSION TOPICS AND QUESTIONS

1. What do social scientists mean when they say that all human behavior is caused? Why is this important to the study of motivation?

2. What is the basic function of any organization? List and discuss the behavioral requirements that allow complex criminal justice organizations to survive and thrive.

3. Define the term *motive*. What are the basic steps in the motivation process? What role do motives play in this process?

4. Explain the difference between content theory and process theory. Why is this distinction important? Are these theories mutually exclusive?

5. Explain Maslow's hierarchy of needs, and show how this theory has been factored into other major content theories. What contribution did the Hawthorne experiments make to Maslow's thinking?

6. Why do motivation theories ordinarily not view a satisfied need as a motivator?

7. What, from Herzberg's perspective, is the difference between a hygiene factor and a motivator? Give an example, and explain why poor hygiene leads to dissatisfaction but good hygiene does not serve as a motivator.

8. Discuss the basic assumptions on which the Theory X and Theory Y continuum is built. How does the theory's self-fulfilling prophecy influence job performance? Is Theory Y always superior to Theory X? Explain your answer.

9. What are the five elements in expectancy theory? What do expectancy theorists mean when they say that the three key elements interact multiplicatively to determine the intensity of motivation? Give an example.

10. How do people ordinarily adapt their job behavior to compensate for a perceived inequity in the way they are being treated vis-à-vis others in the workforce? What can police administrators do to control the equity dynamic in their work unit?

11. Identify the major strategies—beyond "more money"—that have developed for motivating police officers. What is the difference between job enlargement and job enrichment? Which one do you feel would be the best for motivating police personnel? Why?

## FOR FURTHER READING

Curtis Cook and Philip L. Hunsaker, *Management & Organizational Behavior with Power Web* (New York: McGraw-Hill, 2001).

This book has two primary themes—management and organizational behavior. The content is anchored in traditional and emergent organizational behavior subjects. It describes in detail the principles of motivation, including methods of motivating people in organizations. Additionally, it describes issues and practices that every manager needs to know. Of special interest is the summary of behavioral skills listed at the end of each chapter.

William A. Salmon, *The New Supervisor's Survival Manual* (New York: AMACOM, 1998).

The author describes the process of creating a supportive work environment and suggests that when people feel challenged, appreciated, and respected for their efforts they will drive themselves to do exceptional work. A number of techniques are presented, ranging from being spontaneous and honest to understanding the feelings of employees. He stresses the necessity of taking a problem-solving orientation rather than trying to control the situation or the person involved. The author recommends learning to modify your own behavior and ideas when appropriate.

Catherine Truss, Lynda Gratton, Veronica Hope-Hailey, Patrick McGovern, and Philip Stiles, "Soft and Hard Models of Human Resource Management," *Journal of Management Sciences*, Vol. 34 (1997), pp. 68–71.

The authors suggest that no organization has adopted either a pure "soft" (Theory Y) or "hard" (Theory X) approach to human resource management. This study found that individual performance was more important to employees than career development. Employees viewed training as limited to improving skills that allowed them to carry out their duties and that when individual development occurred, it was incidental to organizational performance.

John L. White, "The Work Itself as a Motivator," *FBI Law Enforcement Bulletin*, Vol. 70 (2001), p. 9.

The author discusses ways of using the work that employees perform as a means of reinforcing organizational values. He recommends creating a "video yearbook" containing videotapes of departmental personnel performing routine tasks. Playing these tapes for personnel is a way of displaying the importance of work. In a police department where this was done, the video served as a long-term motivator. The author views the process as a new way to motivate officers.

# NOTES

1. Paul Whisenand, *Supervising Police Personnel: The Fifteen Responsibilities* (Upper Saddle River, NJ: Prentice Hall, 2004), p. 134.

2. Ibid., p. 135.

3. Ibid.

4. Michael L. Vasu, Debra W. Stewart, and G. David Carson, *Organizational Behavior and Public Management* (New York: Marcel Dekker, 1998), p. 61.

5. Gary Dressler, *Management: Principles and Practices for Tomorrow's Leaders* (Upper Saddle River, NJ: Prentice Hall), p. 284.

6. Vasu, Stewart, and Carson, *Organizational Behavior and Public Management*, p. 57.

7. Robert P. Vecchio, *Organizational Behavior: Core Concepts* (Mason, OH: Thompson, 2003), p. 332.

8. Whisenand, *Supervising Police Personnel*, p. 153.

9. James L. Bowditch and Anthony F. Buono, *A Primer on Organizational Behavior* (New York: John Wiley & Sons, 1998), p. 64.

10. Lyman W. Porter, Edward E. Lawler, and J. Richard Hackman, *Behavior in Organizations* (New York: McGraw-Hill, 1975).

11. Dessler, *Management*, pp. 2–3.

12. Ibid., p. 283.

13. Vasu, Stewart, and Carson, *Organizational Behavior and Public Management*, p. 59.

14. Dressler, *Management*, pp. 284–287.

15. F.M. Levine, ed., *Theoretical Readings in Motivation* (Chicago: Rand McNally, 1975).

16. Paul M. Whisenand, *The Effective Police Manager* (Englewood Cliffs, NJ: Prentice Hall, 1981).

17. Stephen P. Robbins, *Essentials of Organizational Behavior* (Upper Saddle River, NJ: Prentice Hall, 2000), p. 44.

18. Ibid.

19. Ronald G. Lynch, *The Police Manager* (Cincinnati: Anderson, 1998), pp. 63–65.

20. Calvin J. Swank and James A. Cosner, *The Police Personnel System* (New York: Wiley, 1983).

21. Robbins, *Organizational Behavior*.

22. Whisenand, *Supervising Police Personnel*, p. 137.

23. Nathan F. Iannone and Marvin P. Iannone, *Supervision of Police Personnel* (Upper Saddle River, NJ: Prentice Hall, 2001), p. 16.

24. Robert B. Denhardt, Janet Vinzant Denhardt, and Maria P. Aristigueta, *Managing Human Behavior in Public & Nonprofit Organizations* (Thousand Oaks, CA: Sage, 2002), p. 151.

25. Ibid., p. 152.

26. Whisenand, *Supervising Police Personnel*, p. 136.

27. Ibid., p. 137.

28. Ramon J. Aldag and Loren W. Kuzuhara, *Organizational Behavior and Management: An Integrated Skills Approach* (Cincinnati: Thomson, 2002), p. 233.

29. Bowditch and Buono, *Primer*, p. 73.

30. Aldag and Kuzuhara, *Organizational Behavior and Management*, p. 274.

31. Bowditch and Buono, *Primer*, p. 65.

32. Abraham H. Maslow, *Motivation and Personality* (New York: Harper & Row, 1970).

33. Lynch, *The Police Manager*, p. 66.

34. Frank G. Goble, *The Third Force* (New York: Pocket Books, 1970).

35. Whisenand, *Supervising Police Personnel*, p. 70.

36. Denhardt, Denhardt, and Aristigueta, *Managing Human Behavior*, p. 152.

37. Dessler, *Management*, p. 289.

38. Aldag and Kuzuhara, *Organizational Behavior and Management*, p. 235.

39. Ibid., p. 236.

40. Lynch, *The Police Manager*, p. 68.

41. Thomas J. Peters and Robert H. Waterman, *In Search of Excellence* (New York: Warner, 1982).

42. Aldag and Kuzuhara, *Organizational Behavior and Management*, p. 236.

43. Clayton P. Alderfer, *Existence, Relatedness, and Growth* (Homewood, IL: Richard D. Irwin, 1981).

44. Aldag and Kuzuhara, *Organizational Behavior and Management*, p. 237.

45. Linda K. Stroh, Gregory B. Northcraft, and Margaret A. Neale, *Organizational Behavior: A Management Challenge* (Mahwah, NJ: Lawrence Erlbaum Associates, 2002), p. 66.

46. Aldag and Kuzuhara, *Organizational Behavior and Management*, pp. 237–238.

47. David McClelland, *The Achieving Society* (New Jersey: Van Nostrand, 1961)

48. Robbins, *Organizational Behavior*, p. 50.

49. Stroh, Northcraft, and Neale, *Organizational Behavior*, p. 54.

50. Douglas M. McGregor, *The Human Side of Enterprise* (New York: McGraw-Hill, 1960).

51. Lynch, *The Police Manager*, p. 72.

52. McGregor, *Enterprise*.

53. Denhardt, Denhardt, and Aristigueta, *Managing Human Behavior*, p. 160.

54. Aldag and Kuzuhara, *Organizational Behavior and Management*, p. 99.

55. Frederick Herzberg, "One More Time: How Do You Motivate Employees?" in Walter E. Natemeyer, ed. *Classics of Organizational Behavior* (Oak Park, IL: Moore, 1978).

56. Whisenand, *Supervising Police Personnel*, p. 143.

57. Herzberg, "One More Time."

58. Lyman W. Porter and Raymond E. Miles, "Motivation and Management," in Joseph W. McGuire, ed. *Contemporary Management: Issues and Viewpoints* (Englewood Cliffs, NJ: Prentice Hall, 1974).

59. Whisenand, *Supervising Police Personnel*. p. 144–148.

60. Aldag and Kuzuhara, *Organizational Behavior and Management*, p. 240.

61. Porter and Miles, *Motivation*.

62. Dessler, *Management*, p. 300.

63. Victor H. Vroom, *Work and Motivation* (New York: Wiley, 1964).

64. Aldag and Kuzuhara, *Organizational Behavior and Management*, p. 261.

65. Ibid., pp. 262–263.

66. J. Stacy Adams, "Inequity in Social Exchange," in L. Berkowicz ed. *Advances in Experimental Social Psychology*, Vol. 2. New York: Academic Press.

67. Aldag and Kuzuhara, *Organizational Behavior and Management*, p. 266.

68. Dessler, *Management*, p. 294.

69. Stroh, Northcraft, and Neale, *Organizational Behavior*, p. 80.

70. Aldag and Kuzuhara, *Organizational Behavior and Management*

71. Whisenand, *Supervising Police Personnel*, pp. 144–145.

72. Dessler, *Management*, p. 305.

73. Ibid., p. 308.

74. Stroh, Northcraft, and Neale, *Organizational Behavior*, p. 314.

75. Dessler, *Management*, pp. 306–307.

76. Herzberg, "One More Time."

77. Stroh, Northcraft, and Neale, *Organizational Behavior*, p. 312.

# 6

# STRESS IN ORGANIZATIONAL LIFE

## Its Nature, Causes, and Control

## LEARNING OBJECTIVES

1. Define *stress*.
2. Compare the two basic forms of stress: frustration and conflict.
3. Identify the types of stress unique to law enforcement.
4. List the operational items identified as stressors.
5. Describe the positive aspect of stress.
6. List the types of psychological reactions possibly caused by stress.
7. Explain the relationship between stress and job performance.
8. Identify the four common elements of the relaxation response.
9. Describe three elements of a stress reduction program.
10. List five benefits of an exercise program.
11. Describe program services that an employee assistance program can offer.
12. Describe the guidelines for the relaxation response.
13. Explain how you can take charge of your life.
14. Describe an indifferent individual.
15. List the two elements of work overload.

In recent decades, organizations have become increasingly concerned with the need for greater flexibility, responsibility, and learning opportunities in the workplace. Dramatic changes have occurred and those changes have far outpaced our understanding of their implications for work life quality. One result of those changes has been increased stress among both managers and working-level employees. Even though stress has been of concern to progressive administrators, it is becoming increasingly accepted that there is a gap in knowledge between what we know about stress and what we should know. It is difficult to imagine a society without stress. It is an integral part of life and can have both positive and harmful effects. In fact, normal stress is always present. Individuals who are well adjusted seem to have no difficulty in handling the everyday stresses of life. In recent years, however, those everyday stresses have come to concern those who study organizational behavior.[1]

Lt. Stanley Clark supervises 12 investigators in the robbery unit of a large police department. He is 51 years of age and has spent most of his career in the investigations unit of the department. Until recently, he has thoroughly enjoyed his work, as reflected in his semi-annual performance evaluations, which have always been excellent. Two years ago, he failed the captains test for the third time. In each instance, he was unable to complete the oral section of the Assessment Center test successfully. No matter how much he studied prior to each examination, the results were negative.

Police work is Lt. Clark's life, and promotion means everything to him. His failure places him in an unfavorable light and hurts him a great deal. Several officers who used to work for him have been promoted to captain, which has frustrated him even more. Lt. Clark had always been a moderate drinker, but since failing the last examination he has begun to drink heavily, and his work performance is becoming increasingly poor. He has been late to work numerous times. During one month he took 12 days of sick leave. He was asked to bring a doctor's report when returning to work after the last of those days, but he failed to do so. In his most recent performance evaluation, he was rated below average and given a list of five ways in which to improve his job performance, but he has not complied with any of the recommendations.

Lt. Clark will face a special performance evaluation at the end of this month. Knowing the probable outcome, he has decided to apply for a disability retirement, which would allow him to retire four years early at a higher pension rate. Clark has obtained reports from three doctors who are ready to testify that his drinking problem is the result of job stress.

*What responsibility does the police department have for reducing job stress? If you were the chief, would you make an effort to salvage Lt. Clark? Why? What should the department do when a police officer becomes an alcoholic? Is police work so unique that job stress is inevitable?*

Stress is a part of organizational life and an inevitable consequence of the relationships between individuals, groups, and the organization as a whole. Stress is a part not only of work, but also of life itself. It can contribute to the personal growth and development of each officer, as well as to his or her good mental health. In the police context, an officer who works at peak efficiency because of stress will be satisfied, have a feeling of well-being, and accept stress as part of the working environment. On the other hand, excessive and prolonged stress in the same situation can cause an officer to perform inadequately because of its negative impact on the body.[2]

It is clear, then, that certain stresses are normal in life. What we have to do is learn how to live with stress. A leading expert suggests three realistic antidotes to the stress problem:[3]

1. Decide what your personal stress levels are.
2. Determine your life goals.
3. Learn how to be needed by others.

This chapter explores some of the ways managers can identify stress, determine its causes, and relieve it in the working environment. We will begin by defining stress, both as a general term and as it applies to organizations.

## DEFINITIONS OF STRESS

Stress creates different problems for each manager. Some handle it very well; others have a great deal of difficulty coping with its effects. If a manager understands stress, he or she will have a better chance of handling it quickly and effectively. Stress in general is defined as *the physical and psychological condition that results from attempting to adapt to one's environment*.[4] This definition makes it clear that stress is partly a function of personality and partly a function of the environment. In order for any environmental stressor to become important to us, it must cause a feeling of uncertainty concerning its potential negative impact. If the uncertainty caused by a stressor inhibits our ability to do something, stress will be rather high, since we do not know whether we are going to win or lose. If the uncertainty is insignificant and winning is not in doubt, then we will feel little stress and will view the stressor as inconsequential. Another factor to consider is *how* important the stressor is. If the situation created by the stressor is not very important, then even if it creates uncertainty, there is little stress. For Lt. Clark (discussed in the introductory case), it was highly important to get promoted to captain, and his continual failure to do so resulted in his becoming an alcoholic. He was unable to cope with the constraints preventing him from achieving his goal.[5] Stress does not need to have such negative results; looking at it from a positive viewpoint, we can speak of "good stress," or *eustress*.[6] The environmental stressor itself is neither good nor bad—all that matters is the importance of the constraints it imposes and how the individual responds to them. Whether that response to stress is positive or negative may depend on the view the individual takes toward various life events.

Our attitude is what determines whether a specific stressor, such as poorly defined departmental policies, is perceived as pleasant or unpleasant, as a challenge or a constraint. By taking a positive view of a stressor, we can convert negative stress into eustress.[7]

This positive approach to stress, if fostered and developed by management, can serve to integrate officers into the department. A certain degree of stress, resulting from the differing value systems of individuals and the organization, can serve, in most instances, as the basis for creating a goal-oriented organizational culture. Managers must accept the fact that different individuals respond to stress differently, so it is important to foster eustress and strive to eliminate those aspects of the work environment that create negative stress.

Organizational stress is defined as *the general, unconscious, patterned mobilization of an individual's energy when confronted with any organizational or work demand*.[8] When an officer is disciplined for violating a regulation (e.g., firing a weapon at a moving vehicle) and is suspended for five days without pay, he or she will react to this stressor either positively or negatively, depending partly on departmental opinion. In some police organizations, the suspension could be a badge of honor for vigorously enforcing the law, while in others it could be seen as the action of a potential troublemaker. Conversely, there is evidence showing that when an officer is promoted, he or she is likely to experience stress even though it is a positive event.[9]

*Organizational stress* can have effects both on individuals and on the organization itself. For the individual, organizational stress can result in problems such as alcohol or drug abuse, psychosomatic disorders, or rigidity of behavior. A person under constant and continual stress may exhibit anger, thoughtlessness, defensiveness, or irritability.[10] At the organizational level, stress effects managers can see include dropping productivity, declining morale, late completion of tasks, an increase in sick leave, or other signs of employee discontent.

# STRESS UNIQUE TO POLICE WORK

Behavioral scientists in recent years have expressed a special concern about the number and types of stressors unique to law enforcement. Emotionally unbalanced people must be dealt with, street people must be confronted every day, alcoholics must be handled repeatedly, domestic disputes must be settled, and child abusers must be arrested. On the other hand, there are positive aspects of the job (such as giving first aid or finding a lost child), but unfortunately they do not occur as often as the negative encounters. Other negative stressors include boredom, danger, shift work, lack of public support, unfavorable court decisions, unfair administrative policies, and poor supervision. Such stressors impede the police task and present a very strong challenge to police managers.

Altogether, research to date supports the following conclusions. First, stress can be extremely costly to a police department. (In many states, a police officer's heart attack will result in early disability retirement. For example, courts in the state of California have repeatedly upheld compensation claims regarding coronary heart disease as occupationally related.) Second, stress is cumulative.[11] A single negative stressor may or may not have serious effects on health, but with each additional stressor such consequences become more likely.

Police departments have struggled for years with the problem of how to treat officers who have become stress victims. A logical first step toward developing an appropriate department policy would be to identify officers vulnerable to stress symptoms and job situations likely to generate stress. An assessment tool that has been used for such early-warning purposes since the 1970s is the life stress inventory devised by T. H. Holmes and R. H. Rahe.[12] This instrument was based on a large number of medical case histories in which specific life experiences were correlated with adjustments required.

The Holmes-Rahe inventory assigns to each of 43 potentially stressful life events a number of points that measures roughly how much adjustment the event is likely to require of a person. Some of these events are positive (marriage, for example, rates 50 points), others negative (death of a spouse rates 100 points). Based on the case histories, Holmes and Rahe estimated that a person who "earns" 200 or more points during a single year has a 50 percent chance of a serious breakdown in health within two years. The risk increases dramatically when the points exceed 300: the potential for serious illness reaches 75 to 80 percent.

Of the 43 life events identified in the scale, six are job-related.[13] They are shown in the list below:

| ITEM | POINTS |
|------|--------|
| Being fired | 47 |
| Retirement | 45 |
| Major readjustments such as reorganization | 39 |
| Major changes in responsibility such as promotions, demotions, or lateral transfer | 29 |
| Trouble with the boss | 23 |
| Major changes in working hours or conditions | 20 |

Not everyone has supported the use of the standardized weights used in the Holmes-Rahe scale. One expert has suggested that life events should be classified as good or bad and rated on how much effect they had on the individual's life (none to great) and how much control the individual had over them (none to complete).[14]

A police-specific stress inventory was devised by James D. Sewell, who constructed a questionnaire of 144 events experienced by police officers and then had officers rate each event on a stressfulness scale of 1 to 100.[15] The highest rating (88) was assigned to violent death of a partner in the line of duty; the lowest (13), to completion of a routine report.

Of the officers who participated in the development of the law enforcement critical life events scale, slightly over half (52.1%) said they had experienced at least one of eight stress-related illnesses. The ailment most frequently cited was digestive disturbances (25.4%); second most frequent was an increased use of alcohol (19.9%).

While the Sewell instrument (see Table 6–1) has received limited testing, it can help managers keep track of critical events in the professional lives of subordinates. When a subordinate experiences events from both this list and

Table 6–1  **Law Enforcement Critical Life Events Scale**

**Life Event**

1. Violent death of a partner in the line of duty.
2. Dismissal.
3. Taking a life in the line of duty.
4. Shooting someone in the line of duty.
5. Suicide of an officer who is a close friend.
6. Violent death of another officer in the line of duty.
7. Murder committed by a police officer.
8. Duty-related violent injury (shooting).
9. Violent job-related injury of another officer.
10. Suspension.
11. Passed over for promotion.
12. Pursuit of an armed suspect.
13. Answering a call to a scene involving non-accidental death of a child.
14. Assignment away from home for a long period of time.
15. Personal involvement in a shooting situation.
16. Reduction in pay.
17. Observing an act of police corruption.
18. Accepting a bribe.
19. Participating in an act of police corruption.
20. Hostage situation resulting from aborted criminal activity.
21. Response to a scene involving the accidental death of a child.
22. Promotion of inexperienced/incompetent officer over you.
23. Internal affairs investigation against self.
24. Barricaded suspect.
25. Hostage situation resulting from a domestic disturbance.
26. Response to "officer needs assistance" call.
27. Duty under a poor supervisor.
28. Duty-related violent injury (non-shooting).
29. Observing an act of police brutality.
30. Response to "person with a gun" call.

Table 6–1 *(continued)*

31. Unsatisfactory personnel evaluation.
32. Police-related civil suit.
33. Riot/crowd control situation.
34. Failure on a promotional examination.
35. Suicide of an officer.
36. Criminal indictment of a fellow officer.
37. Improperly conducted corruption investigation of another officer.
38. Shooting incident involving another officer.
39. Failing grade in a police training program.
40. Response to a "felony in progress" call.
41. Answering a call to a sexual battery/abuse scene involving a child victim.
42. Oral promotion review.
43. Conflict with a supervisor.
44. Change in departments.
45. Personal criticism by the press.
46. Investigation of a political/highly publicized case.
47. Taking severe disciplinary action against another officer.
48. Assignment to conduct an internal investigation on another officer.
49. Interference by political officials in a case.
50. Written promotional examination.
51. Departmental misconduct hearing.
52. Wrecking a departmental vehicle.
53. Personal use of illicit drugs.
54. Use of drugs by another officer.
55. Participating in a police strike.
56. Undercover assignment.
57. Physical assault on an officer.
58. Disciplinary action against partner.
59. Death notification.
60. Press criticism of an officer's action.
61. Polygraph examination.
62. Sexual advance toward you by another officer.
63. Duty-related accidental injury.
64. Changing work shift.

*Source:* This table lists the top 64 critical life events out of the 144 developed by James D. Sewell. A copy of the instrument was obtained from the author. For a detailed explanation of the scale, see also James D. Sewell, "The Development of a Critical Life Events Scale for Law Enforcement," *Journal of Police Science and Administration,* Vol. 11 (1983), or James D. Sewell, "Police Stress," *FBI Law Enforcement Bulletin* (April 1981).

the Holmes and Rahe list (such as divorce, marital separation, or the death of a spouse), a police manager should react by personally providing appropriate support or by seeing that a professional counselor gives support. As an example of the kinds of situations that can arise, Table 6–2 presents a number of critical life events with a combined stress score exceeding 300.

If all these events happened to an employee during one year, the employee's likelihood of having serious psychological or physiological symptoms within the next two years would increase dramatically.

**Table 6–2  Combined Stressful Life Events Occurring in One Year That Require a Managerial Response**

| Event | Value of Life Change Units |
| --- | --- |
| Divorce | 73 |
| Oral promotion review | 57 |
| Written promotional review | 55 |
| Changing work shifts | 50 |
| Reassignment/transfer | 46 |
| Unfair administrative policy | 46 |
| Total | 327 |

Other studies have compared how male and female officers in a large law enforcement agency rated a number of potentially stressful events. Both sexes identified, as the most significant stressors, events that highlighted how important it is for managers to focus on human resources, equipment, and supervision. Interestingly, male officers expressed a greater concern about career issues, whereas female officers had their greatest concern with personal safety issues.[16] In another study, which looked at officers in two states, a researcher found female officers did not generally experience any more work-related stress than white male officers in the same departments. At the same time, the study showed that women police officers felt danger was an important stressor, in contrast to male officers who gave it a low rating.[17]

Danger in police work is real. Every year a considerable number of law enforcement officers are victims of felonious assault or murder. Table 6–3 shows the number of officers assaulted and killed over a four-year period from 1997 through 2000. The number of such incidents per year showed a slight decrease during this period but was higher than a decade earlier.

Francis A. Graf presented some interesting observations in his study of a Canadian police department. Two-thirds of the officers he surveyed felt stressed by never or almost never having successfully handled problems created by work, by feeling that change was not conducted effectively, and by their lack of confidence in their ability to deal with work hassles.[18]

**Transitory Stages of Life**

Another police-focused stress study was carried out in 21 police organizations in western New York State during the early 1980s by John M. Violanti and James R. Marshall. They found that officers' perception of stress typically

**Table 6–3  Law Enforcement Officers Killed and Assaulted**

| Year | Assaulted | Killed |
| --- | --- | --- |
| 1997 | 52,149 | 132 |
| 1998 | 60, 673 | 142 |
| 1999 | 55,026 | 107 |
| 2000 | 58,398 | 135 |

*Source:* Bureau of the Census, *Statistical Abstracts of the United States, 2002,* 121st ed. (Washington, DC: USGPO, 2003), p. 323.

**Table 6–4  Transitory Stages of a Police Career**

| | |
|---|---|
| Alarm | (0–5 years) |
| Disenchantment | (6–13 years) |
| Personalization | (14–19 years) |
| Introspection | (20 years and over) |

went through four stages in the course of a career (see Table 6–4). This result is different from those of earlier studies.[19]

**Alarm Stage (0 to 5 Years)**

The early period of an officer's career involves adjusting to the reality of the street. Life is usually entirely different from circumstances the officer experienced while attending the police academy. Actual police work is also entirely different from what is depicted by police shows on television. Faced with the demands of the job, the new officer has the tendency to question his or her personal ability to handle police work. All these factors cause stress, and stress increases over the five-year period.

**Disenchantment Stage (6 to 13 Years)**

Stress increases further during this stage, as officers learn that not all crimes can be solved—that there is a limit to what can be done. Officers continue to question their ability to do good police work and control their personal destinies.

**Personalization Stage (14 to 19 Years)**

In this stage there is a dramatic decrease in stress. An officer who has been working long enough does not find the demands of police work so great. There is also a lessening of concern because the fear of failure loses its importance. This is a period when an officer becomes more concerned with personal goals.

**Introspection Stage (20 Years and Over)**

With the exception of concern for retirement, stress continues to decrease during this stage, which might even be described as a coasting period. An officer is usually more secure in the job by this time, and failure is of limited concern.

If the longitudinal model just described remains constant under additional scrutiny and replication in other departments, it will prove that police managers should focus stress reduction programs on officers in the early stages of their careers. If a department has a *field training officer* (FTO) program, it is an excellent place to educate new officers about the nature and types of stress they are likely to encounter during a career.

## STRESSORS AT WORK

It is very important for police managers to recognize the varying sources of stress because the impact of stress on an officer can lead to poor health and even injury.[20] Increasingly, managers are becoming interested in stress and its potential impact on job behavior. Given our present level of knowledge, though, it is not yet possible to develop a comprehensive list of stressors and their possible consequences.

It is essential to remember that stress comes in two forms: *malstress* (bad or negative stress) and *eustress* (good or positive stress). One officer can view a specific stressor as being inimical while another finds it rewarding

## Table 6-5  **Stressors Related to Work**

| Job Characteristics | Individual Variables |
|---|---|
| Role ambiguity | Personality |
| Role controversy | Age |
| Nature of work | Relations |
| Work overload | Gender |
| Physical features | Race |
| Use of deadly force | |

| Organizational Characteristics | Group Characteristics |
|---|---|
| Style of leadership | Norms |
| Rules and regulations | Support |
| Policy | Cohesiveness |
| Authority | Informal leaders |
| | Discord |

| External Variables | Human Resources |
|---|---|
| Community | Discipline |
| Persons | Training |
| Victims | Promotion |
| Criminal justice system | Assistance |

*Source:* Adapted from Michael T. Matteson and John M. Ivancevich, *Controlling Work Stress: Effective Human Resources and Management Strategies* (San Francisco: Jossey-Bass, 1987), and Stephen P. Robbins, *Essentials of Organizational Behavior* (Upper Saddle River, NJ: Prentice Hall, 2000).

and enjoyable. In law enforcement, some stressors are easily identified, but others are subtle, emerging only after careful consideration. The first thing for a manager to do in combating malstress is to identify the stressors peculiar to a specific task or assignment and work out a way of modifying the stressful working environment.[21] When one of the stressors identified in Table 6–5 is found to be of concern to managerial and operational personnel, it should be carefully analyzed to see if it is actually causing stress in the organization.[22]

The following sections address many of the work-related stressors peculiar to law enforcement. We will not attempt to discuss all potential stressors, only those important to police management.

## THE JOB

### Role Conflict and Ambiguity

Role conflict and ambiguity represent quite significant sources of stress for law enforcement personnel and problems for their agencies. *Role conflict* occurs when an officer is simultaneously subject to two (or more) sets of pressures, compliance with one of which would hinder or prevent compliance with the other.[23] The roles to be performed by a contemporary police department are certainly not cut-and-dried. Police officers have many responsibilities besides enforcing laws.

If we suggest that the primary function of law enforcement in a democracy is the prevention of crime, we need to define carefully whether we mean keeping crime from happening or merely keeping it from getting out of control. Typically, police are under pressure to do everything at once, and they have to balance roles like maintaining the peace with competing roles like identifying criminals and bringing them to justice. What is an officer to do when an immediate supervisor pushes him or her to spend more time handling inebri-ated individuals on the beat but higher-level management at the same time pushes him or her to provide more comprehensive documentation of daily events (a time-consuming process), and there is not enough time to do both?

These competing expectations of an officer are experienced by him or her as *role pressures*; significant, continuing role pressures constitute role conflict, which is generally recognized as a stressor.[24] The more conflict an officer is subjected to by inconsistent demands, the greater is the potential for him or her to be affected by negative stress.[25]

Another type of role conflict occurs when a supervisor communicates incompatible or conflicting expectations. For example, a lieutenant in charge of a burglary unit expected an improvement in the conviction rate but found it difficult to accept investigators' needs to spend a great deal of time developing informants. The investigators viewed the lieutenant's two demands (more convictions, less developmental time) as diametrically opposed.

*Personal role conflict* occurs when there is a perceived incompatibility between the expectations of one individual and those of others in the organization. This is especially apparent in police work when an officer is pressured by other officers to conform to informal production standards. (He or she may, for example, be urged not to disturb the status quo by writing more tickets than other officers or conducting more field interrogations during a shift.)

All these forms of role conflict contribute to increased stress levels, greater levels of interpersonal tension, a lowering of job satisfaction, and decreased confidence in the organization. Interestingly, research has found that the higher up the chain of command conflicting messages originate, the greater is job dissatisfaction among employees.[26]

*Role ambiguity* is the uncertainty resulting from a lack of clarity about tasks and the way the individual can perform them. Such a situation can be stressful for an officer, especially if a structured environment is very important for him or her. On the other hand, some officers readily accept and actually thrive on ambiguity. Managerial jobs in law enforcement are prone to ambiguity by virtue of the way law enforcement is organized. Line officers control information needed for decision-making, but police managers also need such information to perform their jobs. In an effort to control the discretion of officers, police organizations constantly generate rules and regulations aimed at making outcomes predictable and reducing ambiguity in the working relationships between managers and officers.[27]

Such efforts to reduce role ambiguity can lead to significant problems at the operational level. In one department, for example, police administrators have forbidden use of the chokehold as a means of restraining someone but have never authorized an alternative means of restraint, telling line personnel only to "use restraint appropriate for the situation." Officers at the operational level consider this policy inadequate because it is open to conflicting interpretations and the burden of interpreting it is left to them.

Role ambiguity has been found to decrease satisfaction in general life as well as on the job. It lowers individual self-esteem and can lead to anxiety and feelings of resentment.

From time to time almost everyone has experienced work overload, but it is of special concern when it becomes chronic. It can cause an employee to feel helpless. Time constraints or deadlines can become such a burden to managers that the job seems to be out of control. Almost everyone has felt the stress caused by having too much to do, whether his or her job is dispatcher, sworn officer, clerk, or manager. Work overload can be quantitative or qualitative.[28] More familiar to most of us is *quantitative overload*. There is just too much to do. It is difficult for an investigator to handle a caseload of 123 residential burglaries. Even when cases are prioritized in terms of solvability, there is only so much time that can be devoted to investigating each case.

*Qualitative overload* is best described as a situation in which employees feel they are not competent enough to perform certain tasks or that performance standards are unrealistic and too high.[29] For example, this type of overload can appear when a highly qualified line officer is promoted to a supervisory management position. Though operationally competent, this person does not have the capacity to shift gears and accomplish tasks through the efforts of others.

Finally, work overload can be a stressor when a manager has too many separate types of tasks to perform. If one must constantly shift from one type of task to the next, the adjustment can be frustrating, and this at some point becomes a stressor. Such overloads occur quite often at the middle management level when the incumbent of a position has no sense of the real responsibilities of the job or when he or she fails to delegate tasks to subordinates.[30]

The other side of the coin is seen when there is too little work to do and boredom sets in, especially when the work underload occurs over an extended period.[31] In many police departments, officers working the midnight shift find that the infrequency of calls for service can make the hours drag on endlessly.

Either work overload or work underload can make employees feel frustrated and anxious about the working environment. Work can become a burden rather than a rewarding experience. This detracts from the quality of working life, a concept which, as one expert has pointed out, has received increasing attention in recent years.[32]

## Work Overload and Underload

In an earlier part of this chapter, danger as a component of police work was discussed. We now consider the *use of deadly force*. Our knowledge of shootings by police officers is irregular and sporadic. Killings and assaults *against* police officers in the United States are documented annually in the Uniform Crime Reports, but it is another story when one attempts to determine how many civilian deaths result from legal intervention. The U.S. Public Health Service is the only agency that addresses this matter. They take their data from Standard Death Certificates, but some researchers feel that this source is suspect because of uneven quality in the medical reports and errors in recording the information. Some experts have concluded that civilian deaths by legal intervention are underreported by 50 percent. In one recent year, 315 deaths were recorded; if the estimate of the experts is correct, the police actually killed some 628 civilians, as compared to 132 police officers murdered during the same year. This is a ratio of about 1 to 5.[33]

There are approximately 1,700 police departments in the United States, with nearly half a million sworn police personnel who are confronted with an untold number of violent situations every day. When these statistics are compared to the estimates of killings by police officers, it is evident that very few police officers are involved in civilian deaths by legal intervention. The evidence

## Use of Deadly Force

also suggests that the majority of police shootings occur in large cities; hence, the vast majority of officers are never involved in a police shooting.[34]

When a police shooting does occur, there are serious legal and psychological implications. The officer can suffer from emotional trauma, be sanctioned by the department, and/or be subjected to legal consequences and spend an inordinate amount of time before a grand jury or in court defending the action. Police managers should be fully aware of the need to give officers who have been involved in a shooting the opportunity to deal with the emotional consequences of their actions. It is in the best interests of the department, the community, and the officer to have a psychological debriefing, allows an officer to express feelings about the incident, to become involved in peer counseling, and to receive maximum support from employee assistance programs. Such measures have proven successful in reducing malstress.

## Physical Factors

Police officers can suffer from stress when their working environment extends beyond a reasonable comfort zone. Potential stress factors include temperature, humidity, sunlight, weather, noise, air pollution, and chemicals. For example, a reasonable temperature comfort zone ranges from 65° to 80°F. In one police department in the central valley of California, the police cars were not air-conditioned, even though summer temperatures often exceeded 100°F.

The chief of police in this valley town had a vehicular temperature study conducted. On an average summer day, in a vehicle without air conditioning, the temperature was 135°F. The city manager refused to purchase air-conditioned vehicles for the department until it was pointed out to him that once resale prices were taken into account, the cost difference between air-conditioned cars and non-air-conditioned ones was negligible. In another community, three-fourths of the patrol vehicles had been driven more than 100,000 miles and were in a general state of disrepair. Only through political pressure generated by the police union did the governing body establish a replacement and repair policy for police vehicles. In both instances, morale improved dramatically.

## Shift Work

Law enforcement agencies are in business around the clock and expected to be available every day. The public demands unlimited availability of their unique services. As a result, officers work all hours of the day and night, every day including holidays. This work schedule is a significant source of occupational stress.

Shift work is not normal. The "rotating shift" schedule is very taxing on an officer's life. Our bodies are adjusted on what is called "circadian schedules," that is, repetitive daily cycles. Our bodies like to have a regular eating time, sleeping time, waking time, and so forth. An officer doing shift work never gets a chance to stay on a schedule. This upsets his or her physical and mental balance in life. The changing work schedule also upsets the routine patterns that are needed in healthy marriage and family development. Strong marital and family development is based on rituals, such as dinners together, "inside jokes," and repeated activities. The rotating shift worker has less chance to develop such rituals, and his relationships suffer. This predisposes the officer's family to potential problems ranging from children acting out to divorces.[35]

Police shift work has an especially adverse impact on families. Mothers and fathers may not be available during school hours and often miss important family functions (birthdays, holidays, graduations) due to their work schedules.[36] Night and rotating shift schedules also raise health and safety issues. They can lead to sleep disorders and gastrointestinal ailments and are related to emotional disturbances and increased risk of occupational injury.[37] Research evidence indicates that the stressful impact of shift work equally affects both male and female officers.[38]

Police managers at every level may create situations leading to stress for themselves as well as for their employees.[39] A leader in an organization is in a position to exert a tremendous amount of influence on how tasks are accomplished and the methods used to attain goals.[40]

**Organizational Characteristics**

Dealing with supervisors who have authoritarian leadership styles is difficult for many people. It generally causes tensions and pressures beyond the control of the individual. Some subordinates respond by accepting this type of supervision and suppressing the resulting stress and hostility. Others object to such arbitrary leadership behavior by becoming hostile. The former response, over a period of time, will (in all probability) result in undesirable physiological changes; the latter response will serve to release some tension but at the same time create a stressful environment.[41]

Certainly, some employees function effectively under an authoritarian leadership style, but today most officers respond more readily to expert and referent power than to legitimate and positional power (see Chapter 8 for an extended discussion of power).

---

**CASE STUDY** | Lieutenant Tom Phelps

Lt. Tom Phelps has been a member of the Sycamore Police Department for nine years and has held his present position for two years. He has recently been transferred to field operations and placed in charge of the SWAT unit, with a team of nine officers. During an average month the unit responds to three calls. When not engaged in such operations, the unit works from 7 P.M. to 3 A.M. and may be deployed anywhere within the city limits.

Generally, when the unit is not training, its job is to identify career criminals by placing suspects under surveillance, following them, and attempting to apprehend them while they are committing a crime. The unit has been highly successful in this endeavor and has arrested numerous suspects in the act of committing felonies.

On the two most recent occasions when the SWAT unit was deployed against barricaded subjects, Lt. Phelps found it necessary to have sharpshooters shoot the suspects, who were armed and were threatening hostages. Each of the officers who shot a suspect underwent extensive psychological debriefing, and the departmental psychologist worked with their families in order to reduce their mental strain.

Unfortunately, the press and several pressure groups object to the actions of the team, taking the position that neither life should have been taken. This is part of the public's overall position concerning this aspect of police work—they believe the police should severely curtail the use of deadly force.

Departmental policy holds that an officer may use deadly force to defend others against deadly force, so it is clear that Lt. Phelps, in both instances, acted within the parameters of departmental policy. The opponents of police use of deadly force are demanding a complete revision of departmental policy and calling for the creation of a civilian review board.

At this same time, the city manager is calling for a 10 percent cut in the police department's budget, with one specific recommendation—the elimination of the department's psychological support unit. The city council has responded to public clamor by establishing a special commission to review the departmental policy on using deadly force. Lt. Phelps has been selected by the chief to prepare a position paper setting forth a rationale for the department's use of a psychologist.

*If you were Lt. Phelps, how would you deal with this issue? In other words, is there a real justification for employing a psychologist to provide counseling services, or should officers be expected to handle their own personal problems?*

Leadership studies to date have not supported any one style as being best in terms of creating the least amount of stress. Therefore, we must assume that a style of leadership which might be stressful for one officer to work under might not be stressful for another.[42]

There is some indication that present-day police managers are not effective at providing performance feedback. This is especially true when it is presented in a highly authoritarian manner: employees tend to respond negatively regardless of the content. For the most part, this type of feedback emphasizes one-way communication and is stress inducing. The manager has a far better chance of reducing stress if he or she creates an atmosphere that fosters two-way communication.[43]

If there is anything characteristic of American law enforcement, it is its bureaucratic nature and its extreme reliance on rules and regulations. Carefully delineated policies are a standard feature of police departments. Rules and regulations outline the authority, responsibility, and duties of every individual in a department. In many instances, it seems there is a policy on everything. One police department has six manuals covering everything from how to operate a radio to how to give an informant a control number.

Some policies are just restatements of state law; others are precise and technical, while still others prove to be moral statements. Some policies are only a few sentences long; others ramble on for pages. Of the many police departments in the United States, one can find some agencies with carefully delineated policies and others where it is almost impossible to find written policies.

Agency policies, when they exist, should be written so that they become firm commitments between the agency and its personnel. If correctly written, policies promote uniformity and continuity. A good policy is one that includes enough detail to ensure that desired results are attained but at the same time does not unnecessarily restrict the exercise of discretion.

Rules, regulations, and policies should be developed jointly between management and agency personnel through formal and informal meetings. Guidance documents created with the participation of those who will be responsible for following them have a much better chance of successful implementation. Jointly developed policy can serve as a stress reducer. It also fosters creative decision-making because it acknowledges the need for discretion. Rules and regulations can become stressors when they are exceedingly detailed and circumscribe discretion to the extent that agency personnel feel stifled and suppressed. A manager should monitor supervised employees in order to identify potential sources of stressors and then work to minimize them.[44]

Change is another organizational stressor. In recent years, police have been asked to implement new philosophies and programs such as community policing, problem-solving policing, and CompStat.[45] The aftermath of 9/11 has put police in America on the front lines in the battle against terrorism and the effort to provide homeland security.[46]

## External Factors

In recent years, increasing attention has been given to the relationship between law enforcement and the community. The police managers of tomorrow will have to meet the challenges of unprecedented societal transformations. Numerous communities are changing rapidly because of urbanization, technological advancement, population explosion, changing morality, and transient lifestyles. Approximately 56 percent of the population is under 25 years of age, and the vast majority of people live in metropolitan areas. At the same time, the nation is graying as more people pass the age of 65. These factors will place increasing demands on the police, and their role will have to be increasingly flexible. Laws will have to be enforced in such a way as to ensure that a reasonable balance is maintained between collective needs and individual rights.[47]

Community relations have been a continuing problem in many police departments. For example, in one large agency study, community relations was ranked fourth as an external stress inducer. Slightly more than one-third of the officers studied cited community conflict as contributing to stress.[48] In a more recent study of women police officers, a negative public attitude was cited as a source of stress. As the police are called on to perform different and more numerous tasks and the public increases its scrutiny of police activities, we can speculate that a negative community attitude will continue to prevail in many towns and cities. However, police departments that adopt a community problem-solving orientation may find negative relations with citizens reduced considerably.

The criminal justice system (especially the courts) is a significant stressor for police officers. Many officers feel that courts are too lenient and that judges show a greater consideration toward the defendant than the community does. They also see the courts demonstrating a lack of regard and interest when court appearances are scheduled. Consideration is never given to the shift an officer works or an officer's days off that can conflict with a court appearance.

The police express a similar concern for defense attorneys, public defenders, and the tactics used in court. These concerns are well demonstrated when a defense attorney diligently shops around in order to find a "lenient" judge or plays the postponement game to the hilt in an effort to delay the trial as much as possible. Another tactic of many public defenders is to attempt to discredit officers' testimony and actually do everything possible to put the officers on trial rather than the defendant.[49]

Recent research supports the proposition that the impact of stress on an employee's behavior definitely reflects that person's personality traits, such as tolerance for ambiguity, extroversion, dogmatism, and rigidity.[50] Every person has distinct personality and behavioral traits that are modified and influenced by such variables as gender, age, ethnic origin, and family. The overall life expectancy for women is almost eight years longer than men. Some of this difference might be explained genetically, but researchers believe that much is attributable to men smoking more, consuming more alcohol, and being more apt to exhibit Type A behavior—all typical reactions to stress. As more women enter law enforcement, it seems likely that they will experience and react to stress much as their male counterparts do.[51] In one study, it was found that levels of work anxiety were the same for both sexes. However, as we mentioned, women found danger to be a more important stressor than did male police officers. On the other hand, female officers intervened more often when infractions occurred, possibly because they were more cynical about human behavior. Such interventions (in spite of their greater concern for danger and lesser degree of self-confidence) suggest that policewomen try harder than men.[52]

In another study, women present a different perspective. Out of 19 different stressors, the most common one centered on their status as women. Even after women were in the department for six years, male officers did not fully accept them. The actions of the male officers definitely increased the stress level of the female officers as they were ignored, harassed, watched, gossiped about, and viewed as sex objects.[53]

As women assume more managerial positions in law enforcement, their behavior seems likely to parallel that of women managers in business, that is, they will smoke more and increase their use of alcohol, tranquilizers, antidepressants, and sleeping pills—all in reaction to the new stressors they will be facing.

With affirmative action programs and a broadening recruitment base in many agencies, members of minority groups are entering the managerial ranks and being affected by occupational stress as a result. In some instances, stress is a reaction to racial prejudice. Carried to its extreme, a minority manager can begin to feel inadequate, develop a sense of inferiority, or experience a loss of self-esteem.[54] One study found that African-American police officers tended to rely more on colleagues from other minorities than did Caucasian officers. They also expressed their feelings less often than whites did in an effort to get others to like them. Women officers, the study revealed, tended to cope with stress by using escape mechanisms such as exercise, social activities, peer groups, and written records.[55]

When minority managers are few in number, their access to the "informal organization" is difficult, which limits their ability to obtain information and contacts they may need in order to do their job effectively. In some agencies, even the formal organization does not provide them the support needed for success. This is currently the case in one large department, which is under court order to promote a certain percentage of minority officers to managerial positions. These managers are isolated from the formal organization and denied access to the informal organization. In some instances, their exclusion impairs their ability to perform at an acceptable level. Special training and support are needed if all new managers are to succeed. This is especially pertinent when the new manager is a member of a minority group.[56]

Many groups in an organization try to influence their members, using forms of pressure that can become sources of stress and tension. (For a detailed discussion of groups and their characteristics, see Chapter 7.) Members of a team or a work shift exert pressure on each other in order to bring about certain kinds of behavior. Informal groups can resist the attainment of departmental objectives, reduce individual freedom, and force members to conform to production standards. On the other hand, managers who are knowledgeable enough to understand thoroughly how a group behaves can use the group to build individual members' self-confidence, to provide a channel for self-expression, and to reduce tension within the organization.[57]

Stressors related to the availability or nonavailability of career development opportunities are common in local law enforcement agencies. One nationwide survey discovered that only six percent of all police personnel held administrative positions. This means that most police officers will be very fortunate to attain the rank of corporal or sergeant and that they have only an extremely limited chance of achieving a rank beyond the supervisory management level.[58] Career variables become organizational stressors to an individual when they cause frustration or anxiety. Just the process of pursuing a promotion can prove to be stressful. Officers have to compete for promotion by taking tests, written and/or oral; candidates can fail outright or can pass but be ranked so low as not to be promoted. As officers grow older and remain unpromoted, dissatisfaction with the job increases.[59]

Management training is a necessary function of human resource management. Its nonavailability can contribute to stress felt by managers. When an organization promotes an officer to a managerial position, it has an obligation to provide the training, skill, and knowledge he or she needs in order to achieve organizational goals. Managers need to be given the opportunity to grow, develop, and contribute.

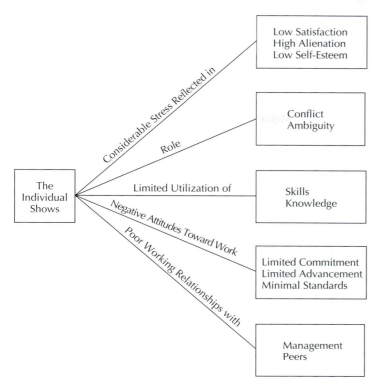

**Figure 6–1**

The Impact of Low Participation.

Adapted from Jerrod S. Greenberg, *Comprehensive Stress Management* (Dubuque, IA: William C. Brown, 1983).

The law enforcement profession is not uniquely subject to occupational stress, but the services it provides to the public are so important that any obstacles to effectiveness—such as stress among employees and managers—need to be dealt with promptly and energetically. As we have seen, one of the causes of stress is exclusion of employees from the decision-making process. Figure 6–1 depicts how the effectiveness of the organization can be impaired by low employee participation in decision-making. Community policing, which emphasizes problem solving by line officers, is one way management can actively solicit officer participation.[60]

A decentralization of tactical decision-making down to the beat level does not imply abdication of executive obligations and functions. It means that first-line supervisors assume greater managerial responsibilities and make every effort to tap the wisdom and experience of line officers. The chief executive, too, must become personally involved in the participative management process from its inception through implementation and subsequent assessment.

## SYMPTOMS OF STRESS

Organizationally induced malstress (bad stress) can be tremendously important to both the individual and the organization. Reactions to stress can be divided into three categories—physiological, behavioral, and psychological—which will

Stress is endemic to police work and is often triggered by situations involving significant others.

Mark Richards

be discussed later in this chapter.[61] Reactions to stress also vary from individual to individual; as a way of understanding these differences, we will divide the employees of a typical police department into three types based on their career attitudes ("ascendant," "indifferent," or "ambivalent") and look at how stress affects each type.

**Ascendant**
The term *ascendant* describes employees who are "on the fast track"; their sole purpose is to move through the ranks as fast as possible. Even if it takes playing musical chairs to accomplish it, ascendant individuals will strive to attain as much rank as soon as possible and then apply for every vacancy occurring in other agencies, with the goal of attaining the rank of chief (generally in a small department) and then moving up to a larger agency.

Ascendant managers relate positively to the job and the department, react favorably to feedback from superiors, and above all are goal oriented. Such individuals are generally known as Type A persons. Work is more important than anything else to them; social and family matters generally take second or third place. Ascendant managers vigorously pursue advanced academic degrees and, in order to become as eligible as possible for promotion to the top, seek to attend the Administrative Officers Course of the Southern Police Institute at the University of Louisville.

Stress is of little consequence to ascendant individuals. In fact, they accept it as an important part of a managerial position—something to thrive on. However, not everyone can make it to the top; those who fall by the wayside suffer extensively from job stress.[62]

**Indifferent**
The indifferent individual typifies most of the regular members of a police organization. Indifferent individuals do not actively seek to attain rank in the organization, and they view power as an interest of others. They perceive change as threatening; their real goal is to maintain the status quo.

In some instances, indifferent officers react to malstress by leaving the organization, either actually or symbolically. Even if they do not actually leave, they escape mentally by daydreaming or just putting in their time (see Table 6–6).

Indifferent officers are apt to seek protection from management decisions by joining and becoming active in a police association or union. They view peers as a primary support group, and the department's informal organization is strengthened by their participation. Both peers and the informal organization help indifferent officers deal with organizational stressors.

**Ambivalent**

The third type of officers is appropriately described as ambivalent. These individuals take the alarm stage of police service (0 to 5 years) in stride, but when the disenchantment stage (6 to 13 years) starts, they become very frustrated with their jobs. As they begin to feel they cannot control their destiny, they become anxious about work. Things are not as clear-cut as they once were—the shadow of doubt enters the picture. Over a period, such individuals become out of step with the organization, and if they attain the level of first-line supervisor, it is usually their highest rank. These individuals find it increasingly difficult to make any decision other than routine ones, and they eventually become less committed to the department. Anxiety about their jobs can create stress that results in one or more behavioral changes.

Table 6–6  **Attitudes Toward Work**

*Ascendant*

Feels strong task orientation
Identifies with the department
Treats work as primary
Thrives on stress
Readily accepts feedback from superiors
Problems can be solved by working harder

*Indifferent*

Never seeks power
Identifies with the informal organization
Obtains support from work groups
Is active in police unions
Accepts change with reluctance
Gravitates toward off-the-job satisfaction
Feels an inability to control own destiny

*Ambivalent*

Resists new rules and regulations
Avoids commitment to the department
Does not like to make decisions
Is frustrated by the inability to do the job well
Eventually develops lessened commitment to the department

**Physiological Symptoms**

A great deal of the early research on stress concentrated on physiological symptoms; as noted by two experts, Leonard Territo and James D. Sewell,[63] they are still of importance. A pioneer in stress research, Hans Selye, set forth a three-stage process of stress damage which he called the *general adaptation syndrome (GAS)*:[64]

1. Alarm reaction
2. Resistance
3. Exhaustion

The initial stage is one of mobilization, as the body responds to a stress-inducing situation. As that first stage subsides, the resistance stage begins, and the body increases its reaction to the threat. The battle for survival begins. When resistance becomes ineffective, the final stage, exhaustion, takes over; adaptive energy lessens and lessens. Eventually the individual dies.

Studies of physiological reactions to stress have centered on the cardiovascular system, with a special emphasis on heart attacks. This is especially applicable in law enforcement. Many cardiovascular irregularities have been determined by several different state court systems to be job related and a reason for retiring on disability. In some police departments, retirement on disability (with various medical reasons) appears to be quite easy for officers to be granted; in others it is very difficult. In one department with more than 1,000 employees, 91 percent of officers retiring were granted a disability retirement. This seems to make a mockery of the intent and purpose of the disability retirement system. One police executive was given a disability retirement because of a bad back, but in fact he was an avid hunter who had no difficulty carrying deer carcasses great distances or performing house remodeling activities requiring him to lift very heavy objects.

By way of contrast, another police chief was in his attic moving some items and thought his wife had turned the lights off by accident. He soon discovered, however, that he was blind from a stroke. Even though he later recovered part of his eyesight, he was unable to continue work. The city vigorously fought his efforts to receive disability retirement, but a court eventually ruled in his favor.

Stress-induced physiological symptoms vary considerably. Some of them appear in Table 6–7 as early warning signs of job stress; they also include such maladies as ulcers, backaches, and changes in metabolism.[65] The link between any specific stressor and particular physiological symptoms is not clear. Various studies have correlated the incidence of certain risk factors with specific occupations, but such statistical correlations have been unable to establish

**Table 6–7  Early Warning Signs of Job Stress**

| | |
|---|---|
| Headaches | Upset stomach |
| Sleep disorders | Job dissatisfaction |
| Difficulty in concentrating | Low morale |
| Short temper | |

*Source:* NIOSH Publication No. 99–101, *Stress at Work* (Cincinnati: National Institute for Occupational Safety and Health, Work Group, 1999), p. 8.

causation for specific symptoms. In time, researchers may be able to measure causal relationships in more detail.[66] Particularly important for police managers to understand are the behavioral and psychological consequences of stress, which we discuss next.

## Behavioral Symptoms

An individual who is experiencing a high level of stress (too intense and too frequent) and is unable to find a suitable outlet may respond by exhibiting behavioral symptoms that can affect performance on the job.[67] Further research is needed in this area. It seems reasonable to assume that stress (with its impact on performance) results from an interaction between the individual's personality, the task being performed, and the working environment.

The relationship between stress and performance is depicted in Figure 6–2. In this inverted-U relationship, it can readily be seen that as we move from a low to a moderate level of stress, productivity increases. At a very low level of stress, employees may not be challenged to perform effectively. As stress increases, most employees are stimulated to perform better and more rapidly. An optimal level of stress exists for each situation and for each individual. Poor performance is the result either when excessive stress drives individuals to the point of agitation or when demands are unrealistic.[68]

Even moderate levels of stress can have a negative influence on employee performance if the stress is so persistent and constant that it reduces the employee's ability to deal with it constructively. Such cumulative effects are especially noticeable in the case of officers assigned to vice or narcotics work, so police administrators have learned to rotate personnel assigned to such units after two or three years.

Behavioral symptoms related to rising levels of stress include an increased use of tobacco products, alcohol abuse, drug abuse, appetite disorders, and (possibly) involvement in accidents. Of special interest are research indications that patrol officers suffer from a higher level of fatigue impairment than the general population and that this fatigue can be controlled administratively, using measures such as shift assignment policies, shift rotation, and shift differential pay.[69]

The excessive consumption of alcohol or the use of other drugs can have severe consequences for both the individual and the organization. Alcohol abuse has always been recognized as a problem. One expert estimated that

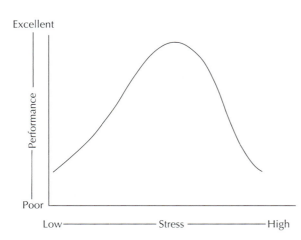

**Figure 6–2**

The Relationship between Stress and Performance.

Adapted from Stephen P. Robbins, *Organizational Behavior*, 3rd ed. (Englewood Cliffs, NJ: Prentice Hall, 1986), and Donald Hellriegel, John W. Slocum, Jr., and Richard W. Woodman, *Organizational Behavior* (St. Paul, MN: West, 1983).

25 percent of police officers in the United States were dependent on alcohol.[70] A study of 500 police officers in 21 police departments determined that police officers used alcohol as a socially acceptable stress reliever.[71] In a recent study, officers anonymously reported that their vulnerability to alcohol abuse had increased during their first 5 years of police employment. They also reported experiencing emotional effects and stress when they attended a police funeral, were the subject of an internal affairs investigation, experienced a needle prick or exposure to body fluids, made a violent arrest, or personally knew victims.[72]

Managers on the lookout for early signs of employee stress should watch for deterioration of work performance as shown in such behaviors as:

1. Excessive absenteeism
2. Unreported absences
3. Late arriving and leaving early
4. Poor quality of work
5. Erratic work performance
6. Failure to meet work standards
7. Friction with co-workers
8. Increased accident rates

Not all these behaviors mean that an officer is under malstress, but they are indications that this possibility should be considered. Managers should of course not limit their monitoring of employee performance to negative indicators; to be fair to employees, managers should also keep track of signs of excellence like high energy levels, alertness, strong motivation, calmness under pressure, thorough problem analysis, sound decision-making, and positive attitudes toward work.

**Psychological Symptoms**

Dissatisfaction with one's job is the most obvious psychological manifestation of malstress. Psychological reactions to stress generally are emotion-laden and involve thought processes rather than some overt behavior. Psychologically based stress is usually characterized by increased tension, irritability, anxiety, procrastination, or becoming bored with the job.

Psychologically, officers usually react to malstress by turning to defense mechanisms in an attempt to reduce the associated anxiety. Officers can engage in such activities as not answering calls rapidly or submitting incomplete reports. They never deal directly with the malstress, and they might not even be aware they are suffering from it.

Psychological problems that can result from malstress include marital discord, family conflict, sleep disturbances, sexual dysfunction, depression, and job burnout.[73]

A good marriage can serve to sustain a police officer when he or she is dealing with job-related stress and can contribute to a successful police career. In this respect law enforcement is no different from other occupational areas. Some relationships end in divorce, but evidence shows that police divorce rates are similar to other professional groups.

When departmental policy encourages sound family relationships, training programs can provide extra support for spouses. Such programs emphasize teaching coping techniques, improving communications, and working out problems. A number of agencies conduct seminars for couples, and some offer the services of a police psychologist.[74] One observer pointed out that although implementing a stress reduction program would initially consume departmental resources, the program would lead to better morale and improved productivity.[75]

Organizational stress can, in some instances, lead to sleep disturbances. Many officers suffer from insomnia caused by a very common stressor—shift work. Other typical work-related problems in law enforcement—such as worries about being promoted, about conflict with a fellow employee, or about testifying in court—can also lead to debilitating sleep disturbances. Excessive use of caffeine and/or alcohol can disrupt sleep patterns. When sleep deprivation becomes chronic, it can have a negative impact on an individual's mood that in turn can affect job performance.[76]

## STRESS REDUCTION

Employees and managers are the most important components of police organizations, and they consume the largest portion of an organization's budget. Their physical and mental well-being contributes directly to the effectiveness of the organization. Having become aware of the impact eustress and malstress can have, both on the individual and on the organization, police organizations are giving increased consideration to developing programs aimed at fostering greater production with less stress and more enthusiasm for work.[77]

**Individual Response to Stress**

Various techniques have been developed that individuals can use to cope with stress effectively. They include exercise, planning, proper nutrition, and mental relaxation. In many instances, stress begins to be recognized by individuals only when things seem to be out of control. Many of us work from day to day and give little consideration to planning. Not only do we fail to consider our life goals realistically, we fail to spend any time contemplating how to deal with job demands, changes in society, and all the other pressures we feel when encountering issues and heading off crisis situations.[78]

**Taking Charge of One's Own Life**

One way individuals can defend against malstress is to review job expectations realistically, comparing them to what is currently happening in the organization. This may, in some cases, enable them to identify and change some counterproductive behavior of their own that is holding them back. In other instances, the process might persuade them to accept the reality of the working environment and quit "fighting the organization." The important thing is for individuals to take charge of their own lives, without waiting for the organization to solve problems they might be able to solve themselves.

Managers may be able to reduce their own exposure to stress by delegating part of their workload to qualified subordinates. Alternatively, they may be able to devise better time management plans. For example, a manager might prepare a schedule at the beginning of each day and follow it as closely as possible. If individuals really take control of their own lives, work can become enjoyable and rewarding. This is a far better response to the malstress problem than relying on addictive substances.[79]

**Relaxation**   Job-related stressors cannot be avoided. Deadlines, interpersonal conflicts, incidents requiring disciplinary measures—there are any number of potentially stressful events. When individuals begin to feel tense or anxious, it should be a signal to employ some type of stress reliever as soon as an opportunity can be found.

Most experts agree that relaxation techniques can play a key role in the control and reduction of stress. In the early 1970s, Herbert Benson and his colleagues discovered what they called "the relaxation response"—a decrease in heart rate, metabolic rate, respiratory rate, and eventually blood pressure that can be brought about by using any of a variety of techniques.[80] Benson and Klipper found that techniques successful in eliciting the relaxation response included four common elements:[81]

1. A place free of distraction, noise, and interruptions.
2. A mental device to help focus thoughts and prevent the mind from wandering. (This mental device can be a word or phrase—even as simple as the number one, monosyllabic and emotion-free—or something in the environment—some people fix their gaze on an object or concentrate on the rhythm of breathing.)
3. A passive attitude (distractions should be countered by refocusing on the mental device being used).
4. A comfortable and relaxed position (not necessarily the classical lotus position; an ordinary sitting position is adequate, but lying down is not recommended because falling asleep is to be avoided).

The authors provided the following instructions for individuals to use in bringing about the relaxation response:[82]

1. Remain in a comfortable position. Sit quietly and refrain from moving or fidgeting.
2. Prevent visual distractions by closing your eyes.
3. Relax all your muscles by starting at the feet and working upward. With practice, total relaxation can be accomplished in one minute or less.
4. Breathe through your nose, and concentrate on the breathing activity. When exhaling, repeat the mental device we discussed.
5. Engage in this activity for 10 to 20 minutes once or twice a day. Upon completion, sit quietly for a few minutes before opening your eyes; stay in the same position, with your eyes open, for a few minutes.
6. Do not be anxious about achieving a deep relaxation. Permit relaxation to occur at its own pace.

A real advantage of the Benson relaxation response is that it does not require any formal training. There is clear evidence for the benefits it provides, which have a practical and realistic application to the workplace. A number of other relaxation techniques, ranging from muscular relaxation to biofeedback, are listed in Table 6–8. Police managers may find any or all of these techniques useful, either in dealing with their own stress or as part of a program aimed at reducing and controlling malstress within the organization.

## Table 6–8 **Mental Relaxation**

Relaxation response
Meditation
Dynamic breathing
Relaxing by exhaling
Alternative nostril breathing
Complete breathing standing
Muscular relaxation
Progressive muscle relaxation
Imagery
Hypnosis
Centering
Prayer
Biofeedback

**Breathing Exercises**

Breathing is so much a part of our life that we seldom take note of it. When an insufficient amount of oxygen reaches the lungs, the flow of carbon dioxide (a waste product) out of the body is diminished; the retention of carbon dioxide can lead over time to the deterioration of body organs and tissues, potentially resulting in headaches, panic attacks, depression, exhaustion, nervousness, and muscle tension. Any of these conditions can intensify stress and make it harder to cope with.[83] Good breathing habits can help counter all these bad effects. Breathing techniques can be easily learned and practiced almost anywhere, by themselves or in combination with other relaxation processes. (Please note that although the techniques can be learned quickly, it may take several months for their full benefit to be felt.)[84]

**Physical Exercise**

It is generally agreed that exercise is one of the best and most helpful means of reducing stress. Individuals committed to reducing stress in their lives should consider participating in an exercise program, which promotes not only physical well-being but peace of mind. It is increasingly common for law enforcement agencies to support physical conditioning programs, including such activities as 10-km runs, the Police Olympics, and the "Pig Bowl" (football).

Numerous agencies now provide their officers with exercise facilities, including bicycles, free weights, weight machines, and treadmills. All this has been in response to an increased awareness of the many values of vigorous exercise:[85]

1. Improves the performance of the circulatory system
2. Delays degeneration of the body
3. Reduces the pulse rate
4. Tones muscles
5. Improves posture
6. Increases endurance
7. Burns calories
8. Strengthens the heart muscles
9. Decreases low-density lipoproteins (harmful cholesterol)

There are three categories of exercise: aerobics, stretching, and toning. Aerobic exercises, which include such activities as running, jogging, brisk walking, swimming, and martial arts, are the most familiar and popular. Performed regularly (three to five times per week) and for a reasonable period of time at each session (30 minutes to an hour), these exercises will increase stamina and strengthen the cardiovascular system. A truly balanced exercise program should include all three categories of exercise.[86]

Different kinds of exercise provide different benefits. For example, individuals who need to lose weight would be well advised to jog, whereas individuals concerned about flexibility would be better off doing calisthenics, yoga, tai chi, or playing handball or squash.

Numerous professional organizations have cautioned that before beginning an exercise program, a medical evaluation is in order. In police departments requiring an annual physical examination, the physician should screen each officer before allowing him or her to engage in vigorous exercise. Aerobics, in the view of some, is almost synonymous with jogging, but there are many other options, and experts encourage individuals to select an exercise they enjoy. Other aerobic exercises include pedaling a stationary bike, jumping rope, running in place, swimming, or playing organized sports such as basketball, water polo, tennis, or racquetball.

The ultimate goal of aerobics is to improve endurance and cardiovascular conditioning (activities like weightlifting bring about excellent benefits of their own, such as building up skeletal muscles, but they have limited aerobic effect). Aerobics is an integral and essential part of a stress reduction program. Whatever aerobic exercise is selected, it must be vigorous enough to raise the heart rate to approximately 80 percent of what has been established as the maximum heart rate. The target rate is easily calculated by subtracting the exerciser's age from 220 and multiplying the result (the maximum heart rate) by 0.8. For example, the target heart rate for someone 25 years of age would be 156 (220 minus 25 equals 195, times 0.8). During workouts, the heart rate should be within 10 beats of the target rate. An exercise program should be designed to ensure what is described as functional fitness. It consists of the following: cardiorespiratory endurance, muscular strength, body composition, and muscular flexibility. Focus 6–1 explains the concept of physical fitness in detail.

## Employee Assistance Programs

The employee assistance program (EAP) concept is new to law enforcement, but it has been a part of many businesses for more than 40 years. Initially these programs concentrated on alcoholism, but in the 1970s, consideration widened to emotional and stress-related problems. Today, some EAPs offer a broad range of services to help employees deal with issues like the family and, more recently, retirement.[87]

An increasing number of psychological services have been offered under the auspices of EAPs (see Focus 6–1). A comprehensive program can address many problems (see Table 6–9). When planning for the implementation of an EAP in a law enforcement agency, a manager should first determine the current conditions in the department. Such a survey should include an analysis of the organization, a detailed study of the need for such a program, and a survey of community resources.[88]

An effective EAP can be of benefit not only to the organization but also to the individual. As organizations become increasingly concerned about the quality of working life, EAPs appear likely to play a very important part in

# FOCUS 6–1

## Physical Fitness

The Albuquerque Police Department, in addition to its academy training curriculum, provides for physical conditioning of all department personnel. The program is designed to keep officers motivated to maintain their fitness level. The goal is to develop greater awareness and emphasize the importance of staying fit. The department conducts annual physical fitness testing, for its 900 officers, including leg press, chest press, sit-ups, sit and reach, a 1.5-mile run, and body composition evaluation. Body fat is measured and included in each officer's health status evaluation but is not used as part of the overall fitness score.

The officers are evaluated utilizing fitness categories and rankings established by the Cooper Institute based on data from over 100,000 individuals considered representative of the U.S. population. The institute's ranking system identifies specific levels of fitness for men and women broken down into ten-year age increments.

The department conducts annual physical assessments during March, April, and May. The incentive program provides compensatory time and T-shirts for the officers as awards. Officers receive specific amounts of compensatory time off depending on how well they perform on the assessment. In 2000, the department awarded over 6,000 hours of time off.

Compensatory time is based on the lowest score on an officer's assessment. If an officer scores in the 40th percentile (of his or her age/gender group within the U.S. population) on one component and scores in the 99th percentile on all the other components, he or she will receive only four hours of compensatory time. The program is designed to encourage officers to focus on their weak areas rather than neglecting them to focus on their strengths. This incentive method encourages "weight lifter" types to work on their cardiovascular fitness and "runner" types to focus more on strength.

This has proven to be an effective method of promoting total fitness within the department. The rules for awarding compensatory time are made public in summary form, and the target percentile rankings allowing some form of compensatory incentive to be issued are designed to be within the reach of most officers.

In addition to the compensatory time, officers who receive scores in the 80th percentile and above on every component receive an APD "Fit for Life" T-shirt. The department and community also provide additional awards for the "most physically fit" officers. These awards are granted to the top male and female officers within each rank level in the department. Awards include plaques, gym apparel, and health club memberships.

The 2000 APD departmental assessment yielded strong performance in a majority of the components that were tested. The departmental assessment average was in the 77th percentile. Officers averaged scores in the 77th percentile or above in all components except the 1.5-mile run.

In the early years of the program, the department offered alternative cardiovascular tests (a sub-maximum bike test and a one-mile walk) as substitutes for the 1.5-mile run. Beginning in 2005, however, the department decided to further promote cardiovascular wellness by requiring all personnel to do the run. The result was that many officers realized how poor their cardiovascular condition was, and it became common to see groups of officers, even entire squads, running together in an effort to improve in this category.

The incentive program is designed for everyone to succeed. In addition to the awards for those who perform well, officers who receive a combined score below the 40th percentile on their overall score are directed to the APD Wellness Unit for a health and fitness consultation. Officers performing poorly are not disciplined but are encouraged to improve their physical condition by participating in a fitness program designed by the Wellness staff. The department allows these officers to work out three hours per week on department time. Their personalized fitness programs can range from a simple walking program to more complex training. They can use any of the department's seven gyms or their own private gym. The Wellness staff monitors program participation, and the officers' supervisors are kept aware of progress.

Two certified experts in the field of exercise science and health education staff the department's Wellness Unit. The experts offer classes in stress management, sleep–shift work adjustments, sports injuries, nutrition, blood pressure management, back care, ergogenic aids, and CPR. Additionally, the unit produces a monthly newsletter, which provides personnel with information about proper nutrition, exercise, injury prevention, and stress reduction techniques. Wellness personnel also offer one-on-one personalized fitness programs and evaluations. A major responsibility of the Wellness staff is the development and implementation of the daily physical training curriculum for the basic cadet class.

## FOCUS 6–1   (*continued*)

Officers and civilian staff have 24-hour access to two gyms that are equipped with state-of-the-art exercise equipment including treadmills, life cycles, free weights, machines, and an aerobics room. The department has five substations throughout the city and a communications center, each of which is also furnished with basic fitness equipment. The department recently completed an all-weather 400-meter running track.

Support from the chief on down ensures the success of the program. All sworn and civilian supervisors and managers, members of the community, and the news media attend award programs. As one recent "Most Physically Fit" officer stated at an award ceremony, "It makes me feel good about the job that I do,

knowing that I am in the best shape possible, knowing that I'm mentally and physically ready for the everyday stresses of police work."

Having a complete, ongoing physical conditioning program in place ensures that department personnel will be more productive while reducing complaints, injuries, and absenteeism. It is the responsibility of administrators that officers have every advantage possible, including the best training, equipment, and physical conditioning.

*Source:* Ray Schultz and Art Acevedo, "Ensuring the Physical Success of the Department," *Law and Order,* Vol. 48 (2000), pp. 34–37.

---

reducing organizational stress and helping officers deal with malstress. This is especially true when officers respond to a critical incident that involves a tremendous loss of life, such as the 2001 terrorist attack against the twin towers in New York City—an unbelievable disaster and a very traumatic experience for the responding officers.[89] Today there is a critical need for law enforcement agencies to provide counseling, rehabilitative, and health promotion services for all personnel.[90]

**Peer Counseling**   Peer counseling has become a part of law enforcement during the last two decades. The first such program, directed by two recovering alcoholics, was offered by the Boston Police Department.[91] The concept spread to other

## FOCUS 6–2

### Standard for an Employee Assistance Program

Standard 22.2.10 is one of the standards promulgated by the Commission on Accreditation for Law Enforcement Agencies:

The agency makes available to employees an Employee Assistance Program (EAP) designed to assist in the identification and resolution of concerns or problems (personal or job related), which may adversely affect an employee's personal or professional well-being or job performance. These personal concerns may include, but are not limited to, health, marital status, family, financial, substance abuse, emotional/stress and other personal matters. The Employee Assistance Program shall include, at a minimum:

  a. a written directive describing program services;

  b. procedures for obtaining program services;

  c. confidential, appropriate and timely problem assessment services;

  d. referrals to services, either workplace or community resources for appropriate diagnosis, treatment, and follow-up;

  e. written procedures and guidelines for referral to and/or mandatory participation; and

  f. training of designated supervisory personnel in the program services, supervisor's role and responsibility, and identification of employees' behaviors that would indicate the existence of employee concerns, problems and/or issues that could impact employee job performance.

*Source:* Commission on Accreditation for Law Enforcement Agencies, *Standards for Law Enforcement Agencies,* 4th ed. (Fairfax, VA: Commission on Accreditation for Law Enforcement Agencies, 2001), p. 22.2. Reprinted by permission of CALEA.

## Table 6–9 Problems That Can Be Addressed by an Employee Assistance Program

| | |
|---|---|
| Alcoholism | Substance abuse |
| Job stress | Job burnout |
| Anxiety | Depression |
| Parent-child conflict | Single parenting |
| Grief | Smoking |
| Nutrition | Exercise |
| Weight control | Divorce |
| Marital separation | Police shootings |
| Family | Health |
| Financial | Critical incident |
| Gambling | Retirement |

*Source:* Adapted from John G. Stratton, "Employee Assistance Programs: A Profitable Approach for Employees and Organizations," in Harry W. More and Peter C. Unsinger, eds., *Police Managerial Use of Psychology and Psychologists* (Springfield, IL: Charles C Thomas, 1987), and Commission on Accreditation for Law Enforcement Agencies, *Standards for Law Enforcement Agencies*, 4th ed. (Fairfax, VA: Commission on Accreditation for Law Enforcement Agencies, 2001).

departments and has been successful because of the general hesitancy of police officers to seek professional assistance. A fellow officer is cut from the same cloth and can be highly successful when counseling colleagues because he or she shares common experiences and special training.

A police psychologist (in those departments where one is available) can train peer counselors and serve as a consultant and referral source.[92] Peer counseling groups in law enforcement have been successful in dealing with clients such as officers injured on duty and widows of slain officers and with issues such as alcoholism, police shootings, retirement, death in the family, and terminal illness.[93]

---

**CASE STUDY** Captain James Stevens

Capt. James Stevens supervises the 12th station house in a large metropolitan police department. There are 221 sworn officers assigned to the station. They are divided into three shifts, with the largest number assigned to the swing shift. Detectives are centralized and work out of headquarters; consequently, Capt. Stevens's primary concern is administering the station house in such a way that called-for services are answered rapidly. The area patrolled is primarily commercial, with some residential sections. The crime rate is very high (when compared to similar-sized cities), averaging 85 felonies to be investigated annually per officer. Besides felonies, there are a large number of misdemeanors.

Even with computers, a state-of-the-art dispatching system, and a large number of civilian support personnel, the station house's workload is excessive. Priority calls become backed up and the paperwork is overwhelming; the officers feel as though they are drowning in reams of paper and entangled in red tape.

Capt. Stevens has been requesting additional personnel for the last five years. Even though his requests have been thoroughly justified, additional officers have never been assigned. The city just does not have the resources to support the police department. The city manager has made the decision to treat all departments in the city alike, even though the police department demonstrates a greater need than any other department. There are no new funds

*(continued)*

and the near future looks quite bleak economically. "Status quo" seems to be the byword of the day.

During the last 18 months, morale has dipped considerably. Many of the officers have always complained, but now complaining seems to be pervasive. Seldom does one hear truly positive statements. In the past, the locker room was a place for jokes and free interchange between officers, but for the most part, it is now quiet and subdued. The primary focus of discussion usually revolves around officers' inability to keep up with the demands of the job.

The captain has noticed that a number of officers are late in attending role call, that sick leave is being used more frequently, and that there is a tremendous increase in what can only be termed sloppy police work. First-line supervisors and watch commanders are spending a great deal of time dealing with the line officers' increasingly poor performance. All these problems seem to be mushrooming.

Capt. Stevens has consulted with all the managers under his command and with other key officers, including staff personnel in headquarters, and finds everyone unanimous: something has to be done to improve working conditions and reduce the stress created by the job.

*The desirable action plan is to conduct a comprehensive survey in order to determine the current conditions in the department and the community resources. Capt. Stevens has been advised it will take 7–8 months to complete the survey. With this in mind, the captain decided to appear at each roll call to discuss the problem. If you were Capt. Stevens, what would you do next? If malstress is the real problem, what should be done while the survey is being conducted?*

# SUMMARY

Stress is unique not only to each situation but to each individual. Some handle stress very well; others have a great deal of difficulty coping with it. Outlook on life is important. A specific stressor, such as a poorly defined policy, can be viewed either as greatly significant or of little importance. If viewed positively, a negative stressor can be converted into eustress (positive stress).

Stress is not unique to law enforcement, but there are certain stressful events and situations especially prevalent in police agencies, such as danger, boredom, lack of public support, unfavorable court decisions, and unfair administrative policies.

An assessment tool used by psychologists for a number of years is the Holmes-Rahe life stress inventory. It provides a rough measure, in points, of how great an adjustment various life events require of an individual over a specified period (e.g., the death of a spouse "costs" the individual 100 points). A somewhat similar scale has been developed that rates 144 critical life events that may be experienced by police officers during their careers. This scale has not been extensively tested but can be used by police managers evaluating the impact of stressful events on their subordinates.

One expert has found there are several transitory stages affecting stress perception: alarm, disenchantment, personalization, and introspection. These stages can be used as benchmarks for the initiation of stress reduction programs. Stressors in law enforcement vary but generally can be categorized as job and organizational characteristics, external factors, personal variables, group characteristics, and resource management issues.

Responses to organizational stress will vary from individual to individual, but they are usually described as taking behavioral, psychological, or physiological forms. Most studies of physiological symptoms have centered on the cardiovascular system, but stress-induced symptoms such as headaches, chronic fatigue, stomach pain, backaches, and chest pains are also widely recognized. Behavioral symptoms are what usually come to the attention of police managers first, because of their impact on job performance. Symptoms related to rising levels of stress include an increased use of tobacco products, alcohol abuse, drug abuse, appetite disorders, and accidents. Managers on the lookout for early signs of employee stress should watch for deterioration of work performance as shown in such behaviors as excessive absenteeism, poor quality of work, erratic work performance, failure to meet work standards, friction with co-workers, and any other type of behavior that seems unusual.

Psychologically, officers usually react to malstress (bad or negative stress) by turning to defense mechanisms in an attempt to reduce the associated anxiety. They may become tense, irritated, anxious, and even bored with the job. When such behavior continues over an extended period of time, it can result in marital discord, family conflict, sleep disturbances, sexual dysfunction, depression, and job burnout. Having become aware of the impact eustress and malstress can have, both on the individual and on the organization, police organizations are giving increasing consideration to developing programs aimed at fostering greater production with less stress and more enthusiasm for work.

## KEY TERMS

alarm stage
ambivalent
ascendant
behavioral symptoms
critical life events scale
disenchantment stage
employee assistance programs
eustress
general adaptation syndrome
indifferent
introspection stage
life stress inventory
malstress
organizational stress

personalization stage
physical factors
physiological symptoms
psychological symptoms
qualitative orientation
quantitative orientation
role ambiguity
role conflict
role pressures
rules and regulations
stressors
stress reduction
use of deadly force

## DISCUSSION TOPICS AND QUESTIONS

1. Compare and contrast eustress and malstress.
2. What are some of the consequences of organizational stress?
3. What can a manager do to reduce the organizational stress felt by women police officers?
4. As a supervisory manager, what types of stress might you expect to see in officers who have been on the force for 6 to 13 years?
5. What are some of the behavioral symptoms a manager should look for that might indicate the presence of malstress?
6. What are some of the things a police manager can do to reduce his or her own personal stress?
7. How do role conflict and ambiguity create stress?
8. Describe the characteristics of an ambivalent officer.
9. Describe stress-induced physiological symptoms.
10. What problems should an employee assistance program address?
11. Describe the alarm stage of a police officer's career.
12. Contrast the personalization stage and the disenchantment stage.

## FOR FURTHER READING

Heith Copes, ed., *Policing and Stress* (Upper Saddle River, NJ: Pearson-Prentice Hall, 2005).

A series of readings provide a thorough review of the latest issues and research on this topic.

Peter Finn, "Reducing Stress: An Organizational-Centered Approach," *FBI Law Enforcement Bulletin*, Vol. 66 (1997), pp. 1–8.

The thesis of this article is that agencies can reduce the organization-based factors that often constitute the most chronic impediments to officers' performance. The author suggests that sources of stress for individual law enforcement officers can be placed into five general categories: issues in the officer's personal life, the pressures of law enforcement work, the attitude of the general public toward police work and officers, the operation of the criminal justice system, and the law enforcement organization itself.

**NIOSH Publication No. 99–101, *Stress at Work* (Cincinnati, OH: National Institute for Occupational Safety and Health, 1999), pp. 1–18.**

This booklet highlights knowledge about the causes of stress at work and outlines steps that can be taken to prevent job stress. It suggests that the effects of stressful working conditions can be reduced by a balance between work and family or personal life, a supportive network of friends and co-workers, and a relaxed and positive outlook. Specific consideration is given to job conditions that may lead to stress, such as the design of tasks, management styles, interpersonal relations, work roles, career concerns, and environmental conditions.

**Dennis J. Stevens, "Police Officer Stress," *Law and Order*, Vol. 47 (1999), pp. 77–81.**

The author studied 415 officers in an effort to examine police stress by comparing critical-incident stressors with general work stressors. It was found that the general work experiences of officers produced more stress than critical-incident experiences. Three of the top five stressors were caused by general work experience and two were produced by critical-incident stressors. The author points out that different job-related situations place different types of officers at risk. The article sets the tone for additional research into causation factors and establishes the need for considering all types of stressors.

**Leonard Territo and James D. Sewell, eds., *Stress Management in Law Enforcement* (Durham, NC: Carolina Academic Press, 1999).**

The authors have gathered an excellent collection of articles on how to develop a comprehensive program to reduce stress in police departments. The text includes sections on the psychological, physiological, and social consequences of stress. This is followed by sections focusing on coping behaviors, suicide and its impact on the family, and the consequences of traumatic events. Finally, consideration is given to psychological services and how the agency can proactively address stress issues.

## NOTES

1. Karl Albrecht, *Stress and the Manager: Making It Work for You* (Englewood Cliffs, NJ: Prentice Hall, 1979), pp. 7–10.

2. Donald Hellriegel, John W. Slocum, Jr., and Richard W. Woodman, *Organizational Behavior*, 7th ed. (St. Paul, MN: West, 1996), p. 568.

3. Hans Selye, *Stress Without Distress* (New York: New American Library, 1974).

4. Lawrence A. Murphy and Theodore F. Schoenborn, *Stress Management in Work Settings* (Washington, DC: National Institute for Occupational Safety and Health, USGPO, 1987), pp. 15–25.

5. Ibid., p. 48.

6. Albrecht, *Stress and the Manager*, pp. 61–63.

7. V.A. Leonard and Harry W. More, *Police Organization and Management*, 9th ed. (New York: Foundation Press, 2000), p. 168.

8. James C. Quick and Jonathan D. Quick, *Organizational Stress and Preventative Management* (New York: McGraw-Hill, 1984).

9. Gregory Moorhead and Ricky W. Griffin, *Organizational Behavior* (Boston: Houghton Mifflin, 1989), p. 198.

10. James D. Higgins, *Human Relations* (New York: Random House, 1982).

11. Stephen P. Robbins, *Organizational Behavior: Concepts, Controversies, and Application*, 6th ed. (Englewood Cliffs, NJ: Prentice Hall, 1993), pp. 91–110.

12. Richard S. Lazarus, *Stress and Emotion: A New Synthesis* (New York: Springer, 1999), p. 49.

13. T.H. Holmes and R.H. Rahe, "The Social Readjustment Rating Scale," *Journal of Psychosomatic Research*, Vol. 11 (1969), pp. 213–218.

14. Lazarus, *Stress and Emotion: A New Synthesis*, pp. 51–52.

15. James D. Sewell, "The Development of a Critical Life Events Scale for Law Enforcement," *Journal of Police Science and Administration*, Vol. 11 (1983), p. 1.

16. Virginia E. Pendergrass and Nancy M. Ostrove, "Survey of Stress in Women in Policing." Unpublished paper presented at the American Psychological Association (1984).

17. Richard M. Davis, ed., *Stress and the Organization* (Los Angeles: University of Southern California Press, 1979).

18. Francis A. Graf, "Police Stress and Social Support," *Journal of Police Science and Administration*, Vol. 14 (3) (1986), p. 41.

19. John M. Violanti and James R. Marshall, "The Police Stress Process," *Journal of Police Science and Administration*, Vol. 11 (4) (1983), p. 4.

20. NIOSH Working Group, *Stress at Work* (Cincinnati: National Institute for Occupational Safety and Health, 1999), p. 5.

21. Kenneth R. Pelletier, *Healthy People in Unhealthy Places* (New York: Delacorte/Seymour Lawrence, 1984), pp. 63–75.

22. J.J. Hurrell, Jr., D.L. Nelson, and B.L. Simmons, "Measuring Job Stressors and Strains: Where We Have Been, Where We Are and Where We Need to Go," *Journal of Occupational Health Psychology*, Vol. 4 (1998), pp. 368–390.

23. Dennis W. Organ and W. Clay Hamner, *Organizational Behavior: An Applied Psychological Approach* (Plano, TX: Business Publications, 1982).

24. Peter Finn and Julie Esselman Tomz, *Developing a Law Enforcement Stress Program for Officers and Their Families* (Washington, DC: Office of Justice Programs, National Institute of Justice, 1997), pp. 6–7.

25. Ellen Kirschman, "Organizational Stress: Looking for Love in All of the Wrong Places," *The Police Chief*, Vol. LXV (10) (1998), pp. 127–135.

26. Dennis J. Stevens, "Police Officer Stress," *Law and Order*, Vol. 47 (9) (1999), pp. 77–81.

27. Gary Johns, *Organizational Behavior: Understanding Life at Work* (Glenview, IL: Scott, Foresman, 1988).

28. J.J. Hurrell, Jr., and L.R. Murphy, "Occupational Stress," in W.M. Rom, ed., *Occupational and Environmental Medicine*, 3rd ed. (New York: Little, Brown, 2001), pp. 36–42.

29. NIOSH Working Group, *Stress at Work*, p. 7.

30. Organ and Hammer, *Organizational Behavior: An Applied Psychological Approach*.

31. Katherine Ellison and John L. Genz, *Stress and the Police Officer* (Springfield, IL: Charles C Thomas, 1983), p. 17.

32. Albrecht, *Stress and the Manager*, p. 135.

33. Vivian B. Lord, "The Stress of Change: The Impact of Changing a Traditional Police Department to a Community-Oriented, Problem-Solving Department," in H. Copes, and M.L. Dantzker., *Policing and Stress* (Upper Saddle River, NJ: Pearson–Prentice Hall, 2005), pp. 48–55.

34. Dennis J. Stevens, "Police Officer Stress and Occupational Stressors: Before and After 9/11," in H. Copes and M.L. Dantzker, eds. *Policing and Stress* (Upper Saddle River, NJ: Pearson–Prentice Hall, 2005), pp. 103–105.

35. Harry W. More, *Special Topics in Policing*, 2nd ed. (Cincinnati: Anderson, 1998), pp. 93–95.

36. James J. Fyfe, ed., *Readings on Police Use of Deadly Force* (Washington, DC: Police Foundation, 1982).

37. Dan Goldberg, "10 Reasons Cops Are Different," *http://www.heavybadge.com/10reason.htm* See also, John M. Violanti, "Dying for the Job: Psychological Stress, Disease, and Mortality in Police Work," in H. Copes, ed., *Policing and Stress* (Upper Saddle River, NJ: Pearson–Prentice Hall, 2005).

38. David A. Alexander and Leslie G. Walker, "The Perceived Impact of Police Work on Police Officers' Spouses and Families," *Stress Medicine*, Vol. 12 (1996), pp. 239–246 and John M. Violanti and Fred Aron, "Police Stressors: Variations in Perception Among Police Personnel," *Journal of Criminal Justice*, Vol. 23 (1995), pp. 287–294.

39. More, *Special Topics*, p. 250.

40. He Ni Zhao and Carol Archibald, "Gender and Police Stress: The Convergent and Divergent Impact of Work Environment, Work-Family Conflict, and Stress Coping Mechanisms of Female and Male Police Officers," *Policing*, Vol. 25 (4) (2002), pp. 687–708.

41. Finn and Tomz, *Developing a Law Enforcement Stress Program for Officers and Their Families*, pp. 126–127.

42. Tony L. Jones, "Autocratic vs. People-Minded Supervisors," *Law and Order*, Vol. 46 (5) (1998), pp. 32–36.

43. L.R. Murphy, "Stress Management in Work Settings: A Critical Review of the Research Literature," *American Journal of Health Promotion*, Vol. 11 (1996), pp. 112–135.

44. Harry More and O.R. Shipley, *Police Policy Manual—Personnel*, (Springfield, IL: Charles C Thomas, 1987), pp. 47–91.

45. Lord, "The Stress of Change."

46. Stevens, "Police Officer Stress and Occupational Stressors."

47. Bureau of the Census, *Statistical Abstract of the United States, 2002*, 121st ed. (Washington, DC: USGPO), p. 322.

48. W.H. Kroes, Joseph Hurrell, and Bruce Margolis, "Job Stress in Policemen," *Journal of Police Science and Administration*, Vol. 11 (1) (1974), pp. 97–102.

49. Ellison and Genz, *Stress and the Police Officer*, p. 49.

50. A.P. Brief, R.S. Schuler, and M. Van Sell, *Managing Job Stress* (Boston: Little, Brown, 1987).

51. Leonard and More, *Police Organization and Management*, p. 166.

52. Finn and Tomz, *Developing a Law Enforcement Stress Program for Officers and Their Families*, p. 10.

53. Judie W. Wexler and Deana Logan, "Sources of Stress Among Women Police Officers," *Journal of Police Science and Administration*, Vol. 11 (1) (1983).

54. Thomas D Kirkpatrick, *Supervision* (Boston: Kent, 1987).

55. Robin N. Harrick, and Merry Morash, "Gender, Race and Strategies of Coping With Occupational Stress in Policing," *Justice Quarterly*, Vol. 16 (2) (1999), pp. 303–328. See also, Robin Harrick and Merry Morash, "Police Coping with Emotions, Gender, and Minority Status," in H. Copes and M.L. Dantzker, eds. *Policing and Stress* (Upper Saddle River, NJ: Pearson–Prentice Hall, 2005).

56. Matteson and Ivancevich, *Controlling Work Stress*.

57. Kirkpatrick, *Supervision*.

58. Brian A. Reaves and Timothy C. Hart, *Law Enforcement Management and Administrative Statistics, 1999: Data for Individual State and Local Agencies with 100 or More Officers* (Washington, DC: Bureau of Justice Statistics, 2000), p. xi.

59. George L. Kelling and Mark H. Moore, *The Evolving Strategy of Policing* (Washington, DC: National Institute of Justice, 1987).

60. Ibid.

61. Stephen P. Robbins, *Essentials of Organizational Behavior*, 5th ed. (Upper Saddle River, NJ: Prentice Hall, 2000), p. 269.

62. Lawrence Steinmetz, H. Ralph Todd, Jr., *First Line Management: Approaching Supervision Effectively* (Plano, TX: Business Publications, 1986), pp. 79–102.

63. Leonard Territo and James D. Sewell, eds., *Stress Management in Law Enforcement* (Durham, NC: Carolina Academic Press, 1999), pp. 210–239.

64. Albrecht, *Stress and the Manager*, pp. 67–68.

65. James Campbell Quick, Lawrence R. Murphy, and Joseph J. Hurrell, Jr., *Stress and Well-being at Work: Assessments and Interventions for Occupational Mental Health* (Washington, DC: American Psychological Association, 1992) pp. 252–291.

66. Robbins, *Organizational Behavior*, pp. 91–110.

67. Quick and Quick, *Organizational Stress and Preventative Management*.

68. Hellriegel, Slocum, and Woodman, *Organizational Behavior*.

69. Bryan Vila, *Tired Cops: The Importance of Managing Police Fatigue*, (Washington, DC: PERF, 2000), p. 31.

70. W. Kroes, *Society's Victim: The Policeman; An Analysis of Job Stress in Policing* (Springfield, IL: Charles C Thomas, 1976), pp. 29–47.

71. John M. Violanti, James R. Marshall, and Barbara Howe, "Stress, Coping, and Alcohol Use: The Police Connection," *Journal of Police Science and Administration*, Vol. 13 (2) (1985), pp. 99–104.

72. Joseph A. Harpold and Samuel L. Feemster, "Negative Influences of Police Stress," *FBI Law Enforcement Bulletin*, Vol. 71 (9) (2002), p. 3.

73. Quick and Quick, *Organizational Stress and Preventative Management*.

74. Grace Kannady, "Developing Stress-Resistant Police Families," *The Police Chief*, Vol. LX (8) (1993), pp. 92–99.

75. Sam Torres, David L. Maggard, Jr., and Christine Torres, "Preparing Families for the Hazards of Police Work," *The Police Chief*, Vol. LXX (10) (2003), pp. 108–114.

76. Quick and Quick, *Organizational Stress and Preventative Management*.

77. Albrecht, *Stress and the Manager*, 173–148.

78. Barry L. Reece and Rhonda Brandt, *Effective Human Relations in Organizations* (Boston: Houghton Mifflin, 1987), pp. 382–387.

79. Ibid., p. 395.

80. Quick and Quick, *Organizational Stress and Preventative Management*.

81. Herbert Benson and Miriam Z. Klipper, *The Relaxation Response*, 2nd ed. (New York: Harper Torch, 2000), pp. 159–160.

82. Ibid., p. 162.

83. Martha Davis, Elizabeth Robbins Eshelman, and Matthew McKay, *The Relaxation & Stress Reduction Workbook*, 5th ed. (Oakland, CA: New Harbinger, 2000), pp. 20–21.

84. J. Barton Cunningham, *The Stress Management Sourcebook*, 2nd ed. (Lincolnwood, IL: Lowell House, 2000), pp. 247–255.

85. George B. Dintiman and Jerrold S. Greenberg, *Health Through Discovery* (Reading, MA: Addison-Wesley, 1980).

86. Peter D. Bullard, *Coping with Stress: A Psychological Survival Manual* (Portland, OR: ProSeminar Press, 1980).

87. Commission on Accreditation for Law Enforcement Agencies, *Standards for Law Enforcement Agencies*, 4th ed. (Fairfax, VA: Commission on Accreditation for Law Enforcement Agencies, November 2001), p. 22.2.

88. Matteson and Ivancevich, *Controlling Work Stress*.

89. Robert D Smithers, *The Psychology of Work and Human Performance* (New York: Harper & Row, 1988).

90. David Kinchin, "The Trauma of Police Work," *Law and Order*, Vol. 48 (3) (2000), p. 43.

91. Edward Donovan, "The Boston Police Stress Program," *The Police Chief*, Vol. 47 (2) (1985), pp. 42–44.

92. Graf, *Journal of Police Science and Administration*, pp. 52–64.

93. Thomas Baker and Jane P. Baker, "Preventing Police Suicide," *FBI Law Enforcement Bulletin*, Vol. 65 (10) (1996), pp. 24–27.

# —7————

# GROUPS AND THE GROUP PROCESS

## Human Dynamics at Work

1. Analyze the behavior of human beings as social animals.
2. Discuss groups and group dynamics.
3. Differentiate between formal groups and informal groups.
4. Identify reasons why people become members of informal as well as formal groups.
5. Compare and contrast leadership in formal and informal work groups.
6. Define *culture* as it applies to groups, subgroups, and cliques in law enforcement agencies.
7. Describe the concept of group culture and the mechanisms used to instill self-control.
8. Identify the elements of the interactionist perspective.

9. Define *socialization* and trace the steps in the socialization process.
10. Compare the categories currently used to classify groups.
11. List and explain the structural components that make a social group a distinct entity.
12. Explain the influence of structural variables on individual and/or group performance.
13. Assess the role of the police administrator in managing group dynamics.
14. Discuss managerial strategies designed to minimize group conflict and maximize individual or group performance.
15. Evaluate the impact of group dynamics on organizational productivity.

Working collectively seems, at first view, to be a natural and effective way to solve problems, but putting the concept into practice poses continuing challenges to managers. A thorough understanding of groups and group dynamics is needed, but in the police world in particular, some administrators have been reluctant to accept the group dynamics approach to management; they have gone to great lengths to maintain the illusion that an organization is little more than an aggregate of individuals performing a common function. There are several reasons why they prefer to deal with their subordinates individually rather than collectively:

1. Their training and experience have accustomed them to handling problems on a person-to-person basis; they are not conditioned to look for systemic variables or interaction patterns that might have contributed to a problem.

Maynard Bear is the chief of police in a large southern city. He was just appointed to the position by the mayor. Chief Bear, a college-educated pragmatist who worked his way up through the ranks, has been ordered by the mayor to streamline the police department's bulky, top-heavy bureaucracy in an effort to make it more efficient, effective, and productive. While the new chief has good intentions, he is having a difficult time overcoming institutional inertia. After a very careful analysis of the situation, he has concluded that his managerial options are limited by legal, organizational, and cultural constraints beyond his immediate control. In a memorandum to the mayor, Chief Bear cites the following limitations:

1. An autonomous civil service commission is in charge of recruiting, screening, ranking, and making de facto appointments (based on a rank order) of all entry-level police personnel.

2. The commission controls promotions because it is in charge of compiling eligibility lists, and a contract exists requiring that promotion selections be based on rank order.

3. All classified positions (including detective) up to the rank of division chief have civil service status.

4. Permanent duty assignments are awarded based on seniority among those officers bidding for them.

5. The department is characterized by a rigid chain of command with an emphasis on control through executive decision-making.

6. The delegation of authority within the department is subject to "traditional" limitations.

7. The police union opposes major changes in police operations.

8. There is little or no support for reform from members of the city council.

9. Budget shortfalls are anticipated for the next several years.

The chief points out that he has little leeway to allocate financial resources or make temporary reassignments of police personnel. While the mayor is sympathetic, he still wants the department to become more efficient, effective, and responsive to the community. This conflict is brought to a head by a series of obviously related and particularly grotesque homicides that are causing panic in the city. After the traditional methods and procedures failed to produce results, the city's leading newspaper decried what it called "bureaucratic bungling" and demanded immediate "action" by the police department. The chief is convinced that inappropriate personnel assignments, organizational rigidity, bureaucratic infighting, and a battle over turf are hindering the investigation. He feels that his job is on the line.

*Although the constraints he identified are real, Chief Bear does have options. What are they? What would someone with a knowledge of groups and group dynamics do in this particular situation?*

---

2. The individual approach to resolving personnel problems is quicker and easier than identifying and analyzing systemic and group factors. Learning to understand and deal with groups requires more time, energy, effort, and expertise than many managers are willing to give.

3. Dealing with individuals rather than groups helps managers retain control over the flow of authority within their organizations. This approach justifies department rules, managerial prerogatives, and limitations on interaction with employees.

According to one police management theorist, it is far less threatening for a manager to condemn individual police officers as lazy, inept, or corrupt than it is to raise substantive questions about the department's structure, operating procedures, and goals.[1] Many police administrators do not have the knowledge, technical expertise, conceptual ability, or human skills needed to understand and deal effectively with group dynamics in the workplace. Competent police managers have a knack for resolving problems and handling personnel. They have learned to appreciate the importance of groups and the group process. They know that people and groups are the human resources on which all social organization is built.[2]

# THE GROUP PHENOMENON

Effective police managers never forget that human beings are social animals.[3] They know that we all need to have interpersonal relationships with other people. Meaningful social interaction is essential for human development and is a very important source of personal fulfillment. Virtually everything we do is in conjunction with or through others. Our unique personality (attitudes, values, and behaviors) evolved in response to the interaction we had with other people in a variety of very different situations.[4] In terms that are more succinct, people do not exist apart from social groups. All people are born into them, transformed through them, and eventually buried by them.

Based on the idea that each person exists and develops a sense of self largely in response to meaningful interaction with important others, many social scientists believe groups are the basic unit of social organization. Groups perform a wide variety of functions, including providing their members with companionship, emotional support, a normative perspective, and a frame of reference for collective behavior. People behave based on how they perceive themselves and how they feel they are perceived by important others within their groups.[5] The interpersonal relationships that police administrators are most concerned with are those found in the work environment, which are normally started and maintained to facilitate the accomplishment of work. In the workplace context, group-based interpersonal relationships are good if they help get tasks accomplished and meet the work-related needs of group members.[6]

A group is more than a mere collection of human beings who happen to be in physical proximity to one another or who share a common interest or characteristic. According to Ronald Smith and Frederick Preston, a group consists of a number of persons who interact with each other in an organized way. They share common traits, views, values, circumstances, and a sense of togetherness.[7] More specifically, a group is composed of (1) two or more people, (2) who are consciously aware of one another, (3) who consider themselves to be a functional unit, and (4) who share in the quest to achieve one or more goals or other common benefit.[8]

Two basic requirements must be met before an aggregate (a number of people who happen to be clustered in one place) qualifies as a group. First, the individuals must interact with each other in some organized manner. Members share norms, role expectations, and social status. Second, there must be "consciousness of kind"—that is, members must recognize themselves as bound together by common traits, perspectives, and circumstances. The combination of these two elements creates a single, dynamic, and goal-oriented social entity.

Groups differ tremendously in size, function, structure, and sophistication. Some groups are one-dimensional, in that they exist for a single purpose. Others have one dominant purpose and various ancillary purposes. Some very complex groups juggle a number of coordinated purposes simultaneously. Without question, groups exhibit their own unique personalities. They can carry on their activities with great vigor and enthusiasm or they may be laid-back, even lackadaisical. They can be as small as just two people or as large as the New York Police Department, the federal government, or the entire United States. Groups also differ with respect to their activity levels and the nature of the interpersonal transactions among their members:

1. *Primary groups.* Primary groups are those in which members develop personal, intimate, and enduring relationships based on frequent and meaningful interaction.

2. *Secondary groups.* Secondary groups are less intense and more segmented than primary groups because the occasional interaction between members is shallow, impersonal, and practical in nature.

Membership in certain social groups (such as families, nations, and sometimes churches) starts at birth. Membership in other groups (such as schools, military services, or juries) comes later in life and may be voluntary or involuntary. The groups that people join voluntarily may be (1) open to everyone, (2) limited to certain categories of people in the population, or (3) open only to those who are willing to go through some type of screening or initiation. Groups can be deliberately organized or may evolve slowly and without conscious intent, through a process of natural selection. Social scientists often describe groups in terms of their positions along various kinds of continuums: groups can be formal or informal, functional or dysfunctional, highly structured or relatively unstructured, related to other groups or unattached, unified or segmented by subgroups, directive (autocratic) or participative (democratic), proactive or reactive, receptive to change or resistant to change, task-oriented or human relations–oriented. Regardless of their characteristics, it is clear that groups provide the context within which almost all human behavior occurs.[9]

It is the police administrator's job to maximize employee productivity within the context of the work group. For our purposes, a work group is defined as a task-oriented group that has been created by formal authority of an organization to transform resource inputs (such as money, material, equipment, ideas, and personnel) into product outputs (reports, decisions, services, and law enforcement activities). A police department, like all other very complex and task-oriented organizations, is composed of an interlocking network of work groups. Police administrators and first-line supervisors perform what Rensis Likert described as the linking-pin function in the network.[10] Through the activities of these officers, each of whom is a senior member of one or more groups and a subordinate member of one or more others, multiple work groups are interconnected in such a way as to create a sense of totality for the organization.[11] Figure 7–1 illustrates the linking-pin principle in supportive relationships.

**Work Groups**

All formal work groups are created as the result of the organizing function inherent in management and through which police officers are assigned to different tasks and task groups by some higher authority (chief executive officer) or the head of a particular subgroup (unit commander). The productivity of any work group depends on how managers handle the division of labor and delegation of authority within the group.

Formal work groups can be temporary or permanent. In either case they are created by management to contribute to the organization's productive purpose as articulated in its mission, goals, and objectives. Permanent work groups are relatively stable and usually appear on organizational charts as departments, divisions, bureaus, or other units. The generic organizational chart presented in Figure 7–2 displays an inverted hierarchy of function based on work-group membership, component interaction, and formal structure. Temporary work groups, on the other hand, are normally created by managers to perform special tasks that existing permanent groups are, for whatever reason, not equipped to deal with efficiently or effectively. Ad hoc committees,

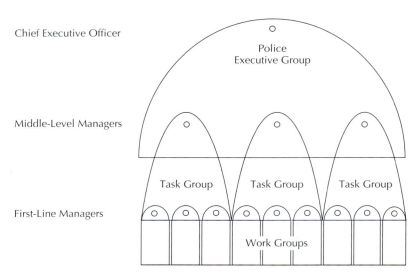

Chief Executive Officer — Police Executive Group

Middle-Level Managers

Task Group     Task Group     Task Group

First-Line Managers

Work Groups

o indicates managerial leaders at various hierarchical levels in the organization. Expectations, instructions, and orders flow down the chain of command to first-line managers who supervise work groups. Administrators below the executive level have overlapping memberships. They are members of superordinate as well as subordinate work groups. As a "linking pin," they serve to integrate and coordinate various groups as they seek to achieve the mission, goals, and objectives of the organization.

**Figure 7–1**

Interlocking and Supportive Relationships in Complex Police Organizations.

Adapted from Rensis Likert, *New Patterns of Management* (New York: McGraw-Hill, 1961).

project teams, and task forces are typical temporary work groups designed to accomplish specific objectives. Once a temporary work group achieves its objective, it is dissolved, and any personnel who were detailed to it are returned to their permanent duty assignments.[12]

Every formal group within an organization has a leader designated by the organization. The leaders who head up groups in police departments normally receive from department senior management the power and legitimate authority needed to coordinate the work of subordinates.[13] Whether they succeed or not, however, depends in large measure on their knowledge, expertise, and leadership skills. The officially designated manager of a work group is not necessarily the group member who exerts the most influence over the job-related behavior of fellow employees. He or she is typically task oriented and eager to get the job done as quickly and effectively as possible even if that means using his or her official position, power, and authority coercively. According to Robert Fulmer, formal leaders—who usually have the institutionalized power and authority to direct, discipline, or fire members of their own particular work group—tend to use negative motivation. They rely on the use of differential status, discipline, and punishment to accomplish their objectives.[14]

**Cliques**   Natural subgroups, or cliques, can be found within nearly all formally designated work groups. When two or more employees come together in an effort to satisfy mutual needs or share common interests, an informal group comes into

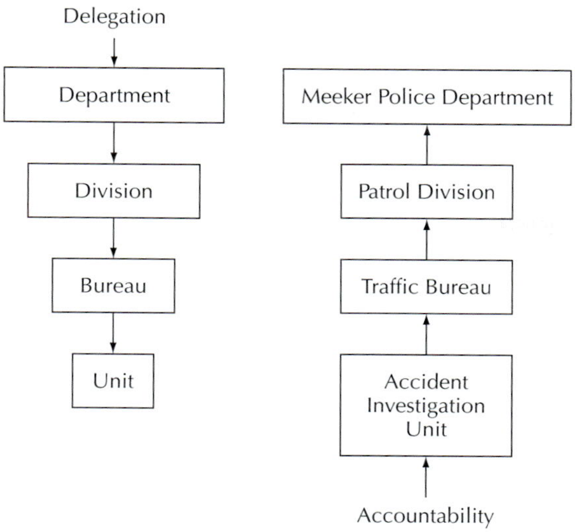

**Figure 7–2**
Formal Work Groups.

being. These informal groups evolve from spontaneous interactions among compatible individuals who are looking for validation as human beings and social reinforcement for appropriate behavior. Informal groups help satisfy member needs for companionship, security, belonging, and self-esteem. Although they are not created by those in authority, seldom have defined goals, and are usually transitory, informal groups are influential in complex organizations. They provide their members with social acceptance, friendship, and an opportunity to develop meaningful interpersonal relationships.[15] They also provide satisfactions that are often denied or thwarted by formal group affiliations.[16] These groups are formed to fulfill very important psychosocial needs for security and camaraderie among members. A formal group can also function as an informal group if members freely choose to associate with each other on and off the job.[17]

Informal groups (or cliques) are shadow organizations; they do not exist officially. They arise out of the interactions, attractions, and needs of individuals. Members are not assigned to these groups. Membership is voluntary and dependent on the mutual attraction the individual and the group have for each other. Informal groups create intricate patterns of influence that extend far beyond the mechanical representations drawn on an organizational chart. Informal groups provide their members with a human infrastructure. They can concern themselves with a broad range of issues ranging from working conditions to policies.[18] Members identify with one another, share common perspectives, and feel a sense of solidarity. They are often able to manipulate the work environment for their own purposes by redefining responsibilities and work relationships within the organization.[19] This may result in the flow of the organization's legitimate authority being altered or circumvented altogether.[20] In other situations informal groups can be supportive of an organization. One officer might, for example, show a fellow member of his or her group how to perform a specific task in a more productive way; this could simultaneously benefit the trained officer, the group the two officers belong to, and the formal organization.[21] Effective administrators know how to recognize and deal with informal groups.

Dalton Melville, in his classic study of industrial organizations, identified three basic types of informal groups, or cliques, that tend to develop within the social environments created by complex organizations: horizontal, vertical, and random (or mixed).[22]

**Horizontal Cliques**  Horizontal cliques are composed of two or more people from the same functional area and the same level (or rank) in the hierarchy. Two or more patrol officers in a department's SWAT (Special Weapons and Tactics) team might become a small informal group because of their shared concern about the team's safety, given their commander's lack of field experience or reluctance to incorporate their ideas into the decision-making process. Due to the nature and complexity of police work, almost all police officers belong to horizontal cliques.

**Vertical Cliques**  Vertical cliques consist of two or more people from the same functional area (or department) who are at different levels in the hierarchy. Police officers at various ranks often socialize with each other. These informal groups are formed and maintained based on similarity of interests and common needs for acceptance, security, self-esteem, and a genuine sense of accomplishment. Many police officers are members of vertical subgroups within their department.

**Random Cliques**  Random or mixed cliques involve two or more people who come from various departments, ranks, and locations. This type of informal network is often made up of individuals who want to get things done and who share a common desire to avoid the red tape normally associated with bureaucracy. Formation of random cliques is often stimulated by a common membership in organizations like the Masons, the Knights of Columbus, or the Southern Police Institute Alumni Association. Many officers become involved in random or mixed cliques in an effort to maximize their overall influence as law enforcers.

Because of the nature of their work, police managers should expect to interact with virtually every type of informal group just described. It must be acknowledged that the activities of influential cliques can lead to disagreement, antagonism, and even challenges to organizational structure and mangement.[23] Managers must learn to identify informal leaders and help them (and their groups) achieve personal goals and objectives that are consistent with those of the organization as a whole.

Every informal group has at least one leader. Informal leaders, unlike formal authority figures, are not appointed; they derive power from their followers. Group members voluntarily accept suggestions, instructions, even direct orders from the informal leader because of their respect for his or her personality, knowledge, abilities, and skills. Since informal leadership is both dynamic and situational, it can almost never be delegated. Formally appointed leaders are seldom, if ever, able to function simultaneously as informal leaders of cliques.[24] The two roles are usually mutually exclusive.

**Membership**  Groups, whether they are formal (created by authority) or informal (spontaneous and goal oriented), can also be classified, based on their criteria for membership, as "open" or "closed."

An *open group* is one that has relatively few restrictions on who is allowed to join. There are few specific requirements. Open groups are constantly adding and losing members. New members can bring enthusiasm, creativity, and eagerness for change. Maintaining a healthy balance between change and stability requires group leaders to spend considerable time and effort socializing new members. Open groups are future oriented, energetic, unpredictable, and usually hard to manage.

A *closed group* restricts its membership to a select few by imposing stringent requirements. Membership is relatively stable. Power and status relationships are well established and fixed. "Groupthink," which will be discussed later in this chapter, is a common characteristic of closed and highly cohesive groups. They tend to lose their flexibility and adopt a single perspective. Elitism tends to mask the absence of critical thinking. Tightly closed groups quickly become "self-perpetuating" cliques.[25]

*Open* and *closed* are maximum terms and represent opposite ends of the continuum. Most groups fall somewhere in between the two extremes. All police organizations are composed of relatively open and relatively closed groups. Once again, it is the manager's job to coordinate the activities of these groups in such a way that they all make positive contributions to the organization.

## GROUPS AS FUNCTIONAL UNITS

The group phenomenon needs to be understood in terms of action as well as structure. From this perspective, a group consists of people acting together as a functional unit. The interaction process allows for a number of officers to coordinate action that is directed, consciously or unconsciously, toward some common objective in anticipation of receiving some type of gratification. Some theorists (known as "social interactionists") place primary emphasis on participation in collective activity rather than on group membership per se. They are not concerned with individuals as total organisms, but with those aspects of their behavior that contribute to the collective enterprise. Group action is regarded as something that is constructed out of the diverse efforts of independently motivated human beings moving together toward some shared goal or objective. According to Robert Albanese, this particular concept of group implies some degree of interdependence, mutual influence, and interaction among those people seeking to accomplish a common purpose.[26]

Social interactionists explore group-based human behavior from the interaction/influence perspective we discuss in Chapter 11. They contend that a group does not really exist until its members are involved in *doing* something together. They define a group as two or more persons who (1) interact with some or all members on an individual or network basis; (2) share one or more goals; (3) allow themselves to be governed by a normative system of attitudes, values, and behavior; (4) maintain stable relationships; and (5) form subgroups based on interpersonal attraction or rejection. Interactionists view groups as synergistic, meaning that people working together within a group are able to produce a greater total effect than would be possible if they worked independently; they form a whole that can be greater than the sum of its parts.[27]

People join and remain in formal and informal groups for a variety of reasons. As noted earlier, human beings are social animals with an innate need to interact with others. In addition, most people—as a condition of employment—are assigned to work with other people in groups. From a utilitarian point of view, people who join groups remain active in them because they have expectations that membership will benefit them in some way. They associate groups with positive outcomes and have formed positive attitudes about group participation. Social scientists argue that most people continue to join and remain in groups because they receive positive reinforcement from group behavior.

Police officers join formal and informal groups within their organizations for exactly the same reasons. They are looking for ways to fulfill their occupational roles while trying to meet personal needs. These personal needs fall into two broad categories: (1) psychosocial and (2) economic. While both of these needs promote purposeful interaction among employees, psychosocial factors (some of which will be discussed in succeeding paragraphs) are the more influential.

## Affiliation

One reason police officers join subgroups (formal and informal) is their need to interact with other people and enjoy the companionship of those with whom they have something in common. These subgroups provide structured environments in which police personnel pursue collective interests and establish lasting friendships. Due to the clannish nature of police work and the 24-hour-a-day rotational scheduling, the requirement for affiliation is often met on the job or not at all.

## Security

All human beings have a basic need for safety and security. People want protection from real as well as imagined external threats. Many police officers experience feelings of insecurity that can only be alleviated through interaction with supportive group members. Probationary police officers sense that there is safety in numbers. By joining a group whose members have already experienced and survived the probationary period, they are able to reduce their anxiety. Rookie police officers can learn the ropes faster and become part of the grapevine information network much more quickly by joining a group than by going it alone. The capacity for informal groups to indoctrinate and socialize new members into the organizational routine gives these groups a great deal of power.

## Self-Esteem

Membership in groups, particularly high-status in-groups, can help police officers develop a sense of worth and self-esteem. In addition to gaining internal satisfaction, they develop close interpersonal relationships that provide them with great opportunities for recognition and praise usually unavailable to those outside the group. Groups provide acceptance, perspective, support, and a milieu in which members feel safe and secure. Self-esteem is a natural by-product of subgroup affiliation.

## Power

Group membership can serve as a source of power in two very different ways. First, subgroup solidarity contributes to an employee's sense of safety and security. Police officers believe in the old adage, "United we stand, divided we fall." There can be little doubt that workers organized into cohesive groups enjoy far greater power than they do as individuals. This is the principle on which the labor union movement was built. Secondly, subgroup membership gives members the opportunity to become leaders. They can exert influence over others in the group even though they do not occupy formal positions of authority within the police department. Informal group leaders normally avoid all the responsibilities that come with positions of formal authority.

**Self-Concept**

Subgroup membership helps individual police officers deal with the introspective question "Who am I?" People have a need to establish an identity and locate themselves as objects in their symbolic environment. According to Charles H. Cooley's concept of the "looking-glass self," people do not see themselves directly, but only as reflected in the behavior of others toward them.[28] In other words, our conception of self is essentially based on what aspects of ourselves we see mirrored in the groups to which we belong. Self-conceptions develop through social interaction in groups. Groups are a very good source of evaluative feedback. Continuous interaction provides a good basis for a collective assessment of each member's personality and behavior, and each member's experience with other members helps him or her measure the credibility of their assessments. Significant others within a group may well be willing to give colleagues candid positive and negative feedback that police managers often try to avoid giving.

**Accomplishment**

Some groups form simply because it takes more than one person to complete a task or because the task is made easier through cooperative effort. Other groups come into being for more complicated reasons. Human beings are social animals who have an innate need to collaborate with one another in order to achieve their individual and collective goals. Police officers join groups to pursue mutual interests. They pool their knowledge, energy, expertise, talent, and tools to accomplish certain tasks. They derive natural satisfaction from achievement, and voluntary interaction with their peers gives them a sense of fulfillment.

**Economics**

Police officers may join groups to pursue their own economic self-interests. They often become members of labor unions, fraternal organizations, professional associations, and (promotion examination) study groups with a utilitarian expectation that they will benefit financially from membership. While economic security can be seen simply as part of a police officer's basic need for safety and security, it also represents a pathway to self-actualization. Driven by years of financial deprivation, police officers' quest for economic security has become one of the most inflammatory issues in American law enforcement. Police officers are now one of the most unionized categories of public employees in the United States.[29]

One of the most important factors leading to interpersonal attraction and group formation in law enforcement organizations is the opportunity to interact. Paul Whisenand and George Rush contend that proximity is a critical variable. Many subgroups form simply because police officers are assigned near one another. All other things being equal, those police officers who live near each other or who work closely together have far greater opportunities for interaction than those officers who are physically separated.[30]

**Group Survival**    Whether or not a particular formal or informal subgroup survives and makes a substantive contribution to the organization depends on its success in (1) achieving goals and objectives, (2) meeting the psychosocial and economic needs of group members, and (3) facilitating smooth, meaningful interaction between those members involved in goal-oriented transactions. The long-term survival of a group is usually contingent on bringing these three factors into a state of dynamic equilibrium.

Groups overlap one another in all complex police departments. As a result, police officers are normally active participants in several subgroups, informal and formal, simultaneously. A police captain, for example, might belong to the chief's staff, the Command Officers' Association (union), the department's precision shooting team, the Black caucus, the Police Athletic League, and the Blue Knights Motorcycle Club all at the same time. Under normal circumstances, the captain plays a variety of different roles (leader, follower, technician, facilitator, counselor, teacher, and so forth) in these groups. Versatility is a key ingredient in successful role playing within an organization.

## TYPES OF GROUPS

As noted earlier, groups can be described in terms of their positions along various kinds of continuums:

1. Primary/secondary
2. Formal/informal
3. Voluntary/involuntary
4. Horizontal/vertical
5. Open/closed
6. Esoteric/utilitarian
7. In-group/out-group

Groups can also be categorized in terms of their principal function. Leonard Sayles has suggested the following four basic functional categories: (1) command groups, (2) task groups, (3) interest groups, and (4) friendship groups.[31]

**Command Groups**    Command groups are vertical groups in complex organizations in which orders are given. A group's structure is determined by a formal organizational chart and chain of command, and it is composed of all subordinates who report to one particular police manager. A captain, a lieutenant, a sergeant, and the sergeant's immediate subordinates form a command group. Activities normally take place on orders from a superior. Even if these orders are phrased as requests, the group is still a command group because of the rank relationships between group members.

**Task Groups**    A task group is a temporary unit created by formal authority to deal with a specific project or task. Police administrators are finding that task forces, being smaller and less formal than most traditional command groups, are also faster and more productive. Task boundaries are not limited to those in the immediate chain of command. In fact, they often cross command boundaries. The activities of task groups and project staffs create situations in which members are able to communicate and coordinate with each other to determine the best way to achieve a goal. If a police officer is suspected of being an alcoholic, for example, communication and coordination among the sergeant, the shift commander, the employee assistance program manager, the personnel director, and the chief may be necessary to resolve the problem. In a command group, emphasis is on following directions. In a task group, on the other hand, emphasis is placed on defining the task and getting it done.

**Interest Groups**

In interest groups, the focus is on the group itself. While they may have a chain of command and assigned tasks, they exist because of the mutual interests of all their members. Police personnel, for example, might band together to have their work schedule changed, to support a colleague who has been disciplined, to protest the establishment of a civilian review board, or to seek improvements in wages, hours, and working conditions; they would be choosing to engage in collective action in order to advance their common interests. Interest groups usually exist for a shorter period than other groups because the objectives that bring them together are likely achieved or abandoned.

**Friendship Groups**

Friendship groups exist primarily because members like being together. Members normally have one or more characteristics in common. Their interaction, which frequently goes beyond work, may be based on sports, hobbies, religious affiliations, interest group activities, professional memberships, or fraternal associations. While members of groups may have met at work or through other groups, real friendship sustains their interpersonal relationships.[32]

These categories are not mutually exclusive. While they often overlap and intertwine, they still provide police administrators with a frame of reference for understanding the structure and function of groups.[33] Every organization has its own constellation of informal as well as formal groups that creates a unique personality or climate that differentiates it from all organizations.

## ANATOMY OF A GROUP

No two groups are the same, and individual groups are never the same over time. They are distinct and evolving entities within an environmental setting. While each group develops a unique personality, all groups have certain structural components that differentiate them from aggregates. Researchers have identified five primary structural components that are common in formal as well as informal groups: (1) role, (2) norms, (3) values, (4) status, and (5) culture. Every police administrator needs to understand these basic sociological concepts because they are often used to analyze group behavior.

One way to analyze groups is to look at the various *roles* played by group members. A role is a set of expectations and behaviors associated with a given position in a social unit (e.g., a group, organization, or institution). The sociological use of this term is similar to its theatrical use. For every function that is performed in a group, there is a role. Most groups, for example, have roles labeled "leader" and "follower." The group also has expectations about how these roles should be performed. As in a drama, a role makes sense only if there is a supporting cast interaction based on a pattern of reciprocal *claims* and *obligations*. A claim consists of those things we expect others to do by virtue of their role; an obligation is what we feel bound to do by virtue of our role. What constitutes a claim by one party to the transaction is an obligation for another member of the group. Without socially defined roles and the regularized behavior these roles produce, collaborative, goal-oriented human behavior would be impossible.

Police personnel play multiple roles within police departments and adjust their roles to the expectations of the group they are part of at a given time. Role playing involves living up to the obligations of the role that has been assumed and insisting that other players do the same. Role behavior can be classified into three categories: (1) task related, (2) maintenance related, and (3) individual related. (These categories were developed more than 50 years ago, but they are still relevant today.)[34] Task-related roles require behavior directly related to establishing and achieving the mission, goals, and objectives of the group. Maintenance-related roles call for those behaviors directly related to the well-being, continuity, and development of a particular group. Individual-related roles—the "joker," "chronic complainer," "hedonist," "opponent," and "troublemaker," for example—are scripted to meet the needs of individual members rather than those of the group. Even though such individual roles can be functional under certain circumstances, they are usually dysfunctional and have a negative effect on the group as a whole.

**Roles within Groups**

Researchers have identified an almost endless array of different roles that can be found in organizations. Whether or not one of these roles emerges will depend on the nature of the group, its task, and the situation involved. Here are some of the most common social roles:

1. The *leader* influences, motivates, and coordinates the goal-oriented activities of other group members.
2. The *follower* does willingly those things the leader asks in order to accomplish the organization's goals and objectives.
3. The *expert* provides technical information and practitioner skills relevant to achievement of the group's task.
4. The *enforcer* sees to it that group norms and values are understood and adhered to and that violations result in appropriate sanctions.
5. The *facilitator* works to avoid destructive intragroup conflict through consensus building and compromise.[35]
6. The *devil's advocate* questions virtually every suggestion or managerial decision affecting the group.
7. The *scapegoat*, for a variety of social and psychological reasons, gets blame for group failures.

As noted earlier, most people occupy several roles simultaneously. Each of these roles belongs to a *role set*, which can be thought of as a theatrical "cast of

## Focus 7–1

Six disabled police officers have sued the city for banishing them to "demeaning" positions within the police department after being injured on the job. The department has 30 "light duty" positions that can be filled by officers who have been injured. The officers (who might be described as an "out-group" or an "interest group") have sued the city for $6 million in damages. After eight years of legal haranguing, a federal appeals court has ruled that the case should proceed. The officers feel that the city has violated federal disability rights laws. In papers filed in the federal court it is alleged that the plaintiffs have been demeaned and that officers working in mainstream units have denigrated them by calling them "snivelers," "cripples," and "fakers." The plaintiffs feel that being placed on light-duty status has denied them the chance for promotion and relegated them to second-class status.

*Source:* Adapted from Howard Mintz, "Cities Keep Eye on S.J. Disabled-Cops Case," *San Jose Mercury News*, December 28, 2003, pp. 1B and 4B.

characters"—all those group members (in other roles) who interact with a given role in some way and have legitimate expectations concerning the behavior of the person playing that role. Role sets are important because they pressure individuals to conform to role-related expectations.[36] The role set of a patrol officer is depicted in Figure 7–3.

Focus 7–1 discusses an instance of *role conflict*, which happens when a person tries to perform two roles that impose contradictory or incompatible demands on him or her. Since most people play a variety of very different roles, and since there will always be varying expectations about how a person should behave in a given set of circumstances, role conflict is inevitable. According to Dean Champion,[37] there are several kinds of role conflicts that managers must learn to deal with. These conflicts arise from (1) the dissimilar demands of two different roles, (2) the simultaneous playing of numerous roles, (3) internal stressors like the time or skill

New York City Police Department Personnel Performing Their Routine Functions.
Courtesy City of New York Police Department Photo Unit

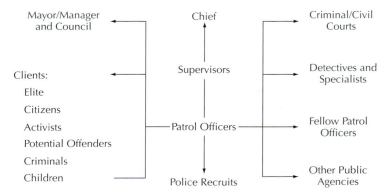

**Figure 7–3**

The Role Set of the Patrol Officer.

Adapted from John J. Broderick, *Police in a Time of Change* (Prospect Heights, IL: Waveland Press, 1987).

required to play roles properly, and (4) different expectations about how a particular role should be carried out. Clearly, role conflict is inherent in group dynamics.[38]

---

**CASE STUDY**   Captain Oliver Dixon

The city of Rinert is located in the northeast United States. The city was founded in 1764 and the police department can trace its history back to the early 1800s. The department is proud that it has employed individuals from the same families from one generation to the next. As a relatively homogeneous group, members of the workforce share similar values, attitudes, norms, and social perspectives. Consensus has become the rule rather than the exception.

Most of Rinert's police officers were trained to use separation and mediation as tools in domestic-violence cases. They viewed domestic conflict as a civil matter. Arrests were infrequent and usually precipitated by truly outrageous behavior or other kinds of aggravating circumstances.

A new law enacted by the state legislature requires arrest in any domestic disturbance involving physical injury or immediate threat of such injury. Capt. Dixon, the department's training officer, immediately distributed a copy of the new law to all police personnel. He also incorporated the information into the basic training curriculum at the police academy. The captain and his staff continually emphasized the importance of the new law and the rationale for arrest in domestic-violence cases. A counselor from the local domestic-violence shelter made an audiovisual presentation and gave an impassioned plea for full enforcement of the new

law. An assistant district attorney was brought in to discuss civil liabilities in these cases. Once rookies graduated from the academy and assumed their duties, a senior police officer, selected at random, was assigned to serve as a field training officer (FTO) and mentor for each rookie.

In order to determine the effect of the new law on arrest rates, the department's planning and research unit did a follow-up study, based on data collected at six-month intervals. The Phase 1 data (first six months after the law took effect) showed a moderate increase in the number of arrests made by veteran officers. For rookies, on the other hand, the ratio of number of arrests to number of domestic-dispute calls answered was very high. In Phase 2, the number of arrests made by both groups declined. Phase 3 data indicated that domestic-dispute arrest rates for veteran officers and rookies had converged and stabilized at a point slightly higher than the departmental average before the new law was passed. Capt. Dixon has been asked to explain why the number of arrests has leveled off and what can be done to increase the effectiveness of the department's training program.

*Based on the concept of groups and group dynamics, how would the captain explain this situation? What could and should be done to make sure this type of cosmetic change does not take place in the future?*

# GROUP-SHARED NORMS AND VALUES

Based on meaningful interaction among members, groups formulate definitions of appropriate and inappropriate behavior. These definitions become normative standards by which all members of the group are judged. Social norms are group-generated, accepted, reinforced, and internalized expectations that are translated into informal as well as formal rules of conduct that guide human behavior in a given situation. Norms require (prescribe) or prohibit (proscribe) certain types of conduct, depending on the circumstances. Members of the group are rewarded if they conform to group-shared expectations and punished if they deviate from the group's norms. Virtually all of our actions are influenced by the norms of one group or another. Most of these have been internalized so thoroughly that people conform to them without being consciously aware that they are conforming. *Norms* are internalized in the subconscious and become part of our very existence.[39] Norms can ordinarily be categorized in terms of the intensity of the feeling, the extent of the social reaction, and the consequences (in terms of sanctions) generated when a group-shared expectation is violated. There are four basic types of social norms: (1) folkways, (2) mores, (3) taboos, and (4) laws.

**Folkways**

Folkways are customs, conventions, or traditions of informal groups that members tend to follow almost automatically. Police officers, for example, learn to use a unique job-related vocabulary. They are also expected to remain calm and collected even in highly stressful situations. Violation of a folkway normally elicits a relatively mild negative reaction from other members of the group.

**Mores**

Mores are the morally binding customs of a group. They are among the strongest norms and comprise the basic ethical behavioral judgments of a particular group. Mores represent those standards of behavior the violation of which elicits intense feelings and very serious consequences. Some mores are considered more important than others and are condemned much more strongly. While "blue coat" crime violates the mores of the average police officer, turning in the officer may be even more repugnant to a loyal group member who has been socialized to believe that maintaining "the code of silence" and supporting "the officers in blue" are more important than eliminating crime or corruption within the police department.

**Taboos**

Taboos represent an absolute prohibition against behavior so atrocious as to be almost unthinkable. Taboos are the strongest norms, and they elicit maximum consequences. Police work has its taboos—lack of courage, for example, or failure to back up an officer who is in danger and needs assistance. Those who break taboos may face ostracism by their group or their society; in extreme cases they may be subject to criminal sanctions.

**Laws**

Laws have been defined as "customs in decay." They represent group-shared expectations that have been translated, for reasons that may or may not be evident, into state demands. The severity of group reaction is measured in terms of the behavior's classification as a summary offense, misdemeanor, felony, or capital crime. Within an organization, policies, procedures, rules, and regulations function as laws do in the world at large. The failure to abide by departmental policies, procedures, rules, and regulations elicits the imposition of sanctions ranging from an oral reprimand to involuntary termination of employment. Legitimate norms are also articulated in civil service legislation, police department accreditation standards, and the Law Enforcement Code of Ethics.

Although we have drawn distinctions among folkways, mores, taboos, and laws, it is important to note that the boundaries between these categories are somewhat arbitrary and often based on selective perception. In reality, norms fall on a continuum in terms of importance and social significance. They do not apply equally to every individual or group. Norms are produced through a dynamic interactive process and continue to change over time. They are best viewed as fluid, shifting guidelines for thinking and behavior.[40]

Group-generated shared values play a crucial role in the personal and professional lives of police personnel. Values are abstract and general beliefs about what is right, good, and desirable. Values are the heart and soul of a group; they provide the philosophical glue that holds the group together. Values are not specific rules for action, but general precepts to which people give allegiance and about which they have strong feelings. Values constitute a general guidance system for thinking and behaving. Interests, attitudes, norms, and behaviors originate in and are reflected by some value or set of values. The word "values" has a variety of meanings. In the most general sense, values are global beliefs concerning what is good (freedom, justice, the "American way") and what is bad (war, poverty, dishonesty). These values provide a cultural base for determining the appropriateness of our behavior. (See Chapter 4 for an extended discussion of values.)

From a managerial point of view, a value is an enduring belief that a specific mode of conduct or goal is preferable to others in a given set of circumstances. Paul Whisenand and George Rush define a value as a fairly stable yet changeable belief that a particular means to a particular end is preferred over the alternatives.[41] Since police officers have more than one value, managers must learn to think and to judge on-the-job behavior in terms of a *value system*.

A value system is a set of beliefs concerning preferred modes of conduct and goals in a hierarchical ranking of relative importance. A value system is a relatively permanent perceptual framework that influences and shapes the general character of each individual's behavior. People are what they value. They discipline themselves and interact with important others according to their personal value system. Values produce attitudes that generate and shape all purposeful human behavior. An attitude represents a state of mind that is focused on an object or event in an individual's psychological world. Attitudes, for police officers as well as other people, are a concrete manifestation of a person's basic values.[42] Fair treatment of a very unpopular minority-group subordinate, for example, is indicative of a commitment to administrative due process and fundamental fairness in the workplace. Values cut across specific situations to which attitudes are tied.

## The Learning Process

While genetics shape broad patterns of human behavior, most value-related behavior is learned. People are exposed to and internalize values throughout life. The most intense learning takes place during the first 20 years and normally consists of three very distinct phases: (1) imprinting, (2) modeling, and (3) socialization.

From a sociological point of view, the mind of each baby at birth is a tabula rasa, a blank slate. Through interaction with important others during the first six or seven years of life, babies learn by osmosis to react to and cope with the exigencies of life. Their personality is formed, setting the stage for virtually all their future mental, emotional, and social development. The principal actors in the imprinting process are parents and other members of the primary group who have a responsibility to nurture children so they can survive, thrive, and move toward far greater autonomy. The infrastructure of a person is the child as formed during these very critical years.

**Imprinting**

During the modeling phase (between ages 7 and 14), children begin to identify with, and pattern their behavior after, an expanding number of family members, peers, and heroes in the outside world. Group membership also begins to play a much more prominent role in their life; they identify with their group as a whole and with significant others within the group. As a result, new values and patterns of behavior are integrated with behavior learned through earlier imprinting. Children construct ego (based on information from a variety of sources) and try to measure the ideal. A child's value system is a composite produced by imprinting and modeling.

**Modeling**

Between ages 14 and 20, social life is organized primarily in terms of friends. Peer influence reaches its zenith and meaningful interpersonal relationships center on common interests or activities. These young men and women spend a great deal of time defining and integrating the beliefs, standards, and values of peers into their own unique personalities. It is during this particular phase of the developmental process that young people achieve physical maturity and adopt a dominant value system. This value system is a guide for internal self-control and molds the individual's personality. Adolescence usually involves experimentation, verification, clarification, and validation of group-shared values.[43] Once a value system is in place, it serves as an internalized set of standards designed to guide human behavior in ambiguous situations.

**Socialization**

From about age 20 on, the value system that was developed during childhood and adolescence locks in and becomes the standard by which people determine what is good and what is bad in a given set of circumstances. While much of the socialization we experience occurs during childhood and adolescence, the inculcation of norms, values, and ethics continues throughout life. New police recruits are taught the values of the police profession and are expected to perform their duties in certain ways. Police officers are rewarded when they conform to group-shared expectations and exhibit appropriate values. They are punished when they fail to do so. Values activate, sustain, and legitimize human conduct.

## STATUS IN GROUPS

Social status is a very important concept in the study of group dynamics. Behavioral scientists point out that each person is involved in a complex web of social relationships. We all interact with other human beings in a variety of group settings. Social groups consist of a number of people whose relationships are based on a set of interrelated roles and statuses. They interact with each other in more or less standardized ways based on the norms and values they accept. They are united by a consciousness of kind and a similarity of interests that enable them to differentiate fellow group members from nonmembers.

In a very general sense, status refers to any position that is held within a group. It also refers to a person's position or rank in relation to other members of the work group. Status is a measure of worth (in terms of prestige or esteem) conferred on a person or on a position by a social group. Persons or positions with high status in a group are considered more valuable in certain respects than most of those to whom they are compared. Many have legitimate authority and real power in the organization of which the group is a part. They also have corresponding duties and responsibilities. This ranking is important because it contributes to the ordering of social interaction and structuring of social relationships. The complex array of roles and statuses that defines the behavior of individuals and specifies their relations with one another constitutes what social scientists call social organization and/or social structure.[44] A police department is a formal organization built on patterned regularity in behavior and interaction.

Few people or positions have universally high status in all situations. In fact, a high-status person or position in one group may have no status at all in another group setting. It is complicated because human beings belong to many groups and occupy different statuses simultaneously. According to behavioral scientists, much of our group-oriented behavior consists of acquiring, enhancing, and preserving social status.

Statuses are designations assigned to individuals and/or positions by the group. They emerge from the process of collective living and are normally broken down into two basic categories: (1) *ascribed status* and (2) *achieved status*. An ascribed status is derived from attributes over which individuals have no control (age, gender, race) or from membership in groups to which they are assigned by others (family, religion, nationality). Based on this ascribed status, the person is expected to acquire and perform certain socially defined roles. Achieved status, on the other hand, is the result of action taken by the individual. Achieved status is earned status. Candidates compete for status and are required to demonstrate that they have the ability to fulfill a particular role. Officially designated leaders, for example, are usually given the respect and esteem due a superior based on the authority inherent in their formal positions within their organizations. Natural leaders, regardless of their rank, earn the respect and esteem of their colleagues—often informally. They share power with followers as well as exercising power over them. Followers do willingly what their leaders ask of them. Ideally—but rarely—formal authority and real leadership come together in the police department's official chain of command. Behavioral scientists refer to this state of affairs as "status congruence."[45]

## GROUP CULTURE

*Social groups*—including work groups—are produced by and reflect certain aspects of the culture in which they exist. Groups also create subcultural milieus of their own. Culture consists of all the knowledge, values, attitudes, norms, behavioral patterns, language, and artifacts that are passed from one generation to the next and form a way of life for those within the group. In the most general sense, culture is a way of life that defines appropriate modes of thinking, acting, and feeling. It exists because human beings are able to share their creations and pass knowledge on to subsequent generations. A common culture is the glue that holds any group together.

Culture is often referred to as the collective personality of the group. Work groups—like the police—develop a distinctive, at times unique, orientation. In fact, the police are frequently described as a culture within a culture.[46] Policing is a vocation somewhat isolated from the rest of American culture. The common knowledge, values, attitudes, norms, and behavioral patterns police officers share may help explain why efforts to reform police departments can arouse extensive opposition from the rank and file.

Police officers also share a common language or argot. There are strong bonds of loyalty and secrecy and a feeling of "us against them" among police personnel. Officers see themselves as "the thin blue line" or "the blue minority." The police academy is the first formal step in the socialization process and is designed to influence the police recruit's values, attitudes, and behaviors. Socialization is the process through which individuals learn proper ways of thinking, acting, and feeling in a particular culture. Academy training serves to separate trainees even further from the society. In addition, various on-the-job experiences provide for continued socialization that draws police officers more deeply into the police subculture.[47] The pillars on which that subculture is built are loyalty, solidarity, esprit de corps, and secrecy. While they do not seem to produce either job satisfaction or equitable law enforcement, they become an integral part of each police officer's working personality.[48]

Most police administrators have been promoted through the ranks. Their friends, colleagues, and on-the-job experiences have shaped their management styles and their approach to discipline, training, and supervision. Knowledge of informal groups and subcultural values, norms, and group dynamics will help ensure the success of contemporary police management. According to Edward Thibault and his colleagues, understanding the subcultural context within which police work takes place may be more important than all other knowledge and administrative skills combined.[49]

# GROUP DYNAMICS

Group dynamics are those forces within the group that affect task performance and member satisfaction.[50] The group process transforms resource inputs into group outputs. Effective police managers learn to harness and deploy the energy created as the result of positive group interaction. Work groups grow and mature just as individuals do. As groups begin to mature, members learn to understand and trust each other. They are better able to work together in making decisions and solving problems. There are four recognizable stages in the group development process: (1) formation, (2) differentiation, (3) integration, and (4) maturity.[51]

## Formation

The group formation begins with a consciousness of kind and/or a recognition of common interests. Prospective members tentatively identify with a group and cautiously enter into a give-and-take relationship with incumbent members. They seek mutual acceptance and focus their attention on the tasks performed, the ways the group can satisfy their psychosocial needs, the ground rules for behavior, and the status a particular group or task has within the larger organization. They derive much of their initial impression of the group through subjective evaluation of the characteristics and behaviors of incumbent members.

**Differentiation**
The differentiation stage in group development involves the process of getting a better feel for the composition of the group and for its assigned tasks. New members learn how to do the job and what to expect in terms of need satisfaction. It is not uncommon for competition and conflict to emerge. Coalitions are often formed to work out strategies for doing the job or to enhance the chances for need satisfaction.[52] As members work together, they learn each other's strengths and weaknesses. Joint problem solving and group decision-making reinforce the team concept. In most cases, meaningful participation cements relationships and promotes efficiency, effectiveness, and participation. As a result, individual members are much more likely to invest their time, energy, effort, and expertise in psychologically satisfying and rewarding group-oriented activities.

**Integration**
The integration stage of group development is the point at which everything comes together. Member motivation changes from primarily hedonistic (attempting to satisfy their own needs) to much more altruistic (internalizing the group's goals). There is a realization that the group can accomplish more as a unit than can individuals acting on their own. Consequently, there is an incentive for members to channel their individual efforts into group solidarity and teamwork. Members receive a psychological as well as a social payoff when they cooperate with each other, encourage others within the group to achieve their full potential, and create an environment in which goal achievement becomes a form of need satisfaction. Under these conditions, the group becomes a goal-oriented and cohesive social entity in which common values, norms, and ethical orientations regulate individual as well as collective behavior. At this stage, the individual member and the group find themselves in a state of dynamic equilibrium.[53]

**Maturity**
The maturity stage of group development reflects group needs for both stability and flexibility. In a mature group, the group assumes the control function from other organizational entities and sets standards for regulating member behavior. Members seek to avoid anomie[54] (a sense of normlessness) and willingly submit to the will of the group as embodied in its values, norms, standards, and other mechanisms designed to guide behavior or ensure conformity. They tacitly agree to abide by informal rules and regulations designed to keep them performing successfully without surrendering their individual autonomy. The group controls itself and individual members control themselves in an effort to benefit the rest of the group. According to Robert Fulmer, mature work groups tend to be self-regulating, self-motivating, and self-directing.[55] They take care of their own needs and are able to solve problems arising within the group. At the same time, mature groups seek to avoid groupthink and try to remain flexible enough to adapt to changing tasks and environmental factors.[56]

Work groups go through life cycles just like all other living organisms. At any given time, some new groups are just forming while others are beginning to come together as distinct and identifiable entities. Some become fully integrated and reach the stage of dynamic equilibrium. While some groups achieve a degree of stability and permanence based on their maturity, others lose their capacity to change and they move toward extinction. Police administrators need to understand the life cycle of groups so they can harness a group's energy and make the adjustments necessary to increase its efficiency, effectiveness, and productivity.

*Within a group* goal-oriented human beings learn relevant knowledge, job skills, and appropriate behaviors. Members interact with one another and communicate their mutual expectations concerning exactly how work is to be performed. Membership in the work group gives participants the opportunity to model correct behaviors, provide instruction or technical assistance to neophytes, and exchange evaluative feedback about job performance. Group members are in a position to exert a direct influence on each other's beliefs and/or predispositions concerning work and how it is to be done. They are in a unique position to encourage interdependence and accomplish work.[57] Functional work groups also provide members with security, emotional support, and an in-group perspective. They give members a sense of identity (vis-à-vis their work) and the opportunity for ego involvement in mutually satisfying activities. An effective work group is multidimensional in that it achieves high levels of task performance and human resource maintenance over a protracted period of time.[58]

## HUMAN RELATIONS AND MANAGEMENT

The human relations school of management and the organizational humanists (discussed in Chapters 4 and 11) emphasize the importance of group dynamics in task performance and human resource maintenance. The human relations movement can be traced back to two pioneering studies that were conducted during the mid-1920s at the Hawthorne Works of the Western Electric Company. The famous Relay Room Experiments and the Bank Wiring Room Study produced concrete evidence that work groups and work-group participation have a direct influence on individual productivity. Elton Mayo and his colleagues discovered that social variables—like interaction patterns, supervisory styles, and group pressure to raise or lower production—played a key role in determining how much effort employees within a particular work group were willing to expend. In one case, these factors operated to increase overall productivity; in the other, they acted to restrain it. In both instances, however, the research team concluded that insight into job performance could be obtained by paying attention to important aspects of human behavior.[59]

Some theorists have a totally negative view of the human relations approach to management. They base this attitude on one or the other of two basic assumptions: (1) social groups do not really exist or (2) groups exist but are a bad thing. Others, such as organizational humanists and group dynamists, take an exactly opposite view. Social groups exist in all complex goal-oriented organizations, theorists say; their reality is demonstrated by the difference it makes to individuals whether they are accepted or rejected by social groups and whether their work groups are healthy or unhealthy. The pro-group theorists also argue that groups are good, because they satisfy deep-seated needs of employees for affiliation, affection, recognition, and self-esteem. Group membership promotes altruism, loyalty, and a sense of belonging; cooperative interaction enables human beings to achieve objectives they could not accomplish by themselves. One researcher found that the theory of cooperation and competition can be useful for identifying the social processes that help teams grapple with problems and work effectively.[60] There are even some pro-group extremists who believe that everything can and should be done by and in groups. They contend that individual responsibility, person-to-person supervision, and even individual problem solving are bad.

Dorwin Cartwright and Ronald Lippit reject the assumption that individual and group interests are incompatible and have challenged it with five assertions about individuals, groups, and group dynamics:[61]

1. *Groups are real.* They are a natural part of the social backdrop. There is dramatic evidence—from a wide variety of different sources—to show that group decisions are often more successful in producing substantive and durable changes in human behavior than are methods dealing with people as isolated individuals.

2. *Groups are omnipresent and inevitable.* Human beings are animals with an instinctive need to interact with one another in a group-generated milieu built around communication and supportive interpersonal relationships. People are incapable of living in geographical proximity without forming groups and/or rewarding group participation in one way or another.

3. *Groups mobilize powerful synergistic forces that produce effects most important to people.* Members' roles in groups affect how others behave toward them and how they feel about themselves. Group membership can be a blessing or a curse. People have been traumatized both by exclusion from groups and by enforced membership in groups. It is also clear that events within a group can have repercussions on others—members and nonmembers—not directly involved in the events.

4. *Groups may produce both good and bad consequences.* The assumption that groups are completely good or bad is likely to lead to selective perception, tunnel vision, and research that tend to be ideological rather than scientific. Groups are multidimensional, and their value always depends on the situation.

5. *The desirable consequences resulting from group interaction can be deliberately enhanced.* Through knowledge gained by researchers into group dynamics theory, managers—including police administrators—can help make work groups more efficient, effective, and productive. (It should be noted that some behavioral scientists find this a cause for ethical concern; they are reminded of the kinds of social manipulation explored in George Orwell's chilling novel *1984.*)

Work groups play a critically important role in attitude formation and provide members with a repertoire of appropriate skills to do the job. Group standards (based on shared values) become the gauge by which to measure individual performance. While group standards may be articulated by management, they are normally internalized by employees via the socialization process. Socialization is designed to promote overall uniformity in thought and action based on the group's values, norms, and ethical orientation. This emphasis on the group—as opposed to the individual—leads to a tendency on the part of work-group members to change their opinions to conform with significant others in the group, to change the opinions of others, and to redefine the boundaries of the group to exclude those individuals holding deviant points of view. The collective success of any work group will have a direct impact on the job performance of individual members.

**Collaboration**

There is ample evidence to demonstrate that when individuals work cooperatively rather than competitively, the work group's cohesiveness increases and the work itself better meets employee needs. Research suggests that both cooperation and group cohesion have a positive influence on an individual's productivity. D. W. Johnson and his colleagues examined the findings of 120 studies designed to evaluate individual productivity in terms of three prevailing reward structures:[62]

1. *Cooperative reward structure.* Goal attainment by each member facilitates goal attainment by others within the work group.
2. *Competitive reward structure.* Goal attainment by one member blocks the attainment of goals by other group members.
3. *Individual reward structure.* Goal attainment by one member is unrelated to the activities of other members.

In most cases, cooperation yielded higher levels of group productivity than competition or individual efforts. This is a much more important factor in small groups than in large groups and in groups where members work interdependently rather than independently.

# INFLUENCES ON BEHAVIOR

Clearly, people's performance in group settings is influenced by a number of factors. These include the task, the work environment, the group's maturity level, ambient stimuli (related to group membership), and discretionary stimuli (such as social acceptance, rejection, and communication). Other relevant variables include complexity, need orientation, size, composition, norms, cohesiveness, and groupthink.

**Complexity**

Simple tasks ordinarily place fewer demands on the group process than tasks that require greater knowledge (technical and other) or social skills. As the overall complexity of tasks increases, it usually becomes more difficult for members of a work group to achieve a productive balance between quantity and quality. Members must distribute their efforts more broadly on increasingly complex tasks that require greater interdependence, cooperation, and coordination. If the group process does not adjust to these demands, individual performance will begin to suffer, with a concomitant reduction in job satisfaction. Conversely, if group members are competent, have needs that are in sync with those of the organization, and can work collaboratively with each other, job satisfaction and performance will tend to increase as the complexity of the task increases. Whether complexity has a negative or a positive effect on the job performance of individual officers will depend on the situation as well as the collective attributes of those involved.

**Need Orientation**    Group members with conflicting needs march to different drummers. The willingness of one individual to exert an effort voluntarily on behalf of the group is always contingent on a variety of factors. A key element in the functioning of a work group is the degree to which there is interpersonal compatibility—based on needs—among its members. William C. Schutz developed his "fundamental interpersonal orientation" theory of behavior (FIRO-B) more than 40 years ago.[63] It is designed to help explain how people orient themselves to each other based on how strongly they need to express and receive feelings of inclusion, affection, and control. Those with a need for inclusion strive for prominence, recognition, and prestige. People with a need for affection manifest it in friendliness and the desire to seek emotional bonding with others in the group. Members with a need to control have a tendency to rebel against those with authority; they resist being controlled by others and refuse to be compliant or submissive. Work groups in which members have reciprocal and compatible needs are usually more efficient, effective, and productive than those groups that are plagued by incompatibilities. Group members who are motivated by very different or conflicting needs are much less likely to work well together.

Antagonistic needs, drives, aspirations, and goals hinder collaboration and have a negative influence on the performance of the group itself and the individuals within it. Symptoms of these debilitating incompatibilities include widespread apathy, open hostility, struggles for control, poor job performance, lowered productivity, and domination of the group by a few powerful and politically adroit members who operate on the "divide and conquer" principle.

**Size**    Formal and informal groups vary greatly in size, as we have seen, but most of the groups with which people interact have fewer than ten members. One approach to the analysis and understanding of behavior in work groups focuses on activities (what each member does), interactions (communication between members individually or between members and the group as a collective entity), and sentiments (personal and group shared and reinforced values, attitudes, beliefs, and feelings).[64]

As the size of a particular work group increases, competing forces are unleashed and the number of potential relationships increases geometrically. These changes may foster better performance or make things worse. On the positive side, an increase in group size increases the human resources available to the group. It may also bring in additional skills that can help accomplish assigned tasks more efficiently and effectively. Finally, expanding the group may make it more representative of the department and thus could offer greater opportunities for affiliation and meaningful participation. On the downside, any real growth in size increases the potential for problems in communication, coordination, and quality control. Expansion may require the imposition of a more formal group structure (well-defined tasks, roles, and statuses), which may in turn make individual members more inhibited and less productive. If the work group gets so large that its internal interactions can no longer be conducted primarily face-to-face, some of its (human and financial) resources will have to be shifted from task achievement to group maintenance functions. The complexity of the coordination problems that must be resolved before a work group can achieve its full potential tends to increase faster than group size. It is very difficult to attain and maintain optimum motivation, morale, performance, and productivity as more and more people join the work group. According to John Schermerhorn and his colleagues, larger groups suffer some real disadvantages in terms of individual performance and group effectiveness.[65] Many of these problems can be overcome in law enforcement through proactive management of the group process.

**Composition**

Job performance, group effectiveness, and group dynamics are all influenced to one degree or another by the demographic, professional, and psychosocial characteristics of individual group members. In order to fulfill their roles and take advantage of their competencies (such as intelligence, maturity, motivation, personality, technical skill, and physical ability), individuals must be capable of functioning in a group setting. This is extremely important because the performance of an individual member can be greatly enhanced or restricted—deliberately or unintentionally—by other members of the work group.

Homogeneous work groups are composed of members who have similar backgrounds, interests, values, attitudes, and other traits. Successful heterogeneous groups, on the other hand, tend to accept and thrive on diversity. Open groups tend by nature to be heterogeneous. They bring a wide variety of skills and perspectives to bear on problems. This diversity can, at times, lead to competition, conflict, and a lack of direction. Closed groups are much more homogeneous. Homogeneity produces common goals and increases the likelihood that there will be relatively harmonious working relationships among group members. Due to their innate similarities, it is easy for individual members to buy into the group's culture. Conformity to group shared values, norms, and ethical orientations becomes the rule rather than the exception.

In spite of government-mandated equal employment opportunity and affirmative action hiring programs, the police profession usually functions near the closed-group end of the continuum. The selection process is designed to identify men and women who possess an affinity for membership in the informal culture as well as the formal organization. According to Jerome Skolnick and Thomas Gray, affinity represents a predisposition to adhere to a distinctive set of sentiments that can be expanded and reinforced through training and socialization.[66] Affinity is the operative concept used to separate those who are technically qualified to become police officers from those who will probably be able to absorb the requirements of the legal system, the formal police organization, and the police subculture.

Managers must exercise judgment in selecting human resources in order to create a healthy balance between homogeneity and heterogeneity. Individual performance and group productivity are directly related to the degree of fit experienced by those involved in a collective enterprise. Police work is undergoing a fundamental transition. It is in the process of moving away from resisting and fearing individual differences and moving toward accepting and utilizing them. The more diverse the membership, the more skilled an administrator must be in reconciling individual differences and managing group dynamics.

**Norms**

As defined earlier, norms are guidelines for accepted and expected social behavior that are inculcated in an individual's subconscious mind through the socialization process. They reflect group-shared ideas about how individual members are supposed to behave inside and outside the group. Group norms not only regulate formal and informal relationships between members of the workforce but also control the overall quantity and quality of the work itself. Socialization is a dynamic process whereby the culture of the group is transmitted from one generation of workers to another through the socialization process. New members learn to identify with, model, internalize, and derive intrinsic social satisfaction from conformity with the values, norms, and ethical standards of the group.

As the result of socialization, the police officer develops a distinct consciousness of kind, a self-concept, and a reaffirmation of personal worth expressed in terms of approval and support.[67] Work groups exert a strong influence on the behavior of their members by providing them with security, support, encouragement, and positive reinforcement for appropriate behavior. Work groups also punish those members who deviate from their group-shared expectations. They use ridicule, shame, and the threat of expulsion to elicit conformity.[68]

Virtually every aspect of a police officer's behavior is regulated by norms. As a result, the norms of the work group determine what is to be done, how it is to be accomplished, who is to do it, and how much value it has to the group as a whole. The work group sets the standard for productivity and quality against which an individual's job performance is judged.

## Cohesiveness

Some work groups are much more cohesive than others. Used in this context, cohesiveness is regarded as a characteristic of a group in which all of the forces acting on members to remain in the group are greater than those forces acting on them to leave it. According to Robert Albanese, cohesive forces—those holding a work group together and strengthening interpersonal relationships among members—can be grouped into two very basic categories: (1) those that positively influence the achievement of the personal goals of group members and (2) those that satisfy group members' needs for meaningful and supportive interaction with significant others in the group.[69] In a best-case scenario, there will be congruence between organizational needs (for efficiency, effectiveness, and productivity) and members' needs (for belongingness, achievement, meaningful participation, and recognition) within a dynamic, synergistic, and hospitable social milieu.

Police officers find themselves in closed and relatively cohesive work groups. They work under hazardous and stressful conditions that draw them into a kind of brotherhood.[70] Confronted with the demands of the public, expectations of administrators, and pressures from their peers, police officers find themselves caught up in a web of insecurity, confusion, and frustration. Since it is almost impossible to resolve these personal dilemmas on their own, they identify with the group and cultivate its support by strengthening interpersonal relationships with other officers. As the police have become more occupationally cohesive, their bonds with the public have grown weaker. These two groups have become polarized and treat each other as adversaries.[71]

Most police officers have now adopted the attitude that "No one can understand me but another cop." Recruits are screened and selected based on how well they will fit the police mold. They are then very carefully socialized to internalize the values, norms, and ethical orientations of the work group. At this point, they become full-fledged members of the police subculture. They think, behave, and operate by the same rationale as their colleagues. Cohesiveness and performance are directly related in several ways: (1) the successful performance of group tasks can increase cohesiveness, (2) even failure can lead to cohesiveness in a threatening or win-lose situation, and (3) cohesiveness can produce an increase in individual and/or group performance. The highest levels of performance are normally found in highly cohesive groups that value productivity and have established uniformly high performance norms.[72] On the other side of the coin, cohesiveness can have a negative effect on performance if there is a conflict between organizational objectives and group members' needs. A high level of cohesiveness coupled with low performance goals promotes low performance. Under these circumstances, both individuality and innovation are discouraged.[73]

Groupthink has become one of the most influential concepts in the behavioral sciences.[74] As just described, group cohesiveness is the degree to which individuals desire and are motivated to maintain their affiliation with a group. Cohesiveness can be a double-edged sword. Although it can have a very positive effect on performance, too much cohesiveness can become pathological. It discourages individuality, critical thinking, and innovation. Groupthink is a common characteristic of excessively cohesive groups. Loyalty to the group (in terms of its values, norms, and subcultural perspectives) becomes the most powerful group-shared expectation. Any behavior—from the inside or the outside—that harms the group or diminishes its solidarity is viewed as divisive, illegitimate, and very unacceptable. It can reach the point where the members' strivings for unanimity override a realistic appraisal of other courses of action.[75] Conformity and consensus replace analysis. It becomes "us" versus "them." "Them" refers to anyone outside of the group, even if that person has legitimate authority and administrative responsibility related to the group's function. Groupthink can foster the belief of invulnerability.

**Groupthink**

Groupthink is a real hazard in police work. It is nourished by an obsession with loyalty, solidarity, esprit de corps, dependability, and secrecy. Many police officers are willing to tolerate incompetence, corruption, brutality, and "blue coat" crime rather than to "blow the whistle" or "hang dirty linen in public." They openly resist civilian control and have deep-seated antipathy for whistle blowers, internal affairs personnel, civilian review boards, and those officers who are induced to break "the code." Police managers must be alert to the following symptoms of groupthink:[76]

1. A false impression of invulnerability.
2. Pressure against those who deviate from the majority viewpoint.
3. Fear of being penalized for deviating from the majority viewpoint.
4. A shared false impression of unanimity and consensus.
5. A perception of outsiders as wicked, unintelligent, or feeble.
6. An unquestioned belief in the principles of the in-group.
7. The presence of self-appointed "mind guards" who shield the leader and other group members from information contrary to the party line.
8. The screening of negative feedback to the group.

Conformity is a natural and normal aspect of group dynamics. Conformity becomes pathological when it manifests itself in groupthink and has a negative effect on individual performance as well as work-group productivity.

# ACCEPTING AND MANAGING WORK GROUPS

The traditional Theory X (autocratic) approach to management is slowly but surely giving way to the kind of participative self-management that McGregor called Theory Y.[77] Experienced administrators understand that groups and the group process are a new part of the landscape in police work. They know that without the group's energy, effort, expertise, and support, the chances of achieving the organization's mission, goals, and objectives are slim. The division of labor and task specialization associated with work in law enforcement organizations place a premium on cooperation, collaboration, and coordination in the workplace. Purposeful interaction and synergy provide an impetus for productivity. A lack of healthy group involvement and support is a kiss of death in those situations requiring collective behavior. Successful administrators see the management of group dynamics as a critical variable in effective task accomplishment. Consequently, they spend a great deal of their time in group development and maintenance. They seek to identify and resolve those problems that make the work group dysfunctional. It is their job to dismantle the barriers that obstruct intergroup as well as intragroup communication, neutralize destructive conflict, and encourage all members to become active participants in the group process.

Participatory management evolved from the concept of organizational humanism espoused by some members of the human relations school of management. It consists of a proactive and integrated strategy designed to increase organizational productivity, as well as individual satisfaction, by giving members of the workforce a substantive role in the decision-making process. Members of the work group are permitted (within the parameters established by management) to establish their own goals and to achieve these goals through a collaborative effort. Once this participatory group process is set in motion, administrators can garner much-needed support by allowing work groups to function with minimum intervention. Under these circumstances, managers assume a different role. They do less directing and more coordinating. They help guide and give substance to the group process by serving as resource persons, role models, teachers, and coaches. Modern police administrators are expected to convert the work group's synergistic effort into productive outputs.[78]

Skillful police administrators utilize their knowledge of groups and group dynamics to meet human needs as well as to motivate their immediate subordinates. They know that membership in a goal-oriented group tends to enhance the satisfaction, performance, and productivity of its members in relatively ambiguous and unstructured situations where they exercise a great deal of discretion. Ethical managers avoid using the group process to manipulate police personnel. They view employees as good and are committed to confirming them as whole persons. Ethical police administrators oppose game playing and cultivate genuine collaboration. They build supportive relationships with individuals and groups based on mutual respect and trust. Mutual respect and trust are part of the glue that holds any productive enterprise together.

**Managerial Strategies**　Richard W. Plunkett has identified seven basic principles he believes managers should follow in order to minimize a work group's tensions and conflicts.[79] He felt this would maximize the group's performance, cooperation, collaboration, coordination, and contribution to the organization:

1. Accept the existence of groups, subgroups, and cliques as a fact of organizational life. These informal groups are allies to be won over and brought to bear on common problems. A manager must work with these groups, not oppose them.

2. Identify informal leaders and seek their cooperation. They have to be reckoned with. The power they possess can be valuable when resolving organizational problems. Informal leaders often recognize the advantage of cooperation and try to avoid conflict. Informal leaders have a strong influence with followers and other informal leaders. They know the opinions and attitudes of their group and represent them when communicating with management.

3. Thwart intergroup rivalry and win-lose situations. Establish achievable standards. Stress—through word and deed—the importance of cooperation and teamwork. Treat all subordinates fairly, without regard to their group, subgroup, or clique affiliation. Ask for input from all groups and, when appropriate, integrate it into the decision-making process.

4. Do not compel people to choose between you and their group. If a manager backs them into a corner, demanding an "either/or" choice, they will usually pick the group. Loyalty to and membership in a subgroup or clique is not necessarily a negative. Members can serve both the organization and the group if their goals are harmonious. People can be loyal and unopposed to a manager as long as that manager is fair, predictable, and loyal.

5. Adopt a mentor's mindset toward all groups, subgroups, and cliques. Team spirit and camaraderie are the trademarks of informal groups that must be cultivated. Be firm, play fair, and demand that subordinates reciprocate. Team players know the value of rules and fair play. Enlist meaningful participation from the groups and allow them to enhance their sense of worth.

6. Appeal to individual group members and to each group's sense of capability. All members have a need to be good at what they do and to know how they are viewed by others. Give people objectives that, when met, will instill a sense of accomplishment, confidence, and pride. By setting organizational objectives and helping subordinates set their own goals, administrators motivate employees to excel and find ways in which to build confidence and self-respect. Point out how poor performance hurts others and makes everyone's job much more difficult.

7. Use the traditional and not-so-traditional levers to encourage cooperation. Levers are tools used to influence people in specific situations. Management levers such as job assignments, overtime, primary action, merit pay, and sincere praise may be effective. Most of them are effective if they are used when subordinates trust and respect the manager. Trust and respect are by-products of the manager's knowledge, ability (technical, interpersonal, and group), skills, and demonstrated concern for the group and its members.

This is a tall order to fill. While it is very difficult to deal effectively with groups, subgroups, and cliques in the workplace, managing groups and group processes now consumes a lion's share of the police administrator's time.

Officer Bob Franklin joined his hometown police department 14 years ago. He was a high school graduate from a working-class family. His fellow officers came from similar backgrounds, and most of them had lived in town all of their lives. They shared many values, attitudes, perspectives, and dreams. The officers felt they belonged and were comfortable interacting with one another. They were a source of mutual support in times of stress.

Bob Franklin, like most of his peers, started out as an idealist. He wanted to be a supercop. His goals were to preserve the peace and to protect people and society from criminals. Bob Franklin placed a relatively high value on individual rights and due process of law. He really wanted to protect and serve.

After three years in the patrol division, Officer Franklin was reassigned. He was placed in an undercover drug enforcement group known as NARCON, which consisted of six investigators and one supervisor who formed a tightly knit work group. They had been together for nearly five years. Bob Franklin's goal—based on his need to belong—was to become a full-fledged member of the group.

NARCON could be described as a subculture within the police department. It consisted of a homogeneous and cohesive group of people who identified with each other and shared a unique set of values, attitudes, and beliefs related to their job. Based on continual face-to-face interaction among themselves and with criminals, they had become cynical reactionaries. They rewarded loyalty, secrecy, and conformity to group-shared expectations. Their highest priority was to get addicts and dealers off the street—at any cost. Members of NARCON were more than willing to lie, deny due process, and violate constitutional rights in order to accomplish their objectives. The end justified the means, as far as the members of NARCON were concerned. Although

Bob Franklin tried to remain neutral and adhere to his set of values, he needed recognition, support, and approval from the group. Subconsciously, he wanted to be a "stand-up guy" and was willing to sacrifice his ethical standards to achieve acceptance and status from the work group. Membership in the group became an end in itself. Abstract notions of right and wrong became irrelevant to him. Virtue consisted of loyalty to and protection of the group.

As Bob Franklin's partner was making a bust for narcotics possession with the intent to distribute, he accidentally shot and killed an unarmed suspect. The officer declared that the suspect was a dealer who deserved to die, and he placed a throw-down gun in the dead man's hand and told Franklin to call the NARCON supervisor. After the three police officers discussed the situation and agreed on a story, the supervisor summoned the department's shooting team.

Members of the shooting team interviewed Officer Franklin and his partner. Bob Franklin was asked to describe what had happened. After a moment's hesitation (during which he thought about his duty to protect and serve and his loyalty to the group), he lied. Even though he knew it was wrong and that he could be fired or prosecuted for providing false information, Bob Franklin told the shooting team member the story that had been concocted to cover his partner. Because the dead man was considered "a lowlife," no further action was taken. Bob Franklin had successfully negotiated a rite of passage. He could now claim to be a full-fledged member of NARCON.

*Using concepts related to groups and group dynamics, explain what happened in this situation. When does group cohesiveness cease to be positive and become pathological? What steps might you take, as a police administrator, to prevent this from occurring?*

## SUMMARY

Human beings are social animals who live, work, and find varying degrees of psychosocial validation in groups. Groups, as the basic unit of social organization, provide people with a cultural milieu in which to satisfy their personality needs as well as their social need for interaction with significant others. Each person develops a social identity, a unique sense of self, and an internalized set of normative controls through meaningful interaction with other people during the socialization process.

Most people belong to and participate in a wide variety of formal organizations and informal cliques. Some groups are task oriented and highly structured. Other groups are much more casual and coalesce around vague (loosely defined) common interests. These groups tend to emphasize the importance of meaningful interpersonal relationships as opposed to the task itself.

Each group develops a distinctive social orientation, or collective persona. New members are socialized to behave in certain ways. They are expected to learn and internalize appropriate roles, norms, values, and cultural perspectives. All members are rewarded for conformity to group-shared expectations and punished if they deviate. Consciousness of kind and internalized self-control reduce conflict and promote collaboration.

Work groups are mechanisms through which goal-oriented human beings learn relevant knowledge, technical skills, and job-related behaviors. Groups have life cycles just like all other living organisms. Group dynamics have an effect on individual performance. Group dynamics also influence the efficiency, effectiveness, and productivity of the organization. Whether these effects are good or bad will depend on member needs, the complexity of the task; the size, composition, norms, and cohesiveness of the group; and the prevailing reward structure.

Experienced police administrators accept that groups, subgroups, and cliques exist within the police department. They understand that groups are inevitable and ubiquitous. They also know that groups unleash powerful synergistic forces that can have either good or bad consequences, depending on the situation. The police administrator's principal job is to manage the department's human resources in such a way as to increase its overall efficiency, effectiveness, and productivity. In order to accomplish this objective, he or she must do the following: (1) accept the group phenomenon as a fact of organizational life; (2) identify and seek cooperation from informal group leaders; (3) prevent dysfunctional competition and the development of win-lose situations; (4) avoid forcing members to choose between allegiance to management and to their group; (5) adopt a coach's attitude toward groups, subgroups, and cliques within the organization; (6) motivate work groups by appealing to their sense of competence; and (7) utilize traditional and nontraditional methods to encourage individual effort as well as group collaboration.

In order to be successful in working with groups, police administrators must have knowledge, good interpersonal skills, and a positive attitude concerning subgroup participation in the organization's decision-making process. This will enable them to channel the energy, effort, and expertise of group members in such a way as to achieve the mission, goals, and objectives of the police department. Truly, knowledge is power and skill is the ability to translate knowledge into action.

## KEY TERMS

affiliation
closed group
cohesiveness
collective behavior
complexity
composition
conformity
culture
folkways
formal groups
friendship group
group dynamics
group growth cycle
group structure
groups and productivity
groupthink
imprinting
individual-related roles
informal groups
initiation
laws
maintenance-related roles

managing group dynamics
modeling
mores
need orientation
norms
open group
primary group
reinforcement
role set
sanctions
secondary group
self-control
self-esteem
size
social animal
social interaction
socialization process
structure and performance
taboos
task group
task-related roles
values

# DISCUSSION TOPICS AND QUESTIONS

1. List and discuss the distinct social functions that groups perform for their members.
2. What is a group?
3. What are the characteristics of formal work groups, and how do they differ from informal groups within law enforcement agencies?
4. How do social interactionists define a group, and why do they place such an emphasis on action?
5. What are the principal psychosocial needs that motivate human beings to join and remain active in informal as well as formal groups?
6. Name and discuss four categories commonly used to classify groups in terms of their function. Which are most often associated with the division of labor in a bureaucracy?
7. Identify and describe the primary structural components that are common to both formal and informal groups.
8. The police are referred to as a subculture. What is a subculture? What are values and norms, and how are they passed on to new members?
9. How does the prevailing reward structure influence individual performance and work-group productivity?
10. Identify, list, and discuss the characteristics of work groups that have a direct effect on individual performance and organizational productivity.
11. If a police administrator accepts the assumptions on which organizational humanism and social interactionism are founded, how would you expect him or her to approach his or her job in a law enforcement agency?

# FOR FURTHER READING

Steve Herbert, "Police Subculture Reconsidered," *Criminology*, Vol. 36 (1998), pp. 343–366.

The author sets forth his concept of normative order as a set of rules and practices oriented around a central value. He suggests that six such orders are crucial to policing: law, bureaucratic control, adventure/machismo, safety, competence, and morality. In his study of the Los Angeles Police Department, he found that aggressiveness and officer safety had long been dominant cultural elements. He suggests that the police subculture can be analyzed by determining which normative orders shape their daily practices. He notes that police organizations are sites of political struggles over how to define different normative orders.

L. Karakowsky and K. McBey, "Do My Contributions Matter? The Influence of Imputed Expertise on Member Involvement and Self-Evaluations in the Work Group," *Group and Organization Management*, Vol. 26 (2001), pp. 70–92.

This article addresses the diversity of expertise in a work team as a critical factor in maximizing group performance. The authors assess sources of influence on group membership perceptions regarding the value of their input to the group and on the level of membership involvement in group activity. They find striking evidence that imputed expertise can clearly affect group member perception and behavior.

Gregory Moorhead, Christopher P. Neck, and Mindy S. West, "The Tendency Toward Defective Decision Making Within Self-Managed Teams: The Relevance of Groupthink for the 21st Century," *Organizational Behavior and Human Decision Processes*, Vol. 7 (1998), pp. 327–351.

It is the position of the authors that groupthink theory has continuing relevance to organizations because of the organizational trend toward self-managing teams. They review the groupthink antecedents (group cohesiveness, structural faults of the organization, and provocative situational context) as key characteristics of groups. Using the foundational approach, they review the variables that tend to give rise to groupthink in self-managed teams. Additionally, they discuss the implications for the prevention of groupthink.

Fran Rees, *How to Lead Work Teams: Facilitation Skills*, 2nd ed. (San Francisco: Jossey-Bass, 2001), pp. 1–240.

The author takes the reader, step by step, through an L.E.A.D. model, showing how one can develop facilitation skills that will help make one an outstanding leader, motivator, and facilitator. She presents methods of articulating group goals and purposes and talks about how to encourage thoughtful discussion (including disagreement), brainstorming, and active listening. She recommends techniques for encouraging team members to communicate in ways that enhance teamwork and achieve results. She reviews means of obtaining consensus by such techniques as summarizing and documenting.

## NOTES

1. Jim L. Munro, *Administrative Behavior and Police Organization* (Cincinnati: Anderson, 1997), pp. 89–93.

2. John R. Schermerhorn, James G. Hunt, and Richard N. Osborn, *Managing Organizational Behavior*, 8th ed. (New York: Wiley, 2002), pp. 199–201.

3. Elliott Aronson, *The Social Animal* (San Francisco: Freeman, 1976), pp. 165–166.

4. Herbert J. Chruden and Arthur W. Sherman, Jr., *Personnel Management*, 3rd ed. (Cincinnati: South-Western, 1976), pp. 8–21.

5. Richard N. Holden, *Modern Police Management*, 2nd ed. (Englewood Cliffs, NJ: Prentice Hall, 1994), pp. 37–45.

6. Robert Albanese, *Management* (Cincinnati: South-Western, 1988), pp. 518–529.

7. Ronald W. Smith and Frederick W. Preston, *Sociology: An Introduction* (New York: St. Martin's, 1982).

8. Richard W. Plunkett, *Supervision: The Direction of People at Work*, 9th ed. (Boston: Allyn & Bacon, 2000), pp. 321–333.

9. Peter I. Rose, *The Study of Society: An Integrated Anthology* (New York: Random House, 1977).

10. Rensis Likert, *Organizational Theory* (New York: McGraw-Hill, 1961), pp. 21–24.

11. Schermerhorn, Hunt, and Osborn, *Managing Organizational Behavior*, pp. 213–214.

12. David H. Holt, *Management: Principles and Practices*, 3rd ed. (Englewood Cliffs, NJ: Prentice Hall, 1993), p. 69.

13. Plunkett, *Supervision: The Direction of People at Work*.

14. Robert M. Fulmer, *Supervision: Principles of Professional Management* (New York: Macmillan, 1982), pp. 338–341.

15. Holt, *Management: Principles and Practices*.

16. Schermerhorn, Hunt, and Osborn, *Managing Organizational Behavior*.

17. Plunkett, *Supervision: The Direction of People at Work*, pp. 213–214.

18. Darrel Ray and Howard Bronstein, *Teaming Up: Making the Transition to a Self-Directed, Team Based Organization* (New York: McGraw-Hill, 1955), p. 80.

19. Thomas A. Kayser, *Mining Group Gold: How to Cash in on the Collaborative Brain Power of a Group* (El Segundo, CA: Serif Publishing, 2001), p. 1.

20. H. Joseph Reitz, *Managing* (Glenview, IL: Scott, Foresman, 1985).

21. Harry W. More, W. Fred Wegener, and Larry Miller, *Effective Police Supervision*, 4th ed. (Cincinnati: Anderson, 2003), p. 211.

22. Dalton Melville, *Men Who Manage: Fusions of Feelings and Theory in Administration* (Cincinnati: Anderson, 1959), pp. 3–12.

23. John Gastil, *Democracy in Small Groups: Participation, Decision Making, and Communications* (Philadelphia: New Society Publishers, 1993), pp. 222–231.

24. Plunkett, *Supervision: The Direction of People at Work*, p. 309.

25. Reitz, *Managing*.

26. Albanese, *Managing: Toward Accountability for Performance*, pp. 520–522.

27. Fulmer, *The New Management*.

28. Smith and Preston, *Sociology: An Introduction*.

29. Reitz, *Behavior in Organizations*.

30. Paul Whisenand and George Rush, *Supervising Police Personnel: Back to Basics* (Englewood Cliffs, NJ: Prentice Hall, 1988), p. 255.

31. Leonard R. Sayles, *Research in Industrial Human Relations* (New York: Harper & Row, 1957).

32. Whisenand and Rush, *Supervising Police Personnel: Back to Basics*.

33. Fulmer, *Supervision: Principles of Professional Management*, p. 93.

34. K.J. Benne and P. Sheats, "Functional Roles of Group Members," *Journal of Social Issues*, Vol. 4 (1959).

35. Fran Rees, *How to Lead Work Teams: Facilitation Skills* (San Francisco: Jossey-Bass, 2001), pp. 13–87.

36. Reitz, *Behavior in Organizations*.

37. Dean J. Champion, *The Sociology of Organizations* (New York: McGraw-Hill, 1976), pp. 119–120.

38. Ely Chinoy and John P. Hewitt, *Sociological Perspective* (New York: Random House, 1975).

39. Smith and Preston, *Sociology: An Introduction*.

40. Charles Zastrow and Lee Bowker, *Social Problems: Issues and Solutions* (Chicago: Nelson-Hall, 1984).

41. Whisenand and Rush, *Supervising Police Personnel: Back to Basics*, p. 93.

42. Albanese, *Managing: Toward Accountability for Performance*, pp. 520–521.

43. Morris Massey, *The People Puzzle: Understanding Yourself and Others* (Reston, VA: Reston Publishing, 1979), pp. 168–187.

44. Chinoy and Hewitt, *Sociological Perspectives*.

45. Schermerhorn, Hunt, and Osborn, *Managing Organizational Behavior*, pp. 444–446.

46. Smith and Preston, *Sociology: An Introduction*.

47. Jerome H. Skolnick and Thomas J. Gray, *Police in America* (Boston: Little, Brown, 1975).

48. Steve Herbert, "Police Subculture Reconsidered," *Criminology*, Vol. 36 (1998), pp. 343–369.

49. Edward A. Thibault, Lawrence M. Lynch, and R. Bruce McBride, *Proactive Police Management*, 5th ed. (Upper Saddle River, NJ: Prentice Hall, 2001), p. 241.

50. Geoffrey P. Alpert and Rodger G. Dunham, *Policing Urban America* (Prospect Heights, IL: Waveland Press, 1997).

51. Broderick, *Police in a Time of Change*.

52. Thibault, Lynch, and McBride, *Proactive Police Management*.

53. Muzafer Sheriff and Carolyn W. Sheriff, *An Outline of Social Psychology* (New York: Harper & Row, 1956).

54. Emile Durkheim, *Suicide* (New York: The Free Press, 1951).

55. Fulmer, *The New Management*.

56. J.S. Heinen and E. Jacobsen, "A Model of Task Group Development in Complex Organizations and a Strategy for Implementation," *Academy of Management Review*, Vol. 1 (1976).

57. Andrew J. Dubrin, *The Complete Idiot's Guide to Leadership* (New York: Alpha Books, 1998), p. 152.

58. Robert A. Sutermeister, *People and Productivity*, 3rd ed. (New York: McGraw-Hill, 1976), p. 243.

59. Robert A. Baron and Jerald Greenberg, *Behavior in Organizations: Understanding and Managing the Human Side of Work*, 3rd ed. (Boston: Allyn & Bacon, 1989), pp. 260–265.

60. Steve Alper, "Interdependence and Controversy in Group Decision Making: Antecedents to Effective Self-Managing Teams," *Organizational Behavior and Human Decision Processes*, Vol. 74 (1) (1989), pp. 33–52.

61. Dorwin Cartwright and Ronald Lippit, "Group Dynamics and the Individual," in Robert A. Sutermeister, ed. *People and Productivity* (New York: McGraw-Hill, 1976), pp. 215–217.

62. D.W. Johnson, et al., "Effects of Co-operative, Competitive and Individualistic Goal Structure of Achievement," *Psychological Bulletin*, Vol. 89 (1981).

63. William C. Schutz, *FIRO: A Three-Dimensional Theory of Interpersonal Behavior* (New York: Rinehart, 1958).

64. Gary Dessler, *Management Fundamentals: Modern Principles and Practices*, 4th ed. (Reston, VA: Reston Publishing, 1985), pp. 264–266.

65. Schermerhorn, Hunt, and Osborn, *Managing Organizational Behavior*, pp. 215–216.

66. Jerome H. Skolnick and Thomas C. Gray, *Police in America* (Boston: Little, Brown, 1975), pp. 12–13.

67. Sam S. Souryal, *Police Administration and Management* (St. Paul: West, 1997), pp. 39–51.

68. Munro, *Administrative Behavior and Police Organization*, pp. 92–101.

69. Albanese, *Managing: Toward Accountability for Performance*.

70. Mark Baker, *Cops* (New York: Pocket Books, 1985), pp. 3–31.

71. Harry W. More, *Special Topics in Policing*, 2nd ed. (Cincinnati: Anderson, 1998), pp. 67–68.

72. J.M. Ivancevich, A.D. Szilagyi, and M.J. Wallace, *Organizational Behavior and Performance* (Santa Monica, CA: Goodyear, 1977).

73. Whisenand and Rush, *Supervising Police Personnel: Back to Basics*.

74. Marlene E. Turner and Anthony R. Pratkanis, "Twenty-Five Years of Groupthink Theory and Research: Lessons from the Evaluation of a Theory," *Organizational Behavior and Human Decision Processes*, Vol. 73 (2/3) (1998), pp. 105–115.

75. Gregory Moorhead, Christopher P. Neck, and Mindy S. West, "The Tendency Toward Defective Decision Making Within Self-Managing Teams: The Relevance of Groupthink for the 21st Century,"

*Organizational Behavior and Human Decision Processes,* Vol. 73 (2/3) (1998), pp. 327–351.

76. Pratkanis and Pratkanis, "Twenty-Five Years of Groupthink Theory and Research." and I.L. Janis, "Groupthink Among Policy Makers," in G.M. Kern and L.H. Rappoport, eds. *Varieties of Psychhistory* (New York: Springer, 1976).

77. V.A. Leonard and Harry W. More, *Police Organization and Management*, 9th ed. (New York: Foundation Press, 2000), pp. 307–308.

78. Holt, *Management: Principles and Practices.*

79. Plunkett, *Supervision: The Direction of People at Work*, pp. 329–330.

# —8—

# POWER

## Its Nature and Use

A sentence quoted extensively in newspapers, magazines, journals, and police training programs is *Power corrupts, and absolute power corrupts absolutely.* The implication is that a person who has an excess of power will use it unwisely.[1] The concern that police managers have too much power is definitely invalid, at least in today's organizations, where in many instances they do not have the power they need in order to function effectively.

The reality is that managers' power is becoming increasingly circumscribed by legal and social constraints. Laws and regulations such as the Civil Rights Act, the Age Discrimination in Employment Act, the Equal Employment Opportunity Act, and rulings by federal courts have resulted in restrictions and limited the power base of police managers.[2]

Managerial power is further reduced by the pressure exerted by interest groups, citizens, city managers or mayors, city councils or boards of supervisors, state legislatures, civic groups, and unions.[3] All these elements combine at different times to limit or restrict the power exercised by police managers. An illustration of this is officer membership in unions or associations, coupled with legislation mandating memorandums of agreement/understanding between police departments and unions.[4]

In addition, the personality of the manager and the characteristics of the organization itself act as modifiers of power. Some police managers are viewed as power hungry; the behavior of others suggests that they do not like to exercise power. This dichotomy is especially apparent in matters involving

Lt. Fred Weaver currently commands the Youth Services Bureau in a medium-sized police department in a city that is primarily a bedroom community, with a large commercial section and no industry. There are a large number of young citizens in the community; thus it is especially important for the police department to emphasize the prevention of crime. This is done through a Police Athletic League that sponsors various sports activities throughout the year.

Lt. Weaver attended the local university, earning a degree in psychology. He was very active in campus activities and earned letters in both baseball and track. As a high school student, he joined a police-sponsored Explorer Scout unit and played baseball in the Police Athletic League. He continued these activities as a college student. He joined the police department after graduation.

He then attended the regional police academy and graduated first in his class. Weaver's first assignment was to patrol, where he served for three years with distinction. In his fourth year of service, he was promoted to sergeant and assigned to the Youth Services Bureau, where he supervised the Explorer Scout unit and coached the baseball team.

In Weaver's seventh year of service he was promoted to lieutenant and became the commander of the Youth Services Bureau. During his three years assigned to the bureau, he has become indispensable

as a fund-raiser. He is an excellent speaker and appears before community groups frequently. Under his leadership the bureau's influence has extended greatly, and many public officials as well as important citizens in the community view Lt. Weaver as the real spokesperson of the department.

During the last three years, Lt. Weaver has quadrupled the unit's income from outside sources and has introduced an annual circus and a youth Olympics program. Both these programs were instant successes and clearly enhanced the reputation of the bureau.

The chief of police is beginning to sense that he has lost control of the bureau and that it is almost becoming an independent police unit. It is a tenuous situation. The chief feels that Lt. Weaver is becoming a threat to his position and is attempting to gain all the power he can.

Lt. Weaver's point of view is that he is only trying to do his job, not searching for power, and that he simply makes decisions to ensure that the bureau stays the primary crime-prevention unit in the community.

*If you were the chief, how would you deal with the potential problem? Could Lt. Weaver have done things differently to avoid being perceived as a power threat? What types of power do both leaders have?*

---

discipline. Some managers will go out of their way to avoid confronting deviant organizational behavior, while others relish the prospects of conflict.

Structurally, the bureaucratic nature of a police organization is such that power is distributed from top to bottom. Power follows the hierarchy of the police organizational structure—the higher the rank, the greater the amount of power.[5]

## DEFINITIONS OF POWER

Power is a concept with negative connotations. Managers who have power deny it. Power seekers do everything possible to camouflage their efforts. Lastly, those who are adept at securing power are reluctant to discuss how they acquired it.[6] From a negative perspective, power implies a master/slave relationship or at the very least, a superior/subordinate relationship. McClelland defines two types of power—dominating and empowering.[7]

1. *Dominating power* seeks to keep individuals weak and dependent on the leader.
2. *Empowering power* aims to promote individuals and build commitment to the organization and its goals.

Empowering power is used for positive ends and is developed through group decision-making. Managers thus face the difficult job of balancing these conflicting types of power in the pursuit of organizational goals.

Researchers who have analyzed the concept of power have defined it in different ways. The following definitions demonstrate the variability:

1. Power is the capacity to translate intention into reality and sustain it. Leadership is the wise use of this power. Vision is the commodity of leaders, and power is their currency.[8]
2. Power is the absolute capacity of an individual agent to influence the behavior or attitudes of one or more designated target persons at a given point in time.[9]
3. Power is to get an individual or group to do something—to get the person or group to change in some way. The individual who possesses power has the ability to manipulate or change others.[10]

Each of these definitions describes either the ability or the capacity to control the behavior of an individual or a group in order to attain some goal. The negative connotations of power can be dealt with best by defining it as *the ability, the vigor, and the strength to influence others and to control one's own destiny.*[11] This definition accepts the premise that everyone in an organization possesses some power giving him or her the capacity to choose between alternatives. In this context, power is viewed as the ability to adapt to a situation, negotiate alternatives, plan for events, or assume responsibility.[12] Needless to say, not everyone in an organization has equal power, and certainly not everyone has the power needed to completely control his or her future. Implicit in the definition is a degree of dependency between members of an organization, as well as some discretion for the individual when responding to efforts to influence his or her behavior.

Power is a paradox. It can be used to achieve organizational goals, group objectives, and individual goals, or it can be used to thwart goal attainment. In recent years a number of pertinent books have received a great deal of attention: *The West Point Way of Leadership;*[13] *Managing with Power;*[14] *Power: How to Get It and How to Use It;*[15] and *Looking Out for Number One.*[16] These texts place a great deal of emphasis on the acquisition of power and, in some instances, its use for personal gain.

It is clear that managerial power, when used correctly, generally involves bringing together resources to accomplish something. Effective managers understand the uses, limitations, sources, and characteristics of power. If power is used to make employees totally dependent, then it is being used ineffectively. If it is used sparingly or in a helping mode, it is more apt to be effective.

As seen in Table 8–1, managers use different techniques to make employees dependent:[17]

1. *The Bureaucrat.* This type of police manager worships the manual. There is a place for everything and everything must be in its place. Exceptions are few and far between. An officer must go by the book. To deviate is to court disaster. Officers being supervised are made dependent and required to conform to every rule and regulation. This type of boss can cite departmental policies in their entirety.

**Table 8–1    Managerial Style and Dependency**

| | |
|---|---|
| 1. The Bureaucrat | 4. The Incompetent |
| 2. The Controller | 5. The Realist |
| 3. The Competitor | |

*Source:* Mardy Grothe and Peter Wylie, *Problem Bosses: Who They Are and How to Deal with Them* (New York: Facts on File, 1987).

2. *The Controller.* This type of police manager is most likely to have had military experience; the tough drill sergeant approach to management typifies the working relationship between the manager and subordinates. Subordinates are never allowed to question the authority of such a manager; dependency must be absolute. The managerial style is autocratic, authoritarian, and in some instances, tyrannical.

3. *The Competitor.* This kind of boss is selective when developing dependency relationships. His or her driving aim is to rise to the top as fast as possible; dependency is used as a tool to achieve promotion and positions of influence. Competitors are the movers and shakers in any organization, and while they have the capacity to be inspirational leaders, they only show that side to their advantage. They are competitive and tend to be risk takers, but when threatened, they can become pushy and overwhelming.

4. *The Incompetent.* Incompetents are always looking for someone who can help them solve a problem, and they become very adept at blaming others for their inadequacies. They clearly are operating at a level beyond their capabilities. This category also includes managers who have become stymied and will never move beyond their present position. They know they are not going anywhere, and everyone else in the organization knows it too. They become negative and preoccupied with how they have been treated unfairly. In terms of dependency they are neutral.

5. *The Realist.* Managers in this category limit employee dependency to emergencies, unusual occurrences, or situations where someone has to be trained in order to achieve an organizational goal. When the realist delegates work, it includes the authority needed to accomplish the task. This leader makes every effort to give each employee a degree of control over his or her own destiny. Realists are risk takers and understand that errors and mistakes are inevitable if employees are allowed to grow and become competent.

Different types of managers, then, use power for different reasons, but to some degree managers are continually using power as a means of influencing others. Influence apparently is the behavioral response to the application of power.[18] When people are convinced to change their behavior, to change their opinion, to complete a certain act or activity, or to support a different position, then a manager can be said to have exerted influence over a follower, a peer, or a superior.

# THE POWER BASE

Power has meaning not only to the individual but also to groups and organizations. At some time or another everyone has heard an individual referred to as powerful, and it is always someone who can influence behavior. Decisions are made, goals attained, or changes instituted. Power involves the interaction between two individuals. This personal interaction is described as consisting of five types of power: reward power, coercive power, legitimate power, referent power, and expert power (see Figure 8–1).[19]

**Reward Power**    Rewarding an employee for performance is one of the best ways a manager can influence behavior. For example, a manager can use pay and promotions to encourage acceptable behavior. In the few police departments that have merit programs, officers can be rewarded monetarily for engaging in acceptable behavior. This has proven to be an excellent tool for motivating employees when they have striven for the recognition accompanying an increase. In other departments the creation of levels for police officers such as Officer I, Officer II, and Officer III (some departments have a Senior Officer position) has provided police managers at every level with another tool useful in the rewards process. Hopefully, other police departments will adopt this system because law enforcement has been constrained for years by the lock-step promotion system wherein an officer receives four salary increments and then remains at the same pay level (other than living raises) until promoted.

Most police officers pursue promotions actively and find them to be one of the best ways, if not the best way, to obtain status and receive recognition, both within the organization and in the greater community. Normally a sergeant can recommend someone for promotion, but the chief takes the action.

In recent years, the reward power of police chief executive officers has extended as typical promotion lists have expanded and chiefs have been given greater latitude in the selection process. For many years a chief was required to select from the top three candidates for promotion, but in recent years this has been increased in many agencies to the top eight candidates.

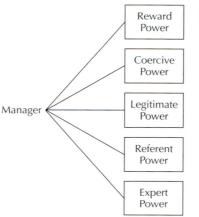

**Figure 8–1**
The Power Base of the Manager.

As police departments have grown in size, the reward power of the chief executive officer has been diluted. It has become increasingly necessary for the chief to rely on recommendations from others. This is in sharp contrast to the situation in smaller police departments, where the chief is personally acquainted with every officer being considered for promotion—except for instances where lateral transfers from other organizations are also being considered.

In law enforcement, intrinsic rewards such as special assignments, praise, and awards have a great deal of importance. Many officers can be motivated because of their desire to be recognized and accepted as productive members of the organization. Managers at various levels within the organization can satisfy such desires by assigning officers to special units such as K-9 or SWAT. In most instances, officers find assignment to these units desirable. In some departments, the same holds true for assignment to crime prevention, traffic (motorcycle), and investigations.

Police managers have a special obligation to acknowledge exemplary action, which can range from apprehending an offender to solving a crime or providing assistance to someone in need. Most agencies have a written policy specifying how police managers will take official notice when an officer deserves commendation. Commendations can be classified as follows:[20]

1. Class A: Outstanding, exceptional work beyond the call of duty.
2. Class B: Meritorious police work, but not outstanding.
3. Class C: Above-average police work of a routine nature.
4. Class D: Ordinary police work of a routine nature, but deserving official notice.
5. Class E: Not requiring official notice.

There are a number of other intrinsic rewards of importance to officers, including a wide range of managerial actions (see Table 8–2). Managers should strive to encourage participation whenever possible.

Thus, power has to be shared. Ways to share power include delegating authority commensurate with responsibility. There is considerable evidence that most people gain satisfaction from exercising power.[21] It is important to remember that some officers are not ready to exercise additional organizational power because they cannot accept the responsibility. Managers are advised to limit delegations to those who potentially can benefit, then monitor their performance, and when necessary teach the employee how to exercise the newly acquired power to support departmental goals.

Whenever possible, a manager should strive for consensus during the decision-making process as a means of increasing mutual trust. The goal is to

Table 8–2 **The Manager's Reward Powers**

| | |
|---|---|
| Promotion | Commendations |
| Increases in pay | Establishing a trusting relationship |
| Special assignments | Participation |
| Additional responsibility | Two-way communications |
| Praise | |

*Source:* James M. Jenks and John M. Kelly, *Don't Do, Delegate!* (New York: Ballantine, 1985).

create an atmosphere whereby subordinates respond to this type of reward by becoming more creative, demonstrating a higher degree of initiative, and exhibiting a greater dedication to the department; this dedication makes for a better operating department. This does not mean that a police manager abandons a leadership position, but the leadership style is facilitative, not repressive. When the situation demands, a police manager must still respond to the situation (especially during emergencies), and orders must be issued and followed without any thought of participation or consensus.

## Coercive Power

Coercive power is at the other end of the continuum from reward power. It is based on fear of punishment and the sanctions police managers can utilize to control the behavior of subordinates. Punishment can take many forms, including suspension, demotion, official reprimand, and more subtle sanctions such as giving an officer an undesirable assignment.

The extreme sanction is termination. Even for a first offense, many departments will dismiss an officer for the following:

1. Soliciting, accepting, or offering a bribe.
2. Being involved in theft of cash or city property.
3. Falsifying city records.
4. Destroying city records.
5. Falsifying time reports, mileage reports, or expense accounts.
6. Deliberately withholding information (relating to work) from supervisors.

In many police departments (because of the 24-hour orientation), the night shift is imposed on officers to punish them or to put them where they are out of sight and mind. The same strategy transfers employees to undesirable locations. For example, an officer can be disciplined by being assigned to a station that is many miles from his or her home and thus requires a long commute.

Not every assignment in law enforcement is sought after. Some officers like to work traffic and others do not. Others enjoy the action of working a crime beat, whereas still others would rather do anything but this task. In most instances a police manager, especially the supervisory manager, will know what an officer likes and dislikes and can use this knowledge for the purpose of punishment.

Overly strict supervision is another way to administer punishment. A recalcitrant officer can have incident reports returned repeatedly for rewriting. Rules and regulations can be enforced down to the crossed *t* or dotted *i*. Every deviation can be written up and documented. Another punishment technique utilized by first-line supervisors is excessive monitoring of the procedures and techniques utilized when stopping someone for a traffic violation. In most instances, the supervisor can find reasons to write a report—for example, the police vehicle was parked incorrectly, the officer's approach to the car was wrong, the radio was not used properly, or the officer detained the offender too long (see Table 8–3).

All this harassment can result in a punishing working environment. The repeated application of negative sanctions can result (at its extreme) in a decision by an officer to quit—or in some instances, to file a grievance against the supervisor. In other cases, an officer can respond to the sanctions by treading water, that is, doing just enough to get by.

Table 8–4 lists forms of behavior considered improper in relation to supervisors, fellow employees, and the public. Potential corrective actions are also

## Table 8–3  Manager's Coercive Powers

| | |
|---|---|
| Termination | Transfer |
| Suspension | Relocation |
| Official reprimand | Strict supervision |
| Undesirable job assignment | Enforcement of rules and regulations |

## Table 8–4  Improper Behavior in Relations with Supervisors, Fellow Employees, or the Public and Potential Corrective Actions

| Offense | First Offense | Second Offense | Third Offense |
|---|---|---|---|
| a. Flagrant refusal to perform reasonable work assignments or cooperate with supervisors or management in the performance of duties (insubordination). | 1 to 6 days suspension | Dismissal | |
| b. Failure to cooperate with or using abusive language toward other employees or the public. | Oral warning or written notice | Written notice to 5 days suspension | 6 days suspension to dismissal |
| c. Unnecessarily disrupting the work of other employees. | Oral warning or written notice | Written notice to 5 days suspension | 6 days suspension to dismissal |
| d. Using threats or attempting to harm another employee or the public. | 6 days suspension to dismissal | Dismissal | |
| e. Making false, vicious, or malicious statements about any employee or city government or department management. | Oral warning to 30 days suspension | 6 days suspension to dismissal | Dismissal |
| f. Unauthorized possession of dangerous weapons, such as firearms or knives, on city or department property. | 30 days suspension to dismissal | 6 days suspension to dismissal | |
| g. Unauthorized use of dangerous weapons, such as firearms, knives, or tools, that could result or results in harm to another employee or the public. | 30 days suspension to dismissal | Dismissal | |
| h. Actions on the job intended to destroy property or to inflict bodily injury (whether or not the destruction or injury actually occurs). | Written notice to dismissal | 10 days suspension to dismissal | Dismissal |
| i. Creating unsanitary conditions. | Oral warning to 5 days suspension | 6–10 days suspension to dismissal | Dismissal |

*Source:* Harry W. More and O. R. Shipley, *Police Policy Manual—Personnel* (Springfield, IL: Charles C Thomas, 1987). Reprinted with permission.

given. In recent years the coercive power of police managers has been reduced because of the influence of police unions and associations.

**Legitimate Power**  Legitimate power is associated with one's position, role, and status in the organization. The incumbent possesses legitimate power as long as assigned to an office or position, and that power is transferred when another individual assumes the position. In law enforcement, rank is closely associated with legitimate power. Power generally increases with each higher rank. For example, a chief executive officer position will usually be described as follows: "The Chief of Police is the chief executive officer of the department and the departmental authority on all matters of policy, operations, and discipline. The chief exercises all lawful powers of the office and issues such lawful orders as are necessary to assure the effective performance of the department."[22]

In law enforcement, the boss has the right to command. The authority identifying that right is usually quite specific, as the following police directive shows:[23]

> *Compliance with Lawful Orders.* The department is an organization with a clearly defined hierarchy of authority. This is necessary because unquestioned obedience of a superior's lawful command is essential for the safe and prompt performance of law enforcement operations. The most desirable means of obtained compliance are recognition and reward of proper performance, and the encouragement of a willingness to serve. However, negative discipline is necessary where there is a willful disregard of lawful orders, commands, or directives.

This directive clearly illustrates that a superior has accompanying reward and coercive powers. Unity of command is also stressed and there is a finite chain of command. All employees are aware of their relative positions in the organization, what tasks they are immediately responsible for, and to whom they are accountable.

In law enforcement, departmental directives will also spell out command responsibilities for handling unusual occurrences. A field commander or the assistant senior officer will have the authority to direct the operation and will be held responsible. A senior commanding officer may make suggestions, but supervision is left up to the field commander. Unless properly relieved, senior command officers will assume command of an unusual occurrence; it is normal for a police department to have a policy specifying that this officer will be held accountable for unfavorable developments even if he or she has chosen not to take command. For example, at a bombing scene departmental policy will specifically state what is the responsibility of the first officer at the scene and what is required of the responding field commander. Procedures for collecting evidence will be specified, and experts will be identified who can assist in the search of the crime scene.

**Referent Power**  Referent power is difficult to define because it is intangible. It is related to the ability of a manager to influence the behavior of subordinates because they identify with him or her. It can be the result of the manager's intelligence or some aspect of his or her personality that subordinates like or admire. When a leader's personal characteristics are seen as exceptional in the eyes of followers, the leader is usually described as charismatic.

Charisma is defined as a personal magic of leadership arousing special loyalty or enthusiasm for a public figure. It is usually used to describe a political leader such as John Kennedy or a military commander such as George Patton. In law enforcement, J. Edgar Hoover at the federal level and O. W. Wilson, Bill Parker, William Bratton, and August Vollmer at the local level are examples of charismatic leaders who had large numbers of supporters.

If a manager is perceived as charismatic, it seems that everything falls nicely into place. Values and attitudes become positive and tasks are accomplished with ease. Such a leader is found to be unusually persuasive and has a vision of the future that subordinates feel is attainable and attractive.[24]

A manager with whom employees identify easily has referent power. A key element of this type of power is trust. When an officer trusts a police manager, it enhances the working relationship. Trust is tied to honesty and dependability. Trust will be lost if followers discover that a leader has exploited or manipulated them in pursuit of self-interest.[25] Trust is a positive variable engendering acceptance and a real desire to follow. When trust is present, the manager is in a position to influence outcomes.

## Expert Power

When managers are able to control the behavior of others because of their knowledge, experience, or judgment, they are said to have expert power. This special information might have been acquired over an extended period of time or as a consequence of special training, but in every instance such expertise provides a base for obtaining subordinate compliance.

When managers have relevant, useful, and important information, they are in a position to exert influence extending beyond their other powers. In recent years, law enforcement agencies have increasingly relied on the expertise of professionals, especially in the areas of law and psychology. It is quite common to find police departments employing police legal advisers and police psychologists.

In addition, as police departments have grown in size, supervisors have developed expertise in numerous areas, including the investigation of auto theft, bunco, forgery, sex crimes, and computer crimes. In other instances managers have been placed in staff positions where they have developed

Washington Police Chief Charles Ramsey meets reporters in Washington to discuss a murder investigation.

Associated Press

unique skills in planning, budgeting, or doing other administrative tasks, giving them additional power.

Expert power (if it is to be of benefit to a department) should not be autocratic, but a process of balancing technical competence and allowing subordinates, superiors, and peers to achieve goals and objectives. We anticipate that technical knowledge will become increasingly important. Experts will have to learn how to manage the complexities of interdependent relationships they encounter if the organization is to be responsive and adapt to changing conditions.[26] Evidence of the five bases of power are presented in Table 8–5.

## POWER SOURCES

An effective manager influences the behavior of others in the work environment. There are distinctions in the five bases of power listed above. Expert and referent power bases are more informal in nature. Legitimate, reward, and coercive power bases are more formal. The extent to which a manager uses one power base can definitely modify power from another base. Unquestionably, when a manager is adept at rewarding, employees respond to a greater extent and prove to be more supportive. On the other hand, when a manager uses coercive power as a consistent managerial style, it can create resentment among subordinates.[27]

The interaction between power sources varies considerably and is modified by how subordinates perceive a manager, whether or not the unit is important to the organization, and whether subordinates are dependent. Legitimate power provides a manager with a supporting base for the utilization of reward or coercive power. This supporting base can be altered. For example, in a large police department, the chief of police could transfer a deputy chief from a position as head of investigations to an administrative position. This is really a disciplinary transfer: by changing the deputy chief's functional location, the chief would be reducing the deputy chief's legitimate power, reward power, and coercive power.

Table 8–5  **Signs of the Five Bases of Power**

If you answer "Yes" to the following questions, then the person has that base of power.

- The person can make things difficult for people, and you want to avoid getting him or her angry. (*Coercive Power*)
- The person is able to give special benefits or rewards to people, and you find it advantageous to trade favors with him or her. (*Reward Power*)
- The person has the right, considering his or her position and your job responsibilities, to expect you to comply with legitimate requests. (*Legitimate Power*)
- The person has the experience and knowledge to earn your respect, and you defer to his or her judgment in some matters. (*Expert Power*)
- You like the person and enjoy doing things for him or her. (*Referent Power*)

*Source:* Stephen P. Robbins, *Essentials of Organizational Behavior,* 7th ed, (Upper Saddle River, NJ: Prentice Hall, 2003), p. 155.

Lt. Luis Gonzales has been a member of the Crater Police Department for 11 years and a lieutenant for 2 years. Crater has a population of 83,000 and is part of a metropolitan area in the northwestern United States. When still a sergeant, Gonzales was assigned to the Support Services Bureau and became involved in the electronic automation of the department.

Lt. Gonzales attended City University where he majored in business administration and minored in computer sciences. This academic preparation, coupled with his intense interest in computers, served as a base of knowledge when the department decided to automate its communications and records center.

Gonzales first surveyed other police departments to determine what computer-aided dispatching systems they used. In addition, he visited state and federal agencies to obtain the latest information on computer applications to law enforcement. Then he wrote a proposal, obtained internal approval for it, and submitted it to various computer vendors.

Once the city selected a vendor, Lt. Gonzales was assigned to work full-time monitoring the installation of the computer-aided dispatch system. This process took nine months; when the system was put online, it proved to be most effective. Problems were solved with dispatch. The chief of police then assigned Lt. Gonzales to head a team to computerize the records system.

With this new assignment, Lt. Gonzales became a real expert in the application of computers to law enforcement. Other departments seek his advice, because he has proven to be very skillful. He runs hands-on training programs for the department, receiving enthusiastic acclaim from all the attendees.

The investigative unit now is capable of accessing computerized criminal records, case files, and field interrogation reports. Patrol units find that their response time for service calls has been reduced drastically, and the immediate access to department records enhances their ability to have the information they need.

Lt. Gonzales is the leading department expert on computers. Other managers in the department have limited computer experience, so they have had to turn to Lt. Gonzales for help. As other departments call on him, his reputation is enhanced and he spends more time away from the department. In every instance, the other departments reimburse the city for Lt. Gonzales's expenses.

During the last two years Lt. Gonzales has become a real power within the department. It seems that everyone relies on him. Since Lt. Gonzales has a unique expertise, there is a great deal of resentment. Part of it can be attributed to a forthcoming promotional examination for captain at the end of the year. Four other eligible lieutenants feel Lt. Gonzales has the inside track because of his expert power.

*The conflict is apparent and known to everyone in the department. Lt. Gonzales is at a loss about what to do. He is perplexed by the whole problem and is considering discussing it with the chief. If you were Lt. Gonzales, how would you deal with this problem? What would you tell the chief? Would you ask to be assigned to another position?*

**Positional Power**

The formal position a police manager holds in an organization provides him or her with positional power. In police organizations, positional power is a matter of the hierarchical relationships identified by the organizational chart. There is a definite division of labor identifying lines of control.

The departmental manual specifically identifies the duties of members of the organization and spells out the legal basis by citing statutes and ordinances. Police departments are especially concerned with command responsibility and specify that police managers will be responsible and accountable for each aspect of their command. A commanding officer is required to work within policy guidelines and legal constraints when coordinating and directing subordinates.

Positional power is further reinforced by policies requiring police managers to enforce department rules and regulations and ensure compliance with department policies and procedures. Because of the potential negative impact of

## Table 8–6  **Notification of Chief of Police**

It is the policy of the police department that the chief of police be notified (by the watch as soon as is practical) concerning any of the following incidents or situations:

1. Any incident where a police officer is injured to the extent it is necessary to consult a physician or medical facility.
2. Any incident where firearms have been used, or where it is reasonable to believe that firearms will be used.
3. Any incident where this department requests assistance (from an outside agency) of an unusual or emergency nature.
4. Any incident where an outside agency requests assistance of an emergency nature.
5. In the event of a major disturbance, or reports are received indicating there may be a disturbance.
6. Any general alerts issued over regular communications circuits requesting the assistance of this department.
7. Any case where a dangerous person is at large in the city or adjacent thereto, particularly by virtue of escape or evasion during pursuit.
8. Any major signal or power failure, either wire, radio, or the transmission line (affecting or potentially affecting the operations of the department).
9. Any matter of an unusual or uncommon nature likely to attract wide public or media attention.

*Source:* Harry W. More and O.R. Shipley, *Police Policy Manual—Personnel* (Springfield, IL: Charles C Thomas, 1987). Reprinted with permission.

certain situations or unusual occurrences, most police departments have policies carefully spelling out when the watch commander will notify the chief of police that such a situation is in progress. Table 8–6 lists a wide range of occurrences requiring such notification. This notification allows the chief executive officer to be present or at least be knowledgeable when something unusual occurs.

Knowledge is power. The higher the position in the department, the greater the amount of information one can process. When we are in the know, we are more apt to be involved in the decision-making process, and when we have the capacity to make or have input prior to a decision, there is an acquisition of power.[28]

Another symbol of power is the ability to obtain resources such as personnel, equipment, and supplies. Resources are important to success, and a manager who obtains the resources needed to accomplish tasks and achieve department goals adds to his or her positional power.

**Personal Power**

Personal characteristics and traits are also a source of power. Personal power is a power an individual develops and is not related to the formal position he or she occupies within the organization. Referent and expert powers provide the base for personal power, and supporting powers can be reward, coercive, and legitimate.

Managers can reinforce personal power by expanding their expert power as much as possible. They should take advantage of every opportunity to attend special training programs. As police departments become more sophisticated, the police manager who has computer and information management expertise will prove to be influential.[29] Specialization reinforces personal power, as can be seen when one develops expertise as, for example, a computer specialist, labor negotiator, or polygraph examiner.

A psychological process is also at work in the attribution of personal power. It involves the subordinate's perception of the actions of the manager. Kelman identified three types of "influence processes":[30]

1. *Instrumental compliance:* The subordinate is influenced by the manager because he or she expects to be rewarded or to avoid punishment. The

level of effort by the subordinate is likely to be the minimal amount necessary to gain the reward or to avoid the punishment.

2. *Internalization:* The subordinate becomes committed to the support and implementation of management proposals because he or she identifies with the values and ideals that are presented. The subordinate is loyal to the ideas themselves, not the individual who presents them. He or she feels that they are right and appropriate.

3. *Personal identification:* The subordinate imitates the behavior of the manager and adopts the same attitudes because he or she wants to please the manager. This kind of behavior can build self-esteem and a stronger personal self-image.[31]

Follower loyalty and responsiveness allow a manager to get things accomplished easily. The manager's desire can be a simple request—the response to which is usually positive. The key is that the followers respond because they want to, not because it is required. When the boss is liked, things just seem to get done. This serves to reinforce a manager-subordinate relationship.

A police manager can enhance and reinforce personal power by becoming an astute observer and participant in the decision-making process whenever possible. Being asked for information provides an opportunity for face-to-face interaction and the potential to influence the ultimate decision.[32]

It is difficult to imagine any manager (other than the most charismatic) being able to rely solely on personal power, without the support of other power bases. In terms of command responsibility, a police manager is obligated to perform a full range of administrative functions, relying on personal initiative in order to ensure the highest level of performance possible.

One can have both positional and personal power. When they are combined, a police manager will have the highest possible level of influence over subordinates, superiors, and peers. Signs of managerial power are presented in Table 8–7.

# UTILIZING POWER

The manner in which a police manager utilizes power sources is important if he or she is to be truly effective. There are times when one technique can be used effectively to influence subordinates or peers and other times that call

Table 8–7  **Signs of Managerial Power**

Signs of the power of the manager include the following abilities:
- To intercede favorably on behalf of someone in trouble with the organization.
- To get a good placement for a talented subordinate.
- To get approval for expenditures beyond the budget.
- To get above-average salary increases for subordinates.
- To get items on the agenda at policy meetings.
- To get fast access to top decision makers.
- To get regular, frequent access to top decision makers.
- To get early information about decisions and policy shifts.

*Source:* Adapted from Ramon J. Aldag and Loren W. Kuzuhara, *Organizational Behavior and Management: An Integrated Skills Approach* (Cincinnati: Thomson, 2002), p. 303.

for the choice of a different tactic. There are seven different techniques managers use to influence others:[33]

1. *Reason*. Persuading or influencing others by the process of reason.
2. *Friendliness*. Showing kindly interest and goodwill as a prelude to a request.
3. *Coalition*. Creating a temporary alliance of distinct parties or persons for joint action.
4. *Bargaining*. Coming to an agreement as to what each gives and receives.
5. *Assertiveness*. Stating a position positively and with force when needed.
6. *Higher authority*. Obtaining the support of departmental superiors.
7. *Sanctions*. Utilizing rewards and punishment that are organizationally derived.

The preferred power tactic used most often when dealing with either superiors or subordinates is reason. Circumscribed by the need to comply and exist in a legal environment, law enforcement officers are prone to utilize rules, regulations, and policies when reasoning with others in the organization. When managers have an abundance of power, they are more apt to use a variety of power techniques than do those who have a limited amount of power.

Assertiveness is a backup strategy that powerful managers use when the situation dictates or when other techniques have proven to be ineffective. A manager can start with a simple request or an effort to reason with someone and then shift to a more forceful, assertive approach in an effort to obtain compliance. If a manager encounters resistance from a subordinate, the technique utilized can indicate the point where sanctions come into play.

When managers attempt to influence subordinates as a means of obtaining compliance and ensuring the attainment of goals, the techniques most frequently used are reason, assertiveness, and friendliness. The normal sequence of occurrences is this—as managers exert both positional and personal power when attempting to influence officers being supervised, there is a greater reliance on personal power.

When managers have had a favorable experience utilizing a power strategy (such as reason), they are more apt to rely on that method in the future. If reason proves to be ineffective, a manager will then try to obtain compliance by using other techniques such as assertiveness or friendliness.

Effective managers are those who utilize power with restraint tailored to the specific situation. They are fully aware of both the positive and negative consequences of power. They apply power with care and concern for personnel as well as for the organization.

An interesting approach to power is to turn it into influence by specifically utilizing power bases. However it is done, it is an effort to obtain true commitment, not just mere compliance. A manager wants employees to work diligently at a task until it is accomplished. It is not a question of just doing one's job, but doing it with dispatch and effectiveness. Workers who just plod along and control the amount of work to a level just barely acceptable are responding to power with compliance, not commitment. When power is used effectively, it results in commitment. Table 8–8 presents legitimate uses of the five bases of power.

Table 8–8 **Guidelines for Using Power**

| Power Base | Guidelines |
| --- | --- |
| Reward | Offer the type of rewards that people desire. |
| | Offer rewards that are fair and ethical. |
| | Don't promise more than you can deliver. |
| | Explain the criteria for giving rewards and keep it simple. |
| | Provide rewards as promised if requirements are met. |
| | Use rewards symbolically (not in a manipulative way). |
| Coercive | Explain rules and requirements and ensure that people understand the serious consequences. |
| | Respond to infractions promptly and consistently without showing any favoritism to particular individuals. |
| | Investigate to get the facts before using reprimands or punishment, and avoid jumping to conclusions or making hasty accusations. |
| | Except for the most serious infractions, provide sufficient oral and written warnings before resorting to punishment. |
| | Administer warnings and reprimands in private, and avoid making rash threats. |
| | Stay calm and avoid the appearance of hostility or personal rejection. |
| | Express a sincere desire to help the person comply with role expectations and thereby avoid punishment. |
| | Invite the person to suggest ways to correct the problem, and seek agreement on a concrete plan. |
| | Maintain credibility by administering punishment if noncompliance continues after threats and warnings have been made. |
| | Use punishments that are legitimate, fair, and commensurate with the seriousness of the infraction. |
| Legitimate | Make polite, clear requests. |
| | Explain the reasons for a request. |
| | Don't exceed your scope of authority. |
| | Verify authority if necessary. |
| | Follow proper channels. |
| | Follow up to verify compliance. |
| | Insist on compliance if appropriate. |
| Referent | Show acceptance and positive regard. |
| | Act supportive and helpful. |
| | Use sincere forms of ingratiation. |
| | Defend and back up people when appropriate. |
| | Do unsolicited favors. |
| | Make self-sacrifices to show concern. |
| | Keep promises. |
| Expert | Explain a request or proposal that is being made and why it is important. |
| | Provide evidence that a proposal will be successful. |
| | Don't make rash, careless, or inconsistent statements. |
| | Listen seriously to the person's concerns and suggestions. |
| | Act confidently and decisively in a crisis. |

*Source:* Gary Yukl, *Leadership in Organizations*, 5th ed., (Upper Saddle River, NJ: Prentice Hall, 2002), pp. 146–152. Adapted by permission of Pearson Education, Inc., Upper Saddle River, NJ.

**Exercising Reward Power**

Most employees respond positively to reward power, and the same holds true for managers. If subordinates have a need for rewards from the organization, the result will be commitment to the department. If organizational rewards are perceived as being used to exploit employees or if rewards are given to employees who do not deserve them, then the reward power has little meaning. When promotions are made, they should be based on measurable performance criteria, not subjective evaluations, and the specific reason or reasons for the promotion should be made known to everyone.[34]

The same principle holds for rewards such as being given a desirable assignment or being assigned to a critical investigative team: inform people why the assignment is being made, and do it publicly at roll call, in a department bulletin, or via a special memorandum.

Other rewards a manager can give range from acknowledgment of a job well done to officially commending an officer. Public recognition should be used whenever the situation allows. The problem is that it takes time. But a manager must make the effort if the officers in the organization feel publicity is important.

The giving of rewards is a pleasurable experience for both the recipient and the manager. One useful technique is to acknowledge police officers' accomplishments publicly every spring during a "Police Week" ceremony.

**Exercising Coercive Power**

The best exercise of coercive power is never to exercise it at all. Unfortunately, situations do occur in which it becomes necessary for a police manager to discipline an officer. There are few managers who enjoy exercising coercive power. It is usually a time-consuming process and can be emotionally exhausting. Disciplined officers can become resentful, minimal performers and at the extreme can become so negative that they are just not pleasant to be around.

Managers are striving to get officers to comply with official procedures or rules and regulations. While commitment is a desirable product of any power source, it is seldom achieved when coercive power is used. Instead, the best result may be mere compliance, and it is very possible to encounter resentment or even obstructionism.

Most police departments have numerous rules and regulations spelling out how tasks should be performed and what can and cannot be done. Infractions are specifically identified, as are punishments. For example, if the infraction is disclosing confidential information, the first offense can result in anything from a one-day suspension to dismissal; for a second offense an employee can be given anything from a ten-day suspension to dismissal; and for a third offense, the punishment is dismissal.[35]

It is imperative for the manager to make sure all employees are aware of policies, procedures, and regulations, especially when procedures are changed or modified. As the old saying goes, Ignorance is no excuse, nor is the failure to advise. The key is to communicate—often and effectively.

There is clear-cut logic requiring a manager not only to inform those supervised of the punishment but (when a violation occurs) to warn them about the action to be taken against them. This action should be documented. A paper trail must be created whenever an employee is warned of possible punishment so that it can serve as a basis for later disciplinary action if needed. It is much more effective to tell an officer, "You were warned of the failure to comply with departmental procedure on July 1, August 5, and August 15," than it is to say, "Well, I warned you."

The same idea applies to performance reviews. The process should be a real dialogue between the employee and the manager, in other words, two-way communication. At the time of a performance evaluation, the boss should never inform employees for the first time of their inability to perform their job properly.[36]

If coercive power is to be used effectively, it should only be administered after a careful investigation to ensure that an actual infraction or violation has occurred. In addition, if there is latitude as to the exact nature or type of punishment to be administered, every effort should be made to ensure that it is appropriate to the situation and commensurate with the seriousness of the infraction or offense.

Lastly, every employee has the right to be warned or reprimanded privately. The manager has this obligation. Punishing in public has the potential of permanently straining a manager's relationship with employees. Punishment is a no-win situation for everyone involved.

Legitimate power represents a type of power a police manager possesses because subordinates believe that he or she has the right to command. It is the same as formal authority, and in law enforcement it is legitimized because managerial duties are usually set forth in legal documents.

**Utilizing Legitimate Power**

Most officers readily accept legitimate power. It is a natural phenomenon to follow the dictates of someone of higher rank when the request is reasonable and clearly authorized by policy or rules and regulations. Legitimate power can be used forcefully, but there is little reason to do so. Forcefulness should be limited to those situations in which it is obvious that it is the only way to obtain compliance.

When a formal request is sent to subordinates, it should be done in a solicitous manner with a concern for those who must respond or react to it. It should be sent through the chain of command, which serves to reinforce its legitimacy. Whenever possible, a formal request should include a reason or reasons for its transmittal in order to set a positive frame of reference for the request.

In every instance, a request should be followed up as a means of ensuring that the recipient understands the request and realizes that the request is not only legitimate but also necessary.

The key element of the effective utilization of referent power is subordinate compliance because the subordinate does not want to disturb the working relationship. Requests are complied with because subordinates like their manager and they identify with his or her personal traits.

**Utilizing Referent Power**

A manager wanting to enhance referent power should do everything possible to create a working relationship based on mutual respect. Fairness and equity are essential when dealing with subordinates. This is best expressed by showing a real concern for subordinate interests and needs.

Finally, whenever the opportunity presents itself, managers should identify individuals who would be most desirable to have in their unit and then actively recruit them.

Managers should make every effort to become knowledgeable in special areas. When they develop special skills needed by others within the organization, they have an expert power base.

**Utilizing Expert Power**

Managers should work diligently at maintaining a specialized skill once it has been attained because it adds to credibility. At the same time, managers should

Capt. Stewart Parsons supervises the mounted patrol unit in a large city. The city has a population of 900,000 and is a tourist mecca. Numerous conventions are held there throughout the year. Parades, rallies, and demonstrations are commonplace, and the mounted horse detail serves at all functions. The police department has 2,232 sworn officers, of whom 27 are assigned to the mounted detail.

The unit was very active during the last calendar year, in terms not only of arrests made but also of the number of traffic citations issued. There were arrests for 129 felonies and 2,657 misdemeanors. The unit also confiscated 102 weapons, including rifles, shotguns, pistols, and knives. Mounted patrol officers issued tickets for 18,921 parking violations and citations for 194 moving violations.

Fines from the traffic violations brought $354,233 into the city's coffers. The mounted unit logged 12,395 hours of patrol. When not working special events, they patrolled the city parks. Currently, the unit has 38 horses, as well as horse carts for transporting the animals.

The city is faced with a large budget deficit, and the mayor's office is recommending that the mounted patrol unit budget allocation be eliminated. Capt. Parsons has always been involved in community activities and holds membership in two civic organizations. He decided to circulate a petition throughout the community asking the city to restore the unit's budget. He obtained the support of both civic groups to which he belonged. Seven police officers assigned to the mounted patrol unit assisted in the circulation of the petition during their off-duty hours.

The petition drive proved to be highly successful, and approximately 21,000 signatures were obtained. Capt. Parsons and the presidents of two civic organizations presented the petition to the city council.

The mayor is really upset about the whole matter—especially because it became apparent that Capt. Parsons had initiated the process and that a number of officers assisted in the gathering of signatures. The mayor called in the chief of police and told him the officers were trying to erode his power base and had no business becoming involved in the political process.

The chief pointed out that in this instance neither Capt. Parsons nor the officers had violated any city or departmental policy. He stated that the officers obtained the signatures when they were off duty. This is the first time this activity has ever occurred. The mayor is convinced that these departmental employees have exceeded their authority and that officers should not attempt to influence budgetary decisions. He asked the chief to develop a department policy prohibiting such activity.

*Should police officers be prohibited from circulating petitions designed to alter budgetary support for the police department? Develop a position paper that prohibits officers from circulating such petitions. Write a policy limiting the way officers can influence budget allocations.*

readily admit any lack of knowledge and never try to bluff their way through. In almost every instance bluffing will catch up with them and jeopardize their reputation. The best position to take is "I will find the answer to the question."

Presenting an image of being an expert can reinforce expert power. When making presentations or discussing issues related to your expertise, it is essential to be direct, decisive, and above all, believable. When explaining things to those less knowledgeable in a specific area, do not use jargon or attempt to impress them with your expertise. Present material at the lowest possible level and make sure everyone understands it. If there is any doubt about whether the material has been understood, go over the material again; make a point of singling out those who appear puzzled, and provide them with the help they need to understand the topic or issue under discussion. Above all, never do anything that would threaten a subordinate's self-esteem.

## SUBORDINATE POWER

Managerial power is never absolute but always seems to be modified. This is also true of subordinate power. In law enforcement, officers in line units have a great deal of power because they are the collectors of a lot of information needed by managers in order to perform effectively. This is especially true in officer-initiated actions, which are seldom monitored by supervisors. Reporting such activities adds to the department's information base. If information is withheld or if incorrect information is put into the system, the power relationship between managers and subordinates will be altered.[37] Information that is unreported—for example, results of field interrogations or background about informants—adds to the power base of the officer.

Subordinates can also exert a definite influence on police managers if they have a skill not possessed by the manager. As police departments grow in size, they are becoming increasingly dependent on specialists, so it is necessary for managers to delegate authority and responsibility.

When officers join unions or associations, they develop a unique base to which police managers must respond if the unit is to exercise a voice. For many years, police associations served a social role. That has changed, for the most part, so that currently these groups function as full-fledged unions. More than three-fourths of all the police departments in the United States are unionized. They are exercising real power in their relationships with police, city managers, and city councils.

In the states that allow collective bargaining for police officers, formal written agreements can be negotiated concerning wages, hours to be worked, and conditions of employment. In the city of Los Angeles, for example, a memorandum of understanding is in effect which lists the following matters that cannot be subjects for grievance or arbitration:

- Transfers, promotions, promotional examinations, and probationary employee terminations.
- Any other matter involving discipline.
- A determination of the fitness of an employee to carry a concealable firearm on or off duty.[38]

These matters are dealt with by general or administrative appeal procedures when discipline of probationary and permanent employees is involved.

It can readily be seen that police associations have definitely altered management-employee relationships. Fortunately, managerial power is decreasing while employee power has increased. This is entirely different, and certainly an improvement, from the days when management possessed all the power.

## SUMMARY

Power is the ability, the vigor, and the strength to influence others and to control one's own destiny. Correct use of power by a manager literally involves bringing together resources to accomplish something. Effective managers are those who understand the uses, limitations, sources, and characteristics of power.

Power has meaning not only to the individual, but also to groups and organizations. When considering power and its implications, we can identify five types of power: reward, coercive, legitimate, referent, and expert. Within police departments, managers will have greater control over reward power in direct proportion to their higher position in the organization. Some common reward powers are praise, commendations, special assignments, additional responsibility, and two-way communication.

Coercive power is based on fear of punishment and the sanctions a manager can utilize to

Table 8–9  **Ways of Acting**

Denhardt and his colleagues ask these questions about the exercise of power in public organizations: "What are we trying to accomplish and for whose benefit?" They offer the following suggestions:

1. Enhance your personal power by considering all of its possible sources.
2. Make yourself visible and indispensable.
3. Take charge of your own empowerment.
4. Use power constructively and effectively.
5. Devote time and energy to clarifying goals.
6. Support and foster the empowerment of others.
7. Think about, plan for, and maintain your awareness of political issues in management and in the implementation process.
8. Whenever possible, be nice.

*Source:* Robert B. Denhardt, Janet Vinzandt Denhardt, and Maria P. Aristigueta, *Managing Behavior in Public and Nonprofit Organizations* (Thousand Oaks, CA: Sage Publications, 2002), pp. 247–249.

control the behavior of subordinates. Punishment may take many forms, including suspension, demotion, and official reprimand, as well as more subtle sanctions such as giving an officer an undesirable assignment.

Legitimate power is associated with one's position, role, and status within the organization. In law enforcement, rank is closely associated with legitimate power, and power generally increases along with rank. All employees in a police organization are aware of their relative positions in the organization, which employees they are immediately responsible for, and to which managers they are accountable.

Managers are said to have referent power when their employees can easily identify with them. A key element of this type of power is trust. When an officer trusts a manager, it enhances the working relationship.

The last power base is expertise. It involves the skill a manager possesses because of knowledge, experience, or judgment. Organization-relevant information gained by an employee increases the power base used to deal with an increasingly complex society and its accompanying social problems.

An effective manager is one who influences the behavior of others in the work environment by using either positional or personal sources of power. Positional power is the power gained from the actual formal position a manager holds in the organization. Personal power is something entirely different. It comes from the personal characteristics and traits a manager possesses.

How police managers use power sources and bases is important if they are to be truly effective. There are times when one technique can be used effectively to influence subordinate or peer behavior, while at other times the choice of a different tactic will be needed. In Table 8–9, Denhardt and his colleagues offer some general guidelines concerning the use of power in public organizations. It is clear that power must be used honestly and with integrity for all parties to be satisfied.

# KEY TERMS

bureaucrat
charisma
coercive power
competitor
controller
expert power
incompetent
legitimate power

personal power
position power
power base
power sources
realist
referent power
reward power

# DISCUSSION TOPICS AND QUESTIONS

1. What distinguishes the bureaucratic managerial style from the realist type?
2. What are the specific rewards police managers can use?
3. What specific measures are available to a police manager using coercive power when strictly supervising an officer?
4. Compare and contrast personal and positional power.
5. What techniques can a manager use to influence others?
6. What can a police manager do to apply expert power?
7. Differentiate between legitimate and reward power.
8. How can a manager utilize referent power?
9. How does a manager deal with subordinate power?
10. What are the limitations of personal power?

# FOR FURTHER READING

Stanley Bing, *What Would Machiavelli Do?—The Ends Justify and Meanness* (New York: Harper-Collins, 2000), and V *The Mafia Manager—A Guide to the Corporate Machiavelli* (New York: Thomas Dunne, 1991).

These authors offer a tongue-in-cheek view of how Machiavelli would advise corporate managers to succeed in business.

Deborah Himsel, *Leadership—Sopranos Style* (Chicago: Dearborn Trade Publishing, 2004), and Anthony Schneider, *Tony Soprano on Management* (New York: Berkley, 2004).

Using examples from America's favorite fictional mobster, these authors analyze the leadership style of Tony Soprano. They do not suggest that you "whack" your adversaries or problem employees, but they do provide lessons on how Soprano exercises power.

Anthony Jay, *Management and Machiavelli—Discovering a New Science of Management in the Timeless Principles of Statecraft* (San Diego: Pfeiffer, 1994).

Jay offers a slightly more serious analysis of how the principles of power developed by Niccolo Machiavelli apply to management and leadership of today's organizations.

# NOTES

1. John P. Kotter, *Power and Influence* (New York: Free Press, 1985) and Rosabeth M. Kanter, "Power Failure in Management Circuits," Harvard Business Review, Vol. 57 (July–August 1979), p. 65.
2. Gary Dessler, *Management* (Upper Saddle River, NJ: Prentice Hall, 2004), pp. 246–248.
3. Jeffrey Pfeffer, "Understanding Power in Organizations," *California Management Review* (Winter 1992), pp. 29–50.
4. Peter C. Unsinger and Harry W. More, *Police Management—Labor Relations* (Springfield, IL: Charles C Thomas, 1989).
5. Max Weber, "Bureaucracy," in Walter E. Natermeyer and J. Timothy McMahon, eds., *Classics of Organizational Behavior* (Prospect Heights, IL: Waveland, 2001), pp. 351–357.
6. Kanter, "Power Failure in Management Circuits."
7. David McClelland, "The Two Faces of Power," *Journal of International Affairs*, Vol. 24 (1970), pp. 36, 41.
8. Warren Bennis and Bert Nanus, *Leaders: The Strategies for Taking Charge* (New York: Harper & Row, 1985), pp. 17–18.
9. Gary Yukl, *Leadership in Organizations* (Upper Saddle River, NJ: Prentice Hall, 2002), p. 142.
10. Fred Luthans, *Organizational Behavior*, 9th ed. (New York: McGraw-Hill, 2002), p. 434.

11. Denis Waitley and Reni L. Witt, *The Joy of Working* (New York: Dodd and Mead, 1985).

12. Ibid.

13. Larry Donnithorne, *The West Point Way of Leadership* (New York: Doubleday, 1993).

14. Jeffrey Pfiffer, *Managing with Power* (Boston: Harvard Business School Press, 1992).

15. Robert J. Ringer, *Power: How to Get It and How to Use It* (New York: Fawcett, 1974).

16. Robert J. Ringer, *Looking Out for Number One* (New York: Fawcett, 1983).

17. Mardy Grothe and Peter Wylie, *Problem Bosses: Who They Are and How to Deal with Them* (New York: Facts on File, 1987).

18. Yukl, *Leadership*, pp. 164–165.

19. John R.P. French and Bertram Raven, "The Bases of Social Power," in Darwin Cartwright, ed. *Studies in Social Power* (Ann Arbor: University of Michigan Press, 1959), pp. 150–165.

20. Harry W. More and O.R. Shipley, *Police Policy Manual—Personnel* (Springfield, IL: Charles C Thomas, 1987).

21. Paul G. Swingle, *The Management of Power* (New York: Lawrence Erlbaum, 1976).

22. More and Shipley, *Personnel*.

23. Ibid., p. 98.

24. Yukl, *Leadership*, p. 241.

25. Ibid., p. 188.

26. Kotter, *Power and Influence*.

27. Robert P. Vecchio, *Organizational Behavior: Core Concepts* (Mason, OH: South-Western, 2003), p. 125.

28. Peter G. Northouse, *Leadership: Theory and Practice* (Thousand Oaks, CA: Sage, 2004), p. 6.

29. Ibid.

30. Herbert C. Kelman, "Compliance, Identification, and Internalization: Three Processes of Attitude Change," *Journal of Conflict Resolution* (1958), pp. 51–60.

31. Ibid, pp. 58–60.

32. Marlene Wilson, *Survival Skills for Managers* (Boulder, CO: Johnson, 1981).

33. D. Kipnis, S.M. Schmidt, C. Swaffin-Smith, and I. Wilkinson, "Patterns of Managerial Influence: Shotgun Managers, Tacticians, and Bystanders," *Organizational Dynamics*, Vol. 4 (1984).

34. Yuhl, *Leadership*, p. 147.

35. More and Shipley, *Personnel*.

36. Maynard M. Gordon, *The Iacocca Management Technique* (New York: Dodd & Mead, 1985).

37. Barry M. Staw, "Organizational Behavior: A Review and Reformulation of the Field's Outcome Variables," in Mark R. Rosenweig and Lyman W. Porter, eds. *Annual Review of Psychology* (Palo Alto, CA: Annual Reviews, 1984).

38. V.A. Leonard and Harry W. More, *Police Organization and Management* (New York: Foundation Press, 2000), p. 48.

# 9

# DECISION-MAKING

## The Essential Element in Applied Management

## LEARNING OBJECTIVES

1. Identify key elements in the definition of a managerial decision.

2. Describe the dynamics involved in the decision-making process.

3. Show the relationship between problem solving and decision-making.

4. Make a distinction between personal and organizational decisions.

5. Discuss what are viewed as the cardinal sins in decision-making.

6. Show correlation in rank to scope of decision-making authority.

7. Identify internal, external, and personal constraints on decision-making.

8. Differentiate between the various types of managerial decisions.

9. Demonstrate the steps involved in the rational decision-making process.

10. Describe the mechanics and utility of comparative analysis.

11. Define the terms *bounded rationality* and *satisficing*.

12. List and explain guidelines to improve individual decision-making.

13. Discuss group decision-making in light of a humanistic philosophy.

14. Consider the advantages and disadvantages often associated with group decision-making.

15. Compare a variety of techniques designed to improve the group decision-making processes.

16. Consider the impact that group decision-making is going to have on the role of tomorrow's police administrator.

In the most general sense, to decide is to make up one's mind. A decision is a choice from among a set of available alternatives. Managerial decisions are choices made between alternative courses of action and translated into administrative behavior that is designed to achieve an organization's mission through the accomplishment of specifically targeted goals and objectives. The key elements in this definition of a managerial decision are (1) choices, (2) alternatives, (3) targets, and (4) purposeful behavior.

Lyndora is a small, relatively affluent community adjacent to a major industrial city in the Midwest. It appeared until quite recently that Lyndora would escape the drug epidemic. The crack cocaine death of a very popular local high school basketball player shattered this illusion, however. The coroner's inquiry into the young man's death concluded that teenage drug abuse was common and represented a serious health problem. Based on the coroner's report, the news media demanded more drug enforcement activity by the police.

Gary Pirsig, the new chief of police who came from outside the department and serves at the pleasure of the city council, was reluctant to act. The chief was, by his own admission, uncomfortable making unanticipated decisions in unsettled circumstances. He was sensitive to the political liabilities inherent in making a "wrong" decision, and he wanted to avoid criticism at all costs. After a particularly nasty editorial in the local newspaper, Pirsig's anxiety level skyrocketed to the point where he became physically ill and had to take three days off from work.

In order to let things cool down, the chief refused all requests for interviews and issued a news release saying that his department's drug enforcement policy was under review. He admitted to a close friend that he was using this stalling announcement in order to avoid making hasty decisions.

The ploy did not work. The media continued to press its demands for action. In an effort to get the media off his back, the chief prepared and circulated the rough draft of a new drug enforcement policy emphasizing full enforcement and user accountability. The draft policy called on police officers, in addition to arresting all drug pushers, to apprehend and prosecute everyone, regardless of age, who possessed illegal drugs or drug paraphernalia. The new "get tough" policy was scheduled to go into effect in ten days.

After receiving some negative feedback on the policy from school administrators, elected officials, and concerned parents, the chief had second thoughts and put the drug enforcement policy on hold for further study. Chief Gary Pirsig's indecisiveness has caused a morale problem in the police department and has strained his relations with members of the city council. In fact, there have been calls for his resignation.

*Chief Pirsig has a big problem. He violated some very basic principles and committed the two cardinal sins associated with decision-making. How should this situation have been handled? Based on the information in this chapter, what process would you have used to decide how to deal with this particular problem? Be specific.*

1. *Choices.* If a police administrator does not have the opportunity or ability to make a choice, there is no real decision. Following rules, obeying orders, or being coerced to act in certain ways cannot—without a great deal of distortion—be construed as making decisions.

2. *Alternatives.* There must be more than one possible course of action available in order for the police administrator to have a choice. Effective managers look for and/or try to create realistic options for resolving problems.

3. *Targets.* Goals and objectives come together to perform a vital function. They activate and give direction to the decision-making process.[1]

4. *Behavior.* Making decisions is irrelevant unless they are translated into action. To quote General George S. Patton: "When a decision has to be made, make it. There is no totally right time for anything."[2]

Decision-making is the complex process of generating and evaluating alternatives and making choices based on relevant knowledge, beliefs, and judgments. Decision-making also involves the application of our own experience and moral orientation in determining what should be done to resolve a particular problem. Logic is used to test our conclusions, and ethics serves to test our judgment.[3]

Decision-making is a natural and ubiquitous human activity. It is, in terms of modern organization and management, one of the most important, if not the most important, of all managerial activities. Virtually every management action is contingent, to one degree or another, on decision-making. Chester I. Barnard[4] identified decision-making as one of the "functions of the executive." Two other management theorists, Claude George[5] and Herbert Simon,[6] go so far as to say that management is, in fact, synonymous with decision-making. While this may be an overstatement, it helps to explain why so much attention is being focused on decision theory and its application in complex criminal justice organizations.

## PROBLEM SOLVING AND DECISION-MAKING

The terms *problem solving* and *decision-making* are used interchangeably in the context of management because managers spend most of their time making decisions to resolve problems. Allison[7] defines the decision-making process as rational, consisting of four steps:

1. Translate goals into objectives, and then translate objectives into payoffs and utility.
2. Choose among alternatives.
3. Consider the consequences.
4. Select the alternative whose consequences have the greatest utility.

Based on these concepts, decision-making can be described as a multistep process through which problems are recognized, diagnosed, and defined. Alternative solutions are generated, selected, and implemented. This process helps produce personal commitment to a given course of action and is manifest in one's willingness to invest energy, effort, expertise, and other resources in order to achieve a desired end state of existence.

All managers are obligated to make decisions designed to resolve problems that fall within the scope of their authority. These decisions can be broken down into two categories: (1) personal decisions and (2) organizational decisions. Personal decisions are those that, due to their nature and complexity, cannot ordinarily be delegated to others. Making a major decision (e.g., to terminate the employment of a high-ranking exempt manager) may require several subsidiary judgment-based decisions that can only be made by the chief executive. In other situations, a major decision (like where to build a new jail) may be announced by the chief of police even though different people acting in their organizational capacity made many subsidiary decisions. Allison calls this the organizational process model.[8] While chief executives do not make all decisions personally, they are ultimately responsible for all of the decisions made by their subordinates.

## ORGANIZATIONAL DECISION-MAKING

While all of us make a wide variety of personal decisions, only certain members of any organized work group have the ability and the desire to exercise formal decision-making authority. Even when people have the ability and desire to make decisions, they are not, under normal circumstances, empowered to make them unless they have been granted specific authority to do so. There must be some type of rationale to stipulate who within a particular organization has the responsibility for which decisions. The lack of specificity in this area produces ambiguity, anxiety, and a sense of anomie.

One generally accepted rationale is based on two factors: (1) the scope of the decision and (2) the designated level of management. The scope of the decision is the proportion of the total organization the decision is likely to affect—the greater the proportion, the broader the scope of the decision. The levels of management are arranged in a hierarchical order indicative of formal authority and/or position power.

1. *Upper-level managers* are the appointed or elected top executives who serve as agency administrators, department heads, and program directors. Executive work is not that of the organization per se, but the specialized work of maintaining the organization in operation. These top executives are expected to establish a sense of purpose, formulate overall policy, and make those decisions that affect the organization as a whole.

2. *Middle-level managers* are located between the top and lower levels of the organization. They are the bureau chiefs and division heads who act on behalf of their superiors to interpret department policies, coordinate the activities of work units, motivate employees, and maintain discipline. Middle-level managers make decisions designed to achieve results. Their decision-making authority is limited and always constrained by preexisting policy.

3. *Lower-level (supervisory) managers* are responsible for the job-related activities of others. They are the work-group leaders charged with getting subordinates to carry out specific tasks as set down by middle managers. Lower-level managers are expected to motivate workers to perform these tasks within a framework of established policies, procedures, rules, and regulations. Consequently, for these managers decision-making is highly structured and related almost exclusively to operational considerations. The rationale is fairly simple: the broader the scope of a particular decision, the higher the level of the manager who is likely to make it.

Nothing just stated precludes any manager who has the primary responsibility for making a decision from seeking the advice of other management personnel or subordinates. Only fools try to make decisions in a vacuum. Top-notch police managers tap every available resource. They also know that it might be desirable to allow members of the work group to make certain decisions. We discuss group decision-making later in this chapter.

## INFLUENCES ON DECISION-MAKING

As we noted, no decision is made in a vacuum. Decisions are made by people at different levels in the organization, and every decision is influenced to one degree or another by the environment, the dynamics of the decision situation, and the personal characteristics of the decision-maker. These factors should not be viewed as independent variables. As a matter of fact, they work in conjunction with one another to produce idiosyncratic decisions. We discuss each of the factors to help you gain more insight into the decision-making process.

Decision theorists frequently discuss what is called the state of nature. State of nature refers to those aspects of a decision-maker's environment that affect choice. Environmental factors can be grouped into two basic categories:

(1) the internal environment and (2) the external environment. Some of the internal factors that affect choice are as follows:

1. The specificity of the organization's mission, goals, and objectives.
2. The delegation of sufficient authority to enable managers to carry out their assigned duties.
3. The degree of autonomy given to management personnel at different levels in the organization.
4. The leeway granted to managers by departmental policies, procedures, rules, and regulations.
5. The availability of valid, reliable, and objective information on which to base decisions.
6. The time and energy used to select, train, and retain well-qualified managers.
7. The nature, extent, and effect of intraorganizational conflict.
8. The restrictions imposed on management via the collective-bargaining process.
9. The adequacy of the reward system in promoting timely and effective decision-making.

The external factors that affect choice include, but are not limited to, the following:

1. Social instability
2. Rising expectations
3. Professional ethics
4. Legal constraints
5. Dwindling resources
6. Political conflict
7. Technological change

Internal and external environmental factors are never under the direct control of the decision-maker. Effective decision-makers learn to accept and cope with this uncertainty, complexity, volatility, and risk. Good managers are willing to take a calculated risk. Since they see decision-making as a challenge, they are seldom immobilized by fear of the unknown in a systematic way.

**Situational Variables**

No two decision situations are exactly the same. There are simply too many variables. Every problem that elicits a decision is unique in terms of its:

1. Nature
2. Extent
3. Difficulty
4. Urgency
5. Seriousness
6. Complexity
7. Solution

Each decision is a unique product of the dynamic interaction between the decision-maker, environmental factors, and situational variables. No one makes correct decisions all the time. Good managers are usually decisive and process information in such a way that they make right decisions more often than wrong decisions. Effective decision-makers dare to be different. They unshackle themselves from the past and use creative problem solving as a ticket to success.

**Personal Variables**

There is a personal dimension to managerial decision-making in all complex criminal justice organizations. Even in the most favorable environment and in relatively stable situations, the personal characteristics of managers have a great influence on the quality of their decisions. Two police administrators evaluating identical data, related to the same problem, based on identical criteria, may reach different conclusions. Decision theorists account for such disparities in terms of unique personal factors such as:

1. *Mental health.* While they do not always make the right choice, emotionally healthy managers tend to be adequate decision-makers. Managers with strong self-concepts know themselves and are inner-directed. Those who see themselves as problem solvers are unlikely to avoid or to postpone decisions. They do not fear that decisions will lead to failure or personal loss. Emotionally unhealthy managers, on the other hand, usually have difficulty in processing information and making decisions. Psychotics are out of touch with reality and neurotics distort it. Impulsive managers become anxious and irritable over delays. They take action without adequate fact-finding or analysis. Compulsive managers are just the opposite. They are detail-minded, cautious people who seek refuge in procrastination. Compulsive managers are very insecure. They allow decision situations to deteriorate due to their emotional need to minimize risks. Understanding the role of the personality in making decisions is important. It has practical value in improving the overall quality of managerial decision-making.

2. *Intellectual capacity.* Because of the formal education usually required of personnel who enter management in the private sector, people with average or below-average intelligence seldom get the chance to test their abilities. Most of the middle- and top-level managers in the private sector are in the upper 10 percent of the general population in terms of intelligence. There is little doubt that this intelligence contributes to their ability to make decisions. Due to the nature of the promotion process in most police departments, police administrators exhibit a much wider range of intelligence. Within this range, the qualitative aspects of a police administrator's intelligence may exert more influence on decisions than his or her intelligence quotient (IQ). A division chief with an IQ of 120 and a great deal of common sense is in a better position to make good decisions than another upper-level manager with an IQ of 130 and little or no common sense. It is likely that the division chief will make even better decisions if he or she is knowledgeable, competent, mature, and emotionally healthy. While intelligence is positively correlated with managerial performance, the relationship is extremely complex.

3. *Education and experience.* The more complex, technical, or global a decision is, the more important it is for the decision-maker to have access to a

broad reservoir of related information. Consequently, education and experience can make a significant contribution to the overall quality of managerial decisions. Decision theorists are quick to point out that the level of relevant knowledge is not necessarily correlated with the years of education or experience, however. It is dependent on the strength of the individual's motivation as well as the nature, extent, and quality of his or her learning experience. In some cases, too much experience can have a negative influence on decision-making. Some managers become experience bound and make major decisions based on past successes even if the current situation calls for creative problem solving and a break with tradition. The effect is also negative when a police administrator's education and experience have led to the development of undesirable managerial practices.[9]

4. *Values, attitudes, and perceptions.* As discussed in Chapter 4, managers bring their beliefs, values, attitudes, and perceptions with them to the workplace. Values are expressions of what a person considers to be worthy and to have a potential for need satisfaction. Attitudes are predispositions to evaluate and act in some favorable or unfavorable way. Values and attitudes are factored into our perception and help to shape it. Perception is our view of the world. Colored by our values and attitudes, perception can short-circuit rational decision-making.[10] Under these circumstances, a manager's values and attitudes have a direct influence on the identification of problems, alternatives, and choice criteria in decision-making. Good police administrators strive diligently to overcome the negative aspects of selective perception. While there is no such thing as objective reality, history is replete with examples of value systems getting in the way of sound decision-making.

5. *Motivation to act.* Managers are unique individuals who are different from one another in terms of their motivation to act. Identifying problems, evaluating data, and searching for solutions require analytical ability as well as creativity. They do not require courage. Making a decision to act based on these processes is another matter altogether. Taking action, which is the essence of decision-making, requires managers to risk their reputations, their positions, and sometimes even their careers.[11] Good managers have confidence in themselves and are motivated to take risks. Police managers who have a healthy need to acquire power usually feel comfortable making tough decisions. They find decision-making pleasurable and self-affirming. Making decisions is an expression of power and a symbol of their value to the organization. Managers with a strong need for affiliation often have a very hard time making organizational decisions. An unhealthy dependence on others detracts from the decision-making task, distorts perception, and lowers their resolve to take unpopular actions. The excessive need for safety or security almost always has the same effect because decision-making involves risk taking. Managers who are offended by constructive criticism, who feel threatened when their subordinates make suggestions, and who fear change frequently make decisions that meet their emotional needs but that fail to solve organizational problems.[12] It is essential for departments to recruit, screen, select, and train managers who have the ability to make correct decisions and to link those decisions with action.

# TYPES OF ORGANIZATIONAL DECISIONS

Management personnel at all levels make many kinds of decisions. Some are fairly simple; others are very complex. Top executives make strategic decisions that affect and guide the total organization. Lower-level managers spend most of their time making operational decisions involving limited actions designed to achieve a work unit's goals and objectives. Middle-level managers play a dual role: They (1) help executives develop long-range strategies and (2) see to it that line managers convert available resources into valuable goods or services.

Another way to categorize organizational decisions is in terms of how routine or well structured they are as opposed to how novel or unstructured they happen to be. Routine decisions include those that recur frequently, involve standardized decision-making procedures, and entail a minimum of uncertainty. Decision-makers rely on policies, procedures, and past precedents. Probably, the majority of all management decisions are routine. Nonroutine decisions, on the other hand, are those that prove to be difficult because of their novel, nonrecurring, and unstructured nature. Their complexity is compounded by incomplete data and the absence of proven methods of resolution. Much more intuition and subjective judgment are involved in nonroutine decision-making.[13]

Some theorists conceptualize managerial decisions on a continuum from those that are well structured to those that are very poorly structured. Partially structured decisions fall somewhere between the two endpoints. Herbert Simon viewed these endpoints as "programmed" and "nonprogrammed." *Programmed decisions* are made repeatedly, on a routine basis and in concert with preestablished alternatives. *Nonprogrammed decisions,* on the other hand, are elicited by new and unique problems.[14] They are normally made in poorly structured situations where there are no preexisting or ready-made courses of action. Programmed and nonprogrammed decisions can ordinarily be distinguished from one another by (1) how unique the problem is, (2) to what degree one solution is specified, (3) who is responsible for making the decision, and (4) in what organizational setting the decision is made. It is clear that deciding how to schedule police personnel is much easier than deciding what to do in a union-initiated work stoppage. Figure 9–1 illustrates graphically the difference between programmed and nonprogrammed organizational decisions.

## Heuristic versus Objective Decisions

Managerial decisions can also be classified in terms of the processes used to make them. *Heuristic decisions* are gut-level choices based on intuition and personal judgment. The most common heuristic approaches to problem solving are rules of thumb and trial and error. Decisions are made on the basis of similar past experiences or the advice of significant others. The essence of the heuristic model is that the criteria used to validate a decision are internal to the personality of the decision-maker, not external to it.[15] Consequently, heuristic decisions—while they may be perfectly rational—are subjective and uniquely personal. Sam Souryal, speaking on behalf of the police management theorists who stress the need for objective or fact-based decision-making, contends that reliance on

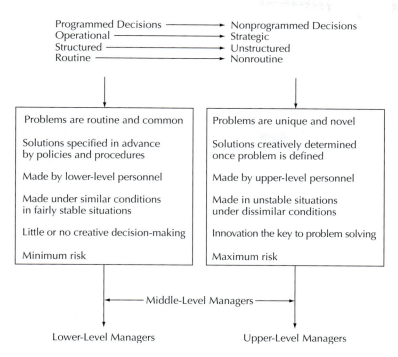

**Figure 9–1**
Programmed and Nonprogrammed Management Decisions.

hunches, rules of thumb, and gut feelings is an indication of organizational underdevelopment, personal immaturity, and lack of training.[16]

*Objective decisions* are logical, fact-based choices that are expected (in terms of probability) to solve problems.[17] Reaching objective decisions is much more difficult than using one's sixth sense. Objective decision-making involves the following:

1. Scanning for problems
2. Identifying problems
3. Listing probable causes
4. Designing solutions
5. Evaluating solutions
6. Choosing an alternative
7. Implementing a decision
8. Analyzing feedback
9. Making adjustments

Here again, organizational decisions are on a continuum, with most decisions falling somewhere between the two endpoints (heuristic and objective). Good police administrators are multidimensional in that they base decisions on affective as well as cognitive input.[18] This is why effective decision-making will continue to be as much of an art as it is a science.

**Reactive versus Proactive Decisions**

Organizational decisions may also be grouped into categories based on one's motivation to act. *Reactive decisions* respond to a perceived problem the decision-maker needs to resolve. The nature of the stimulus and strength of the drive to resolve the problem help establish the urgency of the response. Crisis decisions at either the strategic or the operational level are always made under pressure. Crisis situations are characterized by surprise, urgency, stress, anxiety, and threat to high-priority goals.[19] Crisis decisions are often made heuristically, based on intuition, past experience, instantaneous analysis, and emotional considerations rather than objective rationality. Even though a crisis decision may lack scientific objectivity and can be very difficult to justify on a logical basis, it may actually solve the problem. *Proactive decisions,* on the other hand, are geared toward the future. They are a by-product of the planning process, and they prepare police managers to deal with the problems they could face down the road. Proactive decision-making involves predetermining future courses of action by deciding when, where, how, and by whom a task or set of tasks will be accomplished. Proactive decisions are preparatory in nature and normally made in an orderly manner, under calm conditions, without the pressure generated by time constraints. Contingency plans (products of proactive decision-making) are designed to counteract the chaos generated by fear of the unknown. While a good tactical plan for dealing with hostage situations cannot guarantee successful negotiations, it sets the stage for coordinated response during a crisis.

The authority to make organizational decisions is distributed according to institutional norms. Managers in bureaucratic organizations normally exercise what Max Weber called rational-legal authority.[20] While they may seek advice, bureaucratic managers view themselves as single rational actors when it comes to making decisions that fall within the scope of their authority. Consequently, individual decisions are the rule rather than the exception. Bureaucratic managers equate decision-making with power and resist any encroachment on that power. Under these circumstances, they control the speed of the decision-making process and the content of the decisions. As the humanistic philosophy of management (see Chapter 11) has displaced traditional bureaucratic thinking, emphasis has shifted away from exercising power over subordinates to sharing power with them. As a result, group decisions are much more common. Teams, committees, task forces, and review panels have become well-established aspects of organizational life. Group decision-making helps satisfy workers' need to participate in making those decisions that affect them. While there are a number of disadvantages, there is evidence that in complex situations—where there is no clear-cut solution—groups using a consensus approach tend to be more effective than individuals. Where problems are less complex and special skill is required, individual managers with proper education and training tend to excel. Group decision-making is explored in more detail later in this chapter.

## PROBLEM SOLVING THROUGH RATIONAL DECISION-MAKING

Given the complexity of modern police work and the crucial need for effective decision-making in the administration of justice, decisions can no longer be relegated to seat-of-the-pants best guessing. The basic weakness of intuitive decision-making is that it can lead to overconfidence and cloud objectivity.[21] Rational decision-making refers to a sensible, logical, and objective approach

Rational decision-making entails scanning the environment, identifying significant unresolved problems, designing alternative solutions to those problems, and choosing the one best solution in terms of situational constraints.

1. Awareness of the need to make a decision. Decision-making is activated by the recognition of opportunities as well as problems.

2. Identifying an existing problem. When feedback suggests there is a problem, it must be diagnosed and defined in explicit terms.

3. Listing possible and probable causes. Once the problem has been identified and articulated in succinct terms, all possible causes must be considered.

4. Designing alternative solutions. Good decision-makers are inclined to develop and test a fairly wide range of creative solutions.

5. Evaluating alternative solutions. All viable solutions must be evaluated in terms of probability, effect, importance, feasibility, sufficiency, and realism.

6. Choosing an alternative solution. All viable options must be analyzed and compared to one another in order to select objectively the one best alternative.

7. Implementing a decision. A decision is meaningless unless it is translated into effective action.

8. Analyzing feedback. Managers are obligated to gather and analyze feedback in order to assess the effectiveness of a given solution on a targeted problem.

9. Making necessary adjustments. Good managers are proactive and do not hesitate—based on the analysis of feedback—to make necessary midcourse corrections.

**Figure 9–2**
Nine Steps in Rational Decision-Making.

that is based on investigation rather than heuristic intuition. Rational decision-making is a process involving several very distinct steps designed to help managers discover optimal solutions. It is a structured approach that allows them to identify opportunities and zero in on the real problem to be solved. The problem-solving process we describe here is illustrated in Figure 9–2.

The best organizational decisions are made via a series of steps that leads to a particular conclusion. The steps in the decision-making process follow.

*Step 1. Awareness of the need to make a decision.* Decision-making is activated by opportunities and problems. A prerequisite for effective decision-making is being aware that a decision is required. The most serious situation exists when dire consequences are possible and the decision-maker is unaware that a problem even exists. When police managers are blindsided by an unanticipated problem, it is often very difficult for them to regain their equilibrium. According to an old adage, "forewarned is forearmed." In the final analysis, problem awareness is a function of the manager's knowledge, perception, and motivation to know what is going on. Good police administrators have very sensitive antennae and relish the thought of resolving organizational problems through proactive decision-making.

*Step 2. Identifying an existing problem.* The nature of the problem must be clearly described in all its attributes. Otherwise, the problem will be addressed in an improper fashion. The two cardinal sins in decision-making are procrastination and vacillation. Often, they lead to "crisis management" decisions. Even if managers occasionally make wrong decisions, it is usually better for them to take action when action is needed than to take no action at all. Decisiveness has a stabilizing influence on subordinates. Indecisiveness is easily perceived and generates disrespect, destroys confidence, lowers morale, and adversely affects performance.

When feedback suggests there might be a problem, it is the manager's job to recognize it, examine it, and determine what caused it. A common mistake in organizational decision-making is concentrating on finding the right answer rather than identifying the right problem. Finding the real problem can be difficult. Good managers focus their attention on what is and compare it to what should be. Focusing on the real problem saves time, energy, and effort. It gives managers an opportunity to mobilize the resources needed to correct the problem. Managers often confuse symptoms (indications that there is a problem) with causes; as a result, they may spin their wheels or tilt at windmills. As organizations become more complex and the decision environment becomes more complicated, police administrators are required to gather and analyze more and more information in a concerted effort to ensure an accurate diagnosis. Because of errors in conceptualization, managers more frequently fail to identify the right problem than they fail to solve the problem they eventually take up.

*Step 3. Listing possible and probable causes.* Once managers have identified and articulated the problem in very succinct terms, they are ready to look for the cause or causes of the problem. A cause may be a person, fact, or condition that is responsible for an effect. Good police administrators try to think of all possible reasons that help to explain the existing state of affairs. They may, depending on the importance of the decision, even consider a few that seem impossible. Good managers are creative, imaginative, and resourceful. They have an innate or acquired need to recognize cause and effect, no matter how oblique the relationship might be. This ability is critical because it sets the stage for the development of alternative solutions. Causes are arranged along a continuum from possible to probable. Those at the "probable" end of the continuum become the focus of further inquiry and the catalyst for decision-making.

*Step 4. Designing alternative solutions.* If there is only one solution to a particular problem, managers—no matter how competent they happen to be—are not in a position to devise alternatives, and no decision is required. In most situations, however, police administrators are called on to develop viable solutions. Formulating alternatives is more of an art than a science. The artistry comes from considering an appropriate range of solutions while reaching out for creative ideas not made obvious by scientific investigation. Poor decision-makers settle for the easiest and most available solutions and have little or no desire to find the best possible solution. Poor decision-makers rely very heavily on intuition and similar past experiences to fashion alternative solutions to new problems. They lack both the imagination and the motivation to attempt creative problem solving. Poor decision-makers are victimized by perceptual predispositions (or mindsets) that interfere with the free association of ideas. This prevents new and useful solutions from emerging. Breaking the mindsets produced by experience, education, prejudice, and emotional conflict is the primary task of those who aspire to think creatively. Effective police administrators are aware of the organizational, biological, physical, technological, and economic constraints that limit their discretion in making decisions, and they learn to work creatively within them.[22]

*Step 5. Evaluating alternative solutions.* It is important to consider as many alternatives as time and other resources allow. Their goals should be carefully considered. These goals should be specific. Specificity not only clarifies but also makes it possible to measure and evaluate the extent to which they have been successfully attained. Alternatives should also be tested to determine their feasibility before they are fully implemented. Choices must not be restricted or limited. It takes a certain amount of imagination to develop alternative modes of action. The manager should make use of subordinates and their knowledge during this stage of the process. They can be a great source of imagination.

How alternative solutions are designed and expressed almost always depends on the manager's problem-solving skills, his or her perception of the problem to be solved, and the nature of the problem itself. It is at this stage that decision-makers attempt to assess the advantages (benefits) and disadvantages (costs) of each alternative. All solutions are evaluated in terms of their probability, possible effects, and importance. Solutions are also evaluated in relation to sufficiency, feasibility, realism, and rationality. According to Simon, the psychological act of evaluating alternatives consists of measuring them vis-à-vis certain value indices that are associated with the realization of our values.[23] The correctness of a particular decision is a relative matter. It is correct if it selects appropriate means to achieve desired ends. Rational decision-making is concerned with selecting preferred alternatives based on some system of values whereby the consequences of the police administrator's behavior can be evaluated. There are several types of rationality. A decision is *objectively rational* if it is the correct behavior for achieving maximum results. It is *subjectively rational* if it achieves maximum results in relation to real knowledge of the subject. It is *consciously rational* to the degree that the adjustment of means to ends is an intellectual process. It is *deliberately rational* when the adjustment of means to ends is intentional. A decision is *ethically rational* when it conforms to the moral standards of the individual and is considered proper by those in the appropriate reference group. Decisions that appear to be irrational may be very rational in light of the decision-maker's goals or the dynamics of the situation.

*Step 6. Choosing an alternative solution.* Consensus requires that decision-makers consider all possible alternatives. Decision-makers must also be open-minded and willing to hear dissent in a most tolerant manner. Criticism is to be expected. Criticism is inevitable in complex organizations. Considered positively, criticism means that the manager is doing something worthy of attention. Competent police administrators know it is impossible meet the needs and/or expectations of everyone affiliated with their departments. As part of a management team, they are required to satisfy the expectations of their superiors while trying to earn the respect of their subordinates. Good managers do what they can under the circumstances and put up an umbrella to keep the rain of criticism from running down the back of their neck.[24]

It is a grievous error to make decisions based on inadequate data. Information is the raw material out of which effective decisions are made. Once the real problem is identified and realistic solutions have been designed, managers seek to find the alternative that will maximize results in terms of specific objectives. Good police administrators weigh, measure, or judge the various truly viable alternatives in terms of effort, cost, risk, or other criteria, in order to discriminate among them and rank them in terms of the probability that they will resolve the problem. Comparative analysis is the data-based comparison of viable alternatives, in light of explicit criteria, to select the optimum line of action. This type of analysis is not a substitute for managerial intuition or a denial of its worth. It is a technique for making decisions more effective by reducing imprecision and error. One of the most useful analytical techniques is known as the *decision matrix*. The matrix approach utilizes data, criteria, alternatives, and judgment as the basis for choosing a particular course of action. As illustrated in Figure 9–3, viable alternatives (solutions) are listed horizontally, and the criteria by which alternatives will be judged are listed vertically. Managers assign a numerical weight to each criterion, from most important to least important. For each criterion, managers assign a numerical score to each alternative (from excellent to unsatisfactory) based on how well it satisfies the criterion. The alternative scores are then multiplied by the criterion weights to produce a numerical value for each alternative/criterion relationship, and those values are summed for each alternative. The optimal alternative is the one with the highest sum. If—after very careful analysis—there is no significant difference between the leading alternatives, personal preference becomes the most important factor in the decision.

*Step 7. Implementing a decision.* While analyzing data and making decisions based on the outcome of the analysis are inherent in the manager's role, deciding what to do is only part of the process. The next step is to translate the most beneficial alternative into action. Unless organizational decisions are supported by appropriate managerial action, there is little or no chance that they will be successful. Once the solution has been chosen, it is the police administrator's job to plan its implementation. The decision-maker must determine who will do what, where, when, and how to carry out the decision. In terms of percentage of time, decision-making takes up a relatively small portion of each manager's workday. Much of a manager's time is spent organizing the environment, mobilizing resources, and motivating others to implement his or her decisions. Emphasizing the decision-making activities of police administrators may produce a distorted view of their function.[25] It can be argued that for every decision there must be an implementation strategy. The best decision, left unimplemented, will have no more effect than if the problem was never recognized and a decision never made. This is what some managers mean when they say, "The way to hell is paved with good intentions and no action."

*Step 8. Analyzing feedback.* After a decision has been made and implemented, managers are obligated to do a follow-up evaluation. It is their job to keep track of who is doing what and to gather feedback in a conscientious effort to assess the effect of that particular solution on the targeted problem. Managers need to know whether an action is accomplishing the intended results. While doing something separates dreamers from achievers, action is only part of the equation. It is learning from experience that is important. This

Comparative analysis is the data-based comparison of viable alternatives, in light of explicit criteria, to choose an optimum line of action designed to solve a given organizational problem.

The problem: To determine which semiautomatic pistol will be purchased to replace department-issued service revolvers.

| Criteria | | Alternatives | | | |
|---|---|---|---|---|---|
| | | Pistol A | Pistol B | Pistol C | Pistol D |
| 1. Operation | (05) | 5 [25] | 4 [20] | 4 [20] | 4 [25] |
| 2. Power | (08) | 4 [36] | 4 [36] | 5 [40] | 5 [40] |
| 3. Capacity | (07) | 4 [28] | 4 [28] | 5 [35] | 5 [35] |
| 4. Cost | (03) | 3 [09] | 3 [09] | 3 [09] | 2 [06] |
| 5. Maintenance | (06) | 4 [24] | 3 [18] | 5 [30] | 2 [12] |
| 6. Reliability | (10) | 3 [30] | 4 [40] | 5 [50] | 4 [40] |
| 7. Safety | (09) | 4 [36] | 3 [27] | 4 [36] | 4 [36] |
| Total | | 188 | 178 | 220 | 194 |

Legend: The numbers in parentheses are weights indicating the importance of a criterion. Those in brackets are scores that reflect how well an alternative satisfies a criterion. Totals show how the alternatives compare to one another in terms of all the criteria. All other things being equal, the alternative with the highest total represents the best solution to a particular problem.

**Figure 9–3**
Decision Matrix.

requires evaluation of one's action related to a given decision. Good police administrators keep their eyes and ears open. By understanding the dynamics that produce correct decisions, they can better assess environmental factors, problems, solutions, implementation strategies, and so on, as they prepare themselves to handle subsequent decision situations. Only the naive believe in final solutions. Like the rings created when a rock is thrown into still water, decisions invariably lead to the need for more decision-making somewhere within the organization. Without adequate feedback, decision-makers are doomed to repeat the mistakes of the past.[26]

*Step 9. Making necessary adjustments.* The ability to make reasonable, correct, and timely decisions is an important skill that is normally found in the repertoire of effective managers. Police administrators who know what is happening and what is to be accomplished garner respect from their peers as well as their subordinates. On the other side of the coin, police executives lose confidence in and respect for those lower-level managers who are plagued by indecision or who are unable to forge a link between decisions and actions.

Since decision-making goes with the territory, effective police administrators learn not to waste time or energy worrying about decisions that have already been made. They avoid anxiety by living in "day-tight compartments" and trying not to second-guess themselves.[27] The only time a manager should reconsider a decision is if it is wrong or if there is a genuine need to consider alternative courses of action. Vacillation has often been the kiss of death for managers. While these principles cannot guarantee successful decision-making on the part of each and every police administrator, they provide guidelines for activating and managing the decision-making process.[28]

The quality of a decision is determined by factors such as the (1) sufficiency of data, (2) accuracy of the database, (3) perceptual ability of the decision-maker, (4) problem-solving skill of the manager, (5) adequacy of the implementation strategy, and (6) nature of the follow-up. Proactive police administrators take decision-making in stride. They are not afraid to admit that they have made a mistake or that a solution they have chosen is inadequate to resolve a particular problem under a given set of circumstances. Good managers are eager to take action and do not hesitate—based on feedback discussed in step 8—to make rational midcourse corrections as environmental conditions change or as the unknowable future becomes the experience of the present. Effective decision-makers tend to be intelligent, perceptive, creative, and proactive. Getting the job done right is almost always more important to them than the ego trip associated with being right all of the time. Only fools make decisions and then dismiss them. Good managers track decisions and are prepared to make those adjustments that become necessary to ensure the efficiency, effectiveness, and productivity of the organization.

There is nothing magical about the nine-step decision-making process just discussed. When it comes to routine problems, most managers go through this thought process quickly and without much conscious effort.

## CASE STUDY   Captain Jayson Moore and Lieutenant Royce Strauss

Captain Jayson Moore, a 17-year veteran of the police department, is a colorful character who learned his trade in the "school of hard knocks." While he has had little or no formal training as a manager, he is acknowledged to be a good decision-maker. He uses his experiences as a guide to the future; he chooses among alternative courses of action based on hunches, gut-level feelings, and rules of thumb. He is right most of the time. Captain Moore and the heuristic tradition he represents are anathema to the cadre of college-educated managers who control the department.

In an effort to become more systematic and objective in his decision-making, Captain Moore enrolled in a senior-level management course offered through the police academy. According to the syllabus, the course was to emphasize managerial problem solving based on rational decision-making and comparative analysis.

Concerned that his lack of formal education might put him at a disadvantage for mastering the material, Captain Moore set up an appointment with the instructor (Lt. Royce Strauss). He asked the lieutenant to explain the rational decision-making process and to illustrate it through the use of comparative analysis. Captain Moore also wanted to know at what point decision-making becomes a science rather than an art.

*If you were the lieutenant, how would you explain the mechanics involved in the rational decision-making process to Captain Moore? What steps are required to identify, compare, and choose from among viable alternatives? Define comparative analysis, and give an example of how it might be used in police work. Would you argue that it is always the police administrator's duty to select the best alternative in each and every decision situation? If not, why not? Is there any need for judgment in objective decision-making?*

Unique organizational decisions require more action. Since relatively few organizational decisions require a split-second decision, it may be advisable to move in a deliberate step-by-step fashion in order to arrive at the very best decision. Most administrative problems do not require immediate resolution. Consequently, managers have some flexibility in the timing of their decision-making. In most important decisions, this cushion is measured in terms of hours, if not days. While a rush to judgment can have catastrophic effects, procrastination is an unacceptable alternative. Competent police administrators adapt their decision-making to the situation.

## LIMITATIONS ON RATIONAL DECISION-MAKING

Decision-making lies at the center of the administrative process. Under ideal conditions, police managers are expected to make rational data-based decisions utilizing the model just described. Since organizational decisions are usually made in an environment of uncertainty and risk, by people who differ greatly in terms of their basic values, acumen, knowledge, and problem-solving skills, complete rationality is an unachievable goal. While it is often assumed that decision-makers first investigate and then reach decisions logically, based on their investigations, empirical studies indicate that the decision-making process involves a great deal of competition and even conflict. Some management theorists refer to decision-making as the art of compromise.[29] They reject the so-called economic-man assumptions generally associated with rational decision-making.

Herbert Simon, one of the leading opponents of the economic-man model, argues that the model simply does not describe actual decision-making behavior in complex organizations. Simon contends that instead of searching for and choosing the best option, many managers settle for decisions that are only good enough to get by. Other decision scientists believe that since people are involved, the best possible decision is seldom made.[30]

**Bounded Rationality**

Responding to what he considered to be the unrealistic assumptions of the economic model, Simon developed an alternative set of assumptions. According to him, decision-makers are not guided by perfect rationality but by *bounded rationality*.[31] He argues that all administrators have limitations on their ability to process information and to make rational decisions. Their ability to reason is limited by constraints such as the following:

1. *Organizational anomie.* Conflicting and continually changing goals or objectives.
2. *Lack of relevant data.* Insufficient and often less-than-objective information.
3. *Physiological factors.* Energy levels, reflexes, habits, and physical skills.
4. *Psychological factors.* Beliefs, values, motives, experiences, and perceptions.
5. *Knowledge of the job.* Actual job-related knowledge of the decision-maker.

All organizational decisions are made within these boundaries.[32] Consequently, it is not unusual for police administrators to misread a decision situation, fail to see a problem, recognize only a limited number of alternatives, or miscalculate the consequences associated with a particular solution. When this happens, they are not being irrational. They are simply making the most rational decision possible within a bounded information set. The goal of any organizational decision-maker is to expand these boundaries just as far as he or she can. While it is clear that there is a natural desire to make the best decision possible, the possible and the best are not always compatible concepts.

**Satisficing**     In addition to the constraints just discussed, the capacity of the human mind to formulate and solve complex problems is very small in comparison to the size of those problems. As a result, managers are inclined to settle for adequate solutions to organizational problems. They take the path of least resistance. Instead of searching for and choosing the best possible option, they accept decisions that are good enough in a given situation. This phenomenon is known as satisficing.

Typically, managers strive for rationality, but factors like time limits breed uncertainty and create boundaries. As a result, they satisfice. To reach a decision, they undertake a limited search among alternatives and choose the most satisfactory within the constraints imposed by the situation. Thus, satisficing is best described as decision-making behavior through which police administrators choose an alternative that is considered adequate but not necessarily the best. Managers ask themselves whether the decision is good enough to produce an adequate solution to a particular problem.

This pragmatic approach to decision-making is also discussed by Lindblom, who calls it "muddling through."[33] Lindblom examines how managers actually make decisions. He assumes that they adapt to each situation in a fragmented way that does not presume rationality. Values and feelings also play an important role in decision-making. Satisficing provides flexibility for those managers who want to avoid failure or mistakes that could jeopardize future promotions, pay raises, continued employment, and so forth. Satisficing is a strategy designed to lessen the danger associated with uncertainty and risk. Many management theorists believe that satisficing is necessary, even desirable, in some situations because of the following constraints:

1. Managers have limited time to devote to organizational decision-making.
2. Managers deal with many complex and competing problems simultaneously.
3. Managers have access to only a relatively small amount of the data concerning any given problem.
4. The cost of procuring and utilizing information to make a better decision may be prohibitive.
5. Some data may not be available to the decision-maker regardless of cost.
6. Bureaucratic managers are not necessarily well trained in using research, logic, or advanced reasoning.
7. Public problems are value-laden, and there is no real consensus about how to approach them.
8. Managers do not always have the independence necessary to make objective or impartial decisions.
9. Major decisions often require public funds controlled by independent legislative bodies.[34]

Satisficing occurs in all aspects of decision-making. During the problem identification stage of the process, for example, police managers ordinarily gather just enough data to give them an adequate picture of what is causing the increase in a particular type of crime. Then, based on their knowledge and problem-solving skills, they develop a short list of viable options that appear to be adequate to solve the problem. If the feasible alternatives all have unacceptable negative consequences, administrators will usually not pick the best of the negatives but will continue to search for another alternative with positive aspects.[35] It is better to compromise and make a less-than-optimal decision than to make no decision at all.

Satisficing decisions buy time. While they are not perfect solutions, they do provide an incremental approach to problem solving. At least some progress can be made while managers continue their search for a better decision.[36] Over time, we may get the best results by moving toward perceived and bounded alternatives via incremental steps of reasonable size, rather than by taking great strides based on the rational pursuit of perfect, yet virtually unattainable, solutions. After all, *satisfice* is a combination of two words, *satisfy* and *suffice*.[37]

## BUILDING BLOCKS FOR EFFECTIVE DECISION-MAKING

Robert B. Denhardt and his colleagues offer the following guidelines for effective decision-making:[38]

1. *Smoke out the issue.* Why is a decision necessary? What is or is not the problem? What is, should be, or could be happening?
2. *State your purpose.*
3. *Set your criteria.* What do you want to achieve? What do you want to preserve? What do you want to avoid?
4. *Establish your priorities.*
5. *Search for solutions.* How can you meet your criteria? What are the possible courses of action?
6. *Test the alternatives.*
7. *Troubleshoot your decision.*

But these guidelines only provide direction for the individual manager. What should the manager do to generate consensus and gain the support of his or her subordinates for the chosen decision?

1. Define and verify the problem fully and accurately.
2. Use the problem to generate solutions.
3. Prevent premature evaluation of solutions.
4. Provide a climate that values disagreement.
5. When possible, gain consensus from all of those affected.[39]

The best managerial decision-makers tend to be intelligent, knowledgeable, competent, collegial, decisive, and action-oriented. They respect subordinates and incorporate them into the organizational decision-making process.

## GROUP DECISION-MAKING

For all practical purposes, the unilateral decision-making associated with autocratic management in complex organizations is heading down the path toward extinction. As police departments move away from the quasi-military model to a more humanistic configuration, much more emphasis is placed on delegating authority and nurturing participative decision-making. Many organization/management theorists contend that operational decisions should be made collectively at the "lowest level possible" by people who are directly affected by the decisions.[40] Modern organizations have become so complex that the single-rational-actor (one-person) model of decision-making is gradually being replaced by group approaches to problem solving and decision-making.

Group decisions are collective decisions produced by specifically designated groups such as committees, study teams, task forces, and review panels. Group decision-making occurs when members of the group provide input and positively participate in the problem-solving process. Group decision-making is particularly appropriate for making important nonprogrammed decisions (like how to deal with a unique hostage situation or what to do about police corruption). Since these decisions are likely to be complex, few managers have all the intelligence, acumen, knowledge, skills, and temperament necessary to make the best decision possible. Good managers know their own limitations. They are not afraid to share power to make certain types of decisions with other people in the organization if it will help to produce better decisions.

Many organization/management theorists argue that groups are in a position to make better decisions than individuals. If the potential of group decision-making can be harnessed and its deficiencies avoided, it can attain a level of proficiency that is ordinarily not achieved by solo decision-makers. The key to achieving a high level of performance in any group decision-making hinges on the availability of people-oriented managers who have the ability to maximize the group's assets and minimize its liabilities. With proper training, police administrators can learn to perform this function.

## Advantages of Group Decision-Making

Group decision-making provides the following advantages:

1. *Pooling of information provides diversity and expansion of alternatives for consideration.* There is more knowledge and information in a group than in any one of its members. Consequently, decisions that require knowledge—internal and external to the police department—generally give groups an advantage over individual decision-makers. By pooling the resources of several people, there is much more information on which to base a sound decision.

2. *The social arousal of participants is greater.* Group membership can motivate and inspire individuals. American society values democratic methods. Group decision-making is consistent with democratic ideals. As a result, collective decisions are often perceived as being more legitimate than those made by a single person. When police administrators, as principal decision-makers, fail to consult with significant others before making important organizational decisions, the exercise of complete power may create the perception that decisions are made arbitrarily as well as autocratically. This perception can lead to intraorganizational conflict and poor morale.

3. *Social rewards for participation are provided.* Many decisions fail after the final choice is made simply because people do not accept the solution. As noted earlier, in the discussion of participative management, employees want to be involved in making organizational decisions that affect them.

They become more committed to decisions in which they have invested their time, energy, effort, and expertise. This commitment translates into support for the decision and satisfaction among those required to implement it. When groups solve problems, more people accept and feel responsible for making the solution work. Members of a decision-making group understand the solution. They are aware of the alternatives and know why they were rejected. Communication is maximized when significant others are incorporated into the organizational decision-making process.

4. *Division of labor provides the development and the utilization of expertise present in all members of the group.* In addition to more input, groups tend to bring more heterogeneity into the organizational decision-making process. Since members of the group have different perceptions and unique approaches to problem solving, they contribute to the decision-making process by knocking each other out of old ruts in their thinking. Diversity in thinking gives police administrators the opportunity to choose from an array of creative approaches and innovative solutions.

5. *Solutions tend to be of higher quality.* Groups outperform individuals working in isolation.[41]

Whether group decisions are, in fact, better than those made by a single rational actor depends on personal as well as situational factors. Good managers are flexible. They use the decision-making model that is most likely to produce the best result under the circumstances.

There are drawbacks to group decision-making. They include these five factors:

**Drawbacks of Group Decision-Making**

1. *Social pressure.* The desire to be a good group member and to be accepted by one's peers tends to squelch disagreement and promote consensus.[42] Psychosocial factors may become more important than objective decision-making. Reaching agreement in the group is often confused with finding the right solution and making the correct decision (see Chapter 7 for a more detailed discussion of group dynamics).

2. *Valence of solutions.* Possible solutions (alternatives or options) elicit critical and supportive comments from members of the group. When one proposed solution receives considerably more positive than negative reaction, it may—based on its relative strength, or valence—be acted on regardless of its actual capacity to solve the problem. This is the transition point where idea getting is turned into decision-making via intuition rather than through objective analysis.

3. *Domination by a few.* In most groups, a few dominant individuals emerge and capture more than their fair share of influence on outcomes. They achieve this power through a greater degree of participation, persuasive ability, and/or stubborn tenacity. This has been called the iron law of oligarchy. If the dominant coalition is composed of those members with low to medium ability, the group's overall effectiveness tends to

suffer. The quality of every group decision is influenced to one degree or another by the knowledge, abilities, and interpersonal skills of its (formal and informal) leaders.

4. *Conflicting secondary goal: winning the argument.* When a decision-making group is confronted with a problem, the initial goal is to resolve it, but the formulation of several competing alternatives or options causes another problem. Members have a natural inclination to adopt and support a particular position. They take it upon themselves to sell the favored solution. Converting those with neutral viewpoints and refuting those with opposing views become part of the decision-making process. The goal shifts to having one's own solution chosen rather than finding the best solution possible under the circumstances. This new goal is totally unrelated to objective analysis or the quality of the decision. Ego-centered decisions of this kind can result in lowering the overall quality of managerial decisions in complex criminal justice organizations.

5. *Consumption of time.* It takes time to assemble and lead a productive decision-making group. The dynamic interaction that occurs once the group has been formed is often inefficient. As a result, groups almost always take more time to reach a decision than would be the case if a single rational actor were making the final choice. Unskilled managers may be so concerned with finding a solution that they terminate the discussion before consensus is achieved, or they may be so interested in getting input that they allow the discussion to become redundant and boring. Both of these conditions limit management's ability to act quickly and decisively when the need arises.[43]

Group decision-making, with its assets and liabilities, has become a permanent feature of the landscape of contemporary organization management. In a Delphi study concerning the future of American law enforcement, 20 management experts expressed the belief that police personnel will continue their demand for more meaningful participation in the organizational decision-making process. The experts concluded that real job satisfaction will be seen as linked to shared decision-making.[44] Group consensus will become the dominant characteristic of police administration. As the shared decision model evolves, the distinction between supervisors and subordinates will become much less significant.[45] Police managers will serve as group facilitators who share decision-making power with others.

**Humanistic Approach**

Interest in group decision-making can be traced back to the human relations school of management and to theorists like Mary Parker Follett, Elton Mayo, Abraham Maslow, Keith Davis, Douglas McGregor, and Warren Bennis. Humanism stresses the importance of group dynamics and participative management in achieving an organization's mission, goals, and objectives. They see participation in decision-making as democracy in action, a way of opening communications, diffusing authority, and motivating people to make a greater commitment to the organization.[46] Humanistic managers in America, like their Japanese counterparts, believe that people—not capital spending or automation—are the primary source of productive gain. They see their employeess as their most important asset and treat them as partners, with dignity and respect.[47] They strive to achieve genuine consensus, collaboration, and collegiality. Humanists believe that group decisions are far superior to those made by a single decision-maker exercising formal authority.

Current research tends to support the humanistic approach when it comes to nonprogrammed organizational decisions. Researchers have found that groups make more and better decisions than individuals working alone.[48] Some management theorists argue that controlled conflict between members helps to stimulate better quality in a group's decisions. Skillful police administrators try to create a climate of disagreement (without causing hard feelings) because they know that properly managed disagreement can be a source of creativity and innovation. They adopt a Hegelian perspective and view disagreement as producing ideas rather than generating difficulty or trouble. Managers who perceive those who disagree with them as troublemakers obtain fewer innovative solutions and achieve far less acceptance of group decisions than do managers who see such people as having valuable ideas.[49] Good managers are able to differentiate between the decisions they must make and those that should be made by the group.

Evidence suggests that there are some important differences between group decisions and decisions that might be made by individuals within the group. What appears to happen in group discussions is that members who were leaning in one direction before the discussion began tend to shift further in that direction, toward more extreme positions. In some cases group decisions are more conservative than individual decisions, but more often than not the shift is toward greater risk taking.[50] This can be explained, in part, by the concepts of "spreading the risk" and "defusing responsibility." If a risky nonprogrammed decision turns out poorly, all members of the group share the negative consequences and no individual is likely to be singled out for punishment. Laboratory experiments show that unanimous group decisions are consistently more risky than the average of the individual decisions. When a group endorses a riskier position than would its individual members, it is known as a "risky shift." The positive aspects of group decisions are summarized in Table 9–1.

## Table 9–1  Benefits of Group Decision-Making

| | |
|---|---|
| 1. Broad knowledge base | 10. Synergistic disagreement |
| 2. Access to more information | 11. Generally better decisions |
| 3. Accuracy in diagnosis | 12. More comprehensive decisions |
| 4. Multidimensional analysis | 13. Inclination to take risks |
| 5. Multiple alternatives | 14. Greater creativity |
| 6. Collaborative problem-solving | 15. Increased job satisfaction |
| 7. Ease of acceptance | 16. Sense of self-fulfillment |
| 8. Accuracy in communication | 17. Greater unity of purpose |
| 9. Inherent legitimacy | |

# IMPROVING GROUP DECISION-MAKING

The most common form of collective decision-making takes place in goal-oriented groups where members interact with each other face-to-face. But as our prior discussion of the drawbacks of group decision-making demonstrated (see Table 9–2), interacting groups often censor themselves and pressure individual members to discard their own thoughts and to adopt the group's perspective. This phenomenon is known as "groupthink"; it becomes pathological if it is taken to an extreme.[51]

*Groupthink,* in this context, is the natural tendency for members of a cohesive decision-making group to become emotionally bound to suboptimal decisions, without analyzing them individually or critically.[52] To deal with such problems, measures such as leader training, brainstorming, nominal group techniques, and Delphi technique have been developed. Each of these techniques is outlined in the paragraphs that follow.

**Leader Training**     Group decision-making is bound to increase over the next decade and become the dominant approach to solving organizational problems. As a result, police administrators must now be trained not only as rational decision-makers but also as work-group facilitators. When group decision-making is used, they will be expected to convene the group and guide the discussion. Since this is a new role for most police administrators, they must be trained to facilitate group discussions without trying to manipulate them. As group leaders, they can make or break the decision-making process. If managers act like autocrats and try to sell preconceived decisions, the advantages of participative management will be lost and acceptance of these decisions will almost certainly be reduced. If, on the other hand, managers abdicate their duty to provide adequate guidance for the group, the group may produce low-quality decisions that are inef-

Fostering Community Relations.
Michael Newman, PhotoEdit

## Table 9–2  Negative Aspects of Group Decision-Making

| | |
|---|---|
| 1. More time-consuming | 6. Emphasis on winning |
| 2. Less consistent | 7. Illusion of valence |
| 3. Pressure to conform | 8. Groupthink |
| 4. Domination by a few | 9. Escalation of risk* |
| 5. Interpersonal games | |

*While risk taking can be a very positive attribute, extreme group-generated and reinforced risk is antithetical to rational decision-making. A lynch mob is a group in which the risk shift takes the concept of law and order to an illogical extreme.

fective in meeting the needs of the organization. Managers should follow these guidelines to lead decision group meetings:[53]

- Inform people about necessary preparations for a meeting.
- Share essential information with group members.
- Describe the problem without implying the cause or solution.
- Allow ample time for idea generation and evaluation.
- Separate idea generation from idea evaluation.
- Encourage and facilitate participation.
- Encourage positive restatement and idea building.
- Use systematic procedures for solution evaluation.
- Encourage members to look for an integrative solution.
- Encourage consensus, but don't insist on it.
- Clarify responsibilities for implementation.

These skills are not abstract concepts, but specific behaviors. They can be learned through training and tested in practical situations. There is good evidence to indicate that this training can best be accomplished through the use of simulation and role playing. Leader training improves the overall quality of group decisions and helps to ensure their acceptance by others in the organization.

## Brainstorming

Brainstorming is a special type of group decision-making process that was initially developed in the advertising industry to help trigger creativity and promote innovation. It is an idea-generating technique that encourages consideration of any and all ideas and prohibits criticism of those ideas. Managers who use brainstorming in problem solving have identified several factors that tend to improve the overall effectiveness of brainstorming sessions:[54]

- *No criticism!* Adverse judgments about your own or others' ideas are to be withheld.
- *"Freewheeling"* is invited. No idea is too wild or crazy. The more creative or unusual the idea is, the better.
- *Quantity is desired.* Generate as many ideas as possible. The greater the number of ideas, the greater is the likelihood that one will work.

- *"Piggybacking" is encouraged.* Participants should build on the ideas and suggestions of others. Combining and extending other ideas is a critical aspect of successful brainstorming.
- *Brainstorming sessions* are always structured in such a way as to maximize the group's creativity.

In the typical brainstorming session, 6 to 12 people sit around a table. The manager or designated group leader states the problem in clear and concise terms so that all participants understand it. Members of the group are allowed to "freewheel," generating as many solutions as they can within the allotted time. All of the proposed alternatives are recorded for subsequent discussion and analysis. Once the analysis has been completed and the options have been narrowed down to a reasonable number, the group or an authorized decision-maker selects the option that appears most appropriate given the circumstances. This approach—while it is not always effective—can be useful in dealing with public policy and administrative problems. It is particularly valuable when the problem necessitates trying to find new ways of dealing with a situation.[55]

**Nominal Group Technique (NGT)**

The nominal group technique (NGT) for decision-making represents a refinement of the brainstorming approach. It follows many of the guidelines used in brainstorming but differs in that members of the group function independently. Unlike traditional brainstorming, NGT is concerned with generating ideas and evaluating them continuously throughout the entire decision-making process. Ideas are generated nominally (e.g., without group interaction) in order to prevent inhibition and conformity. Interaction and discussion take place during the evaluation phase, which is structured in such a way as to make sure that each and every idea gets adequate attention. True collaboration occurs when group members consider the merit of each fully articulated alternative collectively. NGT attempts to minimize the biases that arise and that are reinforced in group dynamics. Once the problem has been presented to the decision-making group for resolution, the following steps take place:

- Individuals silently and independently write down their ideas and alternative solutions to a stated problem.
- All members take turns presenting their ideas, and these ideas are recorded on a chart or chalkboard.
- The ideas are discussed only to clarify them. Evaluative comments are not allowed.
- A written voting procedure is used to rank the alternatives.

An effective variation in the NGT process is to go back and repeat the first three steps. This gives the group an opportunity to flesh out new ideas or amplify recommendations prior to taking the final vote. If there is no clear consensus, the entire process can be repeated until the group reaches a mutually acceptable compromise. One variation of the NGT is shown in Figure 9–4.

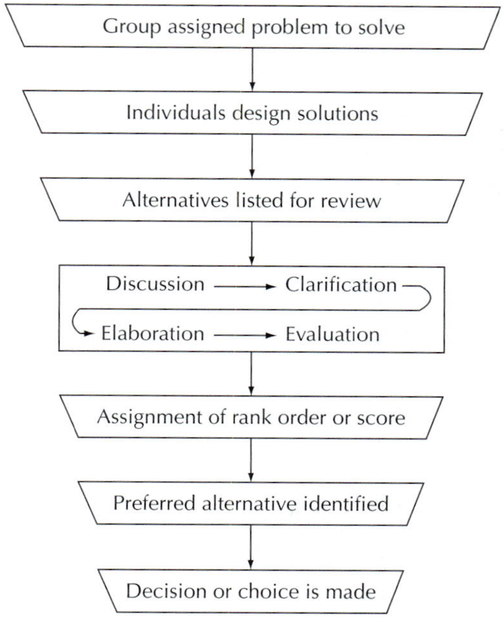

**Figure 9-4**
The Nominal Group Technique.

Group assigned problem to solve

Individuals design solutions

Alternatives listed for review

Discussion ——→ Clarification

Elaboration ——→ Evaluation

Assignment of rank order or score

Preferred alternative identified

Decision or choice is made

## Delphi Technique

The Delphi technique used in group decision-making was originally developed by the prestigious Rand Corporation (a think tank) to make technological predictions. This process is similar to the nominal group technique just discussed except that it does not require the physical presence of the participants. There is, in fact, no face-to-face interaction. Consequently, it is possible to poll a group of experts without bringing them together in the same place at the same time. The people who are selected to serve as members of the group do not actually make final decisions. Their job is to generate conceptually sound alternatives for consideration by organizational decision-makers.[56] The heart of the Delphi approach is to determine expert opinion through a series of questionnaires. This process typically involves the following four sequential steps:[57]

1. The first questionnaire distributed to members of the Delphi group identifies the problem and asks for alternative solutions to it.

2. The Delphi coordinator summarizes the solutions, and the summary is returned to participants along with a second questionnaire specifically designed to identify areas requiring further clarification and consideration.

3. The results of the second questionnaire are presented to the participants, who rate the various alternatives presented.

4. Members' ratings are tabulated, and a summary of the data and resulting decision are returned to the participants.

The Delphi technique is illustrated in Figure 9–5. Like the nominal group technique (NGT), the Delphi approach insulates group members from undue influence of others. It gives police administrators opportunity to explore complex issues without unwieldy analysis. Respected experts are kept on tap

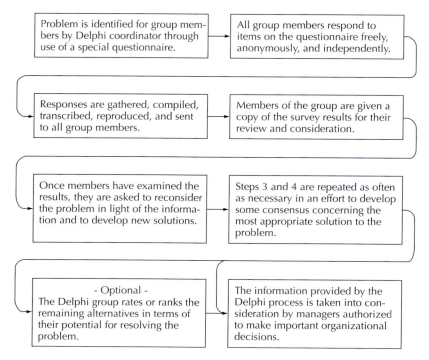

**Figure 9–5**

The Delphi Approach to Decision-Making.

to share their personal beliefs, values, and accumulated knowledge. One drawback to the Delphi method is the lengthy time frame involved in the questionnaire phases. Quick decisions are the exception rather than the rule. Another problem is that consensus can be achieved through compromise. The best solution may be ignored if group opinion shifts toward a compromise decision. Despite these disadvantages, the Delphi technique is an efficient method of drawing on and pooling expert judgment while avoiding the problems of conformity and domination that often occur in interacting groups.

Much more emphasis is now placed on participative management and formal group decision-making in complex criminal justice organizations. Many police organization/management theorists believe that collective decision-making may become the dominant form of organizational problem solving during the next decade. They support this trend and argue that meaningful employee involvement in the decision-making process will increase job satisfaction as well as produce better decisions. Research indicates that because of the synergistic effect of social dynamics, groups tend to be more vigilant than individual decision-makers. They generate more solutions, and better ones, to organizational problems. When employees share power with management and are allowed to make meaningful decisions, they do a more thorough job of evaluating alternatives than do individuals acting alone.

On the downside, group decision-making is complex, time-consuming, and slow. The quality of group decisions can be adversely affected by (1) inherent pressure to conform, (2) undue influence by a few dominant individuals, (3) conflicting personal goals, or (4) an unintended escalation in risk taking.

Lieutenant Karras earned a BA in sociology before he joined the police department in 1969. He continued his education and was awarded an MBA several years later. Lieutenant Karras is an intelligent, caring, and committed person who puts the welfare of the organization ahead of his own interests. During his 20 years with the Metropolitan Police Department, he has served in various capacities. The lieutenant is viewed as a hard-working and self-disciplined professional.

The lieutenant, who until recently was commander of an intensive patrol unit assigned to an inner-city precinct, was reassigned and designated as director of the department's graphic arts bureau. This is a staff position and considered a stop on the fast track to higher rank.

The previous director, an alcoholic, had given bureau personnel little or no direction. Because of the lack of management, the unit was in chaos. It had become the laughingstock of the police department. Lieutenant Karras's job was to clean up the mess. Since he was not familiar with the work of the bureau and had never been in a staff position before, he realized that he was not, by himself, prepared to manage the unit in an efficient, effective, and productive manner.

After seeking advice from other administrators and doing a great deal of introspection, Lieutenant Karras came to the conclusion that, in order to succeed in the new assignment, he needed to share some decision-making authority with his subordinates. He was absolutely convinced that, except in a limited number of situations, the single rational actor model would not work. He viewed participative management and group decision-making as the most realistic approach. Based on his education and training, he was willing to share power with subordinates rather than exercise power over them. Lieutenant Karras was glad to play the role of group coordinator and facilitator.

*If you were Lieutenant Karras's adviser, which of the three group decision-making techniques would you recommend he use in order to identify problems and generate creative solutions to those problems? Explain to the lieutenant how the process works and the results that you would expect him to achieve.*

These negative aspects of group decision-making can be offset, however. More and more emphasis is being placed on the manager's role as a group facilitator. Managers are being trained to become leaders who share power with their subordinates rather than merely exercising power over them. They are learning how to enhance the effectiveness of group decision-making through brainstorming, nominal group techniques, and the Delphi method.

There is absolutely no doubt that group decision-making will play an increasingly important role in police administration. Harry More's Delphi group hit the nail on the head. Collective decision-making is here to stay.

## SUMMARY

A decision is a choice from among a set of alternatives and is intended to accomplish a goal or resolve a problem. The key elements in decision-making are targets, alternatives, choices, and behaviors. Managers continually (1) monitor the environment for problems—conditions that require a decision, (2) design appropriate alternative courses of action for solving the problems, and (3) select the alternatives that they—based on their own knowledge, expertise, and experience—believe will work in given situations.

Good managers avoid procrastination and vacillation. They are decision-makers who expect criticism and refuse to worry about it. They know that external constraints and personal limitations have an influence on the quality of their decisions.

The most challenging part of any police administrator's job is to make proactive, non-programmed decisions. For all practical purposes, modern management has abandoned the heuristic model and embraced the scientific approach, which emphasizes fact-based, objective, and rational decision-making and involves the following:

- Perceiving the need to make a decision.
- Identifying the specific problem.
- Listing all possible and probable causes.
- Designing viable options or alternatives.
- Evaluating alternatives in light of specific and detailed criteria.
- Choosing the most appropriate alternative.
- Implementing the decision in a timely way.
- Analyzing feedback to assess effectiveness.
- Making necessary midcourse corrections.

Since external and personal constraints make absolute rationality impossible, good managers learn how to compromise and are often willing to settle for less-than-optimal decisions that are good enough to get by. These satisficing decisions are considered to be adequate, not the best.

Some organizational decisions are made by single rational actors in positions of authority. In order to do a good job, they need to know what institutional constraints have been imposed on their decision-making power. They must also:

- Distinguish between personal and organizational decisions.
- Minimize the number of decisions made in crisis situations.

- Let subordinates make decisions they are capable of making.
- Anticipate the political fallout that might be generated.
- Realize that beliefs and values influence decision-making.
- Approach decision-making from a problem-solving perspective.
- Assess problems in terms of importance, priority, and status.
- Formulate viable and creative solutions for major problems.
- Select the most appropriate alternative given the situation.
- Monitor their decisions and make all necessary corrections.

Good managers see decision-making as a challenge rather than a chore. They rely on existing policies, procedures, rules, and regulations to solve problems whenever possible. In addition, they make it a policy to consult with significant others prior to making major nonprogrammed decisions. The best decision-makers do not attempt to anticipate every eventuality that might be associated with the choice of a particular alternative, nor do they expect to make the right decision all of the time.

## KEY TERMS

bounded rationality
comparative analysis
decision
decision environment
decision-making
group decision-making
heuristic decision-making
individual decisions
levels of decisions

managerial decisions
nonprogrammed decisions
participative management
personal constraints
programmed decisions
rational decision-making
satisficing decisions
scanning for problems

## DISCUSSION TOPICS AND QUESTIONS

1. What are the four elements in the operational definition of a managerial decision?
2. Why are the terms *problem solving* and *decision-making* used as synonyms in management? Identify the three stages in the problem-solving (or decision-making) process.

3. Discuss the cardinal sins in decision-making. Give an example of how one of these sins has affected you personally.
4. How does a police administrator's level in the managerial hierarchy affect the scope of his or her decision-making authority?

5. Discuss the influence of internal, external, and personal constraints on managerial decision-making. Which do you feel are the most important? Justify your answer.

6. What is the difference between a programmed and a nonprogrammed organizational decision? Give at least three examples to illustrate the point.

7. Why are objective decisions perceived as better than heuristic decisions even when heuristic problem-solving techniques work?

8. What series of steps should a single rational actor follow while making important nonprogrammed decisions? Discuss each of these steps in light of a problem with which you are familiar.

9. Define *comparative analysis*. Explain how it can be used by police administrators.

10. What did Herbert Simon mean by the term *bounded rationality*? How is this term related to the concept of *satisficing*?

11. Discuss the advantages and disadvantages of group decision-making. How does it fit into the humanistic philosophy of management? What role does the manager play in the group decision-making process?

12. Discuss four ways to improve group decision-making. Which one do you think is best? Why? Give an example of how it might be used in a police department.

## FOR FURTHER READING

William Bratton with Peter Knobler, *Turnaround—How America's Top Cop Reversed the Crime Epidemic* (New York: Random House, 1998), and Rudolph W. Giuliani, *Leadership* (New York: Hyperion, 2002).

The two prime movers in the implementation of the CompStat paradigm, Bratton and Giuliani, offer their views on decision-making. Bratton's candid analysis of his management style and Giuliani's views on September 11th are the crucial attributes of these works.

Celia Sandys and Jonathan Littman, *We Shall Not Fail—The Inspiring Leadership of Winston Churchill* (New York: Portfolio, 2003).

Giuliani's model for dealing the September 11th crisis, Winston Churchill, is analyzed in this inspiring work coauthored by Churchill's granddaughter. The authors outline the major attributes of Churchill's decision-making style and discuss its effectiveness.

## NOTES

1. Gary Dessler, *Management* (Upper Saddle River, NJ: Prentice Hall, 2004), p. 80.

2. Alan Axelrod, *Patton on Leadership: Strategic Lessons for Corporate Warfare* (Paramus, NJ: Prentice Hall Press, 1999), p. 129.

3. Charles R. Swanson, Leonard Territo, and Robert W. Taylor, *Police Administration* (Upper Saddle River, NJ: Prentice Hall, 2001), pp. 507–508.

4. Chester I. Barnard, *The Functions of the Executive* (Cambridge, MA: Harvard University Press, 1976).

5. Claude George, *Management in Industry* (Englewood Cliffs, NJ: Prentice Hall, 1964).

6. Herbert Simon, *The New Science of Management Decisions* (Englewood Cliffs, NJ: Prentice Hall, 1977).

7. Graham T. Allison, *The Essence of Decision: Explaining the Cuban Missile Crisis* (Boston: Little, Brown, 1971), pp. 29–30.

8. Ibid.

9. Peter Drucker, *On the Profession of Management* (Boston: Harvard Business Review, 1998), p. 32.

10. Dessler, *Management*, pp. 71–72.

11. Allison, *Essence of Decision*, pp. 29–30.

12. Ronald G. Lynch, *The Police Manager* (Cincinnati: Anderson, 1998), p. 138.

13. Dessler, *Management*.

14. Herbert Simon, *The New Science of Management Decisions* (Englewood Cliffs, NJ: Prentice Hall, 1977).

15. William Gore, *Administrative Decision Making: A Heuristic Model* (New York: Wiley, 1964).

16. Sam S. Souryal, *Police Administration and Management* (St. Paul, MN: West, 1977), p. 319.

17. Irving L. Janis and Leon Mann, *Decision Making: A Psychological Analysis of Conflict, Choice, and Commitment* (New York: The Free Press, 1977), pp. 11–15.

18. Paul M. Whisenand and R. Fred Ferguson, *The Managing of Police Organizations* (Upper Saddle River, NJ: Prentice Hall, 2002), p. 311.

19. Ramon J. Aldag and Loren W. Kuzuhara, *Organizational Behavior and Management* (Cincinnati: South-Western, 2002), pp. 147–149.

20. H.H. Gerth and C. Wright Mills, *From Max Weber: Essays in Sociology* (New York: Oxford University Press, 1946).

21. Dessler, *Management,* p. 66.

22. Robert B. Denhardt, Janet V. Denhardt, and Maria P. Aristigueta, *Managing Human Behavior in Public and Nonprofit Organizations* (Thousand Oaks, CA: Sage, 2002), p. 146.

23. Herbert Simon, *Administrative Behavior: A Study of Decision-Making Processes in Administrative Organization* (New York: Free Press, 1976).

24. Dale Carnegie, *How to Stop Worrying and Start Living* (New York: Pocket Books, 1948).

25. Holden, *Modern Police Management,* pp. 128–130.

26. Swanson, Territo, and Taylor, *Police Administration,* p. 519.

27. Allison, *The Essence of Decision.*

28. Dessler, *Management,* p. 71.

29. Souryal, *Police Administration and Management.*

30. Linda K. Stroh, Gregory B. Northcraft, and Margaret A. Neale, *Organizational Behavior* (Mahwah, NJ: Lawrence Erlbaum and Associates, 2002), p. 97.

31. Joseph H. Reitz, Behavior in Organizations (Homewood, IL: Richard D. Irwin, 1981).

32. Holden, *Modern Police Management,* pp. 113–114.

33. Charles E. Lindblom, "The Science of Muddling Through," *Public Administration Review,* Vol. 19 (1959), pp. 79–88.

34. Ibid.

35. John C. March and Herbert Simon, *Organizations* (New York: Wiley, 1958).

36. Dessler, *Management,* p. 58.

37. Stroh, Northcraft, and Neale, *Organizational Behavior,* p. 94.

38. Denhardt, Denhardt, and Aristigueta, *Managing Human Behavior,* pp. 142–144.

39. Ibid., pp. 144–145.

40. Robert P. Vecchio, *Organizational Behavior: Core Concepts* (Mason, OH: South-Western, 2003) p. 192.

41. Ibid., p. 193.

42. Dessler, *Management,* pp. 359–362.

43. Vecchio, *Organizational Behavior.*

44. Harry W. More, "Delphi Analysis on the Quality of Work Life in the Police Field." An unpublished paper (1984).

45. Harry W. More, W. Fred Wegener, and Larry S. Miller, *Effective Police Supervision* (Cincinnati: Anderson, 2003) pp. 326–327.

46. Fred Luthans, *Organizational Behavior* (Boston: McGraw-Hill, 2002), pp. 376–377.

47. Thomas J. Peters and Robert H. Waterman, *In Search of Excellence: Lessons from America's Best-Run Companies* (New York: Warner Books, 1982).

48. Stroh, Northcraft, and Neale, *Organizational Behavior,* p. 243.

49. Swanson, Territo, and Taylor, *Police Administration,* p. 544.

50. Stephen P. Robbins, *Essentials of Organizational Behavior* (Upper Saddle River, NJ: Prentice Hall, 2000), pp. 98–99.

51. Vecchio, *Organizational Behavior,* p. 190.

52. Stroh, Northcraft, and Neale, *Organizational Behavior,* p. 252.

53. Gary Yukl, *Leadership in Organizations* (Upper Saddle River, NJ: Prentice Hall, 2002), pp. 331–334.

54. Stroh, Northcraft, and Neale, *Organizational Behavior,* p. 240.

55. Swanson, Territo, and Taylor, *Police Administration,* pp. 546–547.

56. Stroh, Northcraft, and Neale, *Organizational Behavior,* p. 241.

57. Ibid., p. 242.

# 10

# MANAGERIAL COMMUNICATION

## The Vital Process

## LEARNING OBJECTIVES

1. Describe why it is important for a manager to become a skillful communicator.
2. Define *communication*.
3. Describe and diagram the elements of a communication system.
4. Identify how the chain of command supports communication.
5. Identify the nature and extent of informal communication.
6. Write a short essay on inhibitors to communication.
7. Describe the critical features of the grapevine.
8. Describe the importance of body language.
9. Identify the key elements of a suggestion system.
10. Compare and contrast survey and feedback techniques used to improve communication.

Effective communication is vital. When communication is faulty, many officers feel they have been left out, rules and regulations can be misinterpreted, rumors overwhelm the communication process, and the transmission of information is inhibited.[1]

One of the major figures in public administration, Chester Barnard, listed several features of communication in his classic work, *The Functions of the Executive:*[2]

1. The channels of communication should be definitely known.
2. There should be a definite formal channel of communication to every member of an organization.
3. The line of communication should be as direct and short as possible.
4. The complete formal line of communication should normally be used.
5. The persons serving as communication centers should be competent.
6. The line of communication should not be interrupted while the organization is functioning.

Barnard's basic concepts outline the need for clear communication in organizations.

Donald Bear has just been promoted to lieutenant and assigned to field operations. In this position, he reports directly to the assistant chief of the department and serves as watch commander on the swing shift.

Lt. Bear has been a member of the department for nine years and prior to his promotion served as a first-line supervisor for three years. His appearance fits the stereotype of a manager. He is 6 feet 4 inches tall, weighs 210 pounds, and keeps himself in top physical shape. He has taken numerous courses at the local university and is currently working on an MBA.

All of Bear's time as a first-line supervisor was spent in records and planning. He gained a world of experience in preparing operational plans and the annual departmental budget. In this capacity, he functioned primarily as a numbers cruncher, so his relationship to line personnel was limited.

Immediately upon promotion he was fortunate enough to attend an 80-hour seminar offered by the Southern Police Institute at the University of Louisville. Armed with theory, he has now reached the time for application. After a "honeymoon" of five and a half months, he has just encountered the first major issue needing his administrative expertise; it involves communication.

Lt. Bear has verbally disciplined Officer George Mandering for engaging in horseplay on two sepa-rate occasions over a three-week period. In each instance Officer Mandering left a typewritten note in the mailbox of another officer, purportedly an order from the assistant chief transferring the officer to the midnight shift. Both officers who received the notes became very upset because the change conflicted with prescheduled vacations.

The lieutenant was caught in the middle in both instances because he was totally unaware of the incidents until the officers came to him and complained. Lt. Bear identified the perpetrator and feels an oral reprimand is sufficient under the circumstances. But when the assistant chief heard about the incidents, he became very upset and expressed the opinion that Officer Mandering should receive formal punishment for unduly harassing other employees.

This is clearly a problem of communication that can be listed under the heading *Why didn't he or she tell me?* It is a question often asked in organizations. Lt. Bear thought he was doing what was right, but his superior disagreed.

*In your judgment, what action should Lt. Bear have taken, or do you agree that oral reprimand was enough? How much and what things should he communicate to the assistant chief? Should all instances of discipline be communicated to one's superior?*

Communication is the process whereby the organization and its managers translate policy and procedures into agreed-on day-to-day decisions and acceptable operational activities. A manager uses communication as a vehicle for motivating, disciplining, and training officers in an effort to achieve organizational goals. In addition, a police manager plans and organizes work, issues directives, gives orders, and evaluates employees' unit and departmental performance, all in an effort to attain objectives and create a safe community.

## DEFINING MANAGERIAL COMMUNICATION

It is difficult to establish a definition of managerial communication acceptable to everyone. The problem is the extensive number of definitions of just the word *communication*, let alone the term *managerial communication*. Luthans provides three elements of communication in organizational behavior: (1) communications media and technology, (2) interpersonal communication, and (3) nonverbal communication. He stresses communication as the use of symbols to transfer the meaning of information.[3]

Thus managerial communication involves two entirely different and distinct functions (see Figure 10–1). The first aspect is organizational communication and includes standard operating procedures, rules, regulations, memoranda, and policy statements. The other element is interpersonal communication, in

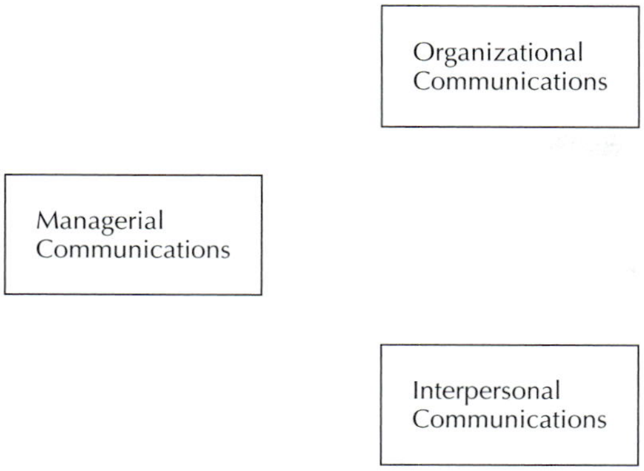

**Figure 10–1**

Components of Communication.

| Organizational Communications |
| :--- |

| Managerial Communications |
| :--- |

| Interpersonal Communications |
| :--- |

which a great deal more is communicated than specific messages. It includes emotions, needs, and feelings modifying and conditioning verbal messages.[4]

There is a critical need for managers to understand the complexity of the communication process and to strive for enhancement and improvement until it is open, continuous, and related positively to goal attainment. Communication among members of an organization is extremely important. When communication is faulty, problems abound and resolving them consumes a major portion of managerial time.

Effective communication between individuals is problematic when one party assumes that everyone concerned is aware of all aspects of the issue, whereas, in fact, many are still uninformed. If the basic assumption is faulty, then (in all likelihood) the results will be defective. Interpersonal communication involves the exchange of information. Not only must information be transmitted—it must be understood.

There are a number of barriers to effective communication:[5]

1. *Failure to listen.* Listening inattentively, passively, or not at all.[6]
2. *Noise in communication.* Interference with the message.
3. *Misuse of language.* Excessively vague, inaccurate, inflammatory, emotional, positive, or negative language.
4. *Lack of feedback.* One-way communication, in which the receiver provides no return of information about whether and with what effect the information came across.

This may sound simple, but it is not. When communication is poor, it can be exceedingly costly and in some cases harmful. If organizations have a vital force, it is communication. It is the binding ingredient of an organization. When a message is not understood, the immediate reaction is to find fault. Generally, blame is placed on a communication gap, or barrier.

Rainey lists even more particular communication barriers between groups:[7]

1. Definition of disagreement between groups as win-or-lose conflict.
2. Attempts by a group to aggrandize its own power and emphasize only its own goals and needs.
3. Use of threats.
4. Disguise of true positions and active distortion of information.

5. Attempt to exploit or isolate another group.
6. Emphasis by a group only of the differences and the superiority of its own position.

Finally, Rainey notes seven specific communication distortions that plague public bureaus:[8]

1. *Distorted perceptions.* Inaccurate perceptions of information that result from preconceived ideas or priorities or from striving to maintain self-esteem or defend cognitive inconsistency.
2. *Erroneous translation.* Interpretation of information by receivers in ways not intended by the senders.
3. *Errors of abstraction and differentiation.* Transmission of excessively abstract or selective information. Underemphasis on differences in favor of similarities or excessive polarization of fairly similar positions.
4. *Lack of congruence.* Ambiguity or inconsistency between elements of a message or between one message and other sources of information.
5. *Distrust of source.* Failure to accept an accurate message because of suspicions about bias or lack of credibility of the source.
6. *Jargon.* Communication difficulties resulting from highly specialized professional or technical language that confuses those outside the specialization (and often those within it).
7. *Manipulation and withholding of information.* Active distortion or withholding of information to support a group's own interests and influence the receiver.

In many instances a great deal of effort is expended to find a scapegoat to blame for inadequate communication. This proves to be a lot easier than dealing with the problem directly. While a common source of organizational problems is faulty communication, the mere act of improving communication will not make up for poor leadership or an inadequately structured organization. Good communication supports and reinforces the managerial processes of planning, organizing, directing, and controlling a law enforcement agency.

## MANAGERIAL FUNCTIONS

The role of communication is distinctly different for each of the major managerial functions. Effective management calls for a different application of communication skills, which vary from level to level within the organization. If communication is to be effective, all levels of management from the top down must nurture it. It is also essential for managers to recognize the human processes involved in communicating and utilize a variety of techniques when dealing with different managerial functions.[9]

**Communication and Planning**

Planning serves as the integrating function for a manager. It ties together separate entities as goals evolve and the objectives of each function are identified. Plans must be developed in a positive and outgoing manner. A useful plan must be based on current information, and in many instances officers at varying levels throughout the organization will have important information to contribute.

One of the problems in some agencies is that plans are developed in isolation and those responsible for plan implementation are never consulted. It seems logical for the preparation of plans to involve the people who will have to implement them, especially when the plans affect the way they will have to do the work.

A police department should continually gather pertinent information, convert it to a usable format, and distribute it to all personnel. The success of a plan depends on how successfully it is implemented, and one of the keys to successful implementation is communication. Put simply, employees can't and won't implement strategies that they don't buy into.[10]

Good planning requires a manager to communicate continually with all information sources (including personnel in other organizations). All information received should be evaluated even if it is not received through the normal chain of command. Rejecting vital information could lead to the failure of a plan when the implementation phase is reached.[11]

An effective police manager should view planning as fulfilling the following communication criteria:[12]

1. Openness within the organization, encouraging communication
2. Organizational climate fostering communication
3. Suggestion system allowing for continuous input
4. Access outside the chain of command so input can be received from all personnel
5. Continuous and responsive feedback

Firm commitment by police managers to an interactive type of planning that involves (as frequently as possible) agency personnel at all levels will lead to a greater degree of effectiveness as the agency deals with a dynamic and constantly changing society.[12]

## Communication and Organizing

The organizing function of police managers brings together various activities and groups, and places them within a structure of authority so that agreed-upon objectives and goals can be attained. Organizational structure provides the framework for transmitting formal communication. The advantage of formal communication is its predictability—it follows the chain of command, which serves as a filtering system as messages are sent and modified at each level of the organization. In some instances the filtering process can dilute a message to the point of distorting the original meaning. Usually, however, formal messages are given serious consideration because they come from known and reliable sources.

## Span of Management

Several factors must be taken into consideration in structuring an organization. One of these is the span of management, sometimes referred to as the span of control. The span of management is the number of subordinates reporting directly to a supervisor.[13] The span-of-control concept was first introduced into the literature by the writers of traditional management theory. *Span of management* is a broader term and includes such factors as the supervisor's capacity (taking into account his or her ability, experience, and level of energy) to oversee the activities of others directly.[14]

In the 1930s, V. A. Graicunas stated, "No executive should attempt to directly supervise the work of more than five, or at most six, immediate subordinates whose work interlocks."[15] Graicunas quantified the relationships between superiors and subordinates. It is interesting to note how rapidly the potential relationships increase as additional subordinates are added to the group (see Table 10–1). When a manager supervises only 2 subordinates, there are a total of 6 relationships among the 3 officers; when the number of subordinates increases to 3, the unit consists of 4 officers and the number of relationships increases to 18; and when there are 8 subordinates, the number of relationships increases to 1,080.[16]

Others have analyzed span of control differently. For example, Dessler states:[17]

> The average number of people reporting to a manager determines the number of management levels in the organization. For example, if an organization with 64 workers to be supervised has an average span of control of 8, there will be 8 supervisors directing the workers and 1 manager directing the 8 supervisors (a *flat* organization). If, on the other hand, the span of control were 4, the same number of workers would require 16 supervisors. 4 managers would in turn, direct the latter. These 4 managers would, in turn, be directed by 1 manager (a *tall* organization).

It is generally accepted that the higher one moves up through organizational levels, the smaller the number of immediate subordinates one should have to supervise. First-line supervisors can interact with a larger number of subordinates than officials at the top of the agency. From the behavioral viewpoint of management and the implementation of problem solving, there is a definite need to be flexible when determining the number to be supervised.

This leads then to the obvious question: "How many subordinates should report to a police manager?" The answer is short and to the point: it depends. Table 10–2 lists factors to be considered when attempting to determine an operational span of management. Each of these factors interacts to either reduce or expand the span of management.

For example, managers must assess their own ability. Those who delegate authority and practice a style of leadership emphasizing trust are capable of supervising more subordinates. Likewise, managers adept at communicating

Table 10–1    **Potential Number of Interactions between Superiors and Subordinates**

| Number of Subordinates | Number of Relationships* |
|---|---|
| 2 | 6 |
| 3 | 18 |
| 4 | 44 |
| 8 | 1,080 |

*The number of relationships can be determined by utilizing the following formula: $r = n(2^{n-1} + n - 1)$.

*Source:* V.A. Graicunas, "Relationship in Organizations," in Luther H. Gulick and Lyndall F. Urwick, eds., *Papers on the Science of Administration* (New York: Columbia University, 1937).

## Table 10–2  **Factors Influencing Span of Management**

1. Complexity of the work to be performed by the subordinate
2. Competence of the manager and the subordinates
3. Value system of the manager and the subordinates
4. Stability of the organization
5. Extent of standardization
6. Nature and number of interactions between the manager and others

*Source:* J. Clifton Williams, Andrew J. DuBrin, and Henry L. Sisk, *Management and Organization,* 5th ed. (Cincinnati: South-Western, 1985), and Robert J. Thierauf, Robert C. Klekamp, and Daniel W. Geeding, *Management Principles and Practices* (New York: Wiley, 1977).

effectively can expand their span of control because they spend less time discussing trivia and clarifying distorted messages.[18]

It is also true that when employees are well trained and self-motivated, a manager can easily supervise a larger number of them. When a community problem-solving program is fully operational, for example, a police manager will find himself or herself able to supervise a greater number of subordinates. If the span is too broad, the following symptoms may occur: communication between managers is poor, feedback fails to provide viable information needed to control operations, and performance standards prove to be unrealistic.[19]

**Line and Staff**

Another organizational problem arises when a law enforcement agency becomes large enough for a distinction to be made between line and staff. Recognizing the line/staff distinction is the initial step to take when a department arranges related functions into specific units. The value of this distinction is that it provides for the proper location of the two major functions of police organizations: preparation for the delivery of police services and the actual delivery of those services.[20]

The key to determining what is line and what is staff is not what specific functions they perform but how directly they contribute to the attainment of departmental goals. The staff serves the line, supplying it with records, data, transportation, and material so that the line can discharge its functions, which are operational.

Smaller organizations do not have separate staff units, but as a department grows, specialization is necessary to provide support services. Initially, functions such as communications, records, and evidence control evolve. As the agency continues to grow, such units as psychological service, crime analysis, and research and development are added.

The concept of line and staff acknowledges that there are two types of managerial authority. To blur this distinction can result in confusion and impede effective communication. One problem that can lead to such blurring is that specialized staff functions become somewhat vague. In most law enforcement agencies, we find three types of authority:[21]

1. *Line authority.* Line managers are always in charge of essential activities and can issue orders down the chain of command.
2. *Advisory authority.* Staff managers can only assist and advise line managers. They run staff departments.
3. *Functional authority.* Here, the manager can issue orders down the chain of command within the very narrow limits of his or her authority.

You can readily see that these three types of authority overlap operationally. In some instances, a single unit can exercise all three types of authority. Problems between line and staff occur in many agencies, generally when staff members exceed their authority by ignoring their advisory position. Thus, rather than recommending, they give orders. What starts out as an advisory function or a service function by a staff member suddenly blossoms into a threat to unity of command when authority is exceeded and there are conflicting orders.

Effective communication can be thwarted when line personnel perceive that line and staff conflicts are ignored and poor conditions are allowed to continue. When the chief supervises an excessive number of immediate subordinates, the office tends to become a bottleneck where effective communication decreases and work is impeded. When a communication network functions at maximum effectiveness, it serves to unify the organization, reduce confusion, and improve efficiency.

**Dual Reporting**     Some police agencies have organized under a matrix system. This type of structure alters the traditional concept of unity of command and allows for multiple supervisors, making it essential for police managers to learn how to function under a dual reporting system (see Figure 10–2). To make this kind of management work calls for the strengthening and formalization of secondary systems.

The problem-solving police department must learn to overcome the barriers to communication that arise under dual reporting. Power and decision-making need to be shared, and this is best handled by formalizing frequent interaction between managers. In other words, talk, but above all, listen.

Lastly, communication becomes increasingly complex when a new unit is created. Both formal and informal lines of communication are changed. It usually takes a considerable period of time before units adapt to each other and communication becomes effective.[22]

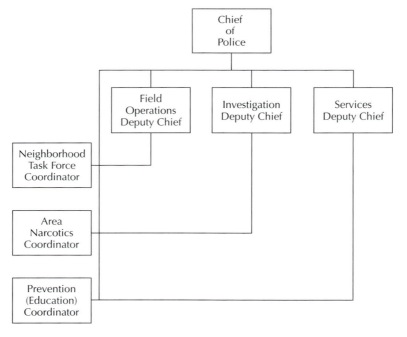

**Figure 10–2**
Dual Reporting System in a Matrix Organization.

A large part of a police manager's time is spent communicating. His or her effectiveness as a manager is tied to his or her ability to send appropriate messages. Communication will be more accurate, undistorted, and effective when it is properly filtered and routed within the organization. This is not always possible, but the police manager should work diligently to maximize attainment of this ideal within the organization.[23]

Establishing and utilizing communication networks in the organization can help bring about positive leadership. When communication networks are managed effectively, information is moved from one point to another within the organization for the greatest benefit of every member.

Communication networks fostering effective attainment of departmental goals serve four main purposes:[24]

1. The department's *regulatory* network serves as a vehicle for transmitting messages providing direction and guidance. Typical content includes policy statements, standard operating procedures, and rules and regulations. It is not uncommon for one department to need six three-ring binders to hold all the detailed procedures.

2. The *innovative* network provides the police manager with a way of adapting to change and meeting the needs of the community. Typical examples of tapping the resources within the organization include suggestion systems, quality circles, and task forces. The changing composition of the typical law enforcement agency places a premium on utilizing the expertise of every employee within the department.

3. The *integrative* network focuses on employee morale and places a strong emphasis on motivating every officer. Examples of communication in this area include praising an individual who does a good job, awarding citations for exceptional accomplishments, and announcing promotions.

4. The *informative* network comprises all types of communication not included under the other networks. Examples are newsletters, training bulletins, annual reports, and bulletin board notices (see Table 10–3).

A positive leadership style can contribute directly to organizational effectiveness by creating an organizational climate that fosters real communication. A manager should view every employee as someone who has the capacity to make a positive contribution to the department. A working relationship should be established, allowing for continuous employee input. Officers should be viewed as genuine assets, and communication should be viewed as the primary process that can ensure that everyone's skills are utilized.

If communication is to be effective, it must be nurtured at every management level—from the chief to the first-line supervisor. A police manager should work diligently at improving communication by utilizing each of the networks just described.

Table 10–3 **Communication Network**

| |
| --- |
| Regulatory |
| Innovative |
| Integrative |
| Informative |

**Communication and Control**

Controlling function is utilized extensively in law enforcement agencies to measure the performance of other managerial functions. Feedback provides a way of assessing the planning process, and (as just indicated) directing emphasizes the control of officer behavior. Finally, the organization is usually structured so as to place responsibility and authority in specific subunits of the department. Control, then, can certainly be viewed as an important ingredient and an integral part of the other managerial functions.

Control involves comparing the actual outcomes with planned outcomes, which can only be accomplished when communication is adequate and reliable. Controls are designed to provide a police manager with information regarding progress. Good communication serves the following four important functions:[25]

1. *Information function.* Communication provides information for decision-making. To make reasoned choices, managers require information concerning alternatives, future events, and potential outcomes of their decisions.
2. *Motivational function.* Communication encourages commitment to organizational objectives, thus enhancing motivation.
3. *Control function.* Communication clarifies duties, authority, and responsibilities, thereby permitting control. If there is ambiguity concerning such things, it is impossible to isolate the sources of problems and to take corrective actions.
4. *Emotive function.* Communication permits the expression of feelings and the satisfaction of social needs. It may also help people to vent frustrations.

Deciding what information is needed in order to have a positive process requires a manager to review the control system constantly and evaluate it in terms of its impact on employees. It has been found that compliance with standards is higher when employees find them to be realistic.

## MANAGERIAL COMMUNICATION

The importance of communication cannot be disputed, but it still serves to confuse and confound some managers. Every manager strives to communicate successfully. Communication must be carefully studied and continuously readjusted for proper clarity in order to avoid confusion. Unfortunately, a poorly written document or a misinterpreted oral message can create serious problems. Frequently managers believe they are communicating when exactly the opposite is true.

Police officers, as they enforce the law, constantly make decisions that deny citizens their freedom. Likewise, law enforcement managers make innumerable daily decisions that have positive and negative impacts on officers as well as citizens. Police managers cannot perform any of the four phases of the managerial process—planning, organizing, directing, and controlling—without communicating either formally or informally.

Communicating with any degree of effectiveness is demanding and time-consuming. It is not easy, nor does it just happen. The process of communicating requires the attention of everyone in the organization. It cannot be turned off and on based on the whim of a manager. It must be constantly refined and adjusted to the current situation.

The chief executive officer of a county law enforcement agency recently was the subject of controversy when a full-page ad publicizing a shopping center appeared in a local newspaper. The heading for the ad read "Crimes of Fashion" and featured a young handcuffed model attired in a tight-fitting black evening gown, leaning forward, with her eyes closed and lips pouting. Off to one side of the ad was a shadowy male figure wearing dark glasses, and a police vehicle was clearly identifiable in the background.

The male figure in the ad was the sheriff, J. Fred Sullivan, who was running for reelection. Two other candidates for the position lost little time in criticizing the sheriff. The ad was depicted by the opposing candidates as anti-feminist and as a vivid expression of sexual bondage.

The sheriff posed for the ad at the request of the shopping center, which contacted him through his campaign manager, Virginia Marsh. Sheriff Sullivan was not compensated for appearing in the ad, but $200 was donated to two different charitable organizations.

Women's organizations are expressing shock over the incident, claiming that the ad is negative toward women and condones violence. Their concern is that the ad damages their years of effort to change the attitudes of the public and law enforcement toward women.

Both the sheriff and his campaign manager say that the ad was done for charity, without intent to insult or demean anyone.

The women's groups find the ad to be so offensive they are considering picketing the sheriff's home and office, as well as the shopping center. The sheriff and his campaign manager have apologized. The shopping center claims the ad will not be used again, and an apology appeared in the following issue of the newspaper. In addition, the shopping center donated money to a women's organization.

*In this instance, the message the sheriff and the shopping center wanted to convey was interpreted by the women's groups as supporting violence against women. Why did the women's groups view the message negatively? Would the ad have had the same negative response if the young model had not been handcuffed? Could the ad have been designed in a way that would have been less controversial? Should a public figure appear in an ad to promote specific business interests?*

Generally speaking, the police chief executive officer serves as the spokesperson for the agency as well as its leader and figurehead (see Chapter 2). The other two managerial levels focus more on internal communication and subordinate interaction. Actually, all the managerial levels have a reasonable amount of contact with citizens and citizens groups, but such contact is least for the supervisory manager. Here is a listing of the communication tasks performed by first-line supervisors in descending order of importance:[26]

1. Provide feedback to subordinates regarding their job performance. This should include such things as identifying strengths and weaknesses as well as calling attention to exceptional or inadequate performance.

2. Prepare written employee performance evaluations.

3. Respond to subordinates' inquiries regarding departmental policy, legal questions, and discretionary decision-making.

4. Meet with and provide direction to subordinates regarding particular violations, investigative techniques, and case processing.

5. Brief subordinates on new or revised policies and procedures.

6. Communicate subordinates' concerns, desires, and suggestions to management.

It can readily be seen that communication defines the nature of a law enforcement agency and is a time-consuming process. Communicating is exceedingly complex, and managerial effectiveness depends on identifying and overcoming communication barriers.

# REALISTIC COMMUNICATION PROCESS

One expert points out that effective communication is built on a free and open exchange among all levels of management. Typical of the communication dilemma is the feeling seemingly shared by supervisors at every level of the organization that the administration gives subordinates everything they need to know but could do a much better job of passing information down to the supervisory level.[27]

Communication in organizations involves three major actors: individuals, groups, and the organization itself.[28] Communicating is a mental maze to be mastered. If it is to be improved, we must become aware of what constitutes effective communication and what should be avoided. Poor communication is a waste of time and energy—so the goal is to avoid inadequate communication at all costs. The sender of a message is responsible for transmitting with clarity and ensuring the message is not only received but understood.[29]

An individual sending a message must do everything possible to affect the behavior of the recipient. One person's communication with another can be effective only if (1) the message is encoded, (2) the message is transmitted, (3) the message is decoded, and (4) the receiver of the message interprets and understands it correctly.[30]

The communication process provides a means of viewing the complexity of making oneself understood in an organizational context. One model of the process involves six stages and two modifiers (see Figure 10–3).

**Sender** The source of a message can be anyone in or outside the organization. It is important to note when someone is trying to function as the sender of a formal or informal message. If the sender has a great deal of expertise and is viewed as knowledgeable, added attention is paid to the communication. This is also true if the sender holds a position of rank. Certainly when the sender is the chief, the message receives immediate attention.

The sender of a message determines not only how important it is but how relevant. This is known as *gatekeeping*. When a police manager is the sender, the chain of command serves as a vehicle of transmission and decisions are constantly made about what messages should be sent.

**Encoding** When the message is converted into a readily understandable form, it is *encoded*. A message can either be verbal or nonverbal. It is desirable to make a choice of symbols (e.g., read the *Miranda* warning) that everyone can understand. Many things influence the encoding process. One of the major variables is the personality of the sender (or organizational members) who actually encodes the message. Every member of an organization has his or her own perception of what a message should accomplish and how it should be encoded.[31]

Vocabulary and expertise can play major roles in the sender's ability to encode data, ideas, or the interpretation of information. Encoding is not easy. It requires a manager to select some type of symbol representing exactly what is to be communicated.

**Message** The specific information transmitted constitutes the message. It might be some type of symbol creating an awareness of need, pointing out a problem, or expressing an opinion about a matter of concern to the department. Whatever

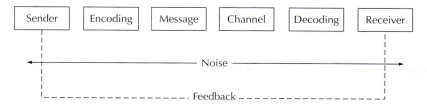

**Figure 10–3**
Realistic Communication Process.

the intent of the message, it is in the sender's best interest to be sure it gets through loud and clear. There is no guarantee that the message as understood by the receiver will be the same as the message intended by the sender.[32]

One of the most difficult tasks for police managers is to write standard operating procedures, rules, regulations, or departmental policies. It seems that such documents have to be written and rewritten several times before every level in the organization places a stamp of approval on them; employees may need training in order to interpret and use them.[33]

Semantics is one of the problems. A single word may have very different meanings to different people. Therefore it is essential that words be carefully chosen and clearly defined for effective communication; jargon aggravates the problem.[34]

Each police manager who prepares a message should seek to answer the following questions:

1. What is the real message I want to send?
2. Is there sufficient information to support the message?
3. Does any word or phrase imply something not intended?
4. Is there any possibility the message can be misinterpreted?
5. What will be the reaction to the message?
6. Will the message produce the intended results?

Good communication means clearly expressing one's intentions in a message. More importantly, when a police manager prepares a message, keep in mind that it must be worded in plain English. The ability to express one's thoughts is one of the most important distinctions separating successful managers from those who prove to be ineffective.[35]

**Channel**

In law enforcement agencies, a number of communications channels are available for transmitting messages, including radio, teletype, computer, teleconferencing devices, telephone, electronic mail, and voice mail. Other potential channels include bulletin boards, departmental newsletters, or, when appropriate, verbal and/or nonverbal communication. In general the supervisory police manager spends more time communicating verbally than managers at higher levels in the chain of command.

As police departments grow and become more decentralized, there is a tendency for communication to become depersonalized. The terminal on the desk or in the police vehicle becomes the major channel for transmitting messages. The screen and the keyboard increasingly dominate the communication process—the in-basket and the mailbox are slowly being replaced. Messages can be sent and received, police records checked, license numbers processed, case files reviewed, and bookings checked without leaving one's vehicle or desk. E-mail and the Internet are enhancing such tasks as recruiting as well as providing yet another form of organizational communication.[36]

**Decoding**   When a message is received, it undergoes decoding—it is interpreted and given meaning by the receiver. If the message is decoded improperly, it will not be understood.

A message becomes significant when meaning is given to symbols (e.g., "book the suspect"). When decoding, a receiver should try to ascertain the following:[37]

1. What the sender *intended* to say
2. What the sender *actually* said
3. What the receiver *heard*
4. What the receiver *thinks* he or she heard
5. What the receiver *said*
6. What the sender *thinks* the receiver said

Each of these factors serves to modify the decoding process, and the accuracy of the receiver's interpretation will depend on his or her ability to respond adequately to each factor.

**Receiver**   The receiver is the person or persons to whom the message is sent. Like the sender, the receiver can inadvertently distort or misinterpret the message in any of several ways. Motives, emotions, and how one perceives a message all have a tendency to impair effective communication. Selective perception will cause the receiver to distort a message in many instances. This is actually a filtering system that prevents messages from being completely understood. Meaning has to be ascribed to a message before it can be followed by a reaction.

Selective perception is more apt to occur when a message is transmitted orally and less apt to occur when the message is written. Personality, previous experience, and some type of stimulus modify perception of the received information. This actually means that different people will react to messages differently.[38]

Miscommunication can also occur because some words allow for different interpretations, some receivers are poor listeners, feedback is inadequate, and nonverbal communication can be interpreted differently.

**Feedback**   Until feedback occurs, communication cannot be described as a two-way process. Feedback only occurs when a receiver responds to the sender, with something as simple as a nod of the head or as complex as the preparation of a detailed report.

Without feedback, the sender will never know whether a message has been received. Feedback in the performance evaluation process has the following characteristics:[39]

1. *Intention.* Effective feedback is directed toward improving job performance and making the employee a more valuable asset. It is not a personal attack and should not compromise the individual's feeling of self-worth or image. Rather, effective feedback is directed toward aspects of the job.

2. *Specificity.* Effective feedback is designed to provide recipients with specific information so that they know what must be done to correct the situation. Ineffective feedback is general and leaves questions in the recipients' minds; it may leave the recipients frustrated in seeking ways to correct the problem.

3. *Description.* Effective feedback can also be characterized as descriptive rather than evaluative. It tells the employee what he or she has done in objective terms rather than presenting a value judgment.

4. *Usefulness.* Effective feedback is information that an employee can use to improve performance. It serves no purpose to berate employees for their lack of skill if they do not have the ability or training to perform properly. Thus, the guideline is that if it is not something the employee can correct, it is not worth mentioning.

5. *Timeliness.* There are also considerations in timing feedback properly. As a rule, the more immediate the feedback is, the better. This way the employee has a better chance of knowing what the supervisor is talking about and can take corrective action.

6. *Readiness.* In order for feedback to be effective, employees must be ready to receive it. When feedback is imposed or forced on employees, it is much less effective.

7. *Clarity.* Effective feedback must be clearly understood by the recipient. A good way of checking this is to ask the recipient to restate the major points of the discussion. Also, supervisors can observe facial expressions as indicators of understanding and acceptance.

8. *Validity.* In order for feedback to be effective, it must be reliable and valid. Of course, when the information is incorrect, the employee will feel that the supervisor is unnecessarily biased or the employee may take corrective action that is inappropriate and only compounds the problem.

When used properly, feedback will not only improve the communication process, it will provide a foundation for better departmental morale and heighten the potential for attaining objectives and goals. Table 10–4 lists some suggestions for improving feedback skills.

## Noise

The last feature of the communication process is noise—defined as anything disrupting communication. It includes not only physical noise but also attitudes and emotions interfering with either interpreting the message or providing adequate feedback. In recent years, substantial job stress has been identified as a type of noise that makes it difficult for some individuals to concentrate on a message.[40]

At the beginning of the communication process, noise can interfere with the conceptualization of the message, making it unclear. When a message is encoded, the wrong symbol may be selected. This can happen when slang, jargon, or unknown technical terms are used. When the message is transmitted, it can be garbled—especially when it is oral rather than written. Decoding can be the next stage at which noise appears when perceptions are different. The receiver's attitude or values can also cause a message to be misunderstood.

**Table 10–4  Suggestions for Improving Feedback Skills**

The following specific suggestions can help managers to be more effective in providing feedback to others:

1. *Focus on specific behaviors.* Feedback should be specific rather than general. For example, instead of saying, "You have a bad attitude," a manager might say, "Bob, I'm concerned with your attitude toward work. You were a half-hour late to yesterday's staff meeting, and then you told me you hadn't read the preliminary report we were discussing. Today you tell me you're taking off three hours early for a dental appointment." This tells Bob why he is being criticized.

2. *Keep feedback impersonal.* Feedback should be job related. Never criticize someone personally because of an inappropriate action. Telling people they're "stupid," "incompetent," or the like is almost always counterproductive.

3. *Keep feedback goal oriented.* If a manager has to say something negative, he or she should make sure it's directed toward the *recipient's* goals. A manager should ask whom the feedback is supposed to help. If the answer is essentially that "I've got something I just want to get off my chest," then he or she should not speak.

4. *Make feedback well timed.* Feedback is most meaningful to a recipient when there is a very short interval between his or her behavior and the receipt of feedback about that behavior.

5. *Ensure understanding.* Is the feedback concise and complete enough so the recipient clearly and fully understands the communication? Managers should consider having the recipient rephrase the content of the feedback to see whether it fully captures the intended meaning.

6. *Direct negative feedback toward behavior that is controllable by the recipient.* There's little value in reminding a person of a shortcoming over which he or she has no control. Negative feedback, therefore, should be directed toward behavior the recipient can do something about.

*Source:* Stephen P. Robbins, *Essentials of Organizational Behavior,* 7th ed., (Upper Saddle River, NJ: Prentice Hall, 2003), p. 127. Reprinted by permission of Pearson Education, Inc., Upper Saddle River, NJ 07458.

Finally, emotional bias plays a very important part in communication noise. The receiver's attitudes, values, and experiences all serve as a filter within the communication process and can cause a message to be altered or misinterpreted. Filtering, whether intentional or unintentional, can result in only part of the message being transmitted or interpreted. An awareness of emotional bias is the first step in working to reduce noise in the communication process.[41]

## FORMAL ORGANIZATIONAL COMMUNICATION

Effective communication within a police organization becomes increasingly difficult as the agency becomes larger and decentralized. Many police organizations have formalized communication channels based on military models—as we have noted, a strict chain of command best describes the typical police organization.

Communication networks within a department reflect both its hierarchical nature and the differentiation of functions within it: communication flows horizontally as well as vertically. The functions performed by police departments require extensive communication. Decisions by managers are generally dependent on information received from operational personnel in various departmental units.

Police bureaucracies are unique in that line personnel are usually the ones at the focal point of activities generating an organizational response to an incident. Consequently the information line officers feed into the communication network is crucial to the department's operations.[42]

## Downward Communication

Downward communication involves messages from senders relatively high in the organizational structure to receivers in lower-level positions (supervisor to subordinate).[43] There are five types of downward messages:[44]

1. *Job instructions.* Directions for doing specific tasks. This type of message is most often given priority in police organizations. Instructions for police officers are communicated to them through direct orders from their supervisors, training sessions, training manuals, and written directives. The objective is to ensure the reliable performance of every police officer in the organization.

2. *Job rationale.* Information about how one task relates to other tasks in the organization. This is designed to provide police officers with a full understanding of their positions and how they are related to other positions in the same organization. Many police officers know what they are to do, but not why. Withholding information on the rationale of the job not only reduces the loyalty of the member to the organization but also means that the organization must rely heavily on job instructions. If officers do not understand why they should do something or how their jobs relate to the organization, then there must be sufficient repetition in the task instructions so that individuals behave automatically.

3. *Procedures and practices.* Messages indicating the "rules of the game" in the organization—the role requirements for its members. In addition to receiving instructions about the job, police officers are informed about other duties and privileges they have as members of the police organization.

4. *Feedback.* Messages telling individuals about their performance on the job. These are necessary to ensure that the organization is operating properly, and they serve as a means to motivate individual performers. As mentioned previously, feedback must be properly given.

5. *Indoctrination.* Messages about overall organizational goals and the relationship of individual goals to organizational goals. The purpose is to implant organizational goals.

Unlike many business managers, who rely on a constant upward flow of information from the bottom of their organizations, police managers devote a great deal of their time to downward communication, with the aim of controlling the discretion of line officers. They do this by issuing orders and developing standard operating procedures.

The chain of command determines the usual flow of messages; priority is given to information that starts at the top and filters down through the organization (see Table 10–5). Except in critical situations, managers give responding to memos from the chief priority over responding to memos from subordinates or other managers.[45]

Generally, in addition to the five types of downward messages listed above, downward communication concerns itself with the following types of messages:

1. Policies
2. Procedures

Table 10–5 **Sample Departmental Policy**

*Officer Duties and Responsibilities at Scene of Air Ambulance Usage*

Officers at the scene of an air ambulance usage should:

1. Clear an area of at least 100 x 100 feet for a helicopter landing pad;
2. Park cruiser in such a manner that the headlights indicate the direction in which the helicopter will come in over the top of the cruiser;
3. Advise the air medical team if the patient received any prior medical treatment at the scene of an emergency;
4. Keep spectators away from the aircraft;
5. Not approach the aircraft from the rear under any circumstances;
6. Not allow a vehicle to be driven closer than 50 feet to the aircraft;
7. Not carry any item in the vicinity of the aircraft that will extend above the height of the individual, such as portable radios with extended antenna;
8. Not assist the aircraft crew with the patient unless requested to do so; and
9. Advise post of the departure of the aircraft.

*Source:* Kentucky State Police, *General Duties, Responsibilities and Guidelines: Chapter 16*, OM-B-7.

3. Rules and regulations
4. Performance feedback
5. Schedules
6. Operational plans
7. Training bulletins
8. Informational memoranda
9. Legal decisions

Even though downward communication has the cloak of power backed by organizational authority, a police executive manager should create an environment that allows for two-way communication. If communication flows only in one direction, then those at lower levels in the organization will resort to modifying or filtering the messages as they come down the chain of command.

Managers must try to avoid the following mistakes when conducting downward communication:[46]

- Pronouncements from "on high"
- Frequent dramatic changes in direction
- Reliance on formal communication
- Policies without explanations
- Ambiguous "bureaucratese"
- Silence

If managers can understand the impact of communication on subordinates and do something about it, communication can become more effective. If employees get the information they need, they perform better as individuals and in groups. Policies and procedures are necessary to guide the downward communication process.[47]

Upward communication involves communication from sources in lower-level positions to receivers in relatively higher positions. It starts with the line officer. As each message goes up through each level of the organization, it is filtered and distorted more than messages are in downward communication. Upward communication is vital because it provides managers with a means of evaluating the messages they have sent down the chain of command. It is a way of identifying problems, and in many instances it is the quickest way of really finding out what is going on in the organization.

Luthans offers the following ways to improve upward communication:[48]

1. *The grievance procedure.* This is provided for in most collective-bargaining agreements in unionized organizations and also in some nonunionized organizations. The grievance procedure allows an employee to appeal upward beyond his or her immediate manager. It protects individuals from arbitrary action by their direct managers and encourages communication about complaints.

2. *The open-door policy.* Taken literally, this means that the manager's door is always open to employees. It is a continuous invitation for employees to come in and talk about anything that is troubling them. Unfortunately, in practice open-door policies often turn out to be more fiction than fact.

3. *The use of e-mail.* The e-mail channel greatly loosens employees' inhibitions about communicating upward. Most employees can and will directly send e-mail to anyone in the organization, including upper-level management.

4. *Counseling, attitude questionnaires, and exit interviews.* Human resources departments can greatly facilitate upward communication by conducting nondirective, confidential counseling sessions; by periodically administering attitude questionnaires; and by holding meaningful exit interviews with employees who leave the organization.

5. *Participative techniques.* Participative techniques can generate a great deal of communication. There is also empirical research indicating that employees who participate in communication networks are generally more satisfied with their jobs, are more committed to their organizations, and are better performers than employees who are not involved in the communication process.

6. *An empowerment strategy.* Closely related to participative techniques are the newly emerging empowerment strategies. Empowerment means different things in different organizations; ideally, though, it should involve giving employees not only the authority to make decisions but also the resources, especially information, to get the job done and satisfy customers. This creates a climate of openness and trust that leads to improved upward communication by empowered employees.

7. *The ombudsperson.* Many organizations have created and used this position to provide an outlet for persons who have been treated unfairly or in a depersonalized manner by a large bureaucratic government.

Generally, two types of information can be supplied by employees: (1) personal information about ideas, attitudes, and performance and (2) more technical feedback about performance. For example:[49]

1. What the persons have done
2. What those under them have done
3. What their peers have done
4. What they think needs to be done
5. What their problems are
6. What the problems of the unit are
7. What matters of organizational practice and policy need to be reviewed

It is very important for managers to determine whether the information received from subordinates is accurate. It will be, provided that there is mutual respect for each other in the working relationship Subordinates must trust a boss and be willing to forward negative information when necessary. Upward communication of a negative type should not place the originator at risk—it should be accepted as a challenge to management to change or fix something that has gone wrong.

The upward flow of communication in police organizations is not noted for spontaneous and objective expression, despite attempts to formalize the process of feedback up the line.[50] As an example of how one can be placed at risk, a deputy chief of police in a medium-sized city publicly criticized how the department handled a situation involving a police officer barricaded in a motel room. The officer was finally talked out of the room without anyone being injured, and after the departmental investigation he was allowed to resign from the department. The deputy chief who voiced his displeasure with the handling of the case was placed on administrative leave, and he retired in short order.

**Horizontal Communication**

Horizontal communication is part of the normal working conditions within a department. For example, two officers talk with each other about a common problem, or an officer discusses a case with a detective or a criminalist, or a records supervisor is consulted about information on a suspect or a defendant. Such communication is initiated in order to coordinate tasks, solve problems, share information, and/or resolve conflict.[51]

Communicating horizontally, across unit boundary lines, is fraught with difficulty. There are a number of reasons why peers may not communicate. For example, rivalry for recognition and promotion may cause reluctance. Subordinates may also have difficulty communicating with highly specialized peers in other divisions.[52]

Whisenand states that "Communicating across and diagonally in a police organization assures it of seamless operations" and offers the following reasons for encouraging such communication:[53]

1. *Teamwork.* Confusion, conflict, and frustration result from a lack of coordination between work units. If teamwork is not emphasized, detectives and the narcotics unit could be investigating the same crime, one patrol unit could be messing up the operations of another, and so on. By helping to coordinate tasks, informal communication contributes to the fulfillment of organizational goals.
2. *Common problems.* Weakness in horizontal and diagonal communication nearly guarantees that the root causes of a police problem will go undetected. Techniques such as brainstorming can help a department engage in problem-oriented policing.

3. *Feedback needed by individuals.* Most of us want to know what others think about our efforts. Some of this feedback occurs within the work unit and meets our ego and esteem needs, which are feelings of value to the organization.

4. *Professional guidance.* The sharing of information among work units increases the probability that the various groups are acting in concert with approved service values and quality standards.

5. *Conflict resolution.* The members of one department may meet to discuss a conflict inherent in the department or between units.

In addition, horizontal communication can improve service delivery to clients by cutting red tape and going directly to the heart of a problem. Such flexibility empowers individuals both inside and outside the organization. As horizontal communication assumes an increasingly important place in the overall communication process, it will bring greater balance to organizations and serve as a major vehicle in improving the delivery of police services.

## COMMUNICATION IN THE INFORMAL ORGANIZATION

As we have observed, a vast majority of the problems in organizations result from faulty communication. Effective police managers become adept at solving such problems by becoming sensitive to one additional communication system—the informal system.

The bureaucratic organization sets forth the communication relations between members of an organization in explicit detail; the informal organization identifies, in most instances, the individuals with whom organizational members prefer to communicate. Whisenand contends that most initial developments of ideas in police departments originate in informal communication channels. The main advantage of developing ideas in this fashion is twofold: they can be withdrawn or changed without fear of official disapproval.[54] When allowed to choose for themselves, people carry on a great deal of communication within informal channels.

In police departments, these informal channels become necessary under certain conditions. Whisenand offers five conditions for their development:[55]

1. The greater the degree of interdependence among activities within the department is, the greater the number and use of subformal channels.

2. The more uncertainty there is about the objectives of the department, the greater the number and use of subformal channels. When the environment is relatively unpredictable, people cannot easily determine what they should be doing by referring to that environment. Consequently, they tend to talk to each other more in order to gain an improved understanding of their situation.

3. When a police organization is operating under the pressure of time, it tends to use the subformal channels extensively because there is often no time to use the formal channels. Thus, police administrators reach out for information whenever they can get it, from whatever channel is necessary.

4. If the divisions of a police organization are in strong competition, they tend to avoid subformal channels and communicate only formally.

Conversely, closely cooperating sections rely primarily on subformal communication.

5. Subformal communication channels are used more frequently if department members have stable relationships with each other than if their relationships are constantly changing.

A word of caution is necessary when considering the informal aspects of organizations, because one individual can belong to more than one group. The membership of any single group is constantly changing. Nonetheless, the informal organization is a vital part of the communication process.

**The Grapevine**    A unique form of informal communication within an organization is the grapevine. In fact, it is an inevitable part of human behavior and an important element of a communication system. It cannot be eliminated, even though it can be harmful as well as helpful.[56] The grapevine never appears on the department's organizational chart, but it carries a number of messages and often works rapidly.

For the most part the messages are oral, although in some instances written messages are sent through this informal communication system. Examples include the selective circulation of a proposal to reorganize the department or an internal affairs investigative report. The grapevine in an organization has no respect for rank or authority and can link members in any combination of directions.

The grapevine functions constantly. Sometimes it is transmitting a great deal of information; in other instances, the messages (of any reasonable importance) are few, and the grapevine performs a more social function. One characteristic of the grapevine is that it usually operates faster than the formal communication system. Another characteristic is distortion. Messages can easily become garbled and ambiguous as they move through the grapevine at a rapid pace.[57]

Rumors are definitely identified with the grapevine. A rumor is an unverified belief flowing freely through the grapevine. A rumor is seldom factual but cannot be refuted easily. As a message moves through the grapevine, the gaps are filled in and embellishment can become significant. If the message is exceedingly complex, the rumor mill will simplify it.

The grapevine cannot be managed, but when it is understood, its negative effects can be minimized or eliminated. When a rumor arises, the following mechanisms can be used to deal with it:[58]

1. Try to wait it out. Some rumors dissipate over time and do little actual harm.
2. If waiting does not work, publicly refute the rumor. Refuting or even ridiculing a rumor in public negates its "news value." This approach may also lead people to distrust those who later attempt to pass the rumor along.
3. Feed valid information into the grapevine to counteract the undesired message.

A police manager should tap into the grapevine by making a sincere effort to know what messages are being carried. The best plan of action is to make relevant inquiries of those who are part of the informal communication network. It is always amazing what different people in an organization know.

Ask the secretaries, clerks, janitors, or active members of employee groups. Any or all of them can help identify current areas of concern.

The grapevine can be an important addition to the formal communication process. It can give a manager insight into employee emotions, attitudes, and concerns. It can also be used to monitor the overall morale of organizational personnel.

## IMPROVING COMMUNICATION

Several techniques are helpful in improving communication. Each of the techniques we describe has both advantages and disadvantages, so a manager should select the technique or techniques appropriate for use within his or her particular organization.

Managers need to develop listening skills. The key is to be sensitive to the purpose of listening. Empathetic listening is called active listening.[59] Table 10–6 lists ten keys to effective listening.

**Listening**

Table 10–6 **Ten Keys to Effective Listening**

| Keys to Effective Listening | The Bad Listener | The Good Listener |
|---|---|---|
| 1. Find areas of interest | Tunes out dry subjects | Opportunizes: "What's in it for me?" |
| 2. Judge content, not delivery | Tunes out if delivery is poor | Judges content; skips over delivery errors |
| 3. Hold your fire | Tends to enter into arguments | Doesn't judge until comprehension is complete |
| 4. Listen for ideas | Listens for facts | Listens for central themes |
| 5. Be flexible | Takes intensive notes using only one system | Takes fewer notes; uses several different systems, depending on the speaker |
| 6. Work at listening | Shows no energy output; fakes attention | Works hard; exhibits active body state |
| 7. Resist distraction | Is distracted easily | Fights or avoids distractions; tolerates bad habits; knows how to concentrate |
| 8. Exercise your mind | Resists difficult expository material; seeks light, recreational material | Uses heavier material as exercise for the mind |
| 9. Keep your mind open | Reacts to emotional words | Interprets color words, does not get hung up on them |
| 10. Capitalize on the fact that *thought* is faster than speech | Tends to daydream with slow speakers | Challenges, anticipates, mentally summarizes, weighs the evidence, and listens between the lines to the tone of the speaker's voice |

*Source:* Linda K. Stroh, Gregory B. Northcraft, and Margaret A. Neale, *Organizational Behavior: A Management Challenge* (Mahwah, NJ: Lawrence Erlbaum Associates, 2002), p. 183.

In sum, listening is a skill that can be developed. To develop active listening skills, take the following steps:[60]

1. Receive the message from the sender.
2. Capture the meaning of the message based on its content and the sender's nonverbal cues.
3. Test your understanding of the message by reflecting it back to the sender.
4. Check whether the sender confirms or corrects your interpretation of the message.

Listening is a skill that is necessary to communication. It must be developed and put into practice.

**Survey Feedback**

Surveys can be useful to managers because they provide information about employee perceptions. Surveys may be conducted by personally interviewing officers and other employees or by using the telephone. Face-to-face interviewing is time-consuming, but it allows the interviewer to ask a large number of probing questions. A telephone survey allows the interviewer an opportunity to talk with a larger number of agency personnel.

It is not necessary to contact every member of the department when conducting a survey. That is why the sampling technique is recommended. A survey can be conducted by dividing the sample by rank, gender, age, ethnic origin, or any other compelling critical element. A random sample results when the manager or a researcher selects each participant in such a way that everyone has an equal chance of being selected.

An employee survey can provide management with information about the communication process as well as serve as an excellent vehicle for improving and increasing the flow of information upward. This information cannot be easily obtained in other ways. Surveys allow employees to express their attitudes about such issues as:[61]

- Communication
- Motivational factors
- Coordination
- Control
- Planning
- Directing
- Satisfaction

This information (obtained by questionnaire) can serve as the basis for a follow-up study and changes in the communication system. The survey-feedback instrument can be used to change and improve the department's communication process. It can prove useful in revealing problems and clarifying issues. However, if superiors ignore the results of an employee survey, the survey project can backfire and result in increased employee frustration, turnover, absenteeism, job apathy, cynicism, an even sabotage.[62]

Jerry Olsen has been with the Seaville Police Department for the last nine years. He is currently assigned to the patrol division and is on the swing shift. He is regarded as an excellent officer and during his service with the department has received 12 commendations for outstanding performance.

Officer Olsen is extremely well liked by his peers and is respected as a real street cop. He attended college for two years and made the decision not to pursue any additional formal education. He really enjoys his job and has no desire to achieve higher rank. In fact, he has been eligible to take the sergeants examination twice but refused both times.

Recently, the department adopted a rewards, gifts, and gratuities policy, which states in part, "Officers shall not solicit, directly or indirectly, any person, firm, or organization for any reward, gratuity, contribution, or gift." This new policy was discussed at length at roll call, and its intent and implications seemed to be understood by everyone.

The officers on Officer Olsen's team always have a coffee break at Lillie's Grill, and they do not pay for their coffee. The manager of the café strongly supports the practice, and it is clear to the staff that the presence of the officers provides added security. The café is located in a high-crime area and is unquestionably an oasis in the desert. Even the patrons like to see the officers come into the café because their presence is calming.

Lt. Cal Germann, watch commander, advised the officers that free coffee is in violation of the new department policy. The officers feel very strongly that a couple of cups of coffee cannot be considered a gratuity or gift. Officer Olsen, serving as the spokesperson for the team, points out that although the officers do not pay for the coffee, they actually leave tips exceeding its price.

Lt. Germann is adamant. He claims that the free coffee is a violation of policy. On the other hand, the officers feel strongly that the policy is not intended to cover such a minor thing as a cup of coffee. All parties involved attended roll call when the policy was discussed, but there is obviously a misunderstanding about the actual intent of the policy.

*How might communication be improved at the roll call meeting other than reading the policy and limiting the discussion to answering questions? The question of a cup of coffee never came up during the original discussion. How can the roll call session be conducted? How should the policy be rewritten to cover Lt. Germann's concern (which actually is interpreted as prohibiting such things as free coffee)?*

**Exit Interview**

Whenever employees retire, resign, or are dismissed, they should be interviewed to obtain information useful for improving the department's communication process. A manager or someone from the personnel unit should conduct the interview. Every effort should be made to obtain accurate information. During the interview, emphasis should be placed on the process and not on the personalities involved. It is also useful to conduct a second interview (after a waiting period) to verify the accuracy of information obtained the first time.[63]

**Gender Differences**

Women have become firmly established in police work, yet it remains a somewhat male-dominated profession. The issue of how well men and women communicate often can be rationalized or ignored.[64] However, difficulties due to differences in communication styles remain. Men speak and hear a language of status and independence; women speak and hear a language of connection and intimacy. For men, conversations are typically a means to preserve independence and maintain status in the organizational hierarchy. For women, conversations are typically negotiations for closeness in which people try to seek and give confirmation and support.[65] Differences such as these must be recognized and kept in the forefront in the communication process between the sexes.

# SUMMARY

Communication is the vehicle that police managers use to translate policy and procedures into day-to-day decisions and acceptable operational activities. Managers utilize communication to motivate, discipline, and train officers and civilian employees for the purpose of achieving organizational goals.

Managerial communication involves two entirely different and distinct types of communication—organizational and interpersonal. The former concerns itself with standard operating procedures; the latter deals with emotions and feelings modifying and conditioning messages.

The role that communication plays is distinct for each of the major managerial functions: planning, organizing, directing, and controlling. The manager must nurture communication at all levels of the organization and learn to recognize the human processes involved in communicating as well as utilize a variety of techniques for each of the managerial functions.

Communication in organizations is performed by three major actors: individuals, groups, and the organization itself. According to one model, each act of communication can be broken down into six elements (sender, encoding, message, channel, decoding, and receiver) and two modifiers (feedback and noise).

Formal organizational communication systems include three types of communication: downward, upward, and horizontal. Each influences the agency differently and places unique demands on police managers at different levels in the organization.

The informal organization identifies the individuals and groups with which members actually communicate. The informal groups include task groups, friendship groups, and other special-interest groups. The grapevine is another supplement to the formal system of communication, making the communication process even more complex.

Finally, a police manager can use several different techniques in an effort to improve organizational communication. Two of these are survey feedback and exit interviews. These techniques can be used to determine employee perceptions. Once information is obtained through one of the techniques, police managers should develop a plan to improve the communication process.

The following guidelines are helpful in the improvement of communication skills:[66]

1. Remember that effective communication involves creating meaning, transmitting meaning, and deciphering meaning. The communication process can break down at any of these stages.

2. Recognize the many barriers that inhibit effective communication.

3. Practice supportive communication.

4. When speaking, consider your audience and make sure that your content, tone, and approach fit the situation.

5. When you wish to persuade someone to your position, consider your credibility and work to improve it.

6. Listen, listen, listen!

7. Remember that body language communicates as much as, or more than, what you actually say.

8. Take advantage of electronic communication, but use electronic channels only when they are appropriate.

9. In specialized forms of communication, always consider the receiver or audience and the norms and expectations embedded in the situation.

10. Remember to consider the ethics of communication. Your ethics and integrity are most clearly on display when you communicate with others.

Finally, it is important to consider the value of face-to-face communication where all verbal and nonverbal cues can be considered and clarification can be asked for and received.[67]

## KEY TERMS

channel
decoding
downward communication

dual reporting
encoding
exit interview

feedback
grapevine
horizontal communication
informal communication
informative network
innovative network
integrative network
interpersonal communication
listening

message
noise
organizational communication
receiver
regulation network
sender
span of management
survey feedback
upward communication

## DISCUSSION TOPICS AND QUESTIONS

1. Compare and contrast organizational communication and interpersonal communication.

2. When a police department operates with a dual reporting–type structure, what are the communication problems?

3. What can a manager do to create an organizational climate fostering *real* communication?

4. Do supervisory managers and middle managers have the same types of communication problems?

5. Differentiate between feedback and noise as parts of the communication process.

6. Is under-communicating more serious than over-communicating?

7. Describe how a manager can deal with a rumor.

8. What is the difference between service and functional authority?

9. Discuss the relationship between superiors and subordinates as conceptualized by V. A. Graicunas.

10. What are the functions of listening?

## FOR FURTHER READING

Arthur Bell and Dayle Smith, *Management Communication* (New York: John Wiley, 1999).

Written by leading experts in the field, this text provides valuable suggestions on how to improve communication within organizations.

Ellen Hochstedler and Christine M. Dunning, "Communication and Motivation in Police

Departments," *Criminal Justice and Behavior*, Vol. 10 (1983), pp. 47–69.

This study reports the results of a survey completed by 1,000 police officers in a large southwestern police department. The satisfaction indicators used in the study showed that the most important kind of communication was vertical.

## NOTES

1. Nathan F. Iannone and Marvin D. Iannone, *Supervision of Police Personnel* (Upper Saddle River, NJ: Prentice Hall, 2001), p. 98.

2. Chester I. Barnard, *The Functions of the Executive* (Cambridge, MA: Harvard University Press, 1938), pp. 175–181.

3. Fred Luthans, *Organizational Behavior* (New York: McGraw-Hill, 2002), p. 334.

4. Iannone and Iannone, *Supervision of Police Personnel*, pp. 99–100.

5. Hal Rainey, *Understanding and Managing Public Organizations* (San Francisco: Josey Bass, 1997), p. 303.

6. Michael L. Vasu, Debra W. Stewart, and G. David Garson, *Organizational Behavior and Public Management* (New York: Marcel Dekker, 1998), pp. 180–183.

7. Rainey, *Managing Public Organizations.*

8. Ibid.

9. V.A. Leonard and Harry W. More, *Police Organization and Management* (New York: Foundation Press, 2000), pp. 234–235.

10. Gary Dessler, *Management* (Upper Saddle River, NJ: Prentice Hall, 2004), p. 115.

11. Harry W. More and Michael O'Neill, *Contemporary Criminal Justice Planning* (Springfield, IL: Charles C Thomas, 1987), p. 113.

12. Leonard and More, *Police Management and Organization,* pp. 469–471.

13. Dessler, *Management,* p. 154.

14. Charles R. Swanson, Leonard Territo, and Robert W. Taylor, *Police Administration* (Upper Saddle River, NJ: Prentice Hall, 2001), p. 181.

15. V.A. Graicunas, "Relationship in Organizations," in Luther H. Gulick and Lyndall F. Urwick, eds. *Papers on the Science of Administration* (New York: Columbia University, 1937).

16. Ibid.

17. Dessler, *Management.*

18. Leonard and More, *Police Management and Organization,* p. 188.

19. Ibid., pp. 187–188.

20. Ibid., pp. 190–191.

21. Dessler, *Management,* p. 140.

22. Brian L. Hawkins and Paul Preston, *Managerial Communication* (Santa Monica, CA: Goodyear, 1981).

23. Robert Vecchio, *Organizational Behavior: Core Concepts* (Mason, OH: South-Western, 2003), pp. 286–287.

24. Norman B. Sigband, *Communication for Management and Business* (Glenview, IL: Scott, Foresman, 1982).

25. Ramon J. Aldag and Loren W. Kuzuhara, *Organizational Behavior and Management* (Cincinnati: South-Western, 2002), p. 189.

26. Harry W. More, W. Fred Wegener, and Larry S. Miller, *Effective Police Supervision* (Cincinnati: Anderson, 2003), p. 82.

27. James L. Lundy, *Lead, Follow, or Get Out of the Way* (San Diego, CA: Avant Books, 1986).

28. Dessler, *Management,* pp. 315–316.

29. Michael L. Vasu, Debra W. Stewart, and G. David Garson, *Organizational Behavior and Public Management* (New York: Marcel Dekker, 1998), p. 160.

30. More, Wegener, and Miller, *Effective Police Supervision,* pp. 78–79.

31. Ibid., p. 80.

32. Aldag and Kuzuhara, *Organizational Behavior and Management,* p. 189.

33. Ibid., p. 199.

34. Ibid., p. 195.

35. Ibid., p. 200.

36. Ibid., pp. 211–217.

37. Naval Education and Training Program, *Human Behavior* (Washington, DC: U.S. Government Printing Office, 1984).

38. Aldag and Kuzuhara, *Organizational Behavior and Management,* pp. 189–190.

39. Luthans, *Organizational Behavior,* pp. 343–344.

40. Iannone and Iannone, *Supervision of Police Personnel,* p. 102.

41. Robert B. Denhardt, Janet V. Denhardt, and Maria P. Aristigueta, *Managing Human Behavior in Public and Nonprofit Organizations* (Thousand Oaks, CA: Sage, 2002), p. 263.

42. Ellen Hochstedler and Christine M. Dunning, "Communication and Motivation in a Police Department," *Criminal Justice and Behavior,* Vol. 10 (1983), pp. 47–69.

43. Aldag and Kuzuhara, *Organizational Behavior and Management,* p. 198.

44. Vasu, Stewart, and Garson, *Organizational Behavior and Public Management,* p. 175 and Paul M. Whisenand, *Supervising Police Personnel: The Fifteen Responsibilities* (Upper Saddle River, NJ: Prentice Hall, 2004), pp. 76–77.

45. Luthans, *Organizational Behavior,* p. 346.

46. Steven Cohen and William Eimicke, *The New Effective Public Manager* (San Francisco: Jossey-Bass, 1995), p. 90.

47. Luthans, *Organizational Behavior,* p. 348.

48. Ibid., p. 349.

49. Ibid., p. 350.

50. Whisenand, *Supervising Police Personnel,* p. 78.

51. Vasu, Stewart, and Garson, *Organizational Behavior and Public Management,* p. 178.

52. Swanson, Territo, and Taylor, *Police Administration,* p. 253.

53. Whisenand, *Supervising Police Personnel,* p. 79 and Luthans, *Organizational Behavior,* p. 353.

54. Ibid., p. 75.

55. Ibid.

56. Vecchio, *Organizational Behavior,* p. 298.

57. Ibid.

58. Ibid., p. 299.

59. Vasu, Stewart, and Garson, *Organizational Behavior and Public Management,* p. 181.

60. Aldag and Kuzuhara, *Organizational Behavior and Management,* p. 206.

61. Leonard and More, *Police Management and Organization,* pp. 234–235.

62. James L. Bowditch and Anthony F. Buono, *A Primer on Organizational Behavior* (New York: John Wiley and Sons, 2001), p. 315.

63. Ibid., pp. 359–360.

64. Whisenand, *Supervising Police Personnel,* p. 89.

65. Bowditch and Buono, *Primer,* p. 125.

66. Denhardt, Denhardt, and Aristigueta, *Managing Human Behavior,* pp. 285–287.

67. Richard N. Holden, *Modern Police Management* (Upper Saddle River, NJ: Prentice Hall, 1994), p. 367.

# 11

## LEADERSHIP

### The Integrative Variable

1. Identify essential managerial tasks.
2. Describe the zone of acceptance.
3. Describe management leadership.
4. Distinguish between power and authority.
5. Contrast knowledge areas with leadership skills.
6. Identify the three components of "the eternal triangle."
7. Compare and select theories of leadership.
8. List the three basic styles of leadership.

9. Describe organizational humanism.
10. Define *participatory management*.
11. Assess adaptive management as an alternative to "the one best way."
12. Compare the Managerial Grid and leadership quadrants.
13. Contrast System 1 and System 4.
14. Distinguish between task-oriented and people-oriented needs.
15. Describe human skills.
16. List the four components of transformational leadership style.

Leadership employment opportunities for police managers in numerous cities usually include characteristics and skills like those displayed in Figure 11–1. They emphasize distinct yet interrelated aspects of police administration. Top executives are expected to have outstanding leadership and administrative skills. They must lead employees as they strive to accomplish the organization's mission, goals, and objectives. They must demonstrate interpersonal and communication skills and be committed to community service. Like the proverbial horse and carriage, interpersonal skills, management, and leadership form a natural unit, or gestalt. Under ideal circumstances, "You can't have one without the other."

The term *motivation* is derived from a Latin word meaning "to move." It involves the use of incentives to encourage or reinforce member behavior that is consistent with and contributes to the organization's purpose. It is incumbent on management to create a hospitable milieu within which police officers are able to satisfy personal as well as organizational needs. Motivation is the key to personal productivity. According to Michael LeBoeuf, good managers have the ability to turn subordinates on and convert collective efforts into productive work.[1] *Things that are rewarded get done!* There is a very direct and inextricable link between motivation and productivity in all complex criminal justice organizations.

## Police Chief Executive Officer*—Multidimensional Leadership

| | |
|---|---|
| Organizational skills | Strong leadership |
| Exceptional communication skills | Two years of relevant postgraduate work |
| Graduation from the Administrative Officers' Course at the Southern Police Institute or the FBI National Academy | Verbal and interpersonal skills |
| | Ability to lead a team |
| Exceptional interpersonal skills | Motivate personnel |
| Self-assured as a leader | Excellent writing skills |
| Abililty to achieve organizational skills | Background in crime prevention |
| Guide and direct staff | Experience in labor relations |
| Background in enforcement | Grant administration |
| Experienced in community policing | Skill in staff development |
| Problem-solving skills | Ability to engage with all segments of the community |
| Administrative skills | |
| Successful in community policing | |

*These items appeared in journal advertisements, describing the desired qualifications wanted for individuals applying for the position of Chief of Police.

**Figure 11–1**
Police Chief Executive Officer—Multidimensional Leadership.

---

**CASE STUDY**   Captain Karl Hammiker

Karl Hammiker, formerly the officer in charge of the police department's planning and research unit, was recently promoted to captain. Based on departmental policy, he was transferred and placed in charge of a medium-sized precinct on the lower east side of the city. While the captain gets along with most of his subordinates, they see him as a desk jockey and have an uneasy feeling that he lacks the leadership skills needed to do the job. A hostage situation occurred late last week that fueled the fire and reinforced these negative perceptions. Capt. Hammiker appeared to be indecisive in dealing with the crisis. Most police personnel—based on the nature of their work—regard decisiveness as an essential leader trait.

Two young males, members of a notoriously violent street gang, had been selling crack to students at a local high school. As an undercover officer from the city's drug task force tried to apprehend them, he was knocked to the ground and stomped. His backup was unable to act without endangering several uninvolved students. The men fled from the scene and took the undercover officer as hostage. Police officers from Capt. Hammiker's precinct cornered the actors in an abandoned house a block away from the school. The men threatened to kill their hostage. All escape routes were sealed off, and the captain was notified of the situation. The captain responded to the scene and quickly established a command post. His objective was to obtain the release of the police officer without

violating the department's policy against making concessions in order to free the hostage.

Capt. Hammiker was committed to the System 4 approach to management and had successfully used it when he was in charge of planning and research. In what could be considered a textbook example of participatory leadership, he sought input from his immediate subordinates before trying to deal with the hostage situation. He and his close advisers worked very diligently to identify the exact problem, to explore alternatives, and to select the best alternative. After what amounted to a two-and-one-half-hour planning session, the captain was ready to take action. The SWAT team was ordered to storm the building, neutralize the offenders, and rescue the hostage. Using a precision timing protocol, the SWAT team entered the building successfully and captured the unarmed gang members without incident. The hostage was in a coma induced by the injuries inflicted during the beating. The officer died three days later. The police union has called for the captain's immediate suspension and asked for an independent investigation of the incident. The union has alleged that Capt. Hammiker is incompetent.

*If you were the chief of police, what would you do? Based on the information you have, what do you think happened in this situation? What can be done to help ensure that it does not happen again?*

Management is the art of getting things done in conjunction with and through others in formally organized task-oriented groups. Truly effective managers use legitimate authority and real power to create a work environment in which police personnel perform as individuals yet cooperate with one another to achieve a common purpose. Such managers devise strategies and use various techniques designed to remove roadblocks to productivity. Experienced managers rely on their knowledge of the behavioral sciences to motivate employees and to enhance the efficiency, effectiveness, and productivity of the organization.

Managers plan, direct, and control police operations. An organization is inert until it is infused with leadership. Then it becomes a dynamic force with a compelling thrust toward the achievement of its overall mission.[2] Proactive leadership is a behavioral transaction that involves the art of influencing, guiding, instructing, directing, and controlling human beings in an effort to gain their willing obedience, cooperation, confidence, support, and respect.[3] Effective management is built on a foundation of trust. Managerial leaders have the ability to elicit productive work that is well beyond the minimum required of employees in a particular job.[4] Police managers are expected to generate a sense of purpose, to motivate and direct the work force, and to lead subordinates so that individual police officers voluntarily make meaningful contributions to the department.

## PERSPECTIVES ON LEADERSHIP

Empirical evidence and common sense suggest that an organization's performance is closely related to the quality of its leadership. While leadership may not be the only important variable in the success or failure of a collective effort, it is an essential one. There is no doubt that inept leaders lower employee morale and hamper police operations. Law enforcement cannot afford leaders who fail to lead.[5] A strong and resourceful leader, on the other hand, can—in the right environment and with proper resources—transform a disparate group of individuals into a cohesive, aggressive, and very successful organization.[6] The leader is the person who energizes the group. He or she knows how to elicit initiative and to draw from employees what they have to give.[7] V. A. Leonard and Harry More contend that leadership is the critical catalyst in this nation's law enforcement agencies.[8] They note that the fundamental basis for success in any police enterprise is found in the energy, effort, and expertise of the chief executive officer.

**Leadership Defined**

*Leadership* is a very difficult term to define. While most people are able to recognize leaders, few can satisfactorily explain exactly what makes a leader different from a non-leader. Defining leadership is even harder since there is no direct relationship between the ability to lead and those who are chosen to provide leadership in any given situation. Scholars have expended considerable time and effort trying to explain the phenomenon of leadership and yet—after more than 50 years of theory construction and research—there are still no provable generalizations.[9] Genuine leadership appears to be something internal to a given individual and is nurtured by the situation. Real leadership (as opposed to formal authority) is not a commodity that can be dispensed by those in positions of power.

The word *leadership* is a recent addition to the English language, in use for only a little over 200 years. It describes the traits, behavior, and/or style of those persons who—either formally or informally—assume responsibility for the activities of a goal-oriented group. In simple terms, leadership is the knack of getting others to follow and to do willingly those things the leader wants them to do.[10] Leadership is a group phenomenon involving interaction between two or more persons. It also involves an influence process whereby the leader exerts intentional influence over followers. The concept of leadership implies that the follower acknowledges that the focal leader is a source of guidance and inspiration.[11]

**Related Concepts**

There is a symbiotic relationship between leaders and followers. They are best viewed as two different sides of the same coin. One view is that leaders—based on their position or power—exert influence on and motivate followers to act in certain ways. Other researchers feel that leadership is not determined by positions of authority but by an individual's capacity to influence peers.[12] At the same time, some experts express the belief that without follower consent, an aspiring leader cannot lead.[13] Followers, on the other hand, have a self-imposed zone of acceptance within which they willingly allow themselves to be activated, directed, and controlled by a leader. They establish psychological parameters and permit leaders to influence personal choices within those limits.[14]

Once a leader follower relationship develops, leaders are thrust into a group maintenance role. Effective leaders focus the group's energy and help members function in such a way that the police department is able to accomplish its mission, goals, and objectives. A leader creates a vision for his or her followers and guides them toward achieving that vision.[15]

The term *leadership* means different things to different people. Our definition evolved from a chain or series of related definitions:

1. *Influence.* To cause some behavior in another human being without the use of authority or physical force, influence is manifest in one's ability to affect the character and actions of others. Influence is the major process, function, or activity involved in the leadership role.[16] The behavior of the leader is also influenced by its consequences. A major consequence of leader behavior is predictable follower behavior. Follower behavior tends to reinforce, diminish, or extinguish leadership.

2. *Power.* The ability of a leader to influence other human beings in such a way as to produce a particular behavior. Whether it is formal (authority) or informal (influence), power carries with it the means necessary to ensure that subordinates respond positively to suggestions, instructions, and orders. According to Richard Plunkett, power is the capacity to command and to get others to do what the leader wants done, when and how the leader wants it done.[17] Leader power comes from different sources (e.g., reward power, coercive power, legitimate power, referent power, and expert power). Power is not a static condition; it changes over time.[18] Real power may or may not coincide with the theoretical distribution of formal authority depicted on an organizational chart.

3. *Authority.* Legitimate power vested in some person for a specific purpose. This is institutionalized power inherent in the position rather than the individual. Authority is the right to act or cause others to act in an

effort to accomplish the organization's mission. Ultimate authority rests with the police chief executive, who delegates appropriate authority down through the formal chain of command to all personnel within the department. Laws, policies, procedures, rules, and regulations control the delegation of authority. Management personnel and supervisors are granted formal authority to determine, direct, control, and regulate the behavior of subordinates. While they are often treated as synonyms, authority and power should be viewed as distinct yet related concepts. There are police administrators who occupy positions with a great deal of formal authority but who have no real power to influence the behavior of the men and women who work for them. Others have no formal authority per se yet exercise a great deal of influence over the people they work with. Effective leaders have the authority and power to fulfill their role in law enforcement agencies.[19]

4. *Reciprocal response.* Mutual influence between parties to a behavioral transaction. Leadership simply cannot exist in a social vacuum. There is a functional relationship between leaders and followers. Mary Parker Follett, a well-known management theorist, noted that a stimulus is always influenced to some degree by the resulting response.[20] Each party to the transaction reacts not just to the other person but to the total situation that he or she helped to create. The result is a situation that neither person could have produced alone. Leadership—much like life in general—is reflected in a series of social situations orchestrated by synergistic relationships. Each situation is dynamic.

5. *Zone of acceptance.* The parameters within which followers are inclined to do willingly what is asked of them by their leaders. This zone or area reflects the exercise of power and formal authority that subordinates voluntarily accept as legitimate (Figure 11–2). The zone of acceptance, which Chester Barnard calls the zone of indifference, is to be found in the mind and behavior of the follower, not in a position or a leader. It represents follower-imposed limitations on the power and authority of superiors.[21] People's zones of acceptance are getting smaller. People do not blindly follow orders today even if they are in religious or military organizations.[22] This makes the job of the police manager more complex and difficult.

Leadership is slowly but surely displacing autocratic control in police departments throughout the nation.

**Functional Leadership**

Emphasis has shifted away from charismatic and autocratic leadership models to a new form of leadership based on function. The evidence is clear. A subordinate's zone of acceptance is flexible. It expands and contracts based on the police administrator's formal authority, real power, managerial know-how, competence, credibility, leadership style, and interpersonal skills.

The origin of the word *leadership* can be traced to early Greek and Latin. It is derived from an archaic term meaning "to act" and/or "to carry out."[23] Every act of leadership consists of two elements: (1) *initiation by a leader* and (2) *execution by followers*. Based on this concept, leadership theorists have developed an almost endless array of definitions. Since leadership is a very complex, multifaceted phenomenon, there is no real agreement on

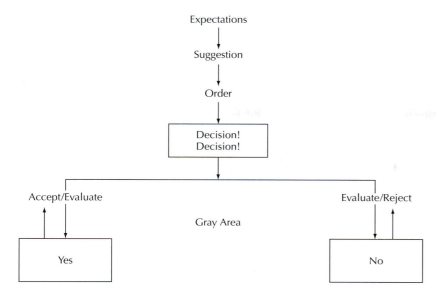

Expectations, suggestions, and orders that fall within the zone of acceptance
are adopted with a minimum of analysis. Those that fall outside of the zone
of acceptance are not easily converted into voluntary or willing behavior;
they may become insurmountable obstacles to human productivity.

**Figure 11–2**
Zone of Acceptance.

what the term means. For our purpose, leadership can be defined as
follows:

> An interactive goal-oriented process through which individual human
> beings are (for a variety of reasons) induced to follow someone and to
> receive psychosocial satisfaction from willingly doing what that person
> wants them to do.

Leader effectiveness is measured by diverse criteria ranging from the
group's performance to the leader's tenure (see Figure 11–3). Two commonly
used measures of leader effectiveness in law enforcement are the degree to
which police officers work and how well they accomplish the department's
mission, goals, and objectives.

## POLICE ADMINISTRATORS AS LEADERS

Police administrators are responsible for providing competent managerial
leadership and are expected to provide it. In fulfilling this role expectation,
they initiate goal-oriented action by others and manage those assigned to do
the work. Executives and other upper-level managers perform the specialized
task of maintaining the organization in operation.[24] As managerial leaders,
police administrators:

**Figure 11–3**

Criteria for Determining Leadership
Effectiveness.

1. Performance
2. Productivity
3. Goal attainment
4. Preparedness .................. Organization
5. Crisis control
6. Growth
7. Development
8. Survival

9. Workmanship
10. Creativity
11. Motivation
12. Satisfaction .................. Personnel
13. Esprit de corps
14. Loyalty
15. Commitment

16. Goal oriented
17. Empathetic
18. Participative .................. Managerial
19. Productive
20. Influence/Power
21. Leader tenure

1. Formulate and refine the department's mission, goals, and objectives.
2. Fulfill the department's mission through goal-oriented and proactive management.
3. Motivate police personnel to invest time, energy, effort, and expertise when engaged in job-related activities.
4. Make police work a fundamentally rewarding and productive profession.
5. Set a moral and professional tone for the organization.
6. Use power and authority to help employees to become more efficient, effective, and productive.
7. Create a working environment in which police officers willingly accomplish tasks.

According to Sam Souryal, the essence of management leadership is for administrators to identify the needs of people in work groups and to meet work-related needs in ways designed to produce optimal productivity.[25]

**Managerial Leadership**    Managerial leaders make an effort to identify and understand the needs of subordinates and to mesh them with those of the organization. While these needs vary from person to person, from one organization to the next, and over time, they are normally separated into two distinct categories:

1. *Task-oriented needs* are work centered and directly related to defining goals, making policy, building programs, establishing process, and creating organizations based on the efficient division of labor. Management organizes the elements of productive enterprise (money, material, equipment, and human resources) to accomplish its stated goals and objectives.
2. *People-oriented needs* are employee centered and related to improving interpersonal relations, facilitating communication, motivating personnel, providing support, generating morale through meaningful participation, and resolving destructive conflict. The task of management is to create

conditions that allow people to achieve their own goals by directing their productive effort toward organizational objectives.[26]

The "task" and "people" dimensions of management leadership are not, and never have been, mutually exclusive. They are interdependent. Effective managers exhibit both orientations simultaneously. They seek to create work environments that are productive as well as satisfying for human beings. People-oriented leadership—interactive behavior based on mutual trust, friendship, support, and respect—is directly related to job performance and employee satisfaction in a wide range of organizations. Those leaders who are more considerate of others usually have the most-satisfied subordinates.[27]

Modern police work is labor intensive. Somewhere between 70 and 85 percent of a typical budget is earmarked for recruiting, screening, training, nurturing, and retaining personnel. Under these conditions, managerial leaders must possess the knowledge and skills required to maximize the efficiency, effectiveness, and productivity of the organization's human resources. Researchers have identified the following major knowledge areas and leadership skills associated with good management:

| Knowledge Areas | Leadership Skills |
| --- | --- |
| 1. Organization theory (workflow) | 1. Conceptual skills |
| 2. Industrial engineering (job) | 2. Human skills |
| 3. Behavioral science (attitudes) | 3. Technical skills |

We now explore these knowledge areas and leadership skills to provide you with a foundation for a more detailed discussion of managerial leadership in law enforcement. Frederick Herzberg refers to organization theory, industrial engineering, and behavioral science as "the eternal triangle."[28] Contemporary managerial leaders utilize organizational theory to structure work in a logical and sequential manner and ensure coordinated efforts by all personnel in order to achieve a work unit's goals and objectives. They function as industrial engineers in the sense that it is their task to create and/or modify individual jobs so that each employee is productive and makes a substantive contribution to the organization. As applied social scientists, managerial leaders use their knowledge of human behavior to motivate employees, nurture positive attitudes toward work, and cultivate appropriate norms, values, and ethical orientations (see Figure 11–4). Good police managers bring the disparate elements of "the eternal triangle" into dynamic equilibrium in order to preserve and strengthen the organization as a consciously coordinated and goal-oriented system of human interaction.[29]

Managerial leaders understand human nature. They know that subordinates learn, participate, and produce best when they are allowed to set some of their own goals, choose activities related to achievement of those goals, and exercise freedom of choice in other important areas of life within the organization. An effective leader acts as a catalyst, a consultant, and a resource person for the work group. The leader's job is to help the group emerge as a collective entity, grow in terms of solidarity, and become less dependent on external direction or outside control. Managers serve the interests of the group best when, as leaders, they are spontaneous, empathetic, direct, open, and honest in dealing with their subordinates. They have a unique ability to apply knowledge readily and effectively in any given situation. In addition to their knowledge, police managers draw on

**Figure 11–4**

Herzberg's "Eternal Triangle."

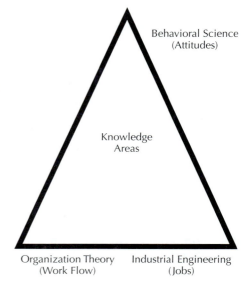

Behavioral Science
(Attitudes)

Knowledge
Areas

Organization Theory
(Work Flow)          Industrial Engineering
(Jobs)

and exhibit a dynamic mix of leadership skills. In this particular context, management leadership requires conceptual skills, human skills, and technical skills.[30] *Conceptual skills* are used to organize and integrate experience. They involve the ability to comprehend and ascribe meaning to bits and pieces of information (data) as they are converted into comprehensive thought. This is not merely an intellectual exercise. It is a part of a process that allows the manager to translate knowledge into action.

Police administrators with well-developed conceptual skills are able to perceive themselves in relation to the department and learn to appreciate how their behavior affects interpersonal transactions and functional relationships within the organization. Effective managers evaluate their own personal worth in terms of their leadership role in the police department, the criminal justice system, and the government itself. While conceptual skills are required at every level in police work, the standards for handling different kinds of information become less clear and the level of abstraction rises when one moves up in the hierarchy of authority.[31]

*Human skills* involve those aspects of behavior and/or personality that influence the individual's ability to interact in a positive way with other persons in the organization. They include, but are certainly not limited to, tolerance for ambiguity, empathetic understanding, and interpersonal communication skills. Tolerance for ambiguity refers to the managerial leader's capacity to deal effectively with problems even though the lack of information might preclude making a totally informed choice from among the available alternatives. Empathy is the ability to position oneself to see a situation or series of situations from the perspective of others. Empathy is a prerequisite for understanding human behavior. Communication represents an "idea transplant" from the mind of one person to the mind of another.[32] Effective communication is a critical variable in the success or failure of any cooperative effort. Tolerance for ambiguity, empathetic understanding, and goal-oriented communication help transform idiosyncratic behavior into coordinated human effort designed to accomplish the police department's mission, goals, and objectives. Managerial leaders have a unique ability to function as members of an organization while fostering a cooperative spirit and guiding its activities.

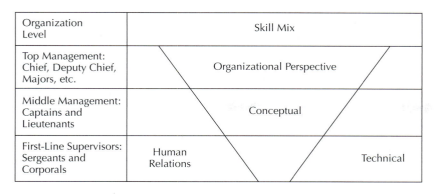

| Organization Level | Skill Mix | | |
|---|---|---|---|
| Top Management: Chief, Deputy Chief, Majors, etc. | Organizational Perspective | | |
| Middle Management: Captains and Lieutenants | Conceptual | | |
| First-Line Supervisors: Sergeants and Corporals | Human Relations | | Technical |

**Figure 11–5**

Rank-Specific Leadership Skill Mix.

Adapted from Charles Swanson et al., *Police Administration* (New York: Macmillan, 1988).

The *technical skills* utilized by police personnel vary depending on the level they have attained within the organization. According to Robert Katz, technical skill represents specialized knowledge, analytical ability related to the specialty, and competence in the use of those tools and techniques associated with police work.[33] The technical skills needed in law enforcement are diverse and normally acquired through job experience or job-related training programs. These skills are more operational than managerial. The techniques and mechanics of arrest, for example, have little or nothing to do with the use of preventive detention to protect the community from potentially dangerous criminals. The ability to shoot a revolver accurately is unrelated to the manager's decision to control the use of deadly force through the imposition of policies, procedures, rules, and regulations.

As police officers attain rank and move up the chain of command, the leadership mix they need in order to function properly changes to reflect the task-oriented and people-oriented demands placed on managerial leaders at higher levels in the hierarchy. Without attempting to split hairs about what constitutes a conceptual, human, or technical skill, Figure 11–5 demonstrates the relative mix of leadership skills needed by line supervisors (corporals/sergeants), middle-level managers (lieutenants/captains), and top managers (division chiefs/deputy chiefs/chief executive officers). Only those officers with leadership skills or the ability to acquire them through education, training, and supervised practical experience should be promoted to higher rank in the police department. Once promoted, they should be judged on their performance as managerial leaders.

## THEORIES OF LEADERSHIP

Many theories have been developed to explain those factors thought to produce leaders and sustain leadership in complex organizations. The conceptual approaches used to study leadership are ordinarily grouped into two basic categories: (1) *universal theories* and (2) *situational theories*. Universal theories search for an explanation of leadership unrelated to follower behavior or the social environment within which it develops. To the extent that these theories are truly universal in nature, they fail to shed much light on managerial leadership in very specific situations.[34] Situational theories, on the other hand, tend to place undue emphasis on contingency variables in an effort to explain the emergence of leaders (and leadership) in particular sets of circumstances. While neither approach has proven to be satisfactory per se, both of them provide us with starting points for further discussion.

Great leaders of the past came to the fore in several different ways. Their personal traits, their leadership styles, and the overall situation came together in such a way as to guarantee them a place in history. Experts in management leadership agree. Gary Dessler contends that there are at least four components in effective management leadership:[35]

1. Positive personal traits
2. Congruent leader style
3. People-oriented approach
4. Meaningful participation

We discuss these factors here in order to describe the ideal type of police administration.

## TRAIT THEORY

Trait theory, one of the earliest approaches used to study leadership, was very popular until the mid-1950s and is still viable in one form or another. Trait theories were formulated by luminaries such as Thomas Carlyle, George Friedrich Hegel, and Francis Galton and are based on the assumption that some people are born leaders. Carlyle saw leaders as unusually endowed and talented people who made history. Hegel took a different approach. He argued that events brought out the latent leadership potential in great men and women. Francis Galton believed that leadership skills were simply inherited biologically.[36]

Trait theory is based on the concept that good leaders always have certain physical, mental, and character traits that poor leaders do not possess. There is an implicit assumption that one's ability to lead develops concurrently with the personality during the formative years of childhood.[37] According to trait theory, leaders differ from followers with respect to several specific key traits that do not change much over time.[38] Persons with these special traits are virtually predestined to exercise informal as well as formal leadership in a variety of situations. Those who worked to refine trait theory and apply it to police administration were confident that adequate leadership could be obtained through a simple two-step process. First, researchers would study good leaders and compare them to non-leaders in order to determine special traits that only the leaders possess. Secondly, police departments would identify officers with these special traits and promote them to managerial positions.

Researchers have been trying to identify the special traits that set effective managerial leaders apart from poor managers for over 50 years. Different researchers—depending on their philosophy and/or academic training—have reached radically different conclusions concerning exactly what constitutes an essential leadership trait. A review of selected research data helps to illustrate this problem.

Based on extensive survey data regarding the qualifications of an executive, Ralph C. Davis found 56 different characteristics or traits that he considered important. While admitting it was unlikely that any manager would exhibit all, he claimed that the following 10 were required for executive success:[39]

1. Intelligence
2. Experience
3. Originality
4. Receptiveness
5. Teaching ability
6. Personality
7. Knowledge of human behavior
8. Courage
9. Tenacity
10. Sense of justice and fair play

Davis did not attempt to rate these factors in terms of their relative importance in determining effective management leadership.

Cecil Goode's research determined that the following traits were essential for successful leadership in complex organizations:[40]

1. Leaders are more intelligent than the *average* follower.
2. Leaders are well-rounded persons in terms of knowledge, interests, and aptitudes.
3. Leaders have an unusual flair for language. They speak and write intelligently, persuasively, understandably, and simply.
4. Leaders are physically, mentally, and emotionally mature.
5. Leaders have a powerful inner drive that compels them to strive for accomplishment.
6. Leaders are fully aware of the need for cooperative effort in order to accomplish tasks and get things done. They practice effective human skills.
7. Leaders rely on their conceptual skills more than on their technical skills.

Goode's list of traits tends to emphasize the people-oriented aspect of managerial leadership.

Typical of later leadership studies is one carried out by Edwin Ghiselli at the University of California, which looked at 306 managers employed by 90 different companies. Several characteristics were found to have a significant relationship to managerial performance: supervisory ability, achievement orientation, intelligence, self-assurance, decisiveness, and the need for self-actualization.[41] In a comprehensive analysis of more than 280 trait studies conducted over 64 years, Ralph M. Stogdill described a managerial leader as someone who acquires status through purposeful social interaction and a demonstrated ability to facilitate efforts of the work group in goal attainment. The traits most often associated with the assumption and performance of this role were intelligence, sensitivity to the needs of others, understanding of the task, initiative and persistence in handling problems, and a desire to accept responsibility and to occupy a position of dominance and control. Based on this research, Stogdill developed a trait profile designed to describe successful managerial leaders. According to the profile, effective leaders exhibit these traits:[42]

1. Strong need to assume responsibility and complete tasks
2. Vitality and perseverance in pursuit of goals
3. Inventiveness in problem solving
4. Drive to exercise initiative in social situations
5. Self-assurance and sense of personal individuality
6. Willingness to accept consequences for their actions
7. Skills in coping with interpersonal stress
8. Patience when dealing with uncertainty and aggravation
9. Skills to influence the behavior of other people
10. Ability to organize a cohesive group

The leader traits (and corresponding leadership skills) emphasized by Stogdill are summarized in Table 11–1.

In a thorough review of the literature on trait theory, Joe Kelly produced what he considered a definitive list of those traits most often identified in research as having a positive correlation with managerial leadership. This list of leader traits included intelligence, initiative, extroversion, sense of humor, enthusiasm, fairness, sympathy, and self-confidence.[43] While these traits seem to be important, there is simply no way to prove whether they are or are not essential elements in effective managerial leadership. There has been and will continue to be an avid interest in those physical, social, and psychological traits that separate leaders from non-leaders and good managers from poor managers. There is, however, no quick and easy test to assess leadership potential. In fact, most management theorists now agree that there are no universal leader traits.[44] Applied research has failed to discover a definite, consistent correlation between genetically determined traits and truly effective leadership.[45]

Table 11–1  **Traits and Skills of Successful Leaders**

| Leadership Traits | Leadership Skills |
| --- | --- |
| Adjusts to the situation | Inventive |
| Aware of the social milieu | Conceptualization |
| Achievement oriented | Creative |
| Has command | Tactfulness |
| Collaborative | Easily uses language |
| Strong-minded | Understands the task |
| Wishes to influence others | Possesses organizational ability |
| Lively and proactive | Believable |
| Assured | Interacts socially |
| Tolerant of ambiguous situations | Understanding |
| Wants to assume responsibility | Motivator |
| "Can do" attitude | Collegial |
| Respects peers | Ability to coach/teach |

Source: Adapted from Gary A. Yukl, *Leadership in Organizations,* 5th ed. (Upper Saddle River, NJ: Prentice Hall, 2002), p. 237. Adapted by permission of Pearson Education, Inc., Upper Saddle River, NJ 07458.

There are inherent methodological problems in defining, identifying, and measuring leader traits. Consequently, no particular set of traits has emerged to differentiate effective leaders from non-leaders in any theoretically meaningful sense.[46] Based on the analysis of available data, the opposite appears to be true. It is clear that situational factors and pressures, rather than innate traits, are critical variables in determining who becomes an effective police manager. Robert Baron argues that different situations require managers with different personal characteristics, leader styles, and leadership skills. In some situations, direct and forceful action by the leader is necessary. It enhances productivity and morale.[47] In others, this type of behavior creates resentment and becomes counterproductive. A flexible, unstructured approach works best. In some circumstances, an autocratic style of decision-making, in which the designated leader gathers information and then acts unilaterally, may be effective. In other circumstances, a participative approach, involving consultation and collaboration with one's subordinates, might be necessary to ensure that important decisions are acceptable to various members of the work group. In short, there is no evidence to support the contention that one particular set of traits produces effective leadership in all situations.

The age-old assumption that leaders are born and develop their conceptual, human, and technical skills independent of situational variables has been completely discredited. The notion that effective managers possess specific leader traits and leadership skills has not been confirmed by research. Consequently, we have been developing a more reasonable and balanced paradigm concerning the importance of traits. It is now believed that certain traits and functional skills increase the likelihood that a given person will be an effective manager. There are no guarantees, however. According to Gary Yukl, the relative importance of the police administrator's personal traits and skills will be determined by the leadership situation.[48]

## LEADER BEHAVIOR APPROACH

Behavioral scientists abandoned trait theory because it provided few clues as to exactly what caused effective leadership. Researchers wanted to identify those proactive leadership strategies that elicited superior performance by human resources and were consistently effective. As a result, they shifted their attention to the study of actual leader behavior. This shift in paradigms had important implications. First, to focus on what leaders do and how they do it (as opposed to who they are) is to make a tacit assumption that there is some best way to lead. Second, in contrast to personal traits (which remain stable over time), leader behavior can be learned.[49] Most management theorists reject the notion that leaders are born and accept the idea that they are created in an interactive social milieu.

Researchers began to study how leader behavior affected follower performance and job-related satisfaction. As a result, leadership came to be viewed as a process of maintaining supportive social relationships in an organized work unit while getting members of that unit to perform assigned tasks at some acceptable level. Although this inquiry did not uncover a list of behaviors that always distinguish leaders from non-leaders, it served to identify major patterns or styles of leader behavior. It also demonstrated that management style has a significant influence on the productivity and morale of personnel within any type of complex criminal justice organization.

**Leadership Styles**

Early studies, using the methodological approach pioneered by Kurt Lewin, Ronald Lippit, and Ralph White, viewed leadership style as an interaction continuum ranging from people-centered to task-centered managerial behavior.[50] The focus of style theory is to determine which leadership style produces the greatest increase in productivity. Three basic styles (autocratic, democratic, and laissez-faire) have been identified:[51]

1. *Autocratic leadership* is power oriented. Autocratic leaders prefer to make decisions and give orders rather than to invite group participation. Loyalty and obedience are rewarded. This style is useful when there is a genuine need for strict control and quick decision-making. While the autocratic approach might be effective in the short run, the organization simply may be unable to function properly when the leader is absent. This type of police management stifles the development of leadership ability in subordinates because they are rarely allowed to make meaningful independent decisions.

2. *Democratic leadership* is people oriented. There is an emphasis on participation and collaboration. Leaders work with subordinates to help them achieve the organization's goals and objectives. These managers strive to establish positive relationships based on mutual respect and trust. Democratic leaders create administrative environments in which they consult with and draw ideas from their personnel. They delegate sufficient authority to accomplish tasks. In crises requiring a highly structured response, a democratic leadership style might prove to be too time-consuming or awkward to be effective. While participative management has merit in police work, it also has its downside.

3. *Laissez-faire leadership* represents a hands-off approach to management in complex organizations. In this style, the leader is actually a non-leader who acts as an information center and exercises almost no control. The organization runs

Chief William Bratton, a Recognized Expert. Associated Press

itself with little or no input from management. This places the entire organization in jeopardy. Many theorists no longer consider this a true style. The laissez-faire approach is now viewed as a form of administrative abdication.[52]

In a somewhat sophisticated approach, Robert Tannenbaum and Warren Schmidt identified four basic leadership styles that they described as "tell," "sell," "consult," and "join"[53] (see Figure 11–6). Phillip Applewhite identified a somewhat different set of four managerial leadership categories, which he named "authoritarian," "democratic laissez-faire," "bureaucratic," and "charismatic."[54] Bureaucratic management is based on the process model of leadership, whereas charismatic management is completely idiosyncratic and fueled by personal magnetism.

One of the problems associated with the leadership style approach is that it does not permit management personnel to rate high at both ends of the continuum. It implies that managers are one-dimensional players who are unable to exhibit people-oriented and task-oriented behavior at the same time. Most leadership theorists now feel that the people and task dimensions of leader behavior are not mutually exclusive. They are, in fact, independent variables that can be exhibited simultaneously.[55] A large body of applied research data suggests that the either/or view of leadership is out of sync with reality.

Much of our knowledge about leadership in police agencies is rooted in studies conducted by Ohio State University and the University of Michigan in the late 1940s. While the researchers used different methodologies and focused their attention on different aspects of leadership, they reached very similar conclusions. They cast doubt on the validity of viewing leader behavior as a single continuum; instead, they developed a two-dimensional independent-factor approach to management. The factors identified in the Ohio State University studies were "consideration" and "initiating structure." The

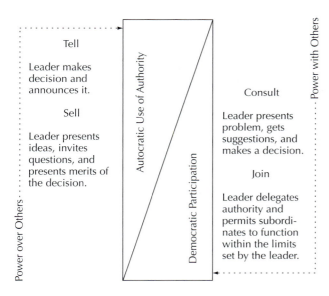

**Figure 11–6**

Leadership Continuum.

Adapted from Paul Hershey and Kenneth H. Blanchard, *Management of Organizational Behavior*,(Englewood Cliffs, NJ: Prentice Hall, 1972).

University of Michigan researchers defined them as "people-oriented" and "production-oriented" aspects of leadership. Regardless of the terminology used, these factors are now considered the two most important dimensions of managerial leadership.[56]

**Leadership Quadrants**

Based on an analysis of extensive survey data, E. A. Fleishman and his colleagues at Ohio State University discovered that subordinates tend to think of leadership in terms of the *consideration* and *initiating structure* provided for them by those in positions of authority.[57] Consideration was measured by behavior items such as openness, communication, consultation, friendship, supportiveness, appreciation, respect, and empathetic understanding. These human relations–oriented behaviors help leaders to establish and maintain positive relationships with their subordinates. Initiating structure was measured by behavior items such as planning, coordinating, monitoring, evaluating, directing, and problem solving. These task-related behaviors promote the efficient utilization of personnel and resources in achieving the organization's mission, goals, and objectives. Effective police administrators are not one-dimensional. They have learned to emphasize both consideration and initiating structure in a concerted effort to influence, motivate, coordinate, and control their subordinates.[58]

The patterns of management leadership described in the Ohio State studies form a composite model with four quadrants plotted along two separate axes. One axis measures a leader's consideration for employees and the other measures his or her emphasis on initiating structure (see Figure 11–7). It is clear, based on an analysis of the research data, that police managers can and often do exhibit concern for their subordinates as well as the task. The underlying assumption is that truly effective managers rank high in both areas.[59] Because leader behavior and leadership skills are learned, police managers might benefit from exposure to leader-effectiveness training. Altering one aspect of their style could lead to an appreciable increase in the productivity of work groups they manage.

Numerous research projects have been conducted to determine what effects consideration and initiating structure have on the performance, productivity, and morale of subordinates. The assumption that managers who adopt leadership styles high in both consideration and initiating structure will be effective in all situations has simply not been proven. Many studies have concluded that no single leadership style is best in all situations. One review of 24 studies related to leadership behavior revealed that 13 found a significant positive correlation between showing consideration and initiating structure for subordinates, 9 found no correlation, and 2 studies found a negative correlation.[60]

Researchers began to realize that what sounds good in theory may not prove so in practice. There is no consistent pattern of research results to demonstrate that one leader style is superior to another.[61]

Even Ralph Stogdill, one of the originators of the Ohio State leadership studies, believes it may be overly simplistic to claim that an effective manager merely needs to behave in a considerate and structuring manner.[62] As stated earlier, an adequate analysis of leadership must take into consideration the leader, the followers, and the situation.

While the Ohio State leadership studies do not provide the aspiring police administrator with a comprehensive "how to do it" explanation of proactive leadership in law enforcement departments, their importance should not be

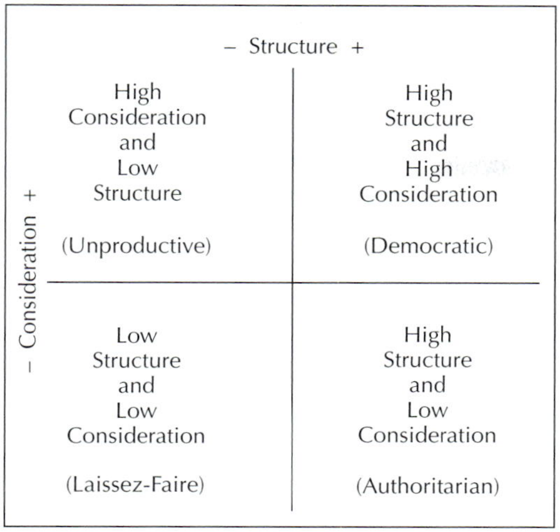

**Figure 11-7**

The Ohio State Leadership Quadrants.

Adapted from Robert M. Fulmer, *The New Management* (New York: Macmillan, 1983).

| | − Structure + | |
|---|---|---|
| **+** | High Consideration and Low Structure | High Structure and High Consideration |
| | (Unproductive) | (Democratic) |
| Consideration | | |
| **−** | Low Structure and Low Consideration | High Structure and Low Consideration |
| | (Laissez-Faire) | (Authoritarian) |

underestimated. The Ohio State research stimulated interest in a systematic study of leaders, leader behaviors, and leadership. The Ohio State studies set the stage for further inquiry and provided a conceptual framework for the well-known managerial grid and the situational leadership theories proposed by Paul Hersey and Kenneth Blanchard.

The University of Michigan launched its own program of research on leadership behavior at about the same time as Ohio State began its program. The focus of the research was to identify relationships between leadership behavior, group processes, and group performance. A major objective of the project was to determine what pattern or style of leadership behavior most often leads to efficient, effective, and productive work by subordinates. Researchers used field studies and survey data in an effort to discover what differences there were between effective managers and ineffective managers. They came up with a two-dimensional leadership profile. Employee-oriented behavior included taking an interest in individual employees and their needs, encouraging two-way communication, developing supportive interpersonal relations, and dealing with conflict. Production-oriented behavior, on the other hand, dealt with planning, establishing goals, giving instructions, monitoring performance, stressing productivity, and assigning people to specific tasks.[63]

The University of Michigan researchers also found that effective managerial leaders do not spend most of their time and effort doing the same kind of work as their subordinates. Effective leaders concentrate on supervisory functions such as planning, scheduling work, coordinating worker activities, and distributing resources (supplies, equipment, and technical assistance). This production-oriented behavior did not detract from their concern for human relations. Effective managers were more considerate, supportive, and helpful with their subordinates than less effective ones. They were likely to use general supervision rather than close supervision. After establishing goals and general guidelines, effective leaders allowed their subordinates some freedom in deciding how to do the work and how to pace themselves while doing the work.[64] While the University of Michigan studies unearthed

Lt. Stern is a shift commander in a relatively large municipal police department. He is a pragmatic, no-nonsense type of person who sets high performance standards for himself as well as for his subordinates. While he does not have an abrasive personality, the lieutenant is aloof and somewhat insensitive to the needs of his personnel. Lt. Stern's management style is definitely located at the task-oriented end of the leadership continuum. He respects competence and rewards achievement.

A probationary patrol officer assigned to Lt. Stern's unit has been lagging behind other members of the work group in the number of traffic tickets issued and is well below the departmental average. In an effort to correct the problem, the lieutenant has placed this person in the marginal performer category and ordered the officer's sergeant to intensify supervision. The sergeant is to monitor the officer's performance and overall productivity on a regular basis. He has been instructed to create a paper trail for use when and if the termination of employment becomes necessary. Since the traditional Theory X approach worked for the lieutenant in the past, he is convinced that it will work again. He subscribes to the authoritarian philosophy summed up in the phrase, "Do it my way or you're fired."

Capt. Harrison Blyler, chief of the patrol division and Lt. Stern's immediate superior, was briefed on the problem and the proposed solution. The captain, who is more personable and people oriented than his lieutenant, agreed with the diagnosis but disagreed with the remedy. He argued that traditional authori-tarianism is passé and counterproductive in most leadership situations.

He urged the lieutenant to become more open, honest, empathetic, and trusting in his relations with subordinates. Capt. Blyler discussed the value of collaboration, mutual goal setting, and joint decision-making. He stressed the manager's role as a motivator, teacher, and team builder.

Capt. Blyler also encouraged the lieutenant to become familiar with various leadership theories and to begin to assess his own strengths and weaknesses in terms of those theories. He placed a great deal of emphasis on the importance of developing supportive relationships throughout the entire organization. What started out as a mere exchange of information quickly became a seminar in the human relations approach to management in complex criminal justice organizations.

Immediately following his meeting with the captain, Lt. Stern removed the probationary patrol officer from the marginal performer program and ordered the sergeant to reduce the level of supervision. The officer's performance continued to deteriorate and he was terminated prior to the completion of his probationary period. Lt. Stern believes that Capt. Blyler's human relations approach made the problem worse and led to the dismissal.

*Which of the two approaches just discussed—authoritarian or human relations—do you feel would work with you if you were the probationary officer? Why? What would you have done differently if you were in the lieutenant's shoes? How did his reaction to the captain's suggestions make the problem worse?*

a great deal of information about leadership, they tell only part of the story. These studies are vulnerable to the same criticisms as were leveled at the Ohio State leadership studies. Leaders are but one element in the mosaic of human interaction.

# THE MANAGERIAL GRID

Robert Blake and Jane Srygley Mouton have also dealt with the task and people dimensions of managerial leadership. They proposed a framework in which leader style is plotted on a two-dimensional grid. The Managerial Grid—a charting technique developed independently of the Ohio State studies—identifies five normative leadership styles based on the relationship between concern for production and concern for people.

Leadership style is determined according to how a particular manager ranks in both of these areas. The Managerial Grid is used as a diagnostic to help individual managers assess their own leadership style.[65] The Managerial Grid is a 9 by 9 matrix. The horizontal axis indicates graduated concern for production. A rating of 9 reflects maximum concern for production. The vertical axis, on the other hand, shows regard for subordinates as human beings. The higher the rating, the greater is the concern. A 9 on this axis is indicative of maximum concern for people.[66] Because the grid is a 9 by 9 matrix, there are 81 possible combinations, or styles of managerial leadership. Only the 5 basic styles are discussed below. This is sufficient to understand the concepts behind grid theory, however.

The 5 basic managerial leadership styles identified by Blake and Mouton are (1) impoverished management, (2) task-oriented management, (3) country club management, (4) middle-of-the-road management, and (5) team management.

People are hired, placed in a job, and left alone. Managers exert minimum effort. They sense little or no conflict between production goals and needs of subordinates. Very little is expected from these managers. They are out of it and seem to be lost among their people rather than actively managing them. A 1,1 style, sometimes referred to as laissez-faire management, represents an abdication of professional responsibility.

**(1,1) Impoverished Management**

The leader exhibits a very strong interest in productivity and almost no concern for employee needs or morale. The manager is a proverbial taskmaster. Human considerations are not allowed to interfere with productivity and/or efficiency. The 9,1 position represents an autocratic management style in which the end justifies the means and the exploitation of personnel becomes the rule rather than the exception.

**(9,1) Task-Oriented Management**

Leaders are overly concerned with creating and maintaining a friendly atmosphere. They spend much of their time placating employees in an effort to meet human needs. The attitudes and feelings of subordinates are their only real concern. People always come first. Managers in the 1,9 position exhibit a low functional concern for productivity. Work becomes a ritualistic exercise designed to sustain the employees' personal lifestyles.

**(1,9) Country Club Management**

Leaders exhibit basic concern for production and people. Their managerial behavior reflects an intermediate level of interest in productivity and a modest concern for subordinates. While they assume that there will be a conflict between organizational goals and personal needs, they seek to strike a balance between the two. The manager's survival often depends on creating and maintaining a state of equilibrium. The 5,5 manager believes that most people are practical and will normally put forth some effort based on self-interest. The middle-of-the-road approach to managerial leadership is very common in modern police work.

**(5,5) Middle-of-the-Road Management**

Managers in the 9,9 position rate high in terms of their concern for both productivity and personnel. They assume there is no conflict between the goals of the organization and the needs of their subordinates. There is an emphasis on meaningful participation. Integration of organizational goals and employee needs is achieved by involving all personnel in determining the goals, methods, and conditions of work.

**(9,9) Team Management**

Blake and Mouton argue that the 9,9 position on the grid represents an ideal leadership style that all managers should try to adopt. They contend that the 9,9 leadership style is the one most positively associated with efficiency, effectiveness, productivity, and employee satisfaction. According to Richard Plunkett, 9,9 managers succeed because they motivate others to join with them in accomplishing the work of the organization. They cultivate a sense of commitment and interdependence by providing their employees with a common stake in the organization. Effective managerial leaders develop goal-oriented relationships with subordinates based on influence, trust, and mutual respect.[67]

Managers ordinarily adopt and retain a dominant mode or style of management that can be described in terms of the grid. Their actions are normally consistent with this grid style unless it fails to work, in which case they may shift into a backup style keyed to the situation. Consequently, where individual managers fit on the grid at any given point in time is not entirely up to them. A variety of factors must be taken into consideration. The demands of the situation as well as the manager's personality, managerial philosophy, administrative acumen, and interaction patterns influence the placement. While police administrators should strive to achieve the 9,9 position on the grid, they must be flexible enough to adapt to changing situations and changes in their personnel when necessary. Truly effective leaders know and have an appreciation for those forces that affect their managerial behavior. They understand themselves, the interpersonal dynamics of the work group, and the situational context within which they function.[68] Due to the paramilitary structure of most police departments, there has not been much of an emphasis on team management in law enforcement. As a result, the grid approach has been used infrequently. In a recent study of 76 police administrators, however, nearly 70 percent of the respondents reported that the team management approach was their dominant leadership style.[69] They identified middle-of-the-road management as their primary backup style. In a study of 25 managers from a large police department, it was discovered that 45 percent of them had 9,9 leadership styles.[70] While these studies are certainly encouraging, they should not be used to make far-reaching generalizations.

In related research, it was found that police managers either tended to have no dominant leadership style or used the "sell" approach to accomplish the organization's goals and objectives.[71] They were most effective when using leadership styles placing an emphasis on the task and least effective in styles requiring delegation of authority and/or work-group participation. According to Roy Roberg and Jack Kuykendall, there is simply no proof to support the assertion by some management theorists that the team management style of leadership is superior to other styles in all situations.[72] While concern for both production and people is important, concern alone cannot ensure effective managerial leadership in complex police organizations.

All behavioral approaches to leadership are based on similar concepts, even though they may be couched in different terms and generate different sets of labels. The notion that effective managerial leaders seek to influence both work output and social factors is a fundamental assumption inherent in all behavior theories. Even though their basic approach was different, Blake and Mouton came to the same conclusions as the Ohio State researchers.

Ohio State used a behavioral model to examine leader actions as perceived by subordinates in the work force. The Managerial Grid, on the other hand, is an attitudinal model that has been designed to measure the predispositions of effective managers. Both discovered a positive relationship between the production-oriented and people-oriented dimensions of proactive managerial leadership. The work of these leader behavior theorists provided the foundation for further study of managerial leadership, because it strongly suggested that the most effective way to lead is a dynamic and versatile process that adapts itself—by way of dominant and backup styles—to unique situations.[73]

Supporters of the Managerial Grid concept believe the 9,9 leadership style is the one best way to lead and to manage. They view leadership as the interaction between two interdependent variables (e.g., concern for production and concern for people). Emphasis is placed on using all available resources to determine the optimum course of action. The 9,9 police leader seeks to achieve coordinated direction through multiloop open communication designed to find the best alternative or course of action congruent with the logic inherent in a given situation. Even in crises, 9,9 managers continue—to the extent possible—to rely on superordinate goals and the processes of participation, conflict resolution, and group problem solving. Their behavior remains consistent with humanistic principles of openness, involvement, and participatory management. The 9,9 leader seeks input, contributions, recommendations, reservations, and doubts from those involved and acts quickly to define problems and devise solutions. According to Blake and Mouton, 9,9 participation is an interaction process predicated on the following:[74]

1. Openness
2. Candor
3. Strong initiative
4. Thorough inquiry
5. Effective advocacy
6. Conflict resolution
7. Delegation
8. Teamwork
9. Two-way critique

If the 9,9 approaches fail, police managers may be compelled to shift into a backup style keyed to the needs of the situation. Once the crisis is over, the 9,9 orientation tends to reemerge as the dominant style of management. This is known as 9,9 versatility.

Some situation theorists discount the importance of philosophical and behavioral continuity in the managerial process. They regard effective leadership as a very complex multidimensional social phenomenon, which can only be understood from an interactionist perspective that emphasizes contingency factors. Managerial leadership is thought to be the product of an interaction/influence system in which leaders exert influence on other people in a concrete situation and are influenced by them.[75] The key variables in the situational approach to leadership are the leaders themselves, the followers, and unique situational factors (see Figure 11–8).

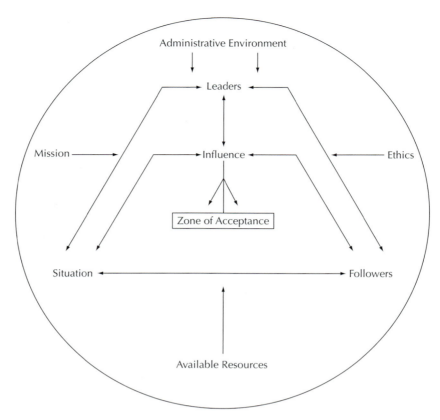

**Figure 11-8**

Leadership Interaction/Influence System.

Adapted from Fred Luthans, *Organizational Behavior*, 10th ed. (New York: McGraw-Hill, 2005).

## SITUATIONAL LEADERSHIP APPROACH

Situational leadership theories attempt to explain effective managerial leadership in terms of the interaction/influence system just discussed. The situational approach is based on the implicit assumption that leadership is always exercised in specific situations that involve real people in a given physical environment.[76] It utilizes contingency variables to explain leader behavior. Contingency variables are those factors within situations or followers that determine the style of management leadership most likely to be effective in a given set of circumstances.[77] In other words, different situations call forth and reinforce different kinds of leadership.

While situational theories cannot explain exactly what causes a human being to become an effective leader, they do provide an analytical frame of reference for thinking about it. Situational theory says, in effect, that managerial leadership is linked to adaptability. Success is contingent on the individual manager's ability to sense, interpret, and deal with various issues shaped by situational forces and unfolding events. According to Robert Fulmer, the situational approach to leadership is expressed symbolically as

$L = f$ (LP, GP, S): leadership (L) is a function (f) of the leader's personality (LP), the work group's personality (GP), and the dynamic situation (S).[78]

Situational approaches are conceptual tools that leaders use to assess circumstances in which their leadership may become an important factor. A careful analysis of each potential leadership situation is of critical importance and is part of the process used by effective managers as they contemplate the most appropriate leadership style. Effective management is dependent on the degree to which the leader's style fits a given situation.

One of the most important aspects of the managerial role is to diagnose and evaluate the disparate factors that could have positive or negative effects on leadership. An accurate assessment of the situation involves identifying and understanding the influences of factors such as individual differences, group dynamics, and organizational policies, procedures, rules, and regulations. As Paul Whisenand pointed out, an accurate diagnosis in a given situation requires police administrators to examine four extremely important areas: (1) managerial characteristics, (2) subordinate characteristics, (3) work-group structure and the nature of the task, and (4) organizational factors.[79]

1. *Managerial characteristics.* Leader behavior in a given situation depends on the forces or personal characteristics of the individual manager. The most important factors seem to be maturity, personality, needs, motives, past experience, and reinforcement.

2. *Subordinate characteristics.* Before managers adopt a particular leadership style, they assess intuitively the personal characteristics and behavioral patterns of others within the work group. Police officers, like their managers, have many internal forces that affect them and that shape their behavior in a given set of circumstances. These factors include maturity, personality, needs, motives, past experience, and reinforcement.

3. *Work-group structure.* Groups are an omnipresent feature in modern society and represent a keystone in the structure of all complex criminal justice organizations. The characteristics of the work group usually have a direct impact on a manager's ability to exercise effective leadership. The significance of the group's influence depends on factors such as its proficiency, cohesiveness, structure, maturity, and work ethic. Work groups that are engaged in ambiguous activities, for example, are much more likely to require a very different kind of leadership than those performing routine tasks. As a rule, the truly effective managerial leader is flexible when it comes to dealing with the collective needs of the group.

4. *Organizational factors.* One of the most crucial yet least understood aspects of a leadership situation is the organization itself. Some of the more important considerations relate to the assigned mission; the influence base (power and legitimate authority) utilized by leaders; the department policies, procedures, rules, and regulations; the skill and professional competence needed to do the job; and the time allotted to make decisions and/or to achieve the goals and objectives of the work group. The complexity of the task, the size of the organization, the work group's interaction pattern, and the reward system help determine the most appropriate leadership style (see Figure 11–9).

Managerial leadership is an art, not a science. Effective managers have the unique ability to create and maintain an interaction/influence system

**Figure 11-9**

Sources of Influence on the Choice of Leader Style.

Adapted from H. Joseph Reitz, *Behavior in Organizations*
(Homewood, IL: Richard D. Irwin, 1981).

based on a dynamic equilibrium between themselves, their followers, and the leadership situation. They derive inner satisfaction from achieving the organization's goals and meeting the psychosocial needs of their subordinates.

It has—after decades of theory construction and research—become apparent that there are no universal leadership traits and no one best way to manage complex goal-oriented organizations. In reality, the effective police manager is one who is able to call on and integrate all of the available leader styles in order to adapt to the demands of a given situation. Good management requires adaptive leadership. In essence, police managers who are able to adjust their styles according to the demands of the situation and the needs of their subordinates are those who will be most effective in achieving personal as well as organizational objectives.[80] Paul Whisenand and Fred Ferguson contend that adaptive leaders are much more likely to be successful than those who remain inflexible in the face of change.[81] Being flexible enough to shift into and out of various leadership styles creates a complete manager. Flexibility is the element in dynamic leadership that permits managers to adjust their style to fit the situation.

## CONTINGENCY MANAGEMENT

The contingency approach to understanding leadership effectiveness attempts to combine elements of both trait theory and situational theory in a single model. It is based on the fundamental assumption that elements in the leadership situation influence the effectiveness of the manager's leadership style. According to the contingency model developed by Fiedler and his associates, the most important situational factors are (1) leader-member relations, (2) task structure, (3) position power of the leader, and (4) favorableness of the situation.[82] Since a manager's personality is set and not easy to change, the way for him or her to be an effective manager is to alter the elements of a particular leadership situation in order to effect a proper fit between leader style and the unique demands of that situation.

According to contingency theory, the effectiveness of groups in achieving organizational goals and objectives ultimately depends on the personalities of their leaders as manifest in their leadership styles and the dynamics of the situations in which they and their subordinates find themselves. The leader's personality, leadership style, and situational control—based on real power and the legitimate authority to reward or punish subordinates—determine exactly what can be achieved through the efforts of others.

Contingency theorists contend that managerial leaders are primarily motivated by either tasks or interpersonal relationships with their subordinates. Task-oriented managers seek accomplishments in order to reinforce their sense of self-esteem and competence. Relationship-oriented managers, on the other hand, seek admiration and respect from subordinates in order to meet their social and esteem needs. The orientation of the manager can be identified through Fiedler's Least Preferred Co-worker (LPC) scale. The LPC classifies leadership orientation by measuring the manager's perceived psychological distance from the least preferred co-worker. The 8-point LPC scale—which rates manager attitudes using a set of bipolar adjectives such as rejecting/accepting and quarrelsome/harmonious—assumes that if managers are inclined to describe in positive terms those persons with whom they work least well, they are motivated by interpersonal relationships. If they describe these people in clearly negative terms, they are task motivated.[83] The LPC measures leader attitudes and values. Low-LPC managers emphasize the task. High-LPC managers are more concerned with establishing and maintaining good relationships in the workplace. They are more cognitively complex than low-LPC leaders and are much more adaptable to changes in the situation.[84]

Whether a task or relationship orientation is more appropriate depends on the nature of the leadership situation. Situational factors determine the power and influence the manager has at any given time. Contingency theory is built on an assumption that all managerial leaders are likely to find themselves in one of three leadership situations: high-control, moderate-control, or low-control situations.

1. *High-control situations.* Managers are allowed by their subordinates—based on positive relationships, task structure, and position power—to exercise a great deal of influence and control. This creates a predictable organizational environment in which to direct the work of their employees.

2. *Moderate-control situations.* Managers are faced with a number of different problems but tend to deal with them all in the same manner. They have either good relationships (with low position power and little emphasis on task structure) or poor relationships (with high position power and high emphasis on task structure).

3. *Low-control situations.* Managers are not permitted to exercise much influence or control because members of the work group do not support them. Neither task structure nor position power gives managers much influence or control. Low-control situations breed chaos.

V. A. Leonard and Harry More emphasize that leader-member relationships, task structure, and position power determine whether a manager has situational control of the job.[85] These three factors are critical and may be described as follows:

1. *Leadership-member relationships* measures how well managers and members of the work group get along. Close leader-follower relationships are normally favorable to the manager. Well-liked and respected leaders can influence a work group far beyond what their legitimate reward and coercive power would suggest.

2. *Task structure* measures how clearly goals, procedures, and performance expectations are defined. Well-defined tasks with minimal ambiguity provide the most favorable situation for the manager. There are four characteristics of structured tasks:

- The goal is clearly understood by members of the group.
- There are relatively few correct solutions to a problem.
- There are only a few ways to accomplish a specific task.
- Decisions about work tasks can be evaluated objectively.

3. *Position power* measures how much authority managers have to hire, reward, discipline, and fire subordinates. Managers who have the real power and formal authority to direct, reward, and punish their employees find themselves in a very favorable leadership situation. Interaction between these factors determines the favorableness of the situation for the leader.

Contingency theory's criterion for organizational effectiveness is productivity. In very favorable situations, those in which the manager has real power, group support, and a well-structured task to accomplish, members of the work force volunteer to be led and they do willingly all that is expected of them. In relatively unfavorable situations, however, the work group tends to disintegrate unless there is active intervention and control by the leader. Consequently, it appears that a more autocratic and task-oriented leadership style is best when situational factors are very favorable or very unfavorable for the leader.[86] A substantial body of research utilizing Fiedler's contingency model has shown a positive correlation between high-LPC (human relations) leadership and productivity in intermediate to moderately difficult situations. Under these conditions, effective leaders seek to create a nonthreatening and much more democratic atmosphere in which subordinates are encouraged to participate in solving the problems faced by the work group. In other words, high-LPC leadership style seems to work well in average leadership situations but not in very favorable (good) or very unfavorable (bad) situations.[87]

Contingency theorists argue that it is often necessary for a manager to change his or her normal leadership style in order to meet the challenges presented by a given situation. They contend that both types of leaders should be able to shift gears and play both kinds of roles. Task-oriented leaders may, under certain circumstances, be required to adopt a human relations approach to motivate their subordinates. On the other hand, a relationship-oriented manager might have to emphasize getting the job done during a crisis or when time constraints demand it but will revert to the high-LPC approach when the situation returns to normal. Richard Plunkett points out that nearly all effective managers are actually situationalists; this flexibility is the hallmark of a true leader.[88] Unfortunately, not everyone has this flexibility. According to Leonard and More, police managers can modify the situation if they find that their leadership style is disharmonious with the demands of the situation in which they are working.[89] Managers can reengineer their jobs by adjusting the three factors involved in situational control (human relations, task structure, and position power). A number of research studies suggest that the contingency approach has practical implications for the training of leaders. Recent research shows, for example, that we can improve organizational performance by teaching managers how to diagnose and modify situational control; this allows them to achieve an optimal match between leadership style and the situation as it unfolds in a constantly changing organizational environment.

While there have been criticisms of the LPC scale and other aspects of Fred Fiedler's contingency model of leadership, it still represents one of the major thrusts in leadership theory. It is a valuable frame of reference that emphasizes the interaction between the manager (based on a consideration of traits), followers, and the leadership situation. The model is antithetical to the notion that there is one best way to manage complex interaction/influence systems like a police department. Successful police administrators learn to adapt their managerial styles to the requirements, constraints, and opportunities presented in the leadership situation (see Figure 11–10).

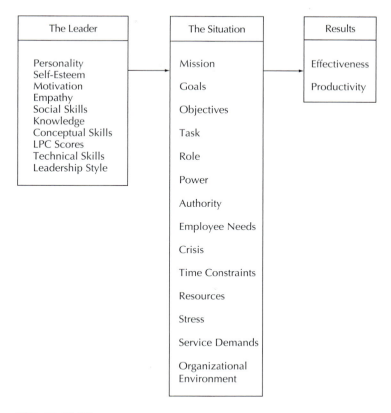

**Figure 11–10**
Contingency Leadership Model.

# PATH-GOAL LEADERSHIP MODEL

The path-goal theory of leadership was formulated by Robert J. House to explain how the behavior of the manager influences the motivation and satisfaction of subordinates.[90] The managerial leader's motivational function consists of increasing the personal payoffs associated with work-goal attainment and making the path to these payoffs easier to follow; he clarifies the path, removes roadblocks, and increases the opportunities for the personal satisfaction of employees while en route. In other words, leaders set goals for their subordinates and clear the path they must take to reach them. The basic assumption underlying path-goal theory is that certain leadership approaches will be much more effective in situations where leader behavior contributes to achievement of the employee's work-related goals. Managers play a supplemental role in the sense that they provide their subordinates with coaching, guidance, and performance incentives that are otherwise not provided by either the organization or the work group.

The path-goal model views leadership as being potentially the most important factor in determining what is to be accomplished (goals) and exactly how it is to be done (job behavior) within the parameters of the situation. Leaders engage in activities designed to identify proper methods (paths) by which their subordinates are allowed to accomplish organizational goals. The key to path-goal leadership is that effective managers create, nurture, and reinforce a meaningful connection between organizational goals and worker goals.[91] These managers affect the relationship between legitimate goals and appropriate means by:[92]

1. Delegating sufficient authority and assigning tasks.
2. Supporting the efforts of subordinates as they strive to accomplish work goals.
3. Determining the amount and kind of extrinsic rewards to be provided.
4. Recognizing, reinforcing, and rewarding goal attainment.
5. Enhancing subordinate satisfaction, reducing stress in the workplace, and removing the barriers that frustrate goal achievement.

Path-goal theorists have identified four very basic leader behavior systems, or styles, commonly found in complex organizations: (1) achievement-oriented leadership, (2) instrumental leadership, (3) supportive leadership, and (4) participative leadership.

1. *Achievement-oriented leadership.* Managers set challenging goals, expect subordinates to perform at the highest level, and constantly seek improvements in job performance. Achievement-oriented managers emphasize excellence and are confident that their subordinates will meet the high standards set for them.

2. *Instrumental leadership.* This type of directive leadership is similar to the initiating structure discussed earlier; it emphasizes planning, organizing, controlling, and coordinating by the manager. The manager lets subordinates know what they are expected to do and controls their job behavior through formal policies, procedures, rules, and regulations.

3. *Supportive leadership.* Supportive leadership is similar to the concept of consideration used in the original Ohio State studies. Supportive managers pay attention to the people dimension of leadership. They are concerned with the social needs of subordinates and exhibit a sincere interest in their well-being.

4. *Participative leadership.* Participative managers share information with subordinates and seek input from them in order to reach group consensus. They consult with their employees and permit them to have meaningful roles in the decision-making process.

The manager's leadership style is an important factor in determining the kinds of rewards that will be used in a given situation. A relationship-oriented manager uses praise, emotional support, encouragement, and various sociopsychological strokes to supplement standard rewards such as pay raises and promotions. They value individual differences and are inclined to tailor reward packages to meet the needs of their employees. Task-oriented managers, on the other hand, use a narrower set of rewards that is normally unrelated to individual psychological needs. They tend to stress pay and job security. In order to be effective managers, police administrators must exercise leadership styles that coincide with the rewards being sought by their subordinates.[93]

There are two very important situational or contingency variables in the path-goal approach. The first one relates to the personal characteristics of subordinates: their individual needs (for achievement, affiliation, and autonomy), their abilities (job skills, knowledge, and experience), and their personalities (emotional stability, self-esteem, and self-confidence). The second variable relates to the nature of the task and the environment in which it is performed. Some tasks are certainly much more demanding and stressful than others. Robert Albanese suggests that three aspects of the organizational environment have a significant impact on leader behavior: (1) the nature and complexity of the task, (2) the formal authority system, and (3) primary group relations.[94] Both the personal characteristics of subordinates and the nature of the task and environment influence the manager's leadership style as it relates to motivating subordinates. Motivation, in turn, is presumed to influence employee satisfaction and job performance. Subordinates perceive leaders' behavior as legitimate and accept it when it is an immediate source of satisfaction or when they anticipate that it will lead to future satisfaction.[95]

Path-goal theory assumes that subordinates respond differently to different leadership styles. Situational factors help determine their preference for certain types of leader behavior. For example, when subordinates are involved in a task that is stressful, tedious, boring, frustrating, time-consuming, dangerous, or otherwise unpleasant, effective managers make the work more tolerable by acting in an empathetic, caring, and supportive manner designed to minimize (moderate) the negative aspects of the job. Supportive relationships tend to increase the intrinsic value (valence) of the task. Increased satisfaction, at least in theory, leads to more effort on the part of most employees.

Directive leadership increases subordinate satisfaction and effort where there is role ambiguity. This condition occurs when the task is relatively unstructured, there is little or no formalization, and employees are inexperienced in relation to the task. Role ambiguity causes subordinates to have a low expectation of success in performing a complex task even if they plan to exert maximum effort. The path-goal model assumes that role ambiguity is dysfunctional, dissatisfying, and counterproductive. Under these circumstances, directive leader behavior will increase employee satisfaction with work and with the leader. Increased satisfaction may lead to an overall increase in productivity.

Directive leader behavior is best at motivating subordinates who have a need for autonomy, responsibility, and self-actualization but who find themselves in very complex and ambiguous situations. They want to know what is expected of them. They need to know the parameters within which they are expected to operate.

In situations where organizational goals and the paths for achieving them are unambiguous, competent workers who have a strong self-image seek autonomy and want to work for a supportive relationship-oriented manager. Less skilled, more passive employees are much more amenable to task-oriented leaders. The trick, of course, is for police managers to make sure that their leadership styles are in harmony with the needs of subordinates and the demands of the situation.

The path-goal model just discussed (see Figure 11–11) is a complex view of leadership. It is designed to deal with the interaction between leader behavior and situational factors. In essence, it views the manager's role as that of motivating employees who are not motivated sufficiently by intrinsic satisfaction or extrinsic rewards. The goal is to increase productivity. The ability of managers to satisfy employee needs and generate increased productivity will be contingent on their leadership style, the moderating effect of subordinate characteristics, and various environmental factors.

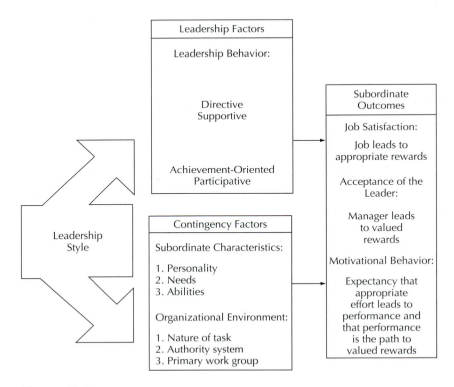

**Figure 11–11**
Path-Goal Approach to Leadership.

As principal actors in the motivation process, managerial leaders are expected to establish legitimate and realistic goals, to identify and clear the most direct path to follow in achieving those goals, and to reward appropriate goal-oriented behavior. A leader style (achievement-oriented, instrumental, supportive, or participatory) that corresponds with employee needs and situational variables will, at least in theory, satisfy subordinates and lead to increased productivity on the part of individual employees and the work group as a whole.

Research on path-goal theory has produced mixed results. Some studies support the concept; others do not. Most support is found for the notion that leader behavior has a direct effect on subordinate satisfaction. In one recent study (of 110 bank employees and 205 manufacturing employees), investigators found that task structure moderated the effects of leader behavior on subordinate satisfaction. When tasks were varied, provided little or no feedback, and offered few opportunities for meaningful social interaction, directive leader behavior (initiating structure) increased employee satisfaction. When tasks were routine, provided feedback, and offered opportunities for social interaction, initiating structure became dysfunctional and dissatisfying. It has been much more difficult to demonstrate the link between satisfaction and increased productivity.

## PARTICIPATORY LEADERSHIP

As noted earlier in this chapter, several leadership studies link managerial style to group performance and have developed classification systems to depict this relationship. These classifications (or ideal types) are usually viewed as elements on a conceptual continuum ranging from completely autocratic to completely democratic leadership. One popular way to illustrate this range of leadership styles is shown in Figure 11–12. The continuum identifies and differentiates among seven styles based on the degree of managerial authority and group involvement. Given the fact that no style is necessarily superior to another, the most appropriate leadership style will depend on the situation and the criteria used to judge what is considered appropriate. If productivity is the criterion, any leader style could be effective. If quick, unambiguous decision-making is the criterion, a leadership style at the leader-centered end of the continuum might be the best one. If, on the other hand, optimizing group participation is the objective, group-centered styles are much more effective than those emphasizing the unilateral exercise of authority by managers in positions of power. Robert Albanese points out that the value of a particular leader's style must be assessed in terms of the desired outcomes.[96]

Group-oriented leadership—known as participatory management—involves the "consults," "joins," and "delegates" styles and is specifically designed to involve employees in the leadership process. Participatory leaders make a sincere effort to get their subordinates involved in the task of creating and maintaining productive work environments. The participatory management model assumes that employees prefer some form of self-governance to autocratic control and that, as achievement-oriented human beings, they have an absolute need to be included in the group decision-making process.

Management by participation is an essential concept for the organizational humanists and an extension of the human relations school of thought.

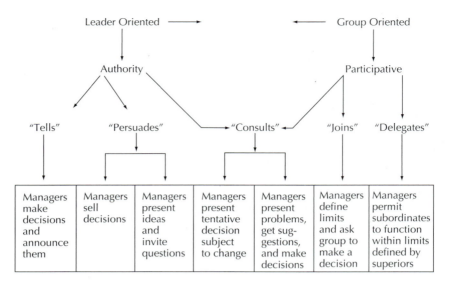

**Figure 11–12**

Seven Leadership Styles.

Adapted and Reprinted by permission of *Harvard Business Review*. From R. Tannenbaum and W. H. Schmidt, "How to Choose a Leadership Pattern," No. 36 (March–April 1958). Copyright © 1958 by Harvard Business School Publishing Corporation, all rights reserved.

It implicitly assumes that full participation in the management process meets employee needs, enhances the satisfaction derived from work, and increases organizational as well as individual productivity. According to the late Douglas M. McGregor, decentralization and delegation are ways of freeing people from the close control of traditional bureaucratic organizations. They give subordinates a degree of freedom to direct their own activities, to assume responsibility, and to satisfy their egoistic needs, which include the following:[97]

1.  Needs related to employee's self-esteem such as knowledge, attainment, self-confidence, competence, and self-sufficiency.
2.  Needs related to the employee's reputation, such as recognition, appreciation, status, and the respect of peers.

In the right circumstances, participatory management encourages employees to direct their creative energies toward organizational goals, gives them a voice in decisions that affect them, and produces significant opportunities for satisfaction of both social and egoistic needs.

The concept of participatory managerial leadership is rooted in the humanistic theories developed by people such as Mary Parker Follett ("power with" versus "power over" in industrial democracy), Elton Mayo (the Hawthorne effect), Abraham Maslow (the hierarchy of needs), Frederick Herzberg (motivation-hygiene theory), and Douglas McGregor (Theory X and Theory Y). These theories are built on the assumption that an increase in participation will usually have a favorable effect on subordinates who have relatively high needs for independence, are ready to assume responsibility, have the necessary knowledge and expertise to deal with problems, and identify with organizational goals.

Participatory management is often touted as the one best way to develop organizational conditions and operational procedures that will motivate individual employees to attain their (social and psychological) goals as they direct their efforts toward achievement of organizational goals and objectives. In fact, some humanist ideologues argue that participatory leadership is the only way to enhance employee satisfaction, performance, and morale in complex organizations. They contend that most people will voluntarily commit to and accept those decisions they helped to make.

The human relations approach to managerial leadership is consistent with the American ideals of equity, democracy, and individual dignity. In a recent study, J. M. Rosow found that 54 percent of all Americans feel they have a right to participate in making decisions that affect their job. Among younger workers the proportion was 62 percent. There is every reason to believe that the demand for worker participation in organizational decision-making will continue to grow.[98]

Organizational humanists have advanced a number of guidelines for enhancing meaningful employee participation. Some of those explanations have been synopsized here:[99]

1. Create an environment in which employees feel they can express their concerns.
2. Propose tentative solutions and encourage officers to improve on them.
3. Make notes in order to ensure that ideas are recorded.
4. Look for positive aspects of suggestions.
5. If concerned about some aspects of a suggestion, work at making them less objectionable.
6. Do not be defensive when listening to a dissenting opinion.
7. Utilize suggestions and deal with expressed concerns.
8. Give people credit for their suggestions and ideas.

Humanist police managers attempt to deal with the people-oriented problems of bureaucracy through an emphasis on management by participation or team management. They try to create organizational environments in which subordinates are kept fully informed and given meaningful roles in the decision-making process. These administrators spend much of their time counseling, training, and developing personnel. Humanists embrace change and stress the human relations approach in which subordinates are treated in an empathetic and supportive manner to enhance morale. Morale is seen as a pathway to efficiency, effectiveness, and productivity.

Once again, the results of the research on participative management have been mixed. While participation is important, some believe that the ideological air of organizational humanism has distorted the true relationship between participation and motivation. Some research indicates that participatory leader behavior is most effective when the tasks being performed are ego-involving, ambiguous, and non-routine. Other studies have concluded that participatory management is most effective when subordinates have enough knowledge and competence to make a meaningful contribution to the organization's decision-making process. According Robert Albanese, the effects of participation on employee satisfaction and performance will depend on the characteristics of the actors, task variables, and situational factors.[100] Consequently, participation should not be considered as a panacea for creating congruence between employee needs and organizational needs. In some situations and for certain types of personnel, participatory leadership techniques might be very effective. In other situations, however, they are definitely inappropriate.

## Management Systems Model

Participative leadership, as espoused by the human relationists and organizational humanists, is predicated on the fundamental assumption that there is a genuine need for power equalization in the management of complex organizations. They argue that it is essential to reduce the power and status differential between superiors and subordinates in order to facilitate meaningful participation. The goal is to deemphasize hierarchical authority, to give workers a collective voice in the decision-making process, to encourage creative responses to change, and to overcome apathy by morale-building approaches in which employees become involved with the organization's mission, goals, and objectives and committed to achieving them.[101]

The late Rensis Likert was a leading advocate of participatory management. Likert's management systems model represents a continuum of styles ranging from autocratic to participatory. The model contrasts traditional management (Theory X) with democratic managerial leadership (Theory Y). Using the well-known Likert scale to measure attitudes and values, he identified four basic management styles, or climates:

1. Exploitive authoritative        System 1
2. Benevolent authoritative      System 2
3. Consultative                          System 3
4. Participative group               System 4

Each of these management systems reflects a different approach to handling major organizational processes like motivation, communication, decision-making, goal setting, coordination, and control. Ronald Lynch, in a book on police management, explored Likert's climate concept. A synopsis of his findings is presented here.[102]

**System 1**

Management is seen as having no confidence or trust in its personnel and seldom involves them in any aspect of organizational decision-making. Top management makes virtually all decisions, sets goals, and issues policies, procedures, rules, and regulations through the chain of command. Employees are kept in line through intimidation and manipulation of the reward system. The emphasis is on meeting what Maslow called basic and security needs. Managerial contacts with subordinates often take the form of disciplinary action aimed at correcting employee mistakes or misconduct. The trend in police work (notwithstanding some pockets of resistance) is to move away from System 1 and toward the other end of the continuum.

**System 2**

Management places some degree of confidence and trust in lower-level police personnel, but the organization retains its rigid paramilitary structure. Most decision-making and goal setting take place at the top and are filtered down through the chain of command. System 2 managers accept some input from lower levels and permit personnel in lower-level positions to make some of the less important decisions. Rewards, punishments, and threats of punishment are used to motivate employees. Managers still instill fear and caution in their employees. While there is some delegation and decentralization, rank-and-file police officers continue to be distrustful of their superiors.

Management exhibits substantial but not total trust between leaders and subordinates. Under this arrangement, most decisions are made at lower levels. Effective leaders tend to manage by exception. Policy-making and high-level decisions remain in the hands of top administrators. Communication flows upward and downward. Rewards and occasional punishments are used to motivate personnel. Since there is more and more interaction between leaders and followers, mutual trust and confidence replace fear and suspicion. Both the higher and lower levels feel a responsibility for increasing productivity and maintaining quality. A System 3 managerial style places emphasis on what Maslow called the belongingness and self-esteem needs of working police officers. **System 3**

Leader behavior and managerial practices demonstrate the total trust and confidence that mid-level and executive-level managers have in their subordinates. Decision-making is widely dispersed and promoted throughout the organization. Communication flows not only up and down within the organization but horizontally among peers as well. Lower-level employees get involved in (1) establishing organizational goals, (2) improving techniques, procedures, and operations, and (3) evaluating the overall success of the organization in accomplishing its mission, goals, and objectives. System 4 managers create a warm and friendly atmosphere in which all levels are fully involved in decision-making and the control process flows from lower units to the top. System 4 leadership is based on empathetic understanding, mutual trust, meaningful participation, and teamwork in very complex interaction/influence structures. **System 4**

According to Daniel Wren, System 4 management style is built on three basic principles:[103]

1. Supportive relationships
2. Group decision-making and supervision
3. High performance goals

The principle of supportive relationships means leaders must ensure that each member of the work group recognizes a sense of personal worth and self-esteem created and maintained for him or her by the group. The principle of group decision-making and supervision involves an overlapping group structure in which individual work groups are linked to the rest of the organization through persons ("linking pins") who are members of more than one group. The principle of high performance goals encourages members of the organization to commit themselves to efficiency, effectiveness, and productivity. These high goals should be keyed to the employee's personal needs as well as to the needs of others within the work group. System 4 management allows personnel at all levels of the organization to move toward what Abraham Maslow described as self-actualization.

Organizational humanists contend that a System 4 management style improves employee morale and that good morale is the harbinger of increased productivity. They are convinced that leadership styles at the System 1 end of the continuum lead to frustration, dissatisfaction, apathy, and decreased productivity. Likert believed that System 2 management styles are the most common.

Buddy Strock is the chief of police in a small municipal police department in the midwestern United States. He was hired to be a change agent and given a mandate for reform. As the first outside chief in the department's history, he inherited a legacy of suspicion, distrust, and outright hostility. Morale was nonexistent, and the local community had lost faith in its nine-person police department.

The chief, a competent, emotionally secure, goal-oriented, and very decisive manager, took immediate action to deal with the chaotic situation. Using emergency powers given to him by the city council and the mayor, Chief Strock fired three veteran officers, suspended a civilian clerk, and put the rest of the employees on notice that they had to pull their load or get out. It was obvious to everyone that the chief was a man with a mission and that he planned to upgrade his department by whatever means necessary. After the smoke cleared, it was obvious that the chief was in charge and that he would determine the rules by which the game would be played.

After the initial flurry of autocratic activity, the chief convened a series of meetings designed to incorporate all of the remaining personnel into the decision-making process. The meetings were held on a regular basis and were designed to reestablish trust through open and honest dialogue. The chief encouraged participation and acted more as a teacher and group facilitator than as a dictator. The officers were given an opportunity to help formulate short-term goals and devise strategies for achieving them. Chief Strock made every attempt to strike an appropriate balance between the needs of the department (for efficiency, effectiveness, and productivity) and the physical, psychological, and social needs of his subordinates. He was convinced that his brand of organizational humanism would lead to more efficiency, effectiveness, and productivity.

Things began to fall apart. The officers rejected Chief Strock's efforts to draw them into the decision-making process. They were content to sit back and complain about things as they waited for the chief to fail. They were used to being spectators, not participants, in the management process. The officers were paranoid and saw participative management as a setup. They did not want to become scapegoats for the administration.

The mayor and city council also expressed concerns about the social experimentation going on in the police department. They wanted their man to be in charge and viewed participative management as an ineffective abdication of authority. The mayor asked Chief Strock to explain what was going on, and the city council demanded a thorough investigation of the police department.

Chief Strock was unable to understand why mature adults acted like a bunch of children. He refused to subject himself to further criticism and resigned. In his letter of resignation, the chief blamed everyone but himself for his failure. He complained that he had not been given a chance to succeed.

*Several factors led to Chief Strock's resignation. He made a number of mistakes. What was his most serious miscalculation? What would you—as an aspiring police administrator—have done differently in this particular situation?*

If we can assume that the actual situation in police organizations reflects prevailing management theories, we would expect to find that most police employees find themselves in a System 2 climate. In one recent study of 18 local police departments of various sizes in 15 different states, Charles R. Swanson and Susette Talarico asked 629 uniformed police officers assigned to field duties to describe their department's management climate. The results were interesting and tended to confirm Likert's management systems model. Some 16.6 percent of the officers assessed their climate as System 1, 42.9 percent reported living under System 2, 35.9 percent identified with System 3, and a mere 4.6 percent thought their departments used the System 4 approach to management.[104]

Research on the participation factor has found that it—much like the other theories discussed in this chapter—produces mixed results. There is no reason to believe that participatory leadership is the one best way to manage law-enforcement agencies.

# TRANSFORMATIONAL AND TRANSACTIONAL LEADERSHIP STYLES

A somewhat newer model of leadership that is receiving increased attention is best described as transformational/transactional. *Transformational leadership* alters employee relationships with, and views of, the organization. It is a process that focuses on building commitment and creating working relationships that allow task accomplishment. Organizational goals and needs become paramount. Self-indulgence and the satisfaction of personal needs become secondary. Subordinate employees are empowered, and in accepting that empowerment they consciously seek higher levels of morality and motivation. Abstract concepts such as equality, justice, liberty, and humanitarianism supercede their baser instincts.[105] The process is two-pronged: at the same time as employees are taking on responsibility for organizational enhancement, their leaders are taking on responsibility to provide for the employees' personal and professional growth. This motivates followers to do more than anticipated—more, in many instances, than they thought possible.[106]

Expectations set so high that they challenge, empower, and stimulate clearly result in improved performance. When leadership addresses the self-worth of subordinates, it provides for commitment that is foundational to the organization. The result is a total and ceaseless process of leader–follower interchange that invokes response from subordinates and modifies their behavior. Conflict is mediated and motivational techniques are paramount.[107] Transformational leadership makes the skills and knowledge of subordinates a means of goal attainment; employee recommendations become a vehicle that enhances transition and realization. Throughout the process, leadership communicates the reasons for decisions and actions. The greater understanding this gives subordinates not only allows them to operate more efficiently, it empowers them to exercise initiative—which is the keystone to operational effectiveness.

Transformational leadership strives to achieve superior results by following these precepts:[108]

1. Present charismatic role models.
2. Motivate and inspire.
3. Stimulate innovation and creativity.
4. Stress individual needs for achievement and growth.

Leadership becomes charismatic when officers strive to identify with the superior and imitate him or her. The true leader is one who is trusted and demonstrates extraordinary capabilities. Because of inspired motivation, the officers respond with enthusiasm and optimism and become committed to such an extent that team spirit is aroused. Transformational leadership encourages innovation and readily allows for the questioning of assumptions without recrimination. Additionally, special attention is given to individual needs, and growth is provided for through coaching and mentoring.[109]

A considerably different approach, taken by some leaders, is the *transactional leadership* style. The specific techniques used by this style range from rewarding officers to disciplining them. Notable achievements are acknowledged through contingency rewards. Tasks are assigned or agreed to, and rewards are given upon successful task achievement. Tasks are assigned in writing and include detailed listings of all rules, regulations, and other guidance that may be relevant. The benefits associated with task achievement and the negative consequences of failure are clearly identified. *Management by exception* is practiced, meaning that leaders focus all their attention on monitoring employee work and looking for errors and mistakes. Monitoring is the byword of the day, and deviance from standards is anticipated.

The leader who relies exclusively on a transactional style takes on a lot of baggage. Subordinate commitment is usually short term, and such things as creativity and innovation become a thing of the past—if they ever existed. Other negative aspects of this style include the absence of room for individual growth and the negative sanctions that can result even from an honest mistake. Transactional leadership can work in some situations, but the leaders who have used it most effectively have selectively used its techniques together with transformational techniques, in combinations tailored to particular situations.[110]

Unfortunately, the promised land of leadership has been and will continue to be an elusive destination. Nevertheless, tremendous progress has been made during the last few decades.

## SUMMARY

There is absolutely no doubt that leadership plays a pivotal role in organizational dynamics. Police administrators are expected to be leaders as well as managers. Management leadership, as we have called it, is a behavioral transaction that involves influencing, motivating, guiding, and controlling human resources in cooperative efforts to accomplish an organization's mission, goals, and objectives. It is an interactive achievement-oriented process through which individual members of the work group are induced to follow a leader; in so doing they receive psychosocial satisfaction from willingly behaving the way the leader wants them to behave. Part of the task of the leader is to get subordinates to participate in the leadership process.

Many types of people make good leaders. No one leadership style has proven to be effective in all situations. Consequently, management theorists tend to define leadership in terms of their own perspective and/or those aspects of the phenomenon that interest them the most. As we have seen, the concept of leadership has been explored in terms of traits, behavior, style, influence, roles, interaction, and situational variables. Five major explanatory paradigms have emerged and dominated the study of leadership in general and managerial leadership in particular. They are (1) the trait approach,

(2) the leader behavior approach, (3) the situational approach, (4) the interaction/influence approach, and (5) the human relations approach. After more than 50 years of contemplation and applied research, theoretical pragmatists have concluded that there is no one best way to manage complex organizations.

While participatory leadership is often touted as the ultimate form of management, the situational approach is much closer to reality. When the chips are down, the most appropriate leadership style will depend on the synergistic interactions among the actors, the task, and the environmental factors that coalesced to create the particular leadership situation. A relatively recent theme is the potential application of transformational and transactional leadership styles to law enforcement agencies.

Many management theorists now believe that adaptive leaders—those who are able to change their style of leadership based on the situation and the needs of their subordinates— will be the most effective when it comes to achieving both personal and organizational objectives. They see adaptive management as a pathway to effective police administration in the 21st century.

# KEY TERMS

adaptive management
authority
autocratic
conceptual
consideration
contingency management model
democratic
"eternal triangle"
human
improvised management
influence
initiating structure
interaction/influence system
knowledge areas
laissez-faire
leader behavior approach
leadership
leadership quadrants
leadership skill mix
leadership skills
leadership styles
least-preferred co-worker
management
management systems model

Managerial Grid
managerial leadership
organizational humanism
participatory management
path-goal leadership model
people-oriented management
people-oriented needs
power
reciprocal response
situational leadership
situational theories
System 1
System 2
System 3
System 4
task-oriented management
task-oriented needs
technical
trait theory
transactional leadership style
transformational leadership style
universal theories
zone of acceptance

# DISCUSSION TOPICS AND QUESTIONS

1. Define *leadership*, and explain its relationship to effective management in complex law enforcement organizations.

2. Why has it been so difficult to identify and describe leader traits common to effective police managers?

3. What two dimensions of leader behavior were identified in both the Ohio State and the University of Michigan leadership studies? What specific terms did they use to describe these particular concepts?

4. Based on the Managerial Grid, what is 9,9 management, and how does it relate to Rensis Likert's System 2 approach?

5. What is the LPC scale, and what does it tell the contingency theorist about the manager who fills it out?

6. Define the *interactionist perspective*, and explain how it relates to L = f(LP, GP, S).

7. Participatory management and organizational humanism are rooted in human relations theory. Name some theorists who are closely identified with these paradigms.

8. Why do most police officers find themselves working in a System 2 climate?

9. What is adaptive police management, and why is it likely to become the dominant approach in the 21st century?

10. Discuss the concept of "the eternal triangle."

11. Discuss transformational and transactional styles of leadership.

# FOR FURTHER READING

Bernard M. Bass, *Transformational Leadership: Industrial, Military and Educational Impact* (Mahwah, NJ: Lawrence Erlbaum Associates, 1998).

A well-written text that conceives of leadership in terms of its transactional or transformational emphasis. Transformational principles are viewed as a new paradigm of leadership allowing for commitment, involvement, loyalty, and performance. Better leaders are transformational more frequently; less adequate leaders concentrate on correction and passivity. Leadership that is passive in nature is seen as least effective and satisfying. The author suggests that leaders use all of these approaches. The book contains a discussion of empowerment and laissez-faire leadership. In addition, the author discusses the implications of transformational leadership for organizational policies.

Donald Griner, "People-Oriented Leadership," *The Police Chief,* Vol. LXX (2003), pp. 10, 30–34.

The author recommends that police leaders focus on work processes much less than they do on the people who work within the processes. People-oriented managers know their employees' strengths and talents, and they place people in positions that take advantage of those positive characteristics. The author suggests that great managers know the mission of the police department and how to accomplish that mission. He stresses that a leader unlocks the potential in each employee to achieve organizational goals. He also discusses the importance of communication and problem-solving models.

Jean Lipman-Blumen, *Connective Leadership: Managing in a Changing World* (Oxford, UK: Oxford University Press, 1999).

Presents nine leadership styles in terms of the connective leadership model, which is a way of analyzing a wide spectrum of leadership strategies. Suggests that the predominant leadership paradigm is shifting from control to connection, from independence to interdependence, and from competition to collaboration. Connective leadership is viewed as having an eye for diversity, accepting ambiguity, and rejecting orthodoxy. This leadership style recognizes subtle connections among people, events, institutions, and ideologies. The book does an excellent job of discussing the changing dynamics of leadership.

Craig L. Pearce and Jay A. Conger, Eds., *Shared Leadership: Reframing the How's and Why's of Leadership* (Thousand Oaks, CA: Sage, 2003).

This book articulates a model of leadership that is called shared leadership. It is viewed as a dynamic, interactive influence process among individuals in groups, whose objective is to lead one another to the achievement of group or organizational goals or both. This influence process is seen as involving both peer (lateral) influence and hierarchical (upward or downward) influence. Leadership of this type is viewed as being broadly distributed among a set of individuals instead of being centralized.

# NOTES

1. Michael LeBoeuf, *GMP: The Greatest Management Principle in the World* (New York: Berkley Books, 1985), pp. 12–18.

2. V.A. Leonard and Harry W. More, *Police Organization and Management,* 9th ed. (New York: Foundation Press, 2000), pp. 256–258.

3. Nathan F. Iannone, and M.D. Iannone, *Supervision of Police Personnel,* 6th ed. (Upper Saddle River, NJ: Prentice Hall, 2001), pp. 81–86.

4. Robert Albanese, *Management* (Cincinnati: South-Western, 1985).

5. Keith D. Bushey, "The Unproductive Executive," *The Police Chief,* Vol. LXVI (3) (1999), pp. 69–73.

6. Justin G. Longenecker and Charles D. Pringle, *Principles of Management and Organizational Behavior* (Columbus, OH: Charles E. Merrill, 1984), p. 214.

7. Mary Parker Follett, "Leader and Expert," in E.M. Fox and L. Urwick, eds. *Dynamic Administration* (New York: Hippocrene Books, 1977).

8. Leonard and More, *Police Organization and Management,* p. 280.

9. Warren G. Bennis, *The Unconscious Conspiracy: Why Can't Leaders Lead,* (New York: AMACOM, 1976).

10. Lester R. Bittel, *What Every Supervisor Should Know: The Complete Guide to Supervisory Management,* 6th ed. (New York: McGraw-Hill, 1990), pp 275–276.

11. Gary A. Yukl, *Leadership in Organization,* 5th ed. (Upper Saddle River, NJ: Prentice Hall, 2002), p. 6.

12. Craig L. Pearce and Jay A. Conger, eds. *Shared Leadership: Reframing the Hows and Whys of Leadership* (Thousand Oaks, CA: Sage, 2003), p. xi.

13. Jean Lipman-Blumen, *Connective Leadership: Managing in a Changing World* (Oxford, England: Oxford University Press, 1999), p. 32.

14. Herbert A. Simon, *Administrative Behavior* (New York: Free Press, 1976).

15. Andrew J. Dubrin, *The Complete Idiot's Guide to Leadership* (New York: Alpha Book, A Simon & Schuster Macmillan Company, 1998), p 5.

16. Ronald G. Lynch, *The Police Manager,* 5th ed. (Cincinnati: Anderson, 1998).

17. Richard Plunkett, *Supervision: The Direction of People at Work,* 9th ed. (Dubuque, IA: William C. Brown, 2000).

18. Yukl, *Leadership in Organization,* p. 189.

19. John R. Schermerhorn, James G. Hunt, and Richard N. Osborne, *Organizational Behavior,* 8th ed. (New York: Wiley, 2002), pp. 71–76.

20. Follett, *Dynamic Administration.*

21. Richard Holden, *Modern Police Management,* 2nd ed. (Englewood Cliffs, NJ: Prentice Hall, 1994), pp. 37–38.

22. David A. Tansik, Richard B. Chase, and Nicholas J. Aquilano, *Management: A Life Cycle Approach* (Homewood, IL: Richard D. Irwin, 1980), pp. 85–90.

23. Hannah Arendt, *The Human Condition* (Chicago: University of Chicago Press, 1958), p. 127.

24. Chester I. Barnard, *The Functions of the Executive* (Cambridge, MA: Harvard University Press, 1868), pp. 216–134.

25. Sam S. Souryal, *Police Administration and Management* (St. Paul, MN: West, 1977), pp. 39–61.

26. Douglas M. McGregor, *The Human Side of Enterprise* (New York: McGraw-Hill, 1960), pp. 23–49.

27. Gary Dessler, *Management Fundamentals: A Framework* (Reston, VA: Reston Publishing, 1979), pp. 420–424.

28. Frederick Herzberg, "One More Time: How Do You Motivate Employees?" *Harvard Business Review,* 46 (1) (1968), pp. 35–41.

29. Barnard, *The Functions of the Executive.*

30. Robert L. Katz, "Skills of an Effective Administrator," *Harvard Business Review,* 52 (5) (1974), pp. 6–12.

31. Edward A. Thibault, Lawrence M. Lynch, and R. Bruce McBride, *Proactive Police Management,* 6th ed. (Upper Saddle River, NJ: Prentice Hall, 2004).

32. Robert M. Fulmer, *The New Management* (New York: Macmillan, 1983), pp. 339–340.

33. Katz, *Skills of an Effective Administrator,* p. 39.

34. Albanese, *Managing: Toward Accountability for Performance.*

35. Dessler, *Management Fundamentals: A Framework.*

36. Charles R. Swanson, Leonard Territo, and Robert W. Taylor, *Police Administration,* 5th ed. (Upper Saddle River, NJ: PrenticeHall, 2001).

37. Holden, *Modern Police Management.*

38. Robert A. Baron, *Behavior in Organizations: Understanding and Managing the Human Side of Work* (Boston: Allyn & Bacon, 1983).

39. Ralph C. Davis, *Industrial Organization and Management,* 3rd ed. (New York: Harper and Brothers, 1957).

40. Cecil E. Goode, "Significant Research on Leadership," *Personnel,* Vol. 18 (3) (1976), pp. 25–29.

41. E.E. Ghiselli, *Explorations in Management Talent* (Pacific Palisades, CA: Goodyear, 1971), p. 139.

42. Ralph M. Stogdill, *Handbook of Leadership* (New York: Free Press, 1974).

43. Joe Kelly, *Organizational Behavior: An Existential Systems Approach* (Homewood, IL: Richard D. Irwin, 1974).

44. Albanese, *Managing: Toward Accountability for Performance.*

45. H. Joe Reitz, *Behavior in Organizations* (Homewood, IL: Richard D. Irwin, 1981).

46. Schermerhorn, Hunt, and Osborne, *Managing Organizational Behavior.*

47. Baron, *Behavior in Organizations: Understanding and Managing the Human Side of Work.*

48. Yukl, *Leadership in Organizations,* pp. 29–32.

49. Tansik, Chase, and Aquilano, *Management: A Life Cycle Approach.*

50. Philip V. Lewis, Ronald Lippit, and Ralph K. White, "Patterns of Aggressive Behavior in Experimentally Created 'Social Climates,'" *Journal of Social Psychology,* Vol. 10 (1939).

51. Philip V. Lewis, *Managing Human Relations* (Boston: Kent, 1983).

52. Holden, *Modern Police Management.*

53. Robert Tannenbaum and Warren H. Schmidt, "How to Choose a Leadership Pattern," *Harvard Business Review,* Vol. 51 (3) (1973).

54. Phillip B. Applewhite, *Organizational Behavior* (Englewood Cliffs, NJ: Prentice Hall, 1965), pp. 130–132.

55. Dessler, *Management Fundamentals: A Framework.*

56. Leonard and More, *Police Organization and Management,* pp. 259–261.

57. Fulmer, *The New Management,* pp. 15–32.

58. Yukl, *Leadership in Organizations,* pp. 46–47.

59. Albanese, *Managing: Toward Accountability for Performance.*

60. Reitz, *Behavior in Organizations.*

61. Longenecker, *Principles of Management and Organizational Behavior.*

62. Stogdill, *Handbook of Leadership.*

63. Reitz, *Behavior in Organizations.*

64. Yukl, *Leadership in Organizations,* pp. 133–136.

65. Bittel, *What Every Supervisor Should Know: The Basics of Supervisory Management,* pp. 275–276.

66. Robert R. Blake and Jane Srygley Mouton, *The Managerial Grid III: The Key to Leadership Excellence* (Houston: Gulf, 1985), p. 29.

67. Plunkett, *Supervision: The Direction of People at Work.*

68. Blake and Mouton, *The Managerial Grid III: The Key to Leadership Excellence,* p. 12.

69. Leonard and More, *Police Organization and Management,* p. 263.

70. Ibid, p. 262.

71. Jack L. Kuykendall and Peter Unsinger, "The Leadership Style of Police Managers," *Journal of Criminal Justice,* Vol. 9 (1982).

72. Roy R. Roberg and Jack L. Kuykendall, *Police Organization and Management: Behavior, Theory and Practice* (Pacific Grove, CA: Brooks/Cole, 1990).

73. Jack L. Kuykendall, "Police Leadership: An Analysis of Executive Style," *Criminal Justice Review,* Vol. 2 (1), (1977), pp. 7–9.

74. Blake and Mouton, *The Managerial Grid III: The Key to Leadership Excellence,* pp. 98–103.

75. Fred Luthans, *Organizational Behavior* (New York: McGraw-Hill, 1977).

76. Longenecker, *Principles of Management and Organizational Behavior.*

77. Albanese, *Managing: Toward Accountability for Performance.*

78. Fulmer, *The New Management.*

79. Paul M. Whisenand, *The Effective Police Manager* (Englewood Cliffs, NJ: Prentice Hall, 1981).

80. Lynch, *The Police Manager: Professional Leadership Skills.*

81. Paul Whisenand and Fred Ferguson, *The Managing of Police Organizations* (Upper Saddle River, NJ: Prentice Hall, 1978), pp. 218–219.

82. Fred Fiedler, "A Contingency Model of Leadership Effectiveness," in L. Berkowitz, ed. *Advances in Experimental Social Psychology* (New York: Academic Press, 1964).

83. Plunkett, *Supervision: The Direction of People at Work.*

84. Reitz, *Behavior in Organizations.*

85. Leonard and More, *Police Organization and Management,* pp. 264–265.

86. Tansik, Chase, and Aquilano, *Management: A Life Cycle Approach.*

87. Longenecker, *Principles of Management and Organizational Behavior.*

88. Plunkett, *Supervision: The Direction of People at Work.*

89. Leonard and More, *Police Organization and Management,* p. 265.

90. Fiedler, *Managerial Control and Organizational Democracy.*

91. Robert J. House, "A Path-Goal Theory of Leadership Effectiveness," *Administrative Science Quarterly* (1971), p. 321.

92. Gary Johns, *Organizational Behavior* (Dallas: Foresman, 1988).

93. Reitz, *Behavior in Organizations.*

94. Albanese, *Managing: Toward Accountability for Performance.*

95. Dessler, *Management Fundamentals: A Framework.*

96. Albanese, *Managing: Toward Accountability for Performance.*

97. McGregor, *The Human Side of Enterprise.*

98. J.M. Roscow, "Quality of Work Life Issues for the 1980s," in C. Kerr and J.M. Rosow, eds. *Work in America The Decade Ahead* (New York: Van Nostrand, 1979).

99. Daniel Wren, *The Evolution of Management Thought* (New York: Wiley, 1987).

100. Albanese, *Managing: Toward Accountability for Performance.*

101. Wren, *The Evolution of Management Thought.*

102. Lynch, *The Police Manager: Professional Leadership Skills.*

103. Wren, *The Evolution of Management Thought.*

104. Swanson, Territo, and Taylor, *Police Administration.*

105. Yukl, *Leadership in Organizations,* p. 324.

106. Bernard M. Bass, *A New Paradigm of Leadership: An Inquiry into Transformational Leadership* (Alexandria, VA: U.S. Army Research Institute for the Behavioral and Social Sciences, 1996), p. 4.

107. Yukl, *Leadership in Organizations,* pp. 325–326.

108. Bass, *A New Paradigm of Leadership: An Inquiry into Transformational Leadership,* pp. 5–6.

109. Bernard M. Bass, *Transformational Leadership: Industrial, Military, and Educational Impact* (Mahwah, NJ: Lawrence Erlbaum Associates, 1998), pp. 4–6.

110. Department of the Army, *Army Leadership: Be, Know, Do,* FM 22–100 (Washington, DC: Headquarters, Department of the Army, August 1999), pp. 3–15–3–18.

# —12—

# CHANGE

## Coping with Organizational Life

We live in a world of kaleidoscopic change—change that is remarkable for its breadth, depth, and accelerating pace. As it is used here, the term *change* refers to any alteration that occurs in the organization of the total environment.[1] According to Alvin Toffler, change is the process by which the future invades our lives and shapes our behaviors. He argues that change is not merely a necessary aspect of life. It is life.[2]

Change is a natural and inevitable manifestation of organizational life. However, the success of any change initiative will ultimately depend on the ability of the executive team to properly implement change and the willingness of employees to alter their behaviors.

Bill Orion is a traditional Theory X manager who has ruled the Smithton Police Department with an iron fist for the last two years. The department has an authorized strength of 17 sworn personnel and 3 civilians. A very weak and easily manipulated civil service system has produced a staffing pattern based on political patronage and nepotism rather than merit. Under the existing circumstances, loyalty to the chief is considered more important than developing professional competence in police work. As a result, routine departmental decision-making has been centralized to the point where virtually all decisions are made by the police chief executive. Subordinates are rewarded for subservience, not creative problem solving.

Several incidents have served to focus media attention on problems within the police department. The most recent incident, involving the suicide of a prisoner, has become something of a cause célébre.

The prisoner, a young man who had been arrested for a relatively minor crime, was placed in a holding cell pending completion of the booking process. The arresting officer observed the prisoner trying to hang himself with a noose made from his own shirt. The officer intervened, took the shirt away, and reported the incident to his immediate supervisor. Sgt. John Caperton talked with the prisoner and concluded that he was emotionally disturbed. Since he did not want to make a decision on how to handle the situation, Sgt. Caperton spent ten minutes on the phone discussing the matter with Chief Orion. When he returned to the holding cell, he found the young man's body. He had hanged himself using a tube stocking attached to a bar in a window opening. It was the second suicide in the holding cell in three months.

According to one political insider, "All hell broke loose!" The dead man's family excoriated the police for failing to provide the proper supervision or care for mentally ill offenders, the media clamored for an objective investigation by a neutral third party, and the Smithton City Council called on Mayor Yarnell to fire Chief Orion.

*If you were the mayor, what would you do in this situation? Why does it often take an incident of this magnitude to precipitate substantive change in complex bureaucratic organizations? What are the most common indicators of the need for planned organizational change? Why is it better to be proactive rather than reactive in circumstances like these?*

Police departments change continuously because they are organic and relatively open social systems. They exchange information, energy, and material with various environments. Police departments are not static structures. They consist of dynamic interrelationships between people performing those functions necessary to achieve the mission, goals, and objectives of the organization. Managers must make their employees understand that there is no penalty for taking risks so long as they are taken for the right reasons.[3]

One of the most important measures of an organization's strength is its ability to adapt to and incorporate change. Aldag and Kuzuhara divide organizational change into two basic categories: (1) Planned change and (2) Reactive change.

1. *Planned change.* occurs when managers develop and install a program that serves to alter organizational activities in a timely and orderly way.
2. *Reactive change.* occurs when managers simply respond to the pressure for change when that pressure comes to their attention. Usually, this is a piecemeal approach because managers are facing problems that need immediate resolution.[4]

Change agents are individuals and/or groups that act as catalysts and assume responsibility for managing the change process. The change agent is defined as someone responsible for coordinating the planning and development of a new program or the revision of an old one. Such an individual will guide the analysis of the problem to be solved, search for causes of the problem and review similar interventions in use elsewhere, and facilitate the collaboration of clients, staff, and consumers involved in the planning process.[5]

A change intervention is an intentional action on the part of someone to make things different. Most planned changes are problem-solving efforts initiated by managers acting in their capacity as change agents (see Chapter 9). For all practical purposes, initiating and coping with change is the essence of the modern police administrator's job.

Unfortunately, most substantive organizational change occurs only when managers find themselves under intense pressure to act. The hard fact is that most individuals and organizations resist change. *Reactive* police administrators try to keep their departments on a fairly steady course. They are wedded to the past and glorify the status quo. They rely on cosmetic changes as they attempt to adjust to new conditions. The problem is that change is synergistic and cumulative. A series of small incremental changes can accumulate to cause a significant alteration in the operation of the organization.[6]

*Proactive* managers, in contrast to their reactive counterparts, are future oriented and much more inclined to embark on a program of planned change. They believe in the systematic approach to initiating and managing organizational change. Planned change involves deliberate actions to alter the status quo. Proactive police administrators set out to change things, to chart new courses rather than maintain the current ones. They want to anticipate changes in the environment and to develop ways of dealing with predicted conditions.

There is absolutely no doubt that the rapidity, intensity, and complexity of change facing law enforcement in contemporary American society require police administrators to learn both to use and to understand planned-change strategies. Learning how to initiate and manage planned change is one of the most important functions of a manager. Part of a manager's job is to manage change—to lead the organization through it productively. Managers in complex criminal justice organizations are no exception. They do not, as a rule, have the option of not initiating and managing substantive change—those organizations that fail to adapt to the changes in their environment almost always fail to accomplish their mission, goals, and objectives. While they may not actually disappear, these organizations tend to wither away and die on the vine. Police administrators face a somewhat paradoxical situation. They must respond both to the need for organizational stability and to the need for change. Good managers create and maintain environments that balance the demands for stability and change.

Whether change is good or bad depends on how it affects the organization. The pace and scope of change are important. There can be too much change or too little. From an organizational perspective, change for the sake of change is not a good thing. A police department that is in a constant state of flux will ordinarily be unable to establish and maintain the regularized patterns of collaborative behavior needed to ensure effectiveness.

## FORCES INFLUENCING ORGANIZATIONAL CHANGE

Police administrators face a variety of factors that dictate the necessity for changes in structural relationships and/or organizational behavior. The most important dimension of each factor is the degree to which it can be influenced or resolved by the intervention of management. Some problems are easily resolved because the solution is apparent. Others are much more complicated and may well be beyond the control of a particular manager. Good managers concentrate their efforts on making needed changes in areas where they have responsibility and in which there is a reasonable expectation of success. Rationality and judgment are critical components in creative problem solving. Creative problem solving is a key to the successful implementation of a planned change.

All organizations are confronted with two basic sources of pressure for change. These sources are usually classified as either external or internal to the organization. While this distinction is somewhat arbitrary, it provides a fairly convenient basis for discussing forces for change.

**Sources of Change**

Modern police departments are open systems that take inputs from the environment, transform some of them into public services, and send those services back into the environment as outputs.[7] Like other organisms, police departments consume external resources in order to survive. This means that they must be able to attract resources—such as capital, personnel, equipment, and knowledge—and must be able to market what they produce in the way of services. External sources of change are those factors outside an organization that modify the organization's ability to attract resources or market its services. These factors include competition and changes in economic conditions, the labor force, public expectations, the physical environment, social norms and values, and legal constraints. Cognizant of these external factors, Dessler argues that it is usually forces outside the organization that trigger strategic changes. Changes are also often required for survival. Dessler warns, though, that strategic changes implemented under crisis conditions are highly risky. Police agencies have consistently demonstrated their ability to change when driven to it by such external forces as legislation, court opinion, media pressure, political figures, commissions of inquiry, the federal government, pressure groups, and high-profile incidents.[8] Often, police departments have had change imposed on them from the outside because their leadership failed to recognize environmental conditions that demanded it.

**External Sources**

The internal sources of pressure to change include conflict, administrative changes, technical changes, declining productivity, changes in key agency personnel, and interpersonal issues such as shifts in workers' attitudes toward their supervisor or their benefits package.[9] A certain amount of intraorganizational conflict is normal and healthy. Under the right conditions, it leads to creative problem solving and produces adaptive change. Administrative changes involve restructuring the organization or revising policies, procedures, rules, and regulations. Technological changes include new paradigms, methods, tools, equipment, and so forth. People changes are concerned primarily with changes in values, attitudes, motivation, skills, and on-the-job behavior. Since change is both synergistic and cumulative, a change in one area leads to changes in others. Problems occur in police organizations because many administrators do not recognize the interdependencies of these internal change areas.[10]

**Internal Sources**

A few of the factors encouraging change warrant special consideration because they have had a major impact on police organizations and management. They are as follows: (1) technological factors, (2) sociocultural factors, and (3) organizational factors.

**Technological, Sociocultural, and Organizational Factors**

**Technological Factors**

Technological change occurs when a new method—such as new machinery, knowledge, tools, or techniques—is used to transform resources into a service.[11] Technological change has had an enormous impact on American law enforcement. The ongoing knowledge explosion has revolutionized modern police work and created a legion of specialists to deal with crime in an enormously complex society. The development and deployment of technology—in such forms as handheld radios, computers, computer-assisted fingerprint identification, offender profiling, infrared surveillance, field drug testing, electronic eavesdropping, voiceprint analysis, thermo tracking, genetic (DNA) fingerprinting, forensic odontology, operations research, mechanical speed detection, and so on—have changed policing forever. If the recent past is indicative of the future, today's mind-boggling technology will become obsolete tomorrow. With our entry into the 21st century, new police administrators must acquire the skills required to keep up with and manage rapidly escalating technological change.

**Sociocultural Factors**

Profound social and cultural changes are taking place in American society as it moves toward a rendezvous with its future. These changes are reflected in our changing values concerning life, human existence, social equity, productive work, and the government's role in dealing with the revolution in rising expectations. As the population has expanded, it has become more diverse. It is aging, becoming more ethnically diverse, and becoming much more litigious in pursuit of social justice. Police departments are beginning to mirror the society at large. Based on changing demographics and Equal Employment Opportunity/Affirmative Action programs, more women and minorities have joined police forces. Some urban police departments are recruiting homosexuals. More and more of these nontraditional employees are moving into supervisory positions. More women have been elevated to executive positions. Organizations are now aiming less for diversity and more for inclusion—a shift in emphasis from employees' differences to their similarities.[12]

**Organizational Factors**

Administrative pressures come from intentional managerially induced chains of goals, practices, procedures, policies, deadlines, and reward systems. Newly appointed police chief executives are likely to be enthusiastic, energetic, and proactive. They are often eager to change things they perceive as creating problems within the organization. They see themselves as change agents.

One of the crucial tasks facing a manager as a change agent is to develop and communicate his or her vision for the organization. This vision should meet several criteria:

1. It should be simple and idealistic, a picture of a desirable future rather than a complex plan with quantitative objectives and detailed action schedules.
2. It should appeal to the values, hopes, and ideals of the members of the organization and its external stakeholders, in order to obtain their support.
3. It should address basic assumptions about what is important to the organization, how it should relate to its environment, and how people (both employees and clients) should be treated.
4. It should present an attainable future grounded in present reality.
5. It should be focused enough to guide decisions and actions, but general enough to allow initiative and creativity.

In sum, the vision statement should convey an image of what is important to the organization, what can be achieved, why it is worthwhile, and how it can be done.[13]

Typically, leaders face the difficult task of changing the culture of their organizations. Organizational culture is made up of the characteristic values, traditions, and behaviors an organization's employees share. A value is a basic belief about what is right or wrong, or what one should or shouldn't do.[14] If the culture promotes divisive values and resists change, there are a number of steps that a manager can take to initiate change:

1. *Clarify expectations.* Make it clear what values you expect your subordinates to follow.

2. *Use signs, symbols, stories, rites, and ceremonies.* They can serve as powerful vehicles to illustrate the values that you wish to inspire and establish.

3. *Deliberately teach, coach, and be a role model for the values you want to emphasize.* "Talk the talk *and* walk the walk." What the manager actually does is what sends the real signals and is thus what ultimately does the most to create and sustain the culture of the organization. People will definitely take note of what things the leader attends to and how they are handled. The leader who institutes a policy or procedure and then fails to act on or in accordance with it is demonstrating that it is not really important or necessary.

4. *Communicate priorities by how you allocate rewards.* Leaders communicate their priorities by how they link raises and promotions (and other nonmonetary rewards) to performance. Those employees who "walk the walk" must be rewarded. Failure to recognize contributions and achievements sends a message that they are not important. The rewards should also be differentially allocated to affirm the importance of some performances over others. The other side of this coin is that people should be disciplined for failing to perform.

5. *React vigorously to crises.* A leader's response to a crisis sends a strong message about values and assumptions. Where was Winston Churchill before World War II? Rudolph Guiliani before 9/11? The leader who supports and communicates values when under pressure clearly communicates that those values are important.[15]

Successful change management is thus predicated on clear and open communication between the leader/manager and the subordinates and stakeholders in the organization.[16]

Intrapersonal pressures are generated by changes in values, interests, attitudes, skills, motivation, and job performance. Some of these changes are elicited and reinforced by managers. They are achieved and nurtured through a strong personnel selection procedure, specialized training, and continuous review in the form of performance appraisals. Other changes occur because of changes in the overall composition of the workforce. New and nontraditional employees bring new values, aspirations, and goals with them into the workplace. While hierarchical bureaucracies require individual employees to accept subordinate status within the organization, people today are less willing to be subordinates. Whether managers are ready for it or not, the ethic of participation has spread across America, bottom-up, and is having a radical impact on the way employees expect to be treated by their employers. People whose lives are affected by managerial decisions are demanding a meaningful role in making those decisions. Participatory democracy has seeped into the core of our value system.[17]

Police officers are the avant-garde of the participatory democracy movement because they have more education than the population at large, place far greater emphasis on achieving self-fulfillment, and exhibit an instinctive need to redesign their jobs or reconfigure organizational relationships in terms of their own values, interests, motives, and abilities. The process of implementing change also involves motivating, supporting, and guiding people. Yukl offers the following guidelines for implementing people-oriented change:[18]

1. Create a sense of urgency about the need for change.
2. Prepare people to adjust to change.
3. Help people to deal with the pain of change.
4. Provide opportunities for early successes.
5. Keep people informed about the progress of change.
6. Demonstrate continued commitment to the change.
7. Empower people to implement the change.

These suggestions may ease the pain and uncertainty of dealing with change at a personal level and thus ensure success.

Internal factors are a powerful force for change in complex criminal justice organizations. The importance of these factors cannot be overestimated. Most organization management theorists subscribe to a synergistic point of view. They contend that a change in any one of the areas just discussed leads to changes in the others. The dynamics that produce change are the same as those in the fabled perpetual-motion machine, and an absence of change is abnormal under any and all circumstances. The realization that change is a natural and inevitable aspect of organizational life has led to a resurgence of interest in initiating and managing planned change (see Figure 12–1).

Two researchers doing DNA sequencing using X-ray with DNA sequence recombinant clones.

Hank Morgan, Science Source

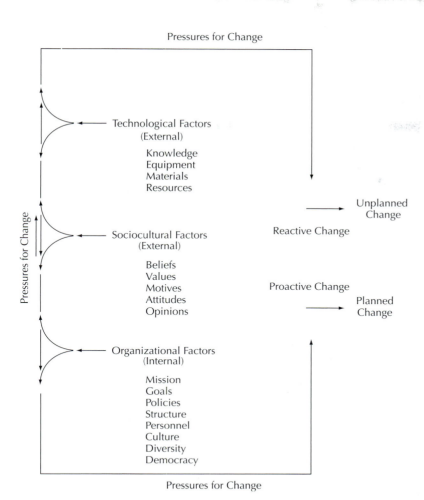

**Figure 12–1**
Forces Affecting the Need for Organizational Change.

## RECOGNIZING THE NEED FOR PLANNED CHANGE

Good police administrators are good because they are multidimensional human beings. They have the ability to process large amounts of abstract information and to learn from their own personal experiences. Competent managers possess better-than-average problem-solving skills. They also exhibit a great deal of flexibility in adjusting their own managerial style to cope with changing conditions. Proactive managers continuously scan the internal as well as the external environment for symptoms calling for some type of organizational change. The remainder of this chapter is designed to create a paradigm that will help police administrators do the following:

1. Recognize the internal indicators that signal the need for some type of planned change.
2. Implement the required change via a planned intervention strategy.
3. Regulate change by monitoring, evaluating, and managing the process.

As stated in Chapter 9, decision-making is a form of problem solving and is, in fact, the essence of management. Police organizations are not static structures. They are organic in the sense that they are entities composed of dynamic interrelationships among people performing those functions necessary to achieve the organization's mission, goals, and objectives. As people or goals change, a need arises for some modification in the organization's structure or functions. In order for police managers to function effectively in their role as problem solvers, decision-makers, and organization change agents, they must perceive problems that exist and have the ability to create solutions to resolve them. Wayne Welsh and Phillip Harris have identified three trends that have increased the need for planned change in police organizations. They are (1) declining resources, (2) increased accountability, and (3) expansion of knowledge and technology.[19]

**Declining Resources**

Declining tax revenues and reductions in funding periodically affect the delivery of public services. Part of the problem resides with increased public concern over high taxes and the resultant reluctance of legislators to increase them even when revenues are insufficient. Partly as a consequence of declining public resources, groups have organized to promote change via advocacy. Inspired by organizations such as Mothers Against Drunk Driving (MADD), groups have arisen in response to such problems as domestic violence, homelessness, and HIV/AIDS.

**Increased Accountability**

Lessened availability of public resources has led to a push for increased accountability. As a result, public managers are now required to demonstrate the cost-effectiveness of their operations. Typically, public managers seek grants to fund new initiatives and operations. Government funding agencies require them to submit plans including evaluations of the anticipated effectiveness of the programs to be funded. Managers must be able to present such evaluations and use their results.

**Expansion of Knowledge and Technology**

Justice information systems have been expanded in recent years. Programs such as CompStat are based on, and make direct use of, information generated by statistical information systems. As discussed previously, CompStat is a clear example of how computers can help generate information to be used to guide program operations. On the downside, the spread of computers has also made possible new forms of crime, especially identity theft.

These trends indicate the need for planned change. Sometimes a crisis, negative feedback about an organization's effectiveness, or routine organizational analysis makes it clear that immediate intervention is required. Emphasis in such interventions is placed on structural change that can be implemented within a relatively short period. At other times, change is the result of a long-range plan of organizational development designed to strengthen the organization by altering certain aspects of its internal environment. The organizational development (OD) approach is discussed in Chapter 14.

## TARGETING CHANGE

Managers can, at least in theory, change just about any aspect of their organizations they wish to change. Since change is such a broad concept, however, it is useful to identify those areas in which planned change has been most common.

Organizations are often compelled by major changes in their external environments to change their goals and the strategies used to reach them. Many police departments, for example, are moving away from the law enforcement model and are placing more emphasis on crime prevention through community-oriented policing.

**Goals and Strategies**

The organizational effect of technological change can be minor or major, depending on the applicability of the innovation. DNA fingerprinting has the potential to revolutionize modern law enforcement when it comes to identifying, apprehending, and successfully prosecuting criminals.

**Technology**

Jobs can be redesigned and enriched in order to offer more variety, autonomy, identity, significance, feedback, and self-fulfillment. The police agent concept focuses on the development and deployment of generalists instead of specialists.

**Job Design**

Structure may be modified in an effort to enhance efficiency, effectiveness, and productivity. Many police departments are revising their policies, procedures, rules, and regulations to broaden spans of control and decentralize decision-making.

**Structure**

The membership of an organization can be changed in terms of its (1) composition (through hiring and firing) and (2) skills and attitudes (through training). Professional police departments, like almost all other successful organizations, have developed sophisticated personnel systems and emphasize the importance of training.[20] Nearly every state has enacted comprehensive legislation establishing minimum qualifications for police personnel and mandating extensive job-related training. The choice of what to change and how to change it is up to management and depends, in large measure, on management's analysis of what internal and external factors are signaling that change is needed.

**People**

Because of their paramilitary nature, police departments have usually imposed change unilaterally (and in all probability will continue to do so). Top police administrators, because they are accountable for efficient and effective operation of their departments, still insist on playing a key role in defining, determining the need for, and directing planned change. Even so, it is now clear that more and more police administrators are beginning to recognize the value and appropriateness of the shared-power approach. Police officers are certainly adaptable to change, and they accept it readily when they become actively involved in the decision-making process.[21]

**The Winds of Change**

## THE PROCESS OF PLANNED CHANGE

Change involves a sequence of psychological adjustments, behavioral alterations, or organizational transformations that occur over time. Most views concerning planned change involving individuals in organizations can be traced back to the work of Kurt Lewin[22] and Edgar H. Schein.[23] They both see all planned change as the result of a very basic three-stage process: (1) unfreezing the status quo, (2) moving to a new state, and (3) refreezing the new state in order to make it permanent (see Figure 12–2).

"J.C." Holleran is administrative captain in a large municipal police department. The department is heading into a budget deficit and must reduce costs or cut services. Capt. Holleran has been ordered by the deputy chief of police to find ways to reduce the amount currently being spent on personnel. They have tentatively agreed to seek a 10 to 15 percent across-the-board reduction in personnel costs.

Adopting the shared-power perspective inherent in participatory management, Capt. Holleran formed a deficit-reduction task force to analyze the available data, determine the cause or causes of the problem, and recommend appropriate solutions. The task force consisted of managers and rank-and-file police officers appointed by the collective-bargaining agent (the union). The task force was authorized to access all of the department's financial data. After excessive deliberations, the task force formulated a cost-containment plan in lieu of recommending cuts in service.

The task force's cost-containment plan called for a temporary freeze on all hiring, restrictions on overtime, a minimal reduction in court-time reimbursement, and an expansion of the telephonic complaint reception/screening program. Once the specifics of the plan were reduced to writing, Capt. Holleran and Deputy Chief Ray Runion met with union leaders as well as the chief in order to elicit support for the proposal.

During the briefing, Chief Bear asked the following series of questions:

1. Who is most likely to be affected by the proposed changes?
2. How will employees, the department, and the public be affected by the proposed changes?
3. What kind of resistance can be expected if the proposed changes are put into effect?
4. What strategies can be used to minimize resistance to the proposed changes?
5. What are the odds of achieving the projected savings in personnel costs?

He asked Capt. Holleran to prepare a position paper outlining answers to these questions.

*Assume that you are Capt. Holleran. Prepare a position paper for submission to Chief Bear. Address each of his concerns to the best of your ability. Use the information presented in this chapter as the basis for your narrative.*

---

The process begins with diagnosis. The accurate diagnosis of organizational problems serves two crucial functions. First of all, it contributes to unfreezing by showing everyone concerned that the problem does, in fact, exist. Secondly, once the unfreezing takes place, further diagnosis helps clarify the problem and suggests what type of change is required. It is one thing to feel that police officer morale has fallen dramatically but quite another to be sure that this is the case and to develop an effective intervention strategy to resolve the problem. Accurate diagnosis ensures that managers have the opportunity to deal with root causes rather than mere symptoms.

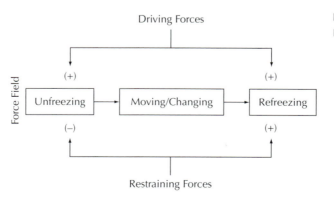

**Figure 12–2**
Planned-Change Process.

Diagnosis takes various forms and can be performed by a variety of individuals. If the problems requiring change are routine, they are best diagnosed by those in the existing chain of command. If the problems are nonroutine or complex, police administrators may be well advised to seek specialized diagnostic help from a change agent. Change agents, whether they are on staff or come from outside the organization, bring an independent, objective perspective to the diagnosis while working with those who are to undergo change. Diagnosis involves analyzing the organization, recognizing performance deficits, and identifying problems. Diagnosticians acquire their information from a variety of sources: (1) observations, (2) interviews, (3) questionnaires, and (4) record reviews. Careful diagnosis is critically important to the success or failure of any planned-change effort. If the diagnosis is done properly, it clarifies the problem, indicates what needs to be changed (in terms of technology, structure, or people), and suggests the appropriate strategy for implementing the change with a minimum of resistance. There are three stages to diagnosis:

1. Problem identification.
2. Isolation of primary causes of the problem.
3. Development of an appropriate and effective solution to the problem.

These three stages can be made more specific as follows:

a. Researching each problem.
b. Documenting the nature of the current police response.
c. Assessing its adequacy and the adequacy of existing authority and resources.
d. Engaging in a broad exploration of alternatives to present responses.
e. Weighing the merits of these alternatives and choosing from among them.[24]

Problem-oriented policing (POP) is a clear example of how to conduct a diagnosis. POP is predicated on the belief that police organizations must develop systematic processes for examining and addressing problems. The POP approach to diagnosing and correcting problems uses a four-stage process called SARA (Scanning, Analysis, Response, Assessment):

1. *Scanning.* Identifying the problem.
2. *Analysis.* Learning the problem's causes, scope, and effects.
3. *Response.* Acting to alleviate the problem and developing an appropriate and effective solution to the problem.
4. *Assessment.* Determining the effectiveness of the response.[25]

Research on police initiatives that won the annual Goldstein award for problem-oriented policing has revealed that the SARA model is having an impact on organizations.[26]

**Unfreezing**

Unfreezing is the process of getting an organization ready for change—recognizing the need for change and overcoming resistance to it. Unfreezing occurs when there is dissatisfaction with the status quo and someone feels the need to alter it. Unfreezing generally involves realizing that an existing technology, job design, or structure is ineffective or that the attitudes or skills of employees are no longer appropriate. Support for current values and behavior is withdrawn, and old ways are seen as no longer desirable or acceptable. Unfreezing is often precipitated by a crisis of some kind, but it may also be produced as the result of a routine organizational analysis. Good managers utilize organizational analysis to scan the internal and external environments for potential problems and initiate planned change before a crisis occurs.[27]

**Moving**  Moving occurs when driving forces overcome restraining forces and a change plan is implemented. The change plan is developed by the change agent to introduce different attitudes and behaviors into the vacuum created during the unfreezing of the status quo. These change efforts range from minor to major. Significant change takes place only when members of the workforce identify with and accept new ideas, approaches, and relationships. The mere introduction of change does not ensure permanent elimination of the prechange condition.[28]

**Refreezing**  Change must be internalized. Internalization is the social/psychological process of trying, adopting, and becoming committed to new attitudes or behaviors. Without some type of positive reinforcement, newly acquired attitudes and behaviors cannot become a permanent part of an individual's normal repertoire. Refreezng is the process of institutionalization—making the change an organizational habit. It stabilizes the change by balancing both driving and restraining forces.[29]

The mechanics of planned change are the same for organizations as for people, because changing people is the critical variable in changing the structure or function of any complex criminal justice organization. Police management training is a very good example of the planned-change process. Trainers (on behalf of the police chief executive) facilitate the unfreezing process by inducing a certain amount of stress in trainees, to make them recognize a need for change. Trainees are then exposed to new ideas, values, and skills. Moving begins when the trainees give credence to these ideas, values, and skills and translate them into new forms of behavior. Once new ideas, values, skills, and behaviors elicit appropriate reinforcements (internal or external rewards and punishments), the refreezing process takes over. Trainees accept, identify with, and internalize the change, incorporating it into their personality structure. It also becomes a recurrent, predictable, and intrinsically rewarding aspect of their job behavior.

While there is great value in being aware of unfreezing-moving-refreezing theory and understanding the dynamics involved in it, good administrators know that using this knowledge effectively requires a tremendous amount of skill. It is not easily accomplished. Yet the manager/change agent concept is applicable to small and medium-sized departments as well as to large urban law enforcement agencies.

## DYNAMICS OF PLANNED ORGANIZATIONAL CHANGE

Based on a study of successful planned change in a number of complex organizations, Larry E. Greiner developed a comprehensive model to explain the dynamics involved in the process.[30] Greiner's model consists of six phases, or steps.

Phase 1 is pressure on, and arousal of, upper-level management to take action. **Phase 1**
Top management perceives a need or pressure to change something. This
pressure is ordinarily caused by one or more significant problems, such as corruption, labor unrest, a sharp decline in performance, or deteriorating community relations. Such crises create a sense of urgency—a need to correct a
wrong and to view the problem as a priority.[31]

Phase 2 is intervention by a respected person (acting as a change agent) and focus **Phase 2**
on the internal problem. In some cases, a new person enters as a change agent.
This person leads a reexamination of past practices and current problems.[32] Outside consultants are often brought in to define the problem and help members of
the organization focus on it. In other situations, internal staff members who are
trusted and considered to be experts may be assigned responsibility for attacking
a particular problem. Such a "guiding coalition" of influential people can mobilize commitment. The change agent must be careful to "choose the right lieutenants." These actions will mobilize political support and ensure success.[33]

Phase 3 is diagnosis of the data and identification of the problem. Information **Phase 3**
is gathered from a variety of sources. The change agent and others analyze the
information in light of their responsibility for initiating and managing planned
change in the organization. The real problem is defined in concrete terms.

Phase 4 is development of a number of creative alternatives and an organiza- **Phase 4**
tional commitment to action. Successful change agents stimulate thought and
avoid using the same old methods. Participatory problem solving is encouraged. Subordinates who are allowed to participate in making decisions that
affect them will probably be much more committed to the course of action that
is finally selected. The change agent must have the active assistance of the
employees to implement the change. But subordinates may not have the tools,
authority, or freedom to implement the change. They must be empowered—
must believe in the change and must believe that they can make it happen.[34]

Phase 5 is experimentation with various alternatives and analysis of results. **Phase 5**
Before the creative solutions developed during the previous phase are implemented organization-wide, they are pilot tested on a limited scale and evaluated in terms of their effectiveness. The structure of large police departments
lends itself to this type of exploration.

Phase 6 is reinforcement from results and acceptance of the planned change. If **Phase 6**
the course of action has been tested and found to be valid, it is likely to be
more willingly accepted by those who will be affected. As an organization
improves, the improvement itself functions as a reinforcement and fosters a
continuing commitment to planned change.

This whole process is outlined in Figure 12–3. Greiner's model provides
police administrators with a convenient list approach to planned change.

Too many managers are inept when it comes to dealing with planned
change. They venerate the status quo and actively resist change. Because of
personal biases, inexperience, and lack of managerial skill, they fall back on
comfortable courses of action fitted to the past. Preexisting solutions seek
problems irrespective of the real problem. This type of tunnel vision creates
and exacerbates organizational problems. Poor police administrators are part
of the problem instead of being part of the solution.

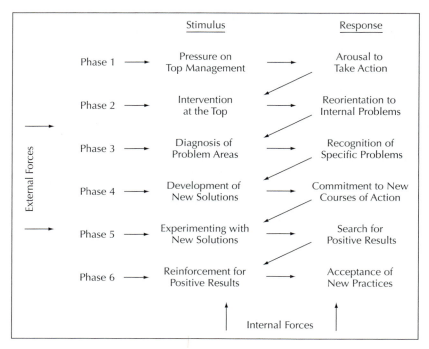

**Figure 12-3**

Dynamics of Planned Change.

Adapted from Larry E. Greiner, "Patterns of Organizational Change," *Harvard Business Review*, No. 5 (1967).

## RESISTANCE TO CHANGE

Resistance to change is ingrained in organizations and the individuals who make them up. Police officers resist change when they fear that its costs outweigh its benefits to them. This resistance takes many forms and ranges from simply ignoring something to open rebellion. There are two sources of resistance to change: individual and organizational.

**Individual Resistance**

Managers should not simply assume that individual resistance to change is the result of stupidity, sloth, arrogance, or ignorance. Rainey asserts that people may have well-justified reasons to resist: "Some ideas are bad ideas. They deserve to be resisted."[35] In addition, some government officials or leaders may become too personally invested in the new programs or initiatives to rationally judge their potential for success. Whatever the source, individual resistance must be overcome if change is to be implemented.

**Habit**

Workers are often captured by *habit*—they do the same things over and over again because these ways are familiar and comfortable.[36] In a complex world, habit reduces the need to make more decisions.[37] People have "sunk cost"— past investments of time, energy, and experience—in their job routines. If there is no obvious need for a change in operations, change will be resisted— especially if no clear evidence is given that there are serious problems in the current mode of operations.

People feel threatened by change. If they have a high need for safety, they will resist it. Change can be personally inconvenient. This is especially true when its nature and the reasons for it are not adequately explained.

**Security**

Change typically introduces ambiguity and uncertainty. Workers often expect the worst. They wonder how the change will affect them in the future and what further changes may result. Such fears are not unfounded. Workers will feel threatened by the proposed change if they think it will render their expertise obsolete. Such fears may apply to certain entire groups or divisions within the organization. This fear extends to the belief that the proposed change is not feasible and is unlikely to succeed. This is especially true in organizations where the failure of previous reform efforts has bred cynicism.[38]

**Fear of the Unknown**

Change often threatens the balance of power in an organization. Changes that are perceived as threats to the autonomy, authority, power, or status of a group or subunit will encounter resistance, regardless of their merit. If people who are currently regarded highly think their status is threatened by the proposed change, they will oppose it. People may also resent interference from others or be reluctant to take orders from others.[39]

**Loss of Status and Power**

Change that is inconsistent with strong values and ideals will be opposed. For this reason, changes that threaten the organizational culture are difficult to implement, even if they are needed.

Clearly, these are all threats to individual self-interest. If proposed changes do not benefit individuals directly, they are likely to be strongly opposed. They threaten changes in skills, power, relationships with others, social status, and self-esteem.

**Threat to Values and Ideals**

As goals, relationships, and people change, the need for modification of organizational structure and function increases. The organization itself often resists change. Dorothy Guyot once likened attempts at police organizational reform as "bending granite."[40]

**Organizational Resistance**

Like individuals, organizations have inertia—they tend to continue in the same direction at the same rate. Denhardt and colleagues assert that public agencies are particularly "risk averse"—they place a high value on not "rocking the boat."[41] The source of inertia may be the *structure*. Some organizations have built-in mechanisms to ensure stability. The hiring process, for example, defines the selection criteria for new members through job descriptions, rules, and operational procedures; applicants are chosen for fit, and the organizational culture may shape their job behavior in certain ways. History and tradition can also serve as impediments to change.[42] *Groups* can also generate inertia through the enforcement of group norms on individuals who may wish to support change. Union opposition to changes is a good example of this form of inertia.[43]

**Inertia**

Organizational units are dependent on one another. Changes can thus affect more than one unit. If proposed changes are aimed at a lower level in the organization, the larger structure may nullify or blunt those changes.

**Limited Focus of Change**

| **Threat to Expertise** | Specialized units may be threatened by organizational change. For example, decentralization (a key feature of community policing) allows beat officers to become generalists and assume some investigatory functions. This could be seen as undermining the need for specialized units (such as detectives). |
|---|---|

| **Threat to Established Power Relationships and Resource Allocations** | If a proposed change threatens the decision-making authority of the organization, resistance will result. Power is tied to resources, so any change in budget allocations or other resources will cause resistance.[44]<br><br>Beer asserts that it is fears like those described above that cause resistance to change. In order to overcome the fears, the organization must make strong efforts to qualify employees in newly required skills. This will require training, counseling, and coaching from human resource professionals as well as supervisors. Input to the planning process will also help to alleviate employee fears and make change less of a threat.[45] |
|---|---|

## CASE STUDY    Chief Charles S. Ahern

Charles Ahern, a veteran law enforcement officer, has been chief of the Johnson County Police Department (JCPD) for a little over three years. This county is a border state and part of a major metropolitan area. With an authorized strength of 272 sworn officers and 37 civilians, it is one of the largest law enforcement agencies in a six-county megalopolis.

The JCPD has long been considered to be one of the most professional police organizations in the state. It has an excellent pay scale and attracts top-notch personnel. As a result, the department has been able to avoid most of the problems and almost all of the criticism leveled at other large police departments in the area. In fact, Chief Ahern was recently elected to serve as the third vice president of the nation's most prestigious professional law enforcement association.

Since personnel complaints were few and far between and the JCPD had never experienced a bona fide case of corruption, management adopted a fairly casual attitude concerning internal discipline. Although it violated generally accepted standards, supervisors in the normal chain of command were assigned to investigate personnel complaints lodged against their own subordinates.

When a high-ranking police official was indicted on a RICO (racketeer-influenced corrupt organization) charge related to drug trafficking, it became obvious that there was a glitch in the system. It was clear there was no objective mechanism to investigate and resolve allegations of corruption. Because of the magnitude of the case and the heat it gener-

ated, Chief Ahern realized that corrective action (in the form of a planned change) was required.

Chief Ahern contacted the executive director of the International Association of Chiefs of Police (IACP) and arranged for its consultants to come in. Their job was to define the problem and help members of the department focus their attention on it. After reviewing the available data, analyzing the organization, and comparing the JCPD with departments of similar size, the consultants recommended creation of an internal affairs unit.

A representative task force was formed and assigned to work with the IACP consultants in an effort to develop structural models congruent with the department's culture. After exploring several different configurations, the task force constructed a model similar in both its structure and its function to the one recommended by the National Advisory Commission on Criminal Justice Standards and Goals. The commander of the internal affairs unit was to report directly to the chief, and unit personnel would remain outside of the normal chain of command. According to the model, the internal affairs unit would investigate all personnel complaints (including corruption) and make recommendations concerning disciplinary action to the chief police executive.

The internal affairs unit became an operational component of the JCPD per Executive Order 6734. It was later upgraded to division status.

*Identify the six phases in the dynamics of a successful organizational change. Are they all accounted for in the case study? If not, which are missing?*

Managing change through shared responsibilities is a comprehensive approach that combines the best aspects of both top-down and bottom-up processes. Top management provides leadership, support, and coordination; lower-level managers and non-management personnel, working in diagnostic problem-solving groups, make and implement operational change decisions.

A climate for planned change is created when recognition of the need for change is coupled with a heightened sense of dissatisfaction and a genuine desire to alter the status quo. Since even the slightest change can be frightening, painful, or disruptive to the employees involved, changes must be initiated carefully and managed with sensitivity. Many well-meaning and necessary changes in criminal justice organizations fail to get off the ground, or to achieve what they are expected to achieve, simply because police administrators are unable to create a win-win atmosphere that is conducive to substantive change.

To become successful change agents, managers must learn to make their subordinates psychologically willing to make an effort to change. This is not nearly as easy as it might appear. One of the key elements of leadership is to establish guidelines for how to implement change. Yukl provides a list of guidelines that may be helpful (see Table 12–1).

It is the police administrator's job to create a positive atmosphere for change by demonstrating that the rational planning of change is superior to seat-of-the-pants decision-making—and far less risky. Police officers will be more inclined to take in stride the ambiguity, confusion, and fear associated with change if they are allowed to participate in the process and to perceive change as an opportunity rather than a threat. Whisenand recommends that managers share with employees both the decision-making responsibility that leads to change and the credit for the eventual success in achieving change.[46]

Table 12–1  **Guidelines for Implementing Change**

*Guidelines for Political or Organizational Actions*

1. Determine who can oppose or facilitate change.
2. Build a broad coalition to support the change.
3. Fill key positions with competent change agents.
4. Use task forces to guide implementation.
5. Make dramatic symbolic changes that affect the work.
6. If necessary, implement change initially on a small scale.
7. Change relevant aspects of the organizational structure.
8. Monitor the progress of change.

*Guidelines for People-Oriented Actions*

1. Create a sense of urgency about the need for change.
2. Prepare people to adjust to change.
3. Help people deal with the pain of change.
4. Provide opportunities for early successes.
5. Keep people informed about the progress of change.
6. Demonstrate continued commitment for change.
7. Empower people to implement the change.

*Source:* Gary Yukl, *Leadership in Organizations,* 5th ed. (Upper Saddle River, NJ: Prentice Hall, 2002), p. 289. Adapted by permission of Pearson Education, Inc., Upper Saddle River, NJ 07458.

The success or failure of a planned change effort can usually be traced back to the attitudes of those to be affected by the change. Police officers must be convinced they will benefit from any proposed change or at least not be adversely affected by it. A history of fair, honest, and competent management lays a foundation for trust and the acceptance of change. The police manager must also present a sense of what the change involves and what employees should do—he or she should provide direction and be patient.[47]

## EVALUATION

Evaluation must not be the "missing link" in planned-change efforts. Ideally, plans for the evaluation of the change effort should be built into the planning process from the beginning. Typically, the following evaluation tasks must be conducted to provide information that will guide the entire planned-change effort:[48]

1. Verify that resources are devoted to meeting previously unmet needs.
2. Verify that planned programs do provide services.
3. Examine (monitor) the results.
4. Determine which services provide the best results.
5. Select the programs that offer the most-needed types of services.
6. Provide information needed to maintain and improve quality.
7. Watch for unplanned side effects.

The evaluation must be designed to provide feedback from program activities. This feedback forms part of an information loop to improve service delivery and performance. The feedback portion of the loop begins with the monitoring function, which determines whether the service has been delivered as designed. It will also determine whether the program has been effective and whether it should be continued, expanded, or terminated.

## SUMMARY

Change is a natural and inevitable aspect of organizational life. Police administrators are expected to cope with spontaneous change as well as to initiate, implement, manage, and evaluate planned change in their departments. Proactive managers are future oriented. They are inclined to change things and chart new courses of action. In order to be effective, proactive managers anticipate change and are prepared to adapt to it. In order to be successful as change agents, managers must understand the internal (organizational) as well as external (environmental) factors pushing for change. Good administrators pay special attention to technological, sociocultural, and organizational factors.

Managers must know how to recognize the need for change. Faulty decision-making, functional failure, poor communication, and lack of innovation should be considered red flags. It is up to management to determine who or what to target for change. They also choose how to effect the change. The shared-power approach to organizational problem solving is gaining in popularity.

No matter which approach is used, the basic change process is the same. Successful change requires unfreezing the target organization, moving it to a new state, and refreezing the change to make it permanent. The dynamics of planned change involve pressure on, and arousal of, top management to take action; intervention by a respected person; diagnosis of the data and identification of the real problem; development of creative alternatives; experiments with the alternatives; and reinforcement of the results.

In order to be effective change agents, police administrators must work on their diagnostic skills. Identifying the right problem is half the battle. Good managers reduce resistance to change by incorporating subordinates into the problem-solving process whenever it is feasible. The unilateral imposition of planned change is being abandoned by some police departments in favor of a combined top-down/bottom-up approach. Participatory management has become one of the most influential concepts in contemporary management theory.

Police administrators have a responsibility to assess the impact of a planned change in terms of member behavior and organizational outcomes. If changes in behavior or outcomes are beneficial, they should be institutionalized through positive reinforcement techniques. Once refreezing has taken place, all changes must be passed on to others through the organization's socialization process. Modern police managers need to acquire an understanding of, and appreciation for, their role in the change process. One thing is certain: police administrators will be spending more of their time initiating, implementing, and managing planned change during the next decade.

## KEY TERMS

administrative pressures
change agent
diagnosis
external forces
internal forces
interpersonal pressures
movement
planned change

proactive management
reactive change
reactive management
refreezing
SARA model
technological change
unfreezing

## DISCUSSION TOPICS AND QUESTIONS

1. Define *change*. Explore the difference between spontaneous change and planned change. Which occurs more often?

2. What is a change agent? Why are proactive managers considered to be change agents? Explain your reasoning.

3. List and discuss the forces or pressures that precipitate the need for planned change in complex criminal justice organizations. Identify those that warrant special consideration.

4. When does a positive climate for planned change exist? What does willingness have to do with it? How would you hedge your bet to ensure that the planned change takes root and is institutionalized?

5. Identify the target areas in which planned change has been the most common. Describe each of these areas. Who is ultimately responsible for determining what is to be changed and how it is to be changed?

6. Describe the unfreezing, moving, and refreezing process as it relates to organizational change as well as personal behavior. Illustrate this process through the use of examples.

7. What are the six phases normally associated with any successful organizational change? Elaborate on each one, and show their dynamic relationship to one another.

8. Why do so many people resist substantive change in the workplace? If resistance is not all bad, what purpose does it serve?

9. What are the elements of the SARA model? How can it help guide the planned-change process?

10. Analyze a change that has occurred in your organization. Consider the following questions:
    a. How did the change come about?
    b. How did the change agent trigger the change? How was it brought forward?

What was done and said? Was it implemented in a participatory or an authoritarian fashion?

c. How did others in the organization react to the change? What was the nature of the resistance? How was it overcome?

d. What was your initial reaction to the change? Did you support it initially, or were you won over?

e. How is the change working out? Looking back, what would you have done differently if you were the change agent?

## FOR FURTHER READING

Dorothy Guyot, "Bending Granite: Attempts to Change the Rank Structure of American Police Departments," *Journal of Police Science and Administration,* Vol. 7 (1979), pp. 253–284.

A classic article on the difficulties of establishing reform and change in police agencies.

Wayne N. Welsh and Phillip W. Harris, *Criminal Justice Policy and Planning* (Cincinnati: Anderson, 1999).

This entire text is based on the planned-change model. It provides key examples of how criminal justice planning can benefit the entire system.

## NOTES

1. Douglas C. Eadie, "Leading and Managing Strategic Change," in James L. Perry ed. *Handbook of Public Administration* (San Francisco: Jossey-Bass, 1996), p. 499.

2. Alvin Toffler, *Future Shock* (New York: Bantom Books, 1972).

3. Robert B. Denhardt, Janet V. Denhardt, and Maria P. Aristigueta, *Managing Human Behavior in Public and Nonprofit Organizations* (Thousand Oaks, CA: Sage, 2002), p. 379.

4. Ramon J. Aldag and Loren W. Kuzuhara, *Organizational Behavior and Management* (Cincinnati: South-Western, 2002), p. 479.

5. Wayne N. Welsh and Phillip W. Harris, *Criminal Justice Policy and Planning* (Cincinnati: Anderson, 1999), p. 5.

6. Gary Dessler, *Management* (Upper Saddle River, NJ: Prentice Hall, 2004), pp. 195–196.

7. Daniel Katz and Robert L. Kahn, *The Social Psychology of Organizations* (New York: Wiley, 1978).

8. Dessler, *Management,* pp. 195–196 and Sheldon Greenberg and Edward A. Flynn, "Leadership and Managing Change," in William A. Geller and Darrel W. Stephens, eds. *Local Government Police Management* (Washington, DC: International City/County Management Association, 2004), p. 67.

9. Robert Vecchio, *Organizational Behavior: Core Concepts* (Mason, OH: South-Western, 2003), p. 356.

10. David A. Tansik and James F. Elliott, *Managing Police Organizations* (Belmont, CA: Wadsworth, 1981), p. 224.

11. Aldag and Kuzuhara, *Organizational Behavior and Management,* p. 482.

12. Stroh, Northcraft, and Neale, *Organizational Behavior,* p. 456.

13. Yukl. *Leadership,* pp. 283–284.

14. Dessler, *Management,* p. 38.

15. Ibid., pp. 38–40; 201 and Yukl, *Leadership,* pp. 279–280.

16. Alan W. Steiss, *Strategic Management for Public and Nonprofit Organizations* (New York: Marcel Dekker, 2003), pp. 278–279.

17. Yukl, *Leadership,* pp. 86–88.

18. Ibid., p. 292.

19. Welsh and Harris, *Criminal Justice Policy and Planning,* pp. 8–11.

20. Fred Luthans, *Organizational Behavior* (New York: McGraw-Hill, 2002), p. 314.

21. Harry W. More, W. Fred Wegener, and Larry S. Miller, *Effective Police Supervision* (Cincinnati: Anderson, 2003), pp. 326–327.

22. Kurt Lewin, *Field Theory in Social Science* (New York: Harper & Row, 1951).

23. Edgar H. Schein, *Organizational Psychology* (Englewood Cliffs, NJ: Prentice Hall, 1980).

24. Herman Goldstein, *Problem Oriented Policing* (New York: McGraw-Hill, 1990).

25. John C. Eck and William Spelman, *Problem Solving: Problem-Oriented Policing in Newport News* (Washington, DC: Police Executive Research Forum, 1987).

26. Jeff Rojek, "A Decade of Excellence in Problem-Oriented Policing: Characteristics of the Goldstein Award Winners," *Police Quarterly,* Vol. 6 (2003), pp. 492–515.

27. Stroh, Northcraft, and Neale, *Organizational Behavior,* pp. 435–436 and Vecchio, *Organizational Behavior,* p. 363.

28. Ibid., pp. 436–437.

29. Ibid., p. 437.

30. Larry E. Greiner, "Patterns of Organizational Change," *Harvard Business Review,* Vol. 45 (1967), pp. 119–130.

31. Dessler, *Management,* p. 206 and Michael L. Vasu, Debra W. Stewart, and G. David Garson, *Organizational Behavior and Management* (New York: Marcel Dekker, 1998), p. 277.

32. Hal G. Rainey, *Understanding and Managing Public Organizations* (San Francisco: Jossey-Bass, 1997), p. 337.

33. Dessler, *Management,* p. 207.

34. Ibid., p. 208.

35. Rainey, *Managing Public Organizations,* pp. 327–328.

36. Linda Stroh, Gregory B. Northcraft, and Margaret A. Neale, *Organizational Behavior: A Management Challenge* (Mahwah, NJ: Lawrence Erlbaum and Associates), p. 425.

37. Stephen P. Robbins, *Essentials of Organizational Behavior* (Upper Saddle River, NJ: Prentice Hall, 2000), pp. 257–258.

38. Yukl, *Leadership,* p. 274 and Aldag and Kuzuhara, *Organizational Behavior and Management,* p. 482.

39. Yukl, *Leadership,* pp. 275–276.

40. Dorothy Guyot, "Bending Granite: Attempts to Change the Rank Structure of American Police Departments," *Journal of Police Science and Administration,* Vol. 7 (1979), pp. 253–284.

41. Denhardt, Denhardt, and Aristigueta, *Managing Human Behavior,* p. 379.

42. Greenberg and Flynn, "Leadership and Change," p. 73.

43. Robbins, *Organizational Behavior,* p. 259.

44. Ibid., p. 275.

45. Michael Beer, "Leading Change," *Harvard Business School,* 9–488–037 (1991), pp. 5–6.

46. Paul M. Whisenand, *Supervising Police Personnel: The Fifteen Responsibilities* (Upper Saddle River, NJ: Prentice Hall, 2004), p. 168.

47. Emil J. Posevac and Raymond G. Carey, *Program Evaluation: Methods and Case Studies* (Upper Saddle River, NJ: Prentice Hall, 2003), pp. 3–6.

48. Whisenand, *Supervising Police Personnel,* pp. 126–127.

# ─13─────────────

# CONFLICT

## Nature, Causes, and Management

───────────────────────

1. Define and discuss the nature of human conflict in complex criminal justice organizations.
2. Describe the dynamics of the collaboration-aggression continuum.
3. Contrast intergroup conflict with interpersonal conflict in organizational settings.
4. List and discuss the recognizable steps involved in the conflict-development cycle.
5. Distinguish the historical phases of management thinking as it relates to organizational conflict.
6. Identify and discuss the most common causes of conflict in complex organizations.

7. Differentiate between functional conflict and dysfunctional conflict.
8. Describe the conflict-management strategies and techniques that are applicable to police work.
9. Describe the management styles that evolved in response to the need for conflict resolution.
10. Define *contingency management* and *economic humanism* as they relate to conflict management.
11. Describe the structure and function of employee assistance programs (EAPs).

Human behavior is diverse and varies tremendously in terms of its interpersonal dimensions. Modes of interpersonal behavior can be pictured as lying along a continuum from collaboration at one end to overt aggression at the other (see Figure 13–1). *Collaboration* exists when, in an effort to help members of a group accomplish their collective goals, mutual assistance is emphasized and personal antagonisms are kept to a minimum. *Cooperation* is a basic form of interaction in which two or more individuals coordinate their behavior in order to achieve a particular objective. *Competition* emerges when individuals attempt to maximize their own advantage while disadvantaging others. Mutual assistance and personal antagonism are both low in healthy competitive situations. *Conflict* arises in those situations where someone or something has thwarted, or is about to thwart, someone else's goals. *Aggression* arises as the result of conflict. It is intentional or unintentional behavior designed to injure the people or things perceived to be the source of the conflict.[1] This chapter examines the nature, causes, and management of conflict in complex criminal justice organizations.

Anson Weller is 54 years old. He is a high school graduate who worked his way up through the ranks at the Harmerville Police Department. Weller has been the chief of police since 1975.

Harmerville is a relatively small, economically depressed town in what is known as the "rust bucket" area of the northeastern United States. The department's authorized strength is 15 FTE (full-time-equivalent) police officers. Most of the officers are part-time. The department's only sergeant, Nick Pason, is in charge of the night shift.

Chief Weller is and always has been an autocratic Theory X manager. He runs an incredibly tight ship and has been dubbed "Captain Hook" because of his propensity to fire people. The city council has always acquiesced and rubber-stamped these personnel actions, even though some of them were of questionable legality.

While there has always been an undercurrent of discontent within the department, most officers kept their complaints to themselves for fear of being fired. Some officers have become much more vocal over the last couple of years.

Some newly hired part-time officers openly criticized the chief's methods and—as a group—urged their colleagues to unionize under the State Labor Relations Act. They also discussed the situation with the executive director of the Fraternal Order of Police. The FOP expressed an interest in organizing the workforce in the department. In order to focus public attention on the issue, the FOP leaked the story to a friendly reporter. The banner headline said it all:

POLICE MORALE PLUMMETS, OFFICERS WANT UNION PROTECTION

The chief was livid. He denounced the unionists as radicals who were trying to destroy the police department. After an internal investigation, Chief Weller fired two of the part-time officers for "conduct unbecoming an officer" and "actions detrimental to the welfare of the department." After a rancorous public hearing in which each side impugned the motives of the other, the tame city council upheld the dismissals. Conflict between the chief and his subordinates continued unabated and got progressively worse.

The FOP filed an unfair labor practice charge with the State Labor Relations Board (SLRB). The SLRB ruled that Chief Weller had, in fact, interfered with the lawful activities of his employees. It ordered its staff to determine if there was sufficient interest in holding an election to select a collective-bargaining agent. An election was held, and the employees voted unanimously to affiliate with the FOP. The city and the FOP are now in the process of negotiating the first collective-bargaining agreement (CBA). Chief Weller is not actively involved in the negotiating process.

Chief Weller and his employees are still at odds with each other. There is no end in sight as far as personal animosity goes. The chief has vowed, on a number of occasions, to "bust the union." Union members continue to attack the chief as a petty dictator who should be forced out of office. While much of this vitriolic rhetoric is designed to influence the ongoing negotiations, it is clear that the conflict is far from over.

*What kind of social dynamics were involved in this conflict situation? How would you classify the chief's basic philosophy as it relates to his reaction to the conflict? Identify the different stages in the development of this conflict episode. What do you feel could have been done by the chief to deal with this conflict before it got out of hand?*

# INTERPERSONAL CONFLICT

Conflict within an organization can be described as the breakdown or disruption of normal activities to a point where individuals or groups experience real difficulty in working with one another and nobody is willing to compromise.[2] In a general sense, interpersonal conflict is a condition in which two or more people have a difference of opinion involving values, goals, perceptions, or scarce resources and one or more of them threaten or attempt to gain advantage over the others by exercising power. Conflict can in some circumstances be positive, because it offers individuals a chance to share information and shed new light on a situation. Conflict begins when one party (person or group) perceives that another party has frustrated or is about to frustrate them in an area they consider important.[3]

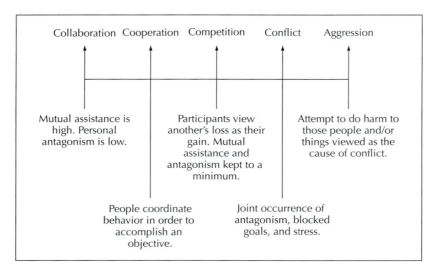

**Figure 13–1**
Collaboration–Aggression Continuum.

Conflict is built into human nature and is exacerbated by intergroup dynamics. It is a pervasive and perhaps inevitable part of human existence.[4] In order to be successful managers, police administrators must learn to understand conflict and develop the skills needed to manage it. This is not an easy task. In fact, learning how to deal effectively with conflict is one of the most challenging aspects of any manager's job.

**Types of Interpersonal Conflict**

Behavioral scientists who specialize in the study of social interaction have identified the following three distinct types of interpersonal conflict: conflict between individuals, conflict between individuals and groups, and conflict between groups.

1. *Conflict between individuals.* Probably the most common type of conflict is conflict between individuals. Some people simply dislike one another— their personalities clash. Two people in conflict tend to disagree with each other concerning role expectations and/or appropriate performance. The intensity of the conflict will depend on issues, personalities of people involved (in terms of intellect, problem-solving skills, mental health, and so forth), internal inhibitions, external constraints, and situational variables.

2. *Conflict between individuals and groups.* Conflicts can also occur between individuals and the groups they interact with. These clashes are normally precipitated by differences in opinion concerning appropriate norms, values, ethical orientations, and behaviors. Individuals who violate group-shared expectations are usually isolated, punished, and labeled as deviant. Conflict over work norms creates special problems. Most work groups establish informal yet binding norms that prescribe certain behaviors and prohibit others. When a person falls short of or exceeds the norms established by the group, social distance is increased. Offenders may be excluded from group-related social activities or cut off from the informal communication process (known as the grapevine). This eliminates a very important source of job satisfaction. If there is a serious conflict between individual behavior and group norms, the group will do everything

within its power to change the individual's "deviant" behavior. Here again, the intensity of the conflict will depend on a wide variety of different factors.

3. *Conflict between groups.* American society can be seen as a collage of social groups, formal and informal, interacting with each other as they pursue their own goals and objectives. Each social group develops an identity reflecting its specialized task, function, structural configuration, location, size, and degree of cohesion. As indicated in Chapter 7, all social groups develop unique personalities based on racial, ethnic, and cultural considerations. Task-oriented work groups generate their own distinct cultures based on their shared beliefs, values, attitudes, interests, and behavioral norms. As a particular group becomes more cohesive, the differences between it and other social groups tend to be accentuated. This often leads to polarization between competing groups. The polarization of competing groups in the same sociocultural milieu (an organization, a society, or a nation) almost always sets the stage for destructive intergroup conflict. The nature, extent, and intensity of the conflict will depend on the specific issue in dispute, relative group strengths, collective rationality, internal control mechanisms, leadership, external constraints, and situational variables.[5]

Police work is an extraordinarily complex goal-oriented human activity and, as such, provides a natural habitat for all three types of interpersonal/intergroup conflict (see Figure 13–2).

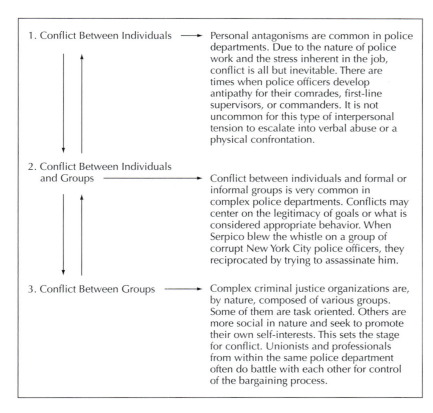

**Figure 13-2**
Types of Interpersonal/Intergroup Conflict.

As we noted, conflict is a disruptive situation between two or more individuals (or groups of people) stemming from substantive disagreements over beliefs, values, attitudes, goals, scarce resources, or normative behavioral expectations. Conflict is ubiquitous. It is also endemic to human nature. From an organizational point of view, conflict is antithetical to development of the collaboration that is needed to achieve collective goals and objectives.

**Conflict-Development Cycle**

It is important that police administrators learn to understand the dynamics of conflict. Conflict does not normally appear suddenly out of the blue. In fact, it passes through a cycle of progressive stages as tension builds. The stages or steps in the conflict-development cycle are as follows:

1. *Latent conflict.* At the latent stage, all of the basic conditions for future conflict exist but have not been recognized as a problem by potential adversaries. The most likely sources of substantive disagreement in an organizational setting are competition for scarce resources, role conflicts, and incompatible expectations.

2. *Perceived conflict.* The cause or causes of the conflict are recognized by one or both of the parties. Some latent conflicts are never perceived as conflicts per se and do not cross the threshold of awareness.

3. *Felt conflict.* At this point, tension starts to build between the participants. Felt conflict differs from perceived conflict in that at least one of the parties begins to experience discomfort, stress, or anxiety.

4. *Manifest conflict.* The struggle begins in earnest, and the behavior of the participants makes the existence of the conflict obvious to others who are not directly involved in the dispute. Manifest conflict takes the form of overt behavior such as apathy, withdrawal, minimum job performance, sabotage, and open aggression.

5. *Conflict resolution.* Attempts to resolve the conflict can range from approaches that simply ignore it to strategies designed to confront it head-on and resolve it in such a way that all parties can achieve their goals.[6]

6. *Conflict aftermath.* The conflict is ended by resolution or suppression. This establishes new conditions that may lead to more effective cooperation or to a new conflict, which could be much worse than the previous one.[7]

From this perspective, conflict is viewed as an unfolding process rather than a discrete event that occurs at one moment in time. The process consists of a series of episodes. Each episode involves an escalation in tension corresponding to the stages of the conflict-development cycle. The resolution of conflict sets the stage—in a dialectical sense—for new life experiences. While this process is fairly simple to understand, it is much more complicated than it might appear, since not all conflict passes through every stage in the cycle. In addition, the participants in the conflict may not be at exactly the same stage. One party might be at the manifest stage (ready to launch attack) while the other is at the latent stage and totally unaware that a confrontation is brewing.[8]

Conflict theorists also use the cyclical approach to illustrate how events in the conflict-development cycle are processed by the participants. In destructive conflict situations, for example, winning becomes the object and is considered far more important than coming up with mutually acceptable solutions to substantive disagreements. The antagonists begin to conceal relevant information or pass on distorted information in an effort to mislead their opponents. Based on psychosocial dynamics, individuals become more committed—at an emotional level—to their original positions. Groups, on the other hand, become more cohesive and may substitute groupthink for rational analysis. Any deviation from the party line results in the imposition of immediate and severe sanctions. Contact with adversaries is discouraged except under controlled circumstances. Contrasting conceptions are formed and projected on opponents through the use of negative stereotypes. These stereotypes fuel the fire of discontent and are used to justify escalation in the level of conflict. Inherently aggressive people, who have the ability to turn others on and the tactical skill needed to exploit conflict, tend to emerge as strategists or group leaders. This usually intensifies hostility and perpetuates the struggle until someone wins.[9] Destructive conflict is almost always a zero-sum equation. "To the victor go the spoils."

## CONFLICT IN FORMAL ORGANIZATIONS

Management theorists often disagree with one another when it comes to defining conflict and assessing its role in organizations. The literature suggests that there have been three relatively distinct phases in the development of thinking about conflict in organizational settings. They are usually referred to as (1) the traditional phase, (2) the human relations phase, and (3) the interactionist phase. Traditionalists viewed conflict as pathological and something to avoid at all costs. Behavioralists perceived conflict as a natural yet resolvable disturbance in the balance or equilibrium of an organization. Modern interactionists contend that a certain amount of conflict is necessary if goal-oriented groups are to perform effectively.

**The Traditionalists**

This early approach to conflict assumed that all interpersonal/intergroup conflict was bad. Traditional theorists believed, for example, that in well-managed organizations there would always be positive cooperation between labor and management. Conflict was viewed as a dysfunctional outcome caused by factors such as poor communication, lack of openness and trust between people, and failure of management personnel to respond to the needs or aspirations of their subordinates. If conflict reared its ugly head, it was management's job—through the use of logic and rational analysis—to determine the cause of the malfunction and to correct it on management's terms. The traditionalists subscribed to a Theory X perspective. Anyone who created conflict within the organization was considered persona non grata. In the past, police officers labeled as disruptive were often fired for the good of the service.

**The Behavioralists**

During the late 1940s, the human relations approach displaced traditionalism as the dominant view of conflict in formal organizations. Behavioralists accepted conflict as an inevitable fact of life whenever people were required to work together. Conflict was seen as a natural yet resolvable disturbance in the balance or equilibrium of an organization. The root causes of conflict were seen as idiosyncrasies in people themselves. Human relations theorists focused their attention on the use of group dynamics (through such mechanisms as encounter groups, T-groups, and guided group interaction) to resolve disruptive interpersonal and intergroup conflict. A modified behavioral approach emerged during the late 1960s. Its proponents maintained that conflict created a paradox in complex organizations. While it often led to serious problems and dysfunctional behavior, it could also be beneficial if it evoked enough anxiety to motivate the parties to resolve their substantive differences through cooperative problem solving and participative management. Emphasis began to shift to the positive aspects of conflict management.

**The Interactionists**     A refinement of the human relations approach is to assimilate conflict when it is beneficial and discourage it only when it becomes harmful. Interactionists actually encourage some forms of conflict on the grounds that harmonious, peaceful, tranquil, cooperative, and collaborative work groups tend to become static, apathetic, and openly resistant to innovation or change. They believe in introducing and maintaining a minimum level of conflict in order to keep the group viable, self-critical, and creative. Conflict can be constructive (or "functional") if it heightens anxiety to the point where the organization is forced to take proactive steps toward a realistic solution to the problem. Dysfunctional conflict, on the other hand, always has a negative influence on group performance and is detrimental to the welfare of all group members. The actual demarcation between functional and dysfunctional conflict is neither clear nor precise; it depends on the situation, the players involved, and the dynamics between the two. However, although some conflict is actually healthy and contributes to overall group performance, most groups and formal organizations try to eliminate it whenever possible.[10]

A police department is not one of Max Weber's ideal organizational types. It is a microcosm of the society at large. Consequently, conflict within departments is the rule rather than the exception. As public officials who are responsible for getting things done through others and managing conflict, police administrators have an affirmative duty to study the causes of conflict and develop strategies designed to control them.

## CAUSES OF ORGANIZATIONAL CONFLICT

Although it is possible to identify a great number of factors that can lead to conflict, much of the conflict in organizations appears to come from one of six sources:

1. Interdependence
2. Differences in power, status, and culture
3. Organizational ambiguity
4. Competition for scarce resources
5. Drive for autonomy
6. Bifurcation of subunit interests

**Interdependence**     Conflict always occurs within a context of mutual interdependence. There is a potential for conflict whenever people or organizational groups are dependent on each other to achieve their own particular goals. Interdependence may be pooled (the output of two relatively independent groups is combined to help the organization achieve its goals), sequential (one group depends on the other for input such as raw materials or clientele, but the dependency is only one-way), or reciprocal (groups exchange inputs as well as outputs). Interdependence sets the stage for conflict in that the participants are required to interact with one another and exercise some power over each other. Large police departments are composed of many specialized work groups that interact to varying degrees in a coordinated effort to accomplish specific goals and objectives.[11]

Intergroup conflict is very likely to erupt when there are significant disparities in power, status, and culture in a particular organization. Because of the complexity of police work, the following factors are important:

**Differences in Power, Status, and Culture**

1.  The real power to influence outcomes for individuals, groups, and the organization as a whole is seldom, if ever, distributed in the manner depicted by the chain of command on the organization chart. There is a very natural tendency for people or groups to acquire disproportionate amounts of power and to use that power to their advantage. Conflict is inevitable whenever there is a struggle for power.
2.  Status, like power, is not shared equally among all persons or groups within a complex organization. In fact, differential status is the rule rather than the exception. Status (the value conferred on someone by significant others) is often related to education, training, assignment, rank, and political influence. Status differences normally do not create interpersonal or intergroup conflict when those with lower status are dependent on those of higher status. This is the way most formal organizations are supposed to work. Group members are socialized to expect and accept this kind of order in work-oriented relationships. Because of the great complexity of modern police work, though, there are times when individuals or groups with technically lower status find themselves in a position to control the action and give orders to persons with higher status. There is, for example, a great potential for status-based conflict in situations where detectives— the so-called prima donnas of the police profession—find themselves under the functional supervision of uniformed patrol personnel. In addition, unbridled competition for status can, in and of itself, degenerate into debilitating conflict in complex criminal justice organizations.
3.  An organization's culture, or way of life (see Chapter 7), consists of shared beliefs, values, motives, norms, and behaviors exhibited by members of a group as they pursue their collective interests, goals, and objectives. Since complex organizations are composed of many work groups, some cultural diversity is normal. When two or more distinct cultures develop within the same organization, the clash in beliefs, values, motives, and behavioral expectations almost always leads to some type of overt conflict. The nature and extent of this conflict will depend on the issue, the emotional responses generated, the resources available, the tactical skills of the combatants, the importance of winning or losing to the various subcultures, and the overall level of reinforcement derived from mindless groupthink. Broderick argues that there is and will continue to be a great deal of conflict between those police officers who subscribe to the due process model of American law enforcement (the idealists) and those for whom crime control is the sole objective of police work (the realists). One group places an emphasis on functioning within constitutional constraints. The other group is utilitarian and operates on the implicit assumption that the end justifies the means.[12]

It is the police administrator's responsibility to manage—not eliminate—the conflict caused by differences in power, status, and culture within complex criminal justice organizations.

## Organizational Ambiguity

Task uncertainty in nonroutine situations, coupled with organizational ambiguity, tends to create a sense of anomie (or normlessness) that exacerbates the potential for serious interpersonal/intergroup conflict. If such things as jurisdictions, goals, behavioral expectations, and performance criteria are not clear and specific, truly spontaneous conflict becomes possible. Under such circumstances, both the formal and the informal rules that govern task-oriented interaction break down. The lack of purposeful interaction makes organizations less efficient, effective, and productive. It also leads to the formation of factions. Once factions (cohesive subgroups) form and develop distinct cultural orientations of their own, they begin to pursue their own interests as opposed to those outlined in the organization's mission statement. Organizational ambiguity of one kind or another is the most frequent cause of substantive conflict between managers and their subordinates. The emphasis on collective bargaining in law enforcement can be traced to the human need to minimize conflict-causing ambiguity in the workplace. Collective bargaining is based on the assumption that a certain amount of controlled conflict (via negotiation) is healthy and represents an appropriate alternative to the spontaneous, often destructive, conflict that is generated by organizational ambiguity.[13]

## Competition for Scarce resources

Every organization operates with finite budget, personnel, equipment, and other resources. What resources one component (or subunit) gets, other subunits do not get. As dependence on the same resource increases, so does the likelihood that competition will degenerate into open conflict. The chances that conflict will occur increase in direct proportion to the degree of scarcity.

Battle lines are drawn and people or groups jockey for the power to capture the resources needed to achieve their own goals. Scarcity has a way of converting dormant or latent hostility into overt conflict—between individuals, between individuals and groups, or between groups.[14] Overt conflict can range all the way from an episodic show of disrespect to intentional sabotage. It is not uncommon for specialized units to siphon resources away from the patrol division. This reduces the patrol division's ability to protect life and property, preserve the peace, prevent crime, and apprehend criminals.[15] Patrol officers feel exploited and become very cynical because they have been denied the resources required to do their job. Cynicism creates and then perpetuates conflict in complex criminal justice organizations.[16]

## Drive for Autonomy

Complex organizations are created, structured, and maintained in order to coordinate the activities of people in the workforce as they pursue mutually acceptable goals and objectives. As a rule, most newly hired employees enter the organization with a fairly broad zone of indifference. In other words, they are willing to accept direction from significant others in the organization who have either the legitimate authority or the power to issue orders and expect compliance.[17] This willingness helps to stabilize interaction patterns within the group. When superiors and subordinates do not agree with each other on the boundaries of the zone, however, the result is often conflict. Conflict erupts when subordinates resist direction and assert their autonomy. Most managers do not fully appreciate the fact that human beings perceive themselves as having certain freedoms (a "set of free behaviors") and that they are—over time—motivated to resist threats to, or abridgment of, those freedoms.[18] If a freedom is eliminated, its former possessor is very likely to try to reestablish it. The most direct way of reestablishing a freedom is to challenge the authority of the manager as a representative of the status quo. Facing such challenges, managers may feel threatened and respond by invoking policies, procedures, rules, and regulations—with the aim of regaining control of the recalcitrant employee's on-the-job behavior. While this response may ensure minimum conformity, it can have dysfunctional consequences. It allows the problem to fester as a continuous source of conflict and perpetuates minimally acceptable performance on the part of the employee.[19] The rigid paramilitary structure in most police departments tends to exacerbate the psychological reactance syndrome that we just outlined.

## Bifurcation of Subunit Interests

The bifurcation of subunit interests is a natural source of conflict in complex organizations. When a subgoal of the organization as a whole is delegated as a task to an organization subunit, it may become that subunit's major or exclusive goal, and that creates the potential for conflict. In the worst case there can be head-to-head competition between subunit goals and the overall goals of the organization. The potential for conflict increases dramatically when two or more specialized work groups with differing goals are functionally dependent on one another. This is a particularly important consideration when one group's success at reaching its goals or accomplishing its tasks depends not only on what it does but on the behavior of other people or groups as well.[20] The desire of a special investigative team to "apprehend dopers and put them behind bars," for example, might become so intense as to cloud their judgment; they might even make a deal to help get a potentially violent burglar (who terrorized a particular neighborhood) out of jail in exchange for information. The detectives in a situation like this would have allowed their own goals to supersede those of the police department, the legislature, and the community at large.

## Dysfunctional Conflict

Interpersonal or intergroup conflict is clearly dysfunctional when it creates intolerable anxiety, disrupts healthy relationships, wastes excessive amounts of time or energy, keeps an organization from accomplishing its lawfully prescribed mission (goals and objectives), or leads to destructive behavior. It is the manager's job to neutralize debilitating conflict and reward those who make positive contributions to the work group. Police administrators must do everything in their power to foster loyalty, cooperation, and a sense of teamwork. They have an affirmative duty to deal with the troublemakers who thrive on creating unnecessary conflict. If large-scale antagonism continues to exist, the reward system probably encourages confrontation and conflict instead of teamwork.[21]

## Functional Conflict

While the destructive effects of dysfunctional conflict are obvious and fairly easy to articulate, the positive effects of functional conflict are far subtler. Good managers have learned to recognize the dual nature of conflict and evaluate it in terms of cost versus benefit. Some of the useful aspects of conflict are as follows:[22]

- It can act as a major stimulant for change.
- It can foster creativity and innovation.
- It can clarify issues and goals.

## Table 13–1    Functional and Dysfunctional Conflict

Conflict is functional when:

1. It turns on and energizes people.
2. It leads to goal-oriented interaction.
3. It helps people sharpen their goals, methods, and procedures.
4. It moves individuals or groups to higher levels of achievement.
5. It opens up channels for more communication.
6. It helps to release pent-up frustration and acts as a healthy catharsis.
7. It leads to more awareness and greater understanding.

Conflict is dysfunctional when:

1. It creates unhealthy and debilitating anxiety.
2. It siphons off energies that could otherwise be spent on productive activities.
3. It disrupts or destroys normal interpersonal or intergroup relationships.
4. It creates a situation in which "might" is used to conquer what is "right."
5. It keeps the organization from accomplishing its assigned mission, goals, and objectives.
6. It focuses on personalities rather than issues.
7. It leads to abnormal frustration, unhealthy anxiety, withdrawal, obstructionism, aggression, and other forms of destructive group behavior such as slowdowns, strikes, and "jungle warfare."

- It can encourage individuality.
- It can enhance communication.
- It can increase energy within a unit.
- It can promote cohesiveness.
- It is psychologically healthy.

The positive value of any conflict episode will depend, to a great degree, on the problem-solving skills of the manager who is responsible for resolving it. Effective police administrators are utilitarian in that they are willing to use any conflict-management strategy they feel is appropriate given the particular conflict situation. Table 13–1 contrasts functional with dysfunctional conflict.

## REACTING TO AND MANAGING CONFLICT

Conflict, like all other elements in the administrative process, must be managed so that it is not allowed to run amok. It is the job of managers to keep conflict functional and within the parameters of organizational necessity.[23] In order to motivate their personnel and increase the overall productivity of the workforce, they must try to stimulate healthy competition while minimizing the negative influence of dysfunctional conflict in the organization. Police administrators react to conflict issues, episodes, and situations in a variety of ways; depending on the circumstances and their own managerial skills, they may either resolve the conflict or make it worse. Conflict-resolution techniques run the gamut from cosmetic to functional.

Based on a review of the literature, it is clear that there are many strategies for dealing with conflict in complex organizations. While each may be effective under certain circumstances or in certain situations, some are of limited value

Lt. Michael "Micky" Parks is a 19-year veteran of the Sparta Police Department. He is a fatherly college-educated man with the demeanor of an empathetic elementary-school teacher. The lieutenant has an easy-going personality and a unique ability to establish almost instantaneous rapport with other police officers. Under normal circumstances, he is an ideal mentor and coach.

Raymond Perkowski, a newly promoted sergeant, was initially assigned to the patrol division. He reported directly to Lt. Parks. They bonded spontaneously and became very good friends. Lt. Parks was the teacher and Sgt. Perkowski was an eager student. He was a protégé who enjoyed picking the brain of his mentor. Sgt. Perkowski didn't object to the fact that the lieutenant called most of the shots and made nearly all of the important decisions. After all, it eased his (Perkowski's) anxiety and made him look good to the brass.

As the sergeant became more comfortable with his role as a supervisor and started to believe in himself as a professional, he began to question his relationship with Lt. Parks. He felt a need to distance himself from the lieutenant.

Since Sgt. Perkowski liked Lt. Parks as a person, he did not want to hurt his feelings. He sent subtle messages designed to tell the lieutenant to back off. When the subtle approach failed and the lieutenant kept interfering in his professional life, Sgt. Perkowski got angry. Since he was unable to vent his frustration, the anger turned to resentment. Sgt. Perkowski began to avoid the lieutenant whenever possible. He cooled their relationship as much as he could.

One night Lt. Parks—without Sgt. Perkowski's knowledge—took disciplinary action against one of Sgt. Perkowski's patrol officers. When Sgt. Perkowski heard about the incident, he got so angry that he initiated a confrontation with the lieutenant. He burst into the lieutenant's office and challenged his authority. After a heated exchange, Sgt. Perkowski told Lt. Parks that he was "sick and tired of being mothered" and that he wanted to be left alone to do his job. He told the lieutenant to "butt out" of his life.

Lt. Parks was mystified by what he saw as Sgt. Perkowski's bizarre behavior and vowed never to talk to the "ungrateful S.O.B." again.

*What would you, as a conflict-management theorist, tell the lieutenant about the cause of his conflict episode? What can he do to ensure that it does not happen again? Be very specific.*

because they fail to get at the sources of the conflict. Others have the potential to be effective but may be very difficult to implement. It is the manager's job to sort through the alternatives and choose the conflict-resolution strategy or technique most likely to succeed, given existing constraints.[24]

Management theorists have identified, described, and analyzed the conflict-management techniques most often used by practitioners. The most common ones are as follows:

**Techniques**

1. Avoidance
2. Dominance
3. Soothing
4. Compromise
5. Resource acquisition
6. Superordinate goals
7. Structural change
8. Behavioral change
9. Use of principled negotiation

Rather than dealing with conflict, many managers choose to close their eyes and pretend that it does not exist. Avoidance may be the most common method of addressing conflict, although what it really does is ignore it. Stalling while a problem is being studied is the administrative equivalent to turning a

**Avoidance**

blind eye to the conflict situation in hopes that things will sort themselves out and the problem will resolve itself. While this does not happen often, it does happen. Avoidance may be reasonable if the consequences of the conflict are perceived as inconsequential, there is little chance of winning, or the costs far outweigh the benefits. However, a pattern of avoidance can lead to crisis management. Crisis management describes what happens when important conflict issues, episodes, or situations are ignored until they become so big they must be resolved immediately, without regard to cost. The most effective managers are inclined to confront conflict head-on; they are least likely to ignore it.[25]

**Dominance**   The autocratic response to conflict is to rely on one's formal authority (i.e., position power) to force others to cease and desist. The hierarchical structure of complex organizations is built on superior-subordinate relationships. Managers occupy strategic positions and are responsible for resolving dysfunctional conflicts. In effect, the manager can force compliance.[26] Due to the paramilitary nature of police work, many police administrators have learned to rely almost exclusively on their formal authority to force decisions on their subordinates. They wield this authority by virtue of their position in the chain of command. This type of autocratic command can be useful in making quick decisions designed to achieve short-term results, but it seems to be a misguided response in most situations. Coercing a cessation of conflict treats only the symptoms, not the cause or causes of the problem. As a result, the unresolved conflict is almost certain to erupt again. It may be even more destructive the second time around.

**Soothing**   Soothing, or smoothing things over, is really not much more than a diplomatic plea for more sensitivity or understanding. It is designed to defuse dysfunctional conflict by calming things down and straightening out ruffled feathers. If there are no substantive conflict issues involved, soothing may, in fact, be the appropriate managerial response. By applying salve to the egos of those who are in conflict with one another, the manager helps eliminate much of the friction. Both sides can focus on points of agreement and downplay differences. The risk in this strategy is that real conflict may go unresolved. It may be pushed under the rug and allowed to fester. Under these circumstances, the conflict may become much worse.[27]

**Compromise**   Compromise is a practical and popular approach to conflict management because it fits in with the realities of life in complex organizations. It consists of the mutual trading of offers, counteroffers, and concessions between those involved or their representatives.[28] The distinguishing feature of compromise is that each party is required to give something up in order to come to a mutually acceptable middle ground. There are no clear winners or losers. Everybody gets a little piece of the action. Compromise is one of the principal techniques used to resolve conflict in police departments throughout the United States. In some ways, though, it is the worst. Compromise puts expediency ahead of principle. As a result, the root cause or causes are ignored and may continue to fester. In addition, compromise decreases accountability and ensures that mediocrity prevails. Two competing good ideas are often merged into one mediocre or bad idea, and everybody loses. Richard Holden argues that organizations are better off if compromise is avoided. He believes that everyone should be allowed to win, as well as lose, on occasion. This will bolster morale and generate better ideas designed to resolve interpersonal or intergroup conflict.[29]

A very important source of conflict in complex task-oriented organizations is unhealthy competition for scarce resources. The best way for managers to defuse this conflict is to acquire additional resources and to distribute them equitably. While this sounds fairly simple, it is often difficult to achieve.[30] Police departments are funded by legislative bodies from a finite and exhaustible tax base, and additional resources may simply not be available. More and more police departments are being confronted by this reality every day. Management by retrenchment and cutback is here to stay. The rank structure in police departments may turn healthy competition into a form of dysfunctional conflict. When the chances for promotion are scarce, competition for it is certain to develop into intense conflict competing for that particular resource. One strategy for managing this kind of conflict is to diversify the rank structure and increase the total number of administrative positions. While the addition of managerial positions may increase morale, job satisfaction is usually temporary because the level of expectation also increases. Top-heavy organizations are seldom, if ever, efficient, effective, or productive.

**Resource Acquisition**

A superordinate goal is a highly valued state of affairs that two or more parties engaged in conflict desire but that cannot be achieved without the cooperation of both or all of them. A manager using this conflict-management technique arranges conditions in such a way that people or groups are compelled to work together to overcome a common threat or achieve shared goals. The creation of superordinate goals is a functional strategy designed to transform "them" (out-group members) into "us" (in-group members). When this strategy works, the overall level of destructive conflict will almost always be reduced.[31] Labor and management, for example, may put aside their deep-seated differences and work together if they are convinced that survival of the organization is contingent on collaboration. Concession and take-back contracts are very common in the hostile world of shrinking resources. The use of superordinate goals should not be viewed as a panacea, however. Since they do not really deal with the causes of conflict, superordinate goals may only delay the conflict. Most police administrators may find that there are real limitations on their ability to generate tailor-made superordinate goals.

**Superordinate Goals**

Reorganization is a common conflict-management strategy. Conflict can be reduced through making transfers, developing new organizational relationships (setting up new departments, creating new coordinator positions, or uncoupling conflicting units), enlarging administrative areas to accommodate different units, and realigning managerial responsibilities within the organization. Transfer is one of the most popular methods used to manage dysfunctional conflict in complex organizations. Difficult employees are frequently reassigned to positions in which the potential for destructive behavior is quite limited. Police administrators often find that it is much easier to isolate recalcitrant personnel in relatively innocuous positions than it is to terminate their employment. Every police department has some very-low-status positions where troublemakers are placed in order to minimize their negative influence on work-group dynamics. There are two basic problems with this strategy, however. Even these low-status positions require personnel who are interested in the work and competent enough to do it. Once a position has been identified as an undesirable disciplinary assignment, good people will avoid it—no matter how important the job is—like the plague for fear that it will destroy their career. This tends to debilitate the whole organization. It should

**Structural Change**

also be noted that transfers do not necessarily resolve conflicts. They may just move them from one location to another within the police department.[32]

**Behavioral Change**  Inducing specific changes in behavior is one of the most difficult conflict-management techniques. One approach involves the use of *planned interventions* to change the beliefs, values, attitudes, and motives of one or more of the antagonists. Managers often try to help those in conflict understand and empathize with one another as they come to grips with personal emotions, values, and behaviors in conflict situations. Quite different from this is the *social learning* approach. In it, the concept of psychosocial motivation is discarded in an attempt to understand and change the behavior that produces conflict. Managers identify the kind, category, or class of behavior (such as verbal, nonverbal, or emotional response) that must be changed. They try to determine what counterproductive "stuff" the persons involved have learned that now controls their behavior. They then factor these bits and pieces of information into a comprehensive diagnosis of the conflict situation and apply techniques (like modeling, direct reinforcement, or persuasive communication) that are likely to produce a desired change in behavior. In other words, by changing the consequences their subordinates expect from their behavior, managers can alter and direct that behavior.[33] But changing behavior is not nearly as simple as it might appear. Resocialization and behavior modification techniques may produce harmful results in the hands of amateurs. They are also costly and time-consuming. Consequently, resocialization and behavior modification have not been used extensively in law enforcement.

**Principled Negotiation**  One way to prevent dysfunctional conflict is to encapsulate it. This is usually done through the formulation of reasonable policies, procedures, rules, and regulations. They specify how group members are to interact with each other. Principled negotiation confronts issues directly. It focuses on identifying and clarifying the cause or causes of the conflict and moving systematically toward its resolution. Emphasis is placed on issues rather than personalities. The objective is to identify mutually acceptable ways of dealing with problems.[34]

> Principled negotiation shows you and your opponent how to obtain what you are entitled to and still be civil. It enables you to be equitable while protecting both of you against being taken advantage of.[35]

Again, the aim of principled negotiation is to decide the issues on their merits rather than resort to a haggling process.

Whisenand outlines six steps involved in "Getting to Yes":[36]

1. *Don't bargain over positions.* This avoids getting yourself locked into your position and forced to defend it.
2. *Being nice is not the answer.* Establish a collaborative context.
3. *Separate the people from the conflict.* Build trust and understanding.
4. *Concentrate on interests, not positions.* Identify where interests overlap and are compatible.
5. *Generate a number of options.* Review the possibilities before deciding what to do.
6. *Adopt objective criteria.* The use of an objective standard will help you to deal with the problem rationally.

If you need to yield in the negotiation process, then choose to yield to principle, not to pressure.[37]

## MANAGERIAL STYLES AND CONFLICT MANAGEMENT

Police administrators, like all other managers, eventually settle into patterns, methods of operation (MOs), or styles of conflict management that reflect their personalities and meet their own unique needs. Based on differing characteristic approaches to conflict resolution, researchers have identified five basic types of managers:

1. *Competitors ("Sharks").* Competitive managers are self-confident, assertive, and aggressive. They use power, intimidation, and domination to achieve their own goals in a win-lose environment. They are driven to win in a zero-sum game.
2. *Avoiders ("Turtles").* Avoiders are lose-lose managers who choose to remain neutral and duck dysfunctional conflict at all costs. They fear the potential damage of confrontation and are willing to limp along within the constraints imposed by the status quo.
3. *Accommodators ("Teddy bears").* These managers formulate and live by a utilitarian lose-win philosophy designed to ensure their survival. Accommodators are not assertive or aggressive; they usually give way to conflict by folding under pressure. They go along to get along.
4. *Compromisers ("Foxes").* Compromise-oriented managers put expediency before principle as they seek short-term solutions to long-term problems. Compromise is a lose-lose strategy that tends to deify the middle ground. Compromisers are always willing to make concessions in order to achieve consensus.
5. *Collaborators ("Owls").* These are win-win managers who accept the premise that conflict is inevitable and—depending on its nature and extent—a potentially positive aspect of life. They look for creative solutions to problems through the purposeful integration of divergent perspectives.[38]

Each style has both positive and negative features. As a result, good managers tend to favor a contingency approach. The contingency view of conflict resolution is based on the fundamental assumption that an effective managerial response is dependent on the synergistic interaction between the manager, the antagonists, and the totality of circumstances inherent in the situation.[39] In other words, they pick and choose the style they feel is most likely to produce a desired result.

## THE PROBLEM EMPLOYEE AS A SOURCE OF CONFLICT

Most police officers are intelligent, hardworking, and helpful human beings. They usually exhibit positive mental attitudes, and they work in concert with their colleagues and managers to accomplish the police department's mission, goals, and objectives. Unfortunately, most work groups have at least one or two members who are continuous sources of dysfunctional conflict.

It is the manager's job to either transform these recalcitrant troublemakers into productive human resources or—as a last resort—purge them from the organization.

Problem employees are usually honest people who—for one reason or another—simply do not fit into the organization and, as a result, engage in disruptive behaviors. They may be suffering from health problems, stress-induced burnout, mental illness, or social malfunctions related to such things as unhealthy romantic relationships, marital discord, drug abuse, and alcoholism. These personal problems can lead to apathy, absenteeism, interpersonal conflict, intergroup antagonisms, overt aggression, and other destructive and dysfunctional forms of behavior.[40]

There is absolutely no doubt that an employee's personal, medical, and emotional problems may seriously affect job performance and can generate a considerable amount of internal organizational conflict. In a police department with 100 or fewer employees, a single employee can create significant problems for the entire organization. A few unhappy, dissatisfied, conflict-oriented workers can—and often do—consume more of a police administrator's time and energy than do the hardworking, productive employees who make up the great majority of the staff.[41]

In the past, troublesome employees were considered to be throwaways. People who were perceived as the cause of organizational conflict were warned, disciplined, or transferred, depending on their willingness to conform to the

A Dallas police officer shouts to onlookers as fellow officers make an arrest in the background after violence broke out after the Cowboys' victory parade in downtown Dallas.
AP/Wide World Photos

expectations of management. Those who could not or would not change their behavior were terminated for the good of the service.[42] Things have changed rather dramatically, however. The human, financial, and organizational costs associated with firing experienced personnel have become prohibitive. Police administrators are now expected, where it is possible and when it is in the best interest of the department, to salvage rather than to fire people.[43] Managers coach and counsel problem employees in an effort to contain dysfunctional conflict and improve performance. This kind of *economic humanism* is on its way to becoming the norm in police administration.

Most managers do not have the clinical training or expertise needed to deal with all of the personal, physical, and emotional problems of their subordinates. Consequently, more and more police departments are establishing employee assistance programs (EAPs). These EAPs are designed to improve personal and organizational performance by making prevention, diagnostic, and treatment services available to ill or troubled personnel.[44]

**Employee Assistance Programs (EAPs)**

The majority of law enforcement agencies with 100 or more officers now have employee assistance programs.[45] They vary tremendously in size, scope, and overall level of sophistication. Comprehensive EAPs usually provide prevention, intervention, and treatment services to those who are at risk or in need:

1. *Prevention.* Prevention (intended to educate employees) is designed to keep potential problems from becoming real problems.
2. *Intervention.* Intervention (stepping into a situation) is a proactive attempt on the part of management to influence the course of events.
3. *Treatment.* Treatment (the application of remedies) represents a concerted effort by a professional staff to cure problems.

Thus, EAPs are designed to help employees cope with their personal and work-related problems, such as alcoholism and drug abuse, sexual harassment, financial planning, child and elder care, depression, and domestic violence.[46] It is estimated that one-fifth of the workforce may occasionally be affected by some kind of problem severe enough to precipitate job and work performance difficulties.[47]

Police administrators play a dual role in an EAP. First, they monitor on-the-job behavior and evaluate actual job performance. If an employee's behavior becomes unacceptable or job performance is below par, it is the administrator's job to determine whether the problem is being caused by organizational or personal factors. Second, if unacceptable behavior or poor performance is caused by personal factors, it is the administrator's job to confront the employee in a constructive manner. As part of this confrontational process, the problem employee should be encouraged to seek help through the EAP.

EAPs establish a clear division of labor. Managers detect problems, confront employees, make necessary referrals, and perform a follow-up function. Prevention, intervention, and treatment services are provided by a professional staff with the training as well as the expertise needed to help troubled employees cope with personal problems that cause disruptive behavior or performance deficits. If problem employees elect not to participate in an EAP or if they fail to benefit from participation in a program, they must—under normal circumstances—be dealt with through the formal disciplinary process. Figure 13–3 illustrates these options.

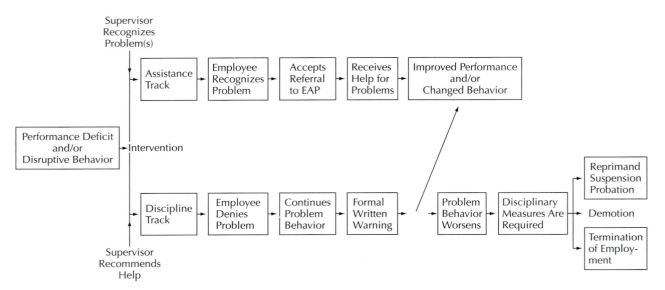

**Figure 13–3**

Dealing with Performance Deficits and Disruptive Job-Related Behavior.

The costs of dealing with troubled employees, both direct (hospitalization, sick leave, severance pay, and so forth) and indirect (lost productivity and managerial time), are phenomenal. It is estimated that personnel matters take up approximately 80 percent of an administrator's time.[48]

While EAPs may not be the panacea some claim them to be, they are tools that police administrators can use to help troubled employees overcome personal, physical, emotional, and social problems that have a negative impact on job performance. The benefits EAPs offer to the employee and the organization include:[49]

1. Increased probability of success.
2. Increased referrals.
3. Joint training sessions.
4. Increased morale.
5. Real help in response to one's "cry for help."
6. Stigma reduction.
7. Feeling of being cared for as a person.
8. Affordable access to help.

Every police department should establish, or have access to, an independent EAP that works with management and for employees. The program must be designed to protect each employee's rights (including the right to privacy) yet provide managers with the information necessary to protect the health and welfare of the citizens being served and of the employees seeking help. Once an EAP is up and running, self-referral should be encouraged. In addition, management should adopt a strong disciplinary policy that incorporates mandatory participation in the EAP as an alternative to punitive action in conflict situations.[50]

Barry Simpson is a bright, street-wise police officer with a degree in human resources management. He was just promoted and has been assigned to the research and planning unit of a fairly large municipal police department. The department has been plagued by personnel problems and has lost a great deal of its credibility. Lt. Simpson's job, as a human resources development specialist, is to pinpoint the cause or causes of the problem and recommend managerial strategies designed to remedy the situation.

Based on an in-depth analysis of over 90 cases that resulted in severe disciplinary action, Lt. Simpson concluded that interpersonal conflict between police officers and civilians was a significant precipitating factor. He also found that much of this dysfunctional conflict was rooted in the physical, emotional, and social problems of troubled employees. It became obvious to him that these personal problems were exacerbated by the stress inherent in police work and the inhospitable psychosocial environment within which police officers ply their trade.

Lt. Simpson's research helped him to understand that interpersonal conflict (induced by unresolved personal problems) exacts an incalculable toll on any complex organization in terms of poor performance, lost productivity, absenteeism, disciplinary action, and turnover. He came to the conclusion that the traditional response—to terminate problem employees—may be "penny wise and pound foolish" in that it is a short-run solution to a long-range problem. The cost of replacing otherwise competent employees for drug or alcohol dependency is often much more costly than salvaging them. The same is true when it comes to dealing with those employees in physical discomfort or emotional distress.

In a preliminary report to the deputy chief in charge of research and planning, Lt. Simpson called for an emphasis on economic humanism in the police department. The deputy chief signed off on Lt. Simpson's report and forwarded it to the chief of police.

*What is economic humanism? Why is it such an important concept? If you were Lt. Simpson, what specific recommendations would you give to your superiors? How should they go about minimizing dysfunctional interpersonal conflict and salvaging troubled employees?*

# SUMMARY

Interpersonal and intergroup conflict is a ubiquitous and normal fact of life in complex criminal justice organizations. Conflict arises in situations where someone or something thwarts, or is about to thwart, someone else's goals. It is an unfolding process rather than a discrete event.

Many police administrators harbor traditionalist views about conflict. They view all conflict as dysfunctional and bad. Their goal is to eliminate it at any cost. Modern-thinking police administrators, on the other hand, view conflict somewhat differently. They accept constructive conflict and try to neutralize destructive conflict. The interactionist school of organizational thought believes conflict is beneficial when it forces the parties to reevaluate situations and to take proactive steps toward realistic solutions to divisive problems.

The common sources of conflict in complex criminal justice organizations are (1) interdependence, (2) differences in power, status, and culture, (3) organizational ambiguity, (4) unbridled competition for scarce resources, (5) drive for autonomy, and (6) bifurcation of subunit interests. Conflict is dysfunctional when it creates too much anxiety, disrupts healthy relationships, consumes an excessive amount of time and energy, keeps the organization from accomplishing its mission, or leads to destructive behavior. Functional conflict, on the other hand, energizes people, enhances communication, provides an outlet for pent-up frustration, and becomes an educational experience.

There are a number of potentially effective conflict-management strategies that can be used in police work; one of the most promising is the use of principled negotiation. Principled negotiation seeks to prevent hardening of attitudes and issues so that the parties involved will work toward true compromise and conciliation.

Problem employees are often a source of dysfunctional conflict in complex criminal justice organizations. Under these conditions, it is management's responsibility to neutralize the conflict or reduce it to an acceptable level. Based on the emerging philosophy of economic humanism, many police departments have established employee assistance programs. These EAPs are designed to improve organizational as well as personal performance by making prevention, intervention, and treatment services avail- able to ill, troubled, or disruptive personnel. Competent police administrators learn how to develop and manage all kinds of human resources rather than waste them.

## KEY TERMS

aggression
behavioralists
causes of conflict
collaboration
competition
conflict cycle
conflict management
cooperation
dysfunctional conflict
employee assistance programs (EAPs)
functional conflict

interactionists
intergroup conflict
interpersonal conflict
management strategies
management techniques
managerial styles
organizational conflict
principled negotiation
problem employees
strategic conflict
traditionalists

## DISCUSSION TOPICS AND QUESTIONS

1. What are the basic behavior modes shown in the collaboration–aggression continuum? Describe them and give an example of each one.

2. Define *interpersonal conflict*. How does it differ from intergroup conflict in an organizational context?

3. List the stages or steps in the conflict-development cycle. Explain how they fit together as a part of a dynamic, unfolding process.

4. Identify the three distinct phases in management thinking as it relates to organizational conflict. How do the interactionists differ from the traditionalists?

5. What are the six primary causes of conflict in complex criminal justice organizations? Give examples.

6. Contrast functional with dysfunctional conflict. Discuss the most useful aspects of organizational conflict.

7. Identify the most common conflict-management techniques used by police administrators. What is the premise of principled negotiation?

8. What are the basic managerial types of police administrators in terms of their approach to resolving interpersonal and/or intergroup conflict?

9. What is the basis of the employee assistance program movement? What is the role of the manager in the EAP process?

## FOR FURTHER READING

Robert B. Denhardt, Janet V. Denhardt, and Maria P. Aristigueta, *Managing Human Behavior in Public and Nonprofit Organizations* (Thousand Oaks, CA: Sage, 2002).

These authors offer a detailed explanation of the causes and results of conflict in public and nonprofit agencies. They cover conflict-resolution strategies in detail and offer their own recommendations.

Paul M. Whisenand, *Supervising Police Personnel: The Fifteen Responsibilities* (Upper Saddle River, NJ: Prentice Hall, 2004).

Whisenand analyzes conflict and its consequences in law enforcement agencies and what administrators can do to address them. Principled negotiation is stressed as a method of conflict resolution.

# NOTES

1. Stephen P. Robbins, *Essentials of Organizational Behavior* (Upper Saddle River, NJ: Prentice Hall, 2000), pp. 167–168.

2. Eric J. Van Sylke, *Listening to Conflict* (New York: AMACOM, 1999).

3. Kenneth W. Thomas, "Conflict and Negotiation Processes in Organizations," in Marvin D. Dunnette and L.M. Hough, eds. *Handbook of Industrial and Organizational Psychology* (Palo Alto, CA: Consulting Psychologists Press, 1992), pp. 651–717.

4. Charles R. Swanson, Leonard Territo, and Robert W. Taylor, *Police Administration* (Upper Saddle River, NJ: Prentice Hall, 2001), pp. 238–239.

5. Linda Stroh, Gregory B. Northcraft, and Margaret A. Neale, *Organizational Behavior: A Management Challenge* (Mahwah, NJ: Lawrence Erlbaum and Associates), pp. 122–127.

6. Elliot M. Fox and Lyndall Urwick, *Dynamic Administration: The Collected Papers of Mary Parker Follett* (New York: Hippocrene Books, 1973).

7. Louis Pondy, "Organizational Conflict: Concepts and Models," *Administrative Science Quarterly,* Vol. 12 (1967), pp. 296–320.

8. Hal G. Rainey, *Understanding and Managing Public Organizations* (San Francisco: Jossey-Bass, 1997), p. 306.

9. Ramon J. Aldag and Loren W. Kuzuhara, *Organizational Behavior and Management* (Cincinnati: South-Western, 2002), p. 472.

10. Robbins, *Organizational Behavior,* pp. 168–169.

11. Aldag and Kuzuhara, *Organizational Behavior and Management,* p. 468.

12. John J. Broderick, *Police in a Time of Change* (Prospect Heights, IL: Waveland Press, 1987).

13. Harry W. More, W. Fred Wegener, and Larry S. Miller, *Effective Police Supervision* (Cincinnati: Anderson, 2003), pp. 430–431.

14. Aldag and Kuzuhara, *Organizational Behavior and Management,* p. 467.

15. V.A. Leonard and Harry W. More, *Police Organization and Management* (New York: Foundation Press, 2000), p. 330.

16. Mark Baker, *COPS* (New York: Pocket Books, 1985).

17. Chester I. Barnard, *The Functions of the Executive* (Cambridge, MA: Harvard University Press, 1976).

18. Jack W. Brehm, *A Theory of Psychological Resistance* (New York: Academic Press, 1966).

19. Aldag and Kuzuhara, *Organizational Behavior and Management,* p. 167.

20. Ibid., p. 468.

21. Robbins, *Organizational Behavior,* p. 169.

22. Paul M. Whisenand, *Supervising Police Personnel: The Fifteen Responsibilities* (Upper Saddle River, NJ: Prentice Hall, 2004), p. 276.

23. Richard N. Holden, *Modern Police Management* (Upper Saddle River, NJ: Prentice Hall, 1986), p. 98.

24. Van Slyke, *Listening to Conflict.*

25. Holden, *Police Management,* p. 100.

26. Gary Dessler, *Management* (Upper Saddle River, NJ: Prentice Hall, 2004), p. 215.

27. Ibid.

28. Stroh, Northcraft, and Neale, *Organizational Behavior,* pp. 128–129.

29. Holden, *Police Management,* pp. 100–101.

30. Ibid., p. 99.

31. Stroh, Northcraft, and Neale, *Organizational Behavior,* p. 133.

32. Holden, *Police Management,* p. 102.

33. Ibid., p. 101.

34. Robert B. Denhardt, Janet V. Denhardt, and Maria P. Aristigueta, *Managing Human Behavior in Public and Nonprofit Organizations* (Thousand Oaks, CA: Sage, 2002), pp. 342–343.

35. Whisenand, *Supervising Police Personnel,* p. 280 and Roger Fisher, William Ury, and Bruce Patton, *Getting to Yes: Negotiating Agreements Without Giving In* (New York: Penguin, 1991).

36. Ibid., pp. 280–282.

37. Denhardt, Denhardt, and Aristigueta, *Managing Human Behavior.*

38. Thomas, "Conflict and Negotiation Processes."

39. Holden, *Police Management,* p. 103.

40. Joseph Wambaugh, *The Choirboys* (New York: Delacorte Press, 1973).

41. Frank E. Williams and Joan E. Bratton, "A Step by Step Guide to Developing Employee Assistance Programs in Small Police Agencies," *The Police Chief,* No. 2 (1990).

42. Leonard and More, *Police Organization and Management,* p. 48.

43. Whisenand, *Supervising Police Personnel,* p. 283.

44. Edward A. Thibault, Lawrence M. Lynch, and R. Bruce McBride, *Proactive Police Management* (Upper Saddle River, NJ: Prentice Hall, 2004), pp. 339–341.

45. Swanson, Territo, and Taylor, *Police Administration,* p. 384.

46. Aldag and Kuzuhara, *Organizational Behavior and Management*, p. 408.

47. James L. Bowditch and Anthony F. Buono, *A Primer on Organizational Behavior* (New York: John Wiley & Sons, 2001), pp. 319–320.

48. Thibault, Lynch, and McBride, *Proactive Police Management*, p. 341.

49. Swanson, Territo, and Taylor, *Police Administration*, pp. 384–386.

50. Williams and Bratton, "Step by Step Guide."

# —14—

# DEVELOPING THE ORGANIZATION

## Techniques for Improving Performance

## LEARNING OBJECTIVES

1. Define *organizational development (OD).*
2. Describe the functions performed by a change agent.
3. List the values that are inherently a part of OD.
4. Describe team building as a technique of planned change.
5. Identify the characteristics of a healthy police organization.
6. List the key characteristics of survey feedback.

Police executives of the 21st century are faced with a rapidly changing world that is placing more and more demands on them and their organizations. As a result, they are constantly thinking about the problems and driving forces that affect their organizations and searching for ways to make those organizations more efficient and effective. Today's police managers must create responsive organizations and must themselves learn to adapt to constantly changing and challenging conditions.

Unfortunately, there is no quick solution to the search for organizational effectiveness. Instead, there is great ambiguity as to what organizational forms, strategies, and tactics organizations should adopt. Ambiguity is not new; it is something all police officers and managers deal with daily. It would be ideal to have everything fall into place, packaged in a neat organizational plan, but this seldom happens. In reality, managing ambiguity is what police managers are paid for, and they must accept the challenge of each contradiction. Today's police manager needs to analyze ambiguous situations (where programs, procedures, regulations, strategies, or tactics need to be changed because they do not work), formulate cross-functional strategies for enabling the organization to achieve its objectives, and then implement and evaluate those strategies.[1] However, this organizational redirection will not happen overnight. In order to prepare their organizations to evolve to a higher, more effective level, police executives will need to employ a comprehensive organizational development (OD) process.

Chief Robert Miller assumed command of the Quail Valley Police Department after being selected via an assessment center. He was previously a captain in another department where he had served for 14 years. It is well known that his predecessor at Quail Valley had a drinking problem and retired early on disability. During the last three years of the former chief's tenure, the morale of the officers in the department had gone down considerably, and the officers performed their duties with a minimum of managerial guidance from the chief's office.

The department has 42 sworn officers and 9 civilians. The city has a population of 37,000 and is governed by a city manager and a weak mayor. The city is located at the edge of a metropolitan area and still has vestiges of open land and some truck farming. In recent years the city has grown because a number of people have opted to live there and commute to other cities to work.

It is anticipated that within 20 years the population of the city will double and the tax base will be improved considerably. The racial mix of the city is currently 12 percent African-American, 26 percent Latino, and the remainder Caucasian. Projections are that the racial mix will remain the same. The city has a moderate crime rate, and the greatest problem is residential burglary.

Mark Rogers, the city manager, has given the chief a mandate to professionalize the department. In the current organization there are three divisions—services, investigation, and uniform—each headed by a lieutenant. In addition there are six sergeants and five detectives; the rest of the force is patrol officers. One-half of the patrol officers have less than three years of service; the other half have an average of 12 years of service. There are two African-American officers and five Latinos; the remainder are Caucasian. The department does not have any policewomen. One was hired three years ago but did not complete the probationary period.

The chief has decided to call a meeting of the lieutenants and sergeants to discuss reorganizing the department and to determine what can be done to improve the organization.

*Prepare an agenda for the initial meeting. Justify the inclusion of each item. How would you involve the lieutenants and sergeants in the meeting? What would be the next thing you would do after the initial meeting? How would you go about involving the other employees? What would be the first organizational development (OD) technique you would use? How would you handle individuals who feel OD is a waste of time?*

## DEFINITION

Organizational development (OD) is a process of systematic planned organization-wide change that is managed by the executive level.[2] It encompasses a collection of change techniques or planned interventions that range from structural reorganization, new reward systems, and cultural change to human development techniques and strategic assessments.[3] OD has various definitions. In its most extended sense, it actually means organizational change. Implicit in this definition is that if OD is to succeed, it has to have the support of top management. It is a long-range process, so those expecting immediate results are probably going to be disappointed. Some have even suggested that it may take seven years from the time organizational renewal begins until significant changes can be observed.

An OD intervention is essentially an attempt to solve an organizational problem by applying knowledge from the behavioral sciences, including psychology, sociology, and cultural anthropology. The focus of an OD intervention is to change the culture of the organization, whether it involves individuals, groups, or the total structure.

OD is goal oriented; its ultimate purpose is to improve organizational effectiveness. It is not surprising that OD is complex, includes a variety of approaches for introducing change, makes assumptions about human behavior, and emphasizes the evaluation and implementation of organizational choices.[4]

# ORGANIZATIONAL DEVELOPMENT OBJECTIVES

A police manager can make better use of OD by being fully aware of its potential for solving current problems and creating an organizational climate that maximizes the effective use of resources. Objectives of OD include the following:

1. Creating an open departmental culture that focuses on problem solving.
2. Building trust between individuals and groups.
3. Moving decision-making responsibilities to the lowest possible level in the organization.
4. Maximizing individual self-control and self-direction.
5. Helping managers achieve organizational objectives.
6. Fostering an organizational climate that stresses a commitment to organizational objectives.
7. Maximizing collaborative efforts.[5]

This process seeks to unfreeze the old ways of doing and thinking, implement a new, more effective way of performing and thinking, and then stabilize this process so that the new ways of thinking and behavior become the organization's normal way of getting things done.[6] Attainment of these objectives creates a working environment that allows for individual and group initiative, builds mutual support, and achieves individual and departmental goals.

# BASIC VALUES OF ORGANIZATIONAL DEVELOPMENT

A manager's ability to contribute significantly to the development of human resources depends not only on having a humanistic view of people but also on building such a view into his or her actual managerial style. There are many police managers who have received excellent management training and know all the latest buzzwords but still operate in the same manner they always have—which in many instances is authoritarian.

OD assumptions about people in organizations are genuinely optimistic; they require managers to be more people oriented and participative with their subordinates.[7] The following are underlying values of OD:

### Individuals

1. People want to grow and mature.
2. Employees have much to offer (e.g., energy and creativity) that is not now being used by the organization.
3. Most employees desire the opportunity to contribute (they desire, seek, and appreciate empowerment).

### Groups

1. Groups and teams are critical to organizational success.
2. Groups have powerful influences on individual behavior.
3. The complex roles to be played in groups require skill development.

**Organization**

1. Participation in groups will help satisfy organization members' needs.
2. Conflict can be functional if properly channeled.
3. Individual and organizational goals can be compatible.[8]

Four further values of OD, to be discussed in the next paragraphs, are openness and trust, feedback, confronting of conflict, and risk taking. All these basic values of OD present a clear-cut challenge to police managers of the future. They call for the redefinition of work and working relationships. They are not a threat to the vast majority of managers but are definitely a menace to autocratic managers who depend on command-and-control tactics to accomplish their objectives.

One of the primary objectives of an OD effort is to develop the organization to the point where the culture is based on *openness and trust* (see Table 14–1). Achieving these things is a significant breakthrough in the relationship between employees and management. It is most difficult to have real communication in a police department when one constantly hears such comments as "I don't trust management," or "She is a manipulator and will do anything to get ahead," or "If anything goes wrong, he will always find someone to blame."

When a manager does not trust his or her officers, it creates resentment and eventually a negative working environment. In a trusting atmosphere, subordinates are allowed to make independent decisions. Trust must be the foundation of any OD effort, but it does not just happen—it has to be cultivated.[9] Trust means allowing subordinates to function with a sense of confidence that they are supported by managers. Trust is based on managers believing that officers have the capacity to contribute to the organization.[10]

*Feedback* is an essential aspect of communicating (see Chapter 10) and helps a manager create a climate where employees feel safe when they share information. It is difficult to underestimate the importance of feedback. Without it, communication does not exist. Inadequate feedback generally leads to performance errors and the need to redo work.[11] Effective feedback is not easily achieved. It requires a manager to be especially sensitive to employees, because many people are uncomfortable when speaking to someone about their performance. A manager should keep in mind that some employees will remain silent rather than share information with someone in a position of power.

In soliciting feedback, managers should use a variety of techniques, including personal discussion or written communication with peers or subordinates, group meetings, and (to obtain candid, anonymous feedback) questionnaires.[12] Whatever technique is used, employees must feel free to express their impressions about work issues. Another value of importance to OD is the desire and ability to *confront conflict*. Whenever individuals interact, there is the potential for conflict. Conflict is inevitable in most organizations, but it can be positive if it is directed constructively.[13] In police departments, discord

Table 14–1 **Foundations of a Successful OD Effort**

Openness and trust
Feedback
Confronting of conflict
Risk taking

arises not only between individuals and groups but also between units and divisions. For instance, traffic units dominate some departments; in others, the detective bureau holds the commanding position. In either instance, if one unit always seems to receive greater support than the other, operational discrepancies can result.

In patrol-dominated police departments, only working the street is viewed as "real" policing; all other specialties are perceived as second-class efforts. When priorities like this surface, conflict is inevitable. Defusing such conflict calls for some type of adjustment by police managers. A potentially effective means of dealing with this particular kind of conflict would be an OD intervention designed to highlight the importance of mutual respect and an integrated organizational effort. This will have the best chance of succeeding if the organization is open and there is a definite feeling of trust between managers and employees.

The last value of importance to OD is *risk taking*. Ambiguity occurs when a police manager takes risks. When responsibilities are delegated, pressure is placed on everyone involved. Mistakes will be made, but they must be turned into learning situations; finding someone to blame (scapegoating) is rarely the right thing to do. People must be allowed to grow, not vegetate. Risk taking means sharing power and letting people learn and grow.

It is important for a police organization to acknowledge the existence of conflict and the need to control it, to create a working environment emphasizing openness and trust, to provide for feedback, and to allow managers to take risks; when it does all these, it is reaching a point where it can maximize organizational productivity.[14]

William F. Walsh, Director of the Southern Police Institute lecturing on organizational development.

# THE HEALTHY ORGANIZATION

When OD is successful, the organization becomes healthier and more responsive to the community it serves. The real purpose of OD is to improve organizations as much as possible. A very healthy organization might be an unattainable ideal, but striving toward it is certainly worthwhile. The healthier the organization, the more it represents the values of OD we have discussed.

In a healthy police organization (see Table 14–2), many goals are established by statute or ordinance, but some goals and most objectives are arrived at jointly by management and employees. Everyone is truly supportive of departmental objectives, and personal objectives are integrated into the organization whenever possible. Departmental objectives are carefully spelled out, and everyone is aware of the relationship between goals and objectives. Managers define a goal as a statement of broad direction, general purpose, or intent, as opposed to an objective, which is defined as a desired accomplishment that can be measured within a given time frame and under specific conditions. For example:

| | |
|---|---|
| *Goal:* | To reduce the opportunities for the commission of crime through preventive patrol and other crime-prevention measures. |
| *Objective:* | To reduce residential burglaries by 33 percent during the next fiscal year as compared to the previous fiscal year. |

The healthy organization has problems, but they are handled effectively, not conveniently ignored. Officers talk about problems when they occur and then work with managers to resolve them. Constructive feedback is a continuing process, and two-way communication is stressed.

Task accomplishment is seen as paramount; thus a reasonable degree of informality in personal relationships is encouraged. Emphasis is placed

## Table 14–2 **Characteristics of a Healthy Police Organization**

1. Objectives are jointly developed by managers and employees.
2. Problems and issues are confronted.
3. Informality in relationships between managers and employees is acceptable.
4. Decision-making is delegated to the lowest possible problem-solving level.
5. Responsibility is shared.
6. Personal needs are considered important.
7. Collaboration between management and employees is considered essential.
8. Conflict is encountered and managed.
9. Feedback is two-way and continuous.
10. Managerial styles vary according to situations.
11. There is an attitude of trust between managers and employees.
12. Risk is accepted when making decisions and conducting operations.
13. Poor performance is confronted.
14. Policy, procedures, and the organizational structure are utilized to support goal attainment.
15. Employees are treated as responsible individuals capable of performing at a high level.

on collaborative problem solving instead of the organizational structure. The chain of command is utilized only as a frame of reference for facilitating communication but is never allowed to disrupt goal attainment. What really counts is achievement rather than a concern with rank, status, or position power.

Employees who have problems are referred to those who have the expertise to help resolve them and can render the most appropriate decision. This process maximizes the participation of those who are both knowledgeable and more apt to be motivated to solve the problems.[15]

In a healthy organization, the managerial approach emphasizes sharing responsibility. It is definitely the opposite of the *we/they* style of management, which takes the position that it is top management's job to tell everyone what to do and how to do it. Shared responsibility improves communication, reduces ambiguity, and creates a support base to facilitate implementation. In addition, sharing responsibility demonstrates the willingness of top management to accept the judgment of lower-level managers and employees.

Personal needs in the healthy organization are given serious consideration. There is a commitment to the integration of personal needs with organizational needs. Job satisfaction is emphasized; managers focus on satisfying subordinates' needs for self-actualization in their work. Motivators such as recognition, achievement, and responsibility are stressed.[16]

In a healthy police department, managers and employees work together to identify objectives, make plans for achieving them, and carry out those plans. This type of collaboration rejects the unit-level and individual competition and petty jealousies quite common in unhealthy police organizations. Information is shared, and the knowledge one possesses (not rank) is what counts. Collaboration is encouraged (regardless of one's position in the organization), and training programs promote the development of expertise and knowledge.[17]

Conflict is viewed as inevitable because of differing attitudes of individuals and groups. It must be managed, not ignored or rejected. Conflict is accepted as a challenge and is dealt with openly and candidly. The goal is to manage conflict with all the resources at the command of the organization (see Chapter 13).

Feedback in the healthy organization is viewed as an integral component of the managerial process. Feedback views performance as essential and never concerns itself with personality. It is a two-way process and is actively sought by employees at all levels and in every rank. Feedback is used in order to help managers and employees grow and meet the challenges of a constantly changing work environment.

Leadership style is flexible. When tasks are varied and complex, the manager utilizes a directive leadership style. When tasks are routine, the manager limits control and utilizes an employee-centered supportive managerial style. During unusual occurrences or emergencies, the leadership style becomes authoritarian (see Chapter 11).

Members of the organization work in an atmosphere of trust. Involvement is emphasized, and employees have the freedom to work for departmental goals and determine work strategies. Control is minimal, and records are limited to those needed for achieving objectives.

In the healthy organization, risk is accepted as a necessary part of the managerial process, something essential to growth and development. When the outcome cannot be controlled, developments are monitored carefully to minimize negative consequences. Risk taking is perceived as a managerial challenge rather than something to be avoided.

When poor performance occurs in the healthy organization, it is dealt with quickly, and the process treats those involved with care and understanding. Standards are clear-cut and known to all. Discipline is used as a last resort, and a strong effort is made to administer it judiciously. Training, coaching, and supervision are used to resolve problems. Expectations are high and mediocrity is not acceptable.[18]

As new situations arise, the healthy organization responds by altering its structure to meet them. Policies and procedures are viewed as flexible guidelines, not absolute dogma. When policies and procedures become dysfunctional, they are reviewed and changed; thus, they are never allowed to become a refuge for incompetent employees.

The healthy organization encourages every employee to develop to the maximum. A job description is never allowed to limit the achievement of objectives. Employees are given wide latitude in their performance and the necessary authority to carry out their work. They are encouraged to support each other in order to achieve teamwork.

Goal attainment by the most effective means possible is what counts. The goal of the contemporary police manager is the creation of a healthy working environment. As change occurs, it is accepted as an inevitable consequence of striving to be more effective. The healthy organization is based on trust and a culture promoting job satisfaction.

## INTERVENTION TECHNIQUES

OD uses a number of techniques to change an organization and influence either individuals or groups. It implies a great deal more than making people happy or teaching them how to get along with fellow employees. OD concentrates on changing conditions so officers can work more effectively and achieve their goals. Intervention techniques utilized in OD have the following common characteristics:

1. They are applied to the total organization.
2. Members of the organization identify the issues and the problems to be solved.
3. Organization members are taught how to solve both immediate and future problems.
4. Emphasis is placed on jointly collecting data, analyzing the data, developing a planned intervention, and evaluating the results of the intervention.
5. An effort is made to create an environment that is committed to change.[19]

Human energy can be focused on specific organizational goals by utilizing OD intervention techniques that deal with the environmental conditions of an organization. Specific intervention techniques can be applied to individuals, groups, or the total organization. Values, attitudes, relationships, and the organizational environment are all issues of great concern to OD consultants and agency personnel.

Once the decision is made to alter the organizational environment, an OD effort usually consists of the following elements:

1. Diagnosis.
2. Planning.
3. Training.
4. Evaluation.

The diagnosis phase of an OD effort can be quite simple or exceedingly complex. It involves the gathering and analysis of data in order to determine what areas need to be improved. Information can be obtained via questionnaires, interviews, meetings, observations, or an examination of rules, regulations, and procedures.[20] The information sought may include how superiors and subordinates relate to each other, how conflict is resolved, how goals are set, or how problems are solved. For example, when determining communication patterns, the following questions might be addressed: Is communication two-way? Who talks to whom, for how long, and about what? Are communications filtered? Who initiates communication? After the diagnosis phase, plans are developed for dealing with the identified problems and issues. These plans might include methods for developing organizational flexibility, providing a frame of reference for decision-making, maximizing employee involvement, or developing ways of measuring individual and unit performance.[21]

Training is the next phase in altering the organizational environment. It consists of sharing information, either one on one or by more traditional methods like group discussion or lecture. The key is to involve everyone who will be affected by the planned change. The training can be done by in-house personnel or by consultants, depending on which method will bring the best results.[22]

The final phase is evaluation, which involves gathering data to determine the effects of the OD effort on the organization. The evaluation includes identifying needs for additional training, as well as determining whether additional information is needed in order to refine the initial OD plan. It may also include fact-finding that could lead to the creation of further change-oriented programs.[23]

**Sensitivity Training**

Sensitivity training, also known as laboratory training or "T-group," is one of the earlier OD techniques. It is an intensive process designed to foster interpersonal awareness and personal growth. Participants share their feelings and receive feedback on their own behavior from group members. In recent years it has been partially supplanted by other intervention techniques such as process consultation.[24]

Sensitivity training is conducted with groups of 8 to 15 members. Meetings are held without an agenda and are leaderless. Normally the group meets away from work, for a period that generally ranges from a weekend up to two weeks. Some groups are composed of co-workers; others are composed of employees from different parts of the same organization or from different organizations.[25]

When a T-group meets, a change agent serves as a catalyst and facilitator. Generally, the change agent starts the first session with a brief introduction, to the effect that the primary objective for the group is to learn more about itself.

As the program moves along, the change agent will take a very passive role, but if needed, he or she can present conceptual material on such topics as interpersonal relations and group dynamics.[26]

The group is process oriented, so the participants learn through observation and participation rather than being lectured by the change agent. If frustration or even hostility arises, it can be directed against the change agent, who in many instances will appear to be inept and ineffective because of the passive attitude he or she has adopted. This seeming ineptness allows the change agent to focus on the specific event, such as hostility, and encourage participants to express their ideas, beliefs, and attitudes.

Even though every effort is made to ensure that feedback is non-evaluative, the process can be quite stressful for some participants. Specialists feel, however, that a certain degree of anxiety helps the participants learn from the process. Generally, the expected outcomes of sensitivity training include the following:

1. A greater awareness and sensitivity to the behavior of others.
2. A better understanding of group dynamics.
3. The ability to analyze one's own behavior.
4. The capacity to act based on what has been learned.
5. Improved diagnostic skills.
6. An ability to improve interpersonal relations.[27]

Sensitivity training has strong supporters as well as a certain number of detractors. It has been difficult to predict how the training will affect an employee. In fact, sensitivity training—particularly the frustration and anxiety caused by the feedback process it includes—has caused psychological problems for some participants. Another problem is the difficulty many former T-group participants have found in transferring the newly acquired knowledge back to the workplace. Effort has been made to solve the psychological problems by a more careful selection and screening of applicants for T-groups. The second problem has been addressed by making the training more job oriented, for example, by having T-group members work on actual organizational problems.

Currently sensitivity training is used by some organizations to increase interpersonal awareness and integrate individuals into the organization. It is the view of many change agents that sensitivity training has its place but that it is only one of a number of intervention techniques that should be considered as part of an overall OD effort.

## Team Building

Team building has become an increasingly popular intervention technique for improving the effectiveness of organizations. Team building is a consensus-building training technique involving both managers and employees. It might involve a team of officers on the same shift, a special unit such as a SWAT team, or a task force created to address a specific problem (for a detailed discussion of groups, see Chapter 7). Team-building efforts by change agents can involve the more traditional emphasis on interpersonal relations, but one major difference is the special weight placed on tasks to be performed.[28]

A properly developed and managed team-building effort offers a variety of benefits to the organization, such as:

Chief Wally Partin has been the chief of police for three years in the city of Popular, which has a population of 113,321. The community has an excellent tax base because of a large number of light industrial plants and two major shopping centers. It is fortunate to have a below-average crime rate (in terms of felonies), with the exception of residential burglaries.

The department has 132 sworn police officers and 42 civilians. There are three major divisions: investigations, field services, and administration. Specialized units include a SWAT team, a traffic unit, a youth bureau, and a crime-prevention unit. In addition, officers are detailed to a metropolitan narcotics unit.

During the last two years the community has been up in arms over the large number of residential burglaries. The situation has reached the point that a number of influential community organizations are pressuring the city administration and the police department. The mayor has told the chief she wants something done about the problem. The research assistant who works in the chief's office has compiled a report on residential burglaries showing that the burglaries occur throughout the city and that the vast majority are committed by youths between the ages of 15 and 20; most of the rest are committed by young persons between 21 and 25. During the preceding calendar year, 16 percent of the reported residential burglaries were solved.

During the weekly staff meeting, attended by the heads of the three major divisions and all special units, the problem is discussed extensively and two recommendations are presented to the chief. The first recommendation is to expand the youth services bureau and use the added personnel to target the burglary problem. The second recommendation is to adopt team policing and restructure the department accordingly.

The chief, with the approval of the mayor and city council, has decided to adopt the concept of team policing, and the department will be allocated 12 new positions. The chief realizes that such a major change in the way the department operates may be resisted by many of the line officers and even some of the managers. Of special concern to the chief is the resistance he anticipates from middle managers. In the past, the lieutenants in the department have resisted all efforts they perceived as diluting their authority. As a group, they were most comfortable in a leadership style relying on the power of their position, and they tolerated little deviation from departmental procedures. The one word best describing their relationship with subordinates can only be "control."

The other group that the chief anticipates will resist team policing consists of 12 senior patrol officers, all of whom work the swing shift. These officers have been in the department for 18 years or more and for the most part are just putting in enough time to retire. As a group, they do not want to do anything that "rocks the boat." The chief has consulted several organizational behavior experts at the local university and has made the decision to institute an OD effort.

*If you were the chief, what type of OD effort do you believe could reduce the anticipated resistance from the two groups? Would you hire an outside consultant or use departmental personnel? How would you present the team policing concept to the public?*

1. Teams provide many perspectives, skills, and resources.
2. Team-building training increases team members' acceptance and understanding of team objectives and their commitment to them.
3. Teams help create a working environment where there is mutual trust among all the components of the organization.
4. Teamwork is stimulating and helps develop leadership skills for resolving conflicts between individuals.
5. Team decisions tend to be more reliable than individual decisions.
6. Participation in teams is a developmental experience that helps individuals learn the skills of planning, setting objectives, controlling activities, budgeting time, solving problems, and soliciting other people's participation.[29]

A team-building effort, to be effective, must be preceded by an OD intervention that includes problem identification, data gathering and analysis,

## Table 14–3  The Team-Building Process

Identification of the problem by all members of the team.

Gathering of data by all available means and methods, including survey-feedback instruments.

Diagnosis of the problem by analyzing the data, determining problem areas, establishing priorities, and developing preliminary recommendations.

Development of an action plan based on the data gathered. The plan should include identification of what should be changed, who is responsible, and a timetable for completion of the effort.

Evaluation of the developmental effort by all of the participants.

---

diagnosis, action planning, implementation, and evaluation.[30] Table 14–3 identifies the sequence and shows how each phase relates to the others.

Team-building work is noteworthy for the high level of participation it requires. Generally, a change agent takes part in the initial steps of the process, but his or her role can be lessened as the team becomes more cohesive and trusting relationships are established. Key factors affecting the success of a team-building endeavor are the changing composition of teams and the continuing need to integrate new personnel into them.[31] In some departments annual personnel turnover (e.g., transfers, retirements, resignations) exceeds 10 percent, so teams continually evolve and may need change agents to work with them over extended periods.

During initial sessions of the team-building process, it is usually beneficial for members of the team to clarify member roles and responsibilities. The change agent should serve as a catalyst and a resource person as goals are established and the team process is analyzed.[32]

Team strengths and weaknesses should be identified and a list of changes compiled. Differing perceptions should be resolved and priorities established. As the diagnosis phase progresses, the training sessions should become increasingly task oriented, with special techniques taught to those who need them in order to deal with the problems identified. Once this skills training is complete, the way the team is performing can be analyzed in an effort to improve the process and maximize effectiveness.

Team building should emphasize teaching individuals how to take their share of team responsibilities so that they can participate in consensual decision-making. In addition, members should be brought to a point where they have a minimal level of relationship skills to accompany their requisite technical knowledge.[33]

Through the team-building process, members learn on the job and become viable parts of the team. Their newly acquired technical, managerial, and interpersonal knowledge makes them more competent as individuals, which in turn improves the team's ability to succeed in accomplishing its tasks.

Team building is most successful when it is an ongoing process. It should never be used as a one-shot operation. Regular training sessions can serve to energize and motivate team members. As new problems are identified, team members get opportunities to grow and respond to new challenges.

**Survey Feedback**

An intervention technique being given increased attention is survey feedback. This involves collecting data from the department through an internal survey, then feeding it back to organization members and groups in a series of meetings convened to identify actions that can correct problems and improve the department.

The survey-feedback method can be used as part of a team-building effort, but when used independently it focuses on the collection of valid data rather than on interpersonal processes. To be totally effective, the surveys must be totally factual and task oriented, with support (and preliminary planning involvement) from top management. Surveys are an excellent way of collecting unbiased officer feedback, including attitudes, beliefs, perceptions, and opinions that cannot be obtained through any other process.[34]

Survey feedback has proven to be most useful when surveys are periodically administered and results are compared from one year to the next. Generally, cost considerations require the change agent to use questionnaires rather than conduct structured interviews with each member of the organization. Most questionnaires ask members for their perceptions and attitudes on a wide range of topics such as communication and decision-making.[35]

Some consultants use prepackaged survey instruments; others design a special instrument for each agency. One standardized survey instrument that can be used to determine the current management style of a police department concerns itself with the following variables:

1. Leadership.
2. Motivation.
3. Communication.
4. Decisions.
5. Goals.
6. Interaction.
7. Control.

Police departments are often described as rigid bureaucracies run by managers who have no confidence in subordinates. Compliance is expected; if necessary, it will be gained by creating an atmosphere of fear with a liberal use of punishment. We can describe this management style as exploitative authoritative (System 1).

One study of police organizations used the standardized survey instrument mentioned earlier to survey 171 officers who were students attending the National Academy of the Federal Bureau of Investigation. Of that number, 83 percent had a college degree or were currently enrolled in a college program. The same officers were surveyed two years later. A comparison of the responses showed that the agencies represented had moved from the upper part of System 2 (benevolent authoritative) to close to the midpoint of System 3 (consultative). Of the eight dimensions measured, the three showing the greatest change were communication, training, and decision-making. This suggests that over the two-year period the departments surveyed had become more open.[36]

Feedback is an essential ingredient of the survey process. It is most effective when done face-to-face. Merely to summarize the data and distribute the results to each participant defeats the whole process. Positive participation, in small groups such as a team of officers or a special unit, is the key. It is also best to have the immediate supervisor of the team or unit conduct the meeting in order to demonstrate interest in the data and commitment to the collection effort.

The change agent should help the manager prepare for the feedback meeting by reviewing the data, suggesting techniques to be used to stimulate discussion, and pointing out how problems can be identified and solved. The change agent can attend meetings and serve as a resource both for the manager and for the other participants.[37]

The meetings should move from analysis to action. Managers should be especially careful not to get bogged down in minutiae. After thoroughly discussing the issues and identifying problems, participants should develop action plans. These plans should include follow-up procedures to see if the desired results are actually attained. One follow-up method is to administer an additional questionnaire, possibly one year later, in order to measure any changes.

## Confrontation Meeting

One means of determining the health of an organization is through a confrontation meeting that involves the total management group of a police organization. A key factor in the effectiveness of such a meeting is how inclusive it is: specialists strongly recommend that the chief executive include first-line supervisors among the attendees. Also critical is commitment on the part of the chief executive to solve a problem. Confrontation need not be very time-consuming—the initial meeting usually takes only one day.

A confrontation meeting has six specific steps (see Table 14–4). At the beginning of the meeting, the chief sets the tone by inviting everyone to express an opinion about the issues under consideration but to focus on issues, not personalities. (If a consultant is used, he or she can address ground rules for problem analysis and resolution.) This tone setting is a key step, which can make or break the confrontation effort; the chief should reinforce it as needed throughout the meeting.

The second step in the one-day meeting is to divide the group into teams of no more than ten members. Each team should include a mix of managers representing different units within the department; the top executives in the organization should meet separately. The major topic of discussion should be the overall health of the organization, including such subjects as morale, job satisfaction, departmental policies, goal achievement, organizational structure, and communication.

After the information is collected by the smaller team, the entire group reconvenes for Step 3, and recorders from each team present the results of their meetings. Normally the chief will combine the items presented by recorders into groups such as leadership, motivation, communication, decision-making, goal attainment, or policy.

The fourth step is most critical—setting priorities and establishing an action plan. The list of items developed in Step 3 is distributed to all involved, and the attendees are divided into normal work groups such as patrol, investigations,

Table 14–4 **Steps in a Confrontation Meeting**

1. Tone setting
2. Information gathering
3. Information sharing
4. Plan development
5. Follow-up by police executive managers
6. Evaluation

traffic, juvenile, and administration. Each group discusses the problem areas and identifies potential situations with which top management will have to deal. Solutions can then be addressed by individual units.

After the confrontation meeting, the top managers in the department meet to discuss what they have learned and to determine what follow-up activities should be taken. The sixth and final step is a progress report, which is typically prepared between one and six months after the confrontation meeting.

The confrontation meeting is most useful in law enforcement. It is inexpensive, practical, responsive, and results oriented. It is an excellent method for determining organizational health and dealing with organizational problems. It opens channels of communication, involves key personnel, and generates a commitment to getting something done.[38]

Quality of work life (QWL) programs are designed to address employee productivity and job satisfaction. QWL is a process used by some organizations in response to employee needs for a share in making the decisions that design their lives at work.[39]

**Quality of Work Life (QWL) Programs**

QWL programs focus on employees in the following areas:

1. Reasonable compensation and fringe benefits.
2. Job security.
3. A safe and healthful work environment.
4. Recognition for achievement through promotion, pay, or other rewards.
5. Due process in the settlement of grievances, separation, and other work-related problems.
6. Participation in decision-making.
7. Some responsibility for, and autonomy in, the immediate work process.
8. Flexible time arrangements such as flextime or the compressed work-week.
9. Emphasis on education, training, and career development.
10. Use of non-bureaucratic forms of work organization.
11. Consideration of social aspects of life on the job.
12. Open communication and adequate feedback.
13. Recognition of the competing demands of work, family, community, and leisure.
14. Redesign of work.[40]

As can be seen in this list, QWL is a very broad concept. Like other OD efforts, QWL programs should be tailored to the specific needs of each police department. This can only be done after a careful diagnosis of the problems unique to that department.

If there is a police union or association, it should be involved in the design and implementation of the program. Otherwise, there is always a possibility that the implementation phase will run into obstacles. It is also essential that plans, once developed, are followed through to completion. Table 14–5 sets out numerous steps managers can take to create working environments that allow employees to increase their job knowledge and fulfill the responsibilities of their positions. Any or all of these may be effective parts of a QWL program.

**Table 14–5  Steps for Improving QWL Programs**

1. Hold meetings with each officer in order to discuss individual skills and goals.
2. Develop a specific plan for each employee that will result in acquiring new skills.
3. Be sure a manager is readily available to meet with employees.
4. Create problem-solving teams that have the responsibility to develop solutions to pressing problems.
5. Review proposals made by problem-solving teams.
6. Reward proven effective performers.
7. Place a notation in the officer's personnel file, when a job is well done.
8. Reward outstanding performance by giving officers special assignments that require the application of special skills.
9. Let people know when they are doing a good job.

The humanistic focus of QWL programs is evident, and researchers have found that the interests of individuals are definitely compatible with organizational interests. When conflicts arise, what is needed is a joint effort between management and employees to understand the issues involved and work toward resolving them. QWL programs tailored to specific organizations have proven to be effective in improving the organizations' overall efficiency.

## SUCCESSFUL IMPLEMENTATION OF OD PROGRAMS

Some OD efforts have been highly successful, but others have failed. The reason for failure varies, so it is definitely more fruitful to review the essential factors for success. First, management must accept the fact that the organization has real problems that must be solved satisfactorily, not carelessly (or deliberately) overlooked. OD efforts are always time-consuming and usually expensive, so they should be considered only when an organization has a problem OD can fix. Police managers should not commission OD projects just because other departments have tried them, but when there is a sense that their organization is not as effective as it could be, they should give OD serious consideration.

Another important characteristic of a successful OD effort is the use of an external change agent, since internal change agents seldom have the equivalent skills and knowledge. Many times, internal personnel have axes to grind, or they are not capable of looking at the big picture. Generally, someone outside the organization is in an exceptional position to gain the support of top management. This is especially true if the external change agent has an excellent track record and his or her credentials are impeccable. An OD effort has a greater potential for success when top management clearly is committed to the program. When top management gives only lip service to an OD program, it is, without a doubt, destined to fail. Managers must not only support the OD in principle, they must become directly involved in the OD effort.

The involvement of top managers in the OD effort sends a direct signal to lower-level managers that the program is important and should be supported by everyone. Managers at all levels must work to improve the effectiveness of the organization. Management must address resistance to change by encouraging those who are participants in the change process;

they should reward organization members who make significant contributions to the OD effort.

Managers should also take a holistic view of the organization and the OD effort. Barriers between subunits should be overcome and the traditional competition between organizational units should be replaced with a working environment that stresses cooperation.

An OD effort will have a better chance of attaining its goal if there is some success during the early stages. This demonstrates to those involved that positive change can occur, and it serves to motivate employees. Without such encouragement, the program has a tendency to bog down. The change agent should deliberately design the OD effort in such a way that early successes are inevitable.

Another characteristic of a successful OD effort is open and continuous communication. As uncertainties and ambiguities arise, they must be responded to with facts readily available to everyone. Rumors should be responded to immediately, and a premium should be placed on the accuracy of information disseminated. During a period of rapid change, every manager should be especially sensitive to the problems created by uncertainty; the watchword should be "Always communicate."

---

## CASE STUDY  Robert Proctor

Robert Proctor became the chief of police after serving 12 years in the department. He replaced a chief who ran the department in a highly autocratic manner, causing departmental morale to reach an all-time low. Proctor assumed his position with widespread organizational support. It is well known that he was as frustrated as the other officers with the authoritarian style of his predecessor.

In his first 2 years as chief, Proctor reorganized the department and added three new captain-level positions to it. Each captain is assigned as the commander of a major unit. Altogether there have been 14 promotions because of personnel changes. During the next 3 plus years of Chief Proctor's tenure, the department added 27 new positions to bring the sworn strength up to 92 positions. (This increase was commensurate with population growth within the city.)

The rapid growth of the department is not without difficulties. The large influx of new officers, along with the many other personnel changes, has caused dissatisfaction among the older patrol officers. The older officers have an average length of service of 11 years and have all been passed over for promotion to sergeant. The frustration this caused was compounded because all six sergeants in the patrol division have assumed their positions within the last few years and are still feeling their way as supervisors.

The newly hired officers are well educated and goal oriented, and they find all the new changes exciting. They appreciate the opportunity to be really involved. However, as a group the younger officers resent the inability of the sergeants to perform effectively; they feel they are not being given the necessary guidance for doing their jobs.

The older officers resent the enthusiasm of the newer officers and feel threatened. There is clearly a we/they schism beginning to hamper the performance of the unit. Capt. Robert Quick (commander of the patrol division) consulted with Chief Proctor and the two agreed that the first-line supervisors need to improve their managerial skills. There is also a need for improving interdepartmental harmony. After hearing the situation described in detail, the chief said that both problems had to be addressed.

It is apparent to all that something should be done as soon as possible to resolve the two problems. Funding has been approved, and a behavioral scientist has been brought in to help.

*The consultant recommends that everyone in the organization complete a questionnaire to be used for determining the exact nature of the problem. An OD effort can then be designed. As the chief, would you suggest using the instrument entitled "Diagnose Your Management"? How would you want to use it? Do you think a confrontation meeting would be helpful? Why or why not?*

# SUMMARY

Organizational development (OD) is a widely accepted method of applying the behavioral sciences to solve organizational problems. It is a normative, goal-oriented managerial process.

OD assumptions about people in organizations are genuinely optimistic and call for managers to be humanistic and participative. One of the primary objectives of an OD effort is to develop the organization to the point where the culture is based on openness and trust—the first of four key OD values.

Feedback is a second important value in OD. Police managers can use a variety of techniques, including personal discussions, written communications, group meetings, and questionnaires to improve communication.

A third important value of OD is that conflict, rather than being avoided at all costs, should be dealt with constructively and turned into something positive.

The fourth important OD value is risk taking. When mistakes are made by subordinates, the mistakes must be turned into learning situations. Officers must be allowed to grow as they accept increasing amounts of responsibility; they should not be punished for exercising the power needed to accomplish a task.

When OD is successful, the organization becomes healthier and more responsive to the community it serves. A healthy police department encourages every employee to develop to the maximum, so that goals can be attained by the most effective means. The changes brought about by an OD effort are viewed with optimism and accepted as an inevitable consequence of striving to become more effective.

Various intervention techniques exist for changing organizations and influencing the behavior of individuals and groups. No matter which technique is selected, using it to alter the working environment will follow a set pattern of steps.

These steps include diagnosis, planning, training, and evaluation.

One of the intervention techniques used extensively is sensitivity training. It can help increase interpersonal awareness as a means of integrating individuals into the organization. Sensitivity training has both supporters and detractors, but it has proven effective when introduced into an organization by a competent change agent.

Another intervention technique, team building, involves both managers and employees. Emphasis is placed on interpersonal relations (as in other techniques), but special attention is given to the tasks to be performed. Team building is most successful when it is an ongoing process. It should never be a one-shot procedure.

Survey feedback is a widely used technique. It involves collecting data from the department and then holding a series of meetings to feed the data back to organization members and groups, with the intent of identifying corrective action.

Another means of determining the health of an organization is through the confrontation meeting. Such meetings are most useful in law enforcement. They are inexpensive, practical, responsive, and results oriented. They involve key personnel and open channels of communication, and they generate a commitment to getting something done.

Quality of working life (QWL) programs are comprehensive efforts that emphasize the need for improving employee productivity and job satisfaction. QWL programs have a humanistic focus and are based on the premise that the interest of each employee is definitely compatible with organizational interests.

Some OD programs have proven to be highly successful, but others have failed. Success seems to reflect top management support, the use of external change agents, and the issue of whether the managers have a holistic view of the organization and the OD effort.

# KEY TERMS

confrontation meeting
confronting conflict
diagnosis
evaluation
feedback

healthy organization
openness and trust
organizational development (OD)
planning
quality of work life (QWL) programs

risk taking
sensitivity training
survey feedback

team building
training

# DISCUSSION TOPICS AND QUESTIONS

1. What are the objectives of a major OD effort?

2. Discuss the importance of the OD assumption that people in an organization want to participate in the decision-making process.

3. How and when should managers take risks when involved in an OD effort?

4. Compare sensitivity training and the confrontation meeting.

5. What would limit the effective use of team building as a training technique?

6. How should a police manager use survey feedback?

7. Discuss the relationship between managers and line officers when developing a QWL program.

# FOR FURTHER READING

Fred R. Davis, *Strategic Management: Concepts and Cases* (Upper Saddle River, NJ: Prentice Hall, 1999).

This excellent text gives a thorough introduction to strategic management.

W. L. French and C. H. Bell, Jr., *Organizational Development: Behavioral Science Interventions for Organization Improvement* (Upper Saddle River, NJ.: Prentice Hall, 1995).

This excellent publication describes the methods and techniques used in the practice of OD. Of special interest are the discussions of such OD intervention techniques as team building, survey feedback, and grid organizational development. There is also a very good discussion of the history of OD.

# NOTES

1. Fred R. Davis, *Strategic Management: Concepts and Cases* (Upper Saddle River, NJ: Prentice Hall, 1999), p. 5.

2. Ramon J. Aldag and Loren W. Kuzuhara, *Organizational Behavior and Management* (Cincinnati: South-Western, 2002), p. 489.

3. Stephen P. Robbins, *Essentials of Organizational Behavior* (Upper Saddle River, NJ: Prentice Hall, 2000), pp. 261–264.

4. J.P. Kotter and L.A. Schlesinger, "Choosing Strategies for Change," *Harvard Business Review* (March–April 1979), pp. 106–114.

5. Jay W. Lorsch, ed. *Handbook of Organizational Behavior* (Englewood Cliffs, NJ.: Prentice Hall, 1987).

6. Charles R. Swanson, Leonard Territo, and Robert Taylor, *Police Administration: Structures, Processes and Behavior* (Upper Saddle River, NJ: 2005), pp. 768–769.

7. John Kotter and Dan Cohen, *The Heart of Change* (Boston: Harvard Business School Press, 2002).

8. John W. Newstrom and Keith Davis, *Organizational Behavior: Human Behavior at Work* (New York: McGraw-Hill, 1993), p. 301.

9. V.A. Leonard and Harry W. More, *Police Organization and Management* (New York: Foundation Press, 2000), p. 230.

10. William G. Dyer, *Contemporary Issues in Management and Organizational Development* (Reading, MA: Addison-Wesley, 1991), p. 34.

11. Michael Hammer and James Champy, *Reengineering the Corporation* (New York: HarperCollins, 1993), pp. 125–126.

12. Leonard and More, *Police Administration and Management*, p. 231.

13. Lee G. Bolman and Terrence E. Deal, *Reframing Organizations: Artistry, Choice, and Leadership* (San Francisco: Jossey-Bass), pp. 183–204.

14. Lyman K. Randall, "Common Questions and Tentative Answers Regarding Organizational Development," *California Management Review,* Vol. 72 (1984), pp. 45–52.

15. Gerard H. Gaynor, *Innovation by Design: How to Keep Your Company on the Cutting Edge* (New York: AMACOM, 2002).

16. Leonard and More, *Police Administration and Management,* p. 133.

17. P.M. Senge, "Sharing Knowledge," *Executive Excellence* (September 1999), pp. 6–7.

18. Steve Buchholz and Thomas Roth, *Creating the High Performance Team* (New York: John Wiley & Sons, 1987).

19. M. Beer, *Organizational Change and Development: A Systems View* (Santa Monica, CA: Goodyear, 1980).

20. W.L. French and C.H. Bell, Jr., *Organizational Development: Behavioral Science Interventions for Organization Improvement* (Upper Saddle River, NJ: Prentice Hall, 1995), p. 171.

21. Bolman and Deal, *Reframing Organizations,* pp. 281–283.

22. Gary Dessler, *Management* (Upper Saddle River, NJ: Prentice Hall, 2004), pp. 240–242.

23. For a discussion of the evaluation process currently being used by many police organizations see: Eli Silverman, *NYPD Battles Crime: Innovative Strategies in Policing* (Boston: Northeastern University Press, 1999) and William Bratton, *Turnaround* (New York: Random House, 1998).

24. Newstrom and Davis, *Organizational Behavior: Human Behavior at Work,* p. 303.

25. Paul M. Muchinsky, *Psychology Applied to Work* (Pacific Grove, CA: Brooks/Cole, 1990), p. 213.

26. French and Bell, *Organizational Development,* pp. 171–193.

27. Gary Johns and Alan M. Saks, *Organizational Behavior: Understanding and Managing Life at Work* (Upper Saddle River, NJ: Prentice Hall, 2000).

28. John R. Schermerhorn, Jr., James G. Hunt, and Richard N. Osborn, *Organizational Behavior* (New York: John Wiley & Sons, 1997), p. 196.

29. Aldag and Kuzuhara, *Organizational Behavior,* p. 562.

30. Schermerhorn, Hunt, and Osborn, *Organizational Behavior,* p. 197.

31. C. Johnson, "Teams at Work," *HR Magazine,* Vol. 44 (1999), pp. 30–36.

32. Robbins, *Essentials of Organizational Behavior,* p. 112.

33. A.V. Carron and L.R. Brawley, "Cohesion: Conceptual and Measurement Issues," *Small Group Research,* Vol. 31 (2000), pp. 89–106.

34. Bureau of Justice Assistance, *A Police Guide to Surveying Citizen and Their Environment* (Washington, DC: National Institute of Justice, 1993), p. 8.

35. Robbins, *Essentials of Organizational Behavior,* p. 265.

36. Gerald W.J. Shanahan, David Hunger, and Thomas L. Wheelen, "Organizational Profile of Police Agencies in the United States," *Journal of Police Science and Administration,* Vol. 7 (1979), pp. 31–38.

37. Swanson, Territo, and Taylor, *Police Administration,* pp. 760–765.

38. French and Bell, *Organizational Development,* pp. 17–21.

39. Robbins, *Essentials of Organizational Behavior,* p. 263.

40. R.E. Walton, "Improving the Quality of Work Life," *Harvard Business Review,* (May–June 1974), p. 12.

# 15

# MANAGERIAL ISSUES

## Considerations for Resolution

## LEARNING OBJECTIVES

1. Describe the current state of police unions.
2. List the types of police unions prevailing in many police departments.
3. Identify five typical categories included in a memorandum of agreement or memorandum of understanding.
4. Identify the key elements of collective bargaining.
5. List three typical managerial rights.
6. Describe three steps when utilizing formal review.
7. Identify the four terms that help to ensure that minorities are not tested out of equal opportunity.
8. Describe the concept of affirmative action.
9. Describe a typical minority-recruiting program based on quota.
10. Describe the reasonable officer standard.
11. Identify the types of brutality committed against civilians by the police.
12. List the problems that women police officers face in their employment.
13. Identify four types of sexual discrimination.
14. Write a short essay describing a hostile work environment.
15. Contrast validity and reliability.

It is widely recognized by contemporary police managers that the scope and complexity of police administration are increasing rapidly. Urbanization, emigration, technological advances, a large youth population, a changing morality, a more educated populace, a greater use of drugs, and the changing nature of crime (which has in recent years come to include identity theft, computer fraud, white-collar crime, financial crime, and gang activity) are all factors changing the way police managers function. A few years back nobody could have imagined that law enforcement would soon be dealing with Russian gangs or threats from Al-Qaida terrorists. Other new challenges to law enforcement include increasing numbers of anti–free trade riots protesting against World Trade Organization meetings and increased violence perpetrated by animal rights groups. In numerous communities, especially on the West Coast, the ethnic mix has changed dramatically and the police find

Bud Fredrickson is a newly appointed sergeant in the patrol division of Mountain Township Police Department. The city covers an area of 18 square miles and may be described as a bedroom suburb located 20 miles from a major metropolitan area. Mountain Township has three major shopping areas and a population of 47,523. The police department has 54 sworn officers. There are 33 officers in the patrol division.

Sgt. Fredrickson supervises a team of seven patrol officers. He graduated from a local community college with a degree in criminal justice and for the past three years he been attending a four-year college part-time. He is married and has two children. He joined the department at the age of 21 and received a promotion to sergeant after just three years. He is the youngest supervisor in the history of the department and has held his current position for nine months. Needless to say, this has generated some animosity from officers with greater longevity who were passed over on the promotion list. He completed the police supervisory course of 80 hours, graduating first in his class. He strives diligently to prove himself and tries his best to lessen "bitching" by performing to the best of his ability. During the last few months, criticism has lessened considerably.

Traditionally, all of the supervisory officers in the department belong to the police union; Fredrickson joined the union when he joined the force, and he is still a member. The current negotiation between Mountain Township and the police union has broken down, and officers are working without a contract. The union has been discussing what should be done to break the impasse. They have considered such measures as the "blue flu" (a work slowdown) or an actual strike. The state in which Mountain Township is located does not provide for collective bargaining,

and strikes are prohibited. Consequently, the relationship between the city and the union is limited to negotiation in an attempt to reach a mutual agreement. Independently of the union, the department's officers have reached the point of being ready to walk off the job.

Sgt. Fredrickson has very strong personal ties with many of the line officers, but he considers himself a part of management. The city's administration has made a serious effort to separate supervisory positions from the union. A number of officers have been talking with sergeants in the department in an effort to get them to walk out, but so far they have not been successful.

Fredrickson feels the officers are being treated unfairly. For years, Mountain Township's administration has ignored the needs of police officers, in terms of not only salary and benefits but also equipment. For example, most of the department's vehicles have been driven more than 100,000 miles, radios are antiquated, and protective vests have never been provided.

Officers in Mountain Township Police Department are poorly paid—the base salary is 22 percent under the amount paid to officers who work for the nearby metropolitan police department. The department loses eight officers each year primarily because of the low pay.

Officers have now scheduled a strike. They intend to leave town and stay in a motel in an adjacent state. This action will make it difficult for the local court to serve a restraining order.

*If you were Sgt. Fredrickson, would you go on strike? Explain your position. Should any officer be allowed to go on strike? Why? Would a state law providing for collective bargaining alleviate such problems?*

themselves dealing with people from numerous cultures. Law enforcement is very different from what it was in the past, when communities were smaller and neighborhoods were cohesive. Another facet of the problem is that because of rapid urbanization, many people do not know their immediate neighbors. In some cities, community policing has worked at reducing the gap between citizens and police departments, but there are many communities across the nation where a great deal of work still has to be done.

Internally, police managers in medium-sized to large agencies currently face challenges requiring increased sensitivity, flexibility, and responsiveness to a rapidly changing organization. Successful managers must accept change within the organization as inevitable. In fact, change must be viewed as a challenge, not as a problem. Other important challenges today for police managers are centered on themes that include:

1. Labor relations
2. Use of force
3. Women officers
4. Discrimination

The nature and extent of each of these challenges vary considerably from city to city. Many of them are not new, and they have been handled with varying degrees of success in the past. One of the themes, the use of force, is a perennial problem. Some segments of some communities use each use-of-force situation as a means of opposing law enforcement and promoting their own political agendas. This is not to suggest that the police have not been wrong in some instances, but one must acknowledge that political rhetoric is rampant. Certainly protest is not new, but it is becoming increasingly sophisticated: the World Wide Web is now frequently used as a vehicle for immediately gathering protest support. Individual incidents that disrupt the tranquility of neighborhoods will become more common as special-interest groups take advantage of use-of-force incidents to generate support for their agenda. At this point in time, it seems likely that issues like those listed above will become increasingly complex problems for local and state law enforcement agencies in the decade ahead—with strong potential to transform those agencies. This is especially true if discrimination is not lessened and police unions become more militant.

## LABOR AND MANAGEMENT

It was almost half a century ago that labor relations became a concern to law enforcement administrators. Since then a majority of the states have passed legislation that allows public employees to participate in collective bargaining.[1] This is very different from earlier times, when unions had no legal standing and were vehemently opposed by business. Today such terms as collective bargaining, bargaining unit, grievance procedures, negotiation tactics, and memorandum of understanding/agreement have become integral parts of the working environment in which administrators find themselves. In a recent study of police agencies with 100 or more sworn officers, 39 percent of the responding agencies reported that they allowed membership in non-police unions, 51 percent (422 out of 831) had police unions, and 88 percent had police associations.[2]

Police managers have an increasingly important part to play in critical aspects of labor relations. In agencies where police managers have demonstrated a continuing interest in the welfare of employees, unions have found limited support. On the other hand, the poor management practices of many law enforcement administrators have almost forced officers to join police unions.[3] Reasons for organizing police unions vary from agency to agency, but in most instances one or more of the following situations apply:[4]

1. Unsatisfactory working conditions
2. Limited opportunity for advancement
3. Lack of a grievance procedure
4. Poor compensation or benefits
5. Limited or nonexistent opportunity to be heard

6. Lack of recognition
7. Meager communication
8. Lack of political clout
9. Excessive turnover of personnel
10. Inadequate equipment
11. Authoritarian management
12. Inadequate means of redress

When line personnel faced with intolerable working conditions, inadequate compensation, or other grievances that are ignored by management have nowhere else to turn, they reach out to internal or external representation (associations or unions). Without question, weak or inadequate management creates a climate that causes officers to try to solve their problems through special-interest groups.[5]

Unions that become an integral part of a police organization deal with a wide variety of issues, depending on the needs and desires of their membership. For example, the Los Angeles Police Protective League (LAPPL) recently supported two bills in the State of California legislature that would block access by managers to complaint records. The police commission and the chief of police strongly opposed the bills. The governor vetoed one of the bills, which would have allowed an officer to delete unfounded complaints from his or her personnel file, but he signed the other bill, which allowed the deletion of "frivolous" complaints.[6] On the other side of the nation, 2,500 Massachusetts police officers recently rallied at the State Capitol in opposition to a bill that would eliminate bonuses for police personnel who earned college degrees. The Massachusetts House later restored funds that would give officers bonuses amounting to 10–24 percent of their base salary for becoming better educated.[7] During the same period the International Brotherhood of Police Officers (IBPO) took a union case to the New Hampshire State Supreme Court. The court sided with the union in a decision that extended employee rights to probationary employees. A probationary police officer, who was a staunch union supporter, had been terminated; he was reinstated with almost three years of back pay and benefits.[8] In another instance a group of LAPD officers said at a press conference that they believed the Teamsters Union would represent them better than LAPPL (which had represented police officers for 76 years and currently represents 8,800 officers). Their reasons for wanting to shift their affiliation to the Teamsters included:[9]

1. *Strong contract.* The LAPD has suffered attrition, as officers have left it for suburban departments that offer better wages and benefits.
2. *Political influence.* The Teamsters have the nation's largest political action committee and maintain extensive relationships with elected officials at all levels of government.
3. *Experience.* The Teamsters represent officers at 297 police departments in 19 states.

While the LAPD ultimately did not shift to the Teamsters, the incident does illustrate how seriously some officers take the topic of union representation. It should be noted that over the years the LAPPL has been very vocal and political, and it has taken very strong positions on issues of interest to its membership. In 2000, the League supported the need for a civilian review board to oversee critical areas of the department's internal investigations. They called for improving the system for investigating personnel complaints against officers. A city councilwoman responded, "That's a historic first, and a welcome one."[10] In recent years, increasing numbers of benevolent associations have become affiliated with more traditional private-sector unions such as the AFL-CIO and the Teamsters. For example, the AFL-CIO has chartered its first police union affiliate, the International Union of Police Associations (IUPA). Although IUPA's exact membership is not publicly known, it is believed to exceed 80,000 police officers. According to best estimates, there are more than 40,000 police officers affiliated with the Teamsters.

The largest police labor organization in the United States is the Fraternal Order of Police (FOP), which has a membership of 310,000 (see Table 15–1). It functions as a fraternal organization for the most part, but some of its local units serve as bargaining units. In addition, the FOP continually updates its membership on the Fair Labor Standards Act and has produced a booklet on collective bargaining. It also conducts labor and grievance seminars from its national office. Like many such organizations, it sponsors a legal fund and an insurance program for its members. In all probability, the most important function performed by the national office of the FOP is its political involvement, which includes formal lobbying of Congress and other legislative bodies.[11]

One study that involved, among other things, a review of police unions in larger cities made several interesting comments:[12]

1. *New York City.* The 29,000-member Patrolmen's Benevolent Association and other police unions and fraternal organizations enjoy a great deal of power.
2. *Minneapolis.* The Police Federation is very strong, and its president has a very high profile in the city.
3. *Portland, Oregon.* The Police Association union is very powerful, according to attorneys, community activists, and press reports.
4. *Philadelphia.* The Fraternal Order of Police is exceptionally powerful—some say it has more control of the police than the police commissioner does.

Clearly, some police unions and associations in their relatively short history have solidified their positions in the community and become "movers and

Table 15–1 **Police Labor Organizations**

| *Unit* | *Number of Members* |
| --- | --- |
| Fraternal Order of Police (FOP) | 310,000 |
| International Union of Police Associations (IUPA) | 80,000 |
| Teamsters | 40,000 |
| National Troopers Coalition | 17,000 |
| International Brotherhood of Police Officers (IBPO) | 300,000 |
| Peace Officers Research Association (PORAC) | 55,000 |
| American Federation of State, County, and Municipal Employees (AFSCME) | 24,000 |
| Patrolmen's Benevolent Association (NYC) | 29,000 |
| Los Angeles Police Protective League | 8,000 |

shakers." They have clearly been adroit at maximizing their political clout. No one should underestimate the power of police unions.[13] With the growth of police unions and benevolent associations, it became increasingly common for municipalities to recognize the right of employees to join unions. In one city, an agreement stated the following:[14]

> Any employee in the City's competitive service may join, organize, or maintain membership in a labor organization if he/she so desires. The City neither encourages nor discourages these activities, nor does membership or non-membership in any labor organization affect the employment standing or right as a City employee. The rights to join, organize or maintain membership in a labor organization is also extended to any association of municipal employees not identified with any labor organization.

In recent years there has been significant growth in the number of rules governing the workplace. As police unions have evolved into meaningful units with considerable power and influence, conflicts have increasingly been resolved through negotiation or some type of mediation process. Management-labor relations govern almost every personnel action taking place in today's police organizations. Actions taken by managers and employees often reflect some aspect of prior labor-management agreements governing the relationship between the two parties.

**Memoranda of Understanding/ Agreement (MOU)**

In a number of agencies, settlements between labor and management are spelled out in documents called *memoranda of understandingt/agreement (MOU)* (see Table 15–2). From the table it is readily apparent that a broad range of categories can be included in a memorandum of understanding/agreement. Such agreements have replaced what in the past was viewed by some police officers as arbitrary and capricious management. On the other hand, many police chiefs view such agreements as reducing their managerial prerogatives. In most instances, the chief of police is excluded from the bargaining process, and the city manager or a designated representative will handle the negotiations. Some view it as wrong for the chief of police to be unable to participate in such a vital process.[15]

An appreciation of what constitutes a memorandum of understanding will allow both managers and union representatives to perform their roles more effectively. An MOU is defined as follows:[16]

> A written agreement reached by management and an employee organization reached through meet and confer procedures that concern wages, hours, or working conditions. The agreement may be submitted to the appropriate determining body or a government official for ratification and implementation.

The typical memorandum of understanding/agreement is a written agreement and generally has a term of from one to three years. In some states, a statute requires the negotiators to prepare a written memorandum:[17]

> If agreement is reached by the representatives of the public agency and a recognized employee organization or recognized employee organizations, they shall jointly prepare a written memorandum of such understanding.

Table 15–2  **Typical Categories Included in a Memorandum of Understanding/Agreement**

| | |
|---|---|
| Working hours | Overtime |
| City rights | Court time |
| Advance notice | Jury leave |
| Dental insurance | Light duty |
| Bereavement leaves | Educational incentive pay |
| Vacation pay | Uniform, maintenance, and salary training allowance |
| Sick leave benefits | |
| Longevity pay | Compensation for medical examinations |
| Family leave | |
| Military leave | Layoffs |
| Work out of class | Pay plan |
| Standby assignment | Notice to correct deficiencies |
| P.O.S.T. certificate bonus | Substance tests |
| Rights representation | Seniority for vacations |
| Employee rights | Life insurance |
| Marksmanship bonuses | Family illness |
| Health insurance | Compensation for firearms qualification |
| Holidays and holiday premiums | |
| Off duty–weekend and holiday premiums | Uniformed field officer |
| Bilingual pay | Police vehicles |
| No labor action | Incentive pay |
| Shift pay | Resignation |
| K-9 pay | |

Preparation to create an agreement requires those involved not only to consider the past but also to take into consideration new laws or ordinances and certainly new programs instituted since the last agreement.[18]

For example, in one community the MOU provides that if an employee is directed to participate in a training program that is related to his or her job, the city shall provide compensation for the following:[19]

1. Regular wages for time away from the job (if during working hours)
2. Overtime or compensatory time off whenever an employee's combined training time and work time exceed the regular assignment in a workweek
3. Costs of tuition and/or registration for the training
4. Reimbursement for authorized transportation costs to and from the training (e.g., mileage reimbursement) if an employee uses his or her personal automobile as allowed by the city
5. Compensable travel time when required by the Fair Labor Standards Act

**Managerial Rights**    When unions negotiate with management, they are usually concerned with such issues as pay, benefits, job security, time off, payment for court time, personal safety, and general fair treatment.[20] In some negotiations, a union might also be concerned with acquiring protection for union officials or administrative support and paid time off to enable them to perform their union duties. Negotiations over items like these become of special concern to police managers when it appears the union is intruding into what they consider managerial prerogatives or rights.[21] Typical rights a city would want to retain include:[22]

1. Planning, directing, and controlling all police operations, and setting departmental policy, goals, and objectives
2. Disciplining and firing employees and establishing disciplinary procedures
3. Determining work and performance standards
4. Determining staffing levels
5. Determining work schedules, tours of duty, and daily assignments
6. Determining transfer policies
7. Hiring employees and determining selection criteria
8. Promoting employees and determining promotion procedures
9. Determining standards of conduct for employees, both on and off duty
10. Educating and training employees and determining criteria and procedures
11. Contracting or subcontracting out for goods and services

In general, police unions are not interested in running departments, but some pushing and pulling is always liable to develop when administrative entities like unions and departments deal with each other. Managers sit on one side of the table and union representatives on the other. Because they are advocates for their respective positions, there is a constant interplay between them. In some instances, unions might deliberately present a proposal that obviously intrudes into managerial prerogatives and use it to bargain for something really wanted as part of a compromise settlement.[23] In some instances, police labor unions have made inroads into management territory by successfully negotiating such things as staffing levels and assignment to specific beats and shifts based on seniority.[24] In Pittsburgh, police officers select their own patrol zones, shifts, and partners based on seniority,[25] and it is not unusual to find two rookie officers working together in a high-crime area. In order to guard against such developments, some cities protect managerial rights by including in every agreement a catchall statement stipulating that all conditions and terms not specifically covered in the agreement are the exclusive province of management.[26] In any case, each manager within a police agency should be fully aware of appropriate managerial rights and prerogatives and guard them jealously in order to retain the ability to function effectively.

**Collective Bargaining**    *Collective bargaining* is a process through which an employees' bargaining agent, usually a union, and the governmental entity responsible for the police department negotiate a labor agreement that considers such things as hours of duty, salaries, and specific conditions of service. Interestingly enough, more than 90 percent of all union contracts emphasize the importance of worker seniority.[27] Both sides have an obligation to bargain, but there is nothing that requires either side to make a concession or accept a proposal. Currently, a majority of police agencies are governed by state laws that provide for collective bargaining, and many states have a Public Safety Officers' Bill of Rights that, among other things, defines the legal relationship between governmental units and employees. There are usually local ordinances that provide further guidance in this area. Some ordinances prescribe what subjects may and may not be negotiated by public employee unions, for example:[28]

1. *Mandatory subjects* clearly relate to working conditions and include such things as wages, hours, disability pay, and other terms of employment.
2. *Voluntary subjects* include such items as stress-reduction programs, health, and club memberships. Negotiators may choose to place these on the table for consideration; they can be accepted or rejected after negotiation.
3. *Illegal subjects* include such things as union shop agreements, binding arbitration, and the right to strike. Public employee bargaining laws specifically prohibit including such items in union negotiations.

The Commission on Accreditation for Law Enforcement Agencies (CALEA) has established a number of standards addressing collective bargaining. Their concern is for the disparity found among agencies that engage in such bargaining. Standard (24.1) includes the following:[29]

1. Establishment of a collective-bargaining team for the agency, with one person designated as the principal negotiator
2. Identification of the bargaining unit or units representing an agency's employees with which it will negotiate
3. Commitment by the agency to participate in good-faith bargaining with the duly recognized bargaining units representing its members
4. Commitment to abide by the ground rules for collective bargaining that arise out of the collective-bargaining process or labor arbitration
5. Commitment to abide, in both letter and spirit, by the negotiated labor agreement that has been signed by management and labor representatives, and ratified by the bargaining unit

A critique of collective bargaining in the police field strongly suggests it has been beneficial to both management and labor. In states with labor laws that encourage bargaining, the vast majority of communities involved in the process have rated it as a positive influence. Contrary to initial fears, unions are not running police departments, but informal or oral procedures have become more formal and contractual in nature.[30] In addition, collective bargaining has provided many police officers with more opportunities to participate in the decision-making process, and this aspect of collective bargaining should not be overlooked. It is a logical extension of the concept of participative management.

## The Negotiation Process

Unquestionably, the negotiation process in the police world is highly visible and receives a great deal of attention. The U.S. Bureau of the Census estimated that in one calendar year about one-half of the police officers in the United States were engaged in some type of negotiations.[31] The negotiations process replaces arbitrary rule making by chiefs of police, civil service commissions, and city managers or other city officials, and it allows for the joint resolution of issues. The initial process generally involves negotiation of a contract or memorandum of understanding to be in force for one to three years.[32] In many instances it is a matter of revising and updating a previous agreement rather than creating a brand-new one. Most labor negotiations result in a written contract that the city and union must live with until the next memorandum is placed under consideration.[33] Another type of negotiation, known as the *sidebar agreement,* involves issues not included in the original contract or memorandum of understanding. Such agreements are often needed because changes in the law or other considerations require more negotiation. Additional negotiation may also be needed to clarify an original memorandum of understanding so that provisions accurately reflect what should have been clear in the beginning. In other words, errors are made, something is left out and needs to be resolved, or a lack of understanding develops as the agreement is interpreted. Successful operation, in many instances, demands resolution because it is impossible to wait until the next time contract negotiation takes place.[34] There can sometimes be day-to-day negotiations between management and labor as the agreement is interpreted and as new problems occur. In addition, grievances have to be resolved and disciplinary cases handled.[35] Ordinarily, a law enforcement negotiation unit will consist of all the non-supervisory sworn personnel of an agency, but this varies considerably. One study found that a major problem in some departments is the inability of both management and labor to distinguish clearly which ranks belong to management and who is a member of the employee bargaining unit. At the extreme, there are jurisdictions where the bargaining unit includes everyone in the department, from the chief on down. In one community, the FOP represents all levels up to captain; in another, the union represents sergeants, lieutenants, and captains. There are cities where only line personnel are represented. Even more complex situations exist. In one agency there is one bargaining unit for lieutenants and below and another unit for command officers. It is not unheard of for a city to have to negotiate with three or four independent police unions. The most accurate summary would be that there is no rime or reason for the plethora of representation.[36]

It seems essential for management to include command personnel and all supervisory personnel as part of the management team. When management personnel belong to bargaining units, there is a tendency for them to look at many contract issues from the viewpoint of line personnel and identify with their needs rather than to take a management perspective. When supervisory personnel are part of management's team, they accept changes more readily, and it is more likely they will support management's perspective.[37] Another dilemma is the part the chief of police plays in the negotiation process. Some chiefs limit their participation to the implementation of the contract after it has been approved by all the interested parties. The role of the chief of police is most difficult in the equation of labor-management relations. The city controls the purse strings, leaving the chief to be concerned with managerial rights. The chief should represent community needs for a safe community by providing for a well-managed police force.[38] At the very least, the chief should serve as an adviser to management's negotiators. Expert input will alleviate many problems that may arise after an agreement has been approved by both sides.[39]

An additional concern for both management and the union is an adequate *grievance mechanism.* This is a formal process for dealing with disputes that may arise relevant to the interpretation or application of personnel ordinances or that concern any rule or regulation governing personnel practices or working conditions.[40] In a typical department, when an employee has a complaint, it should be brought to the immediate attention of his or her supervisor and a serious effort should be made to resolve the problem.[41] If the problem is not resolved, the employee has the right to discuss the issue with the supervisor's immediate superior. Again, every effort should be made to work out a mutually acceptable agreement. If this cannot be done and the employee does not agree with the decision, a formal written appeal should be submitted within 15 days after the initial presentation of the grievance.[42] Following are steps that might typically be required when an employee requests a *formal review:*

## Grievances

> *Step 1.* The employee and/or representative shall explain the situation to the employee's immediate supervisor, who shall render a decision within three working days.
>
> *Step 2.* If the grievance is not settled at the first step, the employee and/or representative may submit the grievance to the department head in writing and/or verbally if necessary. The department head shall notify the employee and the employee's representative of the decision in writing within two working days.
>
> *Step 3.* If the grievance is not settled at the second step, the employee may, within three working days, submit the grievance to the city manager. The city manager shall notify the employee, the department head, and the employee's immediate supervisor of the decision within two days.

Grievances should be resolved at the lowest possible organizational level. It is essential for police managers to adopt a problem-solving approach (extending beyond the immediate resolution of each grievance) in an effort to identify more broadly based actions management should take. This should involve attempting to find answers to the following questions:[43]

1. Is there a need for changes in policies, procedures, rules, regulations, or contract provisions?
2. Is there a need to provide managers with additional training?
3. Is there a need for providing officers with additional training?
4. Is there either a localized or a widespread supervisory problem?
5. Is there a problem attributable to employee misunderstanding of an operational need?

These and similar questions can provide managers with information that, in many instances, can be used to prevent future problems and improve the organization's capacity to respond to emerging problems.[44]

# DISCRIMINATION

Our melting-pot society is changing rapidly. Currently the majority of our citizens are Caucasian; 12.8 percent are African-American and 11.8 percent are Hispanic. These figures will alter significantly in the next 20 years, during which the Census Bureau expects Hispanics to account for 25 percent of the nation's population growth. Even without immigration (legal and illegal) over the next century, the Hispanic population is expected to increase at twice the national rate. A recent study pointed out that more than 90 percent of the growth in the U.S. labor market in the near future will be among minorities and women; only 8 percent will be Caucasian males. This means that minorities and women will be recruited increasingly by police departments, because there will be fewer Caucasian males in the potential recruitment pool.

The presence of many different ethnic groups within the workplace creates the possibility for discrimination against minority employees. (An individual is considered a member of a minority group if the group to which he or she belongs is smaller than other dominant groups in a society.) An individual is discriminated against if he or she is denied treatment or opportunities equivalent to those afforded to members of the dominant group. Discrimination can be manifested in policies related to recruitment, promotion, job assignment, training, or other work-related privileges.[45] Historically, law enforcement agencies have been particularly vulnerable to accusations of discrimination in the area of selection and recruitment: entry requirements not especially related to the actual job to be performed have allowed agencies to tilt their hiring in the direction of non-minority members.[46] Some minority groups, such as African-Americans, Hispanics, Asians, Pacific Islanders, Native Eskimos, and Native Americans may appear to be easily identifiable. Other less obvious minorities, such as those of a different sexual orientation, may also be discriminated against. While the the U.S. Equal Employment Opportunity Commission (EEOC) does not enforce the protections that prohibit discrimination and harassment based on sexual orientation, some state and local agencies do.[47] It should be kept in mind that the civil rights of everyone must be protected, as decreed by Title VII of the Civil Rights Act of 1964, United States Code § 2000-e2[a][1]:[48]

> It shall be an unlawful employment practice for an employer (1) to fail or refuse to hire, or discharge any individual or otherwise to discriminate against any individual with respect to his compensation, terms, conditions, or privileges of employment, because of such individual's race, color, religion, sex, or national origin; (2) to limit, segregate, or classify his employees or applicants for employment in any way which would deprive or tend to deprive any individual of employment opportunity or otherwise adversely affect his status as an employee because of such individual's race, color, religion, sex, or national origin.

It is evident that this section specifically applies to discrimination in personnel practices including recruitment, hiring, promotion, discharge, classification, training, compensation, and other conditions and privileges of employment.[49] The EEOC is the federal agency responsible for administering Title VII, and it has the authority to investigate all charges of discrimination. In the years since Title VII became law, it has been given authority to administer the Age

## Equal Employment Opportunity Commission

The U.S. Equal Employment Opportunity Commission was created by Title VII of the Civil Rights Act of 1964, which prohibits employment discrimination based on race, color, sex, religion, or national origin. Since 1979, the EEOC has also been responsible for enforcing the Age Discrimination in Employment Act of 1967, which protects employees 40 years of age or older; the Equal Pay Act of 1963, which protects men and women who perform substantially equal work in the same establishment from sex-based wage discrimination; and Section 501 of the Rehabilitation Act of 1973, which prohibits federal-sector discrimination against handicapped persons. In 1992, the EEOC became responsible for Title I of the Americans with Disabil-

ities Act, which prohibits employers and unions from discriminating against qualified individuals with disabilities. The EEOC staff receives and investigates employment discrimination charges against private employers and state and local governments. If the investigation shows reasonable cause to believe discrimination occurred, the commission will begin conciliation efforts. If the EEOC is unable to conciliate the charge, it will be considered for possible litigation. The commission's policy is to seek full and effective relief for each victim of employment discrimination, whether such relief is sought in court or in conciliation.

*Source:* The U.S. Equal Employment Opportunity Commission, November 1988, *Commission Enforces EEO Laws*, Office of Communications and Legislative Affairs and EEOC, 2003, *Facts about Age Discrimination*, (Washington, DC: EEOC), pp. 1–2.

Discrimination in Employment Act and the Equal Pay Act, and in 1992 it assumed responsibility for enforcing the Americans with Disabilities Act.[50] Focus 15–1 describes the mandate of the EEOC.

The EEOC issues standards and guidelines for compliance with antidiscrimination laws. Many of the cases filed with this agency have reached various courts where decisions have been rendered that completely altered many police personnel practices.[51] For example, in one appeals court decision, a height requirement for police officers was upheld, even though the requirement resulted in the exclusion of a number of female applicants. This contradicted the result of one of the earlier cases in this area—*Officers for Justice* v. *Civil Service Commission*, San Francisco, 395 F.Supp. 378 (Northern District, Calif., 1975)—in which a federal judge ruled that existing minimum height requirements for the selection of police officers were illegal because they excluded females and certain ethnic groups.[52] The court struck down a weight requirement at the same time.[53] Since those decisions, some agencies have altered or eliminated height requirements, which has allowed women, Hispanics, and Asians to meet one aspect of police employment prerequisites successfully. Another standard that has been altered is the physical agility test that in many agencies had discriminated against women.[54] In another earlier case the court ruled that the state had to hire one African-American trooper for each Caucasian trooper hired until 25 percent of all troopers were African-American.[55]

**Job-Related Standards**

The common element of rulings like these is that applicants can only be held to definitely job-related standards. When standards are arbitrary or are clearly not related to the tasks performed by a police officer, they are discriminatory, and courts have ruled against such standards. Federal law prohibits the use of tests or standards disproportionately disadvantaging minority applicants that are not shown to be job related.[56] The Supreme Court has ruled that *standards* have to be valid, reliable, job related, and based on bona fide occupational qualifications.[57] It is important to understand these terms:

1. *Validity.* The test measures what it is supposed to measure.
2. *Reliability.* The test consistently yields accurate measurements.
3. *Job-relatedness.* The knowledge or skill measured by the screening device is directly related to the actual job to be performed.
4. *Bona fide occupational qualification.* An attribute or skill is actually required in order to do a particular job.

In recent years, affirmative action plans have come into vogue as a means of remedying the effect of past discrimination against ethnic and other minority groups. The U.S. Civil Service Commission and various courts reached the conclusion that simply removing inappropriate standards was not eliminating the reality of discrimination or making up for the many past years of discrimination.

For many years the U.S. Commission on Civil Rights has called for law enforcement agencies to work toward developing police departments that truly reflect the racial and ethnic composition of the communities they serve, including speaking the major language or languages spoken in the community.[58] It must be kept in mind that the central issues in EEOC law are concerned with several types of discrimination, including recruiting, hiring, promotion, employment testing, employment conditions, seniority, layoffs, retaliation, and reverse discrimination. The essential components of a nondiscriminatory employment policy include basic new-employee recruiting and selecting procedures that do not intentionally or inadvertently work to screen out minority group members or other protected groups.[59]

**Quotas**   If there is any issue that immediately arouses the ire of many, it is quota hiring. Title VII explicitly bans quota hiring, but the language of the title has been interpreted to allow, for example, a district court to impose a hiring quota as a remedy for racial imbalance caused by unlawful discriminatory conduct.[60] In reaction to quotas, Caucasian males have filed reverse discrimination complaints challenging employers' affirmative action programs. The major case in this area was decided in 1978. In *The Regents of the University of California* v. *Bakke,* the U.S. Supreme Court found that the university's affirmative action program, which in effect set aside 16 percent of the freshman medical class for non-Caucasian applicants, violated Title VII. It is important to note that the Court's ruling said affirmative action programs *would* be permissible if race was only one of several admission factors; the Court reaffirmed this opinion in deciding a recent University of Michigan admission-policy case.

When the *Bakke* decision was first announced, some people believed it would substantially affect affirmative action programs in the United States, but it has turned out to have limited impact. Note that this decision was made in an educational context and not in police employment.[61]

The U.S. Commission on Civil Rights has taken the position that the use of racial-preference employment techniques, such as quotas, is not properly viewed as pitting the interests of African-Americans against the interests of Caucasians. Rather, each specific preference plan favors members of the preferred group—of whatever race or gender—at the expense of the non-preferred group, which inevitably includes persons of diverse ethnic, religious, or racial groups.[62] The commission also rejects the concept of an operational justification for racial quotas.

One major police department asserted that its promotion quota increasing the numbers of African-American officers at all ranks was necessary in order to achieve more effective law enforcement and reduce discriminatory treatment against African-American citizens. The commission took the position that this amounted to a claim that only African-American officers can effectively provide law enforcement services to African-American citizens or supervise lower-ranking African-American police officers. The commission asserted that such a claim has no place in a free pluralist society made up of many diverse ethnic and racial groups striving to achieve the goal of becoming one nation. If the department's claim were accepted, the commission said, members of any racial or ethnic group could claim that only fellow members of that group could properly serve or treat them.[63]

Table 15–3 lists the ethnicity of officers working in cities of various sizes. In the largest cities, 22.6 percent of the sworn officers in 2000 were members of minority groups. By way of contrast, a survey taken 20 years earlier found that minorities in police departments averaged 7.6 percent. During the decade 1990–2000, the number of officers nationwide who were members of a racial or ethnic minority increased by about 38,000 (61 percent). The largest increase was for Hispanic or Latino officers, whose numbers increased by 17,600 (93 percent) during the period.[64] This is a significant gain in minority representation, and it appears likely that in the years ahead more minority group members will enter law enforcement.

A few court decisions have imposed quotas as a means of achieving greater minority representation in police departments, but this has only been done after careful investigations showed that racial imbalance had been caused by unlawful discrimination. Court decisions vary considerably across the nation. In one community a court took the position that the police department should hire a specific number of employees who were bilingual in Spanish and English. In another, a court issued an order requiring 15 percent of a local police force to be composed of African-Americans and Puerto Ricans. Still another decision by

**Table 15–3   Race of Full-Time Sworn Personnel in Local Police Departments, by Size of Population Served**

| | *Percent of Full-Time Sworn Employees Who Were* | | | |
| Population Served | White | Black | Hispanic | Other* |
| --- | --- | --- | --- | --- |
| 1,000,000 plus | 63.5 | 16.1 | 14.2 | 3.1 |
| 500,000 to 999,999 | 62.4 | 25.2 | 6.8 | 5.6 |
| 250,000 to 499,999 | 67.9 | 19.0 | 10.7 | 2.4 |
| 100,000 to 249,999 | 76.2 | 12.2 | 8.0 | 3.7 |
| 50,000 to 99,999 | 85.2 | 7.3 | 5.7 | 1.8 |
| 25,000 to 49,000 | 87.8 | 6.1 | 4.6 | 1.5 |
| 10,000 to 24,999 | 90.6 | 4.6 | 3.4 | 1.4 |
| 2,500 to 9,999 | 90.1 | 4.5 | 3.9 | 1.5 |
| Less than 2,500 | 87.9 | 5.8 | 3.1 | 3.2 |

*Includes Asians, Pacific Islanders, American Indians, and Alaska Natives.

*Source:* Adapted from U.S. Department of Justice, *Local Police Departments 2000* (Washington, DC: Bureau of Justice Statistics, 2000), p. 4.

a district court imposed quotas based on race for promotions to sergeant and lieutenant.

**Affirmative Action**    The real goal is to use affirmative action techniques as tools to enhance equal opportunity for all citizens rather than as devices to compensate some people (for unequal treatment based on race, gender, or other status) at the expense of others. Appropriate affirmative action techniques include the following:

1. Development of recruitment efforts aimed at increasing the number of qualified minority applicants.
2. Training, education, and counseling programs that target minority participants and aim at enhancing their opportunities to be hired or promoted on the basis of merit but which are open to all applicants and employees.

One way for an agency to meet its equal-opportunity obligations is to develop a recruitment policy and program with specific measurable goals that are evaluated periodically. Law enforcement agencies should have a ratio of minority employees approximately equal to the proportion of such groups within the service area. A police department whose ratio falls significantly short should prepare an affirmative action plan that specifically provides for equal employment opportunity. CALEA has a standard (31.2.1) that addresses this issue; it stipulates that:[65]

> The agency has ethnic and gender composition in the sworn law enforcement ranks in approximate proportion to the makeup of the available workforce in the law enforcement agency's service community, or a recruitment plan pursuant to standard 31.2.2.

The commentary specifies the need for a police agency to direct recruitment steps toward the goal of approximating within the sworn ranks the demographic composition of the community that it serves. Statistics on the composition of the workforce in the agency's service community are available from a variety of sources, including the U.S. Department of Labor's Bureau of Labor Statistics. For the purposes of this standard, the agency may also expand its recruitment efforts beyond the immediate service community.

Another step can be taken: establish an equal employment opportunity grievance process that provides an efficient means for resolving individual or group problems (of a sensitive nature) quickly and with a minimum of formal procedural requirements. This process should deal with allegations of discrimination in regard to application, recruitment, appointment, training, promotion, retention, discipline, or other aspects of employment practice. Grievable cases involve discrimination based on race, color, national origin, ancestry, age, sex, sexual orientation, marital status, physical or mental disability, medical condition (e.g., cured or rehabilitated cancer), religious or political opinion or affiliation, or union activity. Exceptions may be made if the basis for discrimination is a bona fide occupational qualification for the position or if what is alleged as discrimination is an action required to comply with federal or state law.[66] Each agency should have an equal employment opportunity counselor who will respond to a complaint within a specified period and do the following:

1. Consult with the aggrieved person.
2. Discuss civil rights laws and EEOC guidelines.
3. Make necessary inquiries in an attempt to resolve the complaint.
4. Counsel the aggrieved person on the issues of the case.
5. Seek informal resolution of the problem or problems.

If informal resolution of the aggrieved person's problem or problems is not possible, a formal complaint should be filed with the department's affirmative action officer. An investigation of the complaint should be made; its findings and recommendations should be submitted to the city manager or mayor, who should then provide the complainant with a written decision within a reasonable period. An effective affirmative action plan demands a serious and vigorous commitment from top management. A plan must be carried through at every level within the organization, because if lower ranks believe the plan is not really supported, they can sabotage it, ignore it, or relegate it to a very low priority. Top management should demand periodic reports that not only list the minority members hired or promoted but also include an in-depth analysis of the positions filled, rates of advancement, and turnover. Management needs quality information indicating how policies are being carried out and what effect they are having on the organization.[67]

# WOMEN

Women have been employed since approximately 1845 in American police departments, but in past years their participation was limited to specific duties and their law enforcement responsibilities were restricted. Typically, they served as jail matrons and performed in a social service role in juvenile units. As time has passed, women have occasionally served as undercover officers in vice and organized-crime details. Being traditionally limited to these types of functions has relegated women to a secondary status in law enforcement; except for those few women who have risen through the ranks in specialized units, they have had little opportunity for advancement. Since the passing of the federal Civil Rights Act, an increasing number of women have entered law enforcement.

Discrimination based on gender is still a major issue in some police departments, but there has been considerable progress as women have entered what was, for many years, a male-dominated occupation. Males make up the majority of sworn officers, 88.7 percent nationally. In rural counties, 92.1 percent of sworn officers were male and 86.9 percent in suburban counties were male. Females made up 11.3 percent of the nation's sworn officers in 2002.[68] Title VII of the 1964 Civil Rights Act specifically prohibits discrimination based on gender with respect to compensation, terms, conditions, or privileges of employment. Eight years later, the Equal Opportunity Act coverage was extended to include public employees. In other words, women must be treated fairly; if they are not, U.S. law has been broken.[69] The ban on sexual discrimination was inserted into Title VII relatively late in the legislative process, so the act was passed with limited accompanying discussion to clarify the intent of that provision. Consequently, the EEOC has had considerably more difficulty

Police Academy Graduation.
Tom Carter, PhotoEdit

in interpreting the ban on sexual discrimination than with any other aspect of the act. The EEOC has issued guidelines twice, and many issues women have encountered in the workplace—such as maternity leave, breast-feeding at work, grooming standards, and stereotyping—have had to be litigated in federal courts.[70]

**Barriers**  Generally, women employed in law enforcement must overcome three barriers:[71]

1.  The traditional roles females are expected to play
2.  The attitudes of males and females within the organization
3.  The lack of support systems to help women stay on the job

It has not been easy for women to enter male-dominated occupations, especially one like law enforcement, which has long perpetuated the myth that a good police officer is a combination of John Wayne and Rambo—tall, tough, and unyielding when confronting criminals. This macho concept has proven to be one of the most difficult for women to deal with, especially for the first women who broke the barriers and entered the previously all-male world of patrol and traffic regulation.[72]

Often women go through three stages when they enter the police world. The *initial stage* is best described as the honeymoon phase, as women adjust to the police academy and to the close supervision provided by a field training officer. The newly hired policewoman begins to get positive feedback as she adapts to each new challenge successfully and realizes many of her fears were unwarranted. She begins to believe she can handle a career, a home life, and outside interests.

Roberta F. Partin was raised in a police family and always wanted to be a police officer. Her father and two uncles were officers. At family gatherings, there was a great deal of discussion of police activities. Roberta joined the Girl Scouts and as soon as she was eligible became an Explorer Scout. She was also very active in the town's Police Athletic League.

Upon graduation from high school, she enrolled in the local community college, where she majored in police science and administration. She graduated with honors and continued to pursue her education at the local university. As soon as she was 21, she took and passed the police officer test at Riverwide City. She placed second on the selection list, was subsequently hired, and attended the regional police academy. She graduated number one from the academy and received high marks from all her supervising officers. She was then assigned to patrol; she works the midnight shift, where she is the only woman on a team of nine officers. As the first female officer ever hired by the department, she finds herself the object of considerable scorn from the majority of officers on the team. She is the butt of many jokes, and three of the officers on the team refuse to work with her. The team sergeant (Sgt. Tom Rogers) is in a dilemma. Personally, he feels there is no place in law enforcement for women, but the chief of police has taken a very strong position supporting women and has directed Sgt. Rogers to make every effort to ensure that Officer Partin is treated fairly.

The only other women in the department are the clerical staff and the dispatchers, so Officer Partin finds she has nobody she can actually turn to other than her father and uncles, who work in another department. The advice they give her is just to do her job as best she can and wait for everything to work out. At the end of their shift, the other officers go to a nearby restaurant for coffee, but she has never been included in the group. Since she is the only woman officer in patrol, everything she does is carefully scrutinized. She feels as though she is operating in a fishbowl. Some members of the community responded to her negatively also.

On the optimistic side, during the last six months a few of the officers with whom Officer Partin works have realized that she is very competent and professional in the way she conducts herself. In several violent confrontations, she remained poised and more than adequately assisted other officers in subduing suspects who appeared to be on drugs. She is 5 feet 4 inches tall and weighs 131 pounds. She has taken extensive self-defense training, at her own expense, and performs effectively and confidently during violent situations. When she responds to family disputes, she has the interpersonal skills to defuse potentially explosive situations.

Partin knows she is doing a good job, and her six-month evaluation confirmed this view. She continues to be unaccepted by the majority of the officers on her shift and is becoming increasingly negative toward the officers who openly oppose her. There is no one she feels she can turn to for help. Her superior notes that she is treated as an equal whenever he is around, but unfortunately he is not around all the time.

*If you were Officer Partin, how would you deal with the other officers on the team? Would it be helpful to fight back, either verbally or by filing a grievance? How could Sgt. Rogers help Officer Partin? If you were the chief of police, what would you do?*

Next, she enters the *ambivalent stage* as she becomes doubtful about her ability to accept the new role. She suffers from internal conflict as the traditional values inculcated through her growing years compete and conflict with the newly defined role she wants to assume in the working environment, Sometimes a woman becomes a victim of the superwoman syndrome as she strives to meet the demands placed on her by both her family and her employer. With many women, the demand to be all things to all people has led to a variety of pressures, resulting in frustration and exhaustion.

The final stage is called the *transformation time* and begins as internal conflicts are resolved. The working environment begins to provide the working woman with a feeling of status and self-fulfillment. The job becomes meaningful to her, and she becomes increasingly motivated and committed. No longer is the home her sole source of role satisfaction.[73]

All these stages are affected by what might be termed the police personality, which includes traits like a need to control situations (an authoritarian attitude) and a need to be assertive and physically aggressive. These traits go with what our society has traditionally regarded as male, rather than female, roles.[74] Women find themselves having to deal with the stereotype of the male police personality. This is an example of true conflict: women who serve as police officers face a difficult choice between retaining their basic femininity and emulating facets of the male police personality. Doing the latter is generally termed *defeminization*. Women who adjust in this way to the police occupation believe that male officers will accept them more readily and it will become easier to establish more trusting work relationships with them.[75] One researcher found that when women attending a police academy exhibited masculine behavior (rather than feminine), they tended to get along better with their male counterparts.[76] Confronting stereotypes, female police officers are faced with the unique challenge of struggling for acceptance among their co-workers while maintaining their own identity.[77]

This presents a dilemma to women officers: if they decide to retain their femininity, they will, practically speaking, be limiting their careers. In most instances, they will not be assigned to patrol, and that will (in all probability) preclude their consideration for supervisory or managerial positions.[78] In addition, in many instances a woman who becomes a police officer will encounter discrimination not only within the department but from a hostile community still learning to accept women as police officers.[79]

Obstacles women must overcome are numerous, but one of the most significant is the attitude of male officers of all ranks. Through the years they have built numerous barriers into the formal and informal structures of the work organization, prescribing the female role as helping and nurturing. The male attitude can be summed up as "Police work is man's work."[80] The male view has been that women are not physically or psychologically able to handle real police work and should serve in limited capacities even if departments are forced to accept them; women should never be allowed to participate in the violence and sordidness of daily police work.

Not all male officers resist the entry of women into their departments, but when they do, their behavior can become irrational. Some officers will openly discriminate against a woman officer. For example, when serving as field training officers, they can pressure a woman to such an extent that she makes mistakes and gets a poor rating. Supervisors have been known to show partiality to men over women when assigning officers to different shifts, when assigning preferred beats, or when selecting officers for special training. The nature of discrimination varies considerably, depending on the female involved. Male officers can make life miserable for a policewoman by making her the butt of jokes, snide remarks, and sexual innuendoes.[81]

A somewhat more rational argument against hiring women police officers, from the male view, has been that women lack necessary physical qualifications. Current data suggest that by some measures (such as upper body strength and overall strength) women are on average less capable than men. However, experts feel that women can (with careful training) reach a level of fitness well within the demands of police work. Women must be prepared to take tests that include scaling a wall, dragging a 150-pound dummy, or bench-pressing one's weight. Physical tests should be validated, and agencies should provide women applicants with a gender-specific physical conditioning regimen.[82] There is a trend to use a general-fitness approach to test the physical ability of candidates. Potential officers are given tests that measure their general fitness through such activities as running and sit-and-reach. These tests are gender- and age-normed, and it has been found that they do not have an adverse effect on women. Candidates who pass the test during academy training are believed to be capable of successfully completing training and perform law enforcement tasks.[83] Contrary to popular belief, policing is not a physically demanding job. There are certainly times when situations become physically demanding. Every officer, male or female, must have a reserve of strength to provide a positive response to a critical incident. Experts state that an officer can stay physically fit through careful and continuous training. This means that an officer should exercise two or three times a week, with each session lasting from 30 to 45 minutes, to maintain a good level of fitness.[84] Chapter 6 has an extensive discussion of the importance of physical fitness.

Research indicates that women police officers are as capable as male officers, and the National Center for Women in Policing points out that there are six advantages for law enforcement agencies that hire and retain more women:[85]

1. Female officers have been proven to be as competent as their male counterparts.
2. Female officers are less likely than males to use excessive force.
3. Female officers can help implement community-oriented policing.
4. Having more female officers will improve law enforcement's response to violence against women.
5. Increasing the presence of female officers reduces problems of sex discrimination and harassment within an agency.
6. The presence of women can bring about beneficial changes in policy for all officers.

Each of these factors should work to the benefit of officers as well as management.

Obstacles that impede the selection, retention, and promotion of women have to be removed. Clearly, women have made and will continue to make significant contributions to law enforcement. What is needed is a level playing field. A number of studies that have been conducted in recent years refute the view that women cannot serve effectively as officers in a police department's patrol division. When an agency has a carefully thought-out recruitment, selection, and training program, women can perform successfully as patrol officers. Nevertheless, there must be an adequate audit of progress (to ensure that women are not isolated in stereotypical jobs), plus carefully spelled-out policies and procedures defining how all officer assignments in patrol operations are to be made.

**Mentoring**

A number of departments have turned to mentoring as a means of improving the retention of women. It has been found that it is best to create a formal mentoring system. Such a system should start when women are recruited and be maintained throughout each female officer's career. Either men or women can serve as mentors, if they are commited to helping women succeed. The Charlotte-Mecklenburg Police Department created a women's network, which started by giving female recruits the opportunity to interact with rank-and-file women to talk about concerns and problems. The network proved to be successful: it became necessary to create subcommittees on recruiting, retention, promotion, and policy. Since the inception of the network, 35 women have successfully graduated from the academy, and exceptional efforts have been expended to enlist a larger number of women applicants. As for promotions in the department, nine women have been promoted to the rank of sergeant, five to captain, and two to major.[86] Success seems to beget success. As more women have entered police departments, the barriers to their employment have eroded—and, in a few instances, been breached. This is not to suggest that every female police officer will function effectively any more than that every male police officer will.[87]

Of agencies responding to a survey in 1987, only 7.6 percent of the sworn officers were female. By 2002 this figure had increased to 11.3 percent. While this represents growth, it is very different from gender parity. It is interesting to note that the larger the size of the city, the higher the percentage of female police officers. For example, in 70 cities with populations greater than 250,000, the average proportion of female police officers was found to be 16.5 percent. The figure for cities with populations under 100,000 ranged from 8.7 percent to 6.9 percent, and in rural counties it was 7.9 percent. Female officers were more numerous in suburban counties (13.1 percent).[88] The number of female officers nationwide in the year 2000 was estimated to be 46,659, an increase of 59 percent from 1990 (see Table 15–4). These are significant figures and demonstrate the increasing acceptance of women into the sworn ranks. Interestingly, women have made limited inroads into communities with fewer than 2,500 residents and have shown the greatest increase in cities with populations more than 500,000.[89]

There are still relatively few women in police departments, especially in supervisory or higher levels. Their sparseness in the upper ranks can be explained as resulting from the fact that women for the most part are relative latecomers to law enforcement. At the same time, consideration must be given to ensuring that gender bias is not present in promotion systems. A survey of 123 cities in the 1980s found only 39 women in positions of lieutenant or higher, as well as only 196 sergeants and 300 investigators.[90] As the number of women police officers increases, it appears likely that more females will move into management ranks. In a 1990

Table 15–4   **Gender and Race of Full-Time Personnel in Local Police Departments, by Size of Population Served, 2000**

| | | *Percent of Full-Time Sworn Employees Who Were Female* | | | |
|---|---|---|---|---|---|
| *Population Served* | *Total* | *White* | *African-American* | *Hispanic/Latino* | *Other\** |
| All sizes | 10.6% | 6.5% | 2.7% | 1.1% | 0.3% |

*Source:* U.S. Department of Justice, Matthew J. Hickman and Brian A. Reaves, *Local Police Departments 2000* (Washington, DC: Bureau of Justice Statistics, 2003), p. 4.

study, S. Martin identified 123 women who were serving as police chiefs but found that the percentage of women who held command positions in law enforcement was less than the total percentage of women in the field.[91] At the end of 2000, Dorothy M. Schultz positively identified 157 women as chief executive officers and estimated that the total number of female chiefs in the United States was probably 175. Overall, Schultz found, women command smaller police departments; one-quarter of the departments she found headed by females had 10 or fewer officers. Most female chiefs who responded to Schultz's survey were Caucasian. Interestingly, 42 percent of the women chiefs nationwide were in charge of college or university police departments. These chiefs had considerable education: 42 percent held a master's degree and 4 percent held a doctorate or law degree.[92] It seems likely that gender will eventually cease to be a factor in promotion decisions and that increasing numbers of women will assume command and executive positions.

Unlawful harassment remains a pervasive problem in American workplaces. With the employment of more women, sexual harassment in law enforcement agencies has increased. Confronted with this problem, more and more agencies have taken steps to create a working atmosphere that is harassment free.[93] Research indicates that 40 percent of employed women and 5 to 10 percent of employed men have been subjected to some type of sexual harassment on the job.[94]

## Sexual Harassment

The number of harassment charges in all types of employment filed with the EEOC and state fair employment practice agencies has risen significantly in recent years. In fact, over a recent three-year period such charges doubled.[95] In a study of one metropolitan police department, 62 percent of 81 female police officers said they had been subjected to sexual harassment by their male counterparts. One-third of the women officers confronted the offender, 6 percent talked to their supervisors, and 21 percent took no action.[96] This failure to report acts of harassment reflects the fear many female officers have of retaliation, as well as the general code of silence that prevails in many law enforcement agencies. Sexual harassment and gender harassment are two of the top reasons women give for leaving law enforcement. This obviously has a damaging impact on the retention rate for women, and it can also cause debilitating stress on women who do not leave the force.[97] Women officers often feel that they are "between a rock and a hard place," and they make a conscious decision not to report violations.[98]

An exact definition of sexual harassment is not easy to arrive at. It is an event more easily recognized than defined. As it turns out, sexual harassment is a form of sex discrimination that is a violation of Title VII of the Civil Rights Act of 1964. Conduct that constitutes sexual harassment includes:[99]

> Unwelcome sexual advances, requests for sexual favors, and other verbal or physical conduct of a sexual nature constitute sexual harassment when submission to or rejection of this conduct explicitly or implicitly affects an individual's employment, unreasonably interferes with an individual's work performance, or creates an intimidating, hostile or offensive work environment.

Sexual harassment can occur in a variety of circumstances, including but not limited to the following:

1. Both victim and harasser may be either male or female. They do not have to be of opposite sexes.
2. The harasser can be the victim's supervisor, an agent of the employer, a supervisor in another area, a co-worker, or a non-employee.
3. The victim does not have to be the person harassed but could be anyone affected by the offensive conduct.
4. Unlawful sexual harassment may occur even if the victim is not discharged or subjected to economic injury.
5. The harasser's conduct must be unwelcome.

It is appropriate for the victim to directly inform the harasser that the conduct is unwelcome and must stop. The victim should use any employer complaint mechanism or grievance system available. Typically, sexual harassment can be one of two types: quid pro quo sexual harassment and creation of a hostile work environment.

**Quid Pro Quo Sexual Harassment**

Unwelcome sexual advances, requests for sexual favors, and other verbal or physical conduct of a sexual nature constitute quid pro quo sexual harassment when (1) submission to such conduct is made explicitly or implicitly a term or condition of an individual's employment, and (2) submission to or rejection of such conduct by an individual is used as the basis for employment decisions affecting such an individual.

This type of harassment places an employee in a position where it is necessary to choose between keeping the job and refusing to comply with the demands. Sexual conduct becomes unlawful only when it is *unwelcome*. The challenged conduct must be unwelcome in the sense that the employee regards the conduct as undesirable or offensive and did not solicit or incite it.[100]

**Hostile Work Environment**

Sexual harassment also applies if an individual's work performance is unreasonably interfered with, or an intimidating, hostile, or offensive working environment is created.[101] In *Meritor Savings Bank* v. *Vinson*, 106 S.Ct. 2399 (1986), a court decided that sexual harassment does not have to result in economic damage to the victim. It was strongly emphasized that the key to defining sexual harassment in a hostile work environment is that the conduct is *unwelcome*. Thus, sexual flirtation, innuendo, or even vulgar language, if it is trivial or merely annoying, would probably not establish a hostile environment. On the other hand, intentional touching of a plaintiff's intimate body areas is sufficiently offensive to alter the conditions of his or her working environment and constitute a violation.

**Sexual Harassment Policy**

It is essential that police departments deal with sexual harassment by creating procedures delineating conduct that is prohibited. A recent survey indicated that 34 percent of law enforcement agencies do not have a written sexual harassment policy.[102] A typical policy setting forth specifically prohibited conduct is displayed in Figure 15–1 .

Without question, prevention is the best way to manage and control sexual harassment in the workplace. Police executives must create written policy that is meaningful and includes sanctions. Systemic changes of this type will decrease the likelihood that harassment of a sexual nature will occur. Focus 15–2 makes suggestions to help managers prevent sexual harassment.[103]

1. Expressing bias in the workplace includes any behavior that is potentially offensive to any employees on the basis of their protected status. Examples of such expressions of bias include but are not limited to:

   - Degrading words, offensive slang labels or names, or profanity describing a person's protected status.
   - Sexually suggestive, obscene, or lewd "jokes" or comments, or "jokes" or comments about a person's protected status.
   - Inappropriate posters or posted "jokes."

2. Examples of such sexual harassment in the workplace include but are not limited to:

   - Sexually suggestive, obscene, or lewd comments or invitations.
   - Gender-related labels such as "honey," "sweetie," "cutie," "boy," and "girl."
   - Requests for sexual favors and implying that there will be economic or employment benefits.
   - Acts of leering, ogling, or drawing attention to a person's body.
   - Sexual advances.
   - Introduction into the workplace of pornographic pictures or written material, except in the course of official police investigations.

3. Retaliation is against the law and is strictly prohibited. It is a separate and distinct illegal action independent of the merits of any prior employment discrimination complaint.

**Figure 15–1**

Departmental Equal Employment Opportunity (EEO) Policy.

Adapted from Tucson Police Department, 1997, *Police Department Procedures*, Vol. I, 92-F-01, and Tucson Police Department, 2003, *General Orders*, Human Resources, Vol. 4, 4100, pp. 1–2.

## USE OF FORCE

Since at least as early as 1857, the media and the public have expressed concerns over the use of force by police officers. No single issue has been of greater concern (not only to police executives but to the community at large) than police shootings and the use of various types of deadly force. Such critical incidents have occurred repeatedly over the years. The location of incidents might change, but furor has evolved that has threatened the well-being of citizens. It has become clear that police shootings can have extreme societal consequences beyond injury or death of a suspect.[104]

The situations vary, as does the nature of force used. In one recent incident, a subject attacked an officer with a sawed-off shotgun, firing twice before the officer returned fire. The officer was not injured, and both the department and a community activist agreed that the officer was justified in shooting the subject.

In a second incident, police responded to a "man down" call. On arrival, the officer saw a man lying in the grass. The man jumped up and grabbed a club consisting of two 2 × 4 boards nailed together; the officer drew his service revolver. The man advanced in a threatening manner toward the officer, who retreated about 140 feet and then shot the man in the chest.

## Preventing Sexual Harassment in the Workplace

1. Don't mix business and pleasure. Personal relationships with subordinates expose managers not only to possible complaints from the person with whom the relationship exists, but to complaints from other employees that favorable treatment is granted only to persons with whom an intimate relationship develops.

2. Avoid the appearance of impropriety as well as any actual impropriety. Think about how a situation will appear to others in the workplace. One experienced manager always makes sure he's in a group of three, and avoids, if possible, one-on-one after-hours meetings with business associates of the opposite sex.

3. Don't tell off-color jokes with sexual implications in a business situation, even when the day's business is over and it's time to relax.

4. Don't make overly personal comments about an employee's clothing or body.

5. It is impossible to deny that situations occur where men and women become more than business associates. If this happens to you or to people within your sphere of responsibility, a good rule is to separate the individuals into different units. It is important to be equitable to both male and female employees, and not to react by "transferring the woman." To allow a supervisory relationship to be continued between two employees who are involved in a personal relationship exposes your agency to liability that could be translated into litigation if an equal-opportunity complaint were to be brought [against the supervisor].

6. Make sure all managers, supervisors, and employees know what sexual harassment is. Hold a workshop for supervisory staff. Define sexual harassment in plain terms for them. Tell them not to . . . make inappropriate sexual comments to coworkers or subordinates.

7. When complaints are made, investigate promptly, confidentially, and follow departmental policy when violations are found.

*Source:* Reprinted with permission from Toeing the EEOC Legal Line, 1989, available from the Alexander Hamilton Institute, 197 W. Spring Valley Ave., Maywood, NJ 07607.

In a third incident, officers responded to a family dispute after receiving a call from the wife stating her husband was distraught at not being able to see his son. The four responding officers attempted to talk the subject into surrendering, standing within 5 feet of him as he threatened them with a knife. The subject suddenly lunged at an officer and was shot 11 times. A grand jury found no basis for indicting the two officers who fired the shots killing the subject. After the incident the police department, which has very strict standards on the use of deadly force, called for additional training of officers in how to handle violent people. Particularly desired was training in defensive delaying tactics and the idea that officers can retreat from confrontation.

In a fourth incident, an officer shot at a hijacked car, feeling that the carjacker was going to run him down. A two-year-old boy in the backseat was not hurt; the bullet grazed the carjacker. Because of this incident the police department instituted a policy forbidding officers to shoot at vehicles unless they are being fired upon.

In a fifth incident, two uniformed officers driving a marked police vehicle approached a subject, who fired several shots at them with a 9mm pistol, wounding one officer. Both officers returned the fire and wounded the subject, who died during surgery at a local hospital.[105]

The foregoing accounts clearly illustrate the complexity of the problems met by an officer working the street. Cases in which an officer uses deadly force can look very different when reviewed afterwards in the quiet environment of an office where there is plenty of time to consider the alternatives than they do on the spot, when a decision has to be made in a few seconds.

This ongoing dilemma of whether or not to use deadly force is not new to the police field. As early as 1857, an officer using his personal weapon shot a suspect who was fleeing from the scene of a crime. The grand jury declined to indict the officer.[106] During a 23-year period ending in 1998, 8,578 felons were justifiably killed by police officers. On average, 373 felons were lawfully killed by police and 79 officers were murdered by felons each year.[107] Most use-of-force incidents occur at night in public locations within high-crime areas of large cities. These incidents generally involve on-duty uniformed officers shooting at subjects in the crime-prone age range.[108]

The police use of deadly force (civilian deaths by legal intervention) is a given, but to put it in perspective, a number of variables must be considered. One of these is the high frequency of all kinds of encounters, favorable as well as unfavorable, between the police and members of the public. During one year, for example, approximately 45 million Americans age 12 or older were estimated to have had at least one face-to-face contact with a police officer. The most common reasons for contact were asking for assistance and reporting a crime. The most common occasions for officers to use force were arrests; next in frequency came disturbances and traffic stops.[109] Of those who had contact with the police, about 0.2% of the population actually had force used against them. In these instances they were hit, held, pushed, choked, threatened with a flashlight or a gun, restrained by a police dog, threatened or actually sprayed with chemical or pepper spray, or otherwise subjected to force. These figures indicate that the actual use of force is rare in police-citizen contacts.[110]

## Law and the Use of Force

Through the years, the conditions governing the use of deadly force have been established by various states via statutes or court decisions. In most instances, states have followed the English common-law rule that was in place when this nation was founded.[111] This rule soon became known as the *fleeing-felon rule*. Under it, an officer was authorized to use deadly force when it was believed an arrest would be made for a felony. In addition, the officer was required to believe the use of force was necessary for self-protection or to prevent a subject from escaping. Keep in mind that under English law, during the 18th century, all felonies were considered capital crimes punishable by death. It was a logical extension, then, that killing a fleeing felon was not only justified but necessary.[112]

An alternative to the fleeing-felon rule can be found in the *Model Penal Code,* developed by the American Law Institute in 1962. Under this recommended rule, deadly force could be used against a fleeing felon under the following conditions:[113]

1. A felony has been committed.
2. The individual making the arrest is a peace officer or someone assisting a peace officer.

3. The officer believes the use of deadly force creates no substantial risk to bystanders.
4. The officer believes (a) that the felony committed by a suspect included the actual use or threatened use of deadly force or (b) that if the suspect is not harmed, there is a risk that he or she will cause death or serious bodily harm to someone else.

The issue of deadly force was placed in focus when two police officers in Memphis, Tennessee, responded to a night call reporting a residential burglary in progress. As the officers arrived at the scene, a woman told them she had heard glass breaking in the house next door. While one officer radioed in their location, the other officer went to the backyard, heard a door being slammed, and saw someone running. The suspect stopped at a 6-foot chain-link fence; the officer (using a flashlight to see the suspect's face and hands) was reasonably sure the man was not armed.

The officer challenged the suspect: "Police, halt." As the man climbed the fence, the officer fired one shot, killing him. Ten dollars and a purse were found on the body, which was identified as that of Eugene Garner, a 15-year-old eighth grader, 5 feet 4 inches tall, weighing 100 to 110 pounds. The use of deadly force to stop the escaping suspect was based on a Tennessee statute permitting the use of "all necessary means" to prevent the escape of a felony suspect if, "after notice of the intention to arrest . . . he either flees or forcibly resists."[114] The father of the suspect filed a suit in federal court seeking damages, and eventually the U.S. Supreme Court heard the case. In a six to three opinion, the Court ruled that statutory and administrative rules governing shootings of fleeing suspects must restrict officers to firing only when they have probable cause to believe the suspect poses a threat of serious physical harm, either to the officers or to others.

The Court concluded, "If the suspect threatens the officer with a weapon or there is probable cause to believe he has committed a crime involving the infliction or threatened infliction of serious physical harm, deadly force may be used if necessary to prevent escape and if, where feasible, some warning has been given."[115] Interestingly, the Court based its decision on the Fourth Amendment's protections against unreasonable seizures (the officer carried out a seizure by restraining the freedom of an individual to walk away). The Court said there can be no question that apprehension by the use of deadly force is a seizure subject to the reasonableness requirement of the Fourth Amendment and that the mere suspicion that Garner was a burglar could not justify the use of deadly force to prevent his escape. Burglary is commonly characterized by law enforcement agencies as a property crime, the Court noted, and the officer had no reason to believe Garner was armed or otherwise posed a personal threat.[116]

**Reasonable Officer Standard**

Since 1989, the courts have required officers to use force based on the "reasonable officer standard" given the totality of the situation.[117] The reasonable officer standard is defined as:

Would another officer with the same or similar training and experience, given the same or similar circumstances as presented to the officer being evaluated, do the same thing or use similar judgment?

Using this standard, the officer must use objectively reasonable force given the severity of the crime at issue, the immediate threat of the suspect to officers and the public, and attempts by the subject to resist or evade arrest.[118]

This brings into play the use-of-force continuum that for many years has served as a guideline officers can use to select an appropriate level of force to resolve a situation. The continuum can be described using the following stages:[119]

**Use-of-Force Continuum**

1. Physical presence
2. Verbal warning
3. Verbal command
4. Chemical weapon
5. Hands-on control (soft hands/hard hands)
6. Impact weapons
7. Deadly force

Although the continuum has its critics, it provides officers with a handy and flexible guide. Needless to say, whatever force is instituted must be appropriate for the situation. An officer must appraise the immediate situation and begin at the lowest level of force appropriate. If compliance is not forthcoming and if time permits, the officer should escalate, step by step, to the level of force needed to gain compliance and control. If resistance lessens, the officer should de-escalate to a lower level on the continuum.[120]

While many officers can complete a career without ever drawing a weapon, there are enough incidents of police shooting civilians that it is of considerable concern not only to police administrators and the public at large but also to legislative bodies and the courts. Without question, the taking of even one life is regrettable, but this subject should be placed in perspective. One expert has pointed out that even according to the highest estimates of shootings by police, over a recent 15-year period fewer than 1 in 60 officers in the United States killed anyone. Since the vast majority of shootings occur in metropolitan areas, it seems likely that in smaller jurisdictions the rate would be much lower.[121]

The U.S. Commission on Civil Rights has suggested that police officers should receive extensive training in the appropriate use of firearms and other weapons and that such instruction should be sanctioned by a written departmental policy approved by both the executive and legislative bodies of the jurisdiction in question. The commission has criticized fleeing-felon statutes, pointing out that even when it is legally permissible to shoot a person who has just committed a felony (for which the penalty imposed after trial will, in nearly all cases, be much less severe than execution), an officer may have only a few seconds in which to assess the situation and decide whether to fire or not. There is little opportunity to determine the nature of the offense committed, the identity and age of the suspect, the reason for the flight, or whether a weapon is being carried. The commission took the position that the circumstances in which deadly force may be used should be limited to those occasions when it is necessary to protect the officer or another person from death.[122]

One leading expert, William A. Geller, has recommended that the easiest way for police departments to meet the requirements of the Supreme Court's *Garner* ruling (if they are not already in compliance) is to adopt the standards promulgated by the Commission on Accreditation for Law Enforcement Agencies.[123] The commission has a number of standards addressing this critical area:[124]

1. *1.3.1.* A written directive that states personnel will use only the force necessary to accomplish lawful objectives.
2. *1.3.2.* A written directive that states an officer may use deadly force only when the officer reasonably believes the action is in defense of human life, including the officer's own life, or in defense of any person in imminent danger of serious physical injury. Definitions of conditional terms, such as those for reasonable belief, serious physical injury, or similarly used terms that are used to qualify the directive, shall be included.
3. *1.3.3.* A written directive that governs the discharge of "warning" shots.
4. *1.3.4.* A written directive that governs the use of authorized less-than-lethal weapons by agency personnel.
5. *1.3.5.* A written directive that specifies procedures for ensuring the provision of appropriate medical aid after use of lethal or less-than-lethal weapons or other use-of-force incidents as defined by the agency.
6. *1.3.12.* A written directive that requires that all agency personnel authorized to carry lethal and less-than-lethal weapons be issued copies of and be instructed in the policies described in standards 1.3.1 through 1.3.5 before being authorized to carry a weapon. The issuance and instruction shall be documented.

The use of deadly force is a complex issue that police managers should review constantly to see that policy is appropriate to a changing society—as can be seen from the standards just listed. It requires a great deal of serious consideration. When drafting a department's deadly force policy, the constitutional boundaries established by *Garner* and the *Graham* v. *Connor* cases should be carefully considered. A policy more restrictive than common law may actually permit the use of unconstitutional deadly force; conversely, an overly restrictive policy can create increased risks to the lives of police officers and others in the community.[125]

---

**CASE STUDY**  Charles A. Sudac

Charles A. Sudac has been a sworn officer for 17 years, and although he and others in the department feel that if he chose to compete for promotion he would receive serious consideration (and in all probability be promoted to sergeant or higher), he refuses to take promotion examinations. He is very content to remain a patrol officer, and he prefers to work the graveyard shift in the high-crime area of the city. Over the years he has worked in patrol, vice, narcotics, and traffic investigation. He is currently a member of the department's tactical unit. He is the oldest officer in the special unit, which consists of 18 officers, 2 sergeants, and a lieutenant. The primary function of the unit is to target known multiple offenders, place them under surveillance, and apprehend them in the act of committing a felony.

The methods used by the tactical unit have proven most successful, as evidenced by the apprehension of numerous felons and a significant reduction in armed robberies in the city. Assignment to the unit is vigorously pursued, so officers are subject to transfer after three years of service in the unit. This is Officer Sudac's third year in the unit. Because of his long service in the department, he has numerous informants and information sources that are of great value to the unit.

During his service, Officer Sudac has killed three felons as they were leaving the scene of armed robberies. The tactical unit has shot more suspects than any other unit in the police department. In fact, over a period of 22 years, the unit killed 31 suspects and wounded 12. No officer assigned to the unit has ever been wounded or killed. Officer Sudac is considered a model for other officers and is very comfortable in this role. Macho from the ground up, he responds positively to violent confrontations and always gives the appearance of being totally in control of himself.

Critics of the unit's operations express grave concern not only for taking of life but also for allowing the surveillance techniques to reach a stage where the use of force becomes all but inevitable. However, the use of deadly force is strongly supported by members of the unit, and legal experts point out that all the unit's operations are well within legal limits. In every instance of suspects being killed or wounded, both internal investigations and grand jury hearings have cleared the officers of any wrongdoing.

Officer Sudac is very effective in the tasks he performs and has always received outstanding ratings. He (like other members of the unit) believes it is best to postpone arresting offenders until after they have committed a serious felony in order to ensure that the case is prosecutable. The officers of the unit operate on the premise that violence can only be responded to with violence.

*The use of deadly force is truly a dilemma facing officers such as Charles A. Sudac as well as police executives. One dimension of the problem is the spirit of the law as well as the letter of the law. Should a suspect under surveillance be allowed to finish committing a serious felony before an officer intercedes? Does such an action really justify the use of deadly force? Should persons like Officer Sudac be assigned to elite units?*

## SUMMARY

The complexity of police administration is such that modern police managers are currently faced with diverse problems requiring not only a sensitive response but also an ability to deal with competing demands. These challenges include the development of police unions and associations, handling the increasing power they have acquired, managing the conflict created by the police's use of deadly force, and hiring women and minority police officers.

Today most police managers are concerned with a wide range of new activities that include dealing with bargaining units, implementing collective bargaining, learning how to negotiate with unions effectively, and guiding the development of memoranda of understanding. In recent years, as police unions have grown in size and acquired new power, many police managers have found it necessary to change their management style and learn how to negotiate with unions. Recently, a growing number of municipalities have recognized the right of employees to organize or maintain membership in a labor organization.

Normally, cities and municipalities take a position of neither encouraging nor discouraging such activities. Membership or nonmembership in a labor organization is viewed as not affecting an employee's standing or rights. Contracts and memoranda of understanding/agreement have become increasingly common. The latter is a written agreement reached through "meet and confer" procedures and dealing with wages, hours, and other working conditions. The typical agreement runs for one to three years and in most instances contains a section describing how to deal with items not covered in the agreement.

Of concern to most police executives is the issue of managerial rights. These generally include the exclusive right to decide the mission of the department, to determine procedures and standards for employee selection, to take disciplinary action, and to relieve employees from duty because of lack of work or other legitimate reasons.

In dealing with police unions, management (in many agencies) has found it necessary to prepare for collective bargaining by (1) establishing a bargaining team and designating one of the members as the principal negotiator, (2) identifying and recognizing the employee bargaining unit, and (3) developing ground rules prior to negotiation. Ordinarily a police negotiation unit will consist of all the non-supervisory sworn personnel of an agency (sergeants and all higher ranks are considered part of the management team). Unfortunately, this clear-cut distinction has not been drawn in every agency. In one instance, the bargaining unit even included the chief of police; in another department there were three distinct bargaining units representing different ranks.

Another dilemma in the labor-management arena is the part the chief of police should play in the negotiation process. Some chief executive officers have taken the position that they should not be involved in negotiation; they limit their participation to the implementation of approved agreements. Generally, experts in this vital area believe the chief should serve as an adviser to management negotiators. Municipalities should establish formal grievance mechanisms. These offer a process for dealing with disputes that arise concerning the interpretation or application of personnel ordinances or of any rule or regulation governing personnel practices or working conditions.

The number of minority-group members and women in the police field has increased considerably since the passing of the Civil Rights Act of 1964. Title VII specifically prohibits discrimination by employers on the basis of race, color, religion, sex, or national origin. The Equal Opportunity Act that was passed eight years later extended the Civil Rights Act to public employees. The Equal Employment Opportunity Commission is the federal agency that administers Title VII, and it investigates all charges of discrimination.

The laws enforced by the EEOC are those involving discrimination in recruiting, hiring, promotion, employment testing, employment conditions, seniority, layoffs, retaliation, and reverse discrimination. In recent years, in order to comply with laws and court decisions, numerous police departments have developed affirmative action plans; their intent is to recruit officers from all segments of society so that personnel can truly reflect the racial and ethnic composition of the community they serve, including speaking the major languages spoken in the community.

Title VII included a ban on sexual discrimination, and this has increased the numbers of women entering law enforcement. Sexual harassment is a form of sexual discrimination. Two forms of sexual harassment that are of special concern are quid pro quo propositions and the creation of hostile work environments. The barriers to women's entry into law enforcement have eroded somewhat, and currently 10.6 percent of sworn officers in the United States are female. This number appears likely to increase rapidly in the next decade.

During the last 30 years, no single issue has been of greater concern (not only to police managers but to the community at large) than police shootings and the use of other types of deadly force. Through the years, statutes and court decisions have revolutionized the use of deadly force by police officers; the current trend is to limit the application of force to situations where officers or members of the community are threatened with death or serious injury.

## KEY TERMS

affirmative action plans
ambivalent stage
bona fide occupational qualification
collective bargaining
deadly force
discrimination
equal opportunity
fleeing-felon rule
grievances
honeymoon phase
hostile work environment
job-relatedness
managerial rights
meet and confer
memorandum of understanding

minorities
model penal code
negotiation
negotiation process
prevention of sexual harassment
quid pro quo sexual harassment
reasonable officer standard
reliability
sexual harassment
sidebar agreement
transformation time
use-of-force continuum
validity
women

# DISCUSSION TOPICS AND QUESTIONS

1. How does a police manager identify those who are members of the management bargaining unit?
2. What categories of working conditions can be included in a memorandum of understanding/agreement?
3. Compare managerial rights and union rights.
4. What are the steps in a typical grievance procedure?
5. Discuss the concept of collective bargaining.
6. What is the function of the Equal Employment Opportunity Commission?
7. What techniques can be utilized to increase the number of minorities in a police agency?
8. What barriers must women overcome when entering law enforcement?
9. What is the fleeing-felon rule?
10. Compare the fleeing-felon rule with the guidelines provided in the *Garner* case.
11. Discuss the reasonable officer standard.
12. Discuss what constitutes *quid pro quo* sexual harassment.
13. What is the use-of-force continuum?

# FOR FURTHER READING

CALEA, *Standards for Law Enforcement Agencies,* 4th ed. (Fairfax, VA: Commission on Accreditation for Law Enforcement Agencies, November 2001).

This manual, the principal publication of the commission, was initially issued in August of 1983. The standards have evolved over the years and are representative of the "best professional practices" for law enforcement agencies everywhere. It is interesting to note that the use of force is included under the concept of role and authority in the initial chapter. Of special importance to the present chapter of this book are the chapters on collective bargaining and grievance procedures. Additionally the recruitment chapter sets forth the standard for equal employment opportunity.

IACP, *Police Use of Force in America* (Washington, DC: International Association of Chiefs of Police, 2001).

This study is the first substantial aggregation of state, county, and local law enforcement use-of-force data. The police used force at a rate of 3.61 times per 10,000 calls for service. The force used in 1999–2000 was primarily physical, followed by chemical and then impact. The use of OC products was greater than the combined total use for electronic, impact, and firearms force. Arrests were the most frequent circumstances in which force was used, followed by disturbances and traffic stops. In addition, the study presents

data on racial characteristics of use-of-force incidents, and subject use of drugs or alcohol as a use-of-force indicator during traffic stops.

NCWP, *Recruiting and Retaining Women: A Self-Assessment Guide for Law Enforcement* (Los Angeles: National Center for Women in Policing, 2001).

This guide addresses the recruitment and the retention of more women in law enforcement. It considers a wide range of issues, including developing a job description, recruiting quality candidates, and removing obstacles in the selection process. It reviews the concept of mentoring and the implementation of family-friendly policies. Consideration is also given to topics such as assignments and promotions, and to the development of effective awards and recognition programs. Additionally, coverage is given to preventing sexual and gender harassment.

U.S. Commission on Civil Rights, *Revisiting Who Is Guarding the Guardians?* (Washington, DC: U.S. Commission on Civil Rights, 2001).

This study presents a comprehensive set of guidelines and objectives to remedy police misconduct. It also discusses the need to increase diversity in all law enforcement agencies, to implement successful models of community policing, and to improve police training (including teaching cultural sensitivity). The book discusses internal regulation of law enforcement agencies, external controls, and legal developments. It stresses the need to find innovative methods for reducing police misconduct. It states that while things have improved significantly since the initial report was released some 20 years ago, there is still room for further improvement.

## NOTES

1. Richard Stone, "Police Unions Mark 20 Years, Add Members," *Police*, Vol. 22 (6) (1998), pp. 7–10.

2. Brian A. Reaves and Andrew L. Goldberg, *Law Enforcement Management and Administrative Statistics, 1997: Data for Individual State and Local Agencies with 100 or More Officers* (Washington, DC: Office of Justice Programs,1999) p. xiv.

3. Walt H. Sirene, "Labor's Effective Organizer," *FBI Law Enforcement Bulletin*, Vol. 52 (1) (1981), pp. 13–16.

4. Donald P. Crane, *The Management of Human Resources*, 3rd ed. (Belmont, CA: Wadsworth, 1986).

5. V.A. Leonard and Harry W. More, *Police Organization and Management* 9th ed. (New York: Foundation Press, 2000), pp. 45–47.

6. State of California, *Statutes, Chapter 1108* (Sacramento, CA: State of California, 1996).

7. Elizabeth W. Crowley, "Police Rally Against Budget Cuts," *IBPO* (April 28, 2003), pp. 1–4.

8. International Brotherhood of Police Officers, "New Hampshire Supreme Court Backs IBPO: Officer's Union Rights Affirmed," *Police Chronicle, IBPO* (2003), pp. 1–12.

9. Teamsters Online, LAPD Officers Say, "We Want to Be Teamsters!" *Press Release*, Teamsters Joint Council (February 12, 2002), pp. 1–2.

10. David Barry, "L.A. Police Union Calls for Civilian Oversight," *APB News* (October 6, 2000), pp. 1–2.

11. Harry W. More. *Special Topics in Policing*, 2nd ed. (Cincinnati: 1998), p. 176.

12. Human Rights Watch, *U.S.: Shielded from Justice: Police Brutality and Accountability in the United States* (New York: Human Rights Watch, 1998), pp. 15–32.

13. Charles R. Swanson, Leonard Territo, and Robert W. Taylor, *Police Administration* 5th ed. (New York: Macmillan, 2001).

14. Milpitas Police Department, *Memorandum of Understanding* (Milpitas, CA: City of Milpitas, January 1, 2002–June 30, 2005), p. 5.

15. Allen H. Andrews, Jr., "Structuring the Political Independence of the Police Chief," in William A. Geller, ed. *Police Leadership in America* (Chicago, IL: American Bar Foundation (1985), p. 18.

16. Peter C. Unsinger and Harry W. More, *Police Management/Labor Relations* (Springfield, IL: Charles C Thomas, 1989), pp. 1–17.

17. *California Government Code*, 1985, Section 3505.1.

18. Paul Coble, "Memorandum of Agreement/ Understanding," in Peter C. Unsinger and Harry W. More, ed. *Police Management/Labor Relations* (Springfield, IL: Charles C Thomas, 1989), pp. 56–61.

19. Milpitas Police Department, *Memorandum of Understanding*, p. 27.

20. Ian McAndrew, The Negotiation Process, in Peter C. Unsinger and Harry W. More, eds. *Police Management/Labor Relations* (Springfield, IL: Charles C Thomas, 1989), pp. 63–71.

21. George W. Bohlander, Scott A. Snell, and Arthur W. Sherman, Jr., *Managing Human Resources*, 12th ed. (Cincinnati: South-Western, 2001).

22. David Doan, "The Role of the Chief and Why It Does Master," in National Executive Institute Associates, *The Chief and the Union: Building a Better Relationship*, Paper, (Washington, DC: National Executive Institute, 1999), pp. 19–23.

23. McAndrew, *Police Management/Labor Relations*, p. 103.

24. Donald F. Favreau and Joseph E. Gillespie, *Modern Police Administration* (Englewood Cliffs, NJ: Prentice Hall, 1978).

25. Harry W. More, W. Fred Wegener, and Larry S. Miller, *Effective Police Supervision*, 4th ed. (Cincinnati: Anderson, 2003), p. 438.

26. Charles D. Hale, *Fundamentals of Police Administration* (Boston: Holbrook Press, 1977).

27. Bureau of National Affairs, *Collective Bargaining Database* (Washington, DC: BNA, Inc., 2001), pp. 27–34.

28. More, Wegener, and Miller, *Effective Police Supervision*, p. 412.

29. CALEA, *Standards for Law Enforcement Agencies*, 4th ed. (Fairfax, VA: Commission on Accreditation for Law Enforcement Agencies, Inc., November 2001), p. 24–1.

30. McAndrew, *Police Labor/Management Relations*, pp. 121–123.

31. Coble, *Police Management/ Labor Relations*, p. 62.

32. Lester R. Bittel and John W. Newstrom, *What Every Supervisor Should Know,* 6th ed. (New York: McGraw-Hill, 1992), p. 251.

33. Coble, *Police Management/Labor Relations,* pp. 38–59.

34. McAndrew, *Police Management/Labor Relations,* p. 72.

35. More, Wegener, and Miller, *Effective Police Supervision,* p. 408.

36. Doan, *The Chief and the Union: Building a Better Relationship,* p. 19.

37. More, Wegener, and Miller, *Effective Police Supervision,* p. 408.

38. James J. Fyfe, Jack R. Greene, and William F. Walsh, *Police Administration,* 5th ed. (New York: McGraw-Hill, 1997), p. 292.

39. Milpitas Police Department, *Memorandum of Understanding,* pp. 14–17.

40. Joseph Lambert, "Grievance Mechanisms," in Peter C. Unsinger and Harry W. More, *Police Management/Labor* (Springfield, IL: Charles C Thomas, 1987), p. 178.

41. Harry W. More and O.R. Shipley, *Police Policy Manual—Personnel* (Springfield, IL: Charles C Thomas, 1987), pp. 179–180.

42. Lambert, *Police Management/Labor Relations,* pp. 179–181.

43. U.S. Census Bureau, *Resident Population Estimates of the United States by Sex, Race and Hispanic Origin* (Washington, DC: U.S. Bureau of the Census, 2001), pp. 55–92.

44. Barry L. Reece and Rhonda Brandt, *Effective Human Relations in Organizations* (Boston: Houghton Mifflin, 1987).

45. U.S. Equal Employment Opportunity Commission, EOP, *Facts About Discrimination Based on Sexual Orientation, Status as a Parent, Marital Status and Political Affiliation* (Washington, DC: EEOP, 2003), pp. 1–3.

46. U.S. Equal Employment Opportunity Commission, *Title VII Enforces Job Rights* (Washington, DC: USGPO, 1988), pp. 1–12.

47. Howard J. Anderson and Michael D. Levin-Epstein, *Primer of Equal Employment Opportunity,* 2nd ed. (Washington, DC: Bureau of National Affairs, 1984).

48. Ibid.

49. U.S. Equal Employment Opportunity Commission, *Facts About the Americans with Disabilities Act* (Washington, DC: EEOP, 2003), pp. 1–2.

50. Charles R. Swanson, Leonard Territo, and Robert W. Taylor, *Police Administration: Structures, Processes and Behavior,* 5th ed. (New York: Macmillan, 2001), p. 217.

51. Anderson and Levin-Epstein, *Primer of Equal Employment Opportunity.*

52. T. Sass and J. Troyer, "Affirmative Action, Political Representation, Unions, and Female Police Employment," *Journal of Labor Research,* Vol. 20 (4) (1999), pp. 212–218.

53. *NAACP v. Allen,* 340 F. Supp. 703 (M.D. Ala. 1972).

54. U.S. Commission on Civil Rights, *Revisiting Who Is Guarding the Guardians* (Washington, DC: USGPO, 1999), pp. 1–5.

55. *Richmond v. Croson Co.,* 109 S. Ct. 706 (1989).

56. U.S. Commission on Civil Rights, *Police Practices and the Preservation of Civil Rights* (Washington, DC: USGPO, 1980), pp. 1–25.

57. Anderson and Levin-Epstein, *Primer of Equal Employment Opportunity.*

58. Ibid.

59. More, Wegener, and Miller, *Effective Police Supervision,* p. 450.

60. U.S. Commission on Civil Rights, *Statements on Civil Rights Concerning the Detroit Police Department's Racial Promotion Quota* (Washington, DC: USGPO, 1984), pp. 4–20.

61. U. S. Commission on Civil Rights, *Revisiting Who Is Guarding the Guardians,* pp. 6–29.

62. U.S. Commission on Civil Rights, *Statements on Civil Rights Concerning the Detroit Police Department's Racial Promotion Quota,* pp. 21–32.

63. CALEA, *Standards for Law Enforcement Agencies,* pp. 31–32.

64. Milpitas Police Department, *Memorandum of Understanding,* p. 41.

65. Reece and Brandt, *Effective Human Relations in Organizations.*

66. Federal Bureau of Investigation, *Crime in the United States* (Washington, DC: USGPO, 2002), p. 295.

67. Jeffrey Higginbotham, "Sexual Harassment in the Police Station," *FBI Law Enforcement Bulletin,* Vol. 58 (9) (1988), pp. 9–13.

68. Anderson and Levin-Epstein, *Primer of Equal Employment Opportunity.*

69. Reece and Brandt, *Effective Human Relations in Organizations.*

70. Swanson, Territo, and Taylor, *Police Administration,* p. 315.

71. Reece and Brandt, *Effective Human Relations in Organization.*

72. Bruce L. Berg and Kimberley J. Budnick, "Defeminization of Women in Law Enforcement: A New

Twist in the Traditional Police Personality," *Journal of Police Science and Administration,* Vol. 14 (4) (1986), pp. 257–261.

73. S. Martin, "Policewomen and Policewoman: Occupational Role, Dilemmas and Choices of Female Officers," *Journal of Police Science and Administration,* Vol. 7 (3) (1979), pp. 127–131.

74. S. Gross, *Socialization into Law Enforcement: The Female Police Recruit* (Miami: Southeastern Institute of Criminal Justice, 1981).

75. IACP, "Women Policing—IACP, Gallup Assess Recruitment, Promotion, Retention Issues," *The Police Chief,* Vol. LXV (10) (1988), pp. 36–40.

76. Berg and Budnick, *Journal of Police Science and Administration,* p. 260.

77. Daniel J. Bell, "Policewomen: Myth and Reality," *Journal of Police Science and Administration,* Vol. 10 (1) (1982), pp. 45–49.

78. Peter Horne, *Women in Law Enforcement,* 2nd ed. (Springfield, IL: Charles C Thomas, 1980), pp. 35–125.

79. Ibid., pp. 132–145.

80. Joseph Polisar and Donna Milgram, "Strategies that Work: Recruiting, Integrating and Retaining Women Police Officers," *The Police Chief,* Vol. LXV (10) (1998), p. 44.

81. NCWP, *Recruiting and Retaining Women: A Self Assessment Guide for Law Enforcement* (Los Angeles: National Center for Women in Policing, 2001), p. 66.

82. Michael T. Charles, "Women in Policing," *Journal of Police Science and Administration,* Vol. 10 (2) (1982), pp. 51–56.

83. NCWP, *Recruiting and Retaining Women: A Self Assessment Guide for Law Enforcement,* pp. 22–27.

84. Peter Horne, "Policewomen: 2000 A.D. Redux," *Law and Order,* Vol. 47 (11) (1999), pp. 53–62.

85. Kimberly Lonsway and Deborah Campbell, "Retaining Women Officers," *Law and Order,* 50 (5) (2002), pp. 107–111.

86. Roslyn Maglione, "Recruiting, Retaining, and Promoting Women: The Success of the Charlotte-Mecklenburg Police Department's Women's Network," *The Police Chief,* Vol. LXIX (3) (2002), pp. 19–24.

87. Swanson, Territo, and Taylor, *Police Administration.*

88. Federal Bureau of Investigation, *Uniform Crime Reports, 2001* (Washington, DC: USGPO, 2002), pp. 45–46.

89. Matthew J. Hickman and Brian A. Reaves, *Local Police Departments 2000* (Washington, DC: Bureau of Justice Statistics, January 2003), p. 4.

90. Police Foundation, *Survey of Police Operational and Administrative Practices, 1981* (Washington, DC: PERF, 1981).

91. S. Martin, *On the Move: The Status of Women in Policing* (Washington, DC: The Police Foundation, 1990). pp. 22–97.

92. Dorothy M. Schultz, "Law Enforcement Leaders: A Survey of Women Police Chiefs in the United States," *The Police Chief,* LXIX (3) ( 2002) pp. 25–28.

93. Steven E. Heckeroth and Andrew M. Barker, "Police Department Efforts to Deter Sexual Harassment," *USA Today* (July 1997), A2.

94. Daniel A. Thomann, David E. Strickland, and James L. Gibbons, "An Organizational Development Approach to Preventing Sexual Harassment: Developing Shared Commitment Through Awareness Training," *College and University Personnel Association Journal,* Vol. 40 (1) (1989), pp. 34–43.

95. EEOC, *Enforcement Guidance: Vicareous Employer Liability for Unlawful Harassment by Supervisors* (Washington, DC: Equal Employment Opportunity Commission, 1999), p. 1.

96. James M. Daum and Cindy M. Johns, "Police Work from a Woman's Perspective," *The Police Chief,* Vol. LXI (9) (1994), pp. 42–46.

97. NCWP, *Recruiting and Retaining Women: A Self Assessment Guide for Law Enforcement,* p. 133.

98. Jennifer Brown and Frances Heidensohm, *Gender and Policing: Comparative Perspectives* (New York: Macmillan, 2000), p. 184.

99. U.S. Equal Employment Opportunity Commission, *Facts About Sexual Harassment* (Washington, DC: EEOP, 2002), p. 1.

100. U.S. Equal Employment Opportunity Commission, 1992, *Identifying Sexual Harassment* (Washington, DC: EEOP), pp. 1–4.

101. U.S. Equal Employment Opportunity Commission, *Policy Guidance on Current Issues of Sexual Harassment* (Washington, DC: EEOC, 1990), p. 14.

102. Philip E. Carlin and Ferris R. Byxbe, "Managing Sexual Harassment Liability: A Guide for Police Administrators," *The Police Chief,* Vol. LXIII (10) (2000), pp. 124–129.

103. Jane Adams-Roy and Julian Barling, "Predicting the Decision to Confront or Report Sexual Harassment," *Journal of Organizational Behavior,* Vol. 19 (4) (July 1998), pp. 333–335.

104. William A. Geller and Kervin J. Karales, *Split-Second Decisions: Shootings of and by the Chicago Police* (Chicago, IL: Chicago Law Enforcement Study Group, 1981), p. 163.

105. Jodi M. Brown and Patrick A. Langan, *Policing and Homicide, 1976–98: Justifiable Homicide by Police, Police Officers Murdered by Felons* (Washington, DC: Bureau of Justice Statistics, 2001), p. 15.

106. Kenneth J. Matulia, *A Balance of Force* (Giathersburg, MD: IACP, 1982).

107. Brown and Langan, *Police and Homicide, 1976–98: Justifiable Homicide by Police, Police Officers Murdered by Felons*, pp. 15, 43.

108. More, Wegener, and Miller *Effective Police Supervision*, p. 270.

109. IACP, "IACP Report Shows Police Rarely Use Force," *The Police Chief*, Vol. LXV (6) (1998), pp. 18–22.

110. Lawrence A. Greenfeld, Patrick A. Lanham, and Steven K. Smith, *Police Use of Deadly Force: Collection of National Data* (Washington, DC: Bureau of Justice Statistics, November 1997), pp. 1–38.

111. John C. Hall, "Deadly Force: The Common Law and the Constitution, *FBI Law Enforcement Bulletin*, Vol. 53 (4) (1984), pp. 12–17.

112. Ibid.

113. John C. Hall, "Police Use of Deadly Force," Part 1, *FBI Law Enforcement Bulletin*, Vol. 58 (9) (1988), pp. 12–18.

114. *Tennessee v. Garner*, 471, U.S. 1 at 7 (1985).

115. Hall, *Deadly Force: The Common Law and the Constitution*.

116. *Graham v. Conner*, U.S. 386, 109 S. Ct. 1865 (1989).

117. Tony L. Jones, "Tactical Use of Force," *Law and Order*, Vol. 45 (2) (1997), pp. 84–86.

118. George T. William, "Force Continuums: A Liability to Law Enforcement?" *FBI Law Enforcement Bulletin*, Vol. 71 (6) (2002), pp. 14–19.

119. Betsy Vickers, *Memphis, Tennessee, Police Department's Intervention Team*, Practitioner Perspectives, Washington, DC: Bureau of Justice Assistance (2000), p. 8.

120. Williams, *Force Continuum: A Liability for Law Enforcement*, pp. 14–16.

121. James E. Fyfe, *Readings on Police Use of Deadly Force*, 3rd ed. (Washington, DC: Police Foundation, 1991).

122. U.S. Commission on Civil Rights, *Police Practices and the Preservation of Civil Rights* (Washington, DC: USGPO, 1980).

123. William A. Geller, "Deadly Force: What We Know," *Journal of Police Science and Administration*, Vol. 10 (2) (1982), pp. 97–102.

124. CALEA, *Standards for Law Enforcement Agencies*, pp. 1–4–1–7.

125. Hall, *Deadly Force: The Common Law and the Constitution*.

# INDEX